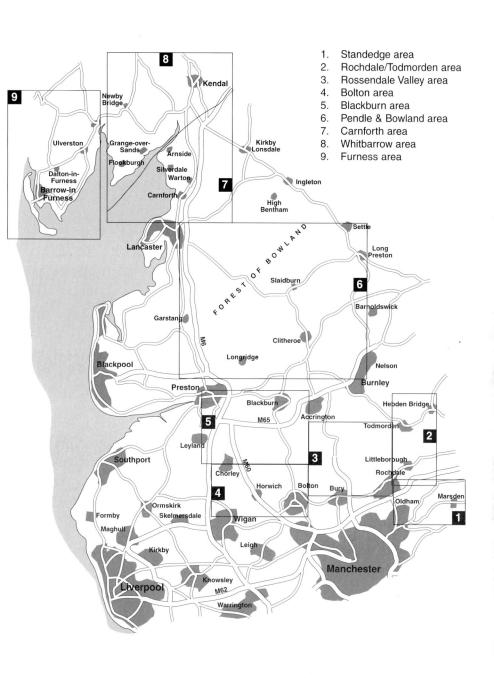

1. Standedge area
2. Rochdale/Todmorden area
3. Rossendale Valley area
4. Bolton area
5. Blackburn area
6. Pendle & Bowland area
7. Carnforth area
8. Whitbarrow area
9. Furness area

Rock Climbs in the Lancashire Area

Series Editor: Geoff Milburn

Volume Compilers and Sub-Editors: Les Ainsworth and Dave Cronshaw

Guidebook Team
Les Ainsworth
Ian Conway
Dave Cronshaw
Brian Cropper
Paul Dewhurst
John Gaskins
Bruce Goodwin
Geoff Hibbert
Paul Horan
Karl Lunt
Al Phizacklea
John Proud

Rob Smitton
Carl Spencer
John Street
Stew Wilson

BMC Guidebook Team
Dave Gregory
Brian Griffiths
Graham Hoey
Geoff Milburn
Geoff Radcliffe
Chris Wright

Illustrated by:
Malc Baxter
Geoff Hibbert
Paul Horan
Mark Griffiths
Al Phizacklea

Tony Powell
Adam Richardson
John Street
Jim Whitham
Dave Wilcock

Produced on a voluntary basis by the BMC
Guidebook Committee for the British Mountaineering Council

1969   *Lancashire. A Guide to Rock Climbs.*   First Edition.   **Ainsworth, L. and Watkin, P.**   Rocksport.

1972   *Lancashire Update. Vols 1, 2 and 3.*   **Ainsworth, L. and Meakin, R.**

1975   *Lancashire. Rock Climbs in the North West.*   Second Edition. **Ainsworth, L.**   Cicerone Press.

1979   *Rock Climbs in Lancashire and the North West. Supplement.* **Ainsworth, L., Cronshaw, D. and Evans, A.**   Cicerone Press.

1983   *Rock Climbs in Lancashire and the North West, Including the Isle of Man.*   Third Edition.   **Ainsworth, L.**   Cicerone Press.

1986   *Rock Climbs in Lancashire and the North West. Supplement.*   **Kelly, P. and Cronshaw, D.**   Cicerone Press.

1987   *Rock Climbs in Lancashire and the North West.*   Fourth Edition. **Kelly, P. and Cronshaw, D.**   Cicerone Press.

This Edition: 1999

ISBN   0 903908 17 4

Prepared by *Synergy*, Royal Oak Barn, The Square, Cartmel, Cumbria, LA11 6BQ in 9/10 Times Roman, using Ventura Publisher for the text and CorelDRAW for the diagrams.

Printed by *The Ernest Press*, 17 Carleton Drive, Giffnock, Glasgow, G46 6NU.

Distributed by *Cordee*, 3a De Montfort Street, Leicester, LE1 7HD.

BMC guidebooks are produced on a wholly voluntary basis and any surpluses raised are re-invested for future productions. In addition a 5% levy is included in the price, which is contributed to the BMC's Access and Conservation Fund. This is used to campaign for access to, and conservation of, crags and mountains throughout Britain and is a vital contribution to climbing.

CONTENTS

(line drawings in italics)

4 CONTENTS

WHITBARROW AREA

FURNESS AREA

Photographs

Front Cover: Geoff Hibbert and Adam Richardson on **Cheat** (E3 5b), Wilton.
Photo: Derek Richardson

First front endpaper: **Aladdinsane** (E1 5a), Trowbarrow
Photo: Ken Wilson

Second front endpaper: Ron Fawcett on the first ascent of **Moonchild** (E4 5c), Chapel Head Scar.
Photo: Al Evans

First colour photo: Keith Phizacklea not wailing on **New Jerusalem** (E4 6a), Anglezarke Quarry.
Photo: Dave Wilkinson

Frontispiece: Adam Richardson's brief respite on **Nobody Wept for Alec Trench** (E5 6a), Egerton Quarry.
Photo: Geoff Hibbert

First Rear Endpaper: Dave Cronshaw finds **Black Gold** (E2 5c), Goldmire Quarry.
Photo: Les Ainsworth

Second Rear Endpaper: An unknown climber examines the impressive top of **Crescendo**, Shooter's Nab.
Photo: Bob Whittaker

Third Rear Endpaper: Bob Whittaker on an early ascent of the **Girdle of Shooter's Nab** (HVS).
Photo: Janet Whittaker

Rear Cover: Paul Cropper on **Aladdinsane** (E1 5a), Trowbarrow.
Photo: Brian Cropper

COLOUR PHOTOGRAPHS

8 PHOTOGRAPHS

An unknown climber makes some magical moves on **Spectral Wizard** (E4 6b), *Page 640*
    Scout Scar.
Photo: Dave Cronshaw

Unknown climber shoots up **Trigger Finger** (E3 6a), Humphrey Head Point. *Page 641*
Photo: Al Phizacklea

Stevie Whittal on **Countach** (E5 6b), Millside Scar. *Page 648*
Photo: Al Phizacklea

Mick Lovatt and Chris Gore spaced out on **Space Buttress** during **Men at** *Page 649*
    Work (E5 6b), White Scar.
Photo: Steve Wilcock

BLACK and WHITE PHOTOGRAPHS
The ever fashion conscious Hank Pasquill at Wilton. *Pages 272 – 273*
Photo: Brian Cropper

A youthful Al Evans on **Pagan** (E1 5b), Lester Mill Quarry.
Photo: Brian Cropper

Eric Robinson making an early ascent of **Frightful Fred** (VS 4c), Wilton One Quarry.
Photo: Ray Evans

This is Nigel Bonnet, utterly **Unjust** (6a), Brownstones Quarry.
Photo: Brian Cropper

Above: The photo that started *Rocksport* magazine. Les Ainsworth on *Pages 336 337*
    The Finger (VS 4b), Anglezarke Quarry.
Photo: George Philips
Below: A motley crew during a Lancashire meet at Brownstones in 1977. From
    left: Nigel Bonnet, Dennis Gray, Ian Lonsdale, Hank Pasquill, the two Moss
    brothers, then ?, Dave Cronshaw at far right.
Photo: Brian Cropper

Les Ainsworth and Les Houlker climbing, belayed by Paul Hamer, on **Orang-Outang**
    (VS 4c), Cadshaw Quarry in 1965 – decades before the route was retro-bolted.
Photo: John Mason

Les Ainsworth on the first ascent of **End of Time** (E2 5b), Denham Quarry.
Photo: George Philips

An amazing early pegging shot entitled, 'On **Main Wall**, Wilton Quarry, near
    Bolton,' *The Climber* magazine ran from November 1962.
Photo: Mr F Redman

Mandarin (E2 5b,5b), Hoghton Quarry. *Pages 644 – 645*
Photo: Leo Dickinson

Christeena (VS, 4c), Wilton One.
Photo: Ken Wilson

Martin Boysen leads **The Golden Tower** (E2 5a,5c) Anglezarke.
Photo: Ken Wilson

Martin Boysen on **Cameo** (E1 5a), Wilton One.
Photo: Ken Wilson

Charlie Vigano

The 1983 edition of the Lancashire Area guidebook was dedicated to Allan Allsopp as *'Father of Lancashire Climbing'*. Since then there has been a feeling that this accolade should pass to Charlie Vigano for his unstinting support and enthusiasm for Lancashire climbing. Therefore, although we know that Charlie would find such recognition a little embarrassing, we intend to dedicate this guidebook to him.

Sadly, Charlie was killed in a climbing accident in Spain as the final work on the guidebook was being completed and so this dedication has become a more poignant tribute to a friend who will be missed by many climbers both in Lancashire and farther afield.

Charlie's climbing started just after the war in Scotland. He made many first ascents, particularly in the Glencoe Area and was a prominent member of the Creagh Dhu. He was also involved in many epics, the most notable of which was when he was benighted during an early winter attempt on Raven's Gully with Hamish MacInnes.

However, in 1958 he ran out of patience with the Scottish winter weather and moved down to Lancashire. Shortly afterwards, he joined the Rock and Ice when members such as Joe Brown and Don Whillans were pushing the limits of climbing.

Charlie played an active role on the Lancashire and Cheshire Area Committee of the BMC and made some valuable contributions over several years. He spent a lot of time on the crags of his adopted Lancashire and obtained an immense amount of pleasure from all his climbing, whether it was on a crag that he had not previously visited, or a route that he had soloed countless times before. Many of us will have seen him in recent years climbing with his wife Sheilgh at Warton Small Quarry, which he considered to be his favourite crag. His unquenchable enthusiasm for climbing and climbers should be an inspiration for all climbers in the area, for by his example he demonstrated very effectively that with a little effort and dedication, age need not be a barrier to enjoying the crags. Furthermore, he also showed that it is possible to maintain a reasonable standard of climbing during retirement – he was hoping to climb Cenotaph Corner on his seventieth birthday. It is to be hoped that many of the climbers reading this guide will follow Charlie's example and will get a lifetime of enjoyment from the crags and the mountains.

Lancashire and Cheshire Area Committee of the BMC

Editorial Introduction

*'Quarries, where climbers try new pegging ideas, climb the
obvious routes and peg the unobvious; where lines are
altered, either by design or mistake. The hagglings and
arguments about whether a climb goes free, or with a peg;
are now down in black and white ...*

*... One cannot help wondering whether Lancashire has more
to offer than people think.'*

Leo Dickinson, Mountain magazine, November 1969

Right up until the early 1960s Lancashire was essentially regarded as a through
route for the majority of climbers who were either going northwards to the
mountain crags of the Lake District and Scotland, or southwards for Wales.
Very few of them diverted to investigate the local crags. Indeed despite
protestations at intervals by the local activists, who insisted that there really was
some good climbing to be had, for many years the red rose county was virtually
a backwater visited only by a relatively few outsiders.

One of the first references to Lancashire climbing (other than on the crags of
the southern Lake District fells) was in 1937 when Allan Allsopp wrote an
article on Cadshaw Rocks for the Mountaineering Journal. Brownstones Quarry
also got a mention in the Lancashire Caving and Climbing Club Journal in 1949
with an article by E Parr. Later, Allsopp enthusiastically introduced Cadshaw
into the Kinder, Roches guidebook of 1951 to draw attention to the possibilities
in Lancashire. By 1960 Edward Pyatt's book 'Where to Climb in the British
Isles' was eagerly received by climbers in many areas, especially where no
guidebook was available. In the Lancashire area it included several small
outcrops such as Quernmore Crag, Hugencroft and Wolf Hole Crag, and there
was mention of a small limestone crag, Fairy Steps. The rather tantalising news
however was that there was a large quarry somewhere between Preston and
Blackburn called Hoghton Quarry and that this had yielded some hard artificial
climbs as well some free routes in the late-Fifties. Another surprise came in
1964 when The Climber magazine carried a front cover picture of an imposing
aid route up the Main Wall of Wilton Quarry.

What actually happened next is known to very few climbers. Early in 1966 an
enthusiastic young student, Les Ainsworth, the Meets Secretary of the Blackburn
Student Climbing Group (B.S.C.G.), wrote a letter to the Peak Committee of the
BMC. The letter, which was a request for a sponsor for an envisaged guidebook
to Lancashire, was received by Dave Gregory who read:

*'It seems that Lancashire has been somewhat shelved away by
the guidebook writers in preference to Yorkshire and
Derbyshire, though I don't know why, because it is highly
populated with climbers (Brown and Whillans for instance)
and it has got many worthwhile routes of all standards from
100 foot XSs at Hoghton, to 25-foot problems at
Brownstones, or from easy peg routes (some now going free),
to a difficult 15-foot overhang on bolts at Hoghton, or from*

> *coarse natural gritstone at Cadshaw to limestone at*
> *Clitheroe. There would be about 250 routes.'*

Dave Gregory, probably rather cautious about such a request from a 'young' unknown climber, replied asking for more detail then passed on the problem to Eric Byne the guidebook Editor of the Peak District asking him to evaluate the material. Byne was curious to know if the guidebook was to stand in its own right or would join the Peak District empire. He wrote:

> *'Do you wish this guidebook to be one of the series of 'Rock*
> *Climbs in the Peak'? – (I suppose that we could stretch the*
> *Peak that far north for an odd volume).'*

Byne was also cautious and referred back to Jack Longland who (as chairman of the Peak Area Committee) according to Byne ruled over the Guidebook Editor. Longland was a man of decision and promptly suggested that they should encourage Ainsworth to get on with the work subject to 'discovery if the B.S.C.G. is competent to produce the guidebook'! Longland commented that they might be in trouble later on if any other group proposed a guidebook to mid- or North Lancashire and pondered the point. Somewhat undecided he commented that:

> *'They sound sensible enough but I don't know much about*
> *them.'*

After further communications between Ainsworth and Byne, the former offered to donate all royalties from the sales of the guidebook to the Mountain Rescue Committee – a noble gesture. In one letter Ainsworth demonstrated his faith in Byne when he wrote:

> *'We were getting a little desperate about managing to get a*
> *guidebook published and had decided not to go ahead until*
> *we had a definite chance of getting it published ...*
>
> *A guidebook can be made or broken by the Editor, and so we*
> *would like you to edit the guidebook.'*

Ainsworth was starting to get enthusiastic by then and estimated that there were about 500 routes in the area (double his estimate to Dave Gregory!). He was also getting 'visions of grandeur' as he said that he was contemplating including Heptonstall Quarry which had an out-of-date typescript guide and as one of the best quarries in Britain ('barring Dovestones and Hoghton'!) it needed publicity. But in the Lancashire guidebook? By June, Byne was told that the team was starting work in earnest and that they aimed to have a finished script ready within twelve months. In addition to working on the guidebook Ainsworth also took on the task of editing the new trendy magazine Rocksport early in 1968. The first edition included an 'Interim Guide to Hoghton Quarry' attributed to Paul Hamer, but mostly written by Ainsworth – to whet people's appetites. There was also an article by Bill Lounds in May 1969, which described a few routes at Warton Crags and Trowbarrow Quarry. Lounds dangled a carrot:

> *'Unknown to most Lakeland climbers who travel via the M6*
> *there are extensive limestone crags close to Carnforth. Indeed*
> *one of the biggest quarries in the area is plainly visible from*
> *a car travelling over the last miles of the motorway.'*

As soon as the magazine came out there were climbers wandering all over the road while craning out of their cars looking for big limestone crags.

Unfortunately by1969 after the death of the Editor Eric Byne, the Peak District guidebook team was starting to have problems with publishing its own guidebooks and with a backlog of guidebooks waiting to be published, there would have been a long delay before the Lancashire guidebook could be printed. Les Ainsworth was faced with a big decision. Finally, he took a deep breath and decided to publish his guidebook under the Rocksport banner. He went for a streamlined factual volume and pruned the text to the bone by omitting Geology, Natural History, and even the climbing History section. The guidebook was reviewed by Leo Dickinson in Mountain magazine in November 1969 and there was a mouth-watering picture of Mandarin to lure the masses.

As a result of the publicity, early in 1970, Dave Gregory and I (as two typical Sheffield climbers who alternated between the Lake District and Wales at weekends) decided to see what Lancashire climbing was all about. Having already swerved all over the motorway while scanning the landscape keenly for large limestone crags, we decided to have a look at some of the local delights starting with Trowbarrow Quarry. Standing under the great blank wall which had not then been rent by cracks caused by explosive charges we stared in amazement at the face wondering what protection could be obtained and after doing Jomo, a nominal tick, we decided that there was a lot of potential – but that the crag was far too loose for our liking. Warton crag was also quickly dismissed, but after raving about Farleton Crag we headed south and ended up at Wilton. After a couple of routes in Wilton Three we walked along the length of Wilton One and we were IMPRESSED! Some of the harder routes looked suicidal, protection seemed to be minimal, rock in places was dangerous and the finishes were mainly loose, vegetated and filthy. Where were all the nice wide jamming cracks? Commenting that only Dukes Quarry near Matlock had impressed us as much we promptly left for home. The crag – and Lancashire – could wait' There were bigger fish to fry.

In the 1970s the grading of many of the routes was regarded with some suspicion as outside Lancashire rumours circulated about parties having epics on routes which should have been well within their capabilities. A feeling was abroad that Lancashire climbing meant having fights with horrendously loose rock and jungle-like vegetation, or dubious pegging in dank underground quarries and so the locals had things more or less to themselves. Which is largely what they wanted, for although between 1968 and 1972 Rocksport carried details about new routes all over the country, they gave away virtually nothing about what they were doing on their home patch. Gradually though, the word spread abroad that there were some gems to be had The splendid Golden Tower of Anglezarke was on people's lips, as was an exceptional route called Mandarin at Hoghton Quarry. Once the cracks appeared at Trowbarrow then classics such as Jean Jeanie and Aladdinsane were put on the itinerary of visiting climbers. Denham meant Mohammed the Mad Monk, while in Wilton One Quarry Wombat threw down the gauntlet.

Eventually the crowds realized that there was a lot of potential and over the next twenty years the tally of routes became ever bigger, especially as new crags were opened up. With the co-operation of Walt Unsworth, the guidebook went to a fourth edition and two supplements were need to keep pace with the development. The impetus for all of this effort came largely from Dave Cronshaw, Phil Kelly and of course Ainsworth himself. For some reason though, whether modesty or merely space saving, the complete history of the area was not recorded for posterity. A project was started in the Peak District in the 1980s when the Peak Guidebook Editor pleaded with Les Ainsworth to do a similar bit of research (for both historical sections as well as first ascent lists) but the Lancashire lads could not be prevailed upon to deliver the goods.

By 1994 when the Peak District Guidebook Committee was approached in a similar vein to that of over twenty-five years earlier the idea of including Lancashire into the Peak District series was welcomed with open arms. After all, despite the fact that the Peak District lies in the centre of the country, Lancashire is perhaps really the warm red heart of Britain. The Lancashire 'triangle' has the Lake District to the North-West, Wales to the south-west and Yorkshire (strategically separated by the Pennines) to the east. The red rose county is also midway between Scotland and the South-West of England. As a wet weather alternative to the mountains it is ideally situated for mobile climbers from all of the great northern cities: Manchester, Leeds, Sheffield, Birmingham, etc. and bearing in mind that the weather on the two sides of the Pennines is often markedly different, the choice of either Lancashire or Yorkshire is often very handy. With a mix of limestone and gritstone, there is now a great variety of climbing especially in the great quarries of Wilton, Anglezarke, Hoghton and Trowbarrow as well as several relatively new discoveries. With greatly cleaned rock and much improved access, Lancashire is now an 'in' place.

Lancashire and the Peak District have always been close neighbours, and in the past many of the crags such as Shooters Nab and Pule Hill have appeared (by agreement) in the guidebooks of both areas. In addition many climbers from Lancashire who climb regularly in the Peak District have contributed towards writing the Peak District's guidebooks. It is thus appropriate that the BMC Guidebook Funds should be used to float a new Lancashire guidebook. Nothing but the best will do. It is to this end that we have worked for the last few months.

Geoff Milburn (Series Editor) April 1998

p.s. The editing for this guidebook was mainly done in an almost continuous concentrated spell over the Easter period during the World Snooker Championships. It was a record year for century breaks and the Editor's loyalties were at times divided and on more than one occasion his concentration 'went to pot'. As John Higgins completed the match with yet another big century-plus break the final corrections were made to the script. If any slight errors remain ...

Lancashire Climbing in the Sixties

Often when talking to climbers I am asked about the early days of Lancashire climbing. Therefore, I felt that it might be appropriate to include a short description of my recollections of that period.

When I started climbing in the early 1960s there were virtually no details available of any climbing in the old county of Lancashire (which then also included Merseyside, Greater Manchester and South Cumbria). In fact the only area within the old county, that was covered in a readily available climbing guidebook, was the F&RCC Dow Crag guidebook. The headmaster at Blackburn Grammar School, Brian Kemball-Cook, had duplicated some descriptions of the routes at Cadshaw Rocks by Allan Allsopp, but apart from that, little was generally known about the other crags dotted about the county that local activists were exploring.

This, added to the poor transport situation at the time, meant that it could be inordinately difficult to get to any crag. For instance, the next crag covered by a guidebook that I visited after I started climbing at Cadshaw, was Dovestones (an hour on a train to Manchester, well over an hour by bus to Greenfield, then about fifty minutes walk). Laddow was out of the question for a day visit without a car, and the only other crag that we could reach for a day's climbing was Widdop, which took just less than three hours each way, provided that the connections worked out.

However, it soon became evident that there were crags closer at hand, though these were only known to local activists. For myself, the first I learned about these other crags was when I met Ray Evans at Cadshaw. He told me of a quarry up to eighty feet high and over half a mile long, split by steep cracks and corners. It seemed a million miles from the short V Diffs at Cadshaw. The next weekend my partner failed to arrive at Cadshaw, but though he had impressed on me that quarry climbing was unsafe, Ray's tales spurred me on and I just could not resist the lure of Cadshaw Quarry. I soloed two climbs that day, but on both, progress was slow, because there was a lot of grass and soil that had to be removed whilst climbing. I soon learned that a peg hammer could greatly improve route cleaning, but at the time it was not really on to abseil down a route first, unless it was in a really bad state. Certainly, if any pegs were fixed, this was virtually always done by the leader. Later that day I met some other climbers from Blackburn and the next weekend we all set off for Hoghton Quarry. I was told that Hoghton was over a hundred feet high and was so steep that it could only be climbed with pegs. Amongst the four of us we had a selection of six pegs and though we only had one 80-foot hemp rope and no idea about where any of the routes went, we felt that we could manage somehow. Anyway, I was sure that the claims about the quarry's height were a gross exaggeration. As we came out of the muddy cutting and first saw the rock, I was amazed – the quarry was every bit as high as I had been told and, even with pegs, it looked an intimidating prospect. We picked an easier line at the left side of the Main Amphitheatre, which later turned out to be Speech Impediment, followed by Easy Route. I then learned that this was to be the first aid route that any of us had done and also that none of us had even led anything before, but the most worrying aspect of our adventure was the pair of wooden étriers that we were using. It was a good job that we picked such an easy line, because it took us most of the day to reach the top in about five pitches, by which time at least one of the étrier steps had broken.

It was a couple of weeks before I could try to reach Ray's quarry (Wilton One) and in the meantime I had read a book on climbing and had bought three spliced slings and some heavy steel ex-War Department krabs, so I then knew about belays and runners. Luckily, when I arrived at Wilton, Ray was already there and so we climbed together. We did quite a few routes, including, if I recall correctly, Fingernail and Great Slab. Soon I was as enthusiastic about the quarries as Ray. The routes were steep and hard, but there were often plenty of good, square-cut holds that could not be seen from below. It was obvious that there was much potential. However, the main thing that I learned that day was that if engineering nuts were threaded on to a sling, these could be jammed into a crack like a chockstone to give protection on these long, otherwise unprotected cracks. Like most climbers at the time, I soon learned which nuts fitted the cracks best and I also found that by filing down some of the faces of the nuts, they could be used in a wider range of cracks. Whilst talking about gear, it is also interesting to record that because pegs were so expensive at the time, we used to get most of our pegs made by the local blacksmith, who simply cut strips of steel of various thicknesses and drilled holes in one end.

During the next couple of years I was to discover that there were several other 'Wiltons' all over Lancashire. None of them as extensive, but each with plenty of potential, which was only known to a few local activists. At nearby Anglezarke Walt Unsworth started the ball rolling, whilst Ray Evans and Ken Powell kept Pilkington's a close-guarded secret for some time. Nearer to Blackburn, at Hoghton, it was Alan Atkinson and John Hamer who were in the know. On the eastern side of the county, Paul Horan recorded the climbing at Summit and Cow's Mouth, whilst Deeply Vale was Mick Pooler's home patch, and Roger Vickers was the Bellmanpark man. Up past Lancaster, it seemed that for some time Stew Wilson and Bill Lounds were virtually the only climbers visiting the Silverdale Crags. My own special patch was Cadshaw Quarry.

Gradually, more climbers visited these quarries, often on exploratory visits and certainly some of the quarries were 'rediscovered' several times, because many of the earliest visitors left no records of their visits, apart from the evidence of rusty pegs. However, guides (often hand-written) were produced and these were circulated amongst friends. At the time these were like gold dust, but, nevertheless, they did much to stimulate further development of many of the crags. This was especially true of Ray Evans's two typescript guides to Wilton, which were freely distributed by courtesy of Hartley's Alpine Sports in Bolton. These typescripts provided both a comprehensive record of the climbing available at Wilton and acted as an impetus to visiting climbers to find quarries nearer to their homes. Wilton became an important meeting point, and during the weekends I would often just turn up there and very soon there would always be someone to climb with. Many of us, who were just starting to climb, did not know of other climbers in our locality, but at Wilton we soon discovered that there were plenty of others eager to get out on to the rock. Many friendships and climbing partnerships were formed from meetings at Wilton, and I am pleased to say that many of these relationships are still strong at the end of the Nineties.

A particularly notable feature of the climbing in the area at that time was an almost complete lack of interest in recording first ascent details. The routes themselves were recorded and there was certainly fierce competition for the plum lines, but somehow it never seemed necessary to actually write down who had done the first ascent. After all, everyone knew who had done the good routes, so writing down your name against a particular route seemed both unnecessary and somewhat egotistical. Al Evans summed up the attitudes of the time, when he commented that:

> '*Everywhere else, in Wales and the Peak, climbers seem pre-occupied with claiming first ascents, even if they are only minor variations. But in Lancashire, climbers have risen above that, and their main aim is the route itself. Satisfaction comes from knowing that it is a good route. There is no need for any further glory.*'

Whilst the friendly rivalry and the low-key approach to new routeing that was prevalent at that time was in many ways laudable, in retrospect it is a great pity that better records were not kept. Much of the historical record of the early days of quarry climbing in the area is based upon recollections from the activists of the time, which were not recorded until many years later, and so it is bound to include some inaccuracies. However, on the credit side, it did spare us for many years from the iniquitous practice of renaming routes after each minor aid reduction.

Before ending this brief excursion back into the Sixties, it is, I believe, interesting to look at climbing ethics at the time. On the Lancashire quarries there were two ethical issues that dominated.

The first of these was the question as to whether it was justified to abseil down a route to clean it prior to a lead. During the early days, the only acceptable form of ascent was from the ground up. If there was a loose block on a climb – and there were several – the leader either had to climb round it, or else manage to remove it whilst leading. Similarly, any soil or vegetation that was encountered on holds or ledges, was generally removed over the leader's shoulder, often whilst maintaining a somewhat precarious position. because the vital holds could not be used. Thus, new routers often finished up looking like coal miners, and on some occasions even followed blocks and debris downwards. Towards the end of the Sixties, a more enlightened attitude, or sense of self-preservation, evolved and it became acceptable to abseil down a potential new route to undertake some limited cleaning. Even so, it was frowned upon if the 'cleaning' was perceived as being mainly to check out the viability of the route, rather than to remove obviously loose blocks.

When considering the early ascents that were made in the Lancashire quarries, it is important to bear in mind that for the majority of these, a ground-up approach was taken. Often, this meant that routes became much easier after the first ascents, as additional holds were uncovered, or as small blocks fell out of the cracks. This also explains why routes that may nowadays seem relatively trivial, were considered to be breakthroughs at the time.

Undoubtedly, the main ethical issue concerned the use of pegs. In many ways the debate was similar to the current bolting concerns, but there were also important differences and it is enlightening to consider how pegs were dealt with. The traditionalists of the time generally wanted no truck with pegs. However, most of them appeared to be willing to accept the use of pegs, provided that they were not placed in traditional crags. In effect, this meant that, even to this group, pegs were acceptable on limestone and in the quarries, where there was little other protection. Remember, that at the time nuts were only just coming in to use (the first purpose-designed nuts were MOACs, which came on sale in about 1966 or 1967) and so protection was limited to rock spikes, natural chockstones and trees – none of which was in great supply in the quarries or the new limestone crags.

At the opposite end of the spectrum were those climbers who wanted to get on to the more overhanging rock that could, then, only be reached by purely artificial climbing. Often, they made their first attempts at artificial climbing on short crack climbs on the less-frequented quarries and buttresses, but these were seen as purely training exercises, which explains why details of first ascents for short peg climbs are particularly scant. Fortunately, the artificial climbers kept to areas that were more amenable to artificial climbing and so there was not a great intrusion into the free-climbers' domain. Indeed, in many cases, the insertion of pegs into previously vague cracks, soon meant that the peg routes could be freed.

In the middle of this debate were the activists of the day who were eager to attack the more difficult and less protected climbs that were characteristic of the Lancashire quarries. Their argument was, that without pegs, many of the climbs on some crags would be virtually unprotectable. Faced with this situation, most climbers agreed that the limited use of pegs for protection, was acceptable. Indeed, there was a remarkable degree of consensus as to where pegs should be used and the extent to which they should be used. Most climbers understood where the boundaries lay, and those few who were considered to have inserted too many peg runners were widely criticised.

Nowadays, when bolts spring up on established VSs, it is worth reminding every climber with strong views on the bolting issue, that climbers have managed to resolve similar issues in the past by exercising a degree of tolerance. In Lancashire in the Sixties, we all knew that to place pegs on some routes would have needlessly upset some climbers, whilst at the same time we appreciated that pegs were justified either for protection or aid, on other crags. Any self-imposed restrictions on the placement of pegs were not seen as limiting the freedom of climbers, but were seen as an acceptable compromise that all climbers could live with. It is my sincere wish, that within the area covered by this guidebook, at least, sport climbers and traditional climbers will maintain a similar degree of tolerance and understanding to that which prevailed in the area on the pegging issue in the Sixties. My personal feeling is that at present we have developed such an understanding about where it is and where it is not acceptable to use protection. However, in some cases, the placement of some bolts appears to have erred on the generous side.

Finally, I would like to end this little sojourn into the Sixties, by thanking all those who were in any way responsible for the early developments in Lancashire, for their efforts in contributing towards cultivating the unique nature of climbing in the area.

Les Ainsworth

General Notes

Safety Advice
Climbing is an inherently dangerous activity with a danger of personal injury or death. All climbers must be aware of and accept that there are risks and therefore take all reasonable precautions so as not to cause accidents to themselves or others.

The details of climbs given in this guide, including their gradings and any references to in-situ or natural protection, are made in good faith. Wherever possible climbs have been checked and their grades debated to give a consensus opinion.

Unfortunately, climbs can change; holds fall off, rock becomes dirty and in-situ gear can deteriorate or disappear. Even small changes can significantly alter the difficulty or seriousness of a route and so, whilst it is believed that the information in this guide was accurate at the time that it was compiled, it is essential that climbers should judge the conditions of each climb before committing themselves.

Definitive Guidebooks
This guidebook, like previous Lancashire guidebooks, attempts to provide a definitive and comprehensive description of all the rock-climbing on the crags and quarries within the area. The BMC and individual authors still wish to retain their rights under copyright law, but are happy for the text and information within this guidebook to be used for future definitive guidebooks to the area. However, the voluntary work that was put into the production of this guidebook was intended to be for the benefit of all climbers in the area and not for the financial gain of a handful of climbers producing a selective guidebook or topo guide to a limited selection of the crags. Therefore, it is a condition of the sale and distribution of this guidebook that the information and route descriptions should not be copied or used in any selective guidebook without the specific written permission of the BMC.

It has been noted that some of the information from the previous Lancashire Area guidebook was used without permission in a Rockfax to the Lake District. This was considered to be a gross abuse of the voluntary efforts of all the workers who contributed to the guidebook, which, incidentally was made even worse by errors introduced in the selective guidebook. Furthermore, the presence of such guidebooks, written solely for a profit motive, undermines the definitive guidebook programme that has been so successful for British climbing. Accordingly, it must be noted that legal redress will be sought if the information and route descriptions from this guidebook are abused in a similar way.

Grades
Adjectival Grades
Throughout the guide adjectival grades have been used to indicate the overall difficulty of the climbs, taking into account all the factors that may contribute to the difficulty or seriousness of the climb. These factors include: the climb's technical difficulty, strenuosity, the sustained nature of the climbing, rock quality and protection. They also assume that the rock is dry. The grades are: Moderate

(M), Difficult (D), Very Difficult (VD), Severe (S), Hard Severe (HS), Very Severe (VS), Hard Very Severe (HVS), and Extremely Severe. The latter grade is subdivided into E1, E2, E3, E4, E5, E6 and E7 etc.

Technical Grades

Technical grades have been given for all pitches of 4a and above, but for some short problems only a technical grade has been given.

Anchor Grades

If a route is reasonably protected, on good rock and is not very sustained, the overall difficulty will be determined solely by the technical difficulty. Thus, for each technical grade, there is an adjectival grade that will normally be expected, provided that all the difficulties are technical. This is known as the *anchor grade*.

Therefore, whilst the technical grade should always directly indicate the technical difficulty of the hardest move on a pitch, the adjectival grade will be reduced if the difficulties are very short, or well protected, for instance, when the only hard moves are getting off the ground. Similarly, a higher adjectival grade than the anchor grade will suggest that a route is poorly protected, very sustained or loose.

The adjectival grade might also be adjusted if the moves were considered to be close to the borderline for a particular technical grade.

The list below gives the anchor grades up to E5 that are used in this guide:

S	4a	HS	4b	VS	4c
HVS	5a	E1	5b	E2	5c
E3	5c/6a	E4	6a	E5	6a/6b

French Grades

There is currently a view that, because 'sport climbs' are virtually free from objective dangers, they cannot be graded adequately within the British grading system and therefore French grades should be used for such climbs. However, the current guidebook writers do not accept this, but believe that a strength of the British grading system (if used correctly) is its ability to differentiate between climbs of similar technical difficulty but differing seriousness. It is considered by a majority of locals that French grades provide no additional information, and that their generally higher numerical values merely give the illusion of a higher technical standard.

Therefore, until a Brussels directive mandates that French grades have to be used, it is intended that we will use the British grading system for all climbs within the North-West. Thus, for most 'sport climbs', the adjectival grade will be based mainly upon an assessment of technical difficulty, though the grade may be slightly increased if a climb is particularly sustained or strenuous. Thus, for instance, a bolt-protected 6a which would receive a French grade of *F6c+*, would probably be graded about E3. This takes account of the fact that protection could be clipped, rather than arranged. However, if it was particularly sustained, it would be raised to E4, 6a. Similarly, if it was short and it eased off to 5c after the first few moves, it would probably be reduced to E2.

Climbers who are used to using French grades will appreciate that similar adjustments are made in that system, in order to balance technical difficulty and strenuosity. For instance a pumpy 6a would probably be raised to *F7a*.

However, because the technical grade is anchored, the change to E4 provides additional information that the climb is more difficult in some way. As it is clear that the route is well-bolted, the climber should appreciate that the climbing is sustained. On the other hand, an *F7a* could also be technically more difficult, but easy to rest between the bolts.

In order to satisfy the requirements of the BMC Guidebook Committee (which has stated that sport grades are now nationally accepted and understood) a French grade is included in brackets for all sport climbs in the text.

However, it is considered to be highly reprehensible to retrobolt existing traditional climbs in order to reduce their difficulty. Therefore, to give sport grades to such climbs is seen as condoning this vandalism and so French grades are not given for routes that were originally done as traditional climbs, regardless of their current bolted status.

Route Descriptions

All the route descriptions are given as if one is facing the rock. The pitch lengths are intended to indicate the amount of climbing, which may sometimes be different from the amount of rope needed. The assumption has also been made that most crags have tops and so, except where it is not possible to climb to the top because of poor rock or to safeguard delicate ecosystems, the climbs are described as going to the top of the crag. Therefore, on some sport climbs, lower-off points may be encountered several metres before the true top of a route is encountered.

First Ascent Details

For the first time in a Lancashire guidebook, it has been decided to include first ascent lists and also to indicate the year of ascent for each route. Unfortunately, probably because of the shy and quiet nature of Lancastrians, this information has not been recorded very well in the past. Therefore, although researches for this guidebook have been extensive, there are bound to be some inaccuracies. **Accordingly, anyone who can provide details of earlier ascents or other historical information is urged to send any relevant information to the BMC offices, 177 Burton Road, Manchester, M20 2BB, for the attention of the Lancashire and Cheshire Area Committee.**

Aid Reductions/Variations

On the title line for a route, if two or more dates are separated by a slash (e.g. 1969/1975), the first date indicates the year that the route was first ascended and subsequent dates are given for significant aid reductions. The dates of any significant variations are given in another set of brackets after the dates of the main route, with alternative starts etc. preceding variation finishes.

Route Names

Although route names are normally chosen by the first ascensionists, a problem arises when the first ascent details were not recorded at the time. Where possible, any route name that has been acquired from a later ascent will then be altered in accordance with the first ascensionist's wishes. However, the primary purpose of naming climbing routes is for identification and so, if a different name has already become well-established, this name will generally be retained, unless the change is relatively small. Thus, *Bettas Wall* at Wilton Three has been corrected to *Betty's Wall*, but at Anglezarke, *Terror Cotta* has become well-established and so it has not been renamed *Ten Pounds Bail*.

Completion of the Historical Record
Unfortunately, some good climbs in the area have in the past been lost, either because of infilling, rockfalls, or climbing restrictions on some parts of the cliffs. Where it was felt appropriate for the historical record, details of these have been included in italics in the first ascent lists.

Other Route Information
Although every attempt has been made to ensure that all the information within this guide is accurate, in some cases the climbs have not been repeated, or verified by the guide-writing team. Such routes are indicated with a dagger (†) to warn climbers to exercise caution when attempting these routes. However, this should not be confused with a black spot ● which is used to indicate climbs where the rock is particularly loose or unstable.

Quality of Climbs
Subjective assessments of the quality of climbs are always likely to be the most contentious ratings in a climbing guidebook. This is especially true in an area such as Lancashire, particularly in the more sheltered gritstone quarries, where some climbs can become vegetated in an amazingly short time, or the less-established quarries where there is still loose rock. For instance, if routes do not have frequent ascents, the natural drainage, especially seepage at horizontal faults, can attract vegetation and wash soil over the rock during the winter months, which then lodges on small incut ledges and in deep cracks. This can enable grasses and ferns to establish themselves very quickly and thereby to completely alter the appearance and character of what was a brilliant crack climb the previous summer. Climbers are encouraged to try to slow down or halt this process by brushing off any loose soil or grass that they may encounter, before it has chance to build up.

Despite these potential difficulties in assessing the quality of climbs within the area, quality ratings have been provided. These are based upon consensus views of local climbers and assume that the routes are in a reasonably clean and dry state. Quality is indicated by a star system, from ★ which indicates a route of above average quality, to the ultimate accolade, which is ★★★.

Aid
It is pleasing to be able to note that local climbers have steadily reduced the number of routes that need any aid so that only a handful of purely artificial routes now remains. Where limited aid is required on a predominantly free climb this has been specifically stated and any lack of reference to a specific aid point means that the climb has been done without it.

Protection
In-situ Protection
As far as possible, all in-situ protection, including threads, pegs and bolts, has been mentioned. However, there can be no guarantee that any protection that is mentioned will still be in place when a route is climbed. It is also essential to remember that all fixed gear will degrade over time. Therefore, it is up to

individual climbers to make their own assessment of any in-situ protection that is encountered, before using it.

All climbers, particularly first ascensionists, are asked to consider carefully the potential life span of any in-situ protection that they may choose to place or replace. They are also asked to try to reduce the environmental impact of such protection. For instance, by avoiding the use of brightly coloured tape and by resisting the temptation to misuse permanent protection to enable a hard section to be reduced to a series of lunges between runners.

Bolts

The use of bolts and staples for protection is a highly controversial issue for climbers. Unlike our continental counterparts, British climbers have decided that it is generally preferable for climbers to rely upon leader-placed, removable protection. Nevertheless, there are some situations where fixed protection is considered acceptable. With specific regard to the placement of bolts for protection, there is a strong consensus view within British climbing that any bolt placements should only be made if the following four guidelines can be met:

(1) **Bolts should only be used on specific crags where local climbers accept their use.**

(2) **Bolts should only be used where other runner placements are impossible or impracticable.**

(3) **Existing routes should not be retrobolted.**

(4) **Bolts should not be placed within clipping distance of existing routes.**

These issues have been discussed at length within this area at well-attended open meetings and there is extremely strong support for the above guidelines. Accordingly, the policy of the Lancashire and Cheshire Area Committee is unanimous in that BOLTS SHOULD NOT BE PLACED IN THE CRAGS WITHIN THE AREA DESCRIBED WITHIN THIS GUIDEBOOK, except in very exceptional circumstances. Recently, two bolts appeared on a short VS pitch that was first climbed in 1966 and to the vast majority of climbers in Lancashire this was seen as needless vandalism that spoiled a good climb. Although this was an isolated incident, it does illustrate the problems and annoyance that insensitive bolting can cause. Therefore, all climbers are asked to adhere to the above guidelines and the accepted climbing ethics on the crags described within this guide.

Apart from the Whitbarrow Area, there has been very little use of bolts and there is virtually unanimous support for the policy of continuing to use bolts very sparingly. Thus, in these areas no additional bolts whatsoever should be inserted, apart from any that are agreed for access purposes by the Area Committee. For instance at Jack Scout Crag bolts have been placed to avoid belay damage to rare trees.

It is important to stress that the owners of the following crags in the Carnforth and Whitbarrow Areas have specifically insisted that no further bolts should be inserted and so any further bolting at these crags could directly jeopardize access:

♦ **Chapel Head Scar**
♦ **Jack Scout Crag**

♦ **Trowbarrow**
♦ **Warton Main Quarry**

There have recently been some alarming failures of bolts and staples. Therefore, on the rare occasions that bolts are placed climbers are asked to take every precaution to ensure that they are safe. If using resin, do not use the first 50mm, take a small sample to check hardening, and if possible re-examine each bolt placement after twenty-four hours.

Abseiling

On some of the Lancashire crags, considerable damage has been done to some routes by abseiling. In order to minimize such damage in future, climbers are asked to avoid popular parts of the crag if they wish to practise abseiling and not to use abseil descents if there are reasonable alternatives.

Access and Conservation

When the original Lancashire guide was produced nearly thirty years ago, there were significant access problems at many of the crags and quarries in the area. Fortunately, this bleak situation has now completely changed and access problems are certainly in the minority. Indeed, many landowners go out of their way to take a pro-active approach to climbers who visit their land.

It is pleasing to note that the old confrontational days have long been replaced by a mutual understanding amongst landowners, climbers and conservation groups. However, these changes have not come about by chance, but have developed by negotiation and by climbers themselves proving time and again that their presence does not represent any threat or inconvenience to the landowners. In fact at some sites it has been shown that the presence of climbers discourages unacceptable behaviour by other visitors at the crag and nearby.

In order that we can all continue to enjoy easy access to the crags in the area and indeed to make further improvements, it is necessary for climbers to continue to play their part by removing all litter from the crags, by parking sensibly and generally acting responsibly.

Climbing Restrictions

Climbers have an excellent record of both honouring seasonal climbing bans that have been implemented to protect nesting birds and also of avoiding parts of the crags where there are rare and vulnerable plants and trees. It is essential that climbers continue to abide by these voluntary agreements, so that we can maintain good relations with landowners and conservation bodies. After all, each group has a mutual interest in the crags and by maintaining a friendly and co-operative approach between the different interests, we can each contribute to achieving something that is beneficial to us all. On the other hand, long-established access could easily evaporate overnight if a minority of us fails to observe these bans or otherwise cause problems, such as thoughtless parking or causing litter.

In the North-West, one of the main environmental concerns is the protection of peregrines, but there are also a few parts of the crags where climbers have agreed not to climb in order to avoid damage to flora. These restrictions are described in the Access sections of the relevant crags, so please read these notes carefully before visiting any crag and if possible refer to the BMC's latest annual pamphlet on bird restrictions. As a general principle, Variable Restrictions are being sought by the BMC in order to provide greater freedom for climbers and to improve protection for important bird species. Therefore, if birds nest late, there may be a site notice indicating that a climbing ban is extended. Such notices should also be honoured.

If you visit a crag that has a ban in force that does not appear to be necessary, please still honour the ban, because there may well still be a valid reason for avoiding the crag. However, contact the BMC Access Representative, who will then investigate and, if necessary, get the situation adjusted for the future.

Up-to-Date Access Information
The latest access information can be obtained from the climbing press, BMC information points, the BMC (0161 445 4747) and from the BMC web site at www.thebmc.co.uk. All these sources of information are regularly updated.

Car Sharing
At some of the crags in this guidebook, parking facilities are limited. Therefore, car sharing is encouraged in order to reduce the pressure for parking spaces at these sites. Obviously, car sharing is also more environmentally friendly and saves brass.

Conservation
By far the best way that climbers can contribute towards conservation at the crags is to remove ALL litter (even if it was not left by themselves). However, climbers can also make a more positive contribution by undertaking limited conservation work at a crag, such as stile erection, or by assisting with bird ringing etc. If you are interested in making such a contribution, please contact the BMC Area Committee via the BMC Office, 177 Burton Road, Manchester, M20 2BB (0161 445 4747).

Access Problems
On many of the crags and quarries within this area the access situation is unknown, or has never been formalised. Even where an access agreement has been made, it is always possible that ownership of the crag may change. Therefore, whilst climbers should check the relevant access notes before visiting any crag it is also necessary to state that the inclusion of any crag or climb within this guide does not necessarily imply that there is a right to climb on it.

If you are challenged on any crag within this guidebook, the golden rule is to remain cool and polite. If a specific access agreement is described in this guidebook, show it to the person concerned and also show them this section if necessary. However, if the person still insists that you should leave, please do so without further aggravating the situation, but if possible try to take a note of their name and telephone number. Then contact your BMC Access Representative as soon as possible. Contact details for the current Access Representatives are listed in *Summit* magazine.

Hopefully, it will then be possible for the Access Representative to approach the landowners and to explain that it would be beneficial to all concerned to discuss and then agree a way that climbing could be managed at that site in a manner that addresses the landowner's concerns.

Theft from Parked Cars

Sadly, it is necessary to warn climbers that there have been several cases of theft from cars parked near many of the crags in the area. When the coast is clear, it only takes a thief a few seconds to break a window and snatch your precious climbing gear, so take sensible precautions. In particular, try to plan your climbing so that you do not need to leave any gear in the car, but if you do leave anything, store it out of sight in the boot.

It must also be stressed that climbing gear would not be stolen if there was not a market for stolen gear. So, if you are offered second-hand climbing gear at a low price from someone whom you do not know, please resist the temptation and if you are really suspicious, contact the police. If you don't, you are only encouraging increased theft and more anguish for your fellow climbers. Remember that if the thief can pass on the gear easily, next week he may well come back for more and you could be the one with broken glass on the back seat of your car and with no climbing gear.

Finally, if you are the victim of car crime, please report it to the Police, because action by them, such as the use of unmarked cars to check on vulnerable sites, will only be taken if they know that there is a problem.

Lancashire and Cheshire Area Committee

Work on the compilation of this guide has been co-ordinated by the Lancashire and Cheshire Area Committee of the BMC. This Committee also deals with ⬧ access problems and other issues of concern to climbers in the area. Any climber is welcome to attend the meetings of this Committee or to make representations about any matter which is of relevance to climbing in the area. Area meetings are advertised in *Summit* and *High* magazines.

BMC Guidebook Committee

Once the guidebook was initially compiled the Guidebook Committee of the BMC, Malc Baxter, Dave Gregory, Brian Griffiths, Chris Hardy, Graham Hoey, Geoff Milburn, Geoff Radcliffe, Keith Sharples, David Simmonite, Dave Turnbull, Mark Turnbull, Andrew Wood and Chris Wright, took over the task of editing, formatting and enhancing the volume so that it would complement the guidebooks that are available for the Peak District.

Acknowledgements

All climbing guidebooks build upon information that has been collated in previous definitive publications to an area. Therefore, sincere thanks must go to all those climbers who through the years have contributed to previous guidebooks to Lancashire and the North-West. In particular, Dave Cronshaw and Phil Kelly must be thanked for all their efforts in editing and collating the information for the previous guidebook, which has certainly stood the test of time.

Climbers may be interested to learn that the idea of a guidebook that specifically covered the Lancashire Area was first mooted with Eric Byne and the BMC in 1967. Unfortunately, these plans had to be scrapped because of funding problems at the time and so the first guidebook was produced by the magazine *Rocksport*. After the demise of *Rocksport*, Cicerone Press stepped in and was responsible for publishing three full guidebooks and two supplements to the area. However, as this guidebook is being published by the BMC it is appropriate to thank Walt Unsworth, his wife Dot and Brian Evans from Cicerone for supporting the area by producing so many guidebooks and also for the friendly way that they were willing to transfer the guide to the BMC's aegis. Without these guidebooks, development of the area would have been severely limited and the area could easily have been without a definitive publication for years.

The main guidebook team members are listed at the front of this guidebook and at the start of the sections to which they contributed most. They must all be thanked for the hard work that they have undertaken in writing the scripts and checking the route descriptions. In many cases this also involved recleaning some of the less-frequented routes and replacing ancient protection pegs and so their efforts have improved the overall quality of the climbing at many crags in the area.

We must also thank all the artists whose diagrams have been included and Jeremy Ashcroft for producing the endpaper map. The old adage that a picture is worth a thousand words is only true if they are prepared skillfully and meticulously. The originals of the diagrams certainly appear to be clear enough and we just hope that they will all reproduce well. All the diagrams have been scanned onto a computer and the route lines and numbers have then been added. This process was a little bit experimental and Geoff Radcliffe must be thanked for his technical assistance with resolving many of the scanning problems.

Thanks must also be given to all those climbers who assisted by proof-reading, or checking the technical information. The attempt to include comprehensive historical information also meant that it was necessary to contact many of the earlier activists and it is pleasing to note that so many of those who contributed to the 1969 guidebook were located and are still climbing. Sincere thanks are given to all of these contributors and to others who helped by checking small sections or by coming on working meets. We must mention in particular: Steve Barker, Dave Bates, John Belbin, Pete Black, Nick Bond, Frank Booth, Ian Conway, Adam Cropper, Brian Davison, Carl Dawson, Margaret Dewhurst, Al Evans, Ray Evans, Rick Graham, Andrew Gridley, Geoff Haigh, Dave Hollows, Tony Howard, Dave Kenyon, Ken Lathom, Mark Leach, Bill Lounds, Mick Lovatt, John Mason, Tony Mitchell, Russ Murray, Dave Musgrove, Ged

O'Sullivan, Duncan Parker, John Parker, Gareth Parry, Hank Pasquill, Keith Phizacklea, Mick Pooler, Paul Pritchard, Jim Ingham Riley, Gary Smith, Jessica Stam, Daniel Waddington, Tom Walkington, Alan White, Bob Whittaker, Dave Wilcock, Steve Wilcock and Wilf Williamson.

We must also thank Geoff Milburn for undertaking the final editing work on the guidebook. Geoff is one of the great unsung heroes of the British rock-climbing scene and has worked tirelessly on the often thankless task of producing both CC and BMC guidebooks. Therefore, we are extremely grateful that he has been able to advise us and let the Lancashire guide benefit from his years of experience. Geoff is a perfectionist and although this often adds to the workload of those producing the guides, in the end it ensures that the highest quality standards are maintained. For this guide, changes have been made in response to requests from Geoff, Dave Gregory and Graham Hoey (who have also read the script in detail), in a way that moves us towards the style used for the BMC Peak District guidebooks, whilst maintaining some distinctive differences. However, whilst these have taken time to implement and may have delayed the guide a little, now that the necessary changes have been made, we are pleased with the results and must thank both Geoff and Graham for their inputs.

Finally. thanks must go to Jean, my wife, for putting up with the reams of scripts and diagrams that have littered my office for several months and for help with the awkward and time-consuming tasks, such as scanning the diagrams, inserting the route lines, re-ordering the first ascent lists and regularly altering the formatting.

Les Ainsworth, Dave Cronshaw (Volume Compilers and Sub-editors), 1998

Standedge Area

Compiled by Brian Cropper, Bruce Goodwin and John Street

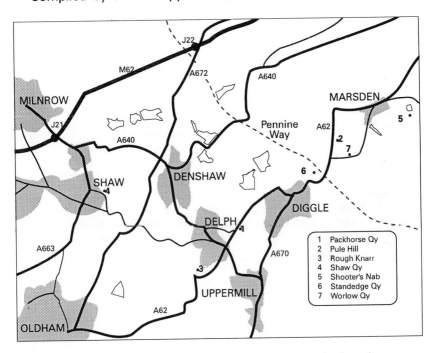

1	Packhorse Qy
2	Pule Hill
3	Rough Knarr
4	Shaw Qy
5	Shooter's Nab
6	Standedge Qy
7	Worlow Qy

This neglected area comprises a series of quarries on the moorlands to the north-east of Oldham. The two major crags, Pule Hill and Shooter's Nab, have to an extent been spared the quarrymen's activities as there are climbs on both quarried and natural gritstone, both giving unusual examples of quarry architecture. Both crags give excellent opportunities for a day's climbing and merit a visit from afar; the natural edge at Pule Hill is an excellent venue for soloing, or for beginners. Shaw Quarry, once billed as an 'enigma to climbing', is becoming increasingly popular as an evening venue and justifiably so.

The smaller crags at Pack Horse Quarry, Rough Knarr, Standedge Quarry and Worlow Quarry compare favourably with minor crags in more popular areas, but they have not generally attracted the attention that they deserve. However, this makes them an ideal venue for climbers who seek a quiet life.

Pack Horse Quarry   O.S. ref.   SD 995 084

Situation and Character
This quarry overlooks the A62 (Oldham–Huddersfield road) a kilometre north-east of the centre of Delph. It is a short gritstone quarry, which is a pleasant venue for an evening visit by middle-grade climbers.

History

Bob Whittaker discovered Pack Horse in the mid-Seventies, but no routes were done until 1982, when Whittaker remembered the quarry during a survey of the crags in the area. He returned with Ralph Pickering and started with *The Riffler*. The sharp end was then handed over to Pickering, who claimed *Times Passed*. Before leaving, they climbed four more lines on the left, including *White Horse* and *Dark Horse*. Whittaker returned a couple of nights later with Alan Noakes to add *Stallion* and three other routes.

In April 1983, shortly after the first guide to the crag had come out, Kev Thaw visited the quarry and soloed three routes, of which the most notable was probably *Ego Trip*. Then in 1984 Bruce Goodwin and John Lord claimed *Kestrel Crack*.

Approach

From Denshaw and the M62 (junction 21) follow the A6052 into Delph and at a sharp right-hand bend just before crossing the river, turn left. Follow this road to the A62, where the top of the quarry can be seen on the moorside, slightly to the right. Turn left and park immediately on the right, below a stone waterworks building. If travelling on the A62 from Oldham, the waterworks building is on the right, just past Delph, shortly after the top of the quarry can be seen. The quarry can be reached by a short walk diagonally rightwards across the moor.

The Climbs

All but one of the climbs are on the back wall and they are described from LEFT to RIGHT, starting at the left side of a grassy terrace.

1.   Keffer HVS 8m 5b   (1983)
Climb the thin crack one metre left of Shaz.

2.   Shaz 8m D   (1982)
The prominent crack in the left side of the wall.

3.   Time Switch 8m S   (1982)
The thin crack two metres to the right.

4.   Grey Donkey 8m HVS 5a   (1983)
Climb the wall between the cracks.

5.   White Horse 9m VS 4c   (1982)
The next crack has a small triangular niche at half-height. Climb this and finish over ledges.

6.   Ego Trip 9m E1 5a   (1983)
The wall one metre farther to the right.

7.   Dark Horse 9m VS 4c   (1982)
The cracks on the right are climbed directly.

8.   Stallion 9m HVS 5a   (1982)
Start up Dark Horse, then follow a right-curving crack to the top.

9.   Roundabout   13m   HS   4b   (1982)
Start as for Dark Horse, but make a rising traverse leftwards to finish up Shaz.

The next route starts at a lower level at a slab below a deep corner.

10.   Mark   10m   VD   (1982)
Climb the left edge of the slab to a grassy ledge, then finish up the crack behind.

★ **11.   Times Passed**   12m   VS   4c   (1982)
Climb the centre of the slab, then finish up a deep corner.

★ **12.   The Riffler**   10m   HS   4b   (1982)
The prominent crack in the steep slab around the arête is gained from the right.
Follow the crack and finish over ledges.

13.   Slabdab   12m   VD   (1982)
Start immediately right of the start of Riffler and follow the obvious weakness
over ledges.

*At right-angles to the back wall the rock is generally broken, but there is one
climb, immediately left of a deep sentry-box at two metres.*

★ **14.   Kestrel Crack**   HVS   5b   (1984)
Climb the appealing, straight crack on the left until it is possible to step left to a
large foothold. Finish directly.

First Ascents at Pack Horse Quarry

1982 Mar   **Shaz, Time Switch, White Horse, Dark Horse, The Riffler**   Bob
              Whittaker, Ralph Pickering
1982 Mar   **Times Passed**   Ralph Pickering, Bob Whittaker
1982 Apr   **Stallion, Roundabout, Mark, Slabdab**   Bob Whittaker, Alan Noakes
1983 Apr   **Keffer, Grey Donkey, Ego Trip**   Kevin Thaw (solo)
1984   **Kestrel Crack**   Bruce Goodwin, John Lord

Pule Hill Rocks   O.S. ref.   SE 032 108

> '*Perhaps more good routes will be discovered when a little
> cleaning up has been done, and the peg man should also be
> able to amuse himself here.*'
>
>   Tony Howard, 1965

Situation and Character

The crag, visible from the road, stretches for approximately 900 metres along
the top of Pule Hill; roughly 500 metres east of the Oldham–Huddersfield road
(A62), where it runs down from Standedge Cutting into Marsden.

The rocks can be divided into two distinct types; the natural rocks and the
quarried rocks. The outcrop has a clean rocky top, reaches a height of up to 12
metres, and gives both strenuous and delicate climbs on rough, sound gritstone.
The routes hereabouts tend to be steep and unusually juggy, though the
occasional '*hollow*' flake adds to the excitement. The quarry attains a height of

15 metres with generally excellent, clean rock, but some of the rock is brittle and fissile.

The hill is a favourite spot with hang-gliding enthusiasts, and strong winds often prevail, which accounts for the quick-drying nature of the rock. The rocks' close proximity to the road, sunny western aspect and numerous soloing possibilities make this an excellent place for an evening visit.

History

The first real climber to leave his mark on the rocks seems to have been George Bower, who scrambled here in the early 1920s. However, considering the natural attraction of the edge, it is surprising to find that its main development as a climbing ground came at a much later date.

Probably the first climbers to give the edge any real attention were the Chew Valley Cragsmen, prominent amongst them being Graham West and Roy Brown, who visited the rocks occasionally during the 1940s and 1950s.

In the summer of 1957 Tony Howard, Alwyn Whitehead and Brian Hodgkinson paid several visits and within a few weekends they had accounted for most of the routes on The Outcrop, although several of these had probably been climbed before. The base for their operations was the infamous cave behind The Flying Buttress, known as the Trog 'Ole, where many pleasant nights were spent.

In October 1960, the quarry was visited by members of the Rimmon M.C. and two routes were added, these being *Tut* by Brian Woods and *Delilah* by Tony Jones. In January of 1962, Malc Baxter of the Manchester Gritstone C.C. added *The Ratcher* and *The Great Scoop*, although the latter route may have been climbed earlier by Howard. A few years later the Rimmon paid another visit, climbing most of the cracks on Leprosy Wall, but kept no records of first ascent details. They did however write-up 55 routes for the 1965 BMC *Saddleworth–Chew Valley Area* guidebook. Several years later Bob Whittaker and Brian Cropper reclimbed all of these cracks, and others, but chose to name and record only a selection for the 1976 *Chew Valley* guidebook.

In the late 1960s, *Krilt* and *Wellington* were added by Bill Tweedale and towards the end of 1969, Howard and Bill Birch climbed, respectively, *Odyssey*, and the girdle of the quarry – *Amazing Revelation*. Shortly after this, someone made a Direct Start to Delilah using one peg, which was dispensed with by Brian Cropper in 1974. Cropper then continued to the top via the final pitch of Amazing Revelation and eliminated the pegs. During this climb he noticed a possible line immediately to the right and so he went on to link this to the Direct Start to Delilah to give a more independent line, which he named *Gold Rush*. On subsequent ascents of the girdle the aid was reduced to three pegs, but it took almost 25 more years before a completely aid-free ascent was recorded by Dave Cronshaw and Les Ainsworth.

The next major additions, climbed in March 1977, were *Spellbound* by Nick Colton and *Godspell* by Jim Campbell, with Con Carey seconding both routes. Within three days these two routes were repeated by Gabriel Regan, who thought that he had just made the first ascents of both lines. Later that year John Smith added *The Bulger*, although this may have been done before.

Brian Middleton on e first ascei (VS 5a), Lumbutts Quarry.   *Photo: Bob Whittaker*

The period 1979–81 was largely dominated by Paul Cropper who found *Midas Direct, Bey Reyt Wall* and *Mega Factor*. Cropper also climbed the previously overlooked *Necronomicon* in April 1980, taking full advantage of the bolt on *Odyssey* which had recently been replaced.

In 1981, Gary Gibson got a look in with *Lethal Lemon* and the vicious *Blood Finger*, as well as confusing issues by renaming variations on existing routes on the first wall of Triple Wall. Virtually all these variations had been climbed before and hence, where possible, the original names have been restored.

Routes continued to appear throughout the Eighties. 1982 saw Mark Kendall produce *Schmarren* and *Star* whilst Brian Cropper added his own *Brian's Route, Sobeit* also appeared that year. Windy Wall saw some activity in 1983, Cropper's *Celtic* passed through the overhangs that *The Swinger* avoided and Con Carey put *Route 1* and *Route 2* up the very steep wall right of *Coffin Corner*. Then in 1983, the crag was completely re-written and appeared in the Lancashire area guidebook. There were however, still lines to be found by the mid-Eighties, *No Exit* and *The 8-Foot Kid* being amongst the better.

Approach and Access
From Oldham follow the A62 Huddersfield road – to the top of Standedge Cutting at the crest of the Pennines. After a further 500 metres, the Great Western Hotel will be seen on the left and just past this is The Carriage House Hotel on the right. Park at a lay-by on the right-hand side of the road, about 400 metres past The Carriage House, two kilometres before Marsden. A short path from this point leads first right, then back left to the first climbs and The Sentinel. The quarry lies more or less directly behind the tunnel ventilation shafts and the main part of the outcrop stretches rightwards from this.

The rocks are the property of the National Trust and climbing is permitted, provided that the Trust's bye-laws are adhered to.

The Climbs
The climbs are described from LEFT to RIGHT, beginning at some broken rocks 30 metres to the left of The Sentinel. On the right-hand side of these rocks, a wrinkled face has a short dog-legged crack at mid-height.

1.   Forerunner 6m S 4a   (Pre-1965)
The wrinkled face is climbed rightwards to finish up the arête.

The Sentinel
The inspiring natural buttress directly above the lay-by is known as The Sentinel.

2.   The Peeler 6m S 4a   (Pre-1965)
At the left-hand end of The Sentinel is a steep crack which is climbed past a small overhang.

Julie-Ann Clyma calm on **Windy Wall** (S 4a), Pule Hill.   *Photo: Roger Payne*

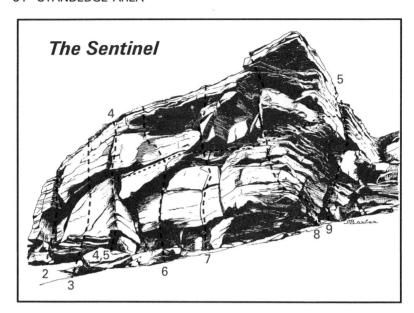

The Sentinel

★ 3.   Overlapping Wall 6m E1 6a   (1966)
A very difficult and necky problem. Start three metres to the right of The Peeler
at an obvious handhold and climb directly, passing the overlap with great
difficulty.

4.   No Traverse 6m HS 4b   (Pre-1965)
Climb the short, stepped arête and finish up a crack.

★ 5.   Tony's Traverse 18m HS 4b   (Pre-1965)
Climb No Traverse until a semi-hand-traverse along the obvious break leads
rightwards for six metres. Move up and across to a comfortable stance (*The
Throne*). Continue traversing around the arête and finish up a short wall.

★ 6.   No Exit 8m VS 4c   (1986-87)
One metre to the right is a short finger-crack. Climb directly up the crack and
steep wall above on surprisingly good holds.

★ 7.   Traverse Not 8m HS 4c   (Pre-1965)
Start to the right at an undercut, faint groove. Climb the fingertip layback and
short crack to reach *The Bed*. Finish direct or slightly rightwards.

★ 8.   Bed End 10m VD   (Pre-1965)
Start at the right-hand side of The Sentinel. Climb leftwards via a Z-shaped
crack to reach *The Throne*, moving up and slightly leftwards to finish.

9.   Sentinel Wall 6m VD   (Pre-1965)
Climb directly up the left-hand edge of the easy chimney on the right side of
The Sentinel.

Pule Hill Quarry
50 metres to the right is the start of Pule Hill Quarry which is divided into three main sections, The Northern Section, Leprosy Wall and The Triple Walls.

Northern Section
At the left-hand end of the quarry, the most obvious feature is a man-made wall halfway up the face. Starting below and two metres left of this is:

10. Schmarren 10m VS 4c   (1982)
Start below a large sandy bowl and climb the wall using a crack on the left. Finish directly above the bowl, taking care with the rock.

11. Star 10m HVS 4c   (1982)
Climb the wall on the right-hand side.

12. Skull Climb 10m VD   (Pre-1965)
Climb the flake crack to reach a cave on the left of the man-made wall, then move rightwards to finish up a groove.

13. The Iliad 10m VS 5a   (1977)
Start about one metre right of the man-made wall and climb directly up the wall via thin cracks and a wide horizontal break.

14. Retreat 8m M   (Pre-1965)
10 metres to the right is a corner capped by a triangular roof. Move rightwards across the slab, then climb up to the overhang which is avoided on the left.

15. Midas 9m VS 4c   (1965-74)
Start on the right-hand side of a sandy bowl. Trend leftwards to a ledge, then go up a short crack to finish up the arête.

★ **16. Midas Direct** 9m HVS 5a   (1981)
Start as for Midas, then gain the shallow scoop with difficulty and finish directly.

★ **17. Lethal Lemon** 9m E1 5a   (1981)
The vague arête one metre to the right is gained and followed directly.

18. Geoff's Groove 8m M   (Pre-1965)
The obvious V-groove on the right.

Spellbound (HVS, 5b) used to follow the overhung arête at the left side of the next buttress. However, there are no records of the route being repeated since the bottom section of the roof collapsed.

★★ **19. The Great Scoop** 15m VS 5a   (1962)
Start at a lower level, below a distinctive orange slab, near a boulder on the ground. Step up and traverse right across a slab to gain a hanging corner, then make a long reach to gain the ledge above and to the right. Step right and finish up the top wall.

★★ **20. Godspell** 12m E2 5b   (1977)
Gain the hanging corner of Great Scoop directly and continue to the ledge above. Traverse left to a flake at the centre of the large roof. Hand-traverse

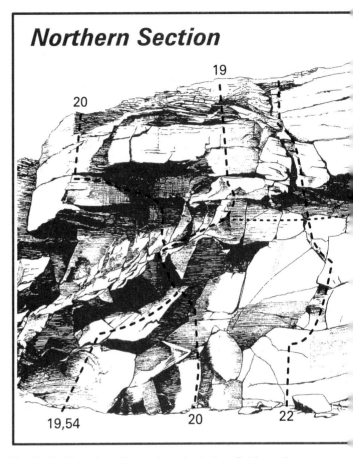

Northern Section

wildly leftwards until a foothold on the arête can be gained, then finish up the steep wall.

21. Sandy Hole 10m HVS 5b   (1986-87)
Climb the short, overhanging crack that leads to a sandy hole three metres farther right, then continue over the blocks above.

22. Annual Route 9m S 4a   (Pre-1965)
Gain a ledge at head-height, then layback the corner to reach an overhung ledge which is quitted by a wide crack on the left.

★ **23. The Bulger** 10m VS 5b   (1977)
Start two metres right of Annual Route. Climb the bulging wall to reach a ledge just below the break. Move right, then finish up Dedfer or its left-hand edge.

24. Dedfer 9m S 4a (Pre-1965)
Start around the arête and climb the hanging corner, passing a ledge to finish up a V-shaped groove. The ledge can also be gained by the arête to the left of the corner.

★ **25. Blood Finger** 10m HVS 5c (1981)
Start just right of Dedfer and climb a short overhanging finger-crack, moving right on a ledge to finish up the wall on the right of a faint rib.

26. So Sew 14m VD (1986-87)
Start about four metres farther right and climb the left-hand side of the slab, then step right to finish up the centre of the wall.

27. Sew 14m VD (Pre-1965)
Climb the right-hand edge of the slab to gain a ledge, then traverse left for three metres and finish up the centre of the wall as for So Sew.

28. Wall and Flake   14m   VS   5a   (Pre-1965)
Start to the right of the arête and follow the cracked wall leftwards past a small
cleft to reach a ledge. Finish up the wide flake.

Leprosy Wall

*This is the long, steep wall on the right, which contains several caves. It is
bounded on its left by a deep chimney.*

29. Tut   15m   HS   4b   (1960)
Start up the chimney, then follow a short crack to gain a cave on the right. Step
up left under the overhang, then stride back right above the cave to a good
foothold. Finish up the arête – exposed.

30. Krilt   14m   HVS   5a   (1966)
Climb the left side of the sandy, ground-level cave to reach a layback flake.
Follow this and finish directly up the wall just left of a short groove.

31. Aquarius   17m   VS   4c   (1970)
From the right-hand side of the sandy cave pull out right to a short crack which
leads to the upper cave. Move out leftwards and finish up the short groove, just
right of Krilt.

★ **32. Mega Factor**   14m   HVS   5a   (1979)
From three metres right of the cave, climb the wall using small ledges, directly
to the right-hand side of the upper cave. Step left and finish directly up the
clean wall.

33. Apollo   14m   VS   4c   (1965-74)
Climb the cracked wall on the right, step right, then finish up a short jamming
crack and a vague flake.

34. Venus   14m   VS   4c   (1979-83)
Start four metres to the right and climb a wide crack to gain an obvious niche
with a triangular roof. Exit left via a flake, and finish up the shattered wall.

35. Space Walk   14m   VS   4c   (1965-74)
Climb Venus to the niche and leave this by a thin crack on the right. Step right
and finish direct.

36. Wellington   14m   VS   4c   (1966)
Start three metres to the right and climb the steep crack to below an ill-defined
chimney, moving right past a '*wobble-block*' to finish direct.

37. Sinbad   14m   VS   4c   (1986-87)
Two metres right of Wellington, climb directly up the crack past a small sandy
cave.

38. Appendix   10m   VS   4c   (1965-74)
Climb the wide crack that leads to the right side of a large cave, then leave this
by the right-hand wall.

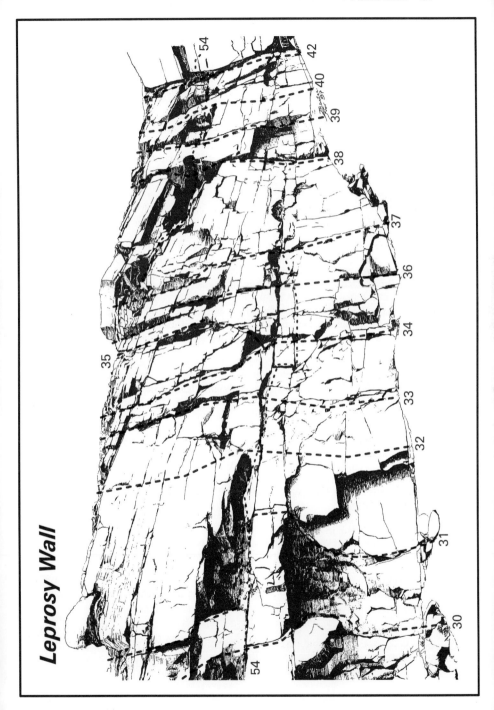

Leprosy Wall

39. Sandman 10m VS 4b   (1976)
Start three metres right of Appendix and climb a short groove and crack which
has a loose finish.

40. Bey Reyt Wall 10m HVS 4c   (1979)
Start two metres right and climb the wall which contains a sandy hole low down.

41. Boozer's Way 11m HS 4b   (Pre-1965)
Climb cracks left of the angle of the wall into a recess, which is in turn vacated
using a crack up its left edge.

42. Fusion Chimney 12m HVS 4c   (1965-74)
This chimney that bounds Leprosy Wall on its right.

First Triple Wall
*The remaining rock in the quarry is known as the Triple Walls The first of these
lies at right-angles to Leprosy Wall and has a deep trough/crevasse directly
below it and a huge sandy cave at two-thirds height.*

★★★ **43. Necronomicon** 17m E3 5c (1 pt)   (1980)
Very well-protected, with some exciting moves above the overlap. Climb Fusion
Chimney to the first horizontal break, then move right and climb a thin, stepped
crack to gain the left-hand side of the large cave. Gain the bolt in the wall
above and use it for aid, then free-climb to the top.

44. Odyssey 15m A1/E1 5b   (1969)
From a metre left of large blocks across the crevasse, make a long reach across
to a peg and use this, then continue past a drill-hole (bong or wooden wedge
also used for aid) to the centre of the sandy cave. Exit from the left-hand side
of this, as for Necronomicon.
Variation (5c): it is possible to join the route just above the large drill hole, by
traversing left from Odyssey Variant, thereby avoiding the peg start.

★ **45. Odyssey Variant** 17m E3 5c   (1979)
From the right-hand side of the large blocks, surmount the jutting nose using a
convenient drill-hole to reach a large ledge. Continue up the thin crack to reach
the right-hand side of the sandy cave. Finish as for Necronomicon.

★★ **46. Delilah** 18m E1 5b   (1960)
An awkward start, but a good route. Start just to the right and thrash up the
narrowing cleft to a ledge on the left. Gain, then climb, the cracked corner on
the right, step right and finish up the centre of the wall.

★★ **47. Gold Rush** 12m E2 6a   (1974)
Climb the steep wall two metres right to a small triangular ledge (peg). Stand on
the ledge and finish diagonally rightwards by a series of deceptively
innocent-looking ledges. Finish easily up the top arête.

★ **48. Sampson** 9m HVS 5b   (1965-74)
Start at the right-hand side of the wall by a protruding piece of iron. Move up
and left to the iron and finish up a thin bulging crackline.

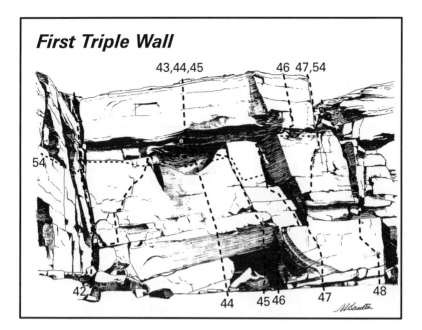

First Triple Wall

43,44,45   46 47,54

54

42   44   45 46   47   48

Second Triple Wall
The Second Triple Wall is parallel to the First and is set well back.

★ **49. The Ratcher** 8m VS 5a   (1962)
Start from below and just right of a sandy cave. Move up then go rightwards
past a sharp fingerhold to reach a flat hold. Stand on this with difficulty, then
go easily to the top.

★ **50. The 8-Foot Kid** 8m VS 5b   (1986-87)
A counter-diagonal to The Ratcher, starting some two metres right at some
well-worn, chipped holds.

Third Triple Wall
*The last of the Triple Walls lies at right-angles to the others and the routes on
it lie facing Leprosy Wall at the end of the trough.*

51. Brian's Route 9m HS 4b   (1982)
Start just left of the chimney and climb directly up the thin crack, followed by a
jamming crack, to the top.

52. Sandy Cleft 9m VD   (Pre-1965)
Climb straight up the chimney.

53. Green Ridge 8m D   (Pre-1965)
Climb the wall right of Sandy Cleft, moving right to finish up the ridge.

★ **54.   Amazing Revelation**   108m   HVS   5a,4b,4c,4a,4c,5a,5a   (1969/1974/1997)
This is a left to right girdle of most of the quarry. It crosses a lot of interesting ground, but the best climbing does not start until close to the right-hand side of Leprosy Wall.
1.   10m.   As for Great Scoop, step up and traverse right across a slab to gain a hanging corner, then make a long reach to gain the ledge above.
2.   12m.   Traverse round the prow into a corner, then cross the right wall past a sandy hollow to belay below the V-groove on Dedfer.
3.   14m.   Make a long reach right for a jug, then follow the undercut foot-ledge round the rib (balancy), to a corner and continue across easy ledges to a belay on a block above the arête of Sew.
4.   13m.   Step across the chimney and go up into the cave on Tut. Continue rightwards to reach another cave and belay on an iron stanchion.
5.   26m.   Follow the gently descending foot-ledge across the shattered wall for 10 metres to the niche with a triangular roof on Venus, then step down on a jammed block and continue the traverse with hands on the ledge for about six metres to a very small cave on Sinbad. Go up the steep cracks of Sinbad to a cave at the top of the crag, then continue right and belay at the right side of a much larger cave. Large Friends useful.
6.   21m.   Swing boldly right on good holds to another cave and continue to the corner. Make an exposed hand traverse right past two pegs to gain a sandy cave and belay at the right side of this.
7.   12m.   Climb down a thin crack to a ledge on Delilah, then make a surprisingly off-balance move to reach the corner crack and climb up and left to the arête. The down climbing can be avoided by following the obvious, short hand traverse. Continue along the break to another ledge and finish up the delightful little arête.

The Outcrop
To the right of the quarry there are several buttresses of natural gritstone.

Crude Crack Area
The first natural buttress on which there are any recorded routes lies about 70 metres right of the end of the quarry, past lesser rocks. The buttress can be further identified by a large hollow in its centre and a very short crack on its left that leads to a ledge:

55.   Crude Crack   9m   D   (Pre-1965)
Climb the crack to gain the ledge on the left, then avoid an escape by climbing the mediocre, shattered crack to the top.

56.   Tariff Wall   9m   HVS   5b   (1979-83)
Climb into the hollow, then move left under the roof to the arête and climb it finishing just right of Crude Crack.

57.   The Token   8m   E1   5b   (1979-83)
A direct finish from the hollow, via the overhang above.

58.   Godsend   9m   HS   4b   (Pre-1965)
Ascend into the hollow, then leave it by moving up and out to the right until a good finishing hold is reached.

59. Dusky Doddle 8m VD (Pre-1965)
Climb directly up the wall on the right-hand side of the hollow via ledges.

Wrinkled Wall Area
The next buttresses lie about 20 metres farther right and can be identified by an obvious overhanging corner. The first climbs lie on a roughly square buttress to the left of the corner.

60. Atlas 9m D (1979-83)
From the top of the sloping-topped block step across and ascend directly up the centre of the square buttress.

61. Whacker's Wall 10m D (1965-74)
Start just left of the overhanging corner. From a short groove, climb the wall and turn the second of two overhangs on the left.

★★ **62. Amen** 10m VD (Pre-1965)
A classic gritstone chimney/crack with superb holds. Climb straight up the overhanging corner-crack. The final three metres are very steep.

★ **63. Sobeit** 10m VS 4c (1982)
Start just right of the right arête of the corner and move up and left to the arête. Then climb this directly on its right-hand side.

64. Wrinkled Wall 10m S 4c (Pre-1965)
As for Sobeit, but avoid a move left by continuing directly up the wrinkled face and passing an overhung ledge.

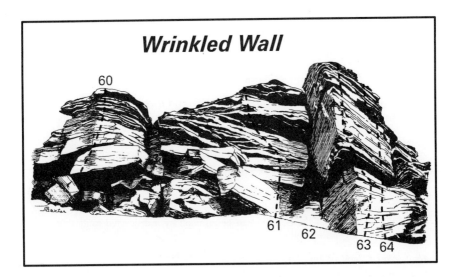

Wrinkled Wall

60

61 62

63 64

Flying Buttress

66 67

68

66 67 68

Flying Buttress Area
The next buttress is characterized by a prominent archway, the front of which forms the renowned Flying Buttress.

★ **65. Minotaur** 9m HVS 5a (Pre-1965)
Start under the left-hand entrance to the archway and bridge up, then swing on to the outer face (exposed) and finish direct.

★★ **66. Flying Buttress** 12m S 4a (Pre-1965)
Interesting rock architecture, excellent climbing and fine positions, make this a must for any visitors, especially on a sunny summer evening. Start at the lowest point of the buttress. Climb a short wall and thin polished crack, then finish up the final wall on good holds.
Variation Finish (4a): make an excellent, exposed traverse left to finish up the arête.

67. Flying Arête 12m VD (1979-83)
The right-hand arête of the buttress can be climbed by a disjointed route that starts two metres farther right.

68. Pilot Crack 12m VD (Pre-1965)
Climb the wide crack on the right to the archway, then finish up the short overhanging corner by some unusual moves.

Windy Wall Area

60 metres right and past some small buttresses (which give many good problems) is the steep wrinkled face that is known as Windy Wall.

★★ **69. Hangover Edge** 8m S 4b (Pre-1965)
Climb the overhanging left arête of Windy Wall on improving holds. Despite being relatively short, this climb gives an unexpected feeling of exposure.

★★ **70. Windy Wall** 8m S 4a (Pre-1965)
A similar, though slightly easier climb up the face a metre to the right, gives steep wall climbing on good holds.

71. The Swinger 12m VD (Pre-1965)
Start four metres left of the obvious corner in the centre of the next buttress. Go up the wall to the overhang, then hand-traverse left and finish up the edge of the buttress.

72. Celtic 9m HVS 5a (1983)
Follow The Swinger to where that route traverses left, then finish directly over the stepped overhangs.

★ **73. Kletterschuhe Capers** 12m S 4a (Pre-1965)
Take a fairly direct line up the wall three metres left of the corner, past a large block near the top and a slight deviation left at mid-height. The line can be straightened out at HVS, 5a.

★ **74. Coffin Corner** 9m VD (Pre-1965)
This follows the obvious corner. Go up the chimney to *The Coffin*, then swing right to reach good holds and continue more easily.

75. Route 1 9m HVS 4c (1983)
Climb the overhanging wall and arête just right of Coffin Corner.

76. Route 2 9m VS 4c (1983)
Climb the steep wall three metres farther right.

77. Blind Buttress 9m VD (Pre-1965)
Start just right of Route 2 and climb the left side of a thin slab on to the face, past two large 'eye-sockets'.

The Tomb

The Tomb is a small cave which is higher up and to the right.

78. Furly 'ard 8m VD (Pre-1965)
Climb directly up the centre of the face on the right, passing several horizontal breaks to the top.

★★ **79. Overhanging Arête** 8m VD (Pre-1965)
Just to the right, the undercut arête is tricky to start; the rest is pure delight.

80. Left Route 8m HS 4b (Pre-1965)
Start two metres right of the left arête of the outer face of the buttress and climb straight up.

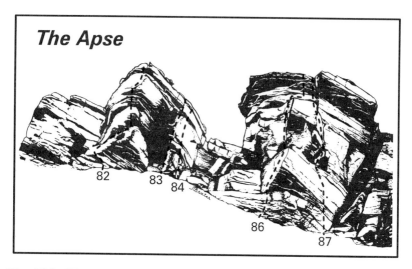

The Apse

81. Right Wall 8m VD   (Pre-1965)
Climb directly up the wall, a little to the right of centre.

The Apse
10 metres to the right, Wizened Wall has a number of short problems. 20 metres right of this is a buttress containing a large cave in its right wall, known as The Apse.

★ **82. Apse Arête Indirect** 9m VD   (Pre-1965)
Climb the arête left of *The Apse* gaining it from the left by a short traverse along an undercut ledge.

83. Apse Crack 6m VD   (Pre-1965)
Climb the crack above the right-hand edge of *The Apse* roof.

84. Apse Wall 6m VD   (Pre-1965)
A barely independent line up the wall just right of Apse Crack.

85. Eel 8m VD   (Pre-1965)
Opposite *The Apse* is a smaller cave with a block at its entrance. From the block, hand-traverse rightwards on improving holds and finish up the wall.

★ **86. S.H.M.** 9m VD   (Pre-1965)
Round to the right is a scooped arête. Move right on to this, then go leftwards until a good hold enables a swing right to be made and so gain a ledge. Finish direct.

87. Has Been 9m VD   (Pre-1965)
Go up the wall two metres right of the arête to a ledge, then climb a short groove and finish up a crack.

88. Ladder Ridge 8m M   (Pre-1965)
Four metres to the right, climb a series of step-like ledges and the scoop above.

Scoop Wall Area

89. Deceit 10m VD   (Pre-1965)
Climb the chimney on the right, passing outside a large chockstone. Avoid
walking off by traversing across the hanging wall, then finish up the arête.

★ **90. Flack** 10m E1 5b   (1965-74)
Start just right of Deceit and climb directly up the left-hand side of an arête,
with a hard move to reach a conveniently-placed chipped hold.

★★ **91. Scoop Wall** 9m VS 5a   (Pre-1965)
A really good problem, demanding faith in friction at the start. On the
right-hand side of the arête, climb the wall via an obvious scoop which is hard
to enter.

92. Cloister Wall 9m S 4b   (Pre-1965)
A three-metre-high block leads to a platform. Climb the short arête to *The
Cloister* (an unusual hole with a pillar inside), which is passed with difficulty
via the overhang on the left or, better, the bulging wall on the right.

93. Suspension 6m S 4c   (Pre-1965)
Climb the severely undercut crack which contains two chockstones and has a
gymnastic start.

94. Cracked Ridge 8m VD   (Pre-1965)
Climb the arête which bounds the wall on the right, then gain the slight scoop
on the right with difficulty and follow it to the top.

50 metres to the right, and past a series of short problem walls, is:

Square Buttress

95. Squaring the Circle 9m HVS 5a   (1983)
Climb the left-hand wall of Square Buttress about one metre left of the arête on the left wall.

★ **96. Bung** 8m HVS 5a   (1975)
Climb directly up the left-hand side of the arête with a long stretch for a ledge at six metres. Very hard to start.

★★ **97. Square Buttress** 8m VS 4c   (Pre-1965)
Trend leftwards up the front face of the buttress to a wide horizontal pocket. The step into the '*eye*' is awkward and is facilitated using a small right fingerhold. From the incut ledge climb the overhangs direct.

Right of Square Buttress are a few broken rocks and then 30 metres farther right is:

98. Last Ridge 6m M   (Pre-1965)
Climb straight up a broken ridge.

99. The Last Fling 6m S 4c   (Pre-1965)
The undercut nose to the right is climbed direct.

First Ascents at Pule Hill

1960 Oct	**Delilah, Tut** Brian Woods, Tony Jones
1962 Jan	**The Great Scoop, The Ratcher** Malc Baxter
Pre-1965	**Tony's Traverse** Tony Howard
Pre-1965	**Geoff's Groove, Forerunner, The Peeler, Annual Route, No Traverse, Traverse Not, Bed End, Sentinel Wall, Skull Climb, Retreat, Dedfer, Sew, Wall and Flake, Boozer's Way, Sandy Cleft, Green Ridge, Crude Crack, Dusky Doddle, Amen, Wrinkled Wall, Minotaur, Flying Buttress, Pilot Crack, Hangover Edge, Windy Wall, The Swinger, Kletterschuhe Capers, Coffin Corner, Blind Buttress, Furly 'ard, Overhanging Arête, Left Route, Right Wall, Apse Arête Indirect, Apse Crack, Apse Wall, Eel, S.H.M., Has Been, Ladder Ridge, Deceit, Scoop Wall, Cloister Wall, Suspension, Cracked Ridge, Square Buttress, Last Ridge, The Last Fling** Members of Rimmon M.C., mainly Tony Howard, Tony Jones, Brian Hodgkinson, Jeff Sykes, Paul Seddon, Brian Woods
1966	**Krilt, Wellington** Bill Tweedale, John Greenwood
1966	**Overlapping Wall** Tony Nichols
1969 Sep	**Odyssey** (A1/E1) Bill Birch, Tony Howard (alts)
1969 Oct 18	**Amazing Revelation** (7pts aid) Tony Howard, Bill Birch (alts)
	3 pts aid on final pitch eliminated by Brian Cropper, Stuart Thirsk, Apr 1974. Aid completely eliminated, Dave Cronshaw, Les Ainsworth, 1997.
1965-74	**Midas, Apollo, Space Walk, Appendix, Fusion Chimney, Sampson, Whacker's Wall, Flack**
1970 Apr 11	**Aquarius** Tony Howard, Bill Birch (alts)
1974 Apr	**Gold Rush** Brian Cropper, Stuart Thirsk
1975	**Bung**
1976 Oct	**Sandman** Brian Cropper, Stuart Thirsk
1977 Mar 5	**The Iliad** Brian Cropper
1977 Mar 12	**Godspell** Jim Campbell, Con Carey
	A fine discovery.

1977 Mar 14	**Spellbound** Nick Colton, Con Carey
1977 Sep 18	**The Bulger** John Smith
1979 Apr	**Bey Reyt Wall** Paul Cropper, Brian Cropper
1979 June 19	**Odyssey Variant** (1 bolt aid) Nick Colton
1979 July 3	**Mega Factor** Paul Cropper, Lawrence Foyle
1980 Apr 25	**Necronomicon** Paul Cropper
	High quality climbing.
1981 Apr 5	**Blood Finger** Gary Gibson
1981 Apr	**Midas Direct** Paul Cropper, Brian Cropper
1981	**Lethal Lemon** Gary Gibson
1982	**Sobeit**
1982	**Schmarren, Star** Mark Kemball
1982	**Brian's Route** Brian Cropper
1979-83	**Venus, Tariff Wall, The Token, Atlas, Flying Arête, Godsend**
1983 May	**Celtic** Brian Cropper
1983	**Route 1, Route 2, Squaring the Circle** Con Carey
1986-87	**No Exit, Sandy Hole, Sinbad, The 8-Foot Kid, So Sew**

Rough Knarr   O.S. ref.   SD 981 071

Situation and Character

These quarries are situated between Delph and Scouthead near the A62, above a minor road which runs parallel to the A62, and about one kilometre west of the centre of Delph.

The views into the Chew Valley are incomparable, so it is well worth a visit.

History

Rough Knarr was visited by members of the Rimmon M.C. in the early 1960s, when Tony Howard, Brian Hodgkinson, Tony Jones, Jeff Sykes and Brian Woods did most of the obvious lines. However, no records were kept and in 1968 the quarry was rediscovered by Bob Whittaker, who climbed the obvious line of *Denshaw*. Though local climbers probably visited the quarry, there were no further recorded ascents at the quarry for 14 years, until Geoff Haigh, Derek Wright and Gordon Mason found the crag. Amongst them, this group added another dozen routes, the most notable of which was the trio of Delph, Dobcross and Diggle, though it is possible that these three lines had been climbed previously.

Activity for the current guidebook has produced five more recorded routes and reports of potential new records (if not new routes) in the Second Bay and to the right of Half Moon. Dave Gregory was involved in three of these ascents, which were his first new routes in Lancashire. It is pleasing to note that even such ardent Peak District devotees as Gregory can find challenges in the Lancashire quarries and it is hoped that during his retirement he makes many more visits.

Approach and Access

From Denshaw and the M62 (junction 21) follow the A6052 into Delph, then a couple of hundred metres after crossing the river, look out for the Bull's Head pub on the left and a wedge-shaped building (Delph Library) in front of you. Fork right on to Stoneswood Road immediately right of the library and follow this for a little over one kilometre to arrive at a bend with a *Road Narrows* sign and a metal gate on the right. There is limited parking by the gate. Through the gate the First Bay is immediately on the left and the path ahead leads past the Second and Third Bays.

The Climbs

The quarry is split into three obvious bays and the climbs are described from LEFT to RIGHT.

First Bay

There has been a rockfall on the left-hand side of this bay and so no routes are recorded, but on the right hand side there are several slanting grooves. At the centre of the quarry is a left-slanting groove with a blue paint splash at its base.

1.   Right Route   9m   VD   (1983-87)
Climb the groove and crack direct. Access to the foot is overgrown.

2.   Golfer's Groove   9m   S   4a   (1983-87)
Start to the right at a groove with an overhang at mid-height, further identified by an arrow and cross painted at its base. Follow the crack and groove to the top.

★★ **3.   Josh's Path**   10m   HS   4a   (1997)
On the right is a deep alcove. Ascend the left wall of the alcove to reach flakes, followed by a crack. Above the crack traverse left to avoid poor rock and ascend to the top (possible escape route right and up from the top of the crack). A very neat route.

4.   Karoshi   10m   HVS   5a   (1997)
Climb the left-leaning, twin cracks at the back of the deep alcove, passing large blocks at the top.

5.   Anit   10m   VD   (1997)
Immediately to the right is a crack/corner. Ascend this directly past a slightly overhanging block to a belay at the top of the groove.

6.   The Printed Page   8m   HS   4a   (1983-87)
Four metres to the right there is a steep slab. Start below an overhang to the left of the slab. Move up and swing right on to the slab, then follow the left edge of the arête to finish.

7.   The Open Book   8m   D   (1983-87)
The wide crack on the right is obvious and pleasant.

8.   Knarrly Groove   10m   VS   4c   (1997)
Two metres to the right is a shallow, slanting groove. Ascend this with difficulty to a ledge. Move up using the corner and the face to the left, to enter a deeper groove and reach a belay in the corner at the top, or scramble to a stake higher up.

Second Bay
At the back of the Second Bay there is an obvious slab.

9.   Pillar Front   10m   E1   5c   (1989)
Climb the overhanging crack right of the slab to a nose, then finish up the front
of the pillar.

Third Bay
*The last and finest of the three bays. It contains a steep 18-metre slab in its
centre. The first routes are situated on this.*

★ **10.   Delph**   12m   VD   (1982)
Climb the groove on the left of the slab until a step left can be made on to the
edge, then follow the edge of the slab all the way.

★ **11.   Delcross**   13m   HVS   5a   (1983)
Start at a groove at the left side of the slab to a small triangular niche, then
climb the wall directly above, crossing a small overlap near the top.

★ **12.   Dobcross**   15m   S   4a   (1982)
Follow the groove as for Delcross, then climb the obvious stepped, right-leading
cracks.

★★ **13.   Diggle**   17m   VS   5a   (1982)
An excellent route, with the crux at the bottom, after which it relents to 4b/c.
Start one metre right and climb over the overlap to an obvious slot and continue
to a triangular niche at four metres (common with Dobcross). Step right on to
the centre of the slab and ascend a parallel line to Dobcross, to the top of the
slab. Care is needed with holds near the top.
Direct Start (5c): start some three metres right of the usual start and climb the
small overhang at four metres to join the normal route two metres above the
right traverse.

★★ **14.   Denshaw**   18m   VS   4c   (1968)
The appealing cleft at the right-hand side of the slab proves to be as good as it
looks, but it is difficult to protect and this can make it feel 5a. Enter the cleft
and follow it awkwardly until it narrows to a series of cracks. Follow these to
the top.

15.   Gardeners' World   15m   VD   (1981)
Climb the V-groove on the right, over several chockstones.

16.   Rough Layback   15m   VD   (1984)
Three metres right is a short layback crack to the right of a fin of rock and
above a small overlap. Climb this, then continue over the blocks above to the
top. A start can also be made on the left of the fin at 4c.

17.   Fireman's Lift   13m   S   4a   (1982)
Immediately right is a short slab with a crack on its left side. Follow this crack
through two overhangs, then step left and pull over the final overhang.
Well-protected.

Third Bay

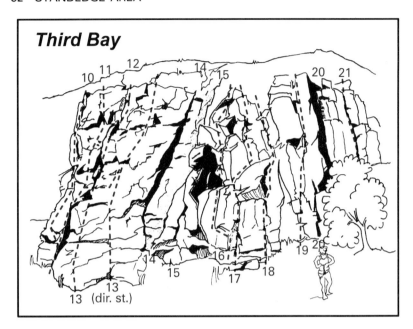

18. Teacher's Pet 13m S 4a (1981)
Follow the crack on the right side of the slab, to the base of a short, narrow
chimney with a chockstone at its top. Once over the chockstone, care is needed
on the last moves.

19. Masons' Lodge 13m S 4a (1982)
Climb the steep, shallow chimney two metres right, until the arête on the right
can be used for the final move.

20. Oak Leaf Chimney 12m HS 4b (1984)
The chimney on the right side of the steep rib.

21. Half Moon 7m VS 4c (1982)
Two metres right is a curving flake. Climb this, taking care near the top.

First Ascents at Rough Knarr

Early 1960s	Quarry visited by Tony Howard, Brian Hodgkinson, Tony Jones, Jeff Sykes and Brian Woods
1968	**Denshaw** Bob Whittaker, John Smith
1981 Sep 19	**Gardeners' World, Teacher's Pet** Geoff Haigh, Gordon Mason
1982 Apr 14	**Masons' Lodge** Gordon Mason, Geoff Haigh
1982 Apr 14	**Half Moon** Geoff Haigh, Gordon Mason
1982	**Delph, Dobcross, Diggle** Geoff Haigh, Derek Wright, Gordon Mason
1982	**Fireman's Lift** Gordon Mason, Geoff Haigh
1983	**Delcross** Bob Whittaker, Ralph Pickering
1984	**Rough Layback, Oak Leaf Chimney**
1983-87	**Right Route, Golfer's Groove, The Printed Page, The Open Book**
1989 summer	**Pillar Front** Bob Whittaker, Phil Latchman
1997 Sep 27	**Karoshi** Dave Cronshaw, Les Ainsworth

1997 Oct 19 **Josh's Path** Dave Gregory, Tina Priestley, Josh O'Grady
1997 Oct 19 **Anit, Knarrly Groove** Dave Gregory, Tina Priestley

Shaw Quarry
O.S. ref. SD 955 103

Situation and Character

Known locally as Buckstones or Pingot Quarry, Shaw Quarry lies on the
western slope of Crow Knoll, in the Crompton Fold area of Shaw. The quarry is
of an open aspect and, being box-shaped, the sun touches all parts of the quarry
at some time during the day.

The excellent climbing hereabouts has been ignored by all but the cognoscenti
for many years, and it certainly deserves more attention. The rock is a
fine-grained gritstone whose compact nature lends itself to small sharp(ish)
holds. Well-developed crack systems are rare and thus the routes need modern
protection and also the skill to use it. A few climbs have little or no protection
– this is indicated in the text. Developments over the past few years have
indicated that the quarry's reputation for loose rock is ill-founded. The quarry is
described in three sections: the Left, Back and Right Walls. The Back and Right
Walls take time to dry after rain, but the Left Wall dries rapidly. Belays above
the Left Wall include stakes, nuts and Friends, the number and position of the
stakes varying according to the whim and strength of local vandals. The belays
on The Back Wall section are quite a way up the easy-angled slab above the
routes. The belays for the Right Wall are assorted fence posts, well up and
farther back.

Shaw Quarry lies in an area under conversion to a country park, thus special
exhortations about behaviour and litter obviously apply.

History

Old pegs greeted the first visits made by the Rimmon Club in 1962–63, which
is when recorded ascents began. First off the mark was Bill Tweedale who made
ascents of *Tweedledum*, its twin, and *Parrot Crack*. An evening visit saw Tony
Nichols solo the excellent *Bugsy* followed by *Perganum* and *T.F.G.*. Apparently,
he was very pleased to complete the latter; the full route name is truly
blasphemous and indicates Nichols' thoughts as he pulled over the top to safety.
Ginger Warburton added *The Pretty Thing* and *Ginger*. A traverse of the Left
Wall was also reported, but *Sting Girdle* remains obscure.

Steve Bancroft, a Shaw resident at the time, climbed three routes in 1970, the
best of which was probably *Crozzle*, though Bancroft was forced to use a point
of aid (dispensed with by Brian Cropper two years later). Phil Booth
free-climbed *The Pretty Thing* with Bancroft and led ascents of *Guano, Red
Revolution* and *A Whiter Shade of Pale*. Bancroft continued his developments
with a bold solo ascent of *The Cynic* in 1974 and the following year John
Hampson soloed *Rattle*. By that time the quarry was becoming known owing to
the efforts of Bancroft who wrote-up the crag for the 1976 BMC *Chew Valley*
guidebook. This phase of development ended in 1978 with Bancroft adding
Cynical, which was then the hardest route on the crag, Chris Johnstone and R.C.
White having climbed the easier *Curig's Corner* and *Flying Pig* the previous
year.

Fresh possibilities were noticed by Ian Conway in 1982 and he returned with Bruce Goodwin, Clive Morton, together with Nichols and Hampson, supplemented at times by John Lord and John Vose. Another Shaw resident, Dougie Hall, also noticed gaps and began working through these, making most of his ascents solo. Pride of place at the time were the two peg cracks on the Back Wall, which Hampson free-climbed and named, only to find later that Hall had soloed both routes the previous year. Conway meanwhile cleaned and re-ascended Red Revolution and added *The Gouk* and the superb *Phosphatic*. Hampson boldly added *Apology* together with *Pull and Go* and *Brandy* amongst others. Nichols led *A Question of Balance* and *Commitment* whilst Goodwin 'Dodged It' and climbed a traverse of the right wall with Morton.

Conway moved north leaving two lines, and Hampson stepped in to lead the aptly named *Sleeping Partner* and *Capital Offence*, plus *Red-Green Eliminate*. The crag was then logically recorded in the 1983 Lancashire Area guidebook. Things started to slow, though Goodwin added *Blusher* and straightened out *A Whiter Shade of Pale* in 1985. In a separate dimension, Hall returned and, with John Smith, climbed *Flaked Maze* up the wall right of Voting Age. Hall also soloed a very hard eliminate between *Ginger* and *Brandy* as well as adding his 'training routes' to The Back Wall. These traverse at various heights and are called 'training routes' because "a fall wouldn't kill you".

Approach and Access
The quarry can be reached from the A663 (Shaw–Newhey road) by turning into Buckstones Road (B6197) about one kilometre north of Shaw. If approaching from the M62, turn off at junction 21 where the A640 leads into Newhey and the A663 leads out past The Jubilee public house. Buckstones Road lies one kilometre ahead on the left. Follow this road until 200 metres past the Park Hotel, a cobbled track, before a church, leads left past Pingot Cottages. The lane ascends to a sharp left turn and the way into the quarry lies straight ahead. There is no access problem.

The Climbs
All the climbs are described from LEFT to RIGHT. The first two routes are hard for their grade.

Left Wall
This is the featureless wall that gains in height from left to right and ends at the waterfall.

1.   Tweedledee 6m HVS 5b   (1963)
A hard layback gains a faint groove which leads to the top.

2.   Rattle 6m HVS 5a   (1975)
Climb to a small square-cut corner at two metres and finish direct.

3.   Blusher 8m HVS 5c   (1985)
The faint blocky arête just left of A Whiter Shade of Pale leads to a short wall.

4.   A Whiter Shade of Pale 8m E1 5b   (1971)
Climb the slab to a ledge. Follow the groove over the overhang to the top, taking care to place some protection.

★ **5. Crozzle** 10m E1 5c (1970/1972)
Climb up to a leaning shot-hole with a thin crack. Make hard moves past an old peg to stand on a small ledge. The top lies just above.

★ **6. Perganum** 10m HVS 5a (1963)
Start as for Crozzle but continue up a corner just right to an awkward move to gain a '*Thank God*' ledge just below the top. An easier start is possible by gaining the small corner from Numbug.

7. Numbug 12m E1 5b (1982)
Climb straight up to a butterfly-shaped overhang. Layaway and bridge, then reach for the top.

★★ **8. Bugsy** 10m E1 5b (1963)
A groove on the blunt arête leads up and left to slabby ledges, then a short crack points the way to a little groove and strenuous pulls to the top. Sustained and thought-provoking.

★★ **9. The Pretty Thing** 14m HVS 5b (1963/1971)(1974)
The obvious diagonal crackline leads to a ledge at six metres. Reach up the wall, then step right to regain the line and hopefully the top. Excellent, steep and bold.
Direct Start (5c): the wall below the ledge gives a desperate problem.

★ **10. Red-Green Eliminate** 12m E3 6a (1983)
Go up easily to a large ledge. Pull up the middle of the red/green wall, then go rightwards to a large foothold. Move up and left to finish. Graded for side-runners, as otherwise it is unprotected.

11. T.F.G. 12m HVS 5b (1963)
As for Red-Green Eliminate but continue and gain a small ledge in the groove above by a '*somehow*' move. Finish direct or (harder) go out right then up.

To the right is a slabby groove leading to an overhang.

12. Apology 12m E3 5b (1982)
Climb direct to the right-hand end of the large ledge of T.F.G. Step right to the groove (which can be reached direct, harder) and go up to its top. Pass the overhang on its left and continue in muscular fashion. Sustained and serious.

To the right is a large low ledge. A grassy mound slopes down rightwards to a drop into some 'slutch' (sludge to foreigners!).

13. Pull and Go 12m E1 5b (1982)
From the low ledge follow a steep thin crack to gain a ledge, then move up and go left to good holds. Continue steeply to the top. Graded for side-runners in Parrot Crack, otherwise there are none where it matters!

14. Parrot Crack 10m VS 4c (1963)
A short blocky groove leads to the ledge on Pull and Go from the right. The obvious corner crack leads steeply upwards.

The wall right of Parrot Crack has two good, though unprotected, routes:

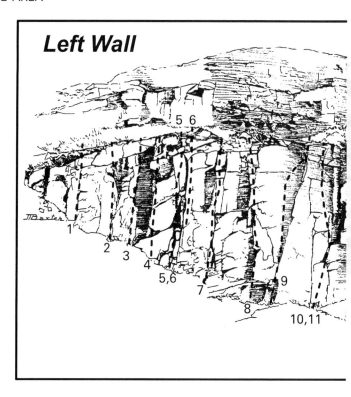

Left Wall

★ **15. Cynical** 14m E4 6a   (1978)
Climb the wall on its left side. A scoop-cum-groove leads above the overhang to
the finishing wall.

★ **16. The Cynic** 14m E4 5c   (1974)
Follow the wall on its right side, at a thin crack; the bulge is overcome at an
obvious shot-hole. Continue in the same line to reach the top.

★★ **17. Ginger** 15m HVS 5b   (1963)
The classic route of the quarry; clean and continuously thought-provoking. From
the foot of Parrot Crack descend the grass rightwards. Traverse across to below
a groove. Follow this weakness to a move right at an old peg, then continue
past two mantels to a heathery finish. A direct start is possible from the sludge
below the groove – ugh!

*The next route goes well with Ginger. This route, and two more, start from a
grassy terrace on the right.*

★ **18. Brandy** 17m E2 5b   (1982)
An excellent climb; bold and poorly-protected.
Gain the grassy terrace. From its left-hand end then step left to below a
triangular overhang. Go up to and over this with difficulty, trending slightly

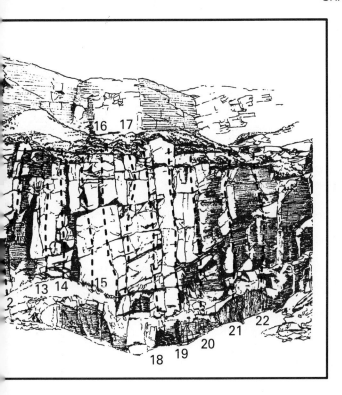

right then go direct to finish. The line may also be started directly from a slabby boulder.

An 'eliminate-eliminate' is possible between Ginger and Brandy. Good moves at 6b.

★★ **19.   Red Revolution**   17m   E2   5c   (1971)
Gain the grassy terrace. Above its left side is a bow-shaped depression which is followed to a bulge (strenuous). A pull or two then lead to the top. A good, sustained route.

★ **20.   The Gouk**   15m   E2   5c   (1982)
A thin crack system above the right-hand side of the grassy ledge provides the route.

★ **21.   Tweedledum**   12m   VS   4c   (1962)(1982)
Go up right of an overhang on the arête. Climb a groove past '*old-timer*'s protection' to a roof. Pull out left to stand on a slabby block, then step right and finish direct.
★ **Variation Start** (VS, 4c): The groove left of the arête gives sustained climbing up to the slabby block.

22. Ledge Way 12m HS 4b (1970)
Climb the broken corner on the right for four metres, step left then go back and up rightwards. Continue over heather for belays. Usually wet with spray from the waterfall.

The waterfall provides a good ice pitch in winter conditions, as can the region between Avoidance and A Question of Balance.

Back Wall

This is the area of rock right of the graffiti-covered slabs. The slabs themselves provide an easy **DESCENT** *from the next few routes. The peg-scarred cracks give two good, sustained and deceptively difficult routes. The right-hand end of the back wall includes the corner of Question of Balance and the routes right of it.*

There is also convenient **DESCENT** *just before the start of the Right Wall.*

★ **23. Back in the Swing** 10m E2 5c (1982)
The left-hand crackline.

★ **24. Voting Age** 10m E2 6a (1982)
The right-hand crackline gives excellent climbing.

★ † **25. Flaked Maze** 10m E4 6b (1986)
Climb the wall past a peg with a sling (sling not in place).

26. Late Finish 9m E2 5b (1982)
Climb a thin crack to a small square-cut overhang. Go over this and continue up ledges in the same line. Bold and poorly-protected.

27. Avoidance 8m VD (Pre-1986)
A line of unstable flakes and blocks lead from right to left starting just right of Late Finish. Probably best avoided!

The Back Wall can be girdled (the once-pegged section).

★★ **28. A Question of Balance** 8m E2 5c (1982)
An interesting technical outing. The obvious corner leads to the overhang. Go over this and up to ledges and a block belay.

★ **29. Commitment** 9m E1 5c (1982)
Climb a wall below a slabby corner. Enter this, then gain a niche and follow a crack to good nut belays on the right.

30. Dodged It 10m HVS 5a (1982)
Climb Commitment for a few metres and deviate right to a good ledge. A delicate move then gains the crack right of the niche, which is followed to a steep finish. Nut belay on left.

A poor unstable route has been climbed up the obvious corner system just to the right; **Rocker** *(HVS, 5a †). Beware, the whole of the top corner block rocks!*

Right Wall
This dark wall starts at the obvious chimney and extends rightwards until it runs out into a steep heathery slope.

31. Guano 21m E1 5b   (1971/1979)(1982)
Start below the line but go rightwards into a wide groove. Go up to a bulge and step left onto the slab, then go up into the chimney which is vacated leftwards. **Direct Start** (5a): climb straight up stepped-rock, pull over on to the slab and continue as for the parent route.

★★ **32. Phosphatic** 21m E2 5b   (1982)
An excellent route that continuously tests the leader. Follow Guano to the bulge, then go straight up to ledges and climb a shallow corner to reach a large ledge. Take the overhang on its left, then continue directly to the top. Spaced protection.

33. Grinder 9m E2 5b   (1982)
The corner on the right leads to a crack which has an awkward move to gain a ledge running across the wall. Finish as for Flying Pig.

34. Flying Pig 18m VS 4c,4c   (1977)
1. 9m. Start four metres right. Follow steps up and left into a niche. Go over the bulge to move left onto a big ledge.
2. 9m. Climb the left-hand corner to the overhang, then pull out left into a groove and hence the top.

35. Too Close for Comfort 19m HVS 5a,4c   (1982)
1. 10m. Climb up stepped rock, right of Flying Pig. A difficult move, right of the niche, leads over a bulge. Delicately gain the ledge and belay.
2. 9m. Finish up Flying Pig, or up rightwards as for One Twin.

36. Curig's Corner 19m VS 4b,4c   (1977)
1. 10m. Climb stepped rock to gain a corner which leads to the ledge and belays.
2. 9m. Finish as for the previous route.

37. One Twin 18m VS 4c,-   (1982)
1. 9m. Climb an overhang below a concave wall then, from ledges, follow the right side of this concavity to the ledge and nut belay.
2. 9m. Climb easily up to steep grass, to fence post belays.

38. Twin Two 17m VS 4c,-   (1982)
1. 9m. Gain the ledges below the concave wall at their right-hand end. Go up past an interestingly-shaped hole and move left to gain One Twin and the large ledge.
2. 8m. Finish as for One Twin.

39. Quadramantel 18m VS 5a   (1982)
Climb up to the overhang on the right and pass it on its left to gain a sloping ledge. Follow a groove system until a way right leads to a grassy slope.

Just right is an obvious V-shaped groove below an open corner.

★ **40. Sleeping Partner** 14m E2 5c (1983)
Climb up and left to the groove. A difficult move leads up to gain the corner which is followed to the top.

★ **41. Capital Offence** 14m E1 5b (1983)
Gain and then follow thin parallel cracks over a bulge. Pull up, gain a niche, then the top.

42. Tripod 9m HVS 5b (1983)
A crack in the wall left of Endymion may be reached in three ways: via ledges on its left, direct (hardest), or from the base of the next route.

43. Endymion 6m VS 5a (1970)
At the right-hand end of the face is a steep groove. The arête on the right provides the route.

A traverse of the Right Wall, from right to left is:

★★ **44. Intuitive Momentum** 36m E1 5a,5b (1983)
The crux move near the start of pitch two gives the name to this interesting and varied route that maintains its interest to the end.
1. 18m. Start as for Sleeping Partner. Go up and gain the wall right of the V-shaped groove. Swing leftwards into the top of the groove, then follow the horizontal break round to join Quadramantel. Go left and up to the large ledge. Walk to its far end. Nut belay. This pitch can be started from Endymion.
2. 18m. Step round on to the face and go across to ledges (Friend above). Descend one move, then go left and enter the base of Guano's chimney. Reverse this route to a block, then go up and leftwards to an overhanging block. Swing round and climb up left using flakes to gain heather-covered ledges. Nut belay six metres farther across the path. Take great care to protect the second man.

First Ascents at Shaw Quarry

1962	**Tweedledum**	Bill Tweedale
	Variation Start by Bruce Goodwin, Tony Nichols, John Lord, 1982.	
1963	**Tweedledee**	Bill Tweedale
1963	**Bugsy, Perganum, T.F.G.**	Tony Nichols (solo)
1963	**The Pretty Thing** (1pt aid)	Bob 'Ginger' Warburton
	Aid eliminated by Phil Booth, 1971.	
	Direct Start by Steve Bancroft, 1974.	
1963	**Parrot Crack**	Bob 'Ginger' Warburton, Bill Tweedale
	There was a peg in place even then.	
1963	**Ginger**	Bob 'Ginger' Warburton
1970	**Crozzle** (1 pt aid)	Steve Bancroft, S. Davies
	Aid eliminated by Brian Cropper, 1972.	
1970	**Ledge Way, Endymion**	Steve Bancroft, G. Davies
1971	**A Whiter Shade of Pale**	Phil Booth, Steve Bancroft
1971	**Red Revolution**	Phil Booth
1971	**Guano** (1 pt aid)	Phil Booth, Steve Bancroft
	Aid eliminated by Steve Bancroft, ? Husdens, 1979.	
	Direct Start by Bruce Goodwin, Simon Wilsher, 1982.	
1974 Sep 12	**The Cynic**	Steve Bancroft (solo)
1975	**Rattle**	John Hampson (solo)
1977 Mar 30	**Curig's Corner**	Chris Johnstone, R.C. White
1977 Apr 4	**Flying Pig**	Chris Johnstone, R.C. White

1978	**Cynical** Steve Bancroft
	The first of the hard routes.
1982 May 11	**Commitment** Tony Nichols, Bruce Goodwin
1982 May 12	**A Question of Balance** Tony Nichols, Bruce Goodwin
1982 May 12	**Dodged It** Bruce Goodwin, Tony Nichols
1982 May 29	**One Twin** Bruce Goodwin, Clive Morton
1982 May 29	**Twin Two** Clive Morton, Bruce Goodwin
1982 May 26	**Quadramantel** Clive Morton, Bruce Goodwin
1982 Sep 9	**Numbug, Brandy** John Hampson, Bruce Goodwin
1982 Sep 11	**Apology, Pull and Go** John Hampson, Bruce Goodwin, John Vose
1982 Sep 11	**Phosphatic** Ian Conway, Pat Duffy, John Vose, John Hampson, Bruce Goodwin
1982 Sep 11	**Too Close for Comfort** Bruce Goodwin, Ian Conway, John Vose
1982	**The Gouk** Ian Conway, Tony Nichols, Bruce Goodwin, John Hampson
1982	**Back in the Swing** Dougie Hall
1982	**Voting Age** Dougie Hall (solo)
1982	**Late Finish** Tony Nichols (solo)
1982	**Grinder** Bruce Goodwin, Pat Duffy
1983	**Red-Green Eliminate** John Hampson, Geoff Thomas, Bruce Goodwin
1983	**Sleeping Partner, Capital Offence** John Hampson, Bruce Goodwin
1983	**Tripod** Bruce Goodwin, John Hampson, Tony Nichols
1983	**Intuitive Momentum** Clive Morton, Bruce Goodwin (alts)
1985 Apr 18	**Blusher** Bruce Goodwin, Andrew Eaton, Gordon Mason
Pre-1986	**Avoidance**
1986 July	**Flaked Maze** Dougie Hall, John Smith
	The hardest route in the quarry.
Pre-1987	**Rocker**

Shooter's Nab

O.S. ref.   SE 065 109

'*During the 1957 visit only the Green Bowl was explored because the remainder of the crag is in direct line with the rifle range and enthusiastic rifle men [of the 'very' Territorial Army] were showing considerable activity ... the great face of Ricochet Wall remains to challenge future tigers.*'

Situation and Character

Shooter's Nab lies within West Yorkshire on Deer Hill Moss, about 10 kilometres south-west of Huddersfield between Marsden and Meltham. It can be seen on the skyline directly above Marsden by anyone approaching on the A62 from Oldham.

It comprises a group of quarried gritstone buttresses and a small outcrop in a pleasant setting on the hillside with excellent views all round. On the left-hand side of the crag the rock is of variable quality and so the climbing is limited to the better sections of rock, but nevertheless the climbs are worthwhile and there are also possibilities for further routes. At the other end of the crag, the main quarry rises to about 20 metres and gives some very impressive climbs that are well worth the effort which is needed to get to this somewhat isolated crag.

History

The first climber to visit the crag was Richard Henry Isherwood, a member of the Rucksack Club, who soloed some of the obvious easy lines in the 1920s.

His explorations remained unknown, but in 1951 he said that he had used nails and thought that the crag had much to offer.

Graham West and Michael Roberts visited Shooter's in 1957 having spotted the crag from a passing train. They found no evidence of previous visits by climbers, and thought the crag to be untouched, even though Tony Howard and Alwyn Whitehead had made a brief recce and done routes a month earlier. The rifle range was in existence even then, and this effectively curtailed their explorations, limiting them to the Green Bowl. Despite the bullets flying around, they managed to climb four fine routes; *Rifleman's Chimney, Elbow Jump, Bull's Eye Crack* and *Sweatyman*. West returned with Clive Barker the following month and this time made ascents of *The Light, Redeemer's Wall* and *Shin Skinner* all in the Green Bowl area, plus three routes on Oval Buttress. The next recorded visit was a whole year later and it was West again who was responsible; he took Bryn Higgins along this time and they attempted *Cream Cracker Crux*, a route which deposited West from the crux at least five times into the mud below. *Panic Knott* was the other route to succumb that day, this time to Higgins.

1959 saw the arrival of the late Barry Kershaw, and the result was a bold lead of *Magpie* together with ascents of *Chimp Crack, S-Bend* and *Cuticle Crack*, the latter being one of his finger-jamming specialities. Graham West prepared a pamphlet guidebook to the crags and passed this on to Eric Byne who recorded 29 routes in the 1961 Journal of the Midland Association of Mountaineers. A lull then followed until the early '60s, when the Rimmon Club came to check the crag for the 1965 guidebook and ended by adding seven routes, including *Trundle Groove* and *Wanderlust* by Howard, and *Barney Rubble* by 'Harpic Harold' Heald. The publication of the 1965 *Saddleworth–Chew Valley Area* guidebook by the Peak Committee of the British Mountaineering Council did little to attract people to the crag; the Peak District and the natural edges of Yorkshire were more attractive to most. This period of quiet gave John Stanger just the opportunity he needed; he now had a free hand to work through the lines still remaining. Over the next few years he soloed *Pisa, Plane Face, Orphic Power, Space Slab, The Shroud, Olympian* and *Lone Stone Buttress*. The latter route then employed a peg for aid until Chris Hardy soloed the line free in 1980.

During a spectacular thunderstorm in 1970, Stanger attacked the most impressive of the quarry's features; the nine-foot roof capping the highest portion of The Rostrum. This route he named *Thunderball* in direct reference to the huge claps of thunder as he hung free in space, dangling from the lip of the roof. From the roof he spotted an obvious traverse line leading leftwards round the arête and he was soon back undeterred, this time with John Earnshaw, to attempt the traverse. Stanger completed the route (*Crescendo*) then belayed to bring up Earnshaw. Once on the hand-traverse, Earnshaw's strength rapidly decreased and eventually his arms gave out and he made a huge pendulum around the arête and into space; quite a climax.

John Hart climbed *Eric the Cosmic Fiend* in 1971 then teamed up with Stanger for the *Girdle Traverse*. Stanger then led *Stimrol* with Julie and John Hart.

Ken Mercer and Brian Cropper put up *Scoop Wall* in 1974, then they switched leads for Cropper to complete *The Long Reach*; a route which had to wait a decade for a second ascent. Despite the publication of the 1976 BMC *Chew*

Valley guidebook things quietened down yet again and remained so until 1981 when Stanger discovered *The Clingon*, a route which had remained tucked away on a hidden buttress opposite Tickle Wall. The buttress is easily visible from the main crag, but looks fairly innocuous until one actually surveys it at close quarters.

In 1975 Bruce Goodwin visited with friends from the Black and Tan M.C. He ascended a route which he then, most uncharacteristically, forgot about. A visit in 1981 jogged his memory and so he named it *Forgotten Wall*, but then forgot it again until work started on this guidebook. Now, 20 years later, it is at last included in a guidebook.

One of the most important influences in Shooter's more recent history was when Paul Cropper was introduced to the crag in 1981. He immediately started to fill in the lines which Stanger had overlooked, and quickly polished off *Cool Man's Wall* and *Slip Arête* with Jeremy Daniels, followed closely by *Light Fantastic* and *Surprise* (originally named Scooping Surprise), the latter with Gary Gibson. Gibson himself made a couple of contributions such as *Yellowcake UFO*. After negotiations with the Peak Area Committee of the BMC it was agreed that Shooter's Nab should be included in the 1983 Lancashire guidebook.

During the summer of 1984, Chris Booth climbed the undercut arête on the buttress left of the Lone Stones, whilst the moors beneath the crag burned away, and named his creation *Smouldering Moors*. The following year Paul Cropper led the right arête of Cuticle Crack to give the serious *Legs*. Phil Kelly made a visit soon after and repeated some of the newer routes, then climbed *Paddington*. Later that year Booth succeeded on the vague seam in the blank-looking wall left of Ricochet Wall, but only managed to complete the problematical moves at the expense of a strained tendon, hence the name; *Born at a Price*. His belayer on that route, Will Steel felt aggrieved at having to spend his time at college, working hard whilst others enjoyed themselves, and so that same day he led a direct line up the wall direct between Elbow Jump and Magpie, *No Time to be 21*.

Approach and Access

From Marsden on the A62 follow the B6107 past the White House public house and about a kilometre farther on, turn right by a bus stop on to Deer Hill End Road. There is a notice '*No Vehicular Access*', so park sensibly somewhere out of the way, between the road and the reservoir. From the left side of the reservoir, go over the stile by the gate, then walk directly up the hillside beside the fence until the old quarry track is reached after two or three minutes toil. Turn right and follow this into the quarry in about 10 minutes (20 minutes from the B6107). From the initial stile a more direct approach can be made, but this tends to be marshy and wet.

If approaching on the B6107 from Meltham, Deer Hill Park Road is on the left, about 500 metres past the Traveller's Rest public house.

A shooting club use the range below the quarry, but the approach and the climbing are a good 200 metres away from the range. Nevertheless, some old shells have been found in the initial bays. Therefore, if the red flag is flying, it may be prudent to leave the track just before crossing the broken wall and to head leftwards, then enter the quarry via the top of the moor.

The Climbs

The climbs are described from LEFT to RIGHT.

After crossing the broken wall, the approach track passes four tiny bays. A landmark to identify these properly is the rib between the second and third bays (Landmark Rib). This lies directly above the white club house on the range and although it is only about three metres high, it is notable for some small rock windows through which daylight can be seen. There are several problems in these bays, but the only recorded route lies 35 metres left of Landmark Rib at the left side of the second bay.

1.   Pisa   8m   S   4a   (1965-76)
A fine route that starts up a wide crack on an obvious leaning pillar. Then use excellent, flat holds and finish up the left edge.

Smooth Buttress

Just past the white club house the crag increases in height. The next climbs lie on a wide buttress about 10 metres high, that is split by a horizontal break and a low cave at half-height. It is further identified by a stack of massive, square-cut blocks directly below its left end.

2.   Plane Face   10m   HS   4b   (1965-76)
Climb the steep face two metres right of the arête then follow a vague, right-trending ramp using holds that are unseen until reached. Stake belay.

3.   Orphic Power   10m   VS   4c   (1965-76)
The right side of the buttress is guarded by three stepped overhangs. Start below the highest of these and move left to gain a shallow, hanging groove. Step left then climb the wall on good holds.

Great Cave Area

The Great Cave is obvious. This area stretches from the left side of an extensive square-cut recess in the moorside that lies immediately to the left of the Great Cave and it ends about 25 metres past the Great Cave where the ground level rises.

★ **4.   Space Slab**   12m   VS   4c   (1965-76)
The left arête of the square-cut recess, some 50 metres before the Great Cave, forms a hanging slab. Start on its left and climb to an overlap, then step right on to the slab and climb this in a pleasant position.

No climbs have been recorded in the square-cut recess itself, but there is some potential.

5.   Zing   13m   S   (Early 1960s)
From just below the left side of the *Great Cave*, move left on to the wall, then climb this, trending right on small holds.

Les Ainsworth on first ascent of **Red Wing** (VS 4c), Worlow Quarry.   *Photo Bob Whittaker*

6.   Fossil Crack 12m VD   (Early 1960s)
The arête below the crack on the left side of the *Great Cave*, then finish up the
top crack.

7.   Eponychial Retreat 12m HVS 5b   (1982)
This route has become considerably harder since a loose block at mid-height
was removed. Start 15 metres right of the *Great Cave* and climb the left arête of
the next buttress, with a hard move above a poor block at mid-height.

★★ **8.   Cuticle Crack** 9m E1 5b   (1959)
An interesting start, which has defeated many and some will also wish that it
relented a bit sooner above this. Start three metres right and climb the
prominent, undercut flake.

★ **9.   Legs** 9m E4 6a   (1981)
Start as for Cuticle Crack, but move out right just above the bulge to gain the
arête. Finish up this. Short, but bold, with a nasty landing.

10.   Dwarf 9m VD   (1965-76)
The oft-damp corner to the right.

Long Wall
Just past Cuticle Crack the ground level rises and the rock height decreases.
This long low section stretches from the rock that faces the Great Cave to a
broken dry-stone wall. Only four climbs have been described on this section, but
there several other possibilities, which are left for climbers to discover for
themselves.

11.   Giant 6m HVS 5c   (1981)
Climb directly up the centre of the wall facing Cuticle Crack. A giant reach is a
distinct advantage on this climb.

12.   Tickle Wall 6m S   (Early 1960s)
Start just right of Giant and climb up trending rightwards, to finish just left of
the arête.

13.   Tickle Arête 6m S 4b   (Early 1960s)
Climb the arête directly.

14.   Tickle Crack 6m S 4a   (Early 1960s)
The kinked crack four metres right of the arête.

Isolated Buttress
About 20 metres in front of Tickle Arête there is a small rock mound capped by
a cubic block. The front face of this is at a lower level and is characterised by
a large roof.

★ **15   The Clingon** 12m E2 6a   (1981)
Start below the crack which splits the roof. Climb up to it, then cross the roof
(hard move on the lip) and finish up the short cracks.

Geoff Hibbert enjoys some winter sun on **Pendulum Swing Direct** (HVS 5a), Blackstone
Edge.   *Photo: Joanne Hibbert*

The Black Bowl

Long Wall ends at the remains of a dry-stone wall, beyond which the height of the rock increases and forms an extensive bay.

16. The Shroud 8m HS 4b (1965-76)
Climb up to an old bolt-hole, in the centre of the first buttress of the bay, then finish up a hanging flake with care.

17. Cream Cracker Crux 12m VS 4c (1958)
Climb to a large sandy hole at the back of the bay, then ascend the slight rib and wall above.

18. Peek Freen 7m VS 4b (1958)
The thin crack in the right wall of the bay, takes the biscuit.

19. Tidos 7m HS 4b (1958-59)
Climb the wall midway between Peek Freen and the arête via an obvious ledge.

20. Ginger 8m VD (1958)
The arête on the right.

Soup Bowl

This is the small, square-cut depression about 20 metres in front of Ginger.

21. Blue Petre 10m HS 4b (1958)
The obvious deep crack in the right-hand corner.

22. Black Crack 10m S (1958)
Climb to a grassy ledge two metres right of the corner, then follow the overhanging crack to the top.

Oval Buttress

Forward of the Soup Bowl and facing Marsden is a natural edge. This is the first buttress.

23. Silly Way 8m VD (1957)
Start three metres right of the left arête. Climb to the break, then step right to finish.

24. Paddington 8m HVS 5b (1986)
The short problem wall immediately right, using a one-finger hole near the bottom. From the break, finish as for Silly Way.

★ **25. Natural Route** 8m S (1957)
Incorrectly known as If Looks Would Kill in the previous guidebook. The thin groove/crack in the centre of the buttress, then the ripply wall above.

26. One Two Wall 9m VS 4c (1957)
The wall immediately right of the crack is undercut, and hard to start.

Overhang Buttress
10 metres to the right is another natural buttress with a hanging arête.

27.   Demerara   8m   D   (Early 1960s)
The centre of the wall left of the arête.

28.   Hard Stair   8m   VS   5a   (1985)
Climb the wall on the right to the break, then finish up the arête above.

★ **29.   Smouldering Moors**   9m   E3   6a   (1984)
A good route, but there is no pro, and the landing is poor. The hanging arête is
climbed on its right-hand side to a small ledge, then easier moves lead to the top.

30.   Tipperary   8m   D   (Early 1960s)
Go up the blocky corner, traverse left then up the prow to finish.

Lone Stone Buttress
*15 metres farther right is a square buttress which contains an old peg at four
metres.*

31.   The Wigan   6m   E1   5c   (1976-78)
Climb the left arête of the square buttress to the overlap and make a long reach
to the top.

★ **32.   Lone Stone Buttress**   6m   E1   5c   (1965-76/1980)
Climb direct to the old peg and pass it with difficulty to reach the top.

33.   Lone Stone Groove   6m   E2   6a   (1981)
The undercut groove on the right.

Green Bowl
*Farther right is the main quarry. This is dominated on its left-hand side by a
huge overhanging buttress named The Rostrum. The continuous section of rock
which contains this is the Green Bowl, and here are the best climbs at Shooter's
Nab. The first routes start on the rock which is set back to the left of The
Rostrum.*

34.   Pocket Route   16m   VD   (1958)
Climb two thin, parallel grooves just right of a deep corner. Finish up a short
chimney.

★ **35.   Panic Knott**   18m   S   (1958)
The fine groove on the right.

36.   S-Bend   24m   S   (1957)
Take the obvious chimney, then climb the arête and hand-traverse into Panic
Knott. Follow this to a horizontal crack which leads round a small overhang.

★ **37.   Cabriole**   20m   VS   4b   (1958)
Climb the undercut diagonal crack which slopes up to the right. Step left and go
up the wall to a platform and an easy exit.

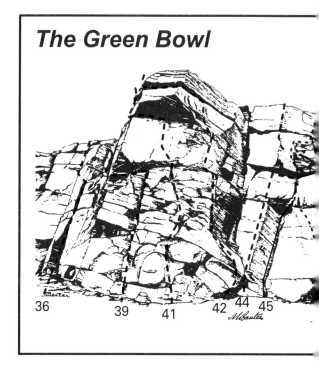

The Green Bowl

36   39   41   42 44 45

38. Shin Skinner 18m HS 4b   (1958)
Follow the curving crack on the right to gain the platform and thus an easy
finish.

★ **39. Wanderlust** 23m VS 4b,4c   (1963)
1. 15m. Climb the deep groove on laybacks, then traverse left below the
overhang to a grassy bay.
2. 8m. Move left and step across on to the arête, then move round on to the
face of the buttress and finish up the centre.

★ **40. Eric the Cosmic Fiend** 20m HVS 5b   (1971)
From the grassy bay on Wanderlust, move back right and climb the thin
bottomless crack. A spacy route.

★★★ **41. Crescendo** 24m E1 5c   (1970)(1970)
Climb the intricate wall directly under the roof of The Rostrum, to gain the base
of an old bolt ladder. Climb the wall just right of this by a confusing sequence
to reach the roof. Hand-traverse sensationally left around the arête to a welcome
foothold and finish direct.
Thunderball A direct finish to Crescendo, tackling the monster roof above on
bolts, with exhilarating moves on the lip. However, the bolts are very old.

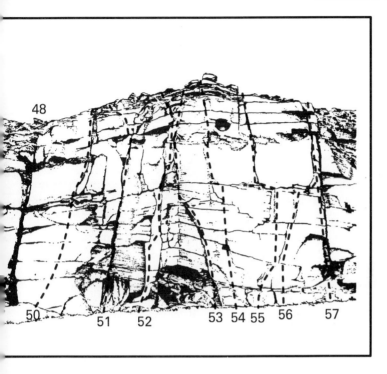

***★★★ 42.   Sweatyman**   23m   HVS   4c,5a   (1957)
After an uninteresting first pitch the second is pure poetry; quarry climbing at its
best. The stomach traverse at the top of The Rostrum is memorable for its fine
position, but the crux is actually slightly lower.
1.   10m.   Pull strenuously out of a deep sandy cave on the right and climb
cracks to a '*proud*' shelf.
2.   12m.   From the middle of the ledge gain the horizontal break above, then
traverse left to the edge. Ascend the slab and traverse to the outermost point of
the overhang, then stomach-traverse through the gap in the overhang and finish
up the front.
★★ Cool Man's Wall   (VS, 4c): is a variation to pitch 2 of Sweatyman. A classic of
its grade, with some thin moves. Good value at 4c. Make a long reach to the
horizontal break above the belay and enter a scoop. Finish direct.

43.   Rifleman's Chimney   20m   HS   4b   (1957)
Despite its name, the chimney on the right is well out of the firing line, so there
are no excuses for avoiding this classic quarry chimney.

★★ 44.   Slip Arête   21m   E2   5b   (1981)
Thin and exposed climbing, with little protection on the arête itself. The
prominent arête on the right is climbed to a large roof, then move right to the
crack of Magpie and climb this for a few metres, until it is possible to go back
left and finish up the arête.

45. Elbow Jump 25m VS 4c (1957)
Climb the corner on the right to below the overhang, then elbow-traverse right to gain a ledge. Move back above the overhang and finish direct.

46. No Time to be 21 20m E3 6a (1986)
Climb the wall between Elbow Jump and Magpie, direct. A long reach comes in useful above the break.

★★ **47 Magpie** 20m HVS 5a (1959)
Start by the arête and rise diagonally left to an overhanging corner crack. Follow this to the top. A good, interesting start, but unfortunately the top can be dirty.

48. Bull's Eye Crack 20m VD (1957)
The broken chimney just right.

49. Forgotten Wall 20 m HVS 5b (1975)
Start a metre right at an obvious small step. Climb the wall past horizontal breaks to a bold step up at two-thirds height. Move more easily to the top.

50. Yellowcake UFO 20m VS 4c (1982)
Start on the right and climb the slab to twin, right-leaning cracks. Finish up these.

51. Redeemer's Wall 20m HS 4a (1957)
Start at a large sandy bowl and take a direct line to the top using the wide crack.

52. The Cuspidor 23m VS 4b (Early 1960s)
Start just left of the arête and ascend to a flake at four metres. Move right and follow the arête until a move left can be made to finish.

★ **53. Tind** 21m HVS 5a (1965-76)
Climb the undercut, diagonal, block-filled crack right of the arête to a hard move on to the arête itself. Finish up this.

★★ **54. Born at a Price** 21m E4 6b (1986)
A fantastic line, but the last protection is at the break and so the top wall requires a high degree of commitment. Start a metre right below a hole and climb up past this to a good break below a vague seam in the upper wall. Follow the pegged-out pockets above by baffling moves, to an easier finish.

★★★ **55. Ricochet Wall** 21m E1 5b (1970)
One of the best climbs in the quarry. The obvious route of the wall; classic. Climb the vague groove in the centre of the wall to its top, then step left to gain a wide, curving crack which leads to the top.

56. Scot's Wall 21m E1 5c (1976)
Start immediately on the right and climb the wall via two slanting cracks to a finish up a wider crack.

★ **57. The Light** 20m VS 4c (1957)
The wide crack on the right. Hard to start.

★ **58. Light Fantastic** 15m HVS 5b (1981)
Climb the wall two metres farther to the right, passing a hole. Traverse right at the break and finish direct.

The next buttress has a slabby front.

59. Second Thoughts 12m S 4b (Early 1960s)
From a sandy block, climb the left edge until it is possible to move right on small holds, then climb the scoop and cracks above.

★ **60. Ball Bearings** 12m HVS 5a (1965-76)
Start to the right, below a small overhang with three tiny cracks above. Climb up to and pass the overhang, then trend right to the top.

★ **61. Surprise** 12m E2 5c (1982)
Climb directly up to a shallow, brandy glass-shaped scoop and enter this with difficulty. Exit via the slab above. A fine route, but get a good runner in before the scoop.

62. Barney Rubble 12m VS 4c (1963)
The dirty corner crack, exiting right at the chockstone.

★★ **63. Stimrol** 12m E2 5b (1971)
The fine arête to the right, passing an old iron, quarryman's spike at half-height.

At the right-hand side of The Green Bowl, a large ledge (The Walk Off) splits the crag into two tiers.

★ **64. The Long Reach** 10m E3 6b (1974)
Climb the groove right of the arête past a roof to reach the left side of *The Walk Off*. Then make a hard move up the thin crack above to gain a good hold on the left, then finish direct.

65. Half Way Climb 7m S 4a (Pre-1998)
Start one metre right and climb the broken cracks to finish at *The Walk Off*.

★ **66. Chimp Crack** 10m VS 5a (1959)
The zigzag crack on the right (old wooden wedge) leads to *The Walk Off*, then the thin rightward-slanting crack above.

67. Olympian 9m HVS 5b (1965-76)
This climb is formed by linking up two boulder problems. Nevertheless, it is well worth doing. Climb the wall two metres right, to reach *The Walk Off*, then walk right and climb the scoop with a good hold in its centre. Beware though, the finishing hold is often full of grit!

Square Buttress
This is the aptly-named, final buttress in the main quarry.

68. Fairy Arête 10m VS 4c (1958)
The left arête, with an easy start and a thin finish.

69. Trundle Groove 9m VD 4a (1963)
The groove to a ledge, then finish up the wall.

70. Scoop Wall 9m VS 4c   (1974)
The flake immediately to the right. Finish direct.

71. Final Corner 9m VD   (Early 1960s)
The cracks in the centre of the buttress, finishing up a groove.

★ **72. Girdle Traverse** 105m HVS 5a,4c,5a,4b,5a,4b   (1971/mid-1990s)
1. 28m. Care is needed with the rope on this pitch. Follow The Long Reach until, just below the ledge of *The Walk Off*, it is possible to traverse left along a good crack to a quarryman's spike on the arête. Continue to the corner and climb this to a large capstone. Traverse left with hands on an obvious ledge until it is possible to climb down on small ledges to a large ledge midway up Second Thoughts. Peg belay (not in situ).
2. 9m. Step down, then move left past a dirty chimney to a large ledge. Belay at a short chimney corner on the left side of this ledge.
3. 20m. Move round on to the front face at an obvious notch, then continue past the hole on Light Fantastic to reach the crack on The Light. Step up, then semi-hand-traverse across Ricochet Wall to reach a belay on the arête of The Cuspidor. Peg belay (not in situ).
4. 21m. Follow the ledges across to the corner of Bull's Eye Crack, then continue across the wall of Magpie using two obvious horizontal cracks to reach a belay in Rifleman's Chimney.
5. 18m. Go along Sweatyman's ledge, then drop down and traverse under The Rostrum to a junction with Wanderlust. Follow this to a belay in a grassy bay at the end of its first pitch.
6. 9m. Step round the edge on the left, then semi-hand-traverse to the corner and finish on a ledge at the same level.

First Ascents at Shooter's Nab

1957 June	**Sweatyman, Bull's Eye Crack** Graham West, Michael Roberts
1957	**Rifleman's Chimney, Elbow Jump** Graham West, Michael Roberts
	Elbow Jump was originally known as Elbow Alley.
1957 July	**Redeemer's Wall, The Light, Natural Route, Silly Way, One Two Wall**
	Graham West, Clive Barker
1957	**S-Bend** Barry Kershaw
1958	**Shin Skinner, Cabriole** Graham West, Tony Jones
1958	**Cream Cracker Crux** Graham West, Bryn Higgins
1958	**Panic Knott** Bryn Higgins, Graham West
1958	**Peek Freen, Ginger**
	Originally climbed as Illegitimate and Passing Arête respectively.
1958-59	**Tidos**
1959	**Cuticle Crack, Magpie, Chimp Crack** Barry Kershaw
Early 1960s	**Tickle Wall, Tickle Arête, Tickle Crack, Zing, Fossil Crack, Blue Petre, Black Crack, Demerara, Tipperary, Pocket Route, The Cuspidor, Second Thoughts, Fairy Arête, Final Corner** Tony Howard, Alwyn Whitehead, Paul Seddon, Tony Jones, Jeff Sykes (varied leads)
	Tickle Wall, Tickle Arête and Tickle Crack were probably originally climbed as Puddin' Wall, Jack Horner Corner and Trog respectively.
1963	**Wanderlust, Trundle Groove** Tony Howard, Harold Heald
1963	**Barney Rubble** Harold Heald, Tony Howard
1970	**Crescendo, Ricochet Wall** John Stanger, John Earnshaw
1970	**Thunderball** John Stanger
1971	**Eric the Cosmic Fiend** John Hart
1971	**Stimrol** John Stanger, Julie Hart, John Hart
1971	**Girdle Traverse** (with rope move) John Hart, John Stanger
	Climbed completely free in mid-1990s.

1974	**The Long Reach** Brian Cropper, Ken Mercer
1974	**Scoop Wall** Ken Mercer, Brian Cropper
1975	**Forgotten Wall** Bruce Goodwin
1965-76	**Ball Bearings, Tind, Dwarf**
1965-76	**The Shroud, Pisa, Plane Face, Orphic Power, Space Slab, Olympian**
	John Stanger (solo)
1965-76	**Lone Stone Buttress** (1 pt aid) John Stanger
	Aid eliminated by Chris Hardy, 11 Sep 1981.
1976 May	**Scot's Wall** Bob Whittaker, Gordon Mason
1976-78	**The Wigan**
1981 June 7	**Light Fantastic** Paul Cropper, Jeremy Daniels
1981 June 18	**Slip Arête** Paul Cropper, Jeremy Daniels
1981 Sep 6	**Legs, Lone Stone Groove** Paul Cropper, Brian Cropper
1981 Sep 6	**Giant** Brian Cropper
1981 Sep 7	**Cool Man's Wall** Paul Cropper, Jeremy Daniels
1981	**The Clingon**
1982 Mar 23	**Eponychial Retreat** Garry Gibson, Neil Harvey
1982 Mar 23	**Surprise** Paul Cropper, Gary Gibson
1982 Mar 28	**Yellowcake UFO** Gary Gibson, Neil Harvey
1984 summer	**Smouldering Moors** Chris Booth
1985	**Hard Stair**
1986 May 1	**Paddington** Phil Kelly (solo)
1986 Sep 3	**No Time to be 21** Will Steel, Chris Booth
1986 Sep 3	**Born at a Price** Chris Booth, Will Steel

Standedge Quarry

O.S. ref. SE 012 103

Situation and Character

The quarry is located about four kilometres north-east of Delph and is easily visible just above and to the north of the A62, Oldham to Huddersfield road. It is directly below the Pennine Way.

The quarry consists of two bands of gritstone. The upper band being harder and much less friable than the lower one. The result is an obvious overhang which runs the length of the quarry. The lower band is loose, giving all the routes a serious air. The traverse below the overhang (**Pennine Way**) is not technically difficult for those who like stomach-traverses on sandy ledges over earthy blocks.

History

Some routes were done by Mick Shaw and Tony Howard in the early 1970s, but no records were kept. The earliest recorded route, *The Flake of the Floating Light*, was climbed by Paul Cropper with Nadim Siddiqui in 1974. Three routes were added on a February day in 1978, Paul Cropper climbing *Thin Line* solo and *Watching the Detectives* with Martin Booth. Brian Cropper soloed *Pennine Arête* that day and later the same year added *Firefrost* with Rehan Siddiqui. Activity at the start of the 1980's saw three additional routes.

Approach and Access

From Oldham or Delph, follow the A62 towards Huddersfield. About four kilometres from Delph is the Floating Light Inn on the left. Half a kilometre beyond this is the watershed of the Pennines and a large car park on the right. Follow the well-marked Pennine Way track north-west to the third stile (in a stone wall). Climb this stile and turn left immediately to descend a short distance when the quarry is immediately to your right (10 minutes from the main road).

A quicker approach is to look out for a hotel on the right of the A62, beyond this the A670 drops off right to Uppermill and soon Globe Farm will be seen on the left. Beyond this turn left into Manor Lane. Where the road widens and joins Standedge Foot Road there is parking space. Follow the public footpath signs towards Rock Farm, go over the stile on the right and directly up into the quarry (four minutes walk from car).

No access problems have arisen so far.

The Climbs
The climbs are described from LEFT to RIGHT.

1.   Wall and Crack 10m S   4a   (1979-83)
Climb the short, broken wall to a grassy ledge and finish up the crack on the right.

2.   Firefrost 10m VD   (1978)
On the right is another right-slanting line of weakness with a slabby upper section. Climb up to the ledge and then finish up the flake crack above and to the right.

3.   Watching the Detectives 14m VS 4b   (1978)
Start at a broken groove 13 metres to the right of Firefrost and continue to the ledge. Take the overhang on its left and finish up an excellent jamming crack.

4.   Footless Oasis 10m VS 4b   (1979-83)
Climb broken rock and the wide jamming crack above.

5.   The Flake of the Floating Light 14m S   4a   (1974)
Climb the flaky crack to the halfway ledge (loose), then step right and follow a right-slanting ramp and crack to the top.

There is some interesting bouldering right of the main crag on boulders directly above the last section of the 'Pennine Way' approach.

200 metres right of the quarry, is a wall and buttress. The wall has two cracks, **Thin Line** *(5b) and* **Short Line** *(5b), which present interesting problems. Beyond the wall, the buttress provides the neat little* **Pennine Arête** *(D).*

First Ascents at Standedge Quarry
1974	**The Flake of the Floating Light** Paul Cropper, Nadim Siddiqui
1978 Feb 4	**Watching the Detectives** Paul Cropper, Martin Booth
1978 Feb 4	**Thin Line** Paul Cropper (solo)
1978 Feb 4	**Pennine Arête** Brian Cropper (solo)
1978	**Firefrost** Brian Cropper, Rehan Siddiqui
1979-83	**Wall and Crack, Footless Oasis**

Worlow Quarry – Lower Pule Quarry

O.S. ref. SE 307 103

Situation and Character

This small gritstone quarry is situated about one kilometre south-east of the southern end of Pule Hill Outcrop. Although it is short, it is easily accessible and the rock is very solid, making it an ideal place for an evening visit.

History

The first climber known to have visited the quarry was Mick Shaw, who led many of the lines in the early 1970s, seconded by Phil Latcham. However, no records were kept and the quarry was rediscovered in 1978 by Al Pierce, Nadim Siddiqui and Paul Cropper, who climbed five lines, including *Swallow Dive* and *Needles and Pins*. The crag was further developed one day in May 1982 by Dave Cronshaw and Bob Whittaker, accompanied by Les Ainsworth. Four new routes fell (and were fallen off), amongst which *Albatross, Eagle* and *Red Wing* perhaps combined with the more recent (1985) additions – *The Bengal Badger* and *Peach Party* by Chris Booth and Will Steel – may provide an evening's entertainment for the jaded connoisseur.

Approach

From Oldham or Delph, follow the A62 towards Huddersfield as far as the Standedge Cutting. Immediately after this the Great Western Hotel will be passed on the left and Pule Hill will be seen directly in front. Take the next turn right (Mount Road) and follow it for just over one kilometre until the quarry can be seen on the left. There is good parking and a short track leads up to the quarry.

The Climbs

The climbs are described from LEFT to RIGHT.

Main Bay

The quarry is composed of two bays, which form a W-shape. This is the left-hand bay.

1.   The Slab 7m D   (1978)
Climb the centre of the easy-angled slab at the left side of the bay.

2.   Bengal Badger 8m E2 5c   (1985)
The faint, curving groove that starts midway up the wall on the right.

3.   Swallow Dive 9m VS 4b   (1978)
Climb the deep groove in the centre of the left wall, then finish up the crack above.

4.   Swallow Dive Right-hand 12m E2 5b   (1998)
From the top of the groove of Swallow Dive, swing right (Friend 1 in horizontal break), then pull up on a series of good ledges (small wire in a horizontal slot) and follow a line of sharp, incut holds to the top.

★ **5.   Two Dead Sheep** 13m E3 6a   (1986-89)
Climb the centre of the next wall past white paint marks to reach a
crescent-shaped hold and thence the horizontal break (Friend 1). Bold moves
then lead to a peg on the wall above, then continue to the top past two more
pegs.

*There are no records of the corner in the angle of the quarry having being
climbed.*

★ **6.   Albatross** 12m HVS 5b   (1982)(1985)
Start immediately right of the corner and climb up to a roof, then move
leftwards to reach good footholds at the foot of a ramp. Finish up the thin,
jagged, left-leading crack.
Shrew to a Kill (E1, 5b): gives a more direct finish from the roof.

★ **7.   Eagle** 12m E1 5b   (1982)
Start as for Albatross and climb to the thin crack that splits the overhang at its
highest point. Continue up a thin crack to a ledge and finish direct.

★ **8.   Red Wing** 12m VS 4c   (1982)
To the right again, a prominent crack is climbed direct.

Small Bay
The small bay starts past a short arête on the right.

9.   Raven 9m HS 4a   (1982)(1985)
Around the arête on the right is a crack three metres off the floor. Gain this
from the right and then follow it to a spacious ledge. Finish up the corner at the
back.
Hot Pants (HVS, 5b): climb the right arête.

10.   Rook 8m S 4a   (1982)
The wide chimney/crack.

11.   Peach Party 7m E2 6a   (1985)
The attractive wall two metres farther right provides an interesting, fingery
problem.

12.   The Corner 7m D   (1978)
Climb the short corner in the angle of the short bay by three mantels.

13.   One More Move 7m S 4a   (1978)
Follow the second crack on the wall right of the corner.

14.   Needles and Pins 7m S 4a   (1978)
The jamming crack a metre farther right.

15.   Thin Line Dynamite 8m HS 4a   (1982)
Gain the small niche two metres right and then finish up the thin crack above.

First Ascents at Worlow Quarry

1978	**The Slab, Swallow Dive, The Corner, One More Move, Needles and Pins** Al Pierce, Nadim Siddiqui, Paul Cropper
1982 Mar	**Albatross, Raven** Bob Whittaker, Ralph Pickering
1982 Apr	**Eagle** Les Ainsworth, Dave Cronshaw, John Ryden, Malc Baxter
1982 Apr	**Red Wing** Dave Cronshaw, Les Ainsworth, John Ryden, Malc Baxter
1982 Apr	**Rook** Dave Cronshaw, Les Ainsworth, John Ryden
1982 June	**Thin Line Dynamite** Paul Cropper
1985	**Bengal Badger** Chris Booth, Will Steel
1985	**Shrew to a Kill, Hot Pants, Peach Party**
1988 Jan 31	**Swallow Dive Right-hand** Brian Cropper, Steve Barker
1986-89	**Two Dead Sheep**

Minor Crags

Grey Stone Quarry   O.S. ref. SE 033 155

This gritstone quarry overlooks the M62 and can be reached in a couple of minutes walk from the B6114. The rock is a little over 18 metres high, but no climbs have been recorded. However, if it were to be developed, it would probably best fit into the area covered by the Yorkshire Gritstone guidebook.

Nab End   O.S. ref. SE 091 118

This gritstone quarry lies on the moorside about one kilometre to the north of Pule Hill and is clearly visible from the A62. It provides only a few short climbs.

Rochdale – Todmorden Area

Compiled by Bruce Goodwin

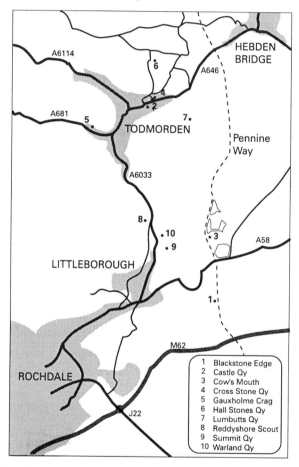

1	Blackstone Edge
2	Castle Qy
3	Cow's Mouth
4	Cross Stone Qy
5	Gauxholme Crag
6	Hall Stones Qy
7	Lumbutts Qy
8	Reddyshore Scout
9	Summit Qy
10	Warland Qy

The Rochdale–Todmorden area is a region of contrasts, with high rolling moors cut deep by narrow, steep-sided valleys. Crags stand proud or are hidden away in man-made quarry holes: the cliffs are cool and sombre contrasting with those of a sunnier aspect.

There are many crags of regional importance, but none of national importance in the area and so solitude is almost guaranteed as one enjoys routes conventional, esoteric, good and excellent. The area contains crags of natural grit and many quarries, which all give steep arêtes, walls, cracks and slabs – in short, a wealth of experience awaits the eager climber.

Blackstone Edge O.S. ref.   SD 973 167

Situation and Character

Blackstone Edge is a natural grit outcrop lying along the north–south ridge of the same name, about three kilometres east of Littleborough. Known locally as 'Robin Hood's Bed', it faces north-west and offers fine views over Littleborough, Hollingworth Lake, Chelburn Moor and the moors and hills to the west. The rock is a dark-coloured, compact gritstone, providing climbs of all grades up to E4. There are relatively few climbs, but most are well worth doing and the crag is an interesting and rewarding venue.

The Pennine Way, a *Roman* road and other popular paths ensure that the area is well used by walkers, ramblers and runners. Sadly, inappropriate use of mountain bikes and, even worse, the occasional motor bike, mean that the delicate peat ecosystems are suffering as a consequence of heavy erosion.

History

Some climbing was recorded on Blackstone Edge as far back as 1827, this date being carved in the upper walls of *South Chimney*, though whether the ascent was completed is not known!

Modern records of first ascents began with the publication of Laycock's '*Some Gritstone Climbs*' in 1913. The easier routes existed then, but little more was done and as late as 1957 '*Climbs on Gritstone*' (volume 3) only added *Central Groove* – although *Pendulum Swing* had been done a little earlier. In the early 1960s *Little Miss Id* was climbed by Alan 'Richard' McHardy and it is also likely that he was responsible for *Pendulum Swing Direct* at around the same time. Paul Horan then contributed *Slim Jim* in 1966 and *Manibus et Pedibusque* the following year, though some tension was used on the latter, which was dispensed with by McHardy shortly afterwards.

Accounts of new routes and aid reductions, etc. are vague, but the Solvé Club members were active here, as well as at the nearby quarries of Summit and Cow's Mouth, and they should probably be credited with ascending most of the routes. *Tryche* dates from that time (with a peg for aid). *Cornflake* had been free-climbed by the end of the decade, though who was first to succeed is not known, and the crag was then put on hold for the nearby Cow's Mouth which attracted (and still attracts) more climbers, with its superior number of routes to enjoy.

In 1977, Bruce Goodwin, together with fellow members of the Black and Tan M.C. began a purge on the lines. All the existing routes received repeat ascents, with Dennis Carr leading *Pots*.

The famous A.N. Other was rumoured to have made a lead ascent of *Tryche* by the early 1980s and the length of some of the locals' noses was seen to grow by the minute! However, 1983 saw Goodwin climb *Master Ego*, a complementary route to Little Miss Id and Tony Nichols' search for a third pebble was the reason for the naming of *No Sign of Three*. Attention then focused on the roof left of Little Miss Id; this hard (and rather artificial) problem has been top-roped by several parties, but has still not succumbed. Finally, in 1994, Goodwin added *Palmistry* and shared leads with Gordon Mason on *Phase Change*.

Approach

Park near the White House on the A58 about three kilometres north-east of Littleborough. Then walk downhill to join a footpath (Pennine Way) and follow this up left to Broadhead Drain. Follow this drainage channel across the *Roman* road until below the crag. Cross the drain and ascend the moor to the crag.

The car park at the foot of the *Roman* road is an alternative starting point. Either approach takes about 20 minutes. An hourly bus service (Rochdale–Halifax) currently runs past the White House.

The Climbs

The climbs are described from RIGHT to LEFT. A short face right of the first climb gives pleasant problems.

1. Pendulum Swing 9m VS 4c (Pre-1957)
Climb a crack to an overhang, then move left and finish up a short chimney. Sadly, this route has been damaged by chipping done by vandals.

2. Pendulum Swing Direct 8m HVS 5a (1962)
The wall to the left of the crack leads with difficulty to the short chimney.

3. Slin and Thippy 8m E4 6a (1988)
The wall left again leads easily to the very hard, and bold, upper section.

Rounding the arête on the left a shallow groove left of an obvious pocket gives:

★ **4. No Sign of Three** 10m E2 5c (1983)
Climb cracks to a horizontal break. Move left and go up the groove with difficulty to ledges. Finish via the obvious weakness.

★ **5. Palmistry** 10m E2 5c (1994)
Climb the wall on the left, then continue, using the arête, to reach ledges, then finish as above, or traverse left.

★ **6. Twin Cracks** 10m D – VD (1913)
The left-hand crack is easier than the right-hand, or they can be combined.

7. South Chimney 10m D (1913)
Climb the crack to an obvious chimney, browse a while, then continue to the top.

★ **8. Outside Edge** 10m VS 4c (1994)
Climb the outside edge of the chimney by bridging and traditional techniques. Protectable, but it feels bold.

9. Pots 10m E2 5c (1997)
Climb the thin crack left of the chimney. At the horizontal break, move left for a couple of metres, then climb up and back right to '*one of those*' finishes.

Right: A rare photo of Ken Powell on his favourite problem, **Somersault** (4c), Brownstones.
Photo: Les Ainsworth
Overleaf: Sheilgh Vigano on **Questionable Stability** (VS 4c), Troy Quarry. *Photo: John Mason*

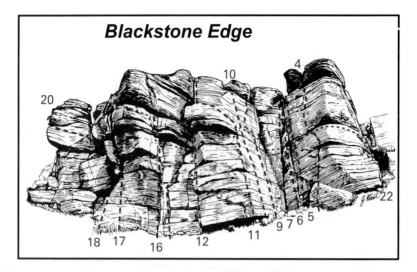

Blackstone Edge

★★ **10. Tryche** 10m E4 6a   (1957-69)
The wall on the left is climbed as directly as possible to a pocket (runner).
Climb the little groove and finish direct. A bold and technical outing.

★★★ **11. Little Miss Id** 12m E1 5c   (1962)
The blunt arête left of Tryche leads to an overhang. Step on to this from the
right and gain a large ledge. Finish up the left side of the short wall.
Variations: (a) Climb the wall left of the usual start to the roof, step right and
finish as usual. (b) From the large ledge, finish rightwards – hard (6a). A fine,
testing route.
Synthesis (Not led, 6b): takes the roof direct, starting up variation (a) above.

12. Master Ego 12m E2 5c   (1983)
The left arête leads to the overhang. Pass it on its left to gain the ledge above
and finish as for Little Miss Id.

*A wide chimney/recess on the left has cracks at either side. The right-hand one
is:*

★ **13. Central Groove** 11m S 4a   (Pre-1951)
A steep and difficult start relents a little, higher up.

14. Central Crack 11m VD   (Pre-1951)
The left-hand crack gives a bold climb.

15. Central Eliminate 11m VS 5a   (Early 70s)
Climb between the two cracks.

Previous page: Dave Cronshaw exhibiting the **Six Nipples of Love** (E1 5b), Pinfold Quarry.
Photo: Les Ainsworth
Left: Geoff Harding needs rigid digits on **Digitation** (5c), Brownstones Quarry.
Photo: Dave Wilkinson

16. Cornflake 11m E2 5c   (1960/1963-69/1969)
The corner left of Central Crack leads to an obvious break. The flake can be
gained with difficulty and leads steeply to the top. Care is needed with
protection. A hard lead.

★ **17. The Mangler** 11m VS 5a   (1960)
The obvious overhanging crack provides a good testing pitch.

18. Belly on a Plate 12m VS 4c   (1992)
Start beneath The Mangler and climb the left-hand crack to an overhang. Pull
left and 'belly' on to a ledge. Climb the right arête of the chimney to the top.
There are other variations at a similar grade.

*The overhanging corner on the left has a hard start (4c) to gain the cave of the
next route.*

19. North Chimney 12m M   (1913)(1913)
Gain the cave from the left and leave it on the right.
Nor Nor' Chimney (VD) leaves the cave leftwards over a chockstone.

★ **20. Manibus et Pedibusque** 12m E4 6a   (1967/Early 1970s)
A difficult traverse across the wall left of Nor' Nor' Chimney leads to a finish
up the arête. A serious route with a controversial history!

The left end of the crag has a widening crack in its upper section.

21. Slim Jim 8m VS 5a   (1966)
A lower wall leads to the foot of the crack. After a bold move the crack eases.

★ **22. Phase Change** 34m E1 5c,5b   (1994)
1. 16m. Begin at the arête right of No Sign of Three. Climb up and traverse
cracks to the arête. Gain Twin Cracks and go up and across South Chimney to a
horizontal foot ledge. Balance across Pots and Tryche, then get across Little
Miss Id (crux) to the large ledge and a sitting belay (small friend and high,
large RP).
2. 18m. Go down and across to Central Groove. gain Central Crack, then go
leftwards and down to join Cornflake below a bulge. Climb up and left and gain
the wide cleft with difficulty, then wriggle (curse or laugh!) along until it is
possible to stand at the upper crack of Mangler. Continue more easily to join
the North Climbs and finish in the same line. For the hardy, it is possible to
join the traverse of Manibus et Pedibusque then finish up that route (E4, 6a).

Bouldering
*The boulders well to the right of the crag (near the trig. point) provide pleasant
bouldering in restful seclusion.*

First Ascents at Blackstone Edge
1913	**Twin Cracks**, *Far South Wall*, **South Chimney**, *South Cracks*, *Central Chimney*, **North Chimney**, **Nor Nor' Chimney** Probably John Laycock
Pre-1951	**Central Groove, Central Crack**
Pre-1957	**Pendulum Swing**
1960	**Cornflake** (with aid)
	Reduced to 1 pt aid, 1963-69.
	Aid completely eliminated in 1969.

1960	The Mangler
Pre-1962	Central Crack
1962	Pendulum Swing Direct
1962	Little Miss Id Richard McHardy
1966	Slim Jim Paul Horan, Ian Butterworth, Stu Halliwell
1967	Manibus et Pedibusque (with tension) Paul Horan
	Done without tension by Richard McHardy, early 1970s.
1957-69	Tryche (1 pt aid)
	First free ascent unknown.
Early 1970s	Central Eliminate Bruce Goodwin
1977 July 16	Pots Dennis Carr, Bruce Goodwin, Tony Cowcill
1983 June 4	No Sign of Three Tony Nichols, Bruce Goodwin, Steve Drewitt
1983 June 14	Master Ego Bruce Goodwin, Steve Drewitt, John Vose
1988 July	Slin and Thippy Ian Cooksey, Mark Radtke
1992 Aug	Belly on a Plate C M Burridge, Clive Barker
1994 Aug 8	Outside Edge Bruce Goodwin (unseconded)
1994 Sep 18	Palmistry Bruce Goodwin, Gordon Mason
1994 Sep 18	Phase Change Bruce Goodwin, Gordon Mason (alts)

Castle Quarry O.S. ref. SD 953 246

Situation and Character
Castle Quarry (or Lobb Mill Delf) stands above the Rochdale canal some two kilometres east of Todmorden. It is very steep and impressive with overhangs everywhere. The routes weave their way through this steep country, rather than attacking it frontally. The rock is surprisingly sound considering the appearance and atmosphere of the crag.

History
The Prow was the first route put up on this impressive (and oppressive) cliff, in 1966, and was pioneered by Bob Whittaker and Ian Butterworth. Whittaker returned in 1968 with Allan Austin and Mike Bebbington and Austin led both *Viking* and *Warrior. Crossbow* was added by Whittaker in 1969

Nothing more was added until 1977 when once again Whittaker paid a visit, this time with Ralph Pickering, to add *Carlite* and *Misty*, and then things rested yet again until Geoff Haigh and Geoff Hamridding climbed *Hooded Raider, Prophylaxis* and *Stealer of Souls* in 1979. The hardest route was added later that same year when Dave Cronshaw and Les Ainsworth claimed *Saxon* then the same pair, followed by John Ryden, found *Norseman* to which Ian Conway and Tony Nichols added a near relative, *Dane* in 1982.

There are several lines left to go, all of which encroach on to impressive territory, but it seems unlikely that it will ever rival its near-neighbour Heptonstall.

Access and Approach
The crag is approached from Haugh Lane (park near the viaduct on the main road). A path leads rightwards below the first house on the right and gains the cliff in 60 metres. Permission to climb has been granted by the owner.

The Climbs
The routes are described from LEFT to RIGHT.

1.   Crossbow   10m   VS   4c   (1969)
Climb the short corner with difficulty, then ledges slightly rightwards lead to a
steep wall just left of the corner. Surmount the overhang direct on to the wall
then a mantel gains the top.

2.   Carlite   10m   S   4a   (1977)
Swing over a prow a couple of metres to the right, and climb into the corner
above. Traverse left across the steep wall to finish up its left edge.

3.   Misty   12m   VS   4b   (1977)
Follow Carlite to the traverse, then gain the groove in the right wall and follow
this to the top.

*Six metres right, past the prow is a flat platform in a corner below huge roofs.
Here starts*:

4.   The Prow   14m   VD   (1966)
Climb diagonally left to the nose and follow the groove above to the top.

To the right is a large, cracked slab.

5.   Hooded Raider   18m   VS   4b,4b   (1979)
1.   10m.   Start from the left edge of the slab and climb the first jagged crack
to a roof, then move right to a break and surmount this to a belay.
2.   8m.   Climb the ramp on the left to finish up a short, wide crack.

6.   Prophylaxis   18m   VS   4c,4b   (1979)
1.   10m.   Climb the second jagged crack to the belay of Hooded Raider.
2.   8m.   Directly above is a wide chimney at the top of the crag. Aim for this
then climb the corner on the left.

7.   Stealer of Souls   18m   VS   4c,4c   (1979)
1.   10m.   As for Prophylaxis pitch one.
2.   8m.   Continue direct and up the wide chimney. Exit out right.

Mediaeval Wall
*This is the very impressive steep buttress on the right that is guarded by several
overhangs, and which strongly resembles parts of Heptonstall. Here are found
the best and hardest routes in the quarry.*

★★ 8.   Saxon   23m   E2   5c   (1981)
A good climb, which compares favourably with the best at the nearby
Heptonstall. Start from the lowest point on the wall at its left side and climb a
flake and shallow groove, then make a hard mantel to gain a standing position
on a small triangular foothold on the left (peg above). Follow the obvious
right-leading crack, then move left round the roof and continue straight up to
grass ledges. Peg belay by the grassy ledges.

9.   Dane   30m   E1   5b   (1982)
Climb Saxon for six metres, then follow the obvious right-slanting ledge for six
metres to its end. Mantel on to the sloping ledge above, then traverse back left
and finish up Saxon. (Peg belay).

★ **10. Longship** 34m E1 5b   (1981)
Start 30 metres right at a higher level, just left of an overhanging corner. Follow the obvious ramp left to a shallow cave, then step back round the nose on the left and continue in the same line to grass ledges overlooking Saxon.

11. Viking 31m VS 4c,4c   (1968)
1. 14m. Start at the same point and climb an overhanging crack just left of the corner for six metres to ledges. Move left for three metres to a cave, then go up to a second cave and belay.
2. 17m. From the left side of the cave climb a steep crack, and the wide crack above to a ledge. Finish up and to the right.

12. Warrior 27m VS 4c,4c   (1968)
1. 12m. Climb the overhanging corner, then move right over blocks and back left to a sloping ledge and belay.
2. 15m. From the right side of the ledge climb on to the slab above, then trend right to an obvious wide crack and finish up Viking.

13. Norseman 20m HS 4a,–   (1981)
1. 12m. 12 metres farther right is a shallow groove leading to a V-shaped niche. Climb this to a large ledge on the right.
2. 8m. Move left and climb up obvious cracks. Loose.

First Ascents at Castle Quarry

1966 Dec 26	**The Prow**	Bob Whittaker, Ian Butterworth
1968 June	**Viking, Warrior**	Allan Austin, Mike Bebbington, Bob Whittaker
1969	**Crossbow**	Bob Whittaker, Ralph Pickering
1977	**Carlite, Misty**	Bob Whittaker, Ralph Pickering
1979 Sep 15	**Hooded Raider, Prophylaxis, Stealer of Souls**	Geoff Haigh, Geoff Hamridding
1981	**Saxon, Longship**	Dave Cronshaw, Les Ainsworth
	Saxon was to be the big, quality route of the quarry.	
1981	**Norseman**	Dave Cronshaw, Les Ainsworth, John Ryden
1982 July 26	**Dane**	Ian Conway, Tony Nichols

Cow's Mouth Quarry   O.S. ref. SD 962 195

Situation and Character
Cow's Mouth Quarry is set beside a gravelled section of the Pennine Way, overlooking the valley about four kilometres north-east of Littleborough. The crag is sheltered and faces west, so it catches the sun. It is mainly composed of solid gritstone. Its slabs, walls, cracks and overhangs give the cliff a fine variety of climbs.

There are excellent views from this crag, which is a popular venue. Walkers and runners alike use the tracks hereabouts. It is possible to follow circuits of three to ten miles depending on one's inclination.

History
The records of climbing at Cow's Mouth stretch back to 1964 when members of the Solvé Club, started visiting the quarry. It appears that the first routes to fall were three easy chimneys, probably climbed by Pete Mustoe After this, Mustoe was tempted by the irresistible lines of *Z Crack*, which he did with John

Lowthian and its neighbour, *Overhanging Crack*, on which he was joined by Jim Schofield. Schofield also followed him up *Sandy Crack* on the same day.

At that time reports were just circulating in the climbing press about the use of bolts in the Dolomites. Suitably inspired, 'Ras' Taylor decided to experiment with bolting and he rawldrilled his way up a short, steep slab using woodscrews, to create *Screwy*. The unaided ascent of this line then became a major challenge, that was resolved a couple of years later by Bob Whittaker.

For some reason, there was very little new route activity in 1965 and the new routes were limited to Jed O'Neill's *Right Corner* and, despite its name, the more interesting *Bore* by Paul Horan. However, in 1966 the pioneering spirit was rekindled and by the end of that year the number of recorded climbs had risen to nearly two dozen. These included the excellent *Route One* by Ian Butterworth, *Cornette* by Lowthian, *Route Right* and the problematic *Flook* by Horan. Towards the end of the year Horan mustered sufficient courage for a head-on attack at the large neb at the right-hand side of the quarry, to produce the memorable *The Bijou*; a route that has seen its fair share of retreats, including one a few months later, when Stu Halliwell sidled off rightwards to create the pleasant but much less intimidating *Variation* to The Bijou.

The remaining years before the first appearance of the first Lancashire guidebook in 1969 some consolidation, with Horan adding *Dessers* and *Groovin'*, in 1967, whilst in 1968 Carl Fletcher added the changeable *Carl's Mark*.

The early 70s saw different groups taking an interest in the quarry. Bruce Goodwin soloed some of the easier routes, and in 1972 members of the Black and Tan M.C. soloed *Groundhog*, whilst Al Evans claimed *Los Endos*. In 1973 Whittaker made several visits, during which he added *Slab Crossing*, *Happy Wanderer* and the excellent *Overlapper*. The 1977 saw Evans and Brian Cropper add *Pavanne, The Romeo Error* and the superb *Daytona Wall*. The latter route caused some controversy at the time, with allegations of resting and dubious tactics being rife; it later transpired that Evans had, in fact, done the route completely free and once the dust had settled, a magnificent route remained. At the same time *Scree? Pain!* was named, when a premature attempt by Goodwin ended with his recumbent form on the scree below, nursing two cracked ribs! The route was led for the first time eight years later, when Andrew Eaton climbed it solo. The year's development ended when Cropper and Ian Lonsdale free-climbed *Three Little Piggies*; a fierce little crack climb that has been the bane of many an able climber.

The only significant event of the next year was Clive Morton and John Vose's traverse from Pavanne to Los Endos. Their route, *Movo*, was extended in 1981 by Whittaker and Geoff Hamridding as *Golden Slipper*, which needed a tension move from Romeo Error. However, it had to wait another two years to dispense with the aid, when Chris Hardy soloed it

The 1980s opened with a hard problem from John Ellis – *The Don*. The impending Lancashire guidebook then brought a rush of activity from Whittaker between 1981 and 1983, who added sixteen routes, the best of which were *King B, Slabmaster, Lapper, Space Invader, Wallin'* and *The Hand-Traverse*. Whittaker returned yet again and climbed *Deadline* in 1987, since when all was quiet until 1991 when Gareth Parry led *Boldness Through Ignorance*, then in 1996 Goodwin and John Lord added *Uncertainty*.

Access and Approach

There are no access restrictions in force here and the quarry can easily be reached from the A58 (Littleborough–Ripponden section). Cars can be parked just below the White House pub. Walk up the hill past the pub to iron gates on the left. Follow the Pennine Way, passing the reservoir, to reach the quarry in around 20 minutes. A good bus service (Halifax–Ripponden–Rochdale) passes the pub.

The White House also serves as an access point for White House Quarry and Blackstone Edge.

The Climbs

The routes are described from LEFT to RIGHT commencing with an obvious and excellent slab. The smaller upper quarried area (Bivouac Wall) has a 4c/5a traverse and some problems, as has the short wall at right-angles to the base of the slab. Most of the slab routes are character-building, with a bold feel to them. All are worth doing.

1.   Cornette   10m   D   (1966)
Climb the corner and the arête above on its left-hand side. Pleasant, but disjointed.

2.   Deadline   10m   VS   5a   (1987)
An eliminate line, starting from the large foothold on Route One. A hard move or two enables the break to be gained. Continue past a pocket and horizontal crack to a rounded finish.

★★ 3.   Route One   10m   HS   4c   (1966)
From a large foothold step up delicately right to holds. Climb directly to the break, then follow the groove above. A fine bold route which requires good footwork.

★ 4.   King B   10m   E1   5c   (1981)
An eliminate line just to the right again. Climb the slab, go over a steepening and on to the break. Finish up the second of three grooves. Delicate and fingery, requiring an honest, if blinkered, approach.

★★ 5.   Route Two   10m   VS   5a   (1966)
Boulder on to the slab below a groove. Continue with a step left then move back right and go up to the break. Finish by climbing the right-hand groove. A thought-provoking crux.

6.   Slabmaster   10m   VS   4c   (1981)
Climb the shallow groove at the right-hand side of the slab to a ledge, then continue direct past slots, or go left from the first slot and pull up the wall steeply (5a) to join Route Two.

7.   Route Right   10m   HS   4b   (1966)
Follow Slabmaster to the ledge, then trend rightwards to finish up Chimney Route.

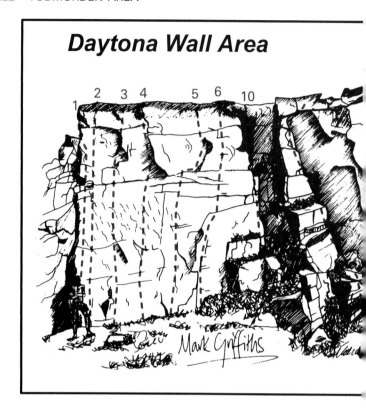

Daytona Wall Area

Mark Griffiths

★ **8.** **Slab Crossing** 12m HS 4b (1973)
The horizontal break can be traversed at foot level in either direction. Various starts and finishes are available. Traversing the break with hands at break level is equally good and is slightly harder (VS, 4b).

There are many variations possible on the slab using different starts, traverses and finishes. The best of these is:

9. **Happy Wanderer** 12m VS 4c (1973)
Climb Route One to the break, then traverse to the third groove on the upper wall and follow this to the top.

A low-level traverse of the slab is possible at 5a.

The grassy area to the right of the slab has two areas of clean rock.

10. **Chimney Route** 10m VD (1964)
Climb left of the grass directly to the final, awkward chimney.

11. **Right Corner** 12m VD (1965)
The disjointed corner right of the grass is climbed to a capstone. Exit right to finish.

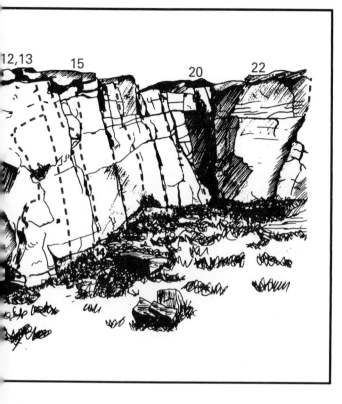

The orange/red wall on the right has been eyed by many and tried by a few. It awaits the future. Starting from the blunt arête however is a good climb.

★★★ **12. Daytona Wall** 10m E5 6a   (1977)(1984)
An excellent, challenging climb that is both bold and technical. On the first ascent a semblance of safety was provided by an old bolt that appeared to be stuck into a rotting piece of wood. In fact, it barely held the weight of a sling and had disappeared by the third ascent a week later! Start at a flake on the left. Traverse right then move up to a standing position. Go over a bulge to a pocket then traverse right until below another pocket. Finish direct. No protection.
Direct Start (6a): follow the faint crackline, then join the parent route.
Direct Finish (6b): climb more, or less, direct from the first pocket to the top.

★★ **13. Boldness Through Ignorance** 10m E7 6c   (1991)
A bold route that takes a direct line up the wall just right of Daytona Wall, joining that route at its last move. Start up the Direct Start to Daytona Wall, but instead of stepping left to the bolt, make some hard and slopy undercut moves past a peg to reach some 'monos' on the upper wall. Crank on these only looking at the bolt runner out to the left, to reach the top.

To the right is a steep wall, split by many cracks.

★ **14. Overlapper** 10m HVS 5b (1973)
Climb the first crack to a groove. Step left and finish direct.

★ **15. Lapper** 10m HVS 5b (1981)
Start as for Overlapper, but continue direct.

16. Dessers 9m HVS 5a (1967)
The crack right of Overlapper has a hard start.

★ **17. Sard** 9m HVS 5a (1981)
Climb the wall to the right of Dessers.

18. Seasy 9m HS 4c (1966)
The third crack. Climb with difficulty past a niche and continue direct.

19. Seasier 8m VD 4a (1966)(1967)
The left-slanting break is followed to its end, then climb directly to the top. The direct start is 5a.

20. Niche Direct 7m HS 4b (1981)
Gain the triangular niche on the right, and leave it by a thin crack.

21. Cracked Wall Chimney 7m D (1964)
The corner chimney is followed to either a left-hand or a right-hand finish.

★ **22. Space Invader** 16m VS 5a (1981)
A traverse from right to left. Climb Cracked Wall Chimney, go past the niche of Seazy and downward to Dessers. Ascend to the hand-traverse into Overlapper and finish as for that route.

23. Cow's Cheek 8m S 4a (1981)
Start at Cracked Wall Chimney, then go rightwards past a nose to a ledge and finish rightwards.

24. Calf 7m VD (1981)
The crack on the right leads to a wider crack above.

★ **25. Cow's Rib** 8m D (1973)
The obvious rib down and right of Calf.

26. Cow's Hide 8m S 4a (1981)
Ascend by laybacking just right of the rib to gain a thin crack and the top.

27. The 'Udder' Way 8m S 4a (1981)
Climb Cow's Hide to the ledge, then finish rightwards.

The steep wall on the right has the remains of an ancient bolt route. It also has a short, fierce free route which has repelled attempts by various notables.

★ **28. Three Little Piggies** 7m E3 6b (1977)
The impending wall leads the climber to a thin crack from which a relenting finish leads, tauntingly, to the top.

At the right-hand end of the wall is a faint arête with flakes above.

29. Carl's Mark 7m E2 5c   (1968)
Gain a ledge on the arête, then continue steeply up the flakes to finish. Some
suspect rock makes this route a serious lead.

30. Bob's Mark 7m HS 4b   (1981)
Climb the overhanging corner on the right. Gain a ledge with difficulty, then
finish up the crack on the left.

31. Mark Bob 6m S 4a   (1981)
Two metres to the right climb the crack then the wall above.

*The quarry floor now drops to a lower level. The next route starts directly
below a vertical bore-hole which is high up, and just right of the arête.*

32. Bore 11m VS 4b   (1965)
Start below the bore-hole. Climb the wall to a ledge then climb just right of the
bore to finish left of the arête.

An easy way down; **Intro** *(M) follows. To the right of this is a prow.*

33. Flake Crack 6m D   (1965)
Climb the flake to a ledge on the left of the prow.

34. Scruff 6m VD   (1965)
A groove on the right, has a jammed block at its base. Follow the groove to a
square-cut groove which leads to the finish.

35. Scruffy 6m D   (1979-83)
The steep wall right of the groove.

*To the right is a square-cut overhang at three metres. The groove to the left of
this is*:

36. Groove 9m S 4a   (1967)
Climb to a ledge, then follow the groove to a second ledge. Traverse left for
two metres and climb the wall.

37. Wallin' 6m VS 5c   (1981)
Make difficult moves up the wall to the overhang, then go more easily direct to
ledges. Traverse off, or follow the groove.

38. Groovin' 6m HS 4b   (1967)
From a slabby boulder, climb the groove to ledges, then finish as for Groove, or
traverse off.

39. The Romeo Error 9m E1 5c   (1977)(1984)
Start up Groovin', then traverse thinly right to below a sloping ledge. Gain this,
then step delicately up to the break and finish direct, or duck out leftwards.
Direct Start (6a): leads to the sloping ledge.

★ **40. Screwy** 10m E2 5c   (1964/1966)
Further right is a line of wood screws. Climb the smooth slab, trusting the
rubber, to the break (old peg above). Finish direct.

★ 41. Groundhog 10m HVS 5b (1972)
A good series of moves up the wall to the left of Sandy Crack, with a runner in the crack.

42. Sandy Crack 9m VS 5a (1964)
The crack left of the chimney is followed, starting awkwardly and easing off higher up. Step right to finish. Bridging to the chimney reduces the grade to 4c.

43. The Hand-Traverse 11m VS 5a (1981)
Climb Sandy Crack to the break, then traverse left.

44. Curving Chimney 8m D (1964)
The obvious chimney gives good practice in wedging, squirming and 'udging. A must for cavers.

45. Jumping Jive 6m HVS 5b (1985)
Gain the large ledge right of the chimney. Continue dynamically just right of the cleft, or make a long reach. Graded for tall leaders who will find protection. For smaller leaders it is a solo.

46. Pavanne 6m HVS 5a (1977)
Mantel or belly-flop on to the large ledge. Go up and right, stepping carefully, until it is possible to finish up Overhanging Crack. Unprotected where it matters.

★ 47. Overhanging Crack 7m VS 4c (1964)
The obvious crack gives sustained climbing to an awkward finish.

★★ 48. Z Crack 8m VS 5a (1964)
Obvious from the shape! Climb awkwardly to a horizontal break, then finish direct from the second crack, or harder (HVS, 5a) by moving left to follow a little groove to the top. Varied, interesting and testing.

49. The Don 7m E1 6a (1980)
The wall to the right of Z Crack. Ascend directly on small holds. No protection.

50. Los Endos 7m HVS 5a (1972)
The arête has a problem start on its left-hand side, though it can also be gained more easily from the right. No runners.

51. Golden Slipper 18m E1 5c (1979/1981/1983)
An extension of a previous route called Movo. Climb Romeo Error to its sloping ledge. Traverse right with difficulty to Sandy Crack, then cross the chimney to the large ledge, and follow Pavanne to Overhanging Crack. Go up and across to Z Crack, then continue more easily to Los Endos. Finish up the arête. Poorly protected on the first section (i.e. a solo).

Just right of Los Endos is an ascending 'scree slope'. A narrow, horizontal slot can be seen in the upper section of the wall.

52. Scree? Pain! 6m E2 6a (1985)
Climb the wall to the slot. Pull on the slot and go for the top. The upper section is easier (5c) using the edge on the left. Sustained, unprotected and with a painful landing.

There is a wall at a higher level which gives a fine collection of routes and problems. Most are protectionless and so it is as well that the landings are good.

53.   Flupper   6m   VS   5a   (1976)
Climb the left side of the blunt arête until forced rightwards. Finish direct.

54.   Flipper   6m   S   4b   (1964)
Start from a footledge right of the arête. Step up, surmount the little bulge and continue daintily.

55.   Flopper   6m   VS   4c   (1980s)
Start at a horizontal flake below a shallow groove. Go up and trend left to finish.

56.   Flapper   6m   VS   5b   (1966)
Start at a foothold and go up, then left and reach for rounded edges. Continue to the big ledge.

57.   Flook   6m   HVS   5b   (1966)
Climb the wall three metres to the left of the right-hand arête on 'slopers' to reach a small protuberant fingerhold. Continue and pull for the finishing holds. Strenuous.

58.   Flak   6m   Not led   6a   (1987)
The sloping, rounded horizontally-flaked arête is followed closely to one of those awful, sloping, rounded finishes. Sustained and usually, very frustrating.

59.   Flooper   10m   D   (1966)
Climb the shallow corner on the arête, moving rightwards. The angle then eases and the ascent continues leftwards over a nose.

Just to the right there are some scrambles and a corner-cum-chimney. The rounded wall on the right leads to the obvious overhang of The Bijou. The wall itself has a good, tricky route:

60.   Uncertainty   9m   E2   5c   (1996)
Start below and left of the overhang. Climb a bulge, then go up left to a ledge. Make a difficult move to gain the large sloping ledge. Above and left is a flat flake on the finishing slab. Gain the flake and the finish is then close at hand.

61.   The Bijou   10m   HVS   5a   (1966)
Climb up on the right side of the roof. Move out left and go up past the roof to gain the break. Finish easily on large holds.

62.   The Bijou – The Variation   8m   HS   4b   (1967)
Climb The Bijou, but avoid that intimidating leftward prospect and continue pleasantly up the breaks.

First Ascents at Cow's Mouth Quarry

1964	**Chimney Route, Cracked Wall Chimney, Curving Chimney** Probably Pete Mustoe
1964	**Z Crack, Flipper** Pete Mustoe, John Lowthian
1964	**Overhanging Crack, Sandy Crack** Pete Mustoe, Jim Schofield
1964	**Screwy** (A1) 'Ras' Taylor
	First free ascent by Bob Whittaker, 1966.
1965	**Flake Crack, Scruff** John Lowthian, Pete Mustoe

1965	**Bore** Paul Horan, Kathleen Meeks
1966	**Seazy** Stu Halliwell, Ian Butterworth
1966	**Seasier** Ian Butterworth, John Lowthian
	Direct Start by Paul Horan, Stu Halliwell, 1967.
1966	**Route One** Ian Butterworth, Stu Halliwell
1966	**Route Two** Paul Horan, Stu Halliwell
1966	**Flapper, Flook, Flooper, Route Right** Paul Horan (solo)
1966	**Cornette** John Lowthian, Pete Mustoe
1965	**Right Corner** Jed O'Neill, Geoff Smith
1966	**The Bijou** Paul Horan, Ian Butterworth
1966	**Screwy** Bob Whittaker
	First free ascent.
1967	**Dessers** Paul Horan, Leonard Bradshaw
1967	**Groovin'** Paul Horan, Ian Butterworth
1967	**Groove** Stu Halliwell, John Lothian
1967	**The Bijou – The Variation** Stu Halliwell, John Lothian
1968	**Carl's Mark** Carl Fletcher, Geoff Smith
1972	**Groundhog** Black and Tan MC members
1972	**Los Endos** Al Evans, Brian Cropper
1973 May 11	**Overlapper** Bob Whittaker, Mick Gorton
1973 May 11	**Cow's Rib** Bob Whittaker (solo)
1973 May	**Slab Crossing** Bob Whittaker (solo)
1973	**Happy Wanderer** Bob Whittaker, Richard Sawicki
1976	**Flupper** Bruce Goodwin (solo)
1977 July	**The Romeo Error, Pavanne** Al Evans, Brian Cropper
	Romeo Error, Direct Start by Andrew Unsworth, 1984.
1977 Sep 29	**Three Little Piggies** Brian Cropper, Ian Lonsdale
1977	**Daytona Wall** Al Evans, Brian Cropper
	Direct Start by Phil Kelly (solo), 15 Mar 1984.
1980	**The Don** John Ellis (solo)
1981 Jan 24	**Bob's Mark, Mark Bob, The Hand-Traverse** Bob Whittaker, Geoff Hamridding
1981 Jan 24	**Golden Slipper** Bob Whittaker, Geoff Hamridding (with tension)
	First ascent without tension by Chris Hardy (solo), 23 June 1983.
	This superseded Movo, which finished at Los Endos, by Clive Morton, John Vose, 1979.
1981 Jan 24	**Wallin'** Bob Whittaker (solo)
1981 May 10	**Sard** Bob Whittaker, Derek Wright
1981 May 10	**Niche Direct** Bob Whittaker (solo)
1981 May 10	**Space Invader** Bob Whittaker, Ralph Pickering, Derek Wright, Les Hardman
1981 May 11	**King B** Bob Whittaker, Ralph Pickering
1981 May 12	**Lapper** Bob Whittaker, Derek Wright
1981 May 12	**Cow's Cheek, Calf, Cow's Hide, The 'Udder' Way** Bob Whittaker (solo)
1981 May 12	**Slabmaster** Bob Whittaker, Ralph Pickering, Derek Wright
1979-83	**Scruffy** Bob Whittaker
Early 1980s	**Flopper** John Hampson
1985 Aug 30	**Jumping Jive** Bruce Goodwin, John Lord
1985	**Scree? Pain!** Andrew lEaton (solo)
1987 Nov 19	**Deadline** Bob Whittaker (solo)
1991 July	**Boldness Through Ignorance** Gareth Parry
1996 Sep 22	**Uncertainty** Bruce Goodwin, John Lord

Cross Stone Quarry

O.S. ref.   SD 951 248

Situation and Character

This quarry, which is known locally as Beanpole Delf, overlooks the
Todmorden–Hebden Bridge road (A6033), about two kilometres from the centre
of Todmorden and almost directly below an obvious church tower on the
skyline. The climbing is limited, but nevertheless, some of the climbs are very
worthwhile and it is a good place for a quiet evening.

History

Bob Whittaker and Ian Butterworth discovered the quarry at Christmas 1966
after they had just climbed the first route in Castle Quarry and to stake their
claim, they put up a solitary route, *Endless Flight*. The quarry was then left until
1980, when Whittaker returned with Geoff Hamridding and added several more
routes, the best of which was *Broken Lance*. A few weeks later Derek Wright
climbed the four 'shifts'.

In March 1997, following successful access negotiations with the new owner,
Dave Cronshaw made a long-overdue attempt to force a route on The Prow, to
give *Bean Stalk*.

Access and Approach

The owner is willing to permit climbing, provided that visitors accept that
climbing is at their own risk. The owner also asks that climbers should park
sensibly and leave no litter.

To reach the quarry from Todmorden, go towards Hebden Bridge for about one
kilometre to the Shannon and Chesapeake pub, then turn left up Phoenix Street
and after a further 150 metres turn right into Shakespeare Avenue. Where the
road turns left, go right then left on to a dirt track. Pass some houses and follow
the track rightwards below the quarry, where cars can be parked just off the
track.

The Climbs

The routes are described from LEFT to RIGHT.

Cross Stone Walls

*This is the section of rock at the far left of the quarry, which ends at a
square-cut prow.*

1.   Stretcher Case   9m   HS   4a   (1981)
The first, overhanging corner in the quarry.

2.   Vulcan   10m   VS   4c   (1981)
Five metres to the right is a groove on the right edge of a blunt arête. Gain the
right side of a large ledge at four metres, then step left and climb the groove
then slabs above.

3.   Vulcan's Variant   11m   VS   4c   (1981)
From the right side of the ledge of Vulcan, climb the continuation groove, then
finish as for Vulcan.

★ **4.** **Endless Flight** 12m VS 5a (1966)
The hanging flake on the wall to the right.

★ **5.** **Bird Lime Corner** 13m HS 4b (1981)
Climb the corner on the right to a belay ledge, then cross the wall on the left to finish.

★★ **6.** **Broken Lance** 13m E1 5b (1980)
A committing route. Even though it avoids the challenge of the top arête, it is nevertheless interesting, with some testing moves. The sharp arête on the right is climbed until a scoop leads left to the belay. Finish as for Bird Lime Corner.

The Prow
This is the obvious square-shaped buttress which projects slightly forward of the other rock.

★★ **7.** **Bean Stalk** 11m E1 5b (1997)
The enticing line up the face of The Prow. Start below a groove in the left arête of The Prow. Climb the groove to a small overhang, then make a balancy move to reach a hidden hold on the wall. Make a delicate move to gain the ramp above, then finish easily.

Back Wall
Farther to the right, the quarry is recessed into a slabby wall.

8. **Recess Crack** 11m S 4a (1981)
The thin crack immediately right of the obvious gully.

9. **Black Crack** 11m HS 4a (1981)
Starting behind a small pinnacle climb the crack on the right.

10. **Crumble Corner** 12m HVS 5a (1981)
The loose corner on the right.

Seamed Wall
The wall to the right has four prominent cracks and ends in a corner.

11. **Redshift** 13m VS 4c (1980)
The first crack.

12. **Whiteshift** 13m VS 4b (1980)
The chimney crack, going leftwards to finish.

13. **Nightshift** 13m VS 4b (1980)
The next thin crack, moving left to finish.

14. **Landshift** 13m VS 4c (1980)
The broken crack on the right to a grass ledge, then the wider crack above.

Geoff Hibbert on **The Bijou** (HVS 5a), a little gem, Cow's Mouth Quarry.

Photo: Joanne Hibbert

15. Gates of Eden 13m VS 4c (1981)

The corner which bound the wall on its right is climbed to a grass ledge. Finish over loose rock.

16. The Jugular 12m HS 4a (1981)

The crack and ledges three metres farther right.

First Ascents at Cross Stone Quarry

1966 Dec 26   **Endless Flight**   Ian Butterworth, Bob Whittaker
              On same day as The Prow at Castle Qy
1980 Sep   **Broken Lance**   Bob Whittaker, Geoff Hamridding
1980   **Redshift, Whiteshift, Nightshift, Landshift**   Derek Wright
1981 May   **Bird Lime Corner**   Geoff Hamridding, Bob Whittaker
1981 May   **Stretcher Case, Vulcan, Vulcan's Variant**   Bob Whittaker,
              Geoff Hamridding
1981 June   **Recess Crack, Black Crack, Crumble Corner, Gates of Eden, The Jugular**
              Phil Conolly
1997 Mar 9   **Bean Stalk**   Dave Cronshaw, Les Ainsworth

Gauxholme Crag   O.S. ref. SD 927 231

Situation and Character

The crag overlooks the Bacup–Todmorden road (A681) about 200 metres from its junction with the A6033 Todmorden–Littleborough road. Its position is a climber's dream – in the '*garden*' of the cottage to its left. The crag is about 25 metres high, of dark gritstone with an obvious roof near its top.

History

Graham Wood did *Wood's Route* in 1966 and the following year Bob Whittaker, Carl Fletcher and Geoff Smith added *Pillar Face*.

Access

Access is with the permission of the owner who lives in the cottage adjacent to the crag. This has readily been given in the past.

The Climbs

The climbs take the centre of the main face. A bracket is bolted to the wall and a ramp drops down leftwards to the ground.

1. Pillar Face 24m VS (1pt) 4c,4a (1967)

1. 15m. Go up the ramp to the overhang and over this with a nut for aid to the ledges above. Move diagonally left to belay under the roof.
2. 9m. Traverse right around the arête. A slabby corner leads to the top.

2. Wood's Route 24m VS/A2 4c,A2 (1966)

1. 15m. As for Pillar Face.
2. 9m. Artificial climbing over the roof on bolts and screws.

Paul Horan on an early ascent of **Order** (HS 4a), in 1967, Summit Quarry.

Photo: Paul Horan collection

First Ascents at Gauxholme

1966	**Wood's Route**	Graham Wood
1967	**Pillar Face**	Bob Whittaker, Carl Fletcher, Geoff Smith

Hall Stones Quarry   O.S. ref. SD 946 263

Situation and Character

Hall Stones (previously incorrectly known as Lower Winsley) is a small delf situated on the edge of the moors about two kilometres north of Todmorden. The climbs are short and the crag is not very extensive, but the rock is excellent and although it is certainly not the place for the hard man, it is a very pleasant setting for a summer evening visit for climbers in the lower grades.

History

Most of the climbs were first recorded by Les Ainsworth, Dave Cronshaw, and John Ryden on three snatched visits during the summer of 1982, but true first ascent details are not known.

Access and Approach

The owners do not currently wish climbers to use the quarry, but it is hoped that access will be permitted in the future.

The quarry is reached from the Todmorden–Hebden Bridge road via Cross Stone Road, which forks left about half a kilometre east of the centre of Todmorden. At the top of the hill, just before the church, turn left into Hey Head Lane and follow this for about 1.5 kilometres to two sharp bends. Cars can be parked out of the way at the second bend. About 100 metres farther up the road, directly opposite the entrance to Hall Stones Green Farm, a public footpath leads through a stile (a bit of a squeeze) and past the foot of the quarry.

The Climbs

The climbs are described from RIGHT to LEFT, starting at the far right, where there is a short buttress with two obvious drill marks at its top. These can be reached by two excellent problems, **Right Drill** (5c) and **Left Drill** (5b).

1.   Soot Juggler 8m HS 4a   (1982)
Climb the left side of the hanging leaf of rock, then step left and finish up the arête.

2.   Blackface 8m VS 5a   (1982)
Start four metres left and climb the thin crack to a grassy ledge, then finish more easily up the wall above.

On the left there is an easy grassy **DESCENT**, *then, at right-angles, is the main buttress.*

3.   Win 8m S 4a   (1982)
Start at the right side of the buttress at a small letter-box and climb straight up to the top.

4.   Roman Letocetum   8m   D   (1982)
Start three metres left at a slightly higher level and climb the slab via a shallow scoop.

★ **5.   Bystander**   9m   HVS   5a   (1982)
Follow the obvious right-slanting fault which is the main feature of the wall.

★ **6.   The Watch**   9m   VS   4b   (1982)
Follow Bystander until a move left leads to ledges and an easier finish.

7.   Hall or Nothing   8m   E1   5b   (1990s)
Climb the rib on the right side of the large overhang to a good slot above the lip, then finish up the wall above past a peg. Peg belay.

8.   Stopwatch   12m   VS   4b   (1982)
Start at a slightly lower level at an inverted triangular niche. Climb the thin crack above to a large ledge, then traverse right with hands or feet on this ledge into a cave-like depression. Finish up the short, shallow corner above. Peg belay.

To the left, after a grassy break, is a more broken section of rock.

9.   Winsley Slab   8m   S   4a   (1982)(1982)
Climb the obvious flake-cum-slab, veering slightly rightwards to gain the upper slab and the top.
Direct Finish (4a): the obvious roof above the first slab can be climbed direct.

10.   First Come   8m   S   4a   (1982)
Start four metres to the left at the back of a small bay. Climb up and slightly left through a break by an awkward mantel to the top.

First Recorded Ascents at Hall Stones Quarry
1982	**Soot Juggler, The Watch**	Les Ainsworth, Dave Cronshaw, John Ryden
1982	**Blackface, Bystander**	Dave Cronshaw, Les Ainsworth, John Ryden
1982	**Win, Stopwatch**	John Ryden, Les Ainsworth, Dave Cronshaw
1982	**Roman Letocetum, Winsley Slab**	Les Ainsworth (solo)
	Winsley Slab, Direct Finish by Dave Cronshaw (solo)	
1982	**First Come**	John Ryden (solo)
Pre-1994	**Hall or Nothing**	

Lumbutts Quarry   O.S. ref.   SD 955 223

Situation and Character
The various quarry faces that collectively constitute Lumbutts Quarry lie along Langfield Edge, which faces north-east, overlooking the village of Lumbutts, about three kilometres south-east of Todmorden.

Excellent views and restful seclusion make Lumbutts a pleasant place to climb, although its north-easterly aspect dictates that good weather is required to fully enjoy the routes. The main quarry is impressive at first sight, but a closer inspection shows otherwise. Perhaps the evolution of a new breed of '*railway navvy*' could make this section climbable (or the development of the portable JCB). There are a few routes, but the best climbing is found on the three buttresses at the left-hand end of the edge, past the Main Wall. There is a little loose rock, but this is usually obvious and is noted in the text. For the middle-grade climber there is much to enjoy at Lumbutts – a curate's egg of a crag.

History

The earliest climbers to visit Lumbutts obviously kept quiet about their discoveries, as when John Taylor and Geoff Bradshaw ascended the first recorded route, *Desperado*, in 1966, *Bolt Route* existed even then!

Fourteen years after Desperado, Bob Whittaker and friends visited the crag and a wave of intense development began. Whittaker put up most of the easier routes and of the hardest, the best were probably *Rojim, Bob's Crack, The Hunter, Deliverance, Tired Digits, Cuckoo's Nest* and *Rings of Saturn. Ron's Crack* was the work of Ron Blunt, whilst Harry Taylor added *Flash Harry*. January 4th 1981 was a particularly productive day, when, despite a snow storm, Haigh and Harry Taylor added *Split Pin, Crumble Corner* and *Cold Digits*. A few months later Dave Cronshaw, with Whittaker and Les Ainsworth, climbed *The Warp* and *Warp Factor* and in 1983 Tony Nichols soloed *Nican*.

In 1986 Gordon Mason and Bruce Goodwin added a good direct finish to *The Hunter* and also put up a complementary route – *The Killer*. Desperado was regardened and in its new and unprotected state it was found to be a little harder than its previous HVS, 4c grade. In the Hidden Wall area, Goodwin added *Goma* and the excellent *Alibob* whilst Andrew Eaton showed good technique on *Digital Abuse* then Goodwin, as a final flourish, ascended the overhanging crack system left of Bolt Route, for the well-named *Power Surge*.

Access and Approach

There are no access problems and there is a right-of-way leading from the Shepherd's Rest up to the edge, linking with a network of footpaths, including the Pennine Way.

The Shepherd's Rest can be reached from the A6033 Todmorden–Littleborough road from Walsden. Follow the Lumbutts and Mankinholes signs, always bearing right until the pub is reached after three kilometres; park opposite. A gate gives access to a footpath leading up the hill and along the base of the rocks. The pub can also be approached from Spring Side, about two kilometres on the Hebden Bridge side of Todmorden; a lane opposite the Rose and Crown pub crosses the canal and leads up to Lumbutts village, and the Shepherd's Rest lies a little over a kilometre farther on. The crag is reached after a pleasantly brisk 20-minute walk.

The Climbs

All the climbs are described from RIGHT to LEFT. The unfortunately named Main Quarry is the large expanse of rock first seen from the approach path. The best climbing is found well to the left of this region. The Pillar is a good reference point and Hidden Wall is up the grass slope to its right. There are some climbs in the Main Quarry, starting at the Solar Slabs Area.

Solar Slab Area
Solar Slab lies part-way along the main cliff, at a lower level and is set at an angle. An obvious wide crack just right of the right arête of Solar Slab is the first route described.

1. Rings of Saturn 12m E2 5c (1981)
Climb the wide crack.

The slab round to the left has a ledge running across it and two cracklines.

2. Lazer Beam 15m HVS 5b (1981)
Gain the ledge and traverse right past both cracks to finish just left of the arête.

3. Star Wars 14m VS 4c (1981)
The right-hand crack is gained from the ledge.

4. Quasar 12 m S 4a (1981)
From the grass ledge follow the right-leaning crack and finish over ledges.

5. Black Hole 12m VD (1981)
The curving corner a couple of metres left.

30 metres left is a crack in a steep slab with a grass ledge.

6. Split Pin 12m VS 4b (1981)
The crack is gained from the left and leads to a difficult finish.

7. Bungalow 12m VS 5a (1981)
Above Split Pin, and slightly to the left, is a low roof which leads leftwards to a corner. Climb over the roof to a small ledge and move right to finish up the slabby corner.

8. Wishbone 14m VS 5a (1981)
Climb out of a shallow corner and go up to a ledge, then continue up a crack on the left.

Hidden Wall Area
The Hidden Wall area is split into two sections, separated by a grassy mound. The right-hand area has a series of steep corners, arêtes and cracks, whilst as a contrast the left-hand side contains mostly slab routes, though with some steeper walls. At the right side of the right-hand area lies a corner with a steep slab.

9. R.P. 8m D (1981)
Climb the series of steps in the shallow groove to the top.

10. Recessed Slab 8m VS 4b (1981)
The right-slanting corner, left of R.P.

11. Flash Harry 9m VS 4c (1981)
Start as for Recessed Slab, then climb the twin cracks in the groove on the left.

12. Daz 9m VS 4c   (1981)
Follow Flash Harry to the overhang, then layback left round this and finish up
an arête.

★ **13. The Warp** 10m VS 5a   (1981)
The steep groove and flake around to the left.

★ **14. Bob's Crack** 10m VS 4c   (1981)
The obvious crack two metres to the left.

The loose corner on the left is best ignored. To its left is:

★ **15. Ron's Crack** 9m HVS 5b   (1981)
Climb the crack which bends left and has a niche in it, to a hard finish.
Sustained.

★ **16. Warp Factor** 9m HVS 5c   (1981)
A couple of metres left of Ron's Crack, climb the thin crack.

17. Armstretcher 8m HS 4b   (1981)
Climb the corner just to the left, traversing left to finish up the arête.

18. Silk Cut 8m S 4a   (1981)
The next arête is taken on its left.

19. Crumble Corner 6m D   (1981)
The next corner.

★ **20. Tired Digits** 6m HVS 5b   (1981)
The arête on the left leads steeply to an awkward upper section.

21. Cold Digits 6m D   (1981)
The last corner.

22. Digit 6m VS 4c   (1981)
The thin crack in the steep wall just to the left.

Slab Area
The Slab Area is over the quarry rise. The slab has a block at its lowest point.
Here starts:

★ **23. Alibob** 9m E1 6a   (1986)
Gain sloping holds, move up and right then delicately step up to the break and
the top. Good.

★ **24. Rojim** 8m VS 4c   (1981)
Climb the slab rightwards to gain a crack/groove, then climb to the left of the
two '*pods*' to finish.

25. Goma 6m HVS 5b   (1986)
A shallow groove on the left gives a hard start which, thankfully, relents on the
upper wall. Low in the grade.

To the left is a large ledge at two-thirds-height. Two crack systems gain this ledge; the right-hand one is **Dry** *(VD) and the left-hand is* **Damp** *(D). Traverse off to finish both of them.* **Waterslide** *(HS, 4c) is the oft-wet corner whilst the flake left of the arête is* **Flaky** *(S). The slab at the end of this section has a corner with a jamming crack (***Sandman** *VD) whilst the rib on the left is* **Blunt Rib** *(S).*

The Pillar

This buttress gives routes of up to 20 metres long. The climbs are usually solid and any loose rock is obvious. The far right-hand side of the buttress has a slabby wall and some grass.

26. Nican 10m HVS 5a (1983)
Gain a grass ledge then step left and climb a slab, finishing rightwards; serious.

27. Desperado 20m E4 5c (1966)
The shallow corner just right of the pillar proper gives unprotected climbing to a ledge (loose block and poor protection on arrival). Follow a left-slanting weakness to a large in-situ peg below the Direct Finish to The Hunter. Either climb this to finish, or skulk off left.

★ **28. The Hunter** 20m HVS 5a (1981)(1986)
From Desperado, follow a ramp leftwards to a flaky crack. Go left and up to a corner which leads to the terrace.
Direct Finish (5a): the wall above the huge in-situ peg gives a steep and airy finish.

★ **29. The Killer** 20m HVS 5a (1986)
Start to the left of the arête. Go right over an overlap to join The Hunter at the flaky crack. Climb this then traverse right and ascend slightly leftwards to a large ledge and the huge in-situ peg. Finish as for the above route or traverse right for three metres and pass a bulge rightwards to an easing finish (4c).

30. True Grit 12m VS 4c (1981)
Follow a bore-hole to a ledge and continue steeply to the grass terrace. A corner above can provide a finish, if desired.

The path passes beneath an orange/brown wall. Above a step in the path are some thin cracks.

31. Digital Abuse 9m E2 6a (1986)
Climb the wall, more or less direct, just left of the cracks; fingery!

There is a chimney at the left end of the wall; three metres to the right is:

32. Deliverance 9m HVS 5b (1981)
Gain the niche three metres above the ground with difficulty, then continue up the crack above.

33. Cuckoo's Nest 8m E1 5c (1981)
From the chimney go up and right to a crack, then the top. Hard.

20 metres farther left is a buttress with 'W. Kershaw' chiselled into the rock.

34. Convoy   9m   HS   4a   (1981)
Climb to a ledge and follow a ramp leftwards to the top.

*A block about 20 metres from the cliff gives some worthwhile problems. The
steep face on the left has a line of rusting ironmongery running its height –*
Bolt Route *(A1). The central weakness of the wall is:*

★★ **35. Power Surge**   12m   E3   5c   (1986)
A sustained and technical outing! Start with difficulty and gain the niche (hard)
then go left and up to a second niche. Exit this and go left and finish direct.
There is a belay stake to the left.

36. Bull's Horns   12m   VD   (1981)
The corner at the left end of the wall leads to a ledge, then finish through the
'Bull's Horns' above.

First Ascents at Lumbutts Quarry

Pre-1966   **Bolt Route**
1966   **Desperado** John Taylor, Geoff Bradshaw
             This was the first recorded route and even then the Bolt Route existed.
1981 Jan 4   **Crumble Corner** Harry Taylor, Geoff Haigh
1981 Jan 11 **Cold Digits** Harry Taylor, Geoff Haigh
1981 Jan 11 **Dry** Ron Blunt, Bob Whittaker
1981 Jan 11 **Sandman, Blunt Rib** Ron Blunt (solo)
1981 May 1   **Rings of Saturn, Lazer Beam, Star Wars** Bob Whittaker, Ralph Pickering
1981 May 2   **Black Hole, Silk Cut, Damp** Bob Whittaker (solo)
1981 May 2   **Recessed Slab, Bob's Crack, Armstretcher** Bob Whittaker, Ralph
             Pickering
1981 May 2   **Bull's Horns** Les Harman, Bob Whittaker
1981 May 23 **The Warp, Warp Factor** Dave Cronshaw, Les Ainsworth, Bob Whittaker
1981 May 23 **Waterslide, Ledgeway** Bob Whittaker (solo)
1981 May 24 **Split Pin, Wishbone** Derek Wright, Bob Whittaker, Ron Blunt
1981 May 24 **Bungalow** Bob Whittaker, Derek Wright, Ron Blunt
1981 May 24 **Flash Harry** Chris ?, Bob Whittaker
1981 May 24 **Daz** Harry Taylor, Chris ?
1981 May 24 **Ron's Crack** Ron Blunt, Bob Whittaker
1981 May 31 **Quasar** Ron Blunt, Bob Whittaker
1981 May 31 **Flaky** Harry Taylor (solo)
1981 Aug 9   **True Grit** Derek Wright, Bob Whittaker, Ralph Pickering
1981 Sep 4   **Convoy** Bob Whittaker, Gordon Mason (both solo)
1981 Sep 4   **Tired Digits, Digit, Rojim, Deliverance, Cuckoo's Nest** Bob Whittaker,
             Gordon Mason
1981 Sep 4   **The Hunter** Bob Whittaker, Gordon Mason
             Direct Finish by Gordon Mason, Bruce Goodwin, Aug 1986.
1981 Dec 26 **R.P.** Ralph Pickering, Bob Whittaker
1983   **Nican** Tony Nichols (solo)
1986 July 10 **Alibob** Bruce Goodwin, Tony Nichols, Gordon Mason
1986 July 10 **Goma** Bruce Goodwin, Gordon Mason
1986 July 24 **The Killer** Gordon Mason, Bruce Goodwin
1986 Aug 18 **Power Surge** Bruce Goodwin, Gordon Mason
1986   **Digital Abuse** Andrew Eaton

Reddyshore Scout

O.S. ref. SD 942 197

Situation and Character

Reddyshore Scout is the series of buttresses that lie on the eastern rim of the moorland plateau overlooking the river Roch and the Rochdale canal, some four kilometres north of Littleborough.

This collection of steep buttresses is in an imposing and exposed position, further enhanced by the angle of the slope beneath. The sense of exposure that this situation engenders gives it that big crag feel and ensures that seconds must belay to the rock. The excellent routes are usually on sound rock, and where there is loose rock it is noted in the text, and does not interfere, usually, with the quality of the climbing. However, all visitors must be aware that rockfalls do occur.

The crags face east and thus are in the shade by the afternoon. Therefore, it is worth waiting for a spell of fine weather before visiting the crag, though the routes dry reasonably quickly. The black wall of Fence Buttress, from Tattersall's Lament to Hidden Gem, contains a fine collection of routes well worth seeking out.

History

The first routes date from 1959, when Rochdale guru Bob Whittaker with Bill Hardacre put up *Layback Corner*. They also added *Tattersall's Lament* in 1961 and added a brace of routes the following year; including the excellent *Blind Panic*. Les Ainsworth, Ian Cowell, Paul Hamer and John McGonagle 'discovered' the crag in 1967 and climbed about ten routes, but sadly their records were subsequently lost. The initial exploration period ended when Jud O'Neill demonstrated that Galileo was wrong, by pulling off a large block whilst attempting a new route; the block fell and so did Jud, though somehow he contrived to reach the ground after the block! Jud's injuries were severe and the crag immediately gained a reputation for loose rock and nothing more was added until 1975 when Whittaker once again took an interest in the crag. With his two long-time partners Gordon Mason and Ralph Pickering, he climbed *Bitter Friends, Beautiful Dreamer, Chasing Dreams* and *Hidden Gem*, which were all fine routes and which brought the crag back towards maturity.

A new face appeared on the scene in 1978, when Ian Lonsdale paid a swift visit with Whittaker, just after Brian Cropper's wedding; the pair celebrated the day by adding *Travellin' Man* and *Wedding Day* and for the occasion they both wore their penguin suits and their EBs had been specially cleaned! Others involved in the development of the crag at that time were Tom Miller and Frank Shaw (who together added *Midnight Express*), Harry Taylor, who was responsible for *Tailor Made*. Another activist at the time was Geoff Haigh, who contributed *Peeler* and *Nailbiter*. Later that year added *Test Piece* and *War Dance* was climbed in the following year. Both of these employed a little aid, though *Test Piece* was free-climbed solo, by Ian Carr in 1983 and Whittaker himself reduced the aid on *War Dance* to a single nut in 1986. Then, in 1980 Derek Wright developed Tower Buttress.

The pace then slowed, and little was done until 1984 when Cropper climbed *Go For Broke* and in 1987, Pickering claimed *Pig Farmer* while Mason added the bold *Sceptre*.

Access and Approach

The crags are reached from Calderbrook Road, which leads off the A6033 Littleborough–Todmorden road at the toll house (an obvious and interesting octagonal building clearly placed on the Littleborough side of the junction). From this road, two tracks lead to the crags; one along the top of the cliff, the other below the grass slope. The upper track is gated, the lower track begins near a ventilation shaft for the Summit railway tunnel. Park off the road and walk to the crag in five to ten minutes. Access is unrestricted.

The Climbs

The usual point of arrival at the crag is Fence Buttress. Pit Buttress lies 100 metres to the left. The climbs are described from LEFT to RIGHT.

Pit Buttress

A small buttress with steep walls that has two routes at present. A ledge above a short drop gives access to the routes. The corner of Pig Farmer is obvious.

1.   Pig Farmer   10m   VS   4c   (1987)
Climb the corner to the overhang. Continue, moving left as required.

2.   Sceptre   10m   E2   5c   (1987)
Climb the arête on its right-hand side to gain a groove. Finish up this. Reachy and poorly protected.

Fence Buttress

A stream runs down the hillside, and a small face on its right has a broken gully to its right. At the base of this face is:

3.   Intro Wall   8m   S   4a   (1978)
Climb the groove, step left then finish up the crack to the left of the arête.

4.   Sidestep   8m   VD   (1981)
As for Intro Wall but step right and finish up the arête.

5.   Night Time   6m   VD   (1981)
Start just to the right. Go over an overhang and finish up a corner.

★★ **6.   Test Piece**   9m   E1   5c   (1978/1983)
A popular, very safe way of warming up for the harder problems. Climb the scoop and gain the horizontal break. Go left to the cracked arête and follow this to an easier finish.

7.   Piece Green   10m   VS   5a   (1981)
The initial difficult scoop of Test Piece leads to a finish up Green Slabs.

8.   Green Slabs   12m   VS   4c   (1962)
Climb the corner on the right, step right then back left on to a slab. From the overhung corner above, swing right to another slab and finish direct.

9.   Tailor Made   14m   VS   4c   (1979)
A V-shaped groove two metres to the right leads to a ledge. A traverse left below an overhang leads to another grassy ledge and the slab above leads to the top.

10. War Dance 15m HVS (1 pt) 5b   (1979/1986)
The arête on the right contains a groove with a small roof three metres below
the top of the crag. Climb to the groove and continue to the roof. Use one nut
for aid to pass this and finish direct.

Right again is a broken chimney with a grassy ledge beneath.

11. Diagonal 18m VD   (1978)
Climb the groove to the grassy ledge. Semi hand-traverse left and follow the
fault to finish up a slab.

12. Green Piece 15m VD   (1978)
Gain and climb the chimney.

13. Midnight Express 15m HVS 5b   (1979)
Climb the left wall of the chimney for eight metres (possible belay).
Hand-traverse left to a small square-cut groove on the arête and go up this to
the top.

*The right wall of the chimney forms a pinnacle. To its right is a grass ledge six
metres above the ground.*

14. Dropover 15m VD   (1978)
Climb cracks on the left to gain the grass ledge. The crack in the left wall leads
to a loose finish.

15. Travellin' Man 15m VS 4c   (1978)
Climb the face just right of Dropover to the ledge, then follow the right-slanting
crack above.

To the right again is a fence and right of this is a blocky groove-cum-crack.

★ 16. Central Crack 18m VS 4c   (1978)
Follow the block-filled crack, step left and follow the crack above to finish up a
little corner.

17. Worthy Venture 18m S 4a   (1978)
Climb the ramp on the right until a swing left leads to a V-shaped groove, up
which a finish can be made.

★ 18. Wedding Day 18m VS 4c   (1978)
The ramp, wall and overhanging crack lead to a ledge (possible belay). The
centre of the slab on the right provides a finish.

19. Go For Broke 18m E1 5b   (1984)
The short groove to the right of Wedding Day is gained direct.

*The rock now becomes grassy and broken for 20 metres then recovers to
become a fine wall with an excellent selection of routes. The prominent arête
has a corner and a cracked wall on its left. The steep slope below this section
creates a definite feeling of exposure.*

20. Layback Corner 12m VD   (1959)
The corner leads to an exit on to easy ledges.

★ **21. Tattersall's Lament** 12m S 4a (1959)
Follow Layback Corner then gain the crack in the right wall and continue direct.

★ **22. Blind Panic** 14m E1 5a (1962)
Climb the arête, then proceed as coolly as possible to the top. No protection on the first section of this good climb.

★★ **23. Bitter Friends** 17m E1 5b (1978)
The shallow groove and cracks a couple of metres right of the arête. A good line with tricky moves.

★ **24. Beautiful Dreamer** 17m HVS 5b (1978)
The overhanging crack three metres to the right, then the thin crack above.

The right-hand end of the wall has a crack to the left of some square-cut overhangs.

★ **25. Chasing Dreams** 17m HVS 5b (1978)
Go left under the roof to the crack. Climb to the break and follow the thin crack above.

★ **26. Hidden Gem** 12m S 4a (1978)
The deep corner on the right leads to the top of a flake. Go up the crack above to a large ledge and step left to a slabby finish.

27. Peeler 8m S 4a (1978)
Follow the groove farther right.

28. Happy Wanderer 24m VS 5a (1978)
From the break on Chasing Dreams, traverse left to finish up Bitter Friends.

★ **29. Wild Goose** 45m HVS 5a,5a,5a (1980)
A girdle traverse of Fence Buttress giving some good climbing.
1. 20m. Follow Happy Wanderer, but continue the traverse to belay on the ledge of Travellin' Man.
2. 10m. Gain the arête then hand-traverse left below the overhang and continue to a belay on the pinnacle of Dropover.
3. 15m. A fault leads across the steep wall to finish up the top slab of Green Slabs.

Tower Buttress

The large buttress on the right has a shaly base. The sounder rock above provides routes which, although relatively easy, can provide problems with route-finding. The buttress is currently neglected and is becoming overgrown. The buttress consists of two bands of loose shale supporting a band of more solid rock. On top of these three bands are set two slabs. The right-hand slab is parallel to the lower bands, whilst the left-hand slab slopes back and up into the hillside. Both slabs end at a ledge, above which lies a four-metre wall leading to the top of the buttress. The top of the left slab is split by an obvious irregular crack. The left edge of the buttress has a crack which provides:

30. Smoker's Satisfaction 14m VD (1980)
Follow grassy ledges to gain the crack and a ledge above. A platform leads to a crack on the left and a loose finish.

31. Piecer 12m VD (1980)
Climb cracks two metres to the left of Smoker's Satisfaction, until a corner above leads to a ledge before a scramble right leads to the finish as above.

32. Reiver 14m VD (1980)
Two grooves three metres to the right of Smoker's Satisfaction lead to rightward-leading steps and a short crack leading to a ledge. Just right of the arête is a hidden chimney which provides a finish.

Six metres below and to the right is a rotting cave, and a grassy ledge leads across the face. A grassy bay four metres right of the cave is the start of the next route.

33. Farrier 18m VD (1980)
Go up steeply to a slab. A groove at its left-hand side veers right to short cracks, the left-hand of which leads to a ledge and a crack above to finish.

34. Hand-loom Weaver 18m VD (1980)
A second bay six metres to the right has a wall which is climbed to a nose of natural rock. Pass this on the left and follow the slab above to join Farrier at its two cracks. Finish up the right-hand crack.

35. 1878 18m VD (1980)
Follow Hand-loom Weaver to the nose. Pass this on the right and climb the slab above to a ledge at the right of the buttress. Go left to a gangway and up left to a crack which leads, with care, to the finish of Hand-loom Weaver.

Chimney Buttress
This buttress has had a serious rockfall and should be ignored for the time being.

36. Nailbiter 12m VS 4b (1979)
The obvious broken groove slants right.

37. Loggerheads 12m VS 4c (1975-79)
The left-hand of two cracks, passing some overhangs en route.

38. Weekend Wonder 12m VS 4c (1975-79)
The right-hand crack, past a flake.

First Ascents at Reddyshore Scout
1959   **Layback Corner** Bob Whittaker, Bill Hardacre
1959 Apr   **Tattersall's Lament** Bob Whittaker, Bill Hardacre
1962 July   **Blind Panic, Green Slabs** Bob Whittaker, Bill Hardacre
1978 Mar   **Intro Wall** Bob Whittaker, Ralph Pickering
1978 Mar   **Test Piece** (1pt aid) Bob Whittaker, Ralph Pickering, Gordon Mason
              Aid eliminated by Ian Carr (solo), 1983.
1978 Mar   **Dropover** Bob Whittaker, Gordon Mason
1978 Apr 4   **Bitter Friends, Beautiful Dreamer, Chasing Dreams, Hidden Gem**
              Bob Whittaker, Gordon Mason, Ralph Pickering

1978 Apr 4	**Peeler, Worthy Venture** Bob Whittaker (solo)
1978 Apr 6	**Happy Wanderer** Bob Whittaker, Ralph Pickering, Geoff Haigh
1978 July	**Diagonal, Green Piece** Derek Wright, Tony Morris
1978	**Travellin' Man, Wedding Day** Ian Lonsdale, Bob Whittaker
1978	**Central Crack**
1979 Apr	**Tailor Made** Harry Taylor, Bob Whittaker, Geoff Haigh
1979 Apr 18	**Midnight Express** Tom Miller, Frank Shaw
1979 Sep 9	**Nailbiter** Geoff Haigh, Bob Whittaker
1975-79	**Loggerheads, Weekend Wonder**
1979 Aug	**War Dance** (aid) Bob Whittaker, Ralph Pickering
	Reduced to 1 pt aid by Bob Whittaker, 1986
1980 Apr	**Wild Goose** Bob Whittaker, Derek Wright, Geoff Haigh
1980	**Smoker's Satisfaction, 1878, Piecer, Reiver, Farrier, Hand-loom Weaver** Derek Wright
1981 Feb	**Sidestep** Bob Whittaker, Ralph Pickering
1981 Feb	**Night Time** Bob Whittaker (solo)
1981 Apr	**Piece Green** Bob Whittaker (solo)
1984	**Go For Broke** Brian Cropper
1987 Sep	**Pig Farmer** Ralph Pickering, Bob Whittaker, Gordon Mason
1987 Sep	**Sceptre** Gordon Mason, Bob Whittaker, Ralph Pickering

Summit Quarry   O.S. ref.   SD 948 196

Situation and Character

The quarry is set on the moor above and east of the A6033
Littleborough–Todmorden road at the village of Summit. The quarry is generally
sound, but there is some loose rock. The text mentions this where necessary.
There are cracks, slabs and walls here and there is a fine variety of climbs to be
enjoyed. The crag does dry slowly, so a day or so of dryish weather is needed
to ensure that most of the climbs are dry.

In addition to the quarry itself, there are a few climbs on Canal Buttress, which
stands just above the footpath leading to the main quarry.

Development and regardening of the crag has shown that this cliff has more to
offer than the nearby Cow's Mouth, though it does not provide the same fine
views. However, it is pleasant enough and as a climbing ground it still awaits
appreciation of its many fine routes.

History

The quarry appears to have been discovered by Ian Butterworth, when taking a
direct route down to the valley from the nearby Cow's Mouth. Butterworth then
staked his claim by soloing *Starters* and *Order*. Shortly afterwards he returned
with Pete Mustoe and added *Double Mantel*. Other members of the Solvé Club
soon followed, and Butterworth started their visit with a mass ascent of *Split
Leg Corner*, followed by *Way Out* and *Buttertoe Wall*. Butterworth then added
Wall Climb whilst Paul Horan then started to explore the deep alcove at the left
side of the crag, where he climbed the prominent *Layback Crack* and the
equally tempting crack of *The Crab*, both with Stu Halliwell. Halliwell then led
an obvious variation, which he named *Creepy Crab*. Many of these climbs were
also repeated and the busy day was eventually completed by Carl Fletcher's
ascent of *Delicatessen*. At about that time some newly-chipped holds were
discovered on a steep slab, and from then on an ascent of this short line

attracted most of the Solvé members at one time or another. Eventually, the problem was solved by Horan on a cold October day to give *Who Dun It?*

During his next visit Horan claimed a trio of fine routes, with *Latentest, Cold* and *Knuclist*, but probably his best route was the bold *Grave's End*, on which he was accompanied by Halliwell a few weeks later. Halliwell then responded with the fine *Cnig's* routes. Other notable ascents during that period were *Epicoff* by John Lowthian and *Hot* by Halliwell. As the year drew to a close Horan and Butterworth completed a Girdle of the Pit. Though they were disappointed to have to resort to two aid wedges on the first pitch, it is interesting to note that it took at least twelve more years before these points of aid were dispensed with.

The early 70s saw different groups in action. Bruce Goodwin soloed some routes on the Wall of Grooves area in 1971, while John Hampson and Steve Cunnis climbed *The Shroud*. Hampson rarely recorded his routes, so he may well have been responsible for more routes in the area. *The Shroud* was named by Bob Whittaker when he made the second ascent. Andrew Eaton did the same on the *Turin Finish* in 1985. Back in 1969 Goodwin soloed *Alexander the Great* in mistake for Cnig's Direct. Members of the Black and Tan M.C. added some of the far right wall routes in the early Seventies and also climbed *Central Corner* on Canal Buttress.

In 1975 Whittaker climbed *Hangman*, but afterwards efforts dwindled, and the only route of any significance was added in 1979 when Clive Morton soloed *Windy Wall*. The crag rested until 1981 when plans for a new guidebook inspired Whittaker, who developed Canal Buttress with Ralph Pickering. He also added *The Coffin* and *Free Spirit*, as well as soloing most of the easier routes in the quarry. Also adding to the total of routes were Ron Blunt, Gordon Mason, Derek Wright and Pickering.

In 1983 Goodwin and Tony Nichols added *Clueless Groove* on Pylon Buttress. The obvious possibilities were left for new routes elsewhere and it was not until 1985 that Goodwin returned and led *First Circle* and *Sunny Day*. Nichols climbed *Groundbait*, which was named after he decked it from eight metres – and got up and walked away unscathed! John Ellis led Goodwin and Hampson across the exciting traverse of *The Chud*. The Pool Area of the main crag also received a vigorous regardening. Mason then soloed *Shorty* (he's a big lad!). Then Goodwin, still suffering from what his friends called an ongoing new route fever added *Sinking Feeling, Comfortable* and a new finish to *Split Leg Corner*. Nichols soloed *Yes* later that year and John Ellis had the 20/20 vision to see *Hawkeye*. Then Goodwin *'Split'* and Ellis showed his *'Personality'*. He had had an early bath on a previous attempt, further, the force of the fall (he's a big lad) dragged Keith Hodgkinson – his second – into the Pool with him. They were on Ellis's big BMW bike and had a chilling ride home! Hampson returned and added the bold and demanding *Laying By*. Also during the mid-80s Dave Hinton visited the crag and traversed the wall above the pool, to give locals *High Tide*.

The crag saw little further development until the late Eighties. Two factors precipitated the next phase. Again a new guidebook was in the process of gestation and Ray Parker arrived from Carlisle. He met and galvanised Goodwin, John Vose and others into action. During 1988 he added a hard problem in *Moroccan Roll*. He also re-ascended Hangman, which had not been climbed since the loss of an important block. Goodwin was spurred into adding *Blinkers*, the wall finish of *Pull Hard* and with Morton added *Combined Ops*. In summer 1989 Parker added *Jaggarnath* and the slightly easier, but no-less committing *Sea Cruise*. He gobbled up *Cheese Balls*, whilst the cleaner (Goodwin) rested from his labours. Parker also showed that not only could he climb, but he could also generate a bad pun with *The Noo*. Goodwin soloed *Tit Bit* and *Ankle Strap*. *Dry Run* was added by Goodwin with John Vose and *Satin Trim* was led by Goodwin, followed by Stan Hodgkinson with his son Mark.

There are still some possibilities – some of these will be very hard, whilst others will require the efforts of a vertical navvy or two. A good place to climb – go there and sample its delights.

Access and Approach

Access is not currently a problem as there is a public footpath up to and alongside the quarry. However, the farmer whose land the quarry lies on is anxious that all litter should be removed.

The best approach is from the Summit Inn, about three kilometres north of Littleborough, where there is a bus stop on the Rochdale–Burnley and Rochdale–Todmorden–Halifax routes. If coming by car, turn down the cobbled lane beside the pub, cross the canal, turn left and park on the left about 50 metres farther on.Then walk along the track to a hairpin bend which leads rightwards. At this point cross the stile on the left and follow the track parallel to the canal, upwards to Canal Buttress. Continue along and round to the right to a fence and another stile. The narrow defile that leads into the quarry lies ahead. This pleasant approach takes about 20 minutes.

Summit may also be approached from Cow's Mouth. A line of pylons across the moor indicates the line to be followed. The round of the three crags (Summit, Cow's Mouth and Blackstone Edge) can also be started (or finished) here.

The Climbs

All the climbs are described from LEFT to RIGHT.

Canal Buttress

There is a belay stake in place at the time of writing.

1.   Short Crack 6m VS 4c   (1981)
The crack up the left-hand side wall.

2.   Fluted Arête 8m VS 4c   (1981)
The arête, climbed on its right side.

3.   Fluted Wall 8m VS 5a   (1981)
The wall and overhang, finishing up a groove.

4.   Central Corner 8m VD   (1972)
The obvious corner is followed, mainly on its right-hand side.

5.   Cracked Wall 6m VS 5a   (1981)
The wall on the right leads to a niche, and the wall right of this leads to the top.

Pylon Buttress

The Main Quarry has an outlying section 40 metres to its left, over a grassy ridge, which is known as Pylon Buttress. There is occasionally a pool below it. Belays are about 20 metres back and left of a large block just above the crag.

6.   Clueless Groove 6m VS 4c   (1983)
The obvious corner system at the left of the face.

★ **7.   First Circle** 10m E2 5c   (1985)
Start three metres to the right of Clueless Groove. Gain a little slab at the bolt holes and follow a thin crack to the break. The flake/block and thin crack lead to the top.

★ **8.   Jaggernath** 11m E4 6b   (1989)
Follow the thin crackline on the right with increasing difficulty until a finger-slot is gained. Pull into the horizontal break of The Chud and continue more or less direct. Protectable provided that you are able to see the placements and are strong enough to place the pro.

The smooth wall to the right has a line of bolt-holes, then the ground starts to rise.

★ **9.   Groundbait** 10m E2 5c   (1985)
Follow the slanting line up right (peg). Go up to the break and continue up the headwall just left of the obvious yellow scar.

10.   Sunny Day 9m HVS 5b   (1985)
Start just left of grassy cracks. Gain a ledge at three metres then continue to the break and on, passing a ledge to gain the top.

★★ **11.   The Chud** 21m E1 5b   (1985)
A traverse of the obvious break from right to left. Climb a little corner right of Sunny Day and traverse left into Clueless Groove, finishing up (or down) that route. Bold and exciting!

Alcove Area

The Main Quarry proper has a little wall, left of a square-cut arête:

12.   Wall Climb 6m VD   (1967)
Climb the centre of the short wall; stiff moves for the grade.

★ **13.   Twixt** 6m HVS 5a   (1967)
The square arête is climbed on its left side. Good.

★ **14.   Windy Wall** 6m HVS 5b   (1979)
The right side of the arête has a hard start.

15.   Double Mantel 8m S 4a   (1967)
Climb the ledges on the right, finishing up the final crack of The Crab.

16.   The Crab 9m VS 4c   (1967)
Climb the two converging cracks from an alcove, to a move left on to a ledge. Finish up the crack above.

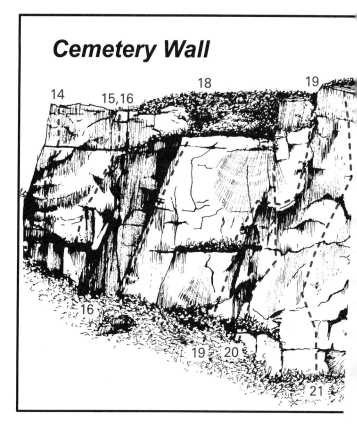

Cemetery Wall

17. Creepy Crab 10m VS 4c   (1967)
Follow The Crab to the large ledge then traverse right to another ledge and
finish via a mantel.

★★ **18.   Layback Crack** 9m VS 5a   (1967)
An attractive line that leads one on. The steep ramp is climbed to hard moves
round the overhang to finish.

★ **19.   Starters** 9m D   (1967)
The obvious stepped corner gives an awkward problem at its grade.

Cemetery Wall
*The steepening, slabby wall right of Starters provides excellent climbing, the
routes being generally better protected than they may appear.*

20.   The Coffin 14m VS 4c   (1981)
Follow a rightward-curving groove just right of the arête to a big ledge on the
left (on Starters). The thin crack in the left wall provides the finish.

★★ 21.   The Shroud   14m   E2   5c   (1971)
A good mantelshelf is reached directly or from lower on the right. Go up
delicately to a ledge and a little groove. The steep wall is the scene of a fingery
climax. An exciting and sustained route.

★★ 22.   The Shroud: Turin Finish   E2   5c   (1985)
From the little groove go left to the arête, pull up and finish on its left side. An
RP gives some illusory comfort, but it is still a bold and committing route.

★★★ 23.   Grave's End   14m   E1   5b   (1967)
A bold route that sees the 'dithers' develop in many a nervous climber. A
groove slants right; climb up to it and move left to footholds. Step up delicately
into the scoop and follow this to a finish up the wall, or step right to finish up
Order.
Direct Start (5c): from a flake on the left, gain a ledge, then go direct to the
runner slot on the parent route. From the slot it is also possible to move left and
continue up The Shroud.

★★ 24.   Laying By   14m   E3   5c   (1985)
An excellent companion route to The Shroud and Graves End. Start as for
Grave's End. Continue up the groove (hard) to gain a standing position (small
nut in slot on the right). Make some exacting moves to gain the blunt arête
above, then a jug, a mantel and a finish *'made to order'*.

A couple of metres right is a deep groove:

★ 25.   Satin Trim   16m   E2   5c   (1989)
Climb Order to a ledge level with the top of the groove of Laying By and
traverse left past an RP slot to gain the top of the groove. Either, continue at
the same level until it is possible to step down to the slot runner on Grave's
End/Shroud and finish up The Shroud, or (bolder) go diagonally left from the
top of the groove to join Grave's End and continue left to a finish up The
Shroud.

★ 26.   Order   14m   HS   4a   (1967)
Follow the groove to ledges, and a shallow corner which leads to the top wall.

27.   Free Spirit   14m   HVS   5b   (1981)
From the groove of Order, climb the wall on the right to a ledge (on Disorder).
The thin crack above leads via reachy moves to a finish just right of the
overhangs. A side runner in Disorder is necessary for this grade, otherwise it
deserves E2.

★★ 28.   Disorder   14m   S   4a   (1967)
Sustained and testing at the grade. The next groove on the right leads diagonally
leftwards to neatly rectify itself and become Order.

Right again is a curving flake in the wall.

29.   Cnig's Direct   14m   VS   4c   (1967)
Climb the groove to the flake and pull over this direct, follow ledges to finish.

30.   Cnig's Underhang   12m   VS   4b   (1967)
Climb to the flake as for Cnig's Direct but follow this rightwards to ledges. A
crack on the right leads to the top.

*On the right is a sloping ledge a couple of metres above the ground. A small
overhang, split by a triangular notch, lies just above.*

★ 31.   Alexander the Great   12m   HVS   5b   (1969)
Gain the left end of the sloping ledge and follow the indefinite crackline above,
which leads delicately to the overlap. Pass this to join Cnig's Direct.

32.   Brightspark   12m   VS   4b   (1981)
A groove above the right-hand end of the sloping ledge leads to the notch in the
overhang; climb through this to finish up the crack on the right.

33.   Laser Beam   12m   S   4a   (1981)
Start as for Bright Spark, but follow a line left of the arête, past a mantelshelf
to an excellent finish.

A wide ledge on the right forms the base of a large open alcove. The roof above is currently unstable and some rockfall has occurred. The routes hereabouts wisely dodge past this upper section.

34.   Delicatessen   10m   VD   (1967)
Go up to the left end of the large ledge, then finish leftwards or up the corner above.

35.   Take Away   10m   D   (1981)
Gain the ledge at its centre then the deep corner on the right leads to a finish rightwards.

36.   Pickwick   9m   D   (1981)
Climb up to the right-hand end of the ledge and take the shallow corner on the right.

37.   Swordfish   12m   HS   4b   (1981)
Start right of Pickwick, at an overhanging corner. Climb up and left to the arête. Gain a ledge above then follow the right-hand side of the sharp arête above to finish.

38.   Squid   12m   VD   (1981)
Follow Swordfish to the ledge then finish up a square-cut corner on the right.

There is an obvious steep slab at a lower level on the right.

39.   Sunstroke   7m   VD   (1969)
Climb up left of the arête, unprotected.

40.   Sunshine   7m   VD   (1974-75)
Start at the bottom left of the slab and follow the arête to the top.

★ **41.   Who Dun It?**   5m   E1   6a   (1967)
The chiselled holds on the slab lead to a very hard move (or a leap sideways to safety) and then the top. Use of the left arête makes the '*tick*' easier; No protection is available whichever route one chooses.

The steep wall on the right is becoming overgrown.

42.   Derek Did It   8m   VD   (1983)
Start just left of the twin cracks and climb up to a groove. Finish up this.

43.   Knuclist   6m   VS   4c   (1967)
The undercut groove on the right, with two cracks.

44.   Hangman   8m   E3   5c   (1975)
The square-cut groove in the arête to the right. Climb easily up this, then make a committing layback up the edge of the groove to a good hold. Finish more easily.

45.   The Noose   8m   HVS   5a   (1981)
From the large ledge on the right, reach a hole in the left wall and finish direct over the blocky overhangs above.

● **46. Gardener's Nightmare** 8m VS 4b   (1969-70)
Gain the large ledge and follow cracks in a green and earthy manner. Eminently forgettable!

Past a dirty chimney lies a steep pillar, just left of a square-cut corner on the arête.

47. Th'way 8m VS 4c   (1967)
Climb the pillar to the horizontal break, follow the wall above slightly left to the top.

Way Out Wall
This is the short compact wall right of the arête almost opposite the quarry entrance. Climbing here is good and the routes are often sustained.

48. Epicoff 8m S 4a   (1967)
Climb the groove to the left of the arête to the overhang then step right to a crack and follow this to the top.

★ **49. Giggle Pin** 8m VS 5a   (1981)
Climb the blunt arête to join Epicoff. Climb down that route to beneath the overhang then stand up in the horizontal crack, step right and follow the little arête.

★ **50. Slight Wall** 6m HVS 5a   (1975-79)
Climb the wall/arête just to the right of Giggle Pin stepping right to finish up a crack.

51. Way Out 8m HVS 5a   (1967)
Two metres to the right ascend the wall to a sloping ledge, then take the thin crack on the left.

★ **52. Combination** 9m VS 5a   (1969)
Start as for Way Out, but traverse left to finish up Epicoff.

A small corner a couple of metres right is the start for the next two routes.

★ **53. Exit** 6m HVS 5a   (1979-83)
Climb the corner and the thin crack above, passing a mantelshelf.

54. L.M.J. 6m HS 4b   (1969)
Climb the corner then move right to a grassy groove which leads to the top.

Wall of Grooves
*Right again is a grassy area, offering an easy **DESCENT** route. The rock soon improves and transforms into a wall gradually increasing in height as it approaches the pool. Just right of the grass is a steep black wall.*

55. Black Wall 8m HS 4a   (1981)
Follow the left edge of the wall.

56. Tit Bit 8m VS 4c   (1989)
Climb the overhang just to the right and continue direct.

57. Tidemark 8m S 4a   (1981)
The right end of the wall, starting under a left-leaning overhang.

58. Kebab 8m S 4a   (1981)
The first groove three metres to the right.

59. Babke 8m VD   (1981)
The next break and corner.

60. Play it Again Sam 8m S 4a   (1981)
The thin crack and right-slanting groove, about one metre right.

61. Hart to Hart 8m VD   (1981)
Farther right start at a heart chiselled into the rock. Climb to a grassy ledge then
take the corner above.

62. Sam 8m VD   (1981)
About one metre to the right, ascend the crack and corner.

63. Mas 8m VD   (1981)
The crack and corner on the right, starting on a higher grass ledge.

Right of the grass ledge is a hanging flake:

64. Casablanca 9m HVS 5b   (1981)
Follow the left-slanting crack through some small overhangs and finish up a
jamming crack above.

★ **65. Buttertoe Wall** 9m HS 4a   (1967)
Climb the crack and hanging flake direct. Strenuous.

66. Ankle Strap 10m VS 5a   (1989)
Start as for Buttertoe Wall and ascend to an obvious traverse line, then follow
this and finish up Latentest.

67. Cheese Balls 9m E1 5c   (1989)
Climb directly up the wall/pillar right of Buttertoe Wall.

Pool Area
*The Wall of Grooves area now merges into the Pool Area. The first route starts
just left of the pool.*

68. Latentest 9m HVS 5a   (1967)
Climb a thin crack to gain a ledge then finish up the corner above. Poor
protection.

★ **69. Split** 8m E1 5c   (1985)
Above the left end of the pool is a ledge with a bolt above; climb up to the
ledge and finish direct. Harder for the short.

★ **70. High Tide** 9m HVS 5b   (1986)
A low-level traverse above the pool. Climb Split until hands are on the obvious
ledge, then traverse rightwards at this level.

★★ 71.   Personality   12m   E2   6a   (1985)
A route that tests the fingers as well as the brain. Gain the ledge as for Split,
then traverse right using bolt holes to make a series of hard and reachy moves
up and right to a ledge (well nigh impossible for the short). The headwall is
something of a relief. An early failure means an early bath!

*Above the right side of the pool is a corner. Left of this is a leftward-slanting
crackline. There is a stake belay hidden in a clump of rushes, in line with Hot
and Cold wall.*

72.   Sea Cruise   9m   E3   6a   (1989)
Follow a line left of Sinking Feeling using carefully placed runners in that route.

★ 73.   Sinking Feeling   9m   E2   5c   (1985)
Step down to a ledge just above the water and follow the crackline above to a
large ledge, then follow the continuation crack to finish.

74.   Split Leg Corner   9m   HVS   5a   (1967)
The obvious corner leads to a large ledge. Either finish direct or via the crack
on the left. It is also possible to traverse left and finish over ledges.

★★ 75.   Hawkeye   9m   E2   5c   (1985)
Climb the wall a couple of metres right of Split Leg Corner. Care is needed
with protection on this bold and fingery route.

76.   The Noo   9m   E2   5c   (1989)
Climb up awkward holds left of Hot. Cracks and runners appear. Continue until
a traverse left can be made to a ledge. The top is just above.

★ 77.   Hot   8m   HVS   5a   (1967)
The diagonal line leads leftwards to a little groove and a mantel to finish.

★ 78.   Comfortable   8m   E1   5b   (1985)
The wall right of Hot gives a bold and testing route.

79.   Cold   8m   HVS   5b   (1967)
The next crack to the right gives a bold outing.

80.   Shorty   6m   VS   5a   (1985)
The wall just to the right again.

★ 81.   Dry Run   18m   HVS   5b   (1989)
Start as for Shorty and gain the obvious traverse line. Step daintily leftwards to gain
the large ledge above the pool, then finish up Split Leg Corner's traverse finish.

*The last routes lie on the short wall at right-angles to Pool Wall. There are no
belays, though a braced, sitting belay is possible in a dip a little farther back.
This is not as insecure as it sounds, but most climbers prefer to solo the routes.*

82.   Gardener   6m   HS   4b   (1975/1979)
Start at the left side, reach a mantel, and thus an easier finish.

83.   Moroccan Roll   6m   E1   6a   (1988)
Start beneath the overhang and surmount it at its left-hand end with great
difficulty, then continue more easily to the top.

84. It's Slippy 6m HVS 5a   (1975-79)
The groove on the right leads with difficulty over an overhang, then climb
directly to the top.

85. Blinkers 6m HVS 5a   (1988)
An eliminate between It's Slippy and Pull Hard gives a pleasant climb.

86. Pull Hard 6m VS 4c   (1975-79)(1988)
Pull strenuously up the wall on the right to gain and follow a little corner.
Wall Finish (4c): an alternative finish from the first ledge is to climb the wall
just right of the little corner.

87. Combined Ops 10m HVS 5b   (1988)
Follow Pull Hard to the ledge, then start to traverse left with a tricky move to
gain Moroccan Roll and finish up leftwards.

88. Yes 6m VS 4c   (1985)
A slabby arête leading to a finishing wall.

89. Maybe 6m HS 4b   (1975-79)
Start on the right of the slab and climb up left to join and finish up Yes.

90. The Pit Girdle 45m HVS 5a,5a   (1967/1979-83)
Start at the left-hand side of the Main Crag.
1. 24m. Start as for Wall Climb, at half-height follow the line as for Creepy
Crab and continue into Layback Crack. Make a worrying hand-traverse to reach
Starters, peg belay (not in-situ, so it may be preferable to continue).
2. 21m. Move delicately down and right on to the slab and follow a line of
holds to join Order and Disorder. This line continues farther, past the Cnig's
routes and a jamming crack on their right which provides a finish.

First Ascents at Summit Quarry

1967 June   **Starters, Order** Ian Butterworth (solo)
1967 June   **Disorder** Pete Mustoe
1967 June   **Double Mantel** Ian Butterworth, Pete Mustoe
1967 July   **Split Leg Corner** Ian Butterworth, Paul Horan, Chris Simpson, Len
               Bradshaw
1967 July   **Way Out, Buttertoe Wall** Ian Butterworth, Chris Simpson, Len Bradshaw
1967 July   **Wall Climb** Ian Butterworth, John Lowthian
1967 July   **The Crab, Layback Crack** Paul Horan, Stu Halliwell
1967 July   **Creepy Crab** Stu Halliwell, Paul Horan
1967 July   **Delicatessen** Carl Fletcher, Ian Butterworth
1967 Aug   **Latentest, Cold, Knuclist** Paul Horan, Ian Butterworth
1967 Aug   **Grave's End** Paul Horan, Stu Halliwell
               Direct Start by Bruce Goodwin, Alan Cowburn, 24 Sep 1997.
1967 Aug   **Cnig's Underhang, Cnig's Direct** Stu Halliwell, Paul Horan
1967 Sep   **Twixt** Paul Horan, Stu Halliwell
1967 Sep   **Th'way, Hot** Stu Halliwell, Ian Butterworth
1967 Sep   **Epicoff** John Lowthian, Stu Halliwell
1967 Oct   **The Pit Girdle** (2pts aid) Paul Horan, Ian Butterworth
               Aid eliminated, 1979-83.
1967 Nov   **Who Dun It?** Paul Horan, Stu Halliwell
1969   **Alexander the Great** Bruce Goodwin (solo)
1969 Sep   **Combination, Sunstroke** Bruce Goodwin (solo)
1969 Sep   **L.M.J.** Bruce Goodwin, Linda Garner, Margaret McClelland, Jackie Hudson
1969-70   **Gardener's Nightmare** Bruce Goodwin

1971	**The Shroud** John Hampson, Steve Cunnis
1972	**Central Corner** Bob Whittaker (solo)
1974-75	**Sunshine** Bob Whittaker (solo)
1975 June	**Hangman** Bob Whittaker, Gordon Mason
	An important block came off and the route was re-ascended by Ray Parker, Bruce Goodwin, 2 June 1988.
1975-79	**Pull Hard**
	Wall Finish by Bruce Goodwin (solo), June 2 1988.
1975-79	**Slight Wall**
1975-79	**Gardener**
1975-79	**It's Slippy**
1975-79	**Maybe**
1979	**Windy Wall** Clive Morton (solo)
1981 Mar 14	**Short Crack, Fluted Arête, Fluted Wall, Cracked Wall** Bob Whittaker, Ralph Pickering, Gordon Mason
1981 Mar 14	**The Coffin** Bob Whittaker, Ralph Pickering
1981 June 28	**Brightspark** Ron Blunt, Ralph Pickering, Bob Whittaker
1981 June 28	**Free Spirit, The Noose** Bob Whittaker, Ralph Pickering
1981 June 28	**Laser Beam** Derek Wright, Ralph Pickering
1981 June 28	**Black Wall, Tidemark** Bob Whittaker (solo)
1981 July 19	**Giggle Pin** Bob Whittaker, Ralph Pickering, Derek Wright
1981 July 19	**Kebab** Ralph Pickering, Bob Whittaker, Gordon Mason
1981 July 19	**Babke** Gordon Mason, Bob Whittaker, Ralph Pickering
1981 July 19	**Play it Again Sam** Derek Wright, Ralph Pickering, Bob Whittaker
1981 July 19	**Hart to Hart** Gordon Mason, Bob Whittaker
1981 July 19	**Sam** Derek Wright, Bob Whittaker
1981 July 19	**Mas** Ralph Pickering, Gordon Mason
1981 July 19	**Casablanca** Bob Whittaker, Gordon Mason, Ralph Pickering, Derek Wright
1981 July 29	**Take Away, Pickwick, Squid** Bob Whittaker (solo)
1981 July 29	**Swordfish** Bob Whittaker, Ralph Pickering
1979-83	**Exit**
1983	**Derek Did It** Derek Wright, Bob Whittaker
1983 July 2	**Clueless Groove** Bruce Goodwin, Tony Nichols
1985 Apr 26	**Sinking Feeling** Bruce Goodwin, Gordon Mason, John Ellis
1985 Apr 26	**Hawkeye** John Ellis, Bruce Goodwin, Gordon Mason
1985 Apr 27	**The Shroud: Turin Finish** Andrew Eaton, Bruce Goodwin
1985 May 7	**First Circle** Bruce Goodwin, John Vose, Andrew Eaton, Geoff Haigh
1985 May 9	**Comfortable** Bruce Goodwin, Gordon Mason
1985 May 9	**Shorty** Gordon Mason (solo)
1985 May 11	**Groundbait** Tony Nichols, Bruce Goodwin, John Warburton
1985 May 11	**Split** Bruce Goodwin, Tony Nichols, John Warburton
1985 May 16	**Sunny Day** Bruce Goodwin, John Hampson
1985 May 20	**The Chud** John Ellis, Bruce Goodwin, John Hampson
1985 May 20	**Laying By** John Hampson, John Ellis, Bruce Goodwin
1985	**Personality** John Ellis, John Warburton
1985	**Yes** Tony Nichols (solo)
1986	**High Tide** Dave Hinton
1988 June 2	**Moroccan Roll** Ray Parker, Bruce Goodwin
1988 June 2	**Blinkers** Bruce Goodwin, Ray Parker
1988 June 26	**Combined Ops** Bruce Goodwin, Clive Morton
1989 June 19	**Jaggernath** Ray Parker, Bruce Goodwin
1989 June 24	**Tit Bit** Bruce Goodwin (solo)
1989 June 24	**The Noo** Ray Parker, Bruce Goodwin
1989 June 29	**Dry Run** Bruce Goodwin, John Vose
1989 July 5	**Sea Cruise** Ray Parker, Bruce Goodwin
1989 July 9	**Ankle Strap** Bruce Goodwin (solo)
1989 July 9	**Cheese Balls** Ray Parker, Bruce Goodwin
1989 July 16	**Satin Trim** Bruce Goodwin, Stan Hodgkinson, Mark Hodgkinson

Warland Quarry

Situation and Character

This pleasant little quarry is situated east of the A6033 some four kilometres from Littleborough. It is clearly visible from the Littleborough–Todmorden road, on the hillside almost opposite the Bird I' Th' Hand pub.

All the routes are on solid gritstone (there being thankfully no climbing on the upper tier). Although the routes are short, they are all worthwhile and Grinning Arête is a minor crag classic. The climbing is on two tiers; the Main Tier has a loose upper tier above it and set back, and the Lower Wall lies hidden in a small hollow in the hillside. A useful addition to the area.

History

When Bruce Goodwin and Tony Nichols 'discovered' the crag at the end of June, 1983 a line of rusting bolts (almost mandatory in Western Pennine quarries) on the lower wall and peg remains in what is now Laughing Crack confirmed that they had been beaten there by unknown climbers. Undeterred, they climbed eight routes during the next two days, the best of which were *Grinning Arête* and *Last Laugh* by Nichols, and *Sickly Smile* and *Laughing Crack* by Goodwin. The girdle, *Laugh a Minute*, was also done at this time.

In 1984 Nichols returned with John Lord and they turned their attention to the Lower Wall, where Lord put up his first new routes with *Lord's* and *Old Trafford*, whilst *Maiden Over* and *Trent Bridge* fell to Nichols.

Access and Approach

The access situation is not clear, but climbers do not appear to have encountered problems in the past. To reach the quarry, leave the A6033 at Warland Gate End, which lies almost opposite the Bird I'Th Hand pub. Follow this lane across the Rochdale canal and left up a hill. A sharp turn right at some houses leads to a steep hill. This can be followed to a parking place on the left. A gate on the other side of the lane opens onto a track which contours past sheds and leads into the quarry. A direct start is possible; cross the canal and go over a fence right of the house. A track leads up from here into the quarry. This approach often renders the hardest moves of the day as a guard dog, living at the house and sometimes unleashed, needs an impromptu body-swerve for success.

The Climbs

The climbs are described from RIGHT to LEFT, using the obvious arête on the Main Tier as a reference point. Right of this is a large ledge. All belays (Friends, nuts etc.) are at the foot of the upper tier.

Main Tier

1.   Sickly Smile 9m   E1   5b   (1983)
Climb a slabby crack, slanting up to the left end of the ledge. The groove above leads to the top. Bold.

★★ 2.   Grinning Arête 14m   HVS   5a   (1983)
Good climbing in a fine position. Climb Laughing Crack for three metres then move right to the arête and follow it to the top.

★ 3. Laughing Crack 12m VS 5a   (1983)
Take the thin crack left of the arête.

4. Smiler 10m VS 5a   (1983)
The wall left of Laughing Crack joining Chuckle Corner at half-height.

5. Chuckle Corner 10m VS 4b   (1983)
The wall below a leaning corner; follow this and move right to finish up the arête.

★ 6. Last Laugh 10m E1 5b   (1983)
A ledge/block at four metres is gained via the wall on its left. Pull up and out left over a bulge to finish.

7. Side Smirk 9m HVS 5b   (1983)
Climb the overhanging groove left of Last Laugh to a grassy ledge. Go up to another ledge then diagonally left into a groove with difficulty. Ascend this to the top to complete a rather disjointed line.

A girdle starting from the large ledge right of the arête is:

★ 8. Laugh A Minute 21m VS 5a   (1983)
Gain the ledge then follow the horizontal crack to the arête. Continue into Chuckle Corner then semi-hand-traverse to finish on the grass slope.

Lower Wall
Below the main part of the quarry is a short wall of smooth gritstone. A bolt ladder runs up its right-hand side.

9. Maiden Over 8m E1 5b   (1984)
The blunt arête right of the bolt ladder is unprotected.

10. The Bolt Ladder 8m A1   (Pre-1983)
Climb the obvious line of bolts. Not really cricket though!

11. Old Trafford 8m VS 4c   (1984)
Follow the right-hand crack of a pair.

12. Lord's 8m VS 4b   (1984)
The left-hand crack of the pair.

13. Trent Bridge 6m HVS 5b   (1984)
The crack at the left side of the wall.

First Ascents at Warland Quarry
Pre-1983   **The Bolt Ladder**
1983 June 30 **Grinning Arête** Tony Nichols, Bruce Goodwin
1983 June 30 **Laughing Crack, Smiler, Chuckle Corner** Bruce Goodwin, Tony Nichols
1983 July 1   **Sickly Smile** Bruce Goodwin, Tony Nichols
1983 July 1   **Last Laugh, Side Smirk, Laugh A Minute** Tony Nichols, Bruce Goodwin
1984   **Maiden Over, Trent Bridge** Tony Nichols, John Lord
1984   **Old Trafford** John Lord, Tony Nichols
1984   **Lord's** John Lord (solo)

Minor Crags

Cliviger
O.S. ref. SD 881 271

The hillside south-west of the A646 Todmorden–Burnley road has many buttresses and exposed rock faces. The crags are spread out over a long distance and whilst some of the rock buttresses are unstable, others would garden into routes, or already have routes on them. Adventurers and explorers can find plenty to enjoy here.

Shore Quarry
O.S. ref. SD 922 171

This quarry lies above the King William pub in Shore, Littleborough. From the left side of the pub walk up Higher Shore Road past Lower Shore Barn, then turn right in front of the next cottages and follow a path which goes through an old gate and up to the quarry. There are many vegetated routes in the easier grades and as a beginner's crag it could have value. The harder and more substantial routes are at the left-hand side; a wide crack provides **Shore Crack** (S), the wall left of the crack is **Wall and Crack** (VS, 4b), whilst farther left, the thin crack line above a niche, widening in the overhanging upper section, gives **Shore Buttress** (HVS, 5a ★). Left again is **Domino Theory** (VS, 5a) which goes up the wall to a broken groove and carefully to the top.

First Ascents at Shore Quarry
1984 July 20 **Shore Crack** Tony Nichols (solo)
1984 July 20 **Wall and Crack** Tony Nichols, Bruce Goodwin, Clive Morton
1984 July 20 **Shore Buttress** Bruce Goodwin, Tony Nichols, Clive Morton
1984 July 20 **Domino Theory** Clive Morton, Tony Nichols, Bruce Goodwin

White House Quarry
O.S. ref. SD 968 175

The small quarry, also known as Blackstone Edge Delf, lies about 100 metres south of the White House pub, on the way to Blackstone Edge. It is a bouldering ground of mainly local interest, which is useful for a workout for an hour or so. However, it could become popular and more important if cleaned!

Winter Climbing in the Cliviger Gorge
O.S. refs. SD 880 273 (Main Area), SD 890 268 (Water Slides)

The Cliviger crags lie on the opposite side of the valley from the bouldering mecca, Kebs, on Bridestones Moor. Its loose and vegetated character discourages all but the most Fowlerish of climbers, but it is a popular winter climbing ground when the conditions are right. The numerous gullies and water courses which split this sprawling crag give steep and in the main, non-serious 'ice-bouldering' possibilities, with three or four longer routes up the slabby hanging gullies of the central section, below the obvious broad grass terrace.

For the main area, park in a lay-by on the left soon after passing through the village. A short walk in the Todmorden direction leads to an unmetalled road on the right, which swings round and passes under the railway line. From beyond this the routes can be seen to the left, past a wooded area. Right of the wooded area, a number of gully lines give shorter pitches.

For the two water slides, continue towards Todmorden for about one kilometre, to a point where the road crosses a stream. From the large lay-by on the right follow the stream into the gorge. The first pitch lies only a few minutes from the road. The second pitch (which comes into condition more often) lies about 175 metres farther up the gorge.

Short pitches begin to form after three to four days of hard frost. A longer period of frost, such as that which occurred in 1986, aided by a snow cover on the terrace, is needed to produce the build-up needed for the longer routes. When these conditions do occur, the resultant pitches rival those on such popular Lakeland crags as Helvellyn and Great End.

The main section of the crag is the central area; an obvious feature to the left of this area is the large hanging icicle which forms an overhang 12 metres from the base of the gully. When complete this gives a testing grade IV problem with pleasant slabby climbing on thin ice above the overhang. To the right, a large triangular grassy mound cuts into the base of the buttress. Beyond this is a deeper gully with a few short pitches. The next route lies slightly right again, taking a less well-defined line up a series of steep steps. At its base hangs a steep icicle-fringed wall (10 metres) and the gully eases off afterwards, only to rear up into a final bulging section near the top: Grade III, though ice build-up does not always make this route easier! Farther right a vague, slabby gully gives similar sustained climbing (grade III) for 40 metres.

Ice climbing in the area is not complete without sampling Todmorden's answer to inner-city bouldering: on the edge of the town and behind the local swimming baths, three to four days of hard frost will freeze two waterfalls hidden in dense vegetation. The second pitch is about 10 metres high and is steep and well worth a visit – a closely guarded secret for some time!

Rossendale Valley Area

Compiled by Paul Dewhurst and Bruce Goodwin

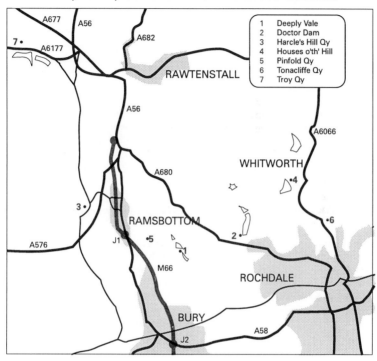

1	Deeply Vale
2	Doctor Dam
3	Harcle's Hill Qy
4	Houses o'th' Hill
5	Pinfold Qy
6	Tonacliffe Qy
7	Troy Qy

The area around the Rossendale Valley contains many quarries of different characters and qualities. Most of these are unworthy of more than the merest passing mention, but the remainder – the ones that are described here – are all good quality, enjoyable climbing grounds.

The most extensive quarry in the area is probably Troy Quarry, above the Haslingden Grane Road, which still contains a little loose rock but it is sound on the whole, and the climbing is good. Deeply Vale on the other hand is a small quarry of excellent rock just outside Bury, which sports some short, traditional gritstone quarry climbs. A recent find nearby is Pinfold Quarry, where some excellent routes cut through large, square-cut roofs.

Deeply Vale   O.S. ref.   SD 823 149

Situation and Character

Deeply Vale is a very solid gritstone quarry above a small reservoir on the moors about four kilometres north-east of Bury, midway between the M66 and the A680 (Owd Betts road). The crag comprises a series of arêtes and corners, between which lie steep, slabby walls, punctuated at times by good cracklines, with the huge roof of Mein Kampf in the centre.

History

The first known recorded routes here were the work of Mick Pooler and friends. By 1961 they had climbed such routes as *The Crack, Central Arête, Crystal Climb* and *Inflexion*, with a peg above the metal hook. Pooler also made an aided ascent of *Leftless* (which was originally called Twilight Crack, because it was finished in the dark). A few days later, Pooler succeeded in soloing to a ledge at mid-height on the arête left of Inflexion and left an old halfpenny on it as evidence of his ascent. Two days later, he led the excellent *Ha'penny Arête* and reclaimed his trophy. Pooler then attempted to climb the central corner of the crag but was repulsed, and the following day Harry Taylor, who had been waiting in the wings, stepped in to snatch *Renegade Corner*. Later that year Pooler and Taylor created the *Girdle*, using some tension to reach the lip of the large overhang. It took just over 20 years before this aid was dispensed with by Phil Kelly in 1982. The year ended with a partially aided ascent of *Scoop and Traverse* by Pooler, though he repeated the route the following year without any aid. Pooler's last addition at the crag was *Nod's Nightmare*, which he climbed in 1965 with Michael Day.

In the Seventies, very little development took place, though Bob Whittaker and Ralph Pickering added *Arête and Slab* in 1974, and two years later Al Evans eliminated the aid peg on *Inflexion*.

On an evening visit in 1983 Dave Cronshaw and Les Ainsworth climbed the bold *Night Out*, whilst Bob Whittaker and Ron Blunt did *Evening Visit*. A couple of weeks later, Derek Kenyon and Pete Wolstenholme claimed the disappearing crackline of *Zanadu* which was originally slightly undergraded; it turned out to be Kenyon's first extreme lead! In 1982 Kelly added *Victim of Changes* and *Watership Down*, then freed *Inflexion Direct*, leaving only *Mein Kampf* with any aid. Mark Leach reduced this to one rest point in July 1982, then Kelly and Mark Griffiths freed it shortly afterwards.

Approach

Deeply Vale is an enjoyable little crag of good quality quarried gritstone. Its easy access makes it ideal for an evening visit. From the centre of Bury, follow the A56 (Walmersley Road) north for about three kilometres to a dip in the road, followed by a short rise to a set of traffic lights. Turn right on to Walmersley Old Road. Continue to the Mason's Arms public house and turn right on to Bentley Road, going under the motorway bridge. Follow the main track to the left, up the hill to a small crossroad. Turn right along a metalled road to a T-junction and turn left. 200 metres farther down on the right there is a gate. Park carefully without blocking the gate or road. Go through this gate and follow the track for about 500 metres, then the crag will be seen set back a little on the right.

The Climbs

The climbs are described from RIGHT to LEFT starting at an arête just right of a large wall set with an iron hook at six metres.

'Tree' – Tree found on **The Reaper** (E6 6c), Egerton Quarry.   *Photo: Photo Games*

Hook Buttress

1.   'Go with Noakes' 8m HS 4b   (1979)
Climb the right side of the short arête to a ledge move right to an obvious handhold then direct up the steep wall to a loose finish.

2.   Arête and Slab 8m VD   (1974)
The left side of the arête to a small ledge then step left and climb the centre of a steep slab.

3.   Deep End 8m VD   (1974)
A poor route. From the corner, traverse the higher breaks left to finish just right of the arête.

4.   Inflexion 12m E2 5c   (1959-61/1976)
The wall is split by a clean diagonal fault line, follow this left to bulging cracks two metres right of the arête. Finish up these by hard moves, crux.

5.   Watership Down 10m E2 5c   (1982)
Mantel on to the traverse line of Inflexion and boldly climb the thin wall above to the bad break of Deep End, finish up that route.

★ 6.   Inflexion Direct 6m E3 6a   (Pre-1975/1982)
The steep hanging cracks left of the hook join Inflexion after six metres.

★★★ 7.   Ha'penny Arête 10m E1 5a   (1961)
The superb and obvious arête left of the iron loop is not for the faint-hearted. Bold climbing and a positive attitude will enable only the most confident of ascensionists to make the crux at the top look its grade. The square-cut arête left of the iron loop. Superb climbing, with the crux at the top.

★★ 8.   Scoop and Traverse 12m VS 5a   (1962)
Start in a short corner groove three metres left of Ha'penny Arête, climb this awkwardly on to a ramp and go up to a horizontal break. Traverse right below the overhangs to finish on the arête.

9.   Evening Visit 9m VS 4c   (1981)
Thin initial moves up the narrow slab left of Scoop and Traverse lead to the overhangs; go over these to finish.

Central Area
On the wall to the left is an obvious right-slanting crack.

10.   Crack Variation 12m HS 4a   (1959-61)
The wall to the right of The Crack.

★ 11.   The Crack 12m VD   (1959-61)
The flake crack offers enjoyable climbing up rock which is becoming rapidly more suspect!

Geoff Hibbert's appeal on **Pigeon Toad Orange Peel** (E5 6b), Ousel's Nest.
Photo: Adam Richardson

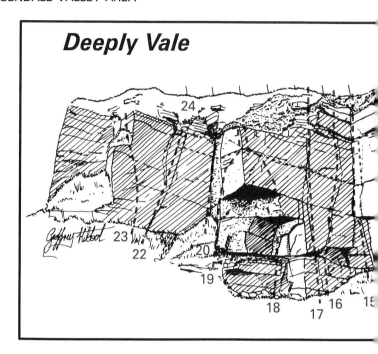

Deeply Vale

An interesting problem can be climbed between The Crack and Central Arête at 6a without using the holds on either route.

Around the arête is an excellent wall with an overlap at half-height.

★ **12.   Central Arête**   12m   VS   4c   (1959-61)
Climb the large, central arête starting on its left-hand side.

★★★ **13.   Slab Dab**   12m   VS   4c   (1961/1968)
The classic route of the Vale. Enjoyable peg pocket climbing up the wall left of the arête with good runners leads to an awkward move at the overlap. Better holds continue to finish up the wall above on good holds.

★ **14.   Victim of Changes**   12m   E2   5c   (Pre-1975/1982)
Start just right of Renegade Corner and climb using old bolt holes up the steep wall to the overlap (peg). Surmount the overlap and continue up the slab above.

★★ **15.   Renegade Corner**   12m   VS   4b   (1961)
The stunning, deep central corner of the crag provide the visitor with some excellent laybacking and bridging moves past a small overhang to gain access to a fine upper groove.

16.   Zanadu   12m   E3   5c   (1981)
The right-slanting fault in the green wall left of Renegade Corner is climbed, to its end, then go direct up the wall. three pegs (not in-situ).

17.   Leftless   9m   E2   5c   (1961/1979)
The peg-scarred crack just right of the cave.

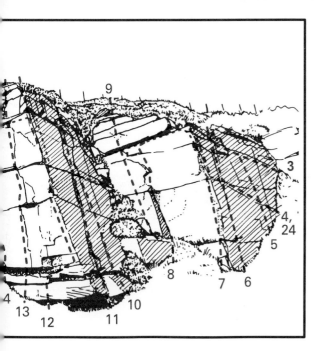

★★★ **18.   Mein Kampf**   12m   E3   5c   (1966/1982)
The route of Deeply Vale. The roof proves strenuous until the holds above are
reached, but then there is still a sting in the tail. Start in the back corner of the
cave and climb to a bolt. Stretch out and gain the lip of the first roof, bolt.
Attain a standing position on the protruding block on the right, (Friend in break
on right), and balance up to a peg. Pull up and left then continue left to finish
up the arête.

★ **19.   Night Out**   8m   HVS   5b   (1981)
Start just right of Nod's Nightmare and climb pockets boldly up and right to
gain the exposed upper arête of Mein Kampf. Finish up this.

20.   Nod's Nightmare   6m   VS   4c   (1965)
The corner on the left side of the main overhang.

21.   Back Seat Rock 'n' Roll   8m   VS   4c   (1982)
Climb up and leftwards from the start of Nod's Nightmare to join and finish up
Crystal Climb.

22.   Crystal Climb   8m   S   4a   (1959-61)
Climb the fault in the wall three metres to the left of Nod's Nightmare.

23.   Second Wall Climb   8m   HS   4b   (1980)
A direct line up the wall left of Crystal Climb, finishing leftwards to the arête.

*There are some interesting boulder problems to be found at the left-hand side of
the crag.*

End Walls

Farther left the crag starts to diminish in height, but there remains a series of arêtes, walls, corners and slabs which all provide good enjoyment should you wish to seek them out. All the obvious lines have been done. A low-level traverse of most of the crag is possible, starting at the left end and continuing rightwards with hard moves to get to Ha'penny Arête.

24.   Girdle Traverse   45m   E2   5c,4b,5a   (1961/1982)
1.   12m.   Climb Inflexion and cross to the top of Ha'penny Arête. Reverse the hand-traverse of Scoop and Traverse and belay.
2.   18m.   Move down slightly and cross The Crack to Central Arête, then climb this to below the top overhangs and traverse into Renegade Corner to belay on the ledge. Nut belay.
3.   15m.   Reverse the corner until a thin crack leads across and up to a hand-traverse on Mein Kampf. Go round the arête and finish up Crystal Climb.

First Ascents at Deeply Vale

1959-61	**Crack Variation, The Crack, Central Arête, Crystal Climb** Mick Pooler	
1959-61	**Inflexion** (1pt aid) Mick Pooler	
	Aid eliminated by Al Evans, 13 June 1976.	
1961 Aug	**Leftless** (A1) Mick Pooler, as Twilight Crack	
	First free ascent by Al Evans, Brian Cropper, 1979.	
1961 Sep 19	**Ha'penny Arête** Mick Pooler (unseconded)	
1961 Sep 24	**Renegade Corner** Harry Taylor, Mick Pooler	
1961 Oct 22	**Girdle Traverse** (with tension at the larger roof) Mick Pooler, Harry Taylor	
	First ascent without tension by Phil Kelly, 1982	
1961	**Slab Dab** (A1) Mick Pooler	
	First free ascent by Mick Pooler, summer 1962	
1962 May 26	**Scoop and Traverse** Mick Pooler	
1965 June	**Nod's Nightmare** Mick Pooler, Michael 'Raz' Day	
1966	**Mein Kampf** (A3)	
	Reduced to 1 rest pt by Mark Leach, 19 July 1982.	
	Aid completely eliminated by Phil Kelly, Mark Griffiths, 8 Sep 1982.	
1974	**Arête and Slab, Deep End** Bob Whittaker, Ralph Pickering	
Pre-1975	**Inflexion Direct** (A1)	
	First free ascent by Phil Kelly, 31 May 1982.	
Pre-1975	**Victim of Changes** (A1)	
	First free ascent by Phil Kelly, 17 Apr 1982.	
1979 Aug	**Leftless** Al Evans, Brian Cropper.	
	First free ascent.	
1979 Dec 26	**'Go with Noakes'** Bob Whittaker, Ralph Pickering, Alan Noakes	
1980	**Second Wall Climb** Clifford Shazby, Mark Leach	
1981 June 23	**Evening Visit** Bob Whittaker, Ron Blunt	
1981 June 23	**Night Out** Dave Cronshaw, Les Ainsworth	
1981 July	**Zanadu** Derek Kenyon, Pete Wolstenholme	
1982 Apr 17	**Victim of Changes** Phil Kelly	
	First free ascent.	
1982 Apr 18	**Back Seat Rock 'n' Roll** Phil Kelly (solo)	
1982 May 31	**Inflexion Direct** Phil Kelly (solo)	
	First free ascent.	
1982 July 17	**Watership Down** Phil Kelly (solo after top-roping)	
1982 July 19	**Mein Kampf** (reduced to 1 rest pt) Mark Leach	
	Aid completely eliminated by Phil Kelly, Mark Griffiths, 8 Sep 1982.	

Doctor Dam

O.S. ref.   SD 854 151

Situation and Character

This quarry which is affectionately known as 'Docky Dam' lies in woods above an old mill lodge, just north of the A680 at Norden, about five kilometres north west of Rochdale. Because the crag is in trees, it is fairly green, but this does not interfere with the climbing and it is often in condition when other crags are not. However, it is mainly of local interest and value.

History

The routes were all ascended by Bruce Goodwin, Tony Nichols and Clive Morton in 1984.

Access and Approach

The quarry is owned by North West Water, whose managers are happy to permit climbing.

From the Bridge Inn on the A680 in Norden, follow Greenbooth Road directly opposite the pub. This is a cobbled road that winds left, then back right and up to an old mill lodge. Park considerately near the lodge. A footpath on the left leads across from the end of the mill lodge to a footbridge. Cross this and the quarry lies ahead in the trees. About two minutes' walk.

The Climbs

The climbs are described from RIGHT to LEFT.

1.   Sparkler 6m HVS 5a   (1984)
The wide, stepped crack at the right side of the wall right of the obvious corner.

★ **2.   Diploma** 14m VS 5a   (1984)
The crack system in the centre of the wall right of the corner.

3.   Touch Right 14m HVS 5b   (1984)
The short crack and wall about one metre right of the corner.

4.   Flybrush 15m HS 4b   (1984)
The corner gives a rather dirty climb.

★ **5.   Shelf and Wall** 17m HVS 5a   (1984)
Five metres left of the corner there is a large shelf at mid-height. Gain this shelf by a weakness on its left, then step right from the right end of the shelf and climb the wall above. Poor protection.

6.   In and Out 18m VS 4c   (1984)
Left of the shelf is a wide angle capped by two overhangs. Climb up to the left side of the first overhang, then move left to a large ledge and tree. Finish up the cracked corner above.

First Ascents at Doctor Dam

1984   **Sparkler, Flybrush** Clive Morton, Bruce Goodwin
1984   **Shelf and Wall** Bruce Goodwin, Clive Morton
1984   **In and Out** Tony Nichols (solo)

Harcle's Hill Quarry
O.S. ref. SD 779 169

Situation and Character
This quarry is situated eight kilometres north of Bury, just above Ramsbottom, and one kilometre from the prominent local landmark of Peel Tower.

There are in fact two quarries on this site; the first (smaller) one has some boulder problems, whilst all the routes described lie in the second (larger) quarry. Climbing here, on the whole, can only be described as mediocre, and mostly for the connoisseur of loose finishes on vegetated rock, but nevertheless, one or two of the routes are worth seeking out.

History
Harcle's Hill was first explored by Dave Cronshaw and Phil Warner in 1977, with Warner soloing first ascents of *Black Maria* and the awkward *Court Jester*, and following Cronshaw up *The Judge, Jailbreak* and the clean arête of *Blue Lamp*.

The next climbers to visit the crag were members of the newly established Mountaineering Club of Bury (the MoB), and between them they accounted for all the other routes. Phil Kelly began, in 1980, with a solo ascent of *Bastille Day* which was then a much easier proposition, but has since lost many holds. Meanwhile, Paul Dewhurst added *Late Night Mob* and *Another Late Night*. Dewhurst's brother Mick led *Sovereign* with Colin Buckley and Bob Spencer, and Pete Wolstenholme climbed *Hammerhead*. Kelly continued the explorations when the others' enthusiasm waned and soloed *Caress of Steel* after top roping it. In 1984 Kelly put up *The Golden Moment* with one rest point which he eliminated the following night. Kelly also laid siege to the overhanging sentry-box to the right on a top rope and eventually managed a lead ascent to give *The Atomic Rooster*.

Since the previous guidebook, the only development at the quarry has been *Bolted Blues*, a short, technical test piece by Gareth Parry.

Approach
To reach the quarry from Bury, take the B6214 north for seven kilometres to a junction at Holcombe Brook (Hare and Hounds pub opposite). Continue up the steep continuation of the B6214 (Lumb Carr Road) for just over one kilometre to the Shoulder of Mutton pub on the right. Opposite the pub is a bridleway marked Moor Road. Park thoughtfully, then walk up the bridleway, past a cattlegrid, to a fork in the track. Go left and follow the track up and round into the quarry.

The Climbs
The routes are described from LEFT to RIGHT with the first route being on the small buttress on the left-hand side.

1.   Black Maria   6m   VD   (1977)
The centre of the first buttress is taken on the left.

2.   Left Chimney   6m   M   (1982)
The loose (as most routes here are!) chimney just to the right.

3.   Lord Foul's Bane 8m   VS   5b   (1981)
A difficult boulder problem. Start up the centre of the next buttress, then easier climbing leads to the break above:

4.   White Maria 8m   HS   4a   (Pre-1986)
The short crack right of Lord Foul's Bane leads to the break, then step left to join and finish up that route.

5.   Time Bandits 8m   VD   (1982)
An unfortunate line which should never have been climbed in the first place, it takes a nondescript line up the choss right of White Maria.

On the right side of the bay is a jutting nose overlooking a step in the quarry floor. On the left of the nose is a shallow corner.

6.   Court Jester 9m   HS   4a   (1977)
Climb the corner and ledges above.

★★ **7.   Caress of Steel** 12m   E2   5b   (1982)
An excellent route that is well worth seeking out. Brave the rubbish to get to the base of the route – there is usually a path. Start to the right of the nose and climb the fingery lower wall just right of the arête and arrange protection at the overlap. Grovel, or swing leftwards, depending upon how resourceful you are, to gain a standing position above the overlap. Finish easily up the slab.

8.   Whoops Apocalypse 12m   S   4a   (1982)
A great route embodying a certain esoteric charisma; it follows the large open corner six metres to the right of the nose.

9.   The Judge 14m   VS   4b   (1977)
Gain the shelf in the wall on the right, and climb twin cracks to a niche. Finish easily.

★ **10.   Blue Lamp** 14m   HVS   5a   (1977)
The sharp arête passing a peg. Good climbing.

The next two routes accept the challenge of the forbidding main wall of the quarry, but unfortunately the climbing ceases after 10 metres and degenerates into a vertical scree slope. A rope hung over this section allows the climber to escape.

11.   Jailbreak 14m   VS   4c   (1977)
Three metres to the right of the arête climb the groove for six metres, then step right to a crack and follow this to the top.

12.   On the Wings of Freedom 12m   HVS   5a   (1982)
Climb straight up to cracks right of Jailbreak and follow these to the bad breaks.

13.   Hallucinogenics 14m   E1   5a   (1984)
You have got to be out of your trees to lead this one! Right of the corner is a sentry-box in a steep '*wall*'. Gain the sentry-box and climb it, carefully!

14.   Late Night Mob 10m   VD   (1982)
The arête just right, starting over a nose.

15. Windbreak 10m S   4a   (1982)
Climb the centre of the wall and finish up a jamming crack.

16. Another Late Night 9m   VD   (1982)
The slab right of Windbreak.

On the right wall of the gully is a steep wall. This turns into the quarry again and has a step at ground level. Starting from the step is:

17. Death Sentence 13m HVS 5a   (1981)
Climb the wall just left of the thin crack, then after about three metres traverse right to a flake on Cinderella and finish on the right.

18. Hammerhead 10m VS 4c   (1982)
Climb the thin crack in the wall to ledges, then finish over these.

19. Cinderella Man 10m HVS 5a   (1982)
Climb directly up the slab via a thin crack to a flake, either step right and finish easily over grass (preferable) or finish directly above the flake.

20. Sovereign 8m S 4a   (1982)
Gain and climb the grooveline on the right side of the slab.

21. Krishna Consciousness 10m VS 4c   (1982)
Start farther right, in the base of the pit. Climb a series of ledges to a move right to gain a finger crack. Follow this to a grassy finish.

Bastille Day Buttress
Bastille Day Buttress is the overhanging sandy-looking wall on the right as one enters the quarry. For safety reasons it would be prudent to hang a rope down the top few metres of the routes Bastille Day and Atomic Rooster to help overcome the loose finish.

22. Bronze Medal 9m HS 4b   (1984)
The left arête of the buttress.

★ **23. The Golden Moment** 10m E3 5c   (1984)
Moves left from the first good holds on Bastille Day, to a sloping jug, then climb the thin crack above (crux), with a move left to join and finish up the arête.
Direct Start (6a): the obvious line.

24. Bastille Day 9m E1 5b   (1980)
Climb cracks six metres right of the arête to a ledge then move up a crack to follow a line of ledges on the right to a loose finish.

25. Bolted Blues 6m E6 6c   (1990)
An eliminate line bouldering out past the second bolt (not in situ).

★ **26. Atomic Rooster** 10m E4 6b   (1984)
Two metres to the right of Bastille Day is an overhanging sentry-box, starting at six metres. Gain and climb this feature, grunting and groaning all the way. It is also possible to start up flakes on the right at a similar grade.

First Ascents at Harcle's Hill Quarry

1977	**Black Maria, Court Jester**	Phil Warner (solo)
1977	**The Judge, Blue Lamp, Jailbreak**	Dave Cronshaw, Phil Warner
1980 Nov	**Bastille Day** Phil Kelly (solo)	
1981 June 18	**Lord Foul's Bane** Phil Kelly (solo)	
1982 Mar 3	**Whoops Apocalypse** Phil Kelly, Colin Buckley, Paul French, Richard Norris	
1982 Mar 3	**Krishna Consciousness** Phil Kelly	
1982 Mar 24	**On the Wings of Freedom** Dave Whittles, Phil Kelly Colin Buckley	
1982 Mar 24	**Cinderella Man** Phil Kelly, Dave Whittles	
1982 June 18	**Death Sentence** Phil Kelly, Dave Whittle	
1982 July 3	**Caress of Steel** Phil Kelly (solo after top-roping)	
1982	**Left Chimney** Bury MC members	
1982	**Time Bandits** Colin Buckley	
1982	**Late Night Mob, Another Late Night** Paul Dewhurst	
1982	**Windbreak**	
1982	**Hammerhead** Peter Wolstenholme	
1982	**Sovereign** Mick Dewhurst, Colin Buckley, Bob Spencer	
1984 July 23	**The Golden Moment** (1 pt aid) Phil Kelly, Dave Whittles *Aid eliminated by Phil Kelly the next day.*	
1984 July 29	**Bronze Medal** Phil Kelly (solo)	
1984 Aug 1	**Atomic Rooster** Phil Kelly – Top-roped several times before leading	
1984	**Hallucinogenics** Phil Kelly (unseconded)	
Pre-1986	**White Maria**	
1990 July	**Bolted Blues** Gareth Parry	

Houses o' th' Hill Quarry   O.S. ref.   SD 876 175

Situation and Character

This quarry is situated only four kilometres north of Rochdale, above Spring Mill Reservoir in Whitworth.

The crag is literally a box-shaped hole in the ground, with a shorter wall above and to one side of the main quarry. The climbs are on sound rock, although the usual care applicable to quarried rock should be observed. The crag is very sheltered, and is at its best during the warmer periods. Some tipping has taken place in the past though this in no way affects the climbing, but the crag has been used little over the past couple of years, and some vegetation is starting to return. Although it now awaits a new generation of cleaners, nevertheless, some of the climbs are still worth doing.

History

The quarry was first visited in the late 1960s when its thick mantle of turf and loose rock presented quite a problem in those far-off days of on-sight leads and 'get up it somehow' techniques. Two corners were climbed by persons unknown, and it is possible that these are the two routes now known as *Cross Bred* and *The Lamb*.

In 1980 Bob Whittaker and his team put up *Return to the Fold* which remains the hardest route to date. Whittaker then introduced Ian Conway, Bruce Goodwin, Clive Morton, Mark Leach and others, and this team (armed with pickaxes, spades, brushes and 'furtling' sticks) rapidly demolished the loose outer skin of rock, soon to begin climbing new routes on the clean, sound rock beneath. Within four months most of the routes were done; Conway produced most of the HVSs, except for *Lonk* (Goodwin) and *Pulpy Kidney* (Morton).

Access and Approach

The quarry is on land owned by North West Water, whose managers are happy to permit climbing.

Two approaches are possible from the junction in Hall Street which is just off the A671 in Whitworth (almost opposite the Dog and Partridge). The junction is just past Whitworth Comprehensive School.

The first possibility is to turn left and go through Wall Bank Estate to a parking place near a mill. Walk up by the wall above the mill for 50 metres, cross it, then a track leads across flat open ground to a rise which leads to the quarry. Alternatively, turn right and go up until a tight left-hand hairpin leads to a narrow lane. The lane ends at an open space near a farm and two houses; Park there. The quarry lies over the wall right of the houses. This approach is quickest if on foot – 10 minutes.

The Climbs

The routes are described from RIGHT to LEFT starting at a corner, just right of a green wall, capped by an overhang.

1.   Scrag-end   8m   VS   4b   (1981)
Climb the corner to a ledge on the right, then ascend the wall just right of a crack.

★★ 2.   The Shepherd   10m   HVS   5b   (1981)
An interesting climb with a deceptively awkward crux at the top. Climb the green wall, or the corner, to the overhang. Follow the leftmost crack over the overhang and continue to the top.

3.   Crossbred   10m   VD   (1981)
From the foot of The Shepherd go left to grass, then climb the corner to just above the overhang. Traverse right and go up to a ledge then the top.

4.   The Lamb   9m   D   (1981)
From the foot of The Shepherd go left to grass then ascend the corner.

5.   Docked   12m   VD   (1981)
Start lower down in a groove behind an elder tree. Climb the groove and step right, then climb up to the obvious crack and follow this to a dirty finish (or traverse right just below the top and finish as The Lamb).

The next climb starts from the floor of the quarry, left of a dirty corner and below an overhang at six metres.

6.   Pulpy Kidney   17m   HVS   5a   (1981)
Start below the overhang. Climb the wall to the overhang, then go over this at the obvious weakness to gain a large ledge (on the girdle). Climb a crack to a ledge on the right arête, and move up into a short corner that leads to the top. An inferior variation using corners to the right then finishing at the same point has been climbed.

7.   Lurcher 17m VS 4c   (1981)
Start as for Pulpy Kidney, but move left to a slight crack, and up this to an
overhung niche. Exit from this to the girdle ledges and then finish up the corner
above.

★★ **8.   Elastrator** 17m VS 4c   (1981)
A sustained climb with an exposed feel. Gain a little rib just left of the quarry
corner, and follow thin cracks to the girdle ledges. The wider crack above leads
to the top.

★ **9.   Come By** 17m VS 4c   (1981)
Starts at the obvious overhanging corner. Climb into the corner, then move left
under the roof, gain the front and ascend to a good ledge. Move right to a small
corner and follow this to an overhanging niche. An awkward move leads out of
the niche and the top is then within reach.

10.   Tess 17m VS 4c   (1981)
Climb a short crack and face to join Come By. The large corner leads past a
tilted block to a steep slab and crack on the left. Ascend the slab to the bulge
and finish over this.

11.   Rough Fell 17m VS 4c   (1981)
Start three metres to the left. An overhung groove leads to a crack system which
leads to the girdle. Follow a groove leading to a V-shaped groove with a crack
in it and follow this to the top.

On the left of the wall is a small cave at three metres.

12.   Spring Bite 17m VS 4c   (1981)
Climb the crack to the right side of the cave, go right to a small groove and
ascend to the girdle ledge. Climb up on to a large yellow block, then gain the
triangular niche on the right and climb more or less direct to the top.

13.   Mutton Swing 17m VS 4b   (1981)
Climb up and left of the cave, then move right and follow cracks and a cracked
slab to a large overhung niche. Swing left and go up to finish.
*The large overhung corner has been climbed below and above the overhang, but
a detached block held together by faith or by skyhooks has deterred attempts at
a complete ascent so far. The next route starts three metres left at a block.*

★ **14.   Dales Bred** 21m HVS 5a   (1981)
Climb into a corner and then gain a flat nose on the right. Continue up the wall
to a roof, then go over this and move up left into a corner with a crack. Climb
this until another crack on the left leads to the top (cave).

★ **15.   Teeswater** 21m HVS 5a   (1981)
From the block on Dales Bred, climb into the first corner and gain a ledge
below an overhang. Climb the crack/groove to good ledges. Ascend to a crack
which leads to an overhang and surmount this with the help of a thin crack on
the left. Finish directly, just right of a sandy cave.

16. Masham 22m VS 4c,4c (1981)
1. 14m. Start six metres to the left. Climb into the right side of the large
recess, then follow the wall to a good ledge overlooking the grassy corner (nut
belays).
2. 8m. Follow the corner to an overhang, pull over this to large sandy holds,
then more easily continue to the top.

17. Asparagus Tarzan 18m HVS 5a (1981)
Climb the wall to a small corner. Ascend this to the large ledge of the girdle.
Move left to a crack, and climb this past a large white-scarred block to a
shallow sandy cave. Finish over the left side of the cave.

18. Reeperbahn Equaliser 18m HVS 5b (1981)
The upper wall has an obvious, short, overhanging crack in it. Take a line up
the wall to below the crack. Follow the crack to bold and exhilarating moves up
the wall to a horizontal fault. A cracked wall then leads to the top.

19. Cloven Hoof 18m S 4a (1981)
The obvious chimney. Climb a short ramp to a corner and go up to a large
ledge below a chimney. Climb the chimney and gain the recess. Move right for
three metres and finish up the wall as for Reeperbahn Equaliser.

20. Acid Flush 20m VS 4c (1981)
Climb the big corner to the crack and follow this to the overhanging vertical
slot. Continue direct to the recess, then traverse right (care needed to protect the
second) and finish as Reeperbahn Equaliser.

*The crag continues round to the left, and the next routes start underneath the
black, cracked, overhanging wall.*

21. Cast Horn 18m D (1981)
Follow ledges up and right to gain a large clean ledge. A long, dirty traverse
leftwards leads to a corner above Derbyshire Gritstone and a finish.

22. Muddy Hoof 15m VS 4b (1981)
The corner leads to a dirty move into the traverse of Cast Horn which is then
followed to join Cast Horn.

★ **23. Derbyshire Gritstone** 14m HVS 5a (1981)
Start just left of the corner. Climb the cracked wall to the overhang, then
continue up the crackline to a large sloping ledge (strenuous). Belay in the little
corner (several nuts) or proceed to stakes on the top.

★ **24. Lonk** 14m HVS 5b (1981)
Climb a corner on the left, to the left of a hole. Move right and go up a steep
rib, then pull up and climb past the large battered flake to gain a jamming crack
then the large sloping ledge. Belay as for Derbyshire Gritstone (not ON
Derbyshire Gritstone or you'll need a very long rope!).

25. Underbelly 14m VS 4c (1981)
Follow Lonk to the hole, then climb the corner to the roof, swing boldly out
two metres left and go up to a ledge. Move up past a flake to gain a ledge with
a large block and then the top.

26. Pot Belly 9m VD (1981)
The grassy groove left of Underbelly.

27. Belly Flop 9m VD (1981)
A line on the left of the wall some eight metres farther left.

At this point the quarry turns left again, and a steep crack is seen in the wall.

28. Return to the Fold 8m E1 5b (1980)
Gain the crack and follow it strenuously to a nasty finish.

29. Sheep Trod 55m VS 4c,4c (1981)
A traverse of the quarry from right to left, starting at the foot of The Shepherd.
1. 37m. Go left on to grass, then left again to a large ledge system which is followed across the walls, crossing the dangerous overhang between Mutton Swing and Dales Bred at foot level. Continue across ledges, then go up to a belay (nuts) on a ledge overlooking the grassy corner rake in the centre of the back wall.
2. 18m. Move up slightly and follow the obvious ledge across the wall until a move down leads across to Cloven Hoof. Go across into the overhanging slot of Acid Flush. Make an awkward move out left on to a large sloping ledge (care needed to protect the second) and follow the earthy traverse of Cast Horn to belay as for Derbyshire Gritstone.

First Ascents at Houses o' th' Hill Quarry

1980   **Return to the Fold** Bob Whittaker
1981 Mar   **Scrag-end** Bruce Goodwin, Ian Conway, Clive Morton
1981 Mar   **Pulpy Kidney** Clive Morton, Ian Conway, Bruce Goodwin
1981 Mar   **Tess** Ian Conway, Bruce Goodwin, Clive Morton
1981 Mar   **Rough Fell, Spring Bite, Mutton Swing** Bruce Goodwin, Clive Morton, Ian Conway
1981 Apr 11 **Teeswater** Ian Conway, Bruce Goodwin, Clive Morton
1981 Apr 13 **The Lamb** Clive Morton, Bruce Goodwin, Ian Conway
1981 Apr   **Dales Bred** Ian Conway, Bruce Goodwin, Clive Morton
1981 May 11 **The Shepherd** Ian Conway, Bruce Goodwin, John Vose
1981 May 13 **Masham** Ian Conway, Bruce Goodwin
1981 June 15 **Docked** Bruce Goodwin, Ian Conway
1981 June 15 **Sheep Trod** Ian Conway, Bruce Goodwin
1981 June 22 **Asparagus Tarzan** Ian Conway, Bruce Goodwin
1981 June 22 **Underbelly** Bruce Goodwin, Ian Conway
1981 June 27 **Acid Flush, Lonk** Bruce Goodwin, Ian Conway
1981   **Crossbred, Lurcher, Elastrator, Come By, Reeperbahn Equaliser** Ian Conway
1981   **Cloven Hoof, Cast Horn, Muddy Hoof, Derbyshire Gritstone, Pot Belly, Belly Flop**

Pinfold Quarry

O.S. ref. SD 807 161

Situation and Character

The quarry is situated across the valley from Harcles Hill, five kilometres north of Bury and about two kilometres south-east of the centre of Ramsbottom. It is less than two kilometres from Deeply Vale and the rock is very similar. However, whilst it is higher and more extensive than Deeply Vale, some sections are a little more broken. Much of the quarry is dominated by large square-cut roofs, which are penetrated by some interesting climbing.

The quarry is a suntrap and like Deeply Vale it is an ideal crag for an evening visit.

History

The quarry was discovered by Gareth Parry, Mike and Chris Preston in 1986. The original route of the quarry was *Necromicon*, by Parry, who soon followed this up with ascents of *Necromicon Arête, Necromicon Right-hand, Madman's Paradise* and *Acid Test*, all solo. Other early ascents were *Bogtrotter's Bench* and *Six Nipples of Love* by Tony Lancashire and *Love Under Will* by Mike Preston. Soon Matt Nuttall and Alan Holden discovered the delights of the quarry and between them, they climbed *Dead as a Door Matt, Central Bowl Crack, Rock On and Roll Off, Hari Kari Hooker, The Phantom Trundler* and *Alan's Route*. Parry then added *Hallucinogenics* (solo) and *Two Scoop or Not Two Scoop*, whilst Nuttall added *Willy Wonker* and the traverse with Holden.

Access and Approach

The farmer, Mr Brown, has granted permission to climb in the quarry, provided that access is made via the white gate, as described below.

The initial part of the approach to the quarry is the same as for Deeply Vale. From the centre of Bury, follow the A556 (Walmersley Road) north out of the centre for about three kilometres until, after a short rise, a church tower appears on the left. Turn right at the traffic lights at the crest of the rise (Walmersley Old Road) and follow this for about 800 metres to the Mason's Arms pub. At this point, instead of turning right (towards Deeply Vale), bear left and continue on cobbles and across the motorway for a further 800 metres to the Lord Raglan. Just less than one kilometre past this is a radio mast on the left and the quarry can be seen through a gate on the right. Continue past a turning to Hillside Kennels and park about 50 metres past a solitary house on the right where the lane widens.

Walk along the lane for about 200 metres to a white gate on the right. Go through the gate and walk along the left edge of the field and into the next field, then turn right and walk by the fence until the quarry can be entered at its left end.

The Climbs

The climbs are described from LEFT to RIGHT, starting at the extreme left end of the quarry.

Mental Block

At the left end of the quarry there is a terrace above an uninspiring pit. The first climbing lies on a short, very clean-cut section of rock capped by a small roof. This gives some excellent problems, of which the left arête (4a), the right arête (5b on left, 4c on right), the wall between (5a at left, 5b at right) and the wall two metres right of the arête via a curious bowl-shaped ledge (5c) are particularly interesting. It is also possible to traverse the Mental Block from right to left at different levels, with the line that follows the break being about 5a.

Layed Back Slabs

This is the short wall at the right side of The Terrace.

1.　Slab Attack　9m　S　4a　(1986)
Climb the wall at the extreme left, to a faint orange depression near the top.

2.　Smear Test　9m　S　4a　(1986)
Start at the right-hand end of the wall. Climb up and left to a shallow groove, then finish up this.

3.　Choss Groove　6m　VD　(1986)
The gruesome corner that limits the wall on its right.

Crystal Wall

This is the higher wall that starts at a slightly lower level than The Terrace, which is characterized by a roof that splits it at two-thirds-height.

4.　Acid Drops　6m　S　4a　(1986)
Start at the extreme left end of Crystal Wall at the edge of The Terrace directly below a saw-toothed arête. Step right around the arête, then climb it directly.

5.　Acid Test　12m　VS　4b　(1986)
Starting at a lower level, follow a direct line up the wall just right of the arête.

★★ 6.　Madman's Paradise　12m　E2　5c　(1986)
Start two metres to the right and climb the wall with a difficult rockover to reach the break. The crux can be reduced to 5b by moving left to a small triangular hold just before the break. From the break, continue in a direct line to finish at an obvious deep bowl.

7.　That Little Bit of Rock Right of David's Route　12m　VS　4b　(1986)
Climb the groove on the right to the break, then move left to a shallow corner and surmount the overhang directly above as for Madman's Paradise.

★ 8.　The Six Nipples of Love　12m　E1　5b　(1986)
Climb the thin flake crack on the right to the break, then pull over the overhang on good holds past a right-pointing rock finger and finish up the wall above, using a hidden hold.

9.　Bog Trotter's Bench　12m　E2　5c　(1986)
Start one metre to the right and climb up to a short, thin crack, then move up and right to reach the horizontal break at another thin crack. Pull over the roof using a suspect block directly above, then step left and finish as for Six Nipples.

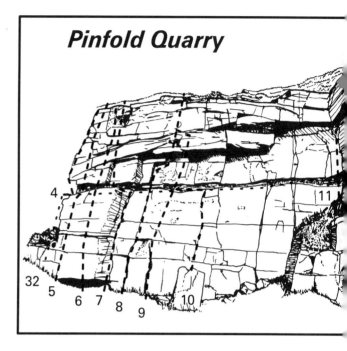

Between a large block and the face there is a small rectangular boulder embedded in the ground at the foot of:

10. Love Under Will 12m E2 5b (1986)
Climb thin cracks to the break, then finish as for the previous route.

Main Overhang Wall
This section of the quarry is characterized by a massive, square-cut overhang at its left side. The first three climbs start from ledges to the left of this.

★ **11. Fearsome** 12m HVS 5a (1986)
From the ledges at the left side of the Main Overhang, climb the corner to the high break, then traverse right to the arête and finish up this.

★ **12. Awesome** 12m E1 5b (1986)
Follow Fearsome for about four metres, then traverse right on smears to reach the arête and finish up this.

★ **13. Hallucinogenics** 8m E4 5c (1986)
From the ledges at the left side of the Main Overhang climb the centre of the wall left of the arête, with the crux at the top overlap. Bold and unprotected unless you start seeing things!

★★★ **14. Necromicon Arête** 12m E2 5c (1986)
After a sensational swing to cross the overhang, there is a good finish in a fine position. Exit from the centre of the left scoop and climb up to the left side of

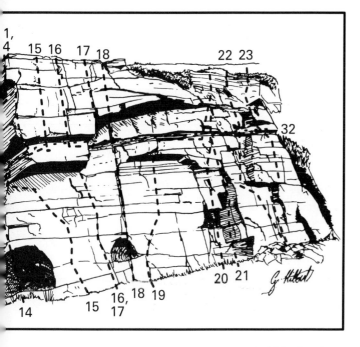

the Main Overhang, then swing right on to the Main Overhang and attain a standing position on the break above the roof (peg). Finish up the arête.

★★★ **15.   Necromicon**   15m   E1   5b   (1986)
An excellent climb, despite the poor rock below the roof. Start between the two scoops and climb up and left to the left side of the Main Overhang. This point can also be reached by climbing to the right side of the Main Overhang, then traversing left. Swing right on to the Main Overhang then gain a standing position above the roof (peg), then finish up the wall about two metres to the right of the arête, between the arête and the crack.

★★ **16.   Necromicon Right-hand**   12m   VS   4c   (1986)
A much easier climb than might at first appear. Climb direct to the right-hand side of the Main Overhang, then step out left on to the lip of overhang and finish up the short crack and wall on the left.

17.   Willy Wonker the Big, Fat Tonker   12m   E2   5b   (1986)
Climb Necromicon Right-hand to the corner above Main Overhang, then surmount the roof directly above and finish direct.

18.   Two Scoop or Not Two Scoop   12m   E3   5c   (1986)
Climb the thin crack that rises from the centre of the right scoop to the roof above, then finish direct.

19.   Suck it and See   12m   E1   5a   (1986)
From the right side of the second scoop, climb up and right, then surmount a
small overlap to reach the horizontal break, Traverse right along this until it is
possible to finish up Phantom Trundler.

20.   Poltergeist   12m   HVS   5a   (1986)
Immediately left of a jumble of blocks on the ground, there is a ramp which is
overlooked by three small overhangs. Take a direct line over the first overhang.

21.   Phantom Trundler   12m   HVS   5a   (1986)
Climb the ramp to the third overhang, then surmount this and climb up and
slightly left to the horizontal break and finish direct as for Poltergeist.
Direct Start (5a): climb the blunt arête on the right.

22.   The Whore   12m   VS   4c   (1986)
Start at the right side of the jumble of blocks and climb to a small roof, then
move left to easy ground.

23.   Hara-kiri Hooker   12m   HVS   5a   (1986)
Starting as for The Whore climb to the right-hand side of the small roof, then
step right to a crack and finish direct. The crack can also be gained direct.

24.   Loathsome   12m   VS   4b   (1986)
The chossy, hanging groove that limits the wall on its right.

Matt's Slabs
*After a short corner, the crag continues with another wall, known as Matt's
Slabs. This is more broken and less impressive than the previous two sections.*

25.   Dead as a Door Matt   11m   E1   5a   (1986)
Climb the wall between two scoops.

26.   Central Bowl Crack   11m   HVS   5a   (1986)
Climb the crack that leads to the next scoop, then follow the crack above, until
it is possible to step right on to a ledge and an easy finish.

27.   Rock On, Roll Off   11m   E1   5a   (1986)
Climb the wall just to the right. Bold and no side runners.

28.   Cardiac Arête   11m   VS   5a   (1986)
Climb the short shallow corner on the right, then move left along the ledge at
its top to an easy finish.

29.   Statement of Marriage   11m   VS   4c   (1986)
Climb the wall about one metre farther right.

30.   Divorce Day Blues   11m   VS   4c   (1986)
A direct line up the wall about one metre right again.

31.   Alan's Route   11m   S   4a   (1986)
From the rock scar climb over easy ledges to the top.

Tiger's Fang
At present there are no routes on this, the final section of the crag.

Traverses
A very enjoyable low-level traverse of the main sections has been done at 6b.

★ **32.** **The Adventures of Willy Wonker Belayed by Matt the Plonker**
   53m   HVS   4a,5b,5a,4a   (1986)
A complete traverse of the three main walls going from left to right.
1. 24m. Round the saw-toothed arête as for Acid Drop, then foot traverse
along the break into the corner and belay on ledges as for Hallucinogenics.
2. 11m. Hand-traverse the Main Overhang to the corner of Loathsome and
belay.
3. 8m. Continue along the break past Poltergeist to a belay in the corner.
4. 10m. Round the arête and continue at the same height until it is possible to
finish up Divorce Day Blues.

First Ascents at Pinfold Quarry

1986	**Slab Attack, Smear Test, Acid Drops, Awesome** Matt Nuttall
1986	**Choss Groove** Alan Holden
1986	**Acid Test, Necromicon Arête, Madman's Paradise, Necromicon Right-hand** Gareth Parry (solo)
1986	**That Little Bit of Rock Right of David's Route** Chris Preston (solo)
1986	**The Six Nipples of Love** Tony Lancashire
1986	**Bog Trotter's Bench** Tony Lancashire, Gareth Parry
1986	**Love Under Will** Mike Preston
1986	**Necromicon** Gareth Parry, Mike Preston, Chris Preston
1986	**Willy Wonker the Big, Fat Tonker, Phantom Trundler, Central Bowl Crack, The Adventures of Willy Wonker Belayed by Matt the Plonker** Matt Nuttall, Alan Holden
1986	**Two Scoop or Not Two Scoop, The Whore, Statement of Marriage** Gareth Parry
1986	**Suck it and See** Rick Marrion
1986	**Poltergeist**
1986	**Hara-kiri Hooker** Matt Nuttall, Alan Holden *Direct Start by Gareth Parry, 1986.*
1986	**Loathsome, Dead as a Door Matt, Cardiac Arête, Fearsome** Matt Nuttall (solo)
1986	**Rock On, Roll Off** Alan Holden (solo)
1986	**Divorce Day Blues** Matt Nuttall
1986	**Alan's Route** Alan Holden, Matt Nuttall
1986	**Hallucinogenics** Gareth Parry (solo)

Tonacliffe Quarry   O.S. ref.   SD 883 166

Situation and Character
Tonacliffe Quarry is situated on the western edge of Roshy Hill, overlooking the
Whitworth Valley just north of Healey. It reaches nine metres in places and is a
quarried gritstone. The rock is reasonable, although the ravages of the past few
winters have caused some rock fall. There is some dubious rock, but this is
obvious and does not usually interfere with the climbs, or the enjoyment thereof.
It is a well-used crag, being popular for evening or 'short day' visits.

History

The original pioneers of the quarry are unknown, except that Derek Clutterbuck has climbed here for many years and still lives below the crag. Many of the problems are traditional, though many should have Derek's name tagged to them. He used to visit the quarry regularly and solo *Layaway Wall* (some say nightly in summer) to prove to himself that he could still do the business.

Modern recorded development began in 1970 when Bob Whittaker and Ralph Pickering visited the crag, climbing *The Corner* and *Overhanging Crack*. Then they left the quarry to Clutterbuck and no new climbs were ascended until 1978 when news of a prospective supplement guidebook spurred Whittaker and Pickering into another visit, this time in the company of Gordon Mason. This trio climbed about twenty new routes, including *Hand-jam Crack, Little Cameo, Hidden Corner* and *Groovin'*.

The pre-guidebook rush saw Whittaker climbing *Paper Tiger* and *Diamond Solitaire* in 1980, though Les Hardman broke Whittaker's monopoly in 1981 when he added *Wazzock*.

A young Mark Leach added *After the Ordeal* and *Icarus Ascending* in 1981. He tried the second ascent of *Icarus* some weeks later in 'traditional' style, with a rope tied round his waist, but slipped near the top and a near decker resulted. In 1985, Andrew Eaton climbed the fine little arête between Central Pillar and Overhanging Cracks. He aptly named it *The Apprentice's Edge* – Master's Edge at Millstone was put up on the same day.

In 1988 Bruce Goodwin began to clean some lines, as did Ray Parker. Blunt Arête and Tonacliffe Pillar were re-recorded, then Goodwin added finishes to the Back Wall routes and ascended *Blues Power*. Parker added *What's Left, Travelling Light* and *Uncertain Feeling*. A final mini-effort saw Goodwin, with brother Phil, add *Plugged*.

Access and Approach

There is no access problem but care must be taken if approaching by car as thoughtless parking will give offence to the local householders.

The quarry is reached from Rochdale by following the A671 until 800 metres north of Healey Corner. Tonacliffe Road leads off right and in turn Highpeak Lane turns off right 800 metres farther on. The steep hill is followed to where it eases off into a level green track which leads back left. Considerate parking is available a little farther on, near the *'public footpath'* sign. The green track leads to the quarry in about 200 metres.

The Climbs

The quarry is best considered in two sections; when entering the quarry the Main Bay is seen first, with the left-hand section making up another bay. With startling originality these have been named from left to right as Bay One and Bay Two. The first climbs start at the extreme left end of Bay One. The climbs are described from LEFT to RIGHT.

Bay One

The first climbs are unstable due to rockfall, but they are included here for completeness.

1.   Andy's Arête 8m VS 4c   (1982)
Climbs to the big ledge and finish up the arête.

2.   Nean 8m VS 4c   (1982)
Climb to the big ledge. The crack in the wall leads to the top.

3.   Snout 8m HS 4b   (1978)
To the right there is a nose of rock. Climb the left edge of this to a ledge, then
finish up the left arête.

★ **4.   Escort** 8m S 4a   (1978)
Climb the wall just right of Snout.

5.   Cavalier 8m HS 4a   (1978)
Just to the right a triangular niche leads to an overhang, then go right to finish
up an arête.

6.   Groovin' 8m D   (1978)
A groove containing jammed blocks.

7.   Wazzock 8m S   (1981)
The wall on the right is climbed direct.

8.   Retreat 8m S   (1978)
Climb the crack to gain a groove with difficulty.

9.   The Arête 8m HS 4b   (1978)
Climb the crack as for Retreat (or direct) then move right and climb the
square-cut groove on the arête.

10.   Lux 9m HS 4b   (1981)
Start below the arête and climb to a ledge on the right then step left and climb
direct to the arête.

★★ **11.   Little Cameo** 9m VS 5a   (1978)
A bold and technical upper section. Start to the right of the arête, gain the large
ledge and crank up the wall above, just left of centre.

★ **12.   Fallout** 9m HS 4c   (1978)
The open corner to the right of Little Cameo provides the substance of this route.

★ **13.   Central Pillar** 9m HVS 5a   (1981)
The pillar is gained direct over an overhang then a narrow wall leads to the top.

14.   The Apprentice's Edge 9m E2 6a   (1985)
Takes the arête of Central Pillar on its right-hand side; fingery. Graded for an
ascent with runners in Overhanging Crack.

★★ **15.   Overhanging Crack** 9m HVS 5a   (1973)
The obvious cracks around the arête give a good climb, that is strenuous and
well-protected, yet it still has a committing feel.

★ **16.   The Corner** 9m VS 4c   (1973)
The obvious corner gives a good route.

★ **17.   Shortie**   9m   HS   4b   (1978)
The crack a couple of metres right of the corner leads to strenuous pulls then
the top.

18.   Flicker   8m   S   4a   (1978)
The wall just left of The Chimney.

19.   The Chimney   6m   D   (1978)
The obvious chimney.

20.   Beginners' Route   6m   D   (1975-79)
The wall to the right of the chimney, finishing left of a pointed block.

21.   Starters' Route   6m   D   (1978)
The wall to the right again finishing right of the pointed block.

Bay Two
Duerdon's Route, *at 4c to 5a, is a disjointed line to the left of Hand-jam Crack.*

★★ **22.   Hand-jam Crack**   6m   VS   4c   (1978)
An awkward outing on good jams. Finger men beware! The obvious crack
taking an overhang en-route. Good.

23.   Paper Tiger   6m   HVS   5b   (1978)
A boulder problem start leads to the wall on the right of Hand-jam Crack.

★ **24.   Layaway Wall**   6m   VS   5a   (Mid-1970s)
Start at the right arête, move up then go left to the middle of the wall and go
over the overhang using flakes and thence the top. Sustained.

★ **25.   After the Ordeal**   6m   HVS   5b   (1981)
Follow Layaway Wall to the end of its block then go up the smooth wall above
via a shallow scoop.

26.   Diamond Solitaire   10m   VS   5a   (1980)
Start as for Layaway Wall. Climb the arête to a hand-traverse line. This leads
leftwards to a finish up Hand-jam Crack.

27.   Icarus Ascending   8m   E1   5c   (1981)
Start as above but continue up the arête on its left-hand side.
*Layaway Wall can also be reached by a direct start (6a), and the wall can be
traversed with hands below the overhang (5b). There is also a low level traverse
at 6a.*

★ **28.   Hidden Corner**   8m   S   4a   (1978)
Ascend the V-groove and a corner groove.

29.   Star of Sirius   8m   VS   4b   (1979-83)
The smooth wall a couple of metres to the right leads to a finish up Hidden
Corner.

30.   The Groove   8m   D   (1978)
Right again is a loose groove leading to a blocky finish.

31. Blunt Arête 8m VS 4c (1988)
The arête is gained and followed closely.

32. Tonacliffe Pillar 9m HVS 5b (1988)
The narrow face right of the arête is followed with a difficult move at the start
and another on the wall

33. What's Left 8m HVS 5b (1988)
The corner and groove to the left of the overhang.

34. Travelling Light 6m E1 5b (1988)
The overhang is tackled as directly as possible.

35. Uncertain Feeling 6m HVS 5b (1988)
The short crack at the right-hand end of the overhanging wall.

Back Wall
On the right there is a corner, then the Back Wall. Left of the first crack is:

★ **36. Blues Power** 10m VS 5a (1988)
Climb the wall to a large ledge, then surmount the overhang above by a layback
and continue to the top.

★ **37. Back Wall Left** 10m VS 4c (1975-79)
Climb the left crack and continue up the wider crack/groove above.

38. Plugged 10m HVS 5c (1988)
Climb in an eliminate fashion between the two cracks. Finish as for the route on
either side.

39. Back Wall Right 10m VS 4b (1978)
The right-hand crack leads to a break. The wall right of the crack/groove of
Back Wall Left provides a good finish.

40. Pop 6m VD (1978)
The end of the wall has a short crack.

Farther right is:

41. The Ceiling 5a (1972)
A good roof problem. The roof has '*Loose*' painted beneath it. It is not, we
hope!!

42. Girdle Traverse 46m VS 5a (1978)
A girdle traverse starting as for Diamond Solitaire or Layaway wall gives 5a
climbing across to the arête left of Hand-jam Crack. Various ways can be
followed to The Corner; high (5c) or low (5a) leads to the ledge of Little
Cameo. Go around the arête and follow the break to finish down (or up)
Cavalier.

First Ascents at Tonacliffe Quarry
1972 Sep   **The Ceiling** Bob Whittaker (solo)
1973 Sep   **Overhanging Crack, The Corner** Bob Whittaker, Ralph Pickering
1973-77   **Layaway Wall** Derek Clutterbuck

1978 Apr 9	**Little Cameo, Fallout** Bob Whittaker, Ralph Pickering, Gordon Mason
1978 Apr 9	**Hand-jam Crack, Back Wall Left, Back Wall Right** Bob Whittaker, Ralph Pickering
1978 Apr 9	**Shortie, Flicker, The Chimney, Beginners' Route, Starters' Route, Pop, Girdle Traverse** Bob Whittaker (solo)
1978 Apr 10	**Hidden Corner** Bob Whittaker, Ralph Pickering
1978 Apr 12	**Paper Tiger, The Groove** Bob Whittaker (solo)
1978 Apr 12	**Groovin', Escort, Cavalier** Bob Whittaker, Ralph Pickering, Gordon Mason
1978 Apr 12	**Snout** Bob Whittaker, Ralph Pickering
1978 Apr 12	**Retreat, The Arête** Bob Whittaker, Gordon Mason
1979	**Duerdon's Route** Mark Duerdon (solo)
1980 Nov	**Diamond Solitaire** Bob Whittaker, Harry Taylor, Ron Blunt, Geoff Haigh
1981 Apr	**Wazzock** Les Harman, Bob Whittaker
1981 Apr	**Lux, Central Pillar** Bob Whittaker, Les Harman
1981	**After the Ordeal, Icarus Ascending** Mark Leach, Andrew Eaton
1982	**Andy's Arête, Nean** Andy Clutterbuck
1979-83	**Star of Sirius**
1985	**The Apprentice's Edge** Andrew Eaton (unseconded)
1988 June 6	**Blunt Arête** Bruce Goodwin, Ray Parker
1988 June 6	**Tonacliffe Pillar, What's Left** Ray Parker, Bruce Goodwin
1988 June 6	**Blues Power,** *Back Wall Left, Groove Finish* Bruce Goodwin, Ray Parker, L Mills, Michael Harrison, M Robertson
1988 June 8	**Travellin' Light, Uncertain Feeling** Ray Parker, Bruce Goodwin
1988 June 17	**Plugged** Bruce Goodwin, Philip Goodwin

Troy Quarry   O.S. ref.   SD 763 235

Situation and Character

Troy Quarry overlooks Haslingden Grane about three kilometres north-west of Haslingden. The quarry is composed of fine-grained grit with many cleavage lines due to the quarry working methods. It is of open aspect, and the south and west-facing walls dry out rapidly after rain. The rock is (generally) sound and the protection usually good. Belay stakes are in place on The West Face, but are limited on The South Face. However, a new fence (please do not damage this) with solid posts provides safe but distant belay points.

On the North Face the climbs are more serious and many have had few ascents. Here it is advisable to belay to a rope hung over the top, again anchored to the fence, as the exits of the climbs here should be viewed with some trepidation. In sunny weather the place is a sun trap.

History

During the 1970s, John Ryden and John Grundy led some routes, but found the character of the rock wanting and abandoned the quarry in disgust.

In 1982, Ian Conway, Tony Nichols and Mark Leach together with Bruce Goodwin and Clive Morton began new explorations with an extensive quarrying campaign. This resulted in many of the main lines being climbed. Collectively, they climbed *Jussy, The Flea, Pink Edge, Tower of Orthank, Huntington's Chorea* and *Rapunzle*, plus several other routes including *One Step Farther* by Mark Leach, which is still the hardest route in the quarry and has seen very few ascents. He also added *Rock Lobster* with Mick Johnston, whilst Bruce contributed *Sounder*. Pete Cain and Greg Rimmer visited once and contributed

Fraser and *Dad's Army*. Alan Cameron and John Mason climbed several routes, including a direct finish to *Sounder* with Dave Etherington and *Shadowfax*.

In 1992 the most prominent part of The Tower collapsed and within 24 hours of discovering this, Matt Nuttall reclimbed the area, retaining the name of Pink Edge, whilst Alan Holden produced *Revenge of the Bendy Ents* from behind the missing *Tower of Orthank*. The area right of Troy Groove also began to collapse and is still doing so.

In preparation for the new guidebook, Paul Dewhurst added *Siam Groove*, which was later extensively cleaned and the hanging flake was removed by Dave Cronshaw. During this period Cronshaw and Les Ainsworth, undertook some major cleaning around Dovetail and Siam Groove then re-ascended the cleaned lines, but the most significant route was a girdle of The West Face by Paul Merrick and Roger Smith, that they named *Golden Thread*.

Approach
From Haslingden follow the Grane Road (B6263) towards Blackburn, past the Duke of Wellington Inn for 200 metres to a lane on the right which is signposted *'Thirteen Stone Hill'*. Follow this lane and park on the right just after some garages. Continue along the road for 200 metres, then turn right at the first gate and follow a track (with a culvert on its right) through three gates into the quarry. About five minutes walk.

Alternatively, the crag can be approached from Junction 5 on the M65 by heading for Haslingden on the B6232. The lane to the quarry lies about five kilometres down this road on the left, opposite the reservoirs and is signed *'Thirteen Stone Hill'*.

The Climbs
The climbing is situated on several buttresses which form an arc, generally overlooking the pool. The most natural approach for most of the climbs is from the right and so they are described from RIGHT to LEFT. However, the climbs on The North Face and Little Buttress are generally approached from the left and so these climbs are described from LEFT to RIGHT, starting from The North Face.

The West Face
At the right-hand side of the pool there is a relatively long area of rock, which is split in two by a loose and more broken bay. The rock between this bay and the steep slope that forms the right end of the area is known as The West Face. At its right side the rock rapidly gains in height to an arête which provides the first route, five metres to the left of the highest point of the ground.

1.   Stilton 6m VS 4c   (1982)
The first arête on the wall.

2.   Open Sesame 7m VD   (1982)
The obvious chimney/grooves just left of the arête. Currently very dirty.

3.   Little Sneak 8m VS 4c   (1982)
Climb cracks in the centre of the wall on the left to a niche and a mantel. Finish just left of the arête.

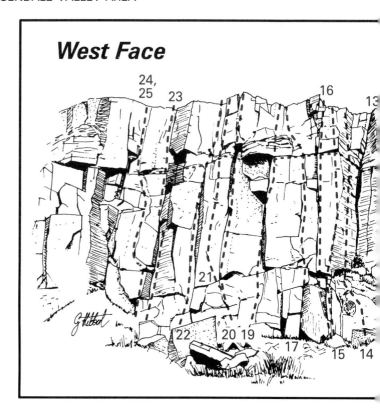

West Face

24,
25 23   16   13

21

22   20 19   17   15 14

4.   One Way Street 8m S 4a   (1982)
The corner is climbed direct. Currently very dirty.

5.   No Right Turn 8m VS 4c   (1982)
Strenuously follow the thin crack left of One Way Street.

6.   Lema 9m HVS 5c   (1982)(1995)
Climb the arête with difficulty to an easier finish.
Saints (E1, 5c): From the midway break, traverse left to gain Bob the Gob and
finish up this.

7.   Nova 9m HVS 5c   (1982)
Boulder up the centre of the steep slab and finish direct.

8.   Bob the Gob 10m VS 4c   (1982)
Follow the deep groove, then the crack in the headwall.

9.   Mucky Pups 11m HVS 5a   (1982)
The recess on the left is climbed via a steep crack at its back.

★★ **10.   Shadowfax** 12m E2 5c   (1986)
Climb the arête. A bold and poorly protected eliminate line which gives
sustained climbing, with a crimpy exit.

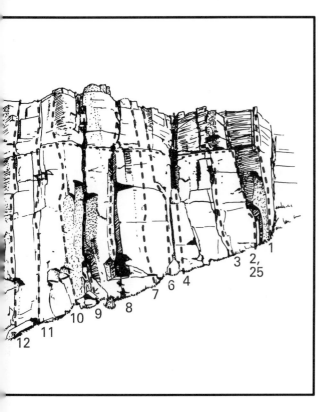

★★ 11. Rapunzle 12m VS 5a   (1982)
The wall on the left contains a prominent feature known as the *'barred window'*. The rock architecture is unique and it is worth a visit, even though the lady has been rescued long ago. Climb thin cracks to gain the window, then finish up the cracks above.

★★ 12. Stacked Deck 12m HS 4b   (1982)
Excellent, positive laybacking with holds on an expanding flake! The fine crack and flake line one metre left.

13. Updraught Corner 12m S 4a   (1982)
The corner on the left is followed to a groove, and the top. Currently very dirty.

14. Jaundice Crack 12m HVS 5a   (1982)
The wall on the left is split by two cracks. Climb the second of these.

★ 15. Siamese Arête 12m VS 4c   (1997)
The arête on the left.

16. Right Siamese Twin 12m S 4a   (1982)
Climb the straight crack immediately left of the arête.

17. Left Siamese Twin 13m S 4a (1982)
Climb over blocks to the more ragged crack in the centre of the wall, then climb this and at the top, finish up the corner on the left.

18. Slow Motion 12m VS 4b (1982)
Take a direct line between the ragged crack and the right arête of the deep groove.

19. Siam Groove 12m VS 4b (1995)
Climb the deep groove to the overhang, then move right to a small hold and finish up the wall above.

20. Cracked Wall 12m VS 4c (1982)
The crack immediately left of the deep groove is climbed via a small pod to an overhang. Finish up the thinner continuation crack.

21. Overlooked Crack 13m HS 4b (1996)
From the foot of Cracked Wall move left to a crack and climb this to a ledge near the top. Step right round the arête and finish up the wall just right of the arête.

22. Troy Groove 12m VS 4b (1982)
Climb the next groove to a tricky move to gain ledges at eight metres. Finish up the corner.

23. Helen of Troy 12m VS 5a (1995)
Two metres left climb the short, shallow groove to a large ledge. Move over blocks (avoiding a loose block) and finish up the corner crack.

24. Gopher 12m HVS 4c (1986)
Climb the flake crack on the left to a ledge, then step left into a bottomless groove and 'go for' the top.

25. Golden Thread 25m VS 4c,4b (1996)
A girdle of the West Face.
1. 14m. Climb Open Sesame to the obvious break, then move left across Bob the Gob and continue past Rapunzel to a belay at Updraught Corner.
2. 11m. Continue leftwards under an overhang, then finish up Gopher.

The South Face
After a loose bay, the climbing continues on the South Face, at the right edge of the pool.

26. Little 'Un 8m S 4a (1982)
At the right side of the small bay and in line with The West Face there is a small buttress with a distinctive grooved notch at its base. Climb the crack and arête to grassy ledges and an escape on the right.

27. Solo Wall 6m VS 5a (1982)
The next section is at a higher level and its left side is split by a horizontal break at half-height. Start two metres to the right of the corner and trend slightly right then go straight up. Unprotected.

28. Grand National 9m   VS   4c   (1982)
Climb the shallow corner just after the ground level starts to fall, to an easier
finish.

29. Aldanite 10m   HVS   5a   (1982)
The crack and shallow groove on the left provide difficult climbing via a
shallow, black, square-cut recess near the top.

30. Tess 12m   HVS   5b   (1982)
Start at an embedded boulder below a blunt arête with a square-cut groove in it.
Climb the crack on the left, move right into the groove and follow it to the top.

⋆⋆ **31. Rock Lobster** 12m   E3   6a   (1983)
A faint crackline up the centre of the wall just left of Tess. Tenacity and a rack
of small wires will enable climbers to overcome its bouldery moves and cruise
to the top. A good pitch.

⋆⋆ **32. Sounder** 12m   HVS   5a   (1983)(1985)(1986)
Good jamming, with a real sinker at half-height. Climb the crack to the
horizontal break near the top, then traverse left and finish up Questionable
Stability. There are two other finishes:
Direct (E2, 5c): straight up the headwall.
Right-hand (HVS, 5a): hand-traverse right and finish up the arête.

⋆ **33. Questionable Stability** 12m   VS   4c   (1982)
The steep corner crack.

The Tower

*This is the narrow projecting buttress on the left. Recent rockfalls have altered
the character of the original routes. A corner crack on its right gives the next
route.*

34. Loose Living 14m   HS   4b   (1982)
The corner crack on the right of the tower leads steeply into a chimney, where a
steep move leads to the top.

⋆⋆ **35. Pink Edge** 14m   E2   5b   (1982/1992)
An excellent route to do as the sun sets. An easy start leads to a steep finish.
Gain the ledge on the front of The Tower, then follow the blocky crack above,
passing an obvious overlap at the top.

⋆⋆ **36. Revenge of the Bendy Ents** 15m   E3   5c   (1982/1992)
This route supersedes the Tower of Orthank, which proved to be attached to the
main face only by a small crescent of lighter rock. The route that remains is
sustained and at the top of is grade. From the lowest point on the front face of
The Tower, climb cracks just right of the left arête of Orthank.

⋆⋆ **37. Pillar Cracks** 14m   VS   4c   (1982)
The crack system on the left leads to a short groove at the top of the wall.

Long Wall
This is the long imposing wall, which is slightly set back from The Tower.

★ **38.   Jussy**   14m   HVS   5b   (1982)
The corner between the buttress and the long wall is followed direct.

39.   Two Dabs   14m   E2   5c   (1982)
Climb Jussy for about five metres, then move left to a crackline and go up this
with two 'dabs' (shallow pockets) right to the top.

★ **40.   The Flea**   14m   E2   5c   (1982)
Climb the next, shallow corner on the left to a niche, then exit via a thin crack.

★★ **41.   Grane Wall**   14m   E1   5b   (1982)
A justly popular climb. Start just left of a sandy recess and follow the wall to a
small overlap, then ascend the fine crack above.

★ **42.   Huntington's Chorea**   14m   E2   5c   (1982)
Start three metres to the left and climb the very thin crack that runs the entire
height of the wall.

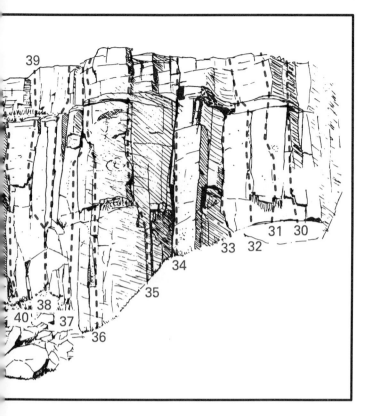

43. Distemper 15m HVS 4c   (1982)
Climb the groove/crack system on the loose rock. Escape from the vegetated
cave any way you can!

44. Deep Throat 15m HVS 4c   (1982)
Climb the obvious overhanging chimney that rises behind a large leaf of rock.
Finish directly at the top.

★ **45. Fallen Friend** 15m E2 5c   (1982)
The wall on the left is climbed direct to a bottomless groove. Go up this and
pull out right at the top to finish.

46. Curlew 14m E1 5b   (1982)
Climb the cracked wall just right of Dovetail, moving right for a runner at six
metres.

★★ **47. Dovetail** 12m E1 5b   (1982)
Climb the V-shaped groove to the top. A good exercise in bridging.

48. Grooved Arête 11m VS 4c   (1982)
Start a couple of metres farther left, at a short groove capped by an overhang.
Climb the left edge of this groove and continue up the blocky arête above.

49.   Troy Corner   9m   V.D   (1982)
The obvious ferny corner at a higher level is climbed via twin cracks to a
V-chimney and the top.

50.   Troy Wall   11m   VS   4c   (1982)
Follow Troy Corner to the horizontal fault, move left to a steep groove above
the sapling and follow this to the top. A poor route.

51.   Annic   9m   HVS   5a   (1982)
Climb the short right-facing corner then move right to a small, pod-like crack in
the upper wall and finish up this.

★ **52.   The Triumvirate**   42m   E2   5a,5c   (1982)
1.   24m.   Climb Annic then follow a line right to the corner, and continue to
the arête. Cross Dovetail, then move right and go up to gain the top of the
chimney of Deep Throat. Descend this to a step right, then move right again to
a belay in the deep corner of Distemper.
2.   18m.   Move right on to a footledge and cross to a crack (on Grane Wall)
and then go down to the niche on The Flea. Continue at this level to Jussy.
Move up the crack system of Pillar Cracks to the second groove, step around
the corner on good handholds on to Revenge of the Bendy Ents and continue to
the ledge on Pink Edge and finish up this route.

*Farther left is an open corner with two large blocks at its base. The next route
starts one metre left of this.*

★ **53.   Pisa**   9m   E1   5b   (1982)
Climb the pillar, trending right at the top.

54.   Dusky   9m   VS   5a   (1982)
Climb the short right-facing, right-angled corner then finish direct.

★ **55.   Conian**   9m   HVS   5a   (1982)
Climb Dusky to a ledge, then step left and climb the wall above.

56.   Nilsar   9m   VS   5a   (1982)
The crack system two metres to the left.

57.   Ventnor   9m   E2   6a   (1982)
Start two metres to the left and follow an indefinite crack up the steep wall to
good holds on a slabby scoop, then finish direct.

58.   Deception   9m   HVS   5b   (1982)
The steep groove and wall immediately left of the slabby scoop.

*Several routes have been done on the broken buttress to the left, which have
sadly become overgrown. They could be cleaned, or left for good placements
when frozen.*

Adam Richardson – 'P' for **Paradox** (E2 5b), Wilton One.   *Photo: Geoff Hibbert*

The North Face

This is the continuous section of rock at the far left side of the pool. At present it is rather vegetated and dirty, but some of the lines are worthwhile and would improve with traffic. As it is usually approached from the left, the climbs are described from LEFT to RIGHT.

59.   Don't Look Down   14m E1   5b   (1982)
Start two metres to the right of a prominent clean-cut groove at the right-hand side of the wall. Follow a crack to the top past a dirty window at three metres. Sustained.

60.   Whoops Apocalypse   14m HVS   5a   (1982)
Start three metres to the right and follow the shallow, stepped groove.

To the right, the height of the rock decreases because of a mound at the foot of the crag. The next climbs start at the foot of this mound.

61.   Penwood Groove   14m HS   4a   (1998)
From the base of the mound, climb the broken groove at the left side of a large block-overhang at mid-height.

62.   Penwood Forge Mill   15m HVS   5a   (1982)
Climb the prominent corner past the large block-overhang at mid-height to reach a large ledge directly above the overhang. Finish on the right.

63.   Sunsalve   15m E1   5b   (1982)
The thin crack in the right wall of the corner.

★ † **64.   One Step Farther**   17m E5   6b   (1982)(1982)
A sustained route. From blocks at the foot of the next corner, traverse left to a deep niche on the arête. Leave this by a crack on its right, then step left and climb a thin crack to a large ledge. Finish easily.   There is also a direct start at 6a.

★ **65.   Anxiety**   15m HVS   5a   (1982)
The steep corner crack, which is currently very overgrown.

66.   What I'd Give for a Friend   15m HVS   5a   (1985)
Six metres to the right is a flake crack below a wide-angled groove. Climb to the base of this via a V-shaped slot then continue up the crack and groove above.

67.   Pike   12m HVS   5a   (1982)
The next deep corner crack to the right is climbed by finger-jams and bridging.

★ **68.   Captain Mainwaring**   12m HVS   5a   (1982)
The arête on the right is climbed on its right.

The next two routes start by the boulder bridge across the pool.

Geoff Hibbert makes wild moves on **Renaissance** (E5 6a), Egerton Quarry.
Photo: Adam Richardson

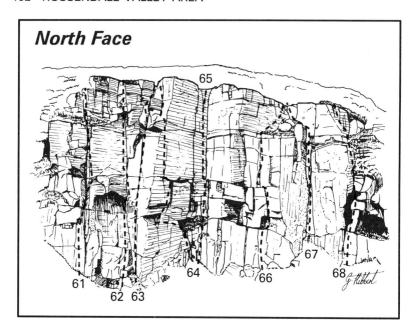

North Face

69. Fraser 12m E1 5b   (Pre-1986)
Immediately before the boulder bridge there is a short pillar. Climb the groove
on the left of the pillar, step up on to the pillar, then step left and climb the
crack immediately above the overlap.

70. Dad's Army 10m VS 4c   (Pre-1986)
The deep groove on the right side of the pillar is climbed to a small triangular
roof, then finish up the wide crack above.

Little Buttress
*This is the small buttress that rises directly out of the pool about 20 metres
farther right.*

71. The Bairn 6m HS 4a   (1982)
The left-hand groove/crackline.

72. Wor Lass 6m VS 4b   (1982)
The right-hand crackline on the front of the buttress.

The Pinnacle
*This is the finger of rock which is obvious on entering the quarry. It has several
climbs, the most notable being the 5a crack on the south side, and the 5c crack
on the north side which leads out of an alcove to a horizontal fault and the top.*

First Ascents at Troy Quarry
1982 Mar 28 **Anxiety** Tony Nichols, Bruce Goodwin
1982 Mar 31 **Questionable Stability** Bruce Goodwin, Tony Nichols, Clive Morton

1982 Apr 3	**Grand National**	Clive Morton, Bruce Goodwin, Tony Nichols
1982 Apr 3	**Tower of Orthank, Curlew**	Tony Nichols, Bruce Goodwin, Clive Morton
1982 Apr 15	**Troy Groove**	Bruce Goodwin, Tony Nichols
1982 Apr 17	**One Way Street, No Right Turn, Bob the Gob**	Clive Morton, Bruce Goodwin, Tony Nichols, Ian Conway
1982 Apr 17	**Grooved Arête**	Bruce Goodwin, Tony Nichols, Ian Conway, Clive Morton
1982 Apr 17	**Pike, Captain Mainwaring**	Ian Conway, Tony Nichols, Bruce Goodwin, Clive Morton
1982 Apr 18	**Troy Corner, Troy Wall**	Bruce Goodwin, Tony Nichols, Ian Conway
1982 Apr 18	**Annic**	Tony Nichols, Bruce Goodwin, Ian Conway
1982 Apr 18	**Solo Wall**	Bruce Goodwin (solo)
1982 Apr 18	**Pink Edge**	Ian Conway, Tony Nichols, Bruce Goodwin
1982 Apr 19	**Aldanite**	Ian Conway, Bruce Goodwin
1982 Apr 19	**Loose Living**	Bruce Goodwin, Ian Conway
1982 Apr	**Stilton**	Clive Morton
1982 Apr	**Open Sesame**	Clive Morton (solo)
1982 Apr	**Little Sneak**	Clive Morton, Bruce Goodwin, Ian Conway
1982 Apr	**Lema**	Mark Leach
	Saints by Adam Dewhurst, May 1995.	
1982 Apr	**Nova**	Mark Leach (solo)
1982 Apr	**Right Siamese Twin**	Bruce Goodwin, Ian Conway, Clive Morton
1982 Apr	**Cracked Wall**	Bruce Goodwin, Clive Morton
1982 Apr	**Little 'Un**	Tony Nichols
1982 Apr	**Pisa**	Ian Conway, Clive Morton, Bruce Goodwin
1982 May 3	**Stacked Deck, Left Siamese Twin**	Bruce Goodwin, Tony Nichols
1982 May 3	**Slow Motion**	Tony Nichols, Bruce Goodwin
1982 May 8	**Rapunzle**	Clive Morton, Bruce Goodwin
1982 May 8	**Updraught Corner**	Bruce Goodwin, Clive Morton, Mark Leach
1982 May 13	**Jaundice Crack**	Bruce Goodwin, Clive Morton
1982 May 13	**Dusky**	Bruce Goodwin (solo)
1982 May 31	**Mucky Pups**	Tony Nichols, Bruce Goodwin, John Lord
1982 June 20	**Two Dabs**	Ian Conway, Tony Nichols, Bruce Goodwin
1982 June 20	**The Triumvirate**	Ian Conway, Bruce Goodwin, Tony Nichols
1982	**Tess, Grane Wall, Huntington's Chorea, Fallen Friend, Conian, Nilsar, Deception, Don't Look Down, Whoops Apocalypse, Penwood Forge Mill, Sunsalve**	Ian Conway
1982	**Pillar Cracks, Dovetail, Ventnor, One Step Farther**	Mark Leach
	One Step Farther Direct Start by Mark Leach (solo), 1982.	
1982	**Jussy, The Flea, Deep Throat**	Tony Nichols
1982	**Distemper**	
1982	**The Bairn, Wor Lass**	Clive Morton
1983 Nov 20	**Sounder**	Bruce Goodwin, Tony Nichols, Mark Leach
	Right-hand Finish by Eric Grindle, Al Cameron, John Mason, September 1985.	
	Direct Finish by Dave Etherington, Al Cameron, 1986.	
1983	**Rock Lobster**	Mark Leach, Mick Johnston
1985 June	**What I'd Give for a Friend**	Al Cameron, John Mason
Pre-1986	**Fraser, Dad's Army**	Pete Cain, Greg Rimmer
1986 Apr	**Gopher**	
1986 Oct 11	**Shadowfax**	Al Cameron, John Mason, Dave Etherington
Pre-1989	**Right-hand**	
1992 Apr 28	**Pink Edge**	Reclimbed after rockfall by Alan Holden, Matt Nuttall
1992 Apr 28	**Revenge of the Bendy Ents**	Matt Nuttall, Alan Holden
	After massive rockfall destroyed Tower of Orthank.	
1995	**Siam Groove**	Paul Dewhurst
	Later extensively cleaned and modified by Dave Cronshaw, Les Ainsworth, John Ryden, July 1996.	
1995	**Helen of Troy**	Dave Cronshaw, Les Ainsworth, John Ryden
1996 July	**Overlooked Crack**	Les Ainsworth, Dave Cronshaw, John Ryden
1996 Aug 5	**Golden Thread**	Paul Merrick, Roger Smith
1997 June	**Siamese Arête**	Dave Cronshaw, Charlie Vigano
1998	**Penwood Groove**	

Minor Crags

Ashworth Moor Quarry   O.S. ref. SD 824 159

A pleasant quarry situated above Croston Close Bottoms. It is about a kilometre
west of the A680 Rochdale–Edenfield road. The quarry is reached by a track
(parking) from the main road, in a dip about 600 metres on the Edenfield side
of the New Inn. The track leads to a derelict mill on the left, the stream is
crossed, and a path leads left and upwards into the quarry.

A spacious grass ledge at the foot of the crag gives easy access to the routes
and problems. There is little for the hard man here as most of the routes are up
to about VS. The lines are obvious and the protection usually good. Climbing
has taken place here for upwards of 35 years and it has always been a place
where one finds one's own way; usually in pleasant solitude.

Britannia Quarry   O.S. ref. SD 880 199

A crag that has modulated from minor to major and now (and this is probably
the final resolution) back to minor again. Recent blasting has blown the best
routes of the upper tier into the hole containing the best routes in the quarry.
Thus, there is little left and the place is best disregarded for the foreseeable
future.

Higher Lench   O.S. ref. SD 824 216

At the top of Lench Road, between Rawtenstall and Bacup a small bulging
buttress has some impressive looking cracks, but the rock looks appalling!
Routes have been climbed in the past, though no details are available.

Lee Quarry   O.S. ref. SD 86 20

On the moor south of Bacup there are numerous old quarry workings that form
tiers of rock lie on the hillsides. Most are shattered and good rock is scarce.
There are some short possibilities and rumours of a 20-metre buttress that can
only be reached by abseil. Would-be explorers should avoid the area between
March and June, because, in recent years, it has been used by peregrines.

Peel Quarry   O.S. ref. SD 779 165

It is situated below the local monument, Peel Tower, just below the crest of
Holcombe Hill. A small eight-metre buttress offers numerous problems on sound
rock. The crag has been visited regularly in the past and all the lines have been
climbed. Routes in the vicinity of the central pillar are especially enjoyable at
around VS.

Bolton Area

Compiled by Les Ainsworth, Dave Cronshaw, Geoff Hibbert and
Carl Spencer

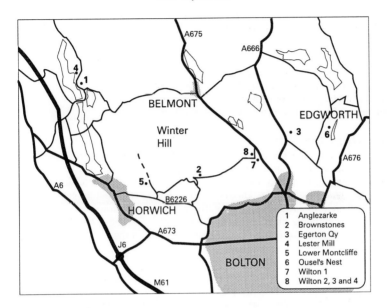

1	Anglezarke
2	Brownstones
3	Egerton Qy
4	Lester Mill
5	Lower Montcliffe
6	Ousel's Nest
7	Wilton 1
8	Wilton 2, 3 and 4

The quarries in the Bolton Area are traditional gritstone quarries that were
mostly formed towards the beginning of the century to provide stone for nearby
reservoirs. The most concentrated of this quarrying was undertaken at Wilton.
Here, four quarries provide well over 350 climbs of all grades, mostly on fine
rock. Wilton One is particularly impressive, with a multitude of classic quarry
climbs on its steep, long walls. The quarry is also famed for a unique wedge of
rock known as The Prow, which beckons an ascent from all visitors at whatever
grade they climb. Just along the road, Brownstones offers a much shortened
version of Wilton, which is ideal for an evening's bouldering.

Directly across from Wilton One, it is just possible to see Egerton Quarry.
Although the rock here is not all of the same high quality as Wilton, the climbs
are nevertheless very worthwhile. Since the previous guidebook the activity here
has been intense, with over 90 new routes, many of which are destined to
become classics.

Overlooking the Anglezarke Reservoir, just north of Horwich the quarries at
Anglezarke and Lester Mill provide another contrast. Here the gritstone is much
more sandy, but most of the climbing is still solid. The slim buttress of The
Golden Tower and the impressive overhangs around Terror Cotta are the
obvious focus at Anglezarke, but unfortunately there have recently been some
small rockfalls elsewhere on the Left Wall Area. Many of the previous gaps in
both of these quarries have now been climbed and Falkland Walls in particular
have seen many new climbs during the final stages of guidework. Recent

cleaning has also improved many of the existing lines, especially in Lester Mill, which now deserves to become more popular.

Between Anglezarke and Brownstones, the small quarry at Montcliffe has been cleaned and now sports a dozen or so climbs.

Anglezarke Quarry   O.S. ref.   SD 621 162

> '*The rock is a kind of flagstone offering incut, as well as the usual pressure holds. Most of the loose material has gone from the popular routes, and what remains is unsound enough to maintain constant interest.*'
>
> Walt Unsworth, 1969

Situation and Character

Anglezarke is one of the larger quarries in the Lancashire area. It is sited on Anglezarke Moor, close to the reservoir, and just across the road lies Lester Mill Quarry. Despite being tree-filled, it is a suntrap and the routes tend to dry relatively quickly after rain. The rock is a sandy gritstone and is generally sound, though it can tend towards brittle in some parts. However, care should be taken when climbing on some parts. Some of the rock above the Left Wall Area, near Terror Cotta, should also be treated with respect.

History

> '*... and Anglezarke Quarry near the Yew Tree Inn, Horwich, has a few climbs and one of the most imposing buttresses on gritstone, the Golden Tower, up which runs a continuous and magnificent virgin crack.*'
>
> Walt Unsworth, '*The English Outcrops*' 1964

Walt Unsworth and Bev Heslop first discovered Anglezarke Quarry late in the 1950s and ascended the first recorded routes. Unsworth and Heslop attacked the lines of least resistance first and climbed a few of the easier routes on *Triple Bob Buttress* as well as one on Grey Buttress (*Pedestal Route*). They also attempted what was later to become Fox's Corner and made ascents of *Plain Bob*, *Tocsin Wall* (the hardest route in the quarry at the time) and a half-dozen others late in the 1950s. *Glister Wall* was soon to follow, which was led by Heslop, though both climbers were amazed to find a peg in situ, which confirmed their suspicions – that other climbers had visited the quarry previously and that routes had been climbed though left unrecorded. This pair also managed to entice other climbers into the quarry, but loose quarry climbing was neither in vogue nor appealing, and so the quarry was forgotten until Les Ainsworth began research into what was to become the first edition of the Lancashire guidebook. Unsworth took on the task of writing the Anglezarke section in 1966 and in order to develop the crag, invited others along. Unsworth introduced Arthur Hassall, Gra' Whittaker and Stu Thomas to the quarry, and these climbers (supplemented at times by others) were the main protagonists of the first major wave of development. Whittaker climbed *Whittaker's Almanac*, Thomas added his *Wall Climb* and Ian Aldred was responsible for his *Original*.

Attention, then moved to Grey Buttress (actually a misnomer, but on their first visit, peering through the mist, Unsworth and Heslop thought it to be grey!) and the atrocious prevailing conditions accounted for the route name *Storm* which was climbed by Hassall and Whittaker, whilst Hassall also led *Elder Groove*, the name being both a reference to the tree and also a pun on his own age! Between them they pioneered a dozen or so routes at that time, including the excellent *Tintinnabulation* and *Edipol*. Whittle co-opted Roger Tweedy into the fray and together this pair climbed one of the more popular routes in the quarry today, the excellent corner groove of *Samarkand*, Whittle had also added *Fleabite* a few weeks earlier.

Things were beginning to hot up a bit with many more climbers 'getting a look in'; Ainsworth was always hungry for new routes and started to visit the quarry on a regular basis, soon resolving the long-standing problem known as *Master's Ledge*. Then, in 1967, he extended it even farther to create *Traumatic Eversion*, on which he employed one point of aid, later freed by Dave Hollows.

The Left Wall was then revisited and Ainsworth climbed a fine crackline which he named *Wedge* and Whittaker raced up *Quickstep*, not daring to hesitate in case all his points of contact fell to the ground! Whittaker then teamed up with John Whittle to create the changeable *Metamorphosis*, or an earlier incarnation of the route, because their route changed with every ascent for the first six months or so of its existence. Ainsworth, meanwhile, became attracted by the curious finger of rock which pointed outwards from the area of rock just right of Glister Wall, and very soon he had exhausted every possible entry to and exit from this; *The Finger, Finger Chimney* and *The Thumb*, whilst Hassall led the stiff *Wedding March* just right again, in reference to Whittaker's impending marriage.

By that time, news of the 'continuous and magnificent' virgin crack had begun to spread and had even reached Yorkshire. At least one Yorkshire team had actually run the gauntlet of border guards and managed to reach the crag undetected. Hassall and Whittaker had attempted the route, unsuccessfully apart from the first pitch, a few weeks earlier and had meant to return for a second bout. Ainsworth heard of the Yorkshiremen's 'ascent' and set off on a second ascent bid with Ian Cowell; Ainsworth led the first pitch, and Cowell the second, though moving slightly right (with two aid pegs) near the top. Soon after, Ainsworth discovered that the Yorkshire team's ascent had only been a top-rope affair, but by then Cowell had moved from the area and was never told of his first ascent of this plum. The forcing of *The Golden Tower* marked the end of the first major wave of development in the quarry.

Just as the first Lancashire guidebook was published, Dave Hollows climbed *Kaibab* on Coal Measure Crag and freed Pyrites, which was renamed *Fool's Gold*. However, both were left unrecorded and were subsequently claimed by other climbers.

When the explorations restarted in the early Seventies, attention shifted to the Left Wall. The rock was steep and sandy and along most of its length it was guarded by a large overhang and so it is not surprising that the first breach was predominantly a peg route, *First Trip* by Bill Cheverst. Hollows then took up the challenge of driving a free route through the overhangs, though he thought that he might need a couple of pegs at the roof. After a mammoth trundle to clear a ledge midway up the initial wall, Hollows arrived at the roof and though he hammered in a knife-blade runner, he was surprised to find that the holds were all there and that no aid was needed. He called the route *Ten Pounds Bail*, after an incident in Holyhead with some of the Bolton lads. However, although this represented a major step forward at Anglezarke, the route was virtually unknown and two years later Stu Thomas claimed it as *Terror Cotta*. The name stuck, and for over twenty years Hollows' accomplishment went unrecognized outside of a small group of climbers from Bolton.

Prior to Thomas's ascent of Terror Cotta, Hassall had been slowly beavering away farther left, climbing *Many Happy Returns* and *Birthday Crack*, while Thomas himself led *Bay Horse* with a bit of aid. Ainsworth added *Zarke* (the Direct Start, *Evil Digits*, falling to Paul Pritchard in 1986.

The magnificent lines on Coal Measure Crag had lain virtually untouched for some time, until Dave Cronshaw and friends began the long, protracted navvying needed to gain access to safe belays above the routes. Many weekends were spent digging an escape path along the bottom of the shale, though this path has been neglected in recent years and has now fallen into a state of disrepair. It was Hollows, however, who started the ball rolling by free-climbing *Sheppey* then Ian Lonsdale and Mick Bullough climbed an alternative start (*Moscow Mule*) which had previously been climbed with aid from a skyhook by Martin Selby. Moscow Mule itself has recently been incorporated into the start of *Age of Reason*, climbed in 1987 by Mark Liptrot.

Cronshaw and Ainsworth attacked Coal Measure Crag proper, climbing *Gritstone Rain* in 1977 and *Vishnu* a couple of years later. In early 1978 Dave Knighton added *Fingertip Control*. Al Evans visited the quarry during guidebook work and due to a mishearing his solo gained recognition for its name at least, with *Get This One in the Guide It's a Gem*. Bill Cheverst had put up several aided lines and July saw Cronshaw and Phil Warner free *Lucky Strike*, the girdle of the Golden Tower. *Double Trip*, another Cheverst aid route was also free-climbed at that time, possibly by Knighton (there being competing claims), who definitely fell off *Gates of Perception* before Jim Moran and Al Cain freed it.

1980 arrived and saw Liptrot and Dick Toon open up Waterfall Buttress (now called Falkland Walls since the waterfall dried up; with a little help from Lonsdale!) with *Superb*. Cronshaw and Lonsdale followed hot on their heels with *Rockin' Horse* and the ever-popular *Tangerine Trip*, which is still one of the most widely used routes in the quarry today. Just round the corner, Cronshaw led John Ryden up *Bellringer* and *Ding Dong*. In 1981 Cronshaw led *Supai* and *Bright Angel Corners,* plus *Anasazi Arête*, with Ainsworth leading *Zoroaster*. 1982 saw him in the Falklands with *Hunter Killer* and *Corned Beef Dictator,* whilst Lonsdale free-climbed *Bay Horse* with Nigel Bonnet.

In 1982, Liptrot took on the modern-day development of the quarry. He began with a solo ascent of *Vishnu Direct Start* and a free ascent of its sister route, *Havasupai,* which he renamed *Lean, Mean Fightin' Machine*. The following year saw Liptrot and Toon open up the steep wall right of *Supai Corner* when he made ascents of *Shibb* and *New Jerusalem*. Over on the Golden Tower area, Liptrot also created *Give Thanks*. The boldness took on another dimension in 1986 when Andrew Gridley climbed a direct start to this route (*Milk Syringe*).

The wall left of the Tower saw Bernie Bradbury climb *Please Lock Me Away* and the next year, Gary Gibson paid a return visit (having climbed *Ain't*

Nothing To It in February 1982) and stole a line from under the nose of Tim Lowe. Lowe had lightly cleaned the wall right of Please Lock Me Away and was about to equip the line, when Gibson stepped in and forced the line, now curiously named *Septic Think Tank*. The second ascent of this route was something of a shocker for Lowe, when he made it to the peg runner, only to find that the peg was a desperate clip, having a small eye and was only clippable in one direction. Also in 1984 Liptrot was back, adding *The Absent Minded Professor*, and *King of Kings*. The latter was the hardest route in the quarry at the time, only surpassed in 1986 when Paul Pritchard climbed the impressive wall of *Karma Mechanic*. 1984 also saw Kev Glass and Neil Hyde's *Skin Game* with Geoff Hope soloing *Snorter*. In 1985 Liptrot climbed *Agrajag* and *Dancing on the Valentine*. The next year Cronshaw and friends ate *Rock Lobster* and in the space of four days in April 1988 four excellent routes were put up by Liptrot – *I'm Spartacus, Schwarzenneger Mon Amour, If You Can't Lick 'em* and *Office Party*. Then in 1990 the young Ian Vickers with Cronshaw added *I Claudius*. Later that year saw the young duo of Ian McDonald and Neil Smith appear on the scene and an attempt to fill in a few of the gaps. *Flyer* was added to the end of Grey Buttress and *The Friable Sausage* on Left Wall.

Activity in the quarry then became rather dormant except for the regular evening top-rope activity on the Golden Tower. As the drought years came and the reservoirs emptied during 1994–1996 the locals moved away to claim dry ascents of the normally green walls at other quarries such as Wilton. Though Ian Conway and Richard Baker added the interesting *Michael Portillo* and *Mu' Azib* in 1995, only to find out much later that Jeff Hope had already climbed much of both routes four years previously as *Peronist* and *Roaring Forties*.

Then in 1996, the sniff of a new guidebook generated a revival of interest. A BMC clean-up at the quarry in the September of 1996 saw another appearance of Cronshaw and Vickers. Whilst the Preston Mountaineering Club and other local groups were picking up bottles, crisp packets and other nasties, Cronshaw and Vickers found a new line next to Tintinnabulation to give *Blueberry Hill*. The summer of 1997 arrived in April and local climber, Carl Spencer armed with the knowledge gained from the writing of the update for Anglezarke, took to the quarry in David Bellamy-style, enlisting help from anyone who hadn't made the bank holiday pilgrimages to Pembroke. A few more gaps were first filled in; *There's More to This* taking the direct line that Cronshaw had missed up the arête of Ain't Nothing To It. A few short routes were found on Beginner's and Triple Bob Buttresses giving a number of names relating to the previous drought – *Thirsty Work, I See No Ships* and *Reservoir Camels* together with *Brick Thick* on Triple Bob. Then, with a major gardening exercise on Falklands Walls, Spencer released a number of routes of surprising quality including *Any Which Way but Loose, Any Which Way You Can* and *To Infinity and Beyond*. With some further gardening this time involving big loose blocks, *Le Mans Finish, Airborne Attack* and *Gardening Leave* were claimed, the names reflecting the regular evening onslaught of the midges. *Botch Weld Job* was then added to the right of Grond with two of its variations. The extent of this activity by Spencer even attracted Alan Atkinson, famous for his aid routes in the 1960s, to defy the mosquitoes for an ascent of the cleaned-up Falklands Wall.

Access and Approach

Both Anglezarke and Lester Mill are owned by North West Water, whose managers have in the past been very climber-friendly. Their only request is that climbers on the Left Wall Area should not belay to the fence posts at the side of the road. Climbers are also asked to avoid abseiling over the Golden Tower and the Left Wall Areas, as this is starting to cause serious erosion.

The quarry lies on Anglezarke Moor, between the M61 and Winter Hill. To reach it from the M61 (Junction 6) follow the A6027 past the Reebok Stadium and continue to the A673 (Bolton–Horwich road) at traffic lights and then turn left. About two kilometres past Horwich, turn right at the Millstone Inn and follow a narrow road to a motorway bridge. Turn right just before this bridge and continue to the Yew Tree Inn. Take the right fork and continue between the reservoirs and past a sharp left-hand bend to a small island where the road forks. Follow the left fork for about 150 metres, past the quarry entrance on the right then drive up the hill and park in either the car park on the right, or a few metres farther on in the large layby on the left.

Both quarries can also be approached from the M61 (Junction 8) for climbers approaching from the north. This is done by following signs for Blackburn, Chorley North (B6228), Heapey and Anglezarke.

The Climbs

All the routes are described from RIGHT to LEFT, i.e. anticlockwise, commencing from the south entrance to the quarry. **PLEASE DO NOT ABSEIL ON THE GOLDEN TOWER AND TERROR COTTA AREAS, as this is causing severe erosion problems**.

Grey Buttress

Grey Buttress is identified by some fallen blocks and its distinctive red colour (though it appeared grey on a misty day to the first explorers). Some belay stakes are in place at the top, well back. The first three routes are found on the shorter wall to the right of the red wall and are slightly higher up.

1.   Just William   9m   VD   (1966)
The prominent crack at the right-hand end of the long low wall. Dirty finish.

2.   Soot Juggler   10m   HVS   5b   (1979)
Start three metres to the left at an obvious sentry-box and follow a direct line to the top.

3.   Thomas's Wall Climb   9m   HS   4a   (1966)
Start slightly left of the large tree which grows above the centre of the wall, and climb a blunt rib to a ledge at three metres, then move up and right to finish through the obvious break.

4.   Years from Now   9m   E2   5c   (1980)
Start left of a tree-filled corner at an obvious finger-crack in the arête. Climb this for six metres, then move left and climb the wall direct over an overlap.

5.   Whittaker's Almanac   8m   S   4a   (1966)
The steep corner groove on the left. Finish direct or on the left.

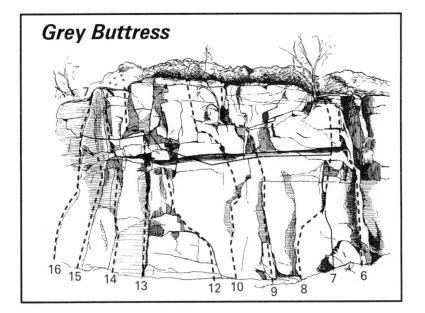

Grey Buttress

★ **6.   Flyer**   12m   E3   6a   (1990)
The arête on the right of the orange wall. Climb the arête directly to a ledge
above mid-height. Finish more easily at a small tree.

★★ **7.   Traumatic Eversion**   39m   E1   5c,4b   (1967/1976-79)
In the Sixties the first moves on this route were one of the major problems at
Anglezarke and devious means were used to reach the natural traverse line.
These are not now needed and the combination of the mantelshelf start, a steep
wall and an impressive hand-traverse make this a great first pitch. Start one
metre left of the arête, at a small ledge about two metres off the ground:
Master's Ledge.
1.   18m.   Mantel on to the ledge, then climb straight up using flake holds on
the left to gain a small ledge below the horizontal break. Step up and
hand-traverse left along the break for four metres to Sheppey, then continue for
another six metres until it is possible to step down onto a pedestal belay.
2.   21m.   Ascend a little, then go easily left and finish up the deep corner of
Elder Groove.
Erratic Traversion (E2, 5c) is a counter-traverse which starts up Turkish
Delight, then traverses right along the horizontal break to finish up the final
arête of Flyer.

8.   Sparrow   14m   E4   6b   (1986-87)
Start on the vague pillar just right of Sheppey, and climb up and right to a peg
(on Traumatic Eversion). Go directly over the small overlap then continue to a
tree belay.

9.   Sheppey   17m   E3   6a   (1967)
One metre left is a steep, peg-scarred crack. Climb this past (long reaches) a
small ledge at two metres to a ledge above the horizontal break, then finish up
the corner and crack on the left.

★ **10.   Age of Reason**   18m   E6   6b   (1980)
Start just to the left and climb a right-leading, blind flake to the break, then
swing out left to holds which lead to a pocket and a peg. Finish direct.
Protection can be found provided some good ropework is employed. An easier
start is possible at 5a, if the flake on the left is used at the bottom.

11.   Splits   18m   E2   5b   (1979)
Follow Storm to the horizontal break, then surmount the overlap on the right
(peg) and continue diagonally rightwards until it is possible to finish up Sheppey.

★★ **12.   Storm**   17m   VS   4c   (1967)
Pleasant, well-protected climbing on good jugs, which provides a good
introduction to the easier climbs at Anglezarke. Climb the prominent pedestal
flake then a fine crackline to a large ledge. Step round to the left and go
through the break in the overhangs to a good stance. Finish up the groove above.

13.   Sunbeam   15m   VS   4b   (1967)
A direct line up the crack which bounds the pedestal flake on its left, then after
the overhang finish up the final groove of Storm. The route contains very little
independent climbing.

14.   Kaibab   20m   HVS   5b   (1969)
The vague weakness $1\frac{1}{2}$ metres left of the prominent flake, finishing direct.

15.   Turkish Delight   15m   VS   5b   (1983)
Start just left of Kaibab. Climb its parallel groove system to a grass ledge then
traverse left to finish up Elder Groove.

★ **16.   Elder Groove**   17m   HS   4b   (1966)
Start two metres to the left and climb a blunt nose diagonally leftwards to a
ledge, then climb the vertical corner crack with a tree stump in it.

*The next four routes are found behind a number of small trees at the base of
the crag.*

17.   Pedestal Route   15m   D   (1962)(1962)
The pedestal lies beneath a large tree at the top of the crag. Climb a groove and
rib, then step left on to a broad flat pedestal. Climb the short crack above and
go left into a V-shaped groove, which is followed to a tree at the top.
Slab Start (VD): climb the slab on the left of the pedestal to reach the upper
ledge.

18.   Rope Thief   10m   HS   4b   (1973)
Five metres to the left is a short corner groove almost directly below a sapling
at the top of the crag. Climb this and the shallow groove above. Peg in
horizontal break.

19. William the Conqueror 12m HS 4b (1967)
The conspicuous shallow corner groove two metres to the left.

20. I'm Spartacus 15m E5 6b (1988)
Start at a short right-trending ramp about six metres right of Flake Out. Climb
up and rightwards to a peg, then go up left to flakes and a second peg. Step
right and finish direct.

21. I Claudius 20m E4 6a (1990)
Start three metres left of I'm Spartacus and right of a thin crack. Climb the wall
directly (peg) to a ledge, then continue past a small, square-cut overhang to
finish up a short groove.

22. The Rapidity of Sleep 18m E1 6a (1982)
The thin crack and wall three metres to the right of Flake Out, traversing into
that route three metres from the top to finish.

Coal Measure Crag
*The long, high wall left of Grey Buttress contains many splendid lines. Most of
the more popular routes now have bolt belays.*

23. Flake Out 17m VS 4c (1967/1976)
A resurrection of the old route Great Flake (which now lies almost buried under
shale) which follows the obvious break behind the fallen flake.

** **24. The Lean Mean Fightin' Machine** 18m E4 6a (1977/1982)
A superb, finger-tearing line up the thin diagonal crackline veering left from the
a ledge just above the start of Flake Out. Finish up Vishnu. Bolt belay, abseil
descent.

25. Vishnu 18m VS 4c (1979)(1983)(1981)
Start at the base of the deep corner and climb the flake on the right to finish up
a groove. Bolt belay at the top of the groove, abseil descent.
Headbanger (E1, 5c): takes the thin crack three metres to the right of the
original start.

26. The Taciturn Boy 18m E4 6b (1986-87)
Climb the cracked left arête of the deep corner.

* **27. Gritstone Rain** 18m HVS 5b (1977)
Start just left of the arête and climb to a small ledge at six metres. Ascend the
groove above to another ledge and exit from this up a short corner. Bolt belay.
Abseil descent.

* **28. Schwarzennegger Mon Amour** 18m E5 6c (1988)
The short, capped groove and wall left of Gritstone Rain. Climb to the
overhang, then pull out left on to the wall (peg). Continue up the wall just left
of the arête to a bolt belay. Abseil descent.

** **29. The Karma Mechanic** 18m E6 6c (1986)
Start at a short diagonal crack in the steep wall on the left. Climb to a thin
break at six metres (peg), then move left and dyno for a large hold. Mantel on
to this and climb the wall above, passing two pegs. Bolt belay on the right.
Abseil descent.

★★ 30. Shibb 18m E3 6b (1983)
The crackline nine metres left of Gritstone Rain. Climb the crack to a small
pod, then move up and go slightly rightwards to a small ledge. Finish up the
flake crack above. Three-bolt belay. Abseil descent.

★★ 31. New Jerusalem 15m E4 6a (1983)
A worrying start leads to a welcome ledge, then good holds appear on the flake,
to give an exhilarating, but strenuous finish. Five metres farther left a thin
crackline trends slightly rightwards to the top. Climb this, passing a ledge and
peg at mid-height. Two-bolt belay. Abseil descent.

32. If You Can't Lick 'em, Lick 'em 13m E5 6c (1988)
The crackline left of New Jerusalem has a peg runner and bolt belay.

33. Supai Corner 11m VS 4b (1981)
The corner which limits the main wall of Coal Measure Crag on its left.

★★ 34. Bright Angel Corner 11m VS 4c (1981)
A much better route than initial appearances might suggest. Climb the next
vague corner groove, two metres farther left, using the cracks in the left wall.
Bolt belay on left. Abseil descent.

★ 35. Anasazi Arête 10m E2 5b (1981)
From the top of the scree slope go up and right to the blunt arête, then continue
on large holds to a ledge at eight metres. Climb the left-hand side of the arête
(crux) to a bolt belay just below the top. Bolt belay. Abseil descent.

36. Son of Dicktrot 10m E2 5c (1986-87)
The narrow wall and thin crack just left of Anasazi Arête, to the bolt belay of
that route. Abseil descent.

37. Zoroaster 10m VS 4b (1981)
Climb the corner formed by two flakes, just to the right of an obvious bush.

38. Kelly's 'i' 11m E2 5c (1988)
Gain and climb the jamming crack to the right of the arête and just above a
bush.

39. The Changeing 11m E1 5a (1984)
Climb the protruding flake just left of the obvious bush. A hanging rope is
essential for a belay. Abseil descent.

40. Thirsty Work 12m E1 5b (1997)
Start just left of the corner and climb the wall on small ledges to gain the
crackline at mid-height. Continue directly to the top. (No belay.)

41. Whiter Shade of Shale 10m HVS 5a (Pre-1979)
The left-hand crack in the back of the square recess. Abseil descent from the
pedestal.

42. Coal Measure Climb 8m HS 4a (1968)
Previously incorrectly known as Tapeats. Climb the left side of the left arête of
the square recess via small ledges and cracks. Abseil descent from the top of the
pedestal.

Low Wall
This the short wall between Coal Measure Crag and Beginner's Buttress.

There is scope for some five or six short routes on this wall. However, only two are recorded. The wall is often wet, dripping water in its middle section. Care should be taken on making an exit from the routes on Low Wall and from those at the far right of Beginner's Buttress.

43. Midgebite Wall 6m VS 5a   (1978)
The wall six metres right of Fleabite, where it gains a respectable height when approaching from the left. Climb the wall and crack.

44. Fleabite 6m HVS 5a   (1966)
Start immediately right of the deep groove at the far left of the wall. Climb to a ledge, traverse left and step up on to a very sloping undercut ledge. Using the crack above, pull on to the overhang and go up to a dirty finish.

Beginner's Buttress Area
The Golden Tower is somewhat obvious. Sixty metres to its right is the easy-angled **Beginner's Buttress;** *A route in the middle of the buttress is often used as a descent from the Golden Tower. The routes to the left of this are often wet.*

45. First Night 8m HS 4b   (1967)
Climb the thin crackline just left of the right arête to a ledge, then finish up the flake on the left, or climb the wall direct (harder).

46. Yapi 6m HS 4b   (1975-79)
The slanting corner which bounds Beginner's Buttress on its left.

47. I See No Ships 8m HVS 5a   (1997)
One metre to the right of the arête and ramp is a thin crack, appearing at mid-height. Climb the shattered groove below then step right to gain the crack. Continue to the top using the crack.

48. Reservoir Camels 8m E1 5b   (1997)
A boulder problem route due to its lack of height and the absence of protection. Start at the far left of the open corner, for I See No Ships. Surmount the ramp on the left of the arête then climb the wall above on small but positive holds.

49. Beginner's Buttress 7m D   (Traditional)
10 metres to the left of an open corner the wall emerges from the undergrowth on the right. Surmount the ledge on the slab and climb the groove above using steps on either side. A popular **DESCENT** from the Tower.

50. Night Before 9m VD   (1967)
The indistinct chimney left of Beginner's Buttress, which is guarded by a pedestal.

★ **51. Stag Party** 9m HS 4a   (1967)
Twin cracks on the left lead to a ledge (*The Bridal Suite*), then climb the right-hand wall to the top.

★ **52. Wedding March** 10m VS 4c (1967)
Climb the fine crack to the left end of the Bridal Suite. Continue up the crack or use the left wall and crack.

Golden Tower Area

The impressive 20-metre high pillar which dominates the quarry from a distance, with a continuous crackline up its middle and the steep yellow wall on its left. The tower dries quickly and displays a distinct golden colour.
In order to prevent serious erosion, please resist the temptation to abseil near the Golden Tower.

★ **53. Finger Chimney** 14m HVS 5a (1967)
Farther left a prominent finger sticks out at six metres. Climb the short hanging chimney below this and on its right, mount the finger, then step right over the chimney to a small ledge and finish direct.

54. The Finger 8m VS 4b (1967)
Climb the finger from the left and mantel on to its end, then go straight up by a crack.

55. The Thumb 9m S 4a (1967)
Starting on the left, climb to the finger, step left and finish up a short blocky crack.

★★ **56. Glister Wall** 10m S 4a (1962)
A pleasant but testing route up the centre of the broken wall on the right of the Tower.

57. Give Thanks 20m E3 5c (1983)(1986)
Start as for Glister Wall, but step left into the thin groove in the wall and climb this to finish just right of Samarkand.
Milk Syringe, E5, 6b, a direct start, takes the lower wall bravely direct past two old bolt holes, to join Give Thanks at the groove.

★★ **58. Samarkand** 20m VS 4c (1966)
A classic route that has stood the test of time and is justifiably popular with VS leaders. The crack which limits the Tower on its right. Finish direct using the crack and holds in the steep wall on the left, or, more easily to the right.

59. The Midas Touch 20m E6 6c (1997)
Start just left of Samarkand at a thin crack below the small overhang. Difficult moves lead over the overhang, then continue with the right hand on the arête, until a rest at a good hold near Fool's Gold and some gear (a side runner protects the start). Move back to the arête and make committing moves to a small ledge. Continue as for Fool's Gold until a final hard move left at the top of the arête, where Fool's Gold goes right.

Right: Alan White daren't look down on **I Shot Jason King** (E5 6a), Egerton Quarry.
Photo: Brian Heywood
Overleaf: Gareth Parry makes big moves on **Gigantic** (E8 6c), Wilton One. *Photo: Alan White*

★ **60. Fool's Gold** 21m HVS 5b,4c (1967/1969)
The awesome hanging crack in the front face of the Golden Tower, then the
bold right arête.
1. 9m. Climb to the ledge at mid-height on the Tower, via a brutal, hanging
groove near its right edge.
2. 12m. Climb the right arête to a point at mid-height in the upper wall.
Move rightwards around the arête and continue up the wall above.

61. Agrajag 24m E3 6a (1985)
Start just left of Fool's Gold and climb the thin crack (runner in Golden Tower)
and wall above on spaced holds (peg not in situ) to the belay ledge of Golden
Tower; finish up that route.

★★★ **62. The Golden Tower** 24m E2 5a,5c (1968)
This is undoubtedly the best known route at Anglezarke and the first ascent did
much to popularise quarry climbing in the late Sixties. Though it is at the lower
limit of its grade, it is nevertheless a memorable climb and when the sun
reflects from the golden rock, the climbing is positively idyllic. It is described
here in two pitches though it is probably better done in one runout.
1. 12m. Start in the small cave at the left edge of the Tower and follow the
jamming crack just right of the arête to a ledge. Step right to a nut belay.
2. 12m. Climb the crack which splits the wall above. Easily protectable.

★★★ **63. Gates of Perception** 24m E4 6a (1978)
Follow Golden Tower to the ledge then climb the crack just right of the left
arête by a series of layback and finger jamming moves. A varied and sustained
pitch.

★★ **64. Septic Think Tank** 18m E5 6b (1984)
Follow Please Lock me Away to the break of Lucky Strike. Move right (peg)
and boldly attack the wall just left of the arête, on spaced finger edges, to a
lo..o..ng reach and a poor peg. Climb the wall above finishing just left of the
arête. Fail to clip the peg at your peril!

★★★ **65. The Italian Job** 25m E5 6b (1989)
A more sustained variant to Septic Think Tank. The start requires some degree
of levitation to get off the ground and is the site of many a slide down the grass
slope. Climb the arête on its left until the break is reached. Continue upwards
using the blocks on the right, until a faint horizontal crack can be reached on
the left. Traverse up and left until the break and pegs of Septic Think Tank can
be reached then continue as for Septic Think Tank.

★★ **66. Please Lock Me Away** 17m E5 6b (1983)
A wonderful route, one of Lancashire's finest, with a puzzling crux low down
and a brilliant, sustained upper crack. The move right to gain the flake requires
a gymnastic reach unique for gritstone quarries. Climb up to the left-hand end of

---

Previous page: Brian Heywood has no time to **Blackout** (VS 4b), Wilton One.
Photo: Alan White
Left: Geoff Mann's no wallflower on **Iron Orchid** (E4 6b), Wilton Two.
Photo: Geoff Hibbert

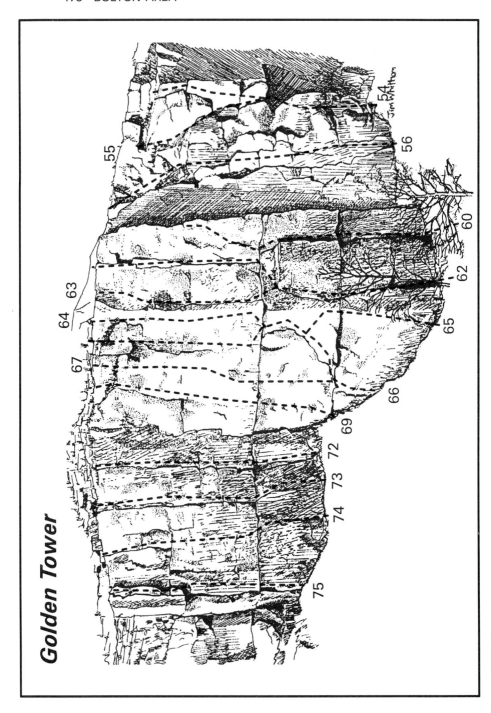

Golden Tower

the undercut flake and follow it rightwards (peg) to the break. Climb the crack above to a ledge and finish on small holds.

Where is My Mind? (E5, 6c): a direct start that takes the faint crack and surmounts the overlap to join the parent route on the undercut flake.

★★★ **67.   King of Kings**   20m   E6   6b   (1984)
Start as for Please Lock Me Away but at the flake climb the hairline crack above, directly to the break. Move slightly rightwards and continue up the technical wall finishing direct. Three pegs. A very sustained route.

68.   The Nausea   25m   E5   6b   (1985)
Climb Klondyke to the overlap then move out right on to the wall and traverse across to finish as for Septic Think Tank.

★★ **69.   Klondyke**   18m   E3   6a   (1966/1975-79)
Crack climbing at its very best. After a searing start, the difficulties relent only to return with a vengeance on the high crux. Halfway up the earthy slope on the left of the Tower is a previously pegged crack. Thin finger jams lead to a good resting ledge. Layback up to the overlap (peg) and make some trying moves to finish.

70.   Dirty Corner   15m   VS   4c   (1976)
The pedestal corner farther left. Traverse off to the right at the top.

★★ **71.   Lucky Strike**   60m   E2   5b,4c,5a   (1971/1978)
The first pitch is noted for its sustained finger traverse. After this, the rest is an anticlimax, but is, nevertheless, well worth doing. A girdle of the Golden Tower Area, starting from the pedestal on Dirty Corner.
1.   24m.   Climb on to the pedestal and traverse right to gain the first ledge on Klondyke. Follow the horizontal break right, around the arête to the front of the Tower. Nut belay as for Golden Tower.
2.   12m.   Traverse right to the arête and continue into Samarkand.
3.   24m.   Go across to the Finger, move round this to gain Wedding March. Descend and make a hard move to reach a willow tree and finish up Beginner's Buttress.

72.   Helical Happiness   15m   HVS   5a   (1978)
Start at the left side of the pedestal and follow the crack to the top.

73.   Gilt Complex   15m   HVS   5b   (1978)
The crack in the middle of the wall on the left is sustained.

★ **74.   Office Party**   15m   E5   6a   (1988)
The wall left of Gilt Complex and Helical Happiness. Peg at seven metres.

75.   The Eight-legged Atomic Dustbin Will Eat Itself   17m   E1   5b   (1992)
Climb the flake crack up to a hanging pillar, then finish up the finger-crack on the front of the pillar.

76.   A Series of Boring Mantelshelves   9m   S   4a   (1975)
15 metres farther left is a short, solid buttress. Start on the left and climb the nose. Steep grass finish.

Falkland Walls

20 metres farther left is the steep back wall of the quarry. Diversion of the old waterfall in the corner has meant that there are now some worthwhile climbs on this part of the quarry, though drainage over parts of the wall can sometimes pose a problem on some climbs. The climbing extends from a blocky ramp on the right, past a deep corner to another short corner at a higher level.

77.   Botch Weld Job   10m   E1   5b   (1997)(1997)(1997)
Start up the grassy slope and two metres right of the blocky ramp. Climb the bubbled wall taking a direct line via the faint crack system.
Iron Start (5b): take the shallow groove on the left and small ledges to the right, to join Botch Weld Job on the small ledge at mid-height.
Steel Start (5b): start as for Grond II then take a rightward rampline to a large ledge and short corner. Climb the corner and step right to join Botch Weld Job at the small ledge.

78.   Rockin' Horse   14m   E2   5c   (1980)
Start at the base of the blocky ramp and follow a direct line up a shallow groove into a very shallow pod near the top, then continue up a crack to the top.

79.   Grond II   ond14m   HVS   5a   (1980)
The obvious block-filled crack two metres to the left.

★ **80.   The Absent Minded Professor**   17m   E4   6a   (1984)
Climb the flaky crack two metres to the left to join Tangerine Trip at the break at eight metres. Continue directly using the crack and small ledges to the top

★★★ **81.   Tangerine Trip**   17m   E3   5c   (1980)
An excellent and strenuous climb, which stays dry even when most of the quarry is wet. From the left side of a sentry-box at the foot of the rock, follow the obvious right-slanting crack in the overhanging wall to the break, move right and climb to a bolt (frequently absent). The ascent of the scree above is now safer than in the past due to traffic, but a preplaced belay is still a wise move.

82.   Hunter Killer   15m   HVS   5a   (1982)
Start as for Tangerine Trip and climb the slightly left-slanting crack.

★ **83.   Falkland Groove**   15m   VS   4c   (1982)
The broken groove three metres to the left provides a good climb which should improve with traffic. Gain the sloping block at the base of the groove with difficulty, then continue up the groove until it is possible to step left on to a large ledge on Mu' Azib. Step back right and finish via the deep cleft.

★★ **84.   Mu' Azib**   15m   E1   5b   (1991/1995)
An interesting line up the rib that forms the left side of Falkland Groove, which gives good, sustained climbing in a steep position. Start on the left side of the rib and climb the short crack, then step right on to a steep slab. Continue to a ledge on the arête, then continue up the shallow groove on good holds.

★★ **85.   Michael Portillo**   15m   E2   5b   (1991/1995)
Although the first ascensionists claimed that Mr Portillo was a little to the right of the infamous Argentinian General, even ardent socialists should enjoy this crack climb. Start at a steep jamming crack one metre farther left and climb this

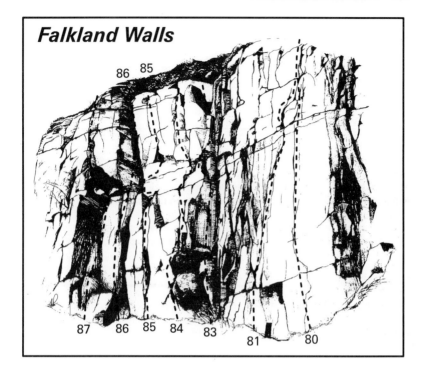

Falkland Walls

to a ledge. The headwall above is steeper than it looks. Climb it via a niche on the right to reach a peg, then finish up parallel cracks.

86. Corned Beef Dictator 15m E1 5a (1982/1991)
The obvious deep chimney on the left provides high quality thrutching at the bottom (devotees of such climbing might argue that it merits three stars), then finish up the continuation chimney above, passing a peg on the right wall.
★ **Peronist** (E1, 5a): an entertaining finish traverse left at the peg to the arête, then use a sloping hold and finish on good holds on the left.

★★ **87. Superb** 17m HVS 5a (1980)
This was the original route of the Falkland's campaign at Anglezarke and is still one of the best. Start one metre left and ascend a corner crack for eight metres, then move left to an obvious notch on the arête. Climb straight up the arête using the crack on the right to finish. Incorrectly identified as Grond in the past.

The next ten-metre section of rock towards the corner has been cleaned-up giving access and some interesting new routes. The wall is more stable than its blotched appearance might suggest. However, care must be taken on exit from each of the routes owing to the unstable ground above. A preplaced belay rope from above is recommended. The routes to the right of and including Le Mans Finish are of good quality and worthy of the effort required in preparing a belay.

88.   Hermes   18m   VS   4c   (1982)
Start one metre left of the arête and climb cracks to a sentry-box and tree at
mid-height, then continue direct to the top.

★ **89.   Any Which Way but Loose**   20m   HVS   5a   (1997)
Two metres to the left of the arête of Superb a broken crack system converges
into a direct line to the top.

★★ **90.   Any Which Way You Can**   18m   E2   5c   (1997)
Not as the name suggests. Start to the right of a small overhang at two metres.
Climb the wall directly by gaining the broken crack system then taking the
vague crackline which finishes in a finger-crack in the steep wall at the top.

★★ **91.   To Infinity and Beyond**   20m   E4   6b   (1997)
A thin line on steep and sustained technical ground, requiring some
concentration. To the left of the small overhang in the base of the cliff a thin
crack gives a direct line to the top. Surmount the overhang to gain the wall and
thin crack. Climb the wall with the assistance of a short crack to the left and
pass the bulge (crux). The crack widens in the steep wall above. Step right to
finish.

★ **92.   Le Mans Finish**   20m   E1   5b   (1997)
Six metres to the right of the overgrown corner a left-facing groove steps
rightwards to the top of the cliff. Climb the groove and crack on its right to a
sloping ledge. Use this to gain the final groove and from the top of this step
right to finish.

● **93.   Airborne Attack**   18m   HVS   5a   (1997)
Start as for Le Mans Finish and climb the first groove of Le Mans Finish, then
continue up the wide crack above directly to the top. A good route, which
unfortunately, loses its appeal at a loose block high up on the left, where it is
necessary to step a long way right to finish safely.

94.   Gardening Leave   17m   VS   4c   (1997)
Three metres to the right of the corner a shattered line can be climbed to a point
just below a small tree. Not the best of routes owing to the unstable top section
of the wall and the dense vegetation in the corner.

Triple Bob Buttress Area
*After the above wall there are two small buttresses then an impressive grey
buttress 40 metres to the left and at right-angles to it. This marks the right side
of the Triple Bob Area, which extends to a complete break in the rock on the
left where there is an easy* **DESCENT** *path. The Triple Bobs themselves are
three perched blocks about six metres left of the grey buttress.*

95.   Gold Digger   14m   VS   4c   (1975-79)
Climb the thin crack just to the right of the right arête of the grey buttress and
finish just left of the arête.

96.   Tinkerbell   15m   VD   (1966)
Start on the right-hand side of the Triple Bobs and climb an easy groove to a
large ledge at mid-height. Step left on to a slab, then climb this and the thin
crack above to a finishing mantel.

97. Triple Bob Major 18m D (1965)
The stability of the Bobs is open to doubt. Either climb the blocks, or the crack
on their left, or a combination of both. In any case arrive at a large grass ledge
at nine metres; cross it and climb another nine metres of easier rocks to the top.

98. Tocsin Wall 8m VS 5a (1965/1975-79)
This route will set a few alarm bells ringing. The steep little wall left of the
Triple Bobs is climbed to an easy finish.

99. Cad Eye the Heather 10m E1 5b (1992)
Climb the wall on the left via a faint crackline to finish at a small terrace.

★ **100. Bellringer** 15m HVS 5b (1981)
Climb the obvious thin crack which splits the wall left of the corner.

101. Ding Dong 15m HVS 5b (1981)
Immediately left, on the arête is an orange groove. Climb this, moving
awkwardly over bulges to ledges, then go directly to the top.

102. Tintinnabulation Direct 15m HVS 5b (1968)
Start from an alcove immediately left and climb direct to join the crack and
finish up the top groove of Tintinnabulation.

103. Tintinnabulation 18m VS 4b (1966)
A line up the shattered wall on the left. Start from a distinctive pedestal and
climb the wide crack for a short way until it is possible to move into a shallow
cave on the right. Finish up the broken groove above.

★ **104. Blueberry Hill** 18m HVS 5b (1996)
From the pedestal, climb the thin, left-leading flake crack on the left by an
interesting start, then continue up to a deep niche. Traverse right across the front
of a square buttress (peg), to a short finishing groove.

● **105. Not In This Life** 15m VS 4c (1997)
Immediately to the left of the pedestal is a shallow groove-cum-crack. Climb
this, passing through two small overhangs, finishing up a short chimney at the
top. Care is needed on unstable rock above the overhangs.

106. Brick Thick 18m HVS 5a (1997)
Start one metre left and climb the leftward-slanting undercut flake/groove (brick
thickness at its lowest point) and the wall above the small overhang to finish to
the left of a small tree.

107. For Whom the Bell Tolls 15m VS 4c (1975-79)
Start three metres left of the groove and climb into a wide alcove. Step left and
finish up a curving crack.

★★ **108. Plain Bob** 15m S 4a (1964)
This was one of the first routes at the back of the quarry, and it remains one of
the best at this grade. A couple of metres left is a sharp rib. Climb the right
face of this to the top, then go easily to a short curving crack and follow this to
the top.

109. Plain Bob Variant   15m   VS   4b   (1964)
The layback crack that forms a groove on the left of the rib.

110. Unappealing   15m   M   (1964)
Left of the previous climb a series of small ledges leads eventually to the top.

Left Wall Area

Between the Triple Bob and Left Wall Areas is the largest break in the quarry,
and the best way down on this side. Along the top of the Left Wall there is a
number of belay stakes. These should be used and it is particularly important
that climbers do not belay to the fence.

111. Fox's Corner   9m   VD   (1964)
The dirty, broken groove and deep-set chimney above.

★ **112. Edipol!**   12m   HS   4a   (1966)
Start below a crack on the left, and surmount the overhang using a large hold
on the left (strenuous), then continue up the crack above to a ledge. Traverse the
ledge to the right and climb the edge of the wall above.

113. Bossa Nova   14m   VS   4b   (1976)
The obvious corner on the left. Traverse right to finish.

114. Bay Horse   15m   E1   5b   (1973/1977)
The first big crack left of the easy way down. Climb for a few metres, then
using a subsidiary crack on the left continue until a hard move can be made on
to a small ledge. To finish, either go right using a flake and mantel on to a
pointed block, or climb the shattered headwall.

115. Rock Lobster   10m   E2   5c   (1986)
The left side of the arête left of Bay Horse is gained from a couple of metres
up that route.

★ **116. Skin Game**   12m   E3   6a   (1984)
Climb the wall left of Rock Lobster, passing a thin crack and a peg. The top
wall feels bold.

117. Terra Firma   15m   HVS   5b   (1977)
Really a variation start to Cotton Terror, taking the thin crack three metres to
the right of Terror Cotta.

118. The Friable Sausage   17m   E3   5b   (1990)
Climb the flake of Cotton Terror, then continue up the yellow wall above taking
the roof at its extreme right-hand end.

★★ **119. Cotton Terror**   17m   E1   5a   (1975-79)
One of the classics of this wall. Although the rock can be friable, it is not as
difficult as it may at first appear. Start as for Terror Cotta, then step right
immediately to a thin flake crack and ascend this to a small ledge. Go up the
grooved wall to a large ledge below the top (peg). Finish straight up.

120. Land   17m   E4   6a   (1986)
The open corner right of Terror Cotta. Climb the open corner direct (peg clipped
on Terror Cotta) and go straight over the capping roof.

★★★ **121. Terror Cotta**   21m   HVS   5a   (1971)
Terror Cotta must rank as one of the big adrenalin surges for anyone moving up
through the grades in the quarries. All the way up the steep bottom wall the
capping roofs look impenetrable, but the holds are there – honestly. On the left
is a big yellow wall with some jutting overhangs above. Start in a short yellow
corner and climb up and left on to a platform. Swing left around the arête, on to
a blank wall and go up (peg) to the overhangs. Pull into the groove above and
finish up this.

★ **122. Terrorific**   20m   E4   6a   (1986)
A direct start to Terror Cotta. Start three metres to the left, below a
crescent-shaped hold; climb directly past this feature and move right to join
Terror Cotta and finish up that route.

123. Mission Impossible   30m   E2   5b   (1983)
A high-level girdle of Terror Cotta Wall; climb this route quickly – like a
volcano it self-destructs from time to time. From the break on Terror Cotta
traverse left beneath the roofs to finish up Zarke.

★ **124. High Revver**   46m   E1   5b,4c   (1977)
An interesting girdle of the main section of Left Wall.
1. 23m. Follow Terror Cotta to the platform, then step on to the front wall
and traverse horizontally to Double Trip (peg). Continue traversing in a more
strenuous manner to the crackline of First Finale. Go up this past an in-situ peg
to the overhang, then arrange protection and semi-hand-traverse left along the
break into the corner of Birthday Crack (peg belay).
2. 23m. Step up and move on to the left wall, continue to an ancient peg,
then step down and move out to the arête. Swing round on to the wall of
Metamorphosis and follow the obvious horizontal break left past Punchline to
finish just right of the broken corner on the left of the wall.

★★ **125. Double Trip**   18m   E3   5c   (1971/1977)
This rather tedious old peg climb now provides one of Anglezarke's gems.
However, bits do sometimes fall off it, so protect yourself carefully. Start in the
centre of the yellow wall, one metre left of a V-shaped groove in the top
overhang. Climb the snappy wall past two pegs to the overhang (peg on right)
and from the break beneath the roof, reach over the roof to reach a good hold
just over the lip and pull boldly on to the upper wall, finishing slightly left. The
shattered holds at the base of the overhang self-destructed just before guidebook
work was completed. This has slightly increased the grade of the route.
However, the route can still be climbed with an alternative exit via the V-groove
on the right, at its previous grade, E2, 5b.

126. Third Party   18m   E3   5c   (1986/1988)
Supersedes Liptrip by adding an independent start. Climb the very faint crack
just to the left to a peg below the roof. Climb over the roof on loose holds to a
good move to finish.

★ **127. First Finale**   18m   E2   5b   (1972/1976)
Climb the thin broken crack two metres to the left, to an overlap and finish up
the shattered groove above.

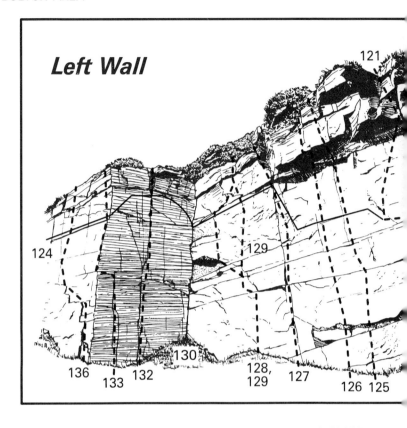

Left Wall

121

124

129

130

136 133 132

128, 129 127

126 125

★★ **128. Zarke** 20m HVS 5a (1973/1975)
An interesting route at the left end of the wall. Although it avoids the
intimidating overhangs and the rock is less friable, there are some exposed and
technical moves. Start as for First Finale. Mantel on to a sloping hold to reach
an overlap at four metres, then move left and go up to a small ledge at the left
side of the overlap. Move left on to a large ledge, and from the right of this
climb up to another ledge. Make an exposed crossing of the wall on the right
until possible to finish straight up through an obvious break.
Evil Digits (6c): is a direct start.

★★ **129. Fingertip Control** 15m E4 5c (1978)
The name says it all – a fine, fingery route. Take an almost direct line up the
bold wall just left of First Finale with a long reach to gain a good hold. The
crux entails leaving this hold to gain the break, way, way above the protection.

130. Birthday Crack 17m VS 4b (1974)
The corner on the left. Traverse out left along the obvious break to finish.

131. Epidural 15m E5 6b (1988)
Climb the centre of the wall to a vague, right-leading crackline and follow this
to the top.

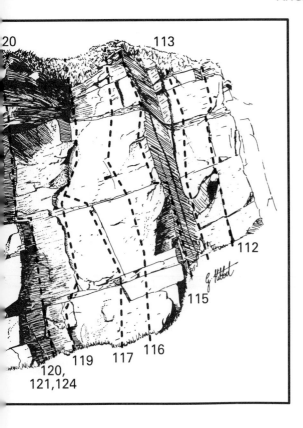

132. Many Happy Returns 15m E1 5a   (1974)
Climb the crack in the middle of the wall on the left.

★★ **133. Ain't Nothing to It** 14m E3 6a   (1982/1991)
Puzzling, reachy, and a little bit bold – this one's a must for connoisseurs of
arêtes. Climb the crack left of Many Happy Returns to its end (peg), then reach
up the arête (crux) to good holds and finish above using holds to the left.
Direct Finish E4, 6a, continues up the wall, instead of the arête.

★ **134. There's More to This** 14m E4 6b   (1997)
Climb the direct line up the nose of the arête, taking advantage of a nut
placement on the left and the peg on ANtI.

135. Dancing on the Valentine 12m E2 5c   (1985)
Climb ledges just left of the arête to gain a thin crack above a peg. Follow this
crack to the top.

★★ **136. Metamorphosis** 17m VS 4c   (1968)
Although this route keeps changing, as the top skin has peeled back over the
years, it still remains a classic. Many VS leaders may well hesitate on the first
steep moves. Climb the previous route to a ledge at three metres, then move left

to a higher ledge (peg). Step right, then go back left and continue directly to the top.

★ **137. Transformation**   15m   VS   4c   (1978)
The thin crack on the left with a loose finish.

138. Punchline   15m   E1   5b   (1977)
Start just to the right of a small niche. Climb the wall until almost level with the porthole, then go diagonally left to the porthole. Finish on the left.

139. Punch-up   14m   VS   5a   (1979-83)
Climb straight up past the niche.

140. Coconino   10m   D   (1978)
The deep corner on the left.

141. Snorter   10m   VS   5a   (1984)
The crack in the left side of the wall to the left of Coconino.

142. Wall and Crack   10m   VS   5a   (1989)
On the left there are two small corners which contain some suspect rock. Climb the wall on the left of these.

143. Telegraph Arête   9m   HS   4b   (1966)
Climb the left edge of the steep, left arête. The telegraph pole has now been moved back and so it can no longer be seen from the bottom.

144. Quickstep   6m   S   4a   (1967)
The next arête, past a dirty corner is at an easier angle, but is still loose.

145. Pandooi   9m   E3   6a   (1986-87)
From a square footledge just left of the arête, climb up and over a bulge, then finish direct.

★ **146. Shorty**   9m   E2   5b   (1978)
Climb the left-slanting weakness three metres to the left of the arête. Where the cracks end move up to a break then go right to finish.

147. Nowhere Man   8m   E1   5b   (1978)
Climb the wall two metres to the left via an obvious flake.

There is a pleasant low-level traverse at 5a between Nowhere Man and Pandooi.

148. Side Track   8m   VS   4c   (1977)
Start at the foot of a groove that leads to the ancient railway sleeper and climb the bulging wall on good holds.

149. Sleeper Bay   8m   VD   (1967)
Climb the dirty groove that leads to the old railway sleeper. Some of the holds are suspect.

Left of the corner is a short wall of excellent rock.

150. Mark   9m   VS   4c   (1975-79)
Climb the groove and crack at the right-hand side of the wall.

** **151. Wedge** 9m HS 4a (1967)
The prominent crack two metres to the left acts as a magnet to lower-grade visitors.

152. Elaine 9m HVS 5c (1983)
The boulder-problem wall and crack that finish just left of Wedge.

* **153. Nightmare** 8m HS 4b (1966)
The converging cracks at the left side of the wall, crossing the break just above mid-height.

154. Minor 6m HVS 5c (Mid 70s)
The wall just to the left gaining the ledge which gives the break in the wall.

155. Mini 6m D (1966)
The short crack at the left edge of the same wall.

156. Writer's Cramp 12m S 4b (1966)
This is the low-level traverse of the wall from Mark to Mini.

Just past the easy way down, there is another wall at a lower level, which can be further identified by a prominent block at its foot.

157. Because 6m HS 4a (1968)
The blunt arête at the right-hand end of the wall.

158. Meanwhile 6m S 4a (1966)
The wall has four cracks. This is the rightmost one.

** **159. Whittaker's Original** 6m HS 4a (1966)
The second crack to the left, is short, but sweet.

160. After The Blitz 6m VS 4b (1974-75)
The wall is taken directly from the small block.

161. Alldred's Original 6m VD (1966)
The third crack, just left of the fallen block. Hard to start.

162. Side Step 6m HS 4b (1966)
The fourth crack is less well-defined. Climb to a bulge which is avoided by a long step left, and escape by a narrow ledge.

163. Get This One in the Guide It's a Gem 6m VS 4b (1978)
The wall just left again is climbed direct.

164. Original Wall Traverse 12m S 4a (1973)
Traverse the wall at mid-height in either direction.

165. Last Post 6m VD (1973)
Hidden by the trees about 50 metres farther left is an isolated buttress, which can be identified by an iron spike low on its right wall. Either climb the front arête, or slightly harder, climb the wall beside the spike.

First Ascents at Anglezarke Quarry

1962	**Pedestal Route, Slab Start** Bev Heslop, Walt Unsworth	
1962	**Glister Wall** Bev Heslop, Walt Unsworth	

Almost certainly climbed before – as a peg was already in place.

1964	**Plain Bob** and **Variant, Unappealing, Fox's Corner** Bev Heslop, Walt Unsworth
1965	**Triple Bob Major** Walt Unsworth, Bev Heslop
1965	**Tocsin Wall** (A1) Bev Heslop, Walt Unsworth

First free ascent by Ian Lonsdale, June 1978.

1966	**Just William** William Jolly
1966	**Thomas's Wall Climb** Stu Thomas
1966	**Whittaker's Almanac, Whittaker's Original, Side Step** Gra Whittaker
1966	**Elder Groove** Arthur Hassall
1966	**Fleabite** John Whittle
1966	**Samarkand** John Whittle, Roger Tweedy

A fine discovery which was soon to become a classic.

1966	**Klondyke** (A2)

First free ascent by Dave Hollows, 1978.

1966	**Mini, Writer's Cramp** Walt Unsworth
1966	**Alldred's Original** Ian Alldred
1966	**Tinkerbell** Arthur Hassall, Walt Unsworth
1966	**Tintinnabulation** Arthur Hassall, Stu Thomas, John Bennison
1966	**Edipol!, Telegraph Arête, Meanwhile** Gra Whittaker, John Whittle, Arthur Hassall, Walt Unsworth and others
1966	**Nightmare**
1967 Apr	**Quickstep** Gra Whittaker
1967 Apr	**First Night, Night Before, Stag Party** Arthur Hassall, Stu Thomas, Walt Unsworth, John Bennison
1967 Apr	**Wedding March** Arthur Hassall
1967 Apr	**Wedge** Les Ainsworth (solo)
1967 Apr	**Storm** (1 pt aid) Arthur Hassall, Gra Whittaker, in a storm

Aid eliminated in 1970.

1967 May	**Sheppey** (S/A1) Arthur Hassall

First free ascent by Dave Hollows, Terry Baker, spring 1971.

1967 May	**Sunbeam** Stu Thomas
1967 May	**Finger Chimney, The Finger, The Thumb** Les Ainsworth, Les Houlker
1967 June	**Traumatic Eversion** (1 pt aid) Les Ainsworth, Ray Miller

Lasso move at the start eliminated by Dave Hollows, summer 1969.

1967	**Flake Out** Les Ainsworth, Paul Hamer as Great Flake

Reclimbed after the flake collapsed, by Roger Walsh, Dave Walsh about 1976.

1967	**Pyrites** (A2)

First free ascent by Dave Hollows as Fool's Gold, 1969.
Line of second pitch altered and made more independent by Ian Lonsdale, Andy Lewandowski, 12 May 1977.

1967	**William the Conqueror** William Jolly
1968	**Tintinnabulation Direct** Arthur Hassall, Stu Thomas, John Bennison
1968	**Coal Measure Climb** Les Ainsworth, Paul Hamer
1968	**The Golden Tower** Les Ainsworth, Ian Cowell (alts)

Slightly right of the present second pitch.
A brilliant discovery, soon destined to become one of the great gritstone quarry classics.

1968	**Metamorphosis** Gra Whittaker, John Whittle
1968	**Sleeper Bay** Les Ainsworth, Roger Vickers
1968	**Because** Stu Thomas
1969	**Kaibab** Dave Hollows
1969	**Fool's Gold** Dave Hollows

First free ascent of Pyrites.

1971 spring	**Sheppey** Dave Hollows, Terry Baker

First free ascent.

1971	**Double Trip** (A3) Bill Cheverst, Colin Dickinson, John Kitchen

1971   **Double Trip**   (A3)   Bill Cheverst, Colin Dickinson, John Kitchen
First free ascent by Dave Knighton, Pete Herridge, 8 Nov 1977.

1971   **Lucky Strike**   (A2/VS)   Bill Cheverst, John. Kitchen, D. Wooliscroft
First free ascent by Dave Cronshaw, Phil Warner, July 1978.

1971   **Terror Cotta**   Dave Hollows, Terry Baker, John Hollows
Originally called Ten Pound Bail.

1972 Feb   **First Finale**   (A2)   Colin Dickinson, Bill Cheverst
First free ascent claimed independently in 1976 by Dave Knighton, Nadim Siddiqui and by Gaz Healey, Phil Davidson.

1973   **Rope Thief**   Dave Cronshaw, Bob MacMillan, Les Ainsworth

1973   **Bay Horse**   (2 pts aid)   Stu Thomas
Aid completely eliminated by Nigel Bonnett, 27 Mar 1977.

1973   **Zarke**   (1 aid pt)   Les Ainsworth, Dave Cronshaw, Bob MacMillan
Aid eliminated by Ian Lonsdale 1975.

1973   **Original Wall Traverse**   Stu Thomas

1973   **Last Post**   Gra Whittaker, John Whittle, Arthur Hassall, Walt Unsworth and others

1974   **Birthday Crack, Many Happy Returns**   Arthur Hassall

1974-75   **After The Blitz**

1975   **A Series of Boring Mantelshelves**   Stu Thomas, Arthur Hassall

1976 Aug 9   **Dirty Corner**   Nigel Bonnett, Steve Marsden

1976   **Bossa Nova**   Dave Cronshaw, Rick Walsham

1976   **First Finale**   Either Dave Knighton, Nadim Siddiqui or Gaz Healey, Phil Davidson
First free ascent. It is unclear which ascent was actually first.

Mid-1970s   **Minor**

1977 Mar 27   **Bay Horse**   Nigel Bonnett
Aid completely eliminated.

1977 May 12   **Punchline**   Ian Lonsdale, Andy Lewandowski

1977 June   **Mark**   Ian Lonsdale

1977   **Havasupai**   (A1)
First free ascent by Mark Liptrot, as Lean Mean Fightin' Machine, 1981 .

1977   **Gritstone Rain**   Dave Cronshaw, Les Ainsworth

1977   **Terra Firma**   Stu Thomas, Phil Davidson, Gaz Healey

1977   **Loco Motion, Side Track**   Stu Thomas, Phil Davidson, Gaz Healey

1977 Nov 8   **Double Trip**   Dave Knighton, Pete Herridge
First free ascent.

1977 Nov   **High Revver**   Dave Knighton (unseconded)

1978 Jan   **Fingertip Control**   Dave Knighton, Eric Dearden
Top-roped many times prior to the lead.

1978 Jan 29   **Transformation**   Paul Cropper

1978 Feb 18   **Gilt Complex**   Nick Colton, Dave Knighton

1978 Feb 19   **Helical Happiness**   Dave Knighton, Eric Dearden

1978 Mar   **Get This One in the Guide It's a Gem**   Al Evans (solo)

1978 June   **Tocsin Wall**   Ian Lonsdale
First free ascent.

1978 July   **Lucky Strike**   Cronshaw, Phil Warner
First free ascent.

1978 Aug 8   **Gates of Perception**   Dave Knighton, Grimshaw

1978 Aug   **Cotton Terror**   Ian Lonsdale, Nigel Bonnett

1978 Sep 26   **Shorty, Nowhere Man**   Ian Lonsdale, Nigel Bonnett

1978   **Klondyke**   Dave Hollows
First free ascent.

1978   **Coconino**   Les Ainsworth, Dave Cronshaw

1975-79   **Flake Out**   Reclimbed by Roger Walsh, Dave Walsh

1975-79   **Whiter Shade of Shale, Yapi**

1975-79   **Gold Digger, For Whom the Bell Tolls**   Phil Davidson

1979   **Fool's Gold**   Dave Cronshaw
First free ascent of entire route.

1979   **Soot Juggler**   Dave Cronshaw (solo with backrope)

1979   **Splits**   John Hart, John Stanger

1979	**Vishnu** Dave Cronshaw, Les Ainsworth
	Headbanger by Ed Peace, Tony Mawer, 1981
1979	**The Changeing** Originally top-roped as Torroweap Overlook
	First lead by Phil Kelly, Paul Pritchard, 5 July 1984.
1980 June	**Superb** Mark Liptrot, Dick Toon
1980 July 3	**Tangerine Trip** Dave Cronshaw, Ian Lonsdale, Mick Brookes
	A great discovery.
1980	**Years from Now** Ian Lonsdale, Dave Cronshaw
1980	**Rockin' Horse** Dave Cronshaw, Ian Lonsdale
1980	**Grond II**
Early 1981	**Bellringer, Ding Dong** Dave Cronshaw, John Ryden
1981	**Supai Corner, Bright Angel Corner, Anasazi Arête** Dave Cronshaw,
	John Ryden, Les Ainsworth
1981	**Zoroaster** Les Ainsworth, Dave Cronshaw
1981	**Lean Mean Fightin' Machine** Mark Liptrot
	First free ascent of Havasupai.
1982 Feb 19	**Ain't Nothing to It** Gary Gibson (unseconded)
	Direct Start by Mark Liptrot (solo), July 1982.
	Direct Finish by Ian Vickers, Dave Cronshaw, 1991.
1982 Aug 4	**The Rapidity of Sleep** Mark Liptrot
1982	**Hunter Killer** Dave Cronshaw, Les Ainsworth, John Ryden
1982	**Falkland Groove, Corned Beef Dictator** Dave Cronshaw, John Ryden
	Peronist by Jeff Hope, Alan Hubbard, July, 1991. This originally started up
	the first section of Michael Portillo.
1982	**Hermes** Dave Cronshaw, Les Ainsworth
1979-83	**Punch-up** Mark Kemball,
1983 May	**Turkish Delight** Mark Liptrot (solo)
1983 July 31	**Mission Impossible** Mark Liptrot, John Dodd
1983 July 31	**Elaine** Mark Liptrot (solo)
1983 Aug 15	**Shibb** Richard Toon, Mark Liptrot
1983 Aug 22	**Give Thanks** Mark Liptrot, Dick Toon
1983 Aug 25	**New Jerusalem** Mark Liptrot, Richard Toon
1983	**Please Lock me Away** Bernie Bradbury
1984 Mar 17	**King of Kings** Mark Liptrot, Dave Vose, Bernie Bradbury
	Gained from PLmA and finished up Klondyke. Liptrot added the direct
	finish later, whilst Ian McMullen forced the direct start to make it
	independent.
1984 Mar	**Skin Game** Kev Glass, Neil Hyde
1984 May 13	**Septic Think Tank** Gary Gibson
1984 June 30	**The Absent Minded Professor** Mark Liptrot, Dick Toon
1984 July 5	**The Changeing** Phil Kelly, Paul Pritchard (led)
1984	**Snorter** Jeff Hope (solo)
1985 Feb 15	**Agrajag, Dancing on the Valentine** Mark Liptrot
1985	**The Nausea** Mark Liptrot (unseconded)
Early 1986	**Terrorific** Andrew Gridley (solo) – Originally called Terrorizer
1986 May	**Rock Lobster** Dave Cronshaw, Phil Kelly, John Ryden
1986 Sep	**The Karma Mechanic** Paul Pritchard (unseconded)
	The appearance of a very talented climber who was to raise the standards
	of British climbing.
1986	**Milk Syringe** Andrew Gridley
1986	**Evil Digits** Paul Pritchard
1986 Nov 16	**Land** Mark Liptrot, Dave Vose
1986 Nov 27	**Liptrip** Mark Liptrip
	Superseded by Third Party.
1986 Nov 29	**Double Trouble** Mark Liptrot (unseconded)
1986-87	**Pandooi**
1986-87	**Sparrow** Mark Liptrot
1986-87	**The Taciturn Boy**

Geoff Hibbert on **Pagan Direct** (HVS 5b), Cadshaw Castle Rocks.   *Photo: Pete Smith*

1986-87	**Son of Dicktrot**
1987	**Age of Reason** Mark Liptrot
1988 Apr 12	**Schwarzennegger Mon Amour, Office Party** Mark Liptrot (unseconded)
1988 Apr 13	**I'm Spartacus** Mark Liptrot (unseconded)
1988 Apr 15	**If You Can't Lick 'em, Lick 'em, Kelly's 'i'** Mark Liptrot (unseconded)
1988	**Third Party** Mark Liptrot
	Straightened out Liptrip by Mark Liptrot, 27 Nov 1987.
1988	**Epidural** Andrew Gridley, Paul Pritchard
1989	**Italian Job** Probably Tim Lowe
	A hard modern classic.
1989	**Wall and Crack** Dave Cronshaw, Ian Vickers, Roger Vickers
1990	**I Claudius** Ian Vickers, Dave Cronshaw
1990 Oct 5	**Flyer** Ian McDonald, Neil Smith
1990	**The Friable Sausage** Neil Smith, R. Arrowsmith
1991 June	**Roaring Forties** Jeff Hope, Andy Stewart. Cath Clunie
	Superseded by Michael Portillo, by Ian Conway, Richard Baker, 1995.
1991 July	**Peronist** Jeff Hope, Alan Hubbard
	Bottom section superseded by Mu' Azib, Ian Conway, Richard Baker, 1995.
1992 May 20	**Cad Eye the Heather** Dave Johnson, P. O'Rourke
1992 June 15	**The Eight-legged Atomic Dustbin Will Eat Itself** Karl Lunt, Barry Rhodes
1995 Apr 8	**Mu' Azib** Ian Conway, Richard Baker
	Climbed the bottom section of Peronist and then straightened out the top of Roaring Forties.
1995 Apr 8	**Michael Portillo** Ian Conway, Richard Baker
	Added an independent finish to Roaring Forties.
1996 spring	**Two Minutes to Midnight** Martin Gibbons
1996 Sep 5	**Blueberry Hill** Dave Cronshaw, Ian Vickers
1997 Mar 30	**The Midas Touch** Andy Farnell
1997 Mar 30	**Erratic Traversion** Andy Harrison
1997 May 4	**Any Which Way but Loose** Carl Spencer, Pete Mayes
1997 May 4	**Any Which Way You Can, To Infinity and Beyond** Carl Spencer (unseconded)
1997 May 5	**Thirsty Work, I See No Ships, Reservoir Camels** Carl Spencer, Pete Mayes
1997 May 24	**Le Mans Finish, Airborne Attack, Gardening Leave** Carl Spencer, Alan Atkinson
1997 May 25	**Botch Weld Job, The Iron Start, The Steel Start** Carl Spencer, Pete Mayes
1997 Aug 8	**Not in This Life** Carl Spencer
1997	**Brick Thick** Carl Spencer
1997	**There's More to This** Carl Spencer, Mark Garratt

Brownstones Quarry   O.S. ref. SD 681 124

'*All the climbs have been given technical gradings, as the
level of seriousness makes Brownstones an excellent place to
introduce climbers to this type of grading. The first part of
this grade is a numerical from 1 to 6 in ascending order of
difficulty. Each number is subdivided into a, b, or c, the
former being the easiest and the latter the hardest. At the
moment the highest grade under this system is 6a.*'

Hank Pasquill, 1969

Adam Richardson on the classic **Wilton Wall** (E3 6a), Wilton Two.   *Photo: Geoff Hibbert*

Situation and Character

Brownstones is situated some seven kilometres from the centre of Bolton and lies conveniently next to Scout Road, within a stone's-throw of ample car parking. The quarry is a fellstone grit of similar nature to (though a finer texture than) Wilton and is generally very clean. The climbs are short and this makes it an ideal spot for bouldering on a summer's evening.

History

The first record of climbing in Brownstones Quarry was published in the journal of the Lancashire Caving and Climbing Club in the spring of 1947 and was written by Eric Parr. That original guide included 47 problems, many of which are still bouldering classics of today. Notable routes which date from that period include *Godwit Groove* and *Crossbill Crack,* now known as *Parr's Crack* and *Layback* respectively, to the modern devotees and both still retain the potential to shock jaded rock-jocks in early season.

The early guide was revised in 1948 and between that date and the publication of the first definitive Lancashire guidebook in the late 1960s, development was spasmodic; during the intervening years all the original problems became known by other names, probably caused by the lack of an available guidebook.

When it finally arrived, the Rocksport guidebook listed 67 routes, along with their technical grades (a new innovation in the area and following the example of Pete Crew's Cloggy guidebook; interestingly the example did not spread to other crags for many years!). *Digitation* became a masterpiece of delicacy, just left of *Ashpit Slab* whilst *Var, Knar* and *Impo* surely rank as some of the hardest additions of a talented Bolton team in the 60s. Pasquill never quite forgot about the place though and with Dave Hollows added *Rusty Wall* in time to make the 'pink' supplement of 1979, and in the early 80s he 'big-booted' his way up Hank's Wall to create a superb technical problem. In 1987 Mark Leach pointed the way to the future with a desperately hard crackline on the Back Wall (*Thunder*) which had previously been tried by many able climbers.

More recently attention focused on the higher section of rock on The Long Back Wall. The first new line to go in this area was the overhanging arête of *Groundhog*, which was done by Geoff Hibbert in 1993. Then, during the final stages of preparations for this guidebook, many of the tops in this area were cleaned and Hibbert claimed *Norma* and *Bill* in 1998. At the same time, Adam Richardson had been attempting to free climb Hangover, the only artificial route at Brownstones. He eventually succeeded a few days before the guidebook work was completed, to create *The Young Pretender.*

Approach

Approaching from Bolton follow the Blackburn signs, A666, about a kilometre from the town centre is a fork in the road. Take the left-hand fork (Blackburn Road carries straight on) and follow Halliwell Road to where it crosses the ring road (Ainsworth Arms pub on corner). Continue straight on up Smithills Deane Road to a crossroads (about two kilometres) and turn left. The quarry is then visible on the right after about 500 metres, set back slightly from the road.

Alternatively, Brownstones can be approached from the Wilton Quarries by following Scout Road for about two kilometres past Wilton Two and Three to a short terrace of cottages on the right. The quarry lies on the right immediately before these.

The Climbs
The climbs are described from RIGHT to LEFT, but no heights are given. Where numbers have previously been painted on the rock, these are listed in brackets after the grade. By tradition only technical grades are given for all the climbs. However, some of the routes on The Long Back Wall are quite serious.

Pool Area
The first rock that is reached starts near a small pool.

1. Pondule D (1974-75)
The small arête on the right of the pool.

2. Ponder 4b (1979-83)
The crack just to the left.

★★ **3. Pond Traverse** 5c (Pre-1965)
An excellent traverse. Start at the arête right of the pond and traverse the pond walls from right to left. Can be extended right round as far as Hernia.

4. Riddle 5c (1984)
From Piddle, traverse right for three metres and climb the wall above.

5. Middle 5c (1984)
Traverse right about one metre from Piddle and finish direct.

6. Piddle 5c (1984)
Climb the wall just right of the right-angled corner of the Pool Walls while contemplating the riddle of the piddle in the middle!

7. The Corner 5a (1979-83)
Traverse left from Pondule into the corner and finish up this.

8. Splosh 5b (1979-83)
The thin crack two metres to the left of the corner.

9. Splish 4c (1975-79)
The twin cracks in the wall on the left.

10. Splash 5b (1975-79)
The third crackline past the corner.

11. Wet Foot 5a (1975-79)
A direct line one metre right of Watery Arête.

12. Watery Arête 4c (Pre-1948)
The left arête of the pond has a slippery start.

13. Slab Variant D (1974-75)
The corner, slab and arête in sequence.

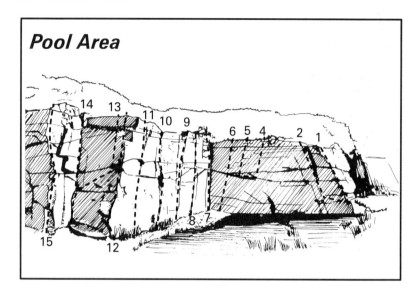

Pool Area

14. Wet Corner VD   (Pre-1948)
Go straight up the initial corner of Slab Variant.

15. Muddy Arête 5c   (Pre-1948)
The next arête is followed above fallen blocks.

16. Muddy Wall 4c   (1979-83)
Climb the wall one metre left of the arête.

17. Chockerblock Corner VD   (Pre-1948)
The corner which contains a jamming flake.

18. Mantelstrug D   (Pre-1948)
Mantel on to a little platform, then climb the wall.

19. Two Step 4b   (Pre-1948)
The wall on the left has three small ledges. Follow these rightwards and finish
on Mantelstrug. 5c if the top is not used.

20. Two Step Left-hand 5b   (Pre-1969)
From the start of Two Step, go slightly leftwards and up.

21. Verdi Wall 4c   (1974-75)
Climb the short wall at a crack.

★ **22. Verdigris** 6a   (1987)
Climb the wall just left, via a good jug in the wall. Use of the jug on the arête
is strictly off limits (it's about 4c with the jug).

★ **23. Verdinand** 6a   (1979-83)
The shallow groove immediately to the left in the same wall, is climbed
avoiding the jug on the previous route.

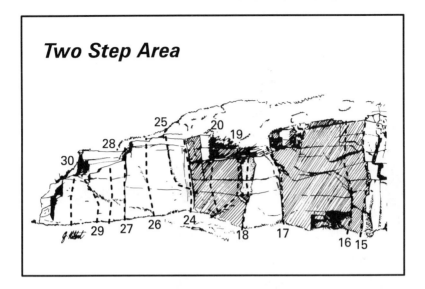

Two Step Area

24. Verdi Corner 4a   (Pre-1948)
The corner crack.

25. Verdi Ramp 4b   (Pre-1948)
From the foot of the corner move left up the obvious scoop.

★ **26. Moss Wall** 4b to 5c   (Pre-1948)
There are at least four ways up the wall on the left.

27. Brownstones Crack VD   (Pre-1948)
The obvious crack.

28. Slimer 5b   (Pre-1948)
The wall on the left.

29. Lobotomy 5a   (1993)
Climb the wall immediately to the left to a notch at the top.

30. Hernia 5a   (Pre-1948)
The left end of the wall.

Long Back Wall

*This is the long steep wall to the left of the easy **DESCENT** route. The first route starts in the centre of the orange, flaky wall at the right-hand side. All the routes on this wall have been led or soloed, but they are higher and more serious than the other routes at Brownstones and so top-ropes are sometimes used, especially where the tops are still poor or the landings awkward.*

In the past, this section of the quarry has been neglected, because of the poor tops. However, these have now been extensively cleaned off and so it is hoped that the interesting test-pieces on this wall will now receive the attention that they deserve.

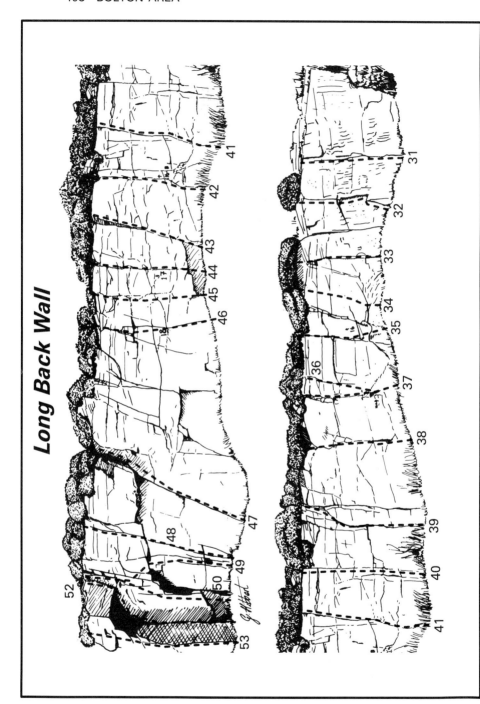

Long Back Wall

31.   Dave's Route   5b   (1982)
Climb the crack that splits the centre of the flaky, orange wall.

32.   Hank   5b   (15A)   (1977)
From a short pedestal at a higher level on the left side of the orange wall, climb
the shallow groove and wall above.

★ **33.   Black Wall**   5c   (15B)   (1979-83)
Start five metres farther left and climb a thin, overhanging, blocky crack.

34.   Rusty Wall   6c   (1977)
Three metres farther left at a slightly higher level is a faint crack. Climb the
wall at this point using shallow pockets.

★ **35.   Stop Butt**   5c   (16)   (Pre-1969)
Climb diverging cracks using two obvious jugs to start, then finish up a thin
crack.

36.   Butt End   6a   (1975-79)
From a low overlap follow the line of two faint cracks that lead rightwards.

37.   Knep   5c   (16a)   (Pre-1969)
From the same point, climb the block-filled crack.

★ **38.   Dave's Other Route**   5c   (1982)
The next crack, passing a small sentry-box.

★★ **39.   The Slanter**   5c   (1979-83)
Start five metres farther left and climb the left-hand of a pair of cracks, passing
a small overlap at half-height.

★ **40.   Thunder**   6c   (1986-87)
The faint crack in the wall two metres farther left. A small block is very helpful
to start the route and it will be much harder if this disappears.

41.   Faintline   5c   (1979-83)
Start two metres farther left at a slightly higher level and climb the crack.

42.   Heartline   5b   (16b)   (1974-75)
Climb the next crack and finish up a short groove.

★ **43.   Hardline**   6a   (1979-83)
The thin crack three metres to the left, that finishes up a slim groove.

44.   Var   5c   (17)   (Pre-1969)
Climb the wall via a large jug in a square hole at half-height.

45.   Lifeline   6b   (1979-83)
The faint crack one metre left.

46.   Knah   5c   (18)   (Pre-1969)
Climb the next thin crack and the small overlap above.

★ 47.   Impo 6a   (Pre-1969)
Start at a lower level directly behind a large rectangular boulder on the floor.
Climb the obvious right-slanting crack to an obvious triangular niche. An
awkward move then gives access to the short corner above.

48.   Norma 5c   (1998)
Climb the wall immediately left of Impo directly to a finish up twin cracks.

49.   Crackle 4c   (Pre-1969)
Start directly behind the left end of the rectangular boulder and climb blocky
cracks to a deep square hole. Step left and finish uo the wall above.

50.   Bill 4c   (1998)
Climb the crack two metres to the left, directly to the top via a dubious-looking
block.

51.   Traverse 6b   (1979-83)
Start from the foot of The Young Pretender and traverse right to Var.

★★ 52.   The Young Pretender 6b   (1974/1998)
Climb the corner crack "with a variety of leverages that would flabbergast major
bridge-building engineers", to a wild, spreadeagled finish rightwards at the roof.
Hangover (A1): finishes directly over the roof on pegs.

★★ 53.   Groundhog 6c   (1993)
The arête and overlap on the immediate left.

★ 54.   The Key 5b (21)   (Pre-1969)
The hand-jam crack on the left.

55.   The Lock 5c   (1979-83)
The crack just to the left.

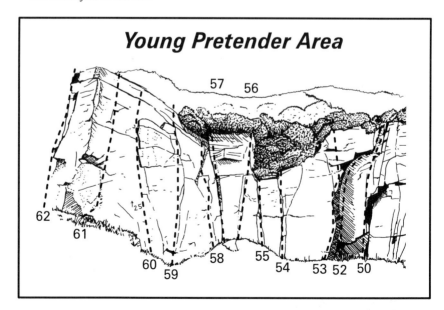

Young Pretender Area

56. The Latch 6a   (1986)
The faint hairline crack just to the left.

57. Finger Crack 5b   (Pre-1969)
Climb directly up the green corner that forms the far left angle of the wall.

Left Wall
The Left Wall is the short section of rock at right-angles to the Long Back Wall,
which ends at a small arête.

58. Y Front 4a   (Pre-1969)
The right end of the wall, via a large ledge, then finish rightwards.

59. Tom 5a   (Pre-1948)
From a small overlap at the foot of the wall climb past a series of small ledges.

60. Jerry 5a   (Pre-1969)
From the left side of the small overlap climb the wall and finish up a thin flake.
Proves if you're a man or a mouse.

61. Butch 6a   (1975-79)
A short problem whose fall potential is quite unnerving; climb the wall just right
of the arête, stepping in from the left.

Ash Pit Slabs
After a small rise on the main path at the arête, the path continues along the
foot of the crag. The rock hereabouts is not very high, but this is more than
compensated for by its high quality. Ash Pit Slab lies roughly halfway along this
wall.

62. Little Man 4a   (Pre-1969)
The first crack to the left of the arête.

63. Crooked Crack 4a   (1979-83)
The next crack.

64. Gullible's Travels 6a   (1983-86)
The overlap and short wall between Crooked Crack and Way Down, without
using either.

65. Way Down 4a (27)   (1979-83)
Climb the wall via the left side of a small overlap. This is (but isn't) the way
down!

66. Vertigo 4a   (Pre-1948)
The next crack.

67. Inferno 4c   (Pre-1969)
Twin cracks then a wall to finish.

68. Dragnet 4b   (Pre-1948)
The next crack, passing on the right of a small overhang.

Ash Pit Slabs

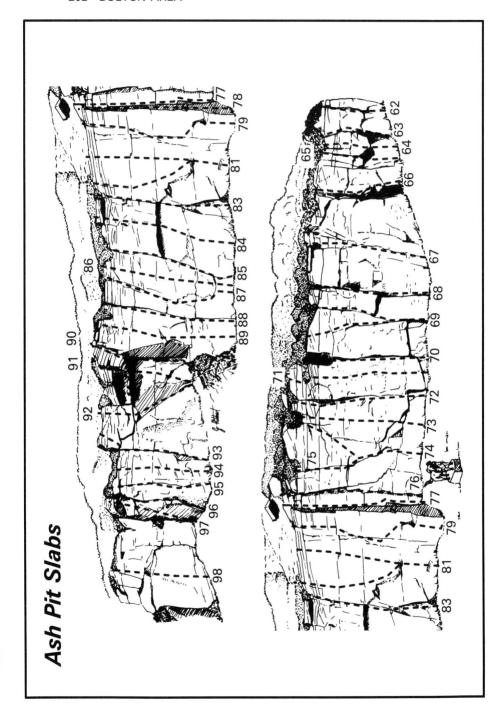

★ **69.   Haskit**   5c   (Pre-1969)
The forked cracks in the wall just to the left.

★ **70.   Layback**   5b   (32)   (Pre-1948)
Climb the crack on the left into a short niche before the top.

★★ **71.   Hank's Wall**   6c   (1979-83)
A strict problem up the wall between Layback and Parr's Crack, avoiding holds
on both those routes.

★★ **72.   Parr's Crack**   5c   (1948-49)
The next crack and slight groove. In the immediate post-Second World War
years this was the ultimate problem. It is still good value.

73.   Pigswill   6c   (1983-86)
The wall between Parr's Crack and Parabola. "If this has been climbed then
'pigs will' fly!" was a quote at the time, but it has had several ascents.

★★ **74.   Parabola**   5b   (Pre-1948)
Follow the flake leftwards to its end, then arc back right across the wall on
small holds to the top of Parr's Crack.

★ **75.   Parabola Direct**   6a   (Pre-1969)
Climb direct to the left end of the flake, then continue up the crack above by
hard moves.

76.   The Chimney   4c   (Pre-1948)
The wide chimney crack immediately to the right of the corner.

77.   Wibble   5a   (Pre-1969)
The corner itself gives a foretaste (hint) of Black Adder to come!

★ **78.   Nexus**   4c   (Pre-1948)
Excellent steep climbing up the wall on the left on good holds.

A pumpy low-level traverse is possible from Y Front to Ashpit Slab (and
farther), in both directions; 6a.

★★ **79.   Ash Pit Slab**   D   (Pre-1969)
Go up the clean arête by a series of ledges that lead slightly left.

80.   Ash Pit Traverse   4c   (Pre-1948)
From the ledge on Ash Pit Slab go left and gain the sloping slab below the
overhang. At its end step down (crux) and continue left to easier ground.

★★ **81.   Digitation**   5c   (Pre-1969)
The centre of the slab left of Ash Pit Slab, with plenty of *'you can't use that'*
and sometimes a sandy finish.

★ **82.   Fraud**   5b   (Pre-1969)
Start up Digitation, then climb the slab on the left using chipped holds. The
same line can be followed without using the chipped holds at 6a.

83.   Analogue   4c   (Pre-1948)
The next crack, just right of an overlap.

★ **84.   Directissima**   5c   (Pre-1969/pre-1948)
Climb the wall on the left, going over a small overlap. This route is getting
much trickier as it becomes more polished.

85.   Degree Crack   5a   (43)   (Pre-1948)
The crack that passes the left edge of the overlap.

86.   Scraper   5b   (44)   (Pre-1948)
A slightly more direct line from the foot of Degree Crack.

87.   Hopper   4c   (45)   (Pre-1948)
Start just to the left and climb first slightly leftwards, then back right at the top.

88.   Corn Mantel   5b   (46)   (Pre-1948)
Climb the wall on the left, with an interesting mantel to start.

★ **89.   Unjust**   6a   (Pre-1969)
The blunt nose either using two small chipped holds or by a long reach for a
poor pinch. A blinkers route that avoids the tempting large holds on either side.

90.   Arur   4b   (Pre-1948)
From a slightly higher level, climb the dirty crack to the right of a nose.

91.   The Nose   VD   (1974-75)
Climb over the jutting prow from the left.

92.   Rambler   D   (Pre-1969)
Climb the little slab to a ledge, then go rightwards up the scoop above.

93.   Climber and Rambler   4a   (1974)
Ascend the crack on the left to join Rambler.

94.   Wall Climb   5c   (1950s)
The wall immediately to the left. Desperate if holds on the two adjacent routes
are strictly avoided.

★ **95.   Noddy's Crack**   5c   (1974-75)
The thin crack on the left.

96.   Groovy   4a   (Pre-1975)
The flaky grooveline just to the left.

97.   Apple   4b   (Pre-1969)
The dirty rock at the left of the wall. In other words it's a rotten apple!

98.   The Thrutch   D   (1974-75)
The isolated problem wall just to the left of the main rocks.

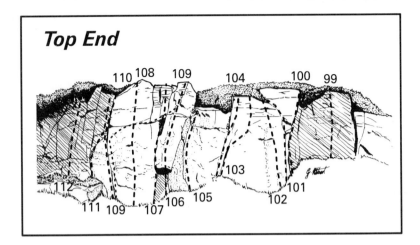

Top End Climbs

The quarry rises slightly at this point, and the first routes are around the
obvious sharp prow of rock.

99. Delicatessen 4b   (1974-75)
The small slab at the right-hand side of the prow.

100. The Prow 4c   (Pre-1969)
The sharply-pointed prow is climbed direct. How now bold prow!

101. Halt 4a   (Pre-1969)
The crack immediately to the left of the prow.

102. Blurt 5a   (Pre-1969)
Climb the blunt nose strenuously.

103. Blurt Variant 5b   (1974-75)
Start at a crack on the left and make a hard move, then move right to finish at
the top of Blurt.

104. Fineline 5c   (1979-83)
Climb the next crack directly to the top avoiding the obvious easy cop-out
leftwards.

105. Diane VD   (Pre-1969)
Climb the awkward, polished corner.

106. Dezertion 6b   (1979-83)
The undercut arête just left of the corner; short but very sharp!

⋆ **107. Dezerit** 5b   (Pre-1969)
Climb the undercut 'desbritt' crack on the left of the arête to a tiny niche.

⋆⋆ **108. Boopers** 6a   (1975-79)
Climb direct up the centre of the wall on the left.

109. Bitto 5c   (1975-79)
Start up the left side of the wall then climb rightwards along the thin horizontal crack to finish up Dezertion.

110. Beano 6a   (1975-79)
The left arête is climbed via an awkward crack, and avoiding the large jug on the arête. Finish in a rather comic way!

111. Grass Groove D   (Pre-1969)
The rightward-curving crack on the left.

112. Dezis Wall 4c   (1979-83)
Start from a block and climb the centre of the next wall direct.

113. Tiptoe 4b   (1974)
Traverse the next slab from right to left (the top must not be used) and continue to the far corner.

114. Slab Direct 4a   (1974-75)
Climb the exact centre of the slab to a ledge and broken wall above.

115. Short Corner D   (1979-83)
The corner on the left.

116. Green Wall 5b   (1979-83)
From a pedestal three metres left of the corner, climb the wall above.

117. Bunnie's Dilemma D   (Pre-1969)
The broken, slanting groove on the wall left of the slab.

★★ **118. Obscenity** 5b   (Pre-1969)
From the foot of Bunnie's Dilemma climb the wall direct.

119. Pocket Hole Wall VD   (1974-75)
Pass the obvious pocket to reach the rib.

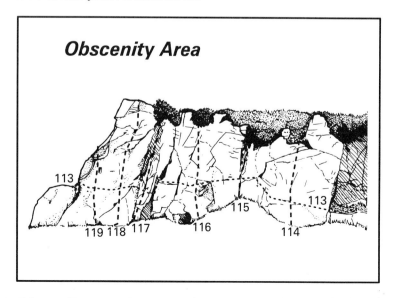

Obscenity Area

120. The Pock 5a (1979-83)
Traverse the wall low from Bunnie's Dilemma to Pocket Hole Wall.

121. Magic Circle 4b (1974)
An eliminate line, but in a horizontal dimension. Around the rib is a tiny amphitheatre of slabby rock. Starting at the right edge of this, traverse left without using the top for hands, to finish at the left arête; good fun.

122. Test Piece 5a (1974-75)
The clean overhanging block left of Magic Circle. Grasp the top and mantel, numerous variations being possible (backwards, etc).

123. Somersault 4c (1966)
Go directly over the jutting roof.

124. Warlon's Wall 4b (66) (Pre-1975)
The steep wall just to the left.

First Ascents at Brownstones Quarry

The names of most of the original routes were lost for some time. Therefore, for the record, the original names of these climbs are given in brackets immediately after the current names.

Pre-1948	**Watery Arête** (The Brink), **Wet Corner** (Water Corner), **Muddy Arête** (The Overhang), **Chockerblock Corner** (Cozy Corner), **Mantelstrug** (Platform Corner), **Two Step** (Three Step), **Verdi Corner** (Cascade Corner), **Verdi Ramp** (The Mantelshelf), **Moss Wall** (2 lines – Juxta and Slab), **Brownstones Crack** (Crock's Crack), **Slimer** (Camlet), **Hernia** (Jerboa), **Tom** (Limpet Wall), **Vertigo** (Ribmot), **Dragnet** (Crex Cracks), **Layback** (Crossbill Crack), **Parabola** (Whinchat Wall), **The Chimney** (Craven Crack), **Nexus** (Nexus), **Ash Pit Traverse** (in the opposite direction as Pirouette), **Analogue** (Long Crack), **Degree Crack** (Nodule), **Scraper** (Scraper), **Hopper** (Musgreave's), **Corn Mantel** (Rogue's Romp), **Arur** (Fescue)
1948-49	**Parr's Crack** (Godwit Groove) Eric Parr and friends
1950s	**Wall Climb** Noddy Farnworth with aid
Pre-1965	**Pond Traverse**
1966	**Somersault** Ken Powell
1968	**Fraud** Hank Pasquill
Pre-1969	**Two Step Left-hand, Stop Butt, Knep, Var, Knah, Crackle, The Key, Finger Crack, Y Front, Jerry, Little Man, Inferno, Haskit, Parabola Direct, Wibble, Ash Pit Slab, Digitation, Directissima, Apple, The Prow, Halt, Blurt, Diane, Grass Groove, Bunnie's Dilemma, Obscenity Impo, Unjust** Hank Pasquill
Pre-1969	**Rambler** Walt Unsworth
Pre-1969	**Dezerit** Des Britt
Pre-1975	**Warlon's Wall**
1974	**Hangover** (A1) Walt Unsworth
	Superseded by The Young Pretender, Adam Richardson, Geoff Hibbert, Apr 1998.
1974	**Climber and Rambler, Tiptoe, Magic Circle** Walt Unsworth
1974	**Noddy's Crack** Noddy Farnworth, Walt Unsworth
1974-75	**Pondule, Slab Variant, Heartline, The Nose, The Thrutch, Delicatessen, Blurt Variant, Slab Direct, Pocket Hole Wall, Test Piece, End Wall, End Crack, Groovy**
1977	**Hank** Hank Pasquill
1977 Apr	**Rusty Wall** Dave Hollows, Hank Pasquill (both solo)
1975-79	**Splish, Splash, Wet Foot, Butch, Bitto, Beano, Butt End**
1975-79	**Boopers** Al Evans, (solo)

1980	**Verdinand** Ian Lonsdale
1982	**Dave's Route** Dave Cronshaw
1982	**Dave's Other Route** Dave Cronshaw (solo)
1979-83	**Ponder, The Corner, Splosh, Muddy Wall, Black Wall, The Slanter, Faintline, Lifeline, Traverse, The Lock, Crooked Crack, Fineline, Dezertion, Dezis Wall, Short Corner, Green Wall, The Pock**
1979-83	**Hank's Wall** Hank Pasquill
1979-83	**Hardline** Jerry Moffatt
1984	**Riddle, Middle, Piddle** Paul Pritchard, Gary McCandish
1983-86	*Dusk*
1983-86	**Pigswill** Hank Pasquill
1983-86	**Gullible's Travels** Paul Pritchard
1986	**The Latch** Geoff Hibbert, Mark Leach
1986-87	**Thunder** Mark Leach, Paul Pritchard
1987	**Verdigris** Geoff Hibbert
1993 June	**Lobotomy** Andrew Gibbons
1993	**Groundhog** Geoff Hibbert
1998 Feb 25	**Norma** Geoff Hibbert, Adam Richardson
1998 Mar	**Bill** Geoff Hibbert
1998 Apr	**The Young Pretender** Adam Richardson, Geoff Hibbert
	Superseded Hangover. The long-awaited free ascent of the only artificial climb at Brownstones, but the line was altered slightly at the top.

Egerton Quarry   O.S. ref. SD 719 143

Situation and Character

Egerton is an extensive gritstone quarry clearly visible across the valley from Wilton. Climbing in the quarry is not concentrated in one area, but is fragmented on a number of sheltered buttresses, which despite initial appearances hide some of the finest routes in the area in terms of quality. As a result of the quarry's layout, there are always some climbs to be found in the sunshine, though the best area, Wood Buttress, has a shady aspect. To aid location of the routes, some have their initials painted at their base.

Since the previous guidebook there has been an explosion of new routes at Egerton and although most have not yet had many ascents, some are certainly destined to become classics. There is also scope for further routes.

History

Hank Pasquill and friends visited Egerton Quarry in 1972 and climbed a handful of routes, of which no records were kept. The first definite record of a first ascent belongs to Jim Fogg who paid a short visit a couple of years after Pasquill, in 1974, and climbed *Thin Crack*. News of a potential guidebook supplement provided the necessary impetus, and the crag was rediscovered by Tony Preston in 1975. Preston climbed *Dickie's Meadow* on the area of rock just right of Wood Buttress proper, a significant route, but something of a flanking attack, leaving the remaining possibilities for later.

Nigel Holmes, who was soon to become one of the prime movers in the race to develop the quarry, added *Red Prow Original* later in 1975, and made the mistake of telling Dave Knighton about the place. Knighton was soon in the thick of things, ever hungry for new rock and new adventures. Together, Knighton and Holmes spent many days in January 1976 clearing away the recent snows and loose rock from, and climbing, *Amphitheatre Terrace, Windchill* and *Dust at Dusk*, Holmes having previously climbed the perfect jamming crack of *White Out* with 'Shed' Makin. Some good routes were done around that time, including *Bridge Crack, God Save the Queen, The Nose* and *Ceremony*, but no-one has claimed them.

The early part of 1976 saw Knighton and Holmes emerging from within the dark recesses behind the Red Prow, and they were drawn ever closer to the steep, almost virgin walls of Wood Buttress. First to fall was *Zoot Chute* round to the left of the wall, and then the race was on again, though this time with Ian Lonsdale to see who would get the first free ascent of *Gallows Pole* (won by Knighton). In one of the closest of new route races Knighton managed to get to the crag ten minutes before the competition to claim the popular *Ten Minutes Before The Worm*. Knighton also led *Wednesday Corner* and *Esmeralda* at that time, whilst Holmes found *Insipidity*. Lonsdale gained his revenge by following the *Pilgrim's Progress* and adding *Chalk Lightning Crack,* which Knighton had already top-roped.

Work for the supplement in 1979 saw a rush for the obvious gaps; Dave Cronshaw climbed *Cherry Bomb* with Bob MacMillan, and attention was turned to the then neglected Lonely Wall, with *Initiation* falling to Tony Brindle, whilst Nigel Holmes claimed *Nasty Little Lonely*. Holmes then introduced a friend to the crag, Dai Lampard, and the development of the crag seemed to become some sort of tortured obsession with these two. Ascents of *Niff-Niff the Guinea Pig, Ice Cool Acid Test* and *Each Way Nudger* were soon on the cards, soon to be followed by the cryptically named *Nobody Wept For Alec Trench* – a route that has taken some notable scalps in the past few years. Later that year Mick Johnson and his brother Ian fired off *I Shot Jason King*, another serious arête opposite Alec Trench.

1983 saw Kev Glass and Neil Hyde's *Lubalin* then in 1984 Paul Pritchard and Phil Kelly took a day's holiday from Wilton to climb *Gnat Attack, Rhythm of the Heat* and *The Lamb Lies Down on Broadway,* up the left arête of Lonsdale's *Neighbourhood Threat*.

Geoff Hibbert then began his campaign to fill in the remaining gaps in the quarry. During 1985 he climbed *One Minute To Midnight* and the cryptically-named *No Screws in Skem* (both with Holmes), and a diagonal traverse across Wood Buttress, *The Disappearing Chip Buttie Traverse* (with Mick Bradshaw), whilst Steve Kirk and Nick Walker made amends for the unfortunate mistake in the 1983 guidebook by following the line shown as Niff-Niff on the diagram; the resultant route is now suitably called *Naff-Naff (The Route)*.

In 1986 Hibbert really set about the quarry with a vengeance, but before he could get a look in that year, Mark Liptrot had climbed two lines up the buttress just left of Esmerelda: *Eleventh Hour* and *Mumbled Prayer*, and these were soon followed by *Dicktrot II: The Movie*. Hibbert restarted his campaign with *Lucky Heather* and *Mental Mantel*, which was dried with a blow-torch before the ascent. Hibbert's other routes bordering on the insane, included *Acme Surplus Overhang* and *Don't Stop Believing* – on sight. As a complete contrast to Acme Surplus and following some twenty days of attempts, Christmas Eve 1986 saw Hibbert finally succeed on the sickle-shaped feature in the smooth wall just right of Zoot Chute, *The Reaper*. The route had to wait almost ten years for a second ascent and subsequent upgrade by Gareth Parry in September 1996, and is the toughest route in the quarry.

To complete work on the 1987 guidebook, Hibbert climbed several problems; *Fathomathon, Bob Bandits, Brittle Fingers* and *The Phantom Zone.*

Interest in the quarry waned, but 1991 saw Hibbert climb a few routes on Red Wall. The most significant being *Red Wall Direct* – all with Andy Moss. Also during 1991, Nick Conway soloed *Tasty* in the Empty Quarter.

An unidentified climber sneaked on to Graffiti Wall and created a route with three pegs and a bolt belay, giving *The Snurcher*. Hibbert returned in 1993 to add two new routes, *After the Goldrush*, a splendid discovery on Graffiti Wall with Mick Bullough and *Long Distance Runner*, with Chris Hemmings and Nigel Poulsom. Other routes done about that time include *Stolen Goods* and *Specific Gravity*, by John Stringfellow and Mike Arnold.

In 1996 Alan White and the ever-present Hibbert spent many hours cleaning and climbing some quite impressive lines. White initially concentrated on the somewhat unexplored Grooved Wall, creating *Sparkin' Bush, The Cutter, Shudabindun* and *Chopper Chimney* with Brian Heywood.

Elsewhere in the quarry, White climbed *Wiad* in the Bridge Area with his brother Duncan. Hibbert climbed *Feeding the Rat* with (Titch) Nick Richardson. Hibbert and White also filled a few gaps in the Red Wall area, as did Michael Jackson, who took a day off his gruelling world tour to climb the rather unstable *Wacko* with Paul Dewhurst. *Step into the Groove* was led by Hibbert, to give a short, but worthwhile route. White then claimed the major crackline of *Saffron* with Nick Richardson and Heywood.

During midsummer 1996 the last great problem fell at a surprisingly low grade. Hibbert had prepared and practised the stunning orange arête on the right of Red Wall, but was undecided as to whether he should lead it. The decision was soon made when Roy Houghton, visiting the quarry for the first time, threatened to do if Hibbert didn't. Not surprisingly, courage emerged and Hibbert led the route, *Renaissance*, with White. Houghton immediately stepped in for the second ascent, after climbing the appropriately-named *Big Mouth,* in the same afternoon.

On the Red Prow, Hibbert produced two good lines with *Roadrunner Pinnacle*, a route which is easier than it feels (hard to believe that it is only 4c, even when you've done it!) and the impressive *Falling off the Edge of the World*. The former was climbed with Adam and Nick Richardson and the latter with Geoff Mann. *Omelette*, the crack bounding this on its left was climbed by White and Heywood, whilst being careful to avoid scrambling some pigeon eggs at the back of the crack.

Graffiti Wall gained a few additions from the renaissance period, the pick of the bunch being *Gollum*, which Hibbert soloed on a typical damp summer's day. In keeping with the soloing fashion, White on-sighted the somewhat easier, but no-less-gripping (because of their shaly top-outs) *Egerton Cavern* and *Scribbles*. *Graffiti Corner* was thoroughly cleaned and climbed in more traditional style by White and Heywood.

The far left of Lonely Wall also saw some activity with White climbing *Alchemy* and *Cracker* with Heywood. Hibbert again took the main prize towards the end of summer by climbing the steep wall between these two with the Richardson brothers. The route was named *Summer Lightning* after a guest ale at The Flag. Later that year Hibbert added a half-dozen more routes, the best of which was probably *Walking on Glass*.

1997 saw Hibbert filling in some of the remaining gaps during guidebook work, with obvious, but previously overlooked lines such as *Spreadeagle, Needle Stick* and *Planet of the Apes*. On many of these, Hibbert was accompanied only by his dog, Basil, who only narrowly missed being flattened during the cleaning of *Bombing Basil*. Perhaps the best route of the summer was *Brightside Revisited*, but a couple of weeks later was an even more fruitful day, with Hibbert soloing four more routes, including *Third Time Lucky*.

As work on this guidebook drew to a close, Cronshaw returned to the quarry and along with Les Ainsworth, Adam Richardson and Hibbert, made a methodical attempt to fill in some of the more obvious gaps. The first route to fall was Cronshaw's *Aethelred Groove*, then over a four-week period at the beginning of 1998, two dozen more climbs were added. Many of these were on previously neglected sections of the quarry, such as the Lower Tier of The Empty Quarter, where Cronshaw added *Empty Arête* and *Organ Grinder*, whilst Richardson claimed *Vulture* and Hibbert did *Street Legal, Swamp Dog* and *Double or Quits*. The latter was so named because the number of routes had then doubled from those previously recorded. Grooved Wall also received some attention, but unfortunately, on that occasion the cleaning generally only uncovered bigger holds and deeper cracks, so that the routes, such as *New Groove, Black Arm* and *Vlad the Impaler*, all turned out to be much easier than they at first appeared. However, on the existing routes in this area, some loose rock was removed and it all became much more attractive. Elsewhere in the quarry, Cronshaw defied some atrocious conditions on two separate visits to add *Whitewater Rafting* and *Unseasonal Weather*, whilst at the same time Hibbert claimed *Three Pint Primer* and the impressive *Changing of the Guards*. This period ended with another fine route by Cronshaw on Lonely Wall, called *Water Margin*, and later in the day, Cronshaw, Ainsworth, Hibbert and Carl Spencer made a mass ascent of *By Hook or By Crook*, an easy climb that brought the final tally of new routes in the quarry since the 1987 guidebook to 92, to draw a line under this busy stage in the quarry's development.

Approach

Egerton Quarry is situated approximately seven kilometres north of Bolton just off the A666 Bolton–Blackburn road. To reach the quarry, turn right off the A666 at the Egerton war memorial and continue along Darwen Road for about 500 metres, until the Dunscar Arms is passed on the right. Turn left up the next side road (Arnold Road) and left again at The Flag public house. A steep hill is then ascended until the last houses on the left have been passed. Cars can be parked at the metal gate on the left. The easiest way to enter the quarry is to follow the path past the metal gate, which leads through undergrowth to a flat area next to Graffiti Wall and – farther along – to an archway leading into the quarry proper.

For climbers approaching along the A666 from Darwen, fork left at the William IV pub, along Cox Green Road and continue to the end of this road. Follow the path that was the old road, for about 200 metres then, just before crossing the bridge, turn left into a track blocked by boulders. After about 30 metres turn right at some more boulders on another path, that leads down into the quarry.

The Climbs

The quarry is effectively split into two parts by Cox Green Road, with the main part on the east side of the road (i.e. farthest from the war memorial). A track beneath the road at the Bridge Area links the two parts. The climbs are described from RIGHT to LEFT, starting in the western part of the quarry.

Graffiti Wall

This is the wall, shattered in its upper reaches, on the right of the approach track. The first routes are situated about 80 metres along the track, at the first reasonable quality quarried rock.

1.   Lucia   5m   VS   5a   (1993)
Climb the crack/arête of the first short buttress.

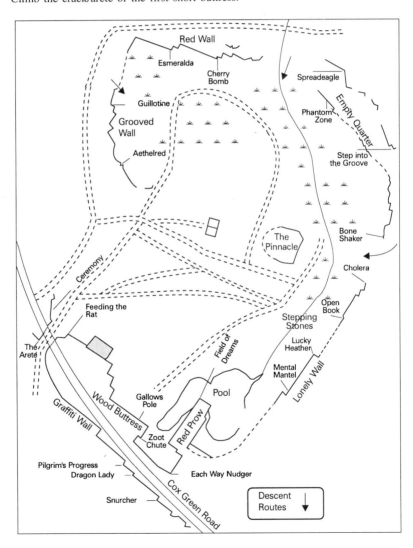

2. Sofia 6m VS 4c (1993)

Six metres to the left, climb the arête with a shot-hole at its base.

3. Spud 11m E1 5b (1993)

Ten metres left, and right of the pegged arête and a bolt lower-off, are two cracks in the wall. The left-hand one is climbed, passing a niche before stepping left to the bolts.

** **4. The Snurcher** 10m E3 6a (1993)

A pumpy clip-up. Technical, sustained and ideal for lost sport climbers. Follow the pegged arête past the bolts and don't get lost.

5. Scribbles 10m HS 4a (1996)

To the left is another sharp arête, which terminates at four metres. Two metres farther left is a black slabby arête. Climb the slab following the ledges until it is possible to step left into a shaky finish.

6. Egerton Cavern 10m VD (1996)

Two metres to the left is a deep chimney which can easily be missed. Ascend this until forced left on to a ledge. Step up and go over the chimney to another ledge to finish up Scribbles.

7. Egerton Arête 8m VS 4c (1998)

The next arête has a shot-hole at its base. Climb the short crack above it to a poor top. Take care with the wall at the top.

8. J.O.B. 12m VS 4c (1996)

30 metres to the left is a pool with a steep wall on its right. Start four metres right of an arête and climb the wall past three drill-holes.

9. Grooved Out 12m HS 4a (1998)

The crack and groove immediately to the right of the arête.

* **10. Dragon Lady** 12m HS 4b (1996)

Climb the middle of the wall left of the arête to a large ledge, then go up the blunt arête in the middle of the face.

* **11. Unseasonal Weather** 12m HVS 5a (1998)

Follow twin cracks in the centre of the next wall to a small overlap. Steep moves then lead to a finishing chimney.

* **12. Pilgrim's Progress** 15m VS 4c (1976)

Gain the left side of the bottom ledge on Unseasonal Weather and continue just right of the arête to the final jutting overhang. Then swing round the arête and finish diagonally left.

* **13. After the Gold Rush** 15m E3 6a (1993)

Climb the centre of the steep wall left of Pilgrim's Progress, then move right to a tree runner and go back left through a bulge. Finish up the jutting overhang on the right arête.

14. Graffiti Corner 15m HS 4a (1996)

The long blocky corner to the left.

The next walls offer good bouldering and a good sustained low-level traverse at 6a, that continues to the left side of the wall containing Gollum.

15.   Stolen Goods   12m   E4   6a   (1993)
The clean arête above a slight rise in the quarry floor is tackled on its right-hand side to the roof (peg), where a swing round the arête leads to an easier finish straight up.

16.   Gollum   12m   HVS   5b   (1996)
The centre of the problematic wall left of Stolen Goods is climbed to a slot and a good runner. Tricky moves up and right lead to a juggy finish. Harder for the short. The top crux can be snivellingly avoided on the left.

17.   Socialist Millionaire   14m   S   4a   (1998)
Climb the corner to a large ledge, then follow stepped ledges rightwards to finish.

Bridge Area

At the end of the wall containing Gollum, the quarry becomes more broken. The next climbs to be described are at the bridge under the old road. The right wall is described first, culminating at a derelict building on the other side of the road, then the routes on the left side are described, working from left to right.

18.   Broken Toe   9m   HVS   5a   (Pre-1993)
Climbs the obvious thin crack in the middle of the red wall, immediately right of the bridge.

19.   Thin Crack   9m   HS   4b   (1974)
The obvious steep crack is climbed past an iron spike.

20.   Markova   9m   S   4a   (Pre-1979)
The crack underneath the bridge, that is capped by an artificial wall. Finish on the right.

21.   Cleft Climb   9m   VS   4c   (1979-83)
Climb the cleft, finishing rightwards up the climbing wall.

★ **22.   Bridge Crack**   12m   VS   5a   (Pre-1979)
A unique situation and good climbing combine to make this a climb a must. Climb the obvious jamming crack to the roof, then hand-traverse or crawl left to finish.

23.   Twilight Crack   9m   S   4a   (1975)
The crack three metres to the left.

★ **24.   Just Out**   9m   S   4a   (1978)
The vague left arête and narrow wall just to the left, with a peg near the top.

★ **25.   Feeding the Rat**   10m   HVS   5a   (1996)
The next arête is climbed on its right to a direct finish on small, but positive, holds.

26. Ludwig 10m S 4a (1996)
Climb the groove just left of the arête.

27. Natural Victim 10m VS 4c (1996)
Climb the wall two metres to the left, passing an obvious orange scar.

28. Dipper 10m E2 5c (1996)
Climb the wall above the first two metal spikes. Don't fall off!
The next routes start on the left wall, facing Thin Crack.

29. Colgy 9m HS 4b (Pre-1993)
Climb the crack just left of The Arête, then continue to the top.

30. The Arête 6m VS 5b (Pre-1979)
The problem arête on the right.

31. Wide Crack 8m VD (1975)
The crack on the right, immediately below the bridge.

32. Toots 8m E2 5c (1996)
The blunt arête that starts at a small upward-pointing, metal spike.

★ **33. The Nose** 8m VS 4c (1979-83)
Just right of centre, under the bridge arch, is a bulging nose which is taken on good holds, with a dubious step right to finish; or, more sensibly, reverse the route.

34. Wiad 10m S 4a (1996)
The jamming crack six metres to the right of The Nose.

35. Hydrophobia 10m HVS 5a (1980)
Start one metre right of Wiad and climb the wall directly, trending right to finish.

36. Rabid 10m HVS 5a (1980)
Start five metres to the right, below an iron spike. Climb leftwards past this to finish as for Hydrophobia.

37. No Screws in Skem 10m E1 5b (1985)
From the iron spike, climb the wall directly.

★ **38. Black Dog** 10m E1 5c (1980)
Start three metres to the right at a crack in the arête. Climb this for six metres, then move left and finish up the thin crack above.

39. The Beauty of Poison 10m E1 5b (1984)
The shattered crack immediately right of Black Dog, starting at a short groove.

★★ **40. Ceremony** 10m VS 4c (Pre-1979)
Looks a bit nasty, but gives delightful climbing on good, hidden holds. Start three metres to the right at the right-hand side of a small overlap, and climb the thin crack direct to the top.

41. Green Thoughts 9m HS 4a (Pre-1979)
Two metres to the right, climb the crack.

Wood Buttress Area

This is undoubtedly the best section of rock in the quarry, and is somewhat reminiscent of Chimney Buttress at Wilton. It is the large buttress about 40 metres left of the far side of the bridge, which starts at a much lower level. However, the first route starts at the higher level on the left of the derelict concrete buildings.

DESCENT: *the best descent from these routes and climbs on the Red Prow, is an interesting route down through the derelict concrete buildings.*

42.   Neighbourhood Threat   10m   HVS   5a   (1979-83)
Step left on to the wall and climb the flake and crack just to the right of the arête (peg).

The next route starts at a lower level.

43.   Shaky Flakes   6m   S   4a   (1979-83)
Climb the right-hand side of the short wall below and right of Neighbourhood Threat.

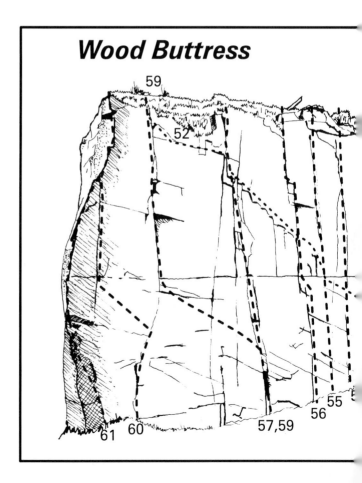

Wood Buttress

44. Dicktrot 8m E1 5c   (1979-83)
Climb the thin crack on the left to a pod finish.

45. The Lamb Lies Down on Broadway 18m E4 6a   (1984)
The long arête is climbed on its right side with runners in Neighbourhood Threat.

46. Temptation 18m E2 6b   (1986)
Climb the wall between the previous route and the corner by a faint groove and
finish rightwards. Side runners in Dickie's Meadow.

47. Dickie's Meadow 17m HS 4a   (1975)
Climbs the obvious corner, just left of the arête.

48. Field of Screams 16m E2 5b   (1996)
Climb the next, short arête to the ledge, then continue up the middle of the
blank-looking wall above on improving holds, to finish up the arête just right of
Insipidity.

★ **49. Insipidity** 15m VS 4c   (1976)
Go up the short corner on the left, then step left and climb the impressive
corner groove, moving left to the arête to finish.

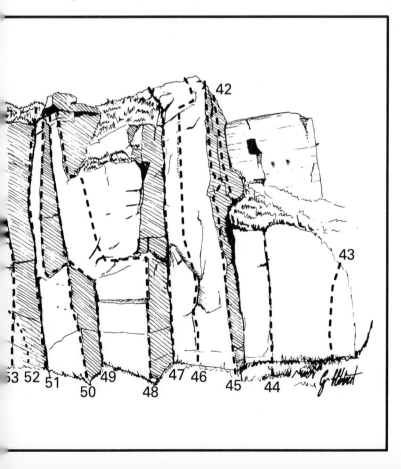

★ **50.   One Minute to Midnight**   15m   E3   5c   (1985)
Climb the technical lower arête, left of Insipidity, to the ledge then follow the
slightly easier upper arête to the top.

★ **51.   Wednesday Corner**   15m   VS   4b   (1976)
Climb the long corner groove, moving right at the top to finish.

★★ **52.   The Disappearing Chip Buttie Traverse**   29m   E1   5b   (1985)
A rising right-to-left traverse across Wood Buttress, that takes in some of the
best climbing. Start just left of Wednesday Corner, move up, and traverse
diagonally left to a peg. Continue towards a second peg (in God Save the
Queen), move left and climb up for a couple of metres to an exit left along a
stiff finger traverse into Ten Minutes Before etc. Worm up that route to finish.

53.   Bag of Bones   15m   HVS   4c   (1979-83)
The obvious crackline which starts from ledges just left of Wednesday Corner.

54.   Naff-Naff (The Route)   17m   E2   5b   (1986)
Climb the crack between Bag of Bones and Niff-Niff.

55.   Niff-Niff the Guinea Pig   17m   E2   5b   (1979-83)
Climb the wall/crack just right of Gallows Pole.

★★ **56.   Gallows Pole**   17m   HVS   5a   (1976)
A typical gritstone quarry climb that combines good moves and interesting
positions. Start directly beneath a wooden sleeper which overlaps the top of the
crag, and follow a vague crackline to finish just left of the pole.

★ **57.   God Save the Queen**   17m   HVS   5a   (1975-79)
All stand and start! Start two metres farther left and follow a crackline to the top.

★ **58.   Lubalin**   17m   E2   5b   (1983)
Three metres to the left of GStQ, up the wall to the ledges on TMBtW. After a
quick step left to protection, go back again before launching up the centre of the
headwall to a thin crack. This is then followed to the top, after clipping the peg
on the right.

★ **59.   Ten Minutes Before the Worm**   20m   VS   4c   (1976)
Follow God but not the Queen for six metres, then take an obvious line of
ledges which lead to a niche. Move past a peg to the arête, then go back right
to finish. A direct start is possible at 5b.

60.   Confusion   20m   E3   5c   (1987-90)
Climb the direct start to TMBtW, then delicately move left and climb the thin
crack right of the arête.

★★ **61.   I Shot Jason King**   18m   E5   6a   (1979-83)
Excellent climbing up the terminal left arête of the buttress, easing in its upper
reaches.

★★★ **62.   The Reaper**   15m   E6   6c   (1986)
Another excellent but rather grim route up the wall right of Zoot Chute direct to
a peg. Then move right to gain a vague groove and desperate moves up the thin
slab above which lead to a welcome ledge. Finish up Zoot Chute (peg).

The Amphitheatre

*The area of rock immediately left of Wood Buttress is known as The
Amphitheatre. It ends at a deep corner on the back wall, known as Dust at Dusk.*

** **63. Zoot Chute** 10m VS 4b (1976)
A pleasant route that covers some impressive ground for its grade. Climb the
recessed slab, then move right across a large ledge and finish up the wall above
(peg).

64. Windchill 10m HS 4b (1976)
Climb the short corner on the left, then step right to a green groove, and go up
this to an awkward exit.

65. Spindrift 10m VS 4c (1996)
Start as for Windchill, but continue directly up the crack through the bulge until
a jug on the right arête can be reached, then finish easily.

66. Saffron 15m E1 5b (1996)
The wall to the left is tackled via the crack system about two metres to the right
of a section of orange rock at half-height.

67. Amphitheatre Terrace 21m VD (1976)
The obvious terrace which splits the back wall from right to left.

68. Life During Wartime 18m HVS 5b (1981)
Follow Amphitheatre Terrace to the grassy bay (old peg), then climb up and
right on large holds until a traverse right can be made to the base of a thin
crack. Finish up this.

69. Bob Bandits 8m HVS 5b (1987)
Left of the start of Amphitheatre Terrace. Climb the obvious off-width crack in
the wall.

70. Fathomathon 8m E2 5b (1987)
Start just to the left and climb the wall to a good though doubtful jug, then
make an '*all-out-mega-span*' and climb direct to join Amphitheatre Terrace.

71. Brittle-Fingers 12m E1 5b (1987)
Left again, climb the crack to gain the bottomless groove. Pass this and finish
up the arête above on its left-hand side.

* **72. Each Way Nudger** 12m E3 6b (1982)
The overhung corner on the left. Desperate bridging moves lead to a long, blind
reach over a bulge before easier ground is reached.

73. Dust at Dusk 12m S 4a (1976)
Climb the deep, left corner at the back of The Amphitheatre.

Red Prow

*This is the obvious sandy prow of rock with a pool on three sides and a
'roadrunner-style' pinnacle on its top. It starts from the left corner at the back
of The Amphitheatre and is bounded on its left by Hidden Wall. At the side
opposite The Amphitheatre, it forms a ridge that comprises two large ledges.
The lower of these is called The Diving Board.*

74.   Specific Gravity   12m   E3   5c   (1993)
Climb the wall left of the corner stepping in from the right above the first
overhang, (peg).

★★ 75.   White Out   12m   HS   4b   (1975)
The wide crack on the left. Although a little loose at the top, the jamming crack
is irresistible.

★★★ 76.   Ice Cool Acid Test   14m   E4   6a   (1982)
Superb wall climbing to the left of White Out. Climb the wall to a ledge at
three metres, then step left from the left side of this ledge to gain a foothold
above an overlap and climb straight up the exposed wall, passing a peg on the
right at two-thirds-height. A large friend (or even a Friend) in White Out, might
inspire confidence to tackle the initial overlap.

★★★ 77.   Nobody Wept for Alec Trench   14m   E5   6a   (1982)
Undoubtedly the centrepiece of the quarry, and one of the finest arêtes on
gritstone. Ascend the striking arête starting on the right, past two pegs of
dubious worth, to a thrilling finish on sloping holds.

★★★ 78.   Chalk Lightning Crack   15m   E2   5b   (1976)
A classic thrutch-and-grope up the off-width crack splitting the buttress. Good
protection but it is still a thought-provoking lead.

★ 79.   Don't Stop Believing   15m   E2   5c   (1986)
Start just left of Chalk Lightning and climb a short wall to a crack. Go up this
to a sloping mantelshelf (crux) and a break above (Friends). Attack the wall
above, trending right at the top.

★ 80.   Roadrunner Pinnacle   15m   HVS   4c   (1996)
Climb the crack/chimney just left on excellent jugs (finish here at VS, 4c),
moving boldly right at the top of the chimney to finish in a superb position up
the right-hand side of the overhanging arête. Photogenic.

81.   Gnat Attack   12m   VS   4c   (1984)
Gain and climb the next groove/chimney to the left, either direct, or from easy
rock on the left.

★★ 82.   Falling off the Edge of the World   12m   E3   5c   (1996)
The outrageously leaning block succumbs to the fast, furious and bold approach.
Climb direct up the overhanging tower from below. A $^1/_2$ Friend protects the top
move.

83.   Omelette   12m   VS   4c   (1996)
Climb Gnat Attack until it is possible to move left and finish up the deep crack
bounding the tower on its left.

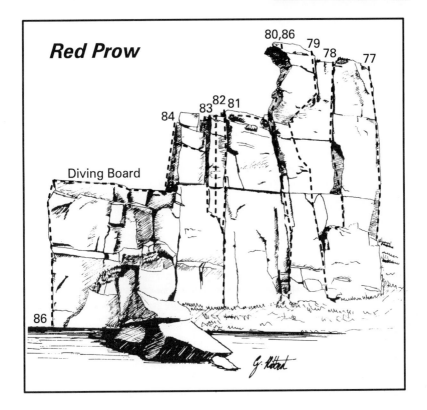

84.   Rhythm of the Heat   8m   E1   5c   (1984)
Situated above the ledge on the end of the prow; climb easily up stepped rock
just left of Gnat Attack on to *The Diving Board*, then spring up the dogleg
crack in the wall above, continuing direct where the crack sneaks off left.

85.   Acme Surplus Overhang   6m   E2   5a   (1986)
A route which completely encompasses the full spectrum of fear. Start from the
upper ledge (the one above *The Diving Board*) and climb the
roadrunner-pinnacle-type roof on the top of Red Prow. To second the route is
not to have lived – but at least you won't risk death!

⋆⋆ **86.   The Field of Dreams**   30m   VS   5a,4c,4c   (1996)
An enjoyable expedition with interesting and varied climbing on each pitch. The
start is reached from a boulder when the pond is low, or by a short traverse at
other times.
1.   10m.   Climb the right-hand arête on the end of Red Prow to a belay on *The
Diving Board*, below a dogleg crack in the wall above.
2.   10m.   Climb the dogleg crack, then traverse airily, but easily, rightwards
round the arête into a corner. Climb this and belay below the formidable
overhang.
3.   10m.   Climb the right-hand arête on its left, then swing right to finish over
the overhanging arête.

87.   Stringbiff   37m   VS   4c   (1986)
Climb the left arête on the end of the Red Prow, then the continuation arête and
finish up the easy ramp left of the previous route.

88.   Red Prow Original   21m   VS   4b   (1975)
Situated round the back of the Red Prow. When the pool is full the start can be
reached by abseil. Start in the corner and climb a rib to a thin crack, then
follow this to a ledge. Step right and go up the crack above to a ledge and large
blocks, then finish easily up a ramp on the left.

Hidden Wall

*Hidden behind the Red Prow is a short, steep wall, which rises directly out of
the pool to a tree-covered terrace.*

89.   Bombing Basil   8m   E1   5b   (1997)
Climb the short wall via two obvious niches.

Lonely Wall

*Farther left, the terrace ends and the rock rises all the way from the pool to the
top. This wall contains much rock that is obviously less-than-perfect.
Nevertheless, some of the routes are well worth doing. This area is best reached
by walking across the stepping stones then walking rightwards along the base of
the crag.*

★ **90.   Initiation**   14m   E2   5c   (1979)
Climb the obvious crack which splits the smooth, grey wall on the right.

★ **91.   Long Distance Runner**   14m   E3   5c   (1993)
Although close to the previous route, the climbing is excellent, being both
technical and exciting. Ascend the blunt arête and crack immediately left, with a
peg at half-height.

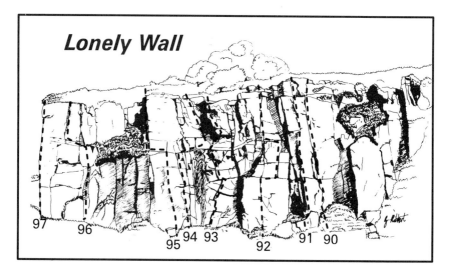

⋆ 92.   Changing of the Guards   14m   E3   5c   (1998)
Climb the steep wall four metres to the left, to a peg runner. Make a long reach
rightwards to a crack and climb this (crux) to gain a groove, then move left
across a large ledge to the base of a thin crack. Finish up this on good finger
jams.

⋆ 93.   Surfin' Bird   14m   E3   5b   (1996)
Start eight metres to the left, past a dirty chimney. Ascend the centre of the
buttress via cracks and ledges to a large ledge beneath prominent roofs.
Surmount the lower roof at its centre, trending slightly left above the next
overhang in a wild position on good holds to a superb finish.

⋆ 94.   The Water Margin   16m   HVS   5a   (1998)
Start at a shallow, flaky groove that forms the right side of a clean wall. Climb
the groove to a large ledge at mid-height, then traverse up and right to a corner.
Step back left to a ragged crack and follow this, trending left up the leaning top
wall.

⋆ 95.   Mental Mantel   17m   E2   5b   (1986)
Technical climbing leads to an interesting mantel, but round the arête there lurks
a sting in the tail. Start two metres to the left, in the centre of the clean wall, at
a small arrow and climb to a difficult mantelshelf on to sloping ledges. Step
left, around the arête and finish up the short jamming crack.

96.   Nasty Little Lonely   18m   HVS   4b   (1979-83)
Start behind a large birch tree at the left side of Lonely Wall. Climb the loose
pillars just right of a smooth red wall. Pass a peg to reach a disintegrating
ledge, then an obvious traverse left leads to a fine finish up a groove. Serious.

⋆⋆ 97.   Lucky Heather   9m   E4   5c   (1986)
A bold proposition, which has seen many top-rope rescues and snivelling
traverses off to the banking. Make a series of boulder-problem-type moves up
the left side of the left arête of the red wall, then swing right to a gripping
heathery finish. It is no place to 'linger'!

Cholera Area
*After a short break, the rock starts again with a broken wall, bounded on its
right by a wide-angled groove, that is almost directly opposite the stepping
stones.*

⋆ 98.   The Open Book   14m   E1   5b   (1998)
Why don't you read it? Start by a series of mantelshelves to reach the open
groove, then climb this and pull over the overhang in a sensational position on
good holds.

99.   Alchemy   14m   VS   4c   (1996)
15 metres farther left at a higher level is a groove on the right-hand side of a
buttress. Follow a line just to the right of this groove, then use the remnants of
a drill-hole to make a quick step into the groove near the top.

★★ **100. Summer Lightning**   14m   E4   6b   (1996)
Climb from the blocks just left of the groove (three pegs and a Friend). The
right arête is used near the top before a move left on to the final slab. A
strenuous effort.

101. Cracker   14m   HVS   5a   (1996)
Start off the blocks and gain bottomless parallel cracks, which can then be
followed to the top.

★★ **102. Cholera**   8m   HVS   5a   (1988)
First climbed the day after a cholera jab that rendered the leader's left arm
barely operational. Although the jab is not compulsory, the route should be, for
visitors who wish to sample the highlights at Egerton. Start four metres left of
the blocks and climb the off-width crack to a sloping mantelshelf finish. Not as
easy as it looks.

Empty Quarter – Lower Tier
80 metres left of Cholera, past an easy **DESCENT** *slope, the rock arcs back
left and forms two tiers. The Lower Tier offers some good climbing. At the right
side of this section the first wall is split by a thin finger-crack.*

103. Just for the Finger Jam   10m   S   4a   (1998)
Climb the thin finger-crack with big ledges on the left and finish over a block.

104. Bone Shaker   12m   VS   4c   (1998)
Eight metres farther left, climb the wide flake crack.

105. Lazy Bones   12m   S   4a   (1998)
Just to the left climb the arête on juggy holds.

106. Kamikaze Coconut   9m   HS   4b   (Pre-1979)
10 metres farther left ascend the right-facing corner.

★★ **107. Precious Cargo**   10m   E1   5b   (1998)
A difficult couple of moves up the left-hand side of the arête on the left leads
to an enjoyable finish in a fine position.

108. Alvin's Wild West Rodeo Show   10m   S   4a   (1998)
The cracks in the wall immediately to the left, starting up the right-hand crack
of the block.

★ **109. Swamp Dog**   10m   S   4a   (1998)
Pleasant bridging up the corner on the left past an overlap.

110. Space Between my Ears   12m   HS   4a   (1977)
The stepped arête on the left. Climb the crack on the right of the arête, then
finish on the left using a large detached flake.

*On the left there is a bramble-infested slope that ends 12 metres farther left at a
taller buttress characterized by an open corner at its top.*

Dennis Gleeson on **Constable's Overhang** (E5 6b), Wilton Three.   *Photo: Geoff Hibbert*

111. Empty Arête 11m HVS 5a (1998)
Start from blocks at a slightly higher level, then climb the arête on its right on widely-spaced holds. Step right using an 'interesting' block, then continue to the top via a very short chimney.

★ **112. Organ Grinder** 12m HVS 5b (1998)
Start in the centre of the wall, directly below the open corner. Climb the bottom wall until it is possible to gain the initial groove by an awkward, balancy move. The groove above eases, but footholds are widely spaced.

113. Monkey Trick 12m VS 5a (1992)
Three metres farther left there is a wide-angled corner. Climb the obvious corner crack (ledge at its base) to an overhanging headwall past an obvious thread (in-situ).

The next routes lie 30 metres to the right at a much higher level, on a wall split by a horizontal crack at two-thirds height.

114. Vulture 8m HVS 5a (1998)
Climb the right-hand side of broken blocks and make delicate moves up the wall just left of some paint streaks.

115. Double or Quits 9m HVS 5b (1998)
Climb the left-hand side of the broken blocks to an interesting mantelshelf move one metre left of the paint streaks.

116. Street Legal 9m E1 5c (1998)
Climb the left arête on its right-hand side, with good protection on the crux.

Phantom Wall
Phantom Wall is a steep, compact wall of red rock about 25 metres farther left that forms the left end of The Empty Quarter. A steep bank on its left leads up to the Upper Tier and this directly faces the bridge.

117. Return of the Native 9m E1 5c (1986)
A problem start on the right of the wall, about two metres to the left of a short corner, leads to easier ground above.

118. Tasty 9m E4 6b (1989)
Climb the very faint crack in the blank wall immediately to the left, to finish up the previous route.

★★ **119. Phantom Zone** 9m E2 5c (1986)
A steep, varied climb, with an intimidating crux at the top. The steep wall is climbed up the middle via a hairline crack to reach good finger-jams at mid-height, with the crux layback to finish.

★★★ **120. Phantom Zone Left-hand** 10m E3 5c (1986)
An even better alternative to Phantom Zone. Climb the parent route to a traverse-line going diagonally leftwards, just above the horizontal crack. Follow this until a rockover can be made, then finish up the wall above.

Dave Cronshaw walks like an Egyptian in the **O-Zone** (E3 5c), Cadshaw Quarry.

Photo: John Ryden

Empty Quarter – Upper Tier

The Upper Tier is located at the top of a grassy bank directly above Phantom Wall. It can be easily identified from a distance by some graffiti in the form of a bird with outstretched wings. The wall is mainly suitable for bouldering, but it does provide the following climbs, which it is more convenient to describe from LEFT to RIGHT.

121. Spreadeagle 8m S 4a   (1997)
From the centre of the slab, take a diagonal line leftwards to the top.

122. Lost in Egerton 10m VS 4c   (1998)
Start 10 metres to the right and climb the narrow rib just left of a protruding block.

123. Dribbles 10m HVS 5b   (1986)
Two metres farther right climb the thin crack in the clean slab to a finish on poor rock.

124. Cancer 9m VS 4c   (1982)
Climb the wall just to the right to finish up a tight, left-facing chimney.

★ **125. Step into the Groove** 10m E2 5c   (1996)
About 90 metres farther right, where the ledge widens. Start just left of the final arête and climb to the right side of a small overlap, then finish up the wall above.

Red Wall

Back on the floor of the quarry, the rock that stretches leftwards into the corner is called Red Wall. This begins as a series of impressive arêtes and corners:

★★★ **126. Renaissance** 14m E5 6a   (1996)
A must for aspiring hardmen. The striking orange arête with a peg at two-thirds-height is climbed on the left-hand side to the peg (don't blow the 5c move below the peg), then swing round the arête and layback to the top.

127. Red Shift 12m VS 4c   (1979-83)
15 metres to the left. Start just right of a blunt, stepped arête, at a block and climb the shallow groove. Finish via a flake on the left.

128. Proper Gander 12m VS 4b   (1996)
Have a 'good look' at the blunt arête itself, starting on the right.

★ **129. Whitewater Rafting** 15m VS 4b   (1998)
Start just to the left of the arête and climb a flaky crack to a small ledge at mid-height. Climb up and go right to a large ledge on the arête, then step left in an exposed position and use a flake to finish.

130. Planet of the Apes 12m HVS 5a   (1997)
Climb the flake crack just left of the next corner.

★★ **131. Brightside Revisited** 18m E3 6a   (1997)
Reminiscent of the Froggatt classic. Climb Cherry Bomb to the roof, then step right round the arête, following the break to a good handjam just before the corner. Finish direct up the wall (crux).

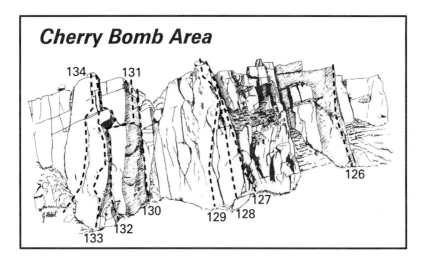

Cherry Bomb Area

★★★ **132. Cherry Bomb**   14m   VS   4c   (1977)
An excellent route, up the blatantly obvious corner that is capped by an
overhang. Once above the overhang finish on the left arête. A fine exercise in
bridging. The roof proves easier that it first appears.

★★★ **133. Satin Sapphire**   14m   E3   5c   (1978)
The fine arête to the left of Cherry Bomb is climbed in its entirety. A serious
and sustained route of great quality.

134. Silk Cut   10m   E2   5c   (1986)
Climb the thin crack just to the left to a horizontal break, then move right along
this until it is possible to finish up another crack, immediately to the left of the
arête.

*The next section of rock appears distinctly unstable and generally lives up to its
appearance.*

● **135. The Razor's Edge**   10m   HVS   4b   (1997)
The short knife-edged arête six metres to the left. Scary owing to the brittle
nature of the edge.

136. Crack   15m   VD   (1990)
Eight metres to the left is the shallow right-facing corner/groove beside
Wormhole. A couple of metres to the right of this climb the easy wall.

137. Wormhole   15m   HVS   4c   (1990)
Two metres to the left, immediately right of a corner groove, close inspection
should reveal a curious drill-hole running the height of the crag. Climb the wall
via this and the shallow corner/groove above. Worth doing, if only to inspect
the wormhole.

138. Think Light   15m   VS   4c   (1997)
Seven metres to the left is a vertical crackline formed by a large block/pedestal
on its left. Finish up the flake and groove above.

139. State of Awareness   12m   HVS   5a   (1997)
Climb the groove formed by the left side of the block, until a step left enables a
ledge on the arête to be gained. Continue up the arête.

140. Dodger   15m   S   4a   (1996)
Left of the arête is a deep crack. Climb this, dodging the loose blocks.

★ **141. Malvinas**   15m   HS   4b   (1982)
The original grade of the climb is in the name of the route. Sink your jams into
this one! Climb the wall just to the left into the obvious leaning corner.

142. Centre of Gravity   15m   HS   4b   (1997)
As for Malvinas to the ledge, then move left and finish up the arête.

143. Desert Dust   15m   HS   4b   (1985)
Three metres to the left is another corner. Climb this then finish up a wide crack.

★★ **144. Dizzy the Desert Snake**   15m   E1   5b   (1985)
Long reaches lead to a thin crux, which will sort out the men from the boys. On
the left there is a thin crack at four metres. This is gained by a jug on the left
and is then followed to a large platform. Finish up the wall above.

★ **145. Third Time Lucky**   15m   E3   5c   (1997)
A pleasant and technical slab route with a good landing. Start just left of a
grotty crack. Climb the hairline crack until a move right brings a good footledge
for a rest. Traverse left for three metres to reach a thin ledge, then mantel on
this and make a thin pull to gain the ledge above and an easy finish.

146. Why Climb Right?   15m   VS   4c   (1978)
Four metres farther left is a slab. Start in the middle of the rubble cone and
mantel at two metres, then traverse right to finish.

147. Why Climb Left?   15m   VS   4c   (1978)
From the initial mantelshelf on Why Climb Right, trend leftwards to finish.

148. Three Pint Primer   14m   VS   4b   (1998)
Climb the right-hand arête of Red Wall using a flake crack.

149. By Hook or by Crook   15m   HS   4b   (1998)
Start one metre left of the arête and climb the obvious stepped groove to the
second large ledge. Mantel on to the ledge on the left, then finish up the short
crack in the top block.
Variation Finish (4a): swing left and finish up a wide crack.

150. Esmeralda   15m   HVS   5a   (1976)
Red Wall proper starts at a slightly lower level. Climb the blocky crack that
forms a pillar on the right side of Red Wall, then finish up a short corner.
Belays well back.

★ **151. Red Wall Direct**   18m   E1   5b   (1990)
Climb the obvious wide crack directly to the top.

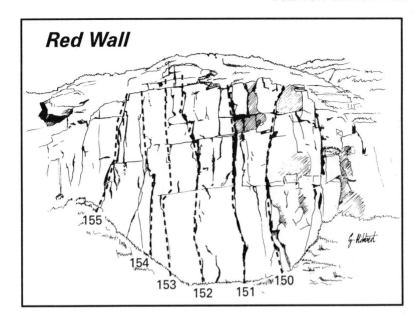

Red Wall

155
154
153
152 151 150

★★ **152. The Eleventh Hour** 18m E4 6a (1985)
Steep and sustained climbing gives a powerful route. Just before the ground
level starts to rise, twin cracks lead to the right side of a ledge. Follow these to
the ledge, then continue up the shallow groove and headwall above.

★ **153. Mumbled Prayer** 18m E3 6a (1985)
Climb the wall at a thin crack, passing the left side of the ledge on Eleventh
Hour. Good climbing.

154. Dicktrot II – The Movie 17m E2 5c (1985)
Starting at a slightly higher level climb the wider, but more indefinite, crack.

155. Needle Stick 15m HVS 4c (1997)
The line of left-facing grooves just to the left.

Grooved Wall

*The final section of rock arcs back towards the Bridge Area. For the most part
the rock is of poor quality. However, there are still several routes that are well
worth seeking out. The first climbs to be described lie some way farther to the
left, at three prominent corners just left of a* **DESCENT** *scramble and the
gravel banking.*

156. Big Mouth 10m VS 4c (1996)
The broken cracks in the steep wall right of the first corner, starting at a small
triangular niche.

★ **157. Sham '69** 15m VS 4c (Pre-1979)
Climbs the first corner which has some excellent hand-jams.

★ **158. Shudabindun**   15m   E1   5b   (1996)
Two metres to the left is a rotten arête with a large slabby scoop to its left.
Climb the scoop to a very thin crack, then follow this to an easier finish.

★ **159. That's Life**   15m   VS   4c   (1983)
Climb the next corner and finish on the right at the top.

160. The Cutter   15m   VS   4c   (1996)
The third corner, starting just to the right, then climb to the overhang with a
drill-hole in it and step right to finish.

★★★ **161. Guillotine**   15m   E3   5c   (1981)
The finger crack which opens into a peapod-like feature contains a wedged
block at its top. A classic struggle, but low in its grade.

162. Chopper Chimney   12m   S   4a   (1996)
The crack/chimney behind the detached tower two metres to the left. Move right
up the blunt arête to finish.

163. Blue Strawberry   12m   VD   (1996)
Climb the outside face of the detached tower.

★ **164. Sparkin' Bush**   15m   VS   4b   (1996)
The 'cleaned' narrow face four metres to the left. Surmount the initial bulge, to
place good protection in the left crack, then continue up the face on hidden
holds. A surprisingly good route.

165. New Groove   12m   HS   4b   (1998)
The right-leaning chimney/groove in the centre of the next wall.

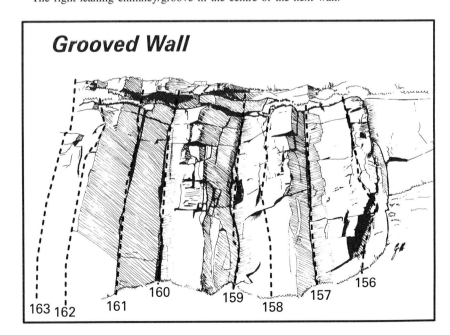

Grooved Wall

166. Black Arm 11m S 4a   (1998)
The deep corner groove that starts three metres farther left.

167. Cutting Edge 13m VS 4c   (1998)
Just round the arête on the left there is a prominent, square-cut overhang at
mid-height, with a wide crack on its right. Scramble over ledges and finish up
the wide crack.

★ **168. Walking on Glass** 15m E4 6b   (1996)
An excellent climb, which gives strenuous and technical, but well protected,
climbing. Climb to the prominent, square-cut overhang, step left on to a block,
then climb directly up to a peg at a small overlap. Undercut the break
rightwards to another peg and finish direct, slapping wildly up the right arête.

169. Vlad the Impaler 12m S 4a   (1998)
The blocky groove on the left.

170. All in the Mind 14m E2 5b   (1997)
Five metres to the left a detached tower forms a deep V-groove on its right.
Climb the wall to a ledge below the V-groove, then step right to gain the arête
and follow this to the top. Worthwhile.

171. Headspin Cleft 12m VS 5a   (1998)
Start up All in the Mind, then continue straight up the V-groove above.

172. Letter-box 15m HVS 5b   (1997)
Three metres to the left. Pleasant climbing up the front face of the detached
pillar. A problem start leads to good holds up the wide face of the detached
tower.

15 metres farther left is a very deep V-groove with a large roof at its top.

173. The Creaking Fossil 14m HVS 4c   (1986)
Climb the blunt right arête of the V-groove via an unattractive crack.

★ **174. Aethelred Groove** 14m HS 4b   (1998)
Climb the deep V-groove using the wide crack in the left wall.

★ **175. Aethelred** 14m E2 5b   (1978)
Climb the poorly-protected left arête of the V-groove.

176. Trumpton 14m S 4a   (1978)
Climb the chimney crack immediately right of the next corner, then step left and
finish up the corner, past a small tree.

First Ascents at Egerton Quarry

1974	**Thin Crack** Jim Fogg	
1975 Apr 5	**Dickie's Meadow** Tony Preston, Nigel Holmes,	
1975 June 13	**Red Prow Original** Nigel Holmes, G. Good	
1975 Sep	**White Out** Nigel Holmes, Ian Makin	
	May have been done earlier.	
1975-76	**Twilight Crack, Wide Crack**	
1976 Jan	**Dust at Dusk** Dave Knighton, Nigel Holmes	
1976 Jan 31	**Windchill** Dave Knighton, Nigel Holmes	
1976 Jan 31	**Amphitheatre Terrace** Nigel Holmes, Dave Knighton	

1976 Mar 3	**Wednesday Corner, Zoot Chute**	Dave Knighton (unseconded)
1976 Mar 30	**Ten Minutes Before the Worm**	Dave Knighton, Nigel Holmes
1976 Apr 1	**Pilgrim's Progress**	Ian Lonsdale, Dave Cain
1976 Apr 4	**Chalk Lightning Crack**	Ian Lonsdale
1976 Apr 7	**Insipidity**	Nigel Holmes, Dave Knighton
1976 Apr 7	**Gallows Pole**	Dave Knighton, Nigel Holmes
1976	**Esmeralda**	Dave Knighton, Nigel Holmes
1977 May	**Space Between my Ears**	Nigel Holmes (solo)
1977	**Cherry Bomb**	Dave Cronshaw, Bob MacMillan
1978 Feb 8	**Satin Sapphire, Why Climb Right?**	Nick Colton
1978 Mar 8	**Aethelred**	Nick Colton (solo with backrope)
1978 Apr 23	**Why Climb Left?**	Nick Colton
1978	**Just Out**	Nick Colton, Dave Knighton
1978	**Trumpton**	Nick Colton
Pre-1979	**Markova, Bridge Crack, Ludwig, The Arête, God Save the Queen, Kamikaze Coconut**	
Pre-1979	**Ceremony**	Originally climbed as Wet Dreams
Pre-1979	**Green Thoughts**	Nigel Holmes
Pre-1979	**Sham '69**	Hank Pasquill
1979	**Initiation**	Tony Brindle, Brendan Conlon
1981	**Broken Toe**	Ian Lonsdale, Nigel Holmes, Laura Holmes
1980 Oct	**Black Dog, Hydrophobia, Rabid**	John Monks, Nigel Holmes, Al Mason
1981 June	**Life During Wartime**	John Monks, Nigel Holmes, Chris Fletcher
1981	**Guillotine**	John Monks, Mick Blood, Nigel Holmes
1982 Apr 19	**Malvinas**	Ian Makin, Chris Fletcher
1982 May 27	**Nobody Wept for Alec Trench**	Dai Lampard, Nigel Holmes
1982 July 20	**Ice Cool Acid Test**	Dai Lampard, Nigel Holmes
1982	**Cancer**	Nigel Holmes, N. Kenny
1982	**Each Way Nudger**	Dai Lampard
1979-83	**Cleft Climb, Colgy, The Nose, Shaky Flakes, Red Shift, That's Life**	
1979-83	**Neighbourhood Threat**	Ian Lonsdale
1979-83	**Dicktrot**	Mark Liptrot, Dick Toon
1979-83	**Bag of Bones**	Geoff Mann, Chris Fletcher, Nigel Holmes, Dai Lampard
1979-83	**Niff-Niff the Guinea Pig**	Dai Lampard, Nigel Holmes
1979-83	**I Shot Jason King**	Mick Johnson, Ian Johnston
1979-83	**Nasty Little Lonely**	Nigel Holmes
1983 June 8	**Lubalin**	Kev Glass, Neil Hyde
1984 May 29	**The Lamb Lies Down on Broadway, Gnat Attack**	Paul Pritchard, Phil Kelly
1984 May 29	**Rhythm of the Heat**	Paul Pritchard, Phil Kelly
	Direct Start added on a later visit by Paul Pritchard and Andrew Gridley.	
1984	**The Beauty of Poison**	Nigel Holmes (solo)
1985 May 5	**Desert Dust, Dizzy the Desert Snake**	Dave Etherington, Dave Clunas
1985 June 2	**No Screws in Skem**	Geoff Hibbert, Nigel Holmes
1985 Aug	**Dicktrot II – The Movie**	Mark Liptrot (unseconded)
1985 Sep 7	**The Eleventh Hour, Mumbled Prayer**	Mark Liptrot
1985	**Talk to me Boggart**	Mark Liptrot (unseconded)
1985	**One Minute to Midnight**	Geoff Hibbert, Nigel Holmes
1985	**The Disappearing Chip Buttie Traverse**	Geoff Hibbert, Mick Bradshaw
1986 May 11	**Temptation**	Geoff Hibbert
1986 Aug	**Naff-Naff (The Route)**	Steve Kirk, Nick Walker
1986 Sep 9	**Don't Stop Believing, Acme Surplus Overhang**	Geoff Hibbert, Phil Kelly
1986	**Stringbiff**	Geoff Hibbert (solo)
1986 Sep 17	**Lucky Heather**	Geoff Hibbert, Mick Bradshaw, Phil Kelly
1986	**Return of the Native**	Geoff Hibbert, Nigel Holmes
1986	**Phantom Zone, Phantom Zone – Left-hand, Dribbles**	Geoff Hibbert
1986	**Silk Cut**	Ian Vickers, Dave Cronshaw
1986 Oct 29	**Mental Mantel**	Geoff Hibbert, Phil Kelly
1986	**The Creaking Fossil**	Geoff Hibbert
1986 Dec 23	**The Reaper**	Geoff Hibbert (unseconded)
1987	**Bob Bandits, Fathomathon, Brittle-Fingers**	Geoff Hibbert (solo)

1988	**Cholera** Geoff Hibbert, Pete Smith
1989	**Tasty** Nick Conway (solo)
1987-90	**Confusion**
1990 Aug	**Crack, Wormhole, Red Wall Direct** Geoff Hibbert, Andy Moss
1992 Nov 2	**Monkey Trick** Mark Indes (unseconded)
1993 Apr 27	**Specific Gravity** John Stringfellow, Mike Arnold
1993 May	**After the Gold Rush** Geoff Hibbert, Mick Bullough
1993 July	**Spud** Craig Entwistle, Nikki Ruane
1993	**Stolen Goods** John Stringfellow,
1993	**Lucia, Sofia** Geoff Hibbert (solo)
1993	**The Snurcher** Craig Entwistle, Nikki Ruane
1993	**Long Distance Runner** Geoff Hibbert, Chris Hemmings, Nigel Poulsom
1996 July 9	**Falling Off the Edge of the World** Geoff Hibbert, Geoff Mann
1996 Sep 19	**Surfin' Bird** Geoff Hibbert, Adam Richardson
1996 Oct 7	**Field of Screams** Geoff Hibbert, Adam Richardson
1996	**Scribbles**
1996	**J.O.B., Dragon Lady** Geoff Hibbert, Mick Bradshaw
1996	**Graffiti Corner** Alan White
1996	**Gollum** Geoff Hibbert (solo)
1996	**Feeding the Rat** Geoff Hibbert, Nick Richardson
1996	**Natural Victim** Geoff Hibbert (solo)
1996	**Dipper** Geoff Hibbert, Adam Richardson
1996 Sep 19	**Toots** Geoff Hibbert (solo)
1996	**Wiad, Egerton Cavern** Alan White
1996	**Spindrift** Geoff Hibbert (solo)
1996	**Saffron** Alan White, Nick Richardson, Brian Heywood
1996	**Roadrunner Pinnacle** Geoff Hibbert
1996	**Omelette, Cracker** Alan White, Brian Heywood
1996	**The Field of Dreams, Step into the Groove** Geoff Hibbert (solo)
1996	**Alchemy** Alan White, Brian Heywood
1996	**Summer Lightning** Geoff Hibbert, Adam Richardson, Nick Richardson
1996	**Renaissance** Geoff Hibbert, Alan White
1996	**Proper Gander, Blue Strawberry** Alan White
1996	**Big Mouth** Roy Houghton, Alan White,
1996	**Shudabindun, The Cutter, Chopper Chimney, Sparkin' Bush** Alan White, Brian Heywood
1996	**Walking on Glass** Geoff Hibbert (second did not follow)
1996	**Dodger** Alan White
1997 June	**Planet of the Apes** Geoff Hibbert (solo)
1997 June	**Brightside Revisited** Geoff Hibbert, Nick Richardson
1997 Aug 7	**Think Light, State of Awareness, Centre of Gravity, Third Time Lucky** Geoff Hibbert (solo)
1997	**Bombing Basil** Geoff Hibbert (unseconded)
1997	**Spreadeagle, The Razor's Edge** Geoff Hibbert (solo)
1997	**Needle Stick, All in the Mind, Letter-box** Geoff Hibbert, Adam Richardson
1997	**The Razor's Edge**
1998 Feb 5	**Aethelred Groove** Dave Cronshaw, Geoff Hibbert
1998 Mar 15	**Empty Arête, Organ Grinder** Dave Cronshaw, Les Ainsworth
1998 Mar 21	**Vlad the Impaler** Geoff Hibbert, Dave Cronshaw
1998 Mar 22	**New Groove, Cutting Edge** Dave Cronshaw, Les Ainsworth
1998 Mar 22	**Black Arm** Les Ainsworth, Dave Cronshaw
1998 Apr 1	**Headspin Cleft** Geoff Hibbert (solo)
1998 Apr 2	**Open Book** Geoff Hibbert, Dave Cronshaw, Chris Fletcher
1998 Apr 2	**Bone Shaker** Dave Cronshaw, Geoff Hibbert, Chris Fletcher
1998 Apr 2	**Lazy Bones, Precious Cargo, Swamp Dog** Geoff Hibbert (solo)
1998 Apr 2	**Alvin's Wild West Rodeo Show** Geoff Hibbert (solo)
1998 Apr 5	**Whitewater Rafting** Dave Cronshaw, Les Ainsworth, Geoff Hibbert
1998 Apr 12	**Vulture** Adam Richardson, Geoff Hibbert
1998 Apr 12	**Street Legal, Double or Quite** Geoff Hibbert, Adam Richardson
1998 Apr 13	**Three Pint Primer** Geoff Hibbert, Adam Richardson, Rob O'Hara
1998 Apr 13	**Changing of the Guards** Geoff Hibbert, Adam Richardson

Lester Mill Quarry
O.S. ref.   SD 619 164

Situation and Character

The quarry lies on the opposite side of the Rivington–White Coppice road to Anglezarke Quarry and is of similar rock. However, it was worked up until the 1930s and does not see a lot of activity, so some suspect rock is still present. This is localised and should improve with traffic. Special care should be taken with Cheese Buttress, The Set Back and the Upper Right Tier. However, recent cleaning has improved these areas considerably and many of the climbs deserve to become more popular, particularly on the higher section at Evil Wall. It is a pity that many climbers who visit Anglezarke across the road do not also spend a short time here.

History

Lester Mill Quarry ceased to be worked in the 1930s and previous to this, stone was taken (along with that from Anglezarke) to pave the city of Salford. The quarry's name derives from Robert Lester, who once owned a small mill that stood nearby and in fact both this quarry and Anglezarke were collectively known as Lester's Mill Quarries.

Much of the early development is still locked securely away in the memories of the participants and it is doubtful as to whether anything more will ever emerge.

The earliest known route is the classic arête of *Lester Rib* which was climbed by Ray Evans and Paul Hancock in 1960 at the age of fourteen. This was a couple of years before Evans started climbing properly and they were armed only with a clothes-line that they hung from their waists whilst they both soloed the climb. Evans admits that *'Halfway up we used our knees on a mantel and we had a real struggle with it'*. There were no further developments until 1970, when John Bennison, Arthur Hassall, Walt Unsworth and Bev Heslop led a more organized assault on the quarry. During that period an educational report known as the Newsom Report was published and as most of the aforementioned climbers were teachers, they were soon acting on its recommendations in taking pupils out of the classrooms to give 'instruction through experience', and so one of their early routes was, naturally, called *Newsom Slab*.

Bennison was working at Southland's School and visited the quarry one afternoon a week with his students and almost certainly added such routes as *Southland's Scoop, Introductory Crack, Caerphilly, Small Oak Crack* and *Lester Corner*. Hassall climbed *Blossom* with one peg and *Stilton* was pegged by unknown climbers.

Later, towards the end of the decade (and into the next), Les Ainsworth and Brian Cropper were active and the Upper Buttress was developed. The first route on Evil Wall was *Doomsday*, which was climbed by Geoff Rigby and Bernie Bradbury and then came Al Evans's *Pagan* and Dave Walsh's *Heretic*, up the right-hand side of the wall. Roger Walsh also freed two aid routes – *Mixed Veg* and *Jane's Route*.

In 1978 there was renewed interest in the back walls and Jim Wyllie and friends put up *Bat Out of Hell* and *Neon Shuffle* whilst Paul Cropper added *P.C.2*. In '82 Dave Sanderson and Roger Bunyon did several routes in the same area, including *Lancashire Crumbly, Fool's Paradise* and *Resolute Roc*. However, the main section of the wall remained untouched, mainly due to its oft-wet character, though this problem was soon to be resolved when in 1982 Ian Lonsdale persuaded North West Water to divert the drainage away from the face. The result was a complete success and the wall dried out totally, paving the way for Lonsdale and Cronshaw to make incursions on to the wall the following year, to produce a series of excellent routes.

Cronshaw led *The Beast, Return to Fantasy* and *Non-Stop Screamer*, since when there has been little farther interest in development on the upper walls.

In 1996 Ian McDonald made a notable ascent of *Don't Think* to free the previous aid route, The Rurper. Then, in 1997, just prior to the publication of this guidebook, Carl Spencer moved over the road from Anglezarke, having been there in situ for the summer whilst working on the guidebook and spent three evenings removing more loose rocks and brambles, to the interest of many a dog-walker. The following weekend, Spencer returned along with Mark Garratt to create the bold line of *To Infinity and Chuck a Left* – the first new line on Evil Wall for fifteen years.

Access and Approach

The quarry is owned by North West Water. In the past the company has diverted a stream to improve climbing at the crag and they continue to be happy to permit climbing.

Park as for Anglezarke and from the opposite side of the road to Anglezarke walk down for about 50 metres to a fence just above the top of the quarry. The foot of the quarry can then be reached by a scramble down about 50 metres farther on, which leads to the right-hand side of Introductory Bay. Alternatively, from the lower car park, follow the tarmac path that leads through a kissing gate at the bottom end towards the reservoir. About 40 metres after the junction with another path, there is a grassy path on the right that leads to the quarry entrance and Introductory Bay is the first rock to be encountered. To reach Evil Wall, it is best to continue along the main path for a short way until the rock can be seen.

To gain a proper orientation of the quarry it is best to view the crag from the hill above the tarmac path alongside the reservoir. The upper section of the quarry, Introductory Bay to the Upper Right Tier is described first. Evil Wall is the main wall that starts directly below the Upper Tier and Jane's Buttress is low on the left of Evil Wall.

The Climbs

The climbs are described from RIGHT to LEFT.

Introductory Bay
This is characterized by a sharp arête at the base of a conical-shaped banking and the leaning wall of Stilton.

1.   Introductory Crack 10m   VD   (1970)
Where the rocks first gain a respectable height there is a wide, broken crack.
Follow this and the rib above.

2.   Southland's Scoop 15m   S   4a   (1970)
A deep scoop five metres to the left. Climb to a big grass ledge on the left, then
go up the wall, working right to a short, wide crack to the top. Or climb direct
to the top from the scoop at HS.

3.   Stilton 12m   HVS   5b   (1970/1975-79)
Three metres left of the scoop, twin cracks lead to the ledge, then finish up a
short wall.

4.   Blue Stilton 14m   E2   5c   (1987)
Climb Stilton to a pegged break on the left. Traverse left and finish for Double
Gloucester.

5.   Double Gloucester 12m   HVS   5a   (1975-79)
Two metres to the left climb the crack in the leaning wall to reach the large
ledge, then finish as Stilton.

6.   Caerphilly 12m   VS   4b   (1975-79)
The broken groove on the left leads to a triangular block just below the large
ledge, then pull right on to the ledge and finish as for Stilton.

7.   Puff Pastry 11m   HS   4a   (1997)
Climb the broken groove which forms the angle of the bay, then finish up the
short corner above.

8.   Flaky Pastry 9m   VS   4c   (1986-87)
A direct line up the centre of the wall just to the right of Flake Wall's start.

★ **9.   Flake Wall** 15m   VS   4c   (1970)
This is the short wall at right-angles to the previous climbs, and facing the
quarry entrance. Start at the left arête and go slightly right to gain a detached
flake above a horizontal crack. Climb this, then move left to a ledge on the
arête and finish on the right of this.

10.   Blossom 14m   HVS   5a   (1970)
Climb cracks in the right wall of the gully.

Lester Buttress
*This is the next buttress, at the other side of the conical banking. A small ledge
at three metres running out from the banking marks the start of the first route.*

11.   Jughandle Wall 6m   VS   4b   (1977)
Climb up the centre of the small wall just left of the grassy banking, crossing
the overlap on excellent holds.

12. Small Oak Crack 9m HS 4b   (1970)
A wide crack with jammed blocks and an oak tree at its top, just beyond the
grassy hummock.

13. Lester Corner 8m VD   (1970)
Start as for Lester Rib, but go right using a flake, into the corner and up this to
a grass ledge. Scrappy.

14. Sleeping Genie 14m VS 4c   (1986-87)
Climb Lester Corner to the flake, then go directly up the overhanging wall to a
niche then finish up the slabby wall above.

★ **15. Lester Rib** 15m VD   (1960)
At the end of the wall climb the prominent rib and a short corner above.

★ **16. Lester Eliminate** 14m VS 4c   (1972)
Start just round the rib and climb past two overhangs into a hanging crack
which leads to the top.

17. Silent Solace 14m E3 6a   (1992)
Start as for Lester Eliminate and climb the thin crack that rises directly from the
left side of the overhang.

18. Wirebrush Crack 10m VS 4c   (1976)
The crackline one metre left of the roof.

★ **19. Newsom Slab** 9m HS 4b   (1970)
10 metres farther left and at right-angles is a steep, grey slab. Use the thin
finger crack to climb the slab until a step right can be made. Step up then go
left on good finishing holds.

Pinnacle Buttress
*Left of Newsom Slab is a short break, before the next buttress, which is split on
its right by a large ledge and is limited on its left by a broken corner gully past
some large flakes.*

20. Pina Colada 10m VS 4c   (1985)
From the trees ascend leftwards over ledges to the right-hand side of a pinnacle,
then climb the thin diagonal crack to the large ledge and finish easily.

21. Pinnacle Route 12m S 4a   (1976-77)
Follow Left Twin Groove until a wide crack on the right can be started. Follow
this to the top of a pinnacle, then finish up the short wall above.

22. Right Twin Groove 12m VD   (1972)
The right-hand groove next to the flake.

23. Left Twin Groove 12m S 4a   (1972)
The left-hand groove, then step left and go up a short crack to finish.

Cheese Buttress

After a grotty, corner groove on the left above a grass-covered rubble cone, the
rock increases slightly in height. This section which forms the remainder of the
bay, is known as Cheese Buttress.

24.   Klink   12m   HS   4a   (1975-79)
This route takes the wide crack which starts where the ground levels out. The
top is loose.

25.   Lancashire Crumbly   14m   HS   4a   (1982)
Start one metre to the left and climb the slab via a scoop directly to a ledge.
Step right and climb the upper crack of Klink to a ledge, then finish up an arête.

26.   Cheese Spread   15m   S   4a   (1979-83)
Climb the wall just right of the left arête to reach the second ledge. From the
next ledge finish up the wall above.

27.   Wensleydale   15m   S   4a   (1975-79)
The corner is taken direct.

28.   Bat Out of Hell   14m   VS   4c   (1978)
Start just left of the corner. Climb the wall and a wide curving crack to a finish
up the obvious slanting chimney above.

29.   Delta Dawn   15m   VS   4b   (1975-79)
Start at the next crack left and trend left, then back right to a flake and finish as
for Bat Out of Hell.

30.   Big Eyed Beans from Venus   12m   VS   4c   (1975-79)
Four metres left of the corner is a slanting chimney groove at the top. Starting
at the right side of 'TG' chipped in the rock, climb directly to this groove, then
to the top. Care is needed with the rock.

31.   Forte Dicks   12m   E2   5c   (1986-87)
Start at a crack just left of where 'TG' has been chipped out of the rock. Climb
the crack to a ledge then climb direct to the top using the continuation crack in
the wall. From the top ledge, finish up a short crack. This route could become
much easier if a couple of loose blocks in the initial crack fall out.

★ **32.   Neon Shuffle**   10m   HVS   5a   (1978)
Climb the arête directly using the thin crack for protection.

The Set Back

This is the name given to the continuation walls on the left of the arête, past a
rise in the ground level that form the next bay.

★ **33.   P.C.2**   8m   HVS   5b   (1975-79)
Three metres to the left of the arête climb the thin crack direct.

34.   Fool's Paradise   8m   S   4a   (1982)
Two metres to the left climb the broken groove for six metres to a ledge, then
finish up a short wall.

35.   The Other Man's Alternative 9m S 4a   (1979-83)
Climb the next crack to a ledge. Traverse three metres right and finish up a
short corner.

36.   Juggernaut 9m VS 4b   (1982)
Climb a pedestal and wall to a break, then ascend the buttress above via a niche
on the face and finish direct. Poor protection on the crux.

37.   Hit by a Lorry HS 4a   (1982)
Climb to the break on Juggernaut, then traverse four metres left and finish as
for Moorland Tooth Highway.

★ **38.   Resolute Roc** 9m VS 4b   (1982)
The flake crack two metres to the left is followed to a break, then climb the
steep wall above using a crack to finish.

39.   Moorland Tooth Highway 8m HS 4a   (1982)
Climb the crack on the right of a detached tooth to a break, then finish up the
corner. Loose.

40.   Gully Climb 10m VD   (1979-83)
Start immediately to the left and climb left over blocks to finish up the gully.

41.   Gully Variant 10m S 4a   (1985)
Gain the gully via the corner crack on the left.

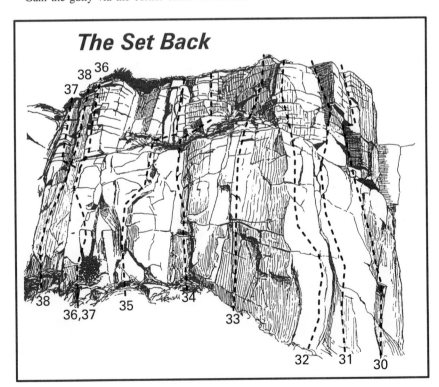

The Set Back

★ 42.   Mythical Madonna   10m   VS   4c   (1978)
Gain the large pedestal on the right via a crack on its left, then make a hard finish directly up a crack in the nose.

43.   Las Vegas Turnaround   10m   VS   4c   (1978)
On the other side of the rib is a crack. Climb this and the corner on its left.

44.   Red Leicester   10m   HS   4a   (1975-79)
The steep, pod-shaped crack in the narrow wall just to the left.

45.   Cheddar   10m   VS   4c   (1975-79)
In the centre of the wall on the left is a crack. Climb this directly over a small overlap at the top to an airy finish.

46.   Camembert   10m   E1   5b   (1985)
Start one metre to the left and follow leaning, twin cracks.

47.   Lead Penguin   10m   HS   4b   (1975-79)
The next arête is followed directly. Peg (not in-situ).

Orange Bay
The aptly-named bay immediately to the left contains the next routes: The bay ends at the deep flake crack of Brian's Route.

48.   The Blimp   10m   HVS   5a   (1975-79)
The thin crack one metre to the left of the arête.

49.   Mirror Man   9m   HVS   5a   (1975-79)
Climbs the wall just to the left of The Blimp, on small flakes.

50.   Woolly Bully   9m   VD   (1975-79)
From the corner a flake crack leads easily rightwards. Loose.

51.   Black Betrayal   12m   VS   4c   (1975-79)
Start behind a tree and climb the thin flake crack two metres to the right of Brian's Route, finishing as for that route.

52.   Brian's Route   10m   VS   4b   (1974-75)
The prominent wide flake crack.

Upper Right Tier
Beyond Brian's Route the terrace at the foot of the crag begins to narrow and becomes the Upper Tier to Evil Wall. Eventually it becomes very narrow and precarious, especially if it is overgrown.

53.   Blue Tile   10m   HVS   5a   (1975-79)
Start up the blunt arête just to the left, then climb to a small ledge and finish up the arête (peg not in situ).

54.   Walk Up   9m   S   4a   (1975-79)
Climb the flake just to the left, then step left and finish up the continuation flake.

★ 55. 10-Metre Crack 10m VS 4c   (1974)
Two metres to the left is an open corner with a thin flake crack in it. Climb the
flake to the top.

56. On Reflection 10m VS 4c   (1975-79)
Start at the arête on the left, where the path begins to narrow, and climb it
directly to a poor finish.

57. Kentaxnip 10m VS 5a   (1975-79)
Climb the next corner to a ledge and a doubtful block at half-height, then go up
the groove to the top.

58. Barnstorm 10m VS 4c   (1975-79)
The next arête is taken direct (peg).

59. Grit Salad Surgery 12m HVS 5b   (1975-79)
Ascend the flake just left of the arête, then traverse left and go up the overhang
to the top, to an exciting finish.

Evil Wall

*In the middle of the quarry below the Upper Right Tier, is a huge shattered
wall at a much lower level, which is named Evil Wall.*

DESCENT: for all routes, except Doomsday, is rightwards along the terrace
below the Upper Tier.

60. The Corner 15m HS 4b   (1974-75)
The right-hand corner, with a tree at mid-height.

★ 61. Heretic 21m E1 5c   (1978)
Follow The Corner, then step left just below the tree and ascend a crack to a
ledge. Continue directly up the wall on small holds (peg).

★ 62. Pagan 21m E1 5b   (1978)
Start three metres to the left of Heretic. Move round the overhang on good
holds and go up to an in-situ peg, then continue to a higher horizontal break
and traverse left to a good resting ledge. Move up right to another ledge and
climb a crack to the top of a huge flake. The thin crack above leads with
increasing difficulty (peg) to the top.

63. Mixed Veg 24m HVS 5b   (1974/1976-77)(1983)
Just right of an overhanging groove is a block-overhang. Climb this using a thin
crack, to a ledge on the left. Move up to a second ledge, then step left and
climb the corner crack above to finish.
Direct Start (HVS, 5b): climb the overhanging groove direct to the corner.

★★ 64. To Infinity and Chuck a Left 21m E4 6a   (1997)
A bold companion route to Evil Crystal, which takes the steep wall and bulge to
the right of the cave stance on Evil Crystal. Two metres left of the overhanging
groove of Mixed Veg a steep and very shallow corner is capped by two small
overhangs. Climb the corner (peg) to pass the second overhang on its left (crux).
Mantel on the ledge and ascend the wall and crack on the right of the cave to

gain a large flake. Continue upwards, then follow the obvious diagonal line of flakes and ledges on the left, to finish at the same point as Evil Crystal. An alternative finish at the same grade is possible by climbing slightly upwards from the large flake, then moving slightly right to finish at a thin crack. A direct finish has also been climbed, but is not recommended, because of loose blocks at the top.

★★ **65.   Evil Crystal**   21m   E1   5b,4c   (1979)

A must for the first time visitor to Evil Wall. Start six metres to the left, below a niche/cave. Better done in one pitch.

1.   9m.   Up the flake crack until it peters out, and continue to a poor stance in a cave.

2.   12m.   Follow the crack on the left to a ledge, then go up the wall (peg) and climb flakes to the top.

★★ **66.   The Beast**   25m   E3   6a   (1983)

A worthy companion to Evil Crystal, with some technical, but well protected, moves to gain the niche. Start just left of Evil Crystal. Climb up to the overhang and traverse left to a small ledge. Gain the niche above with difficulty and finish directly to a small tree.

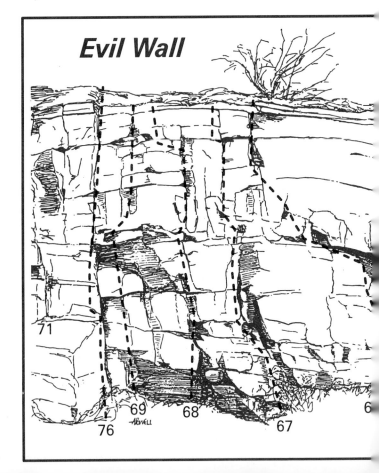

★ **67. Escharchado** 21m E3 5c (1982)
Four metres to the left is a flake crack. Climb this to a break at half-height, then climb the groove above to a small overhang three metres from the top. Move up and left to finish. Two in-situ pegs.

★ **68. Non-stop Screamer** 23m E2 5b (1983)
Start six metres to the left of Escharchado and climb blocks and a thin crack to gain a groove. Follow the groove to a sloping ledge on the left and finish up a short wall.

69. Don't Think 24m E5 6b (1974/1996)
Free climbs the aid route previously known as The Rurper. Start just right of Return to Fantasy at an old ring peg below an overhang. Follow a thin crackline to the overhang, then continue up the steep wall and thin crack above.

★ **70. Return to Fantasy** 21m E2 5c (1983)
Start in the corner on the left with a sloping ledge at six metres. Climb the corner to the ledge and gain the crack above. Follow this with increasing difficulty to the top.

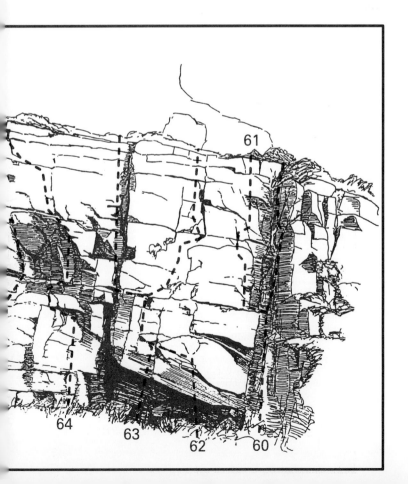

★ 71. Doomsday 23m   VS   5a   (1970)
The route takes the obvious large corner which rises from the large sloping
ledge at the left side of Evil Wall. Gain the ledge (possible belay) and climb the
corner. A recent rockfall over the top of this route has made it difficult to exit.
Therefore, it would be best to abseil from the top of the corner.

Jane's Buttress
*The final routes are located on a small buttress with a prow-shaped overhang at
its centre, which lies about three metres left of Doomsday.*

72. Gorgonzola 9m   VS   4c   (1977)
Climb the crackline just right of Jane's Route and finish up a short corner.

73. Jane's Route 10m   E1   5b   (1974/1977)
Start directly below the prow-shaped overhang and climb a crack to a sapling.
Pull up to good holds and finish direct (peg).

On the left side of the next bay are some short easy climbs and a traverse.

First Ascents at Lester Mill Quarry

1960	**Lester Rib** Ray Evans, Paul Hancock (both solo)
1970	**Introductory Crack, Southland's Scoop, Flake Wall, Small Oak Crack, Lester Corner, Newsom Slab** John Bennison
1970	**Stilton** (A1)
	First free ascent by Dave Cronshaw, Bob MacMillan, 1975-79.
1970	**Blossom** Arthur Hassall
1970 July	**Doomsday** Geoff Rigby, Bernie Bradbury
Pre-1972	**Right Twin Groove, Left Twin Groove**
1972	**Lester Eliminate** Les Ainsworth, Dave Cronshaw
1974	**10-Metre Crack** Brian Cropper, John Tout
1974	**Mixed Veg** (1pt aid) Brian Cropper, John Phillips
	Aid eliminated by Roger Walsh, Ken Linkman, 1976-77.
	Direct Start by Dave Cronshaw (solo), 11 Sep 1983.
1974	**The Rurper** (A2) Brian Cropper
	First free ascent by Ian McDonald, as Don't Think, June 1996.
1974	**Jane's Route** (A1) Brian Cropper
	First free ascent by Ken Linkman, Brian Cropper, 1976
1974-75	**Brian's Route** Brian Cropper
1974-75	**The Corner**
1976 Aug 18	**Wirebrush Crack** Dave Knighton, Allan Whalley
1976-77	**Mixed Veg** Roger Walsh, Ken Linkman
	Aid eliminated.
1976-77	**Pinnacle Route** Roger Walsh, Ken Linkman
1977 Feb 7	**Gorgonzola** Roger Walsh, Ken Linkman
1977	**Jughandle Wall** Stephen Lee
1978 Mar 11	**Pagan** Al Evans, Paul Cropper
1978 Mar	**Mythical Madonna, Las Vegas Turnaround** Nadim Siddiqui, Jim Wylie, Steven Beresford
1978 Apr 16	**Bat Out of Hell, Neon Shuffle** Jim Wyllie, Steven Beresford, Nadim Siddiqui, Brian Cropper
1978	**P.C.2** Paul Cropper, Rehan Siddiqui
1978	**Heretic** Roger Walsh, Dave Walsh
1978	**Evil Crystal** Ian Lonsdale, Dave Knighton (alts)
1975-79	**Stilton** Dave Cronshaw, Bob MacMillan
	First free ascent.
1975-79	**Double Gloucester** Bob MacMillan, Dave Cronshaw
1975-79	**Caerphilly** Bob MacMillan, Dave Cronshaw

1975-79	Klink, Wensleydale, Delta Dawn, Big Eyed Beans from Venus, Red Leicester, Cheddar, Lead Penguin, The Blimp, Mirror Man, Woolly Bully, Black Betrayal, Blue Tile, Walk Up, On Reflection, Kentaxnip, Barnstorm, Grit Salad Surgery
1982 Apr 18	Escharchado Dave Cronshaw, John Ryden
1982	*Whip Me! Whip Me!*, Lancashire Crumbly, Fool's Paradise, Juggernaut, Hit by a Lorry, Resolute Roc, Moorland Tooth Highway Dave Sanderson, Roger Bunyan
1979-83	Cheese Spread, The Other Man's Alternative, Gully Climb
1983 Aug 23	Non-stop Screamer Dave Cronshaw, Dave Hetherington, John Ryden
1983 Aug 25	Return to Fantasy Dave Cronshaw, Greg Rimmer
1983 Sep 1	The Beast Dave Cronshaw, John Ryden
1985	Pina Colada, Camembert Dave Sanderson
1985	Gully Variant
1986-87	Flaky Pastry, Sleeping Geenie, Forte Dicks
1987	Blue Stilton Chris Marshall (solo)
1992 Nov 19	Silent Solace Mark Indes (solo)
1996 June	Don't Think Ian McDonald (unseconded) *First free ascent of The Rurper.*
1997 July	Puff Pastry Dave Cronshaw, Les Ainsworth
1997 Aug 6	To Infinity and Chuck a Left Carl Spencer, Mark Garratt

Lower Montcliffe Quarry   O.S. ref. SD 653 121

Situation and Character
This small quarry lies on Rivington Moor, overlooking Horwich, about one kilometre north-east of the town. The rock is steep and very fractured gritstone, that attains a maximum height of about 14 metres. The Horwich Wall often stays dry when all else in the area is sodden.

There are further routes to be done in the quarry, but these will require some cleaning.

History
The quarry has been climbed on since at least the early 1966 when Ray Evans did a couple of climbs on the back wall, but these cannot now be identified. However, no details were recorded, though *Show us Yer Topos* and *The 10p Giro* were reported in the 1987 guidebook. Almost certainly, most of the climbs that are now recorded, were done earlier, but no records were kept.

Approach
To reach the quarry from Wilton or Brownstones, follow Scout Road for about one kilometre to the B6226 (Horwich–Bolton road) at Bob's Smithy, then turn right towards Horwich. Just over one kilometre farther on, fork right along George's Lane, and park about 500 metres along this, where the road narrows and directly below the far end of the working quarry at Montcliffe. Walk along the road for about 100 metres to a signed footpath on the left, which arcs leftwards to the quarry entrance after a couple of minutes walk.

George's Lanes can also be reached from junction 6 of the M61, by turning towards the Reebok Stadium, then at the A673 (Bolton–Horwich) roundabout, turn left. After 400 metres turn right immediately before the second set of pedestrian lights into Ainsworth Avenue, which eventually becomes New Chapel Lane. Continue up this road, keeping left at a fork after 400 metres, then after a sharp right bend, the road turns into a narrow twisting lane. This meets the main road at Ye Jolly Crofters. Turn right, then immediately left along George's Lane.

The Climbs

The quarry forms a horseshoe, within which the routes are described from LEFT to RIGHT.

The Pillar

The first two climbs lie on an isolated section, characterized by a deep corner, just left of the quarry entrance.

1.   Entrance Corner   6m   VD   (Pre-1997)
The deep corner.

2.   Montcliffe Pillar   6m   VD   (Pre-1997)
The right side of the corner forms a pillar. Climb the front face of this, keeping right of the arête.

Horwich Wall

After a short grassy gap, the main section starts at a clean wall known as Horwich Wall. There is a belay stake well back.

3.   Wanderers' Return   8m   VS   4b   (1997)
Follow the prominent flake in the centre of the wall to a ledge then finish up a short jamming crack.

4.   Formula One Bribery   8m   E1   5c   (1998)
Climb the cracked wall directly, starting at a short, deep crack one metre right.

★ **5.   Horwich Eliminate**   8m   E1   5b   (1997)
Climb directly up the wall between Formula One Bribery and Horwich Groove.

6.   Horwich Groove   8m   S   (1997)
The flaky groove that forms the right side of the wall.

7.   Cracked Pillar   8m   HS   4b   (1997)
Climb the pillar on the right via an obvious, ragged crack.

Rivington Wall

This is the back wall of the quarry, which lies roughly parallel to George's Lane. Some climbs have been done, but more cleaning is still needed and so they are not currently recorded.

Bolton Wall

The right-hand section of the quarry comprises two higher and more compact walls, separated by a deep alcove.

8.   Step Left   10m   E2   5c   (1998)
Start below a neb above the crag and climb the thin crack, then step left at half-height.

9. Inverted Y 10m VS 4c (1997)
Climb twin cracks in the centre of the first wall until they join, then finish up
the flake crack above.

10. Slim Corner 10m VS 4b (Pre-1987)
Two metres farther right climb the right-facing groove.

★ **11. Show us yer Topos** 10m E1 5b (Pre-1987)
The prominent, overhung groove between the two walls, which has a peg low
down, proves difficult at the bulge. Follow the slabby upper section and exit on
the left.

★ **12. Stadium** 10m HVS 5a (1998)
Three metres to the right of the alcove there is a thin, curving crack that widens
at its top. Climb this, then finish easily over blocks.

13. The 10p Giro 10m E1 5b Pre-1987
Two metres to the right is a thin peg-scarred crack. Climb this to a finish up
Stadium.

14. Letter-box Wall 10m E1 5b (Pre-1994)
Start two metres farther right and climb the cracked wall above the right-hand
side of a letter-box at three metres.

15. Bolton Staircase 12m HS 4a (Pre-1997)
Start three metres to the right. Climb up to a ledge, then move right to a short
corner and climb the blunt rib on the right using sloping holds. This route may
become easier with cleaning.

First Ascents at Lower Montcliffe Quarry

These are all first recorded ascents. It is highly likely that many were done
much earlier.

Pre 1987	**Show us yer Topos, The 10p Giro**
Pre-1994	**Letter-box Wall**
Pre-1997	**Entrance Corner, Montcliffe Pillar, Bolton Staircase**
1997	**Wanderers Return, Horwich Eliminate, Horwich Groove, Cracked Pillar,**
	Inverted Y, Slim Corner Dave Cronshaw, Les Ainsworth
1998	**Stadium, Step Left, Formula One Bribery** Dave Cronshaw, Les Ainsworth

Ousel's Nest
O.S. ref. SD 731 142

Situation and Character

The quarry offers good climbing in a very pleasant situation just west of
Jumbles Reservoir and about five kilometres north of Bolton. It is a only a short
walk from Bromley Cross station.

The crag is short, but steep and most of the climbs are strenuous. In the past,
vegetation and a pool at the foot have dissuaded many from climbing at Ousel's
Nest. However, the crag has now been cleaned and there is better access to the
rock, which has considerably improved the crag. The reward for visitors will be
many good, hard routes, including a few excellent lines, that have not yet been
climbed.

History

Ancient pegs greeted Carl Dawson and John Spencer when they 'discovered' Ousel's Nest on New Year's Day in 1968. Spencer returned later with Steve Jones and this pair ascended and named *Hogmanay Slab*, though it is now obvious that Jim Fogg and many others had in fact climbed it earlier. Jones himself had paid an earlier, forgotten visit to the crag and had climbed a line over on the right-hand side of the crag that he named *The Peeler*, though no details are now available. Spencer teamed up with Phil Bond that April and climbed a route which they named *Freak-Out*, though it is now known as *Metropolis*.

In May, Spencer and Dawson finally managed to entice the Wilton lads over to Ousel's, telling them tales of 75-foot overhanging walls, clean grooves and soaring arêtes. Amongst that team was Hank Pasquill, who left a calling card in the shape of *The Crucifix*, which retains its two points of aid to this day. Dave Kenyon and Ian Lonsdale climbed *Resurrection* over on the right-hand extremity of the main wall, whilst 'Little Sid' Siddiqui cleaned the wall just to its left, which Nick Colton inadvertently pinched and called *Sorry Sid*. Pete Grimshaw climbed *Please Ring the Plumber* later that year and *Anarchy*, then Nick Colton added *Earwig*. Siddiqui meanwhile followed Paul Cropper up *Angel Delight* and thus things remained until Geoff Hibbert began to explore the untapped potential of the crag in 1984.

Beginning with *Prayer Battery*, climbed with Mick Bradshaw, Hibbert began to systematically work through all the remaining gaps, in May adding *Pigeon Toad Orange Peel*, then the 'big cherry' at the crag and later succeeded on *Gauntlet Route*, again with Bradshaw, and also a direct line up Hogmanay Slab, entitled *Chasing Rainbows*.

In 1986, Mark Liptrot paid a short visit and happened to encounter Hibbert at the crag. Eliciting some information from Geoff, he later used it for his own gain (naughty). Firstly he repeated Pigeon Toad Orange Peel, describing it as 'hard', then he broke out left to create the fine and aptly-named *A Thief in the Night*. His other routes included *Exile and The Kingdom, Mr and Mrs Liptrot Go to the Seaside, Napoleon Solo* and a girdle of the left-hand section of the main wall – *The Hollow Men*. Then in 1990, Andy Griffith soloed the impressive *Faith and Energy*.

Access and Approach

The quarry is in the Jumbles Country Park which is owned by Bolton Council. Currently the Council take a pro-active approach that encourages climbing at the crag.

The easiest approach is from the A666 at Dunscar war memorial. Follow the B6472 towards Bromley Cross and turn left past Bromley Cross railway station (on Bolton–Blackburn line), immediately before a railway bridge. Follow this road (Chapeltown Road) for one kilometre to Prospect Hill Cottages on the left. Turn right and go down to a parking area. On foot follow the path down from the car park and go down into the quarry

The Climbs

When walking across lush green fields to the rock face, a wall will be seen on the extreme right of some trees. The first route starts on an overgrown slab just to the right. The routes are described from RIGHT to LEFT.

Main Wall

1. Little Wall 8m VD 5a (1990)
Climb the middle of the slab, with a technical move to get off the ground.

2. Captain Hookleg 10m HVS 5a (1986)
Climb direct past the tree stump and follow thin crack above to big ledges.

3. Resurrection 10m HVS 5a (1978)
Just left of a tree stump in the rock three metres above the ground climb the obvious crack.

4. Sorry Sid 10m HVS 5a (1978)
Start three metres to the left in an overhung niche and climb direct, stepping right at three-quarters-height, then finish direct.

5. Angel's Kiss 10m E2 5a (1979-83)
The unprotected off-width crack one metre to the left.

6. Wiggerley Worm 10m HVS 5a (1985)
Start a couple of metres right of Please Ring the Plumber, at an obvious crack, and climb this.

7. Please Ring the Plumber 9m VS 4c (1978)
The often-damp groove just right of the point at which the trees finish.

8. The Red Rose 9m E2 5b (1986)
A couple of metres to the left, climb twin cracks to the wide upper crack. Layback this to the top.

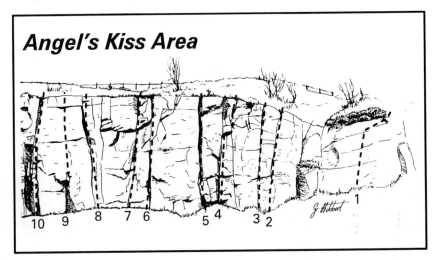

Angel's Kiss Area

9.   Faith and Energy 10m E4 6a   (1990)
Climb the wall just left of Red Rose, with the crux low down.

10.   Lace 9m HVS 5a   (1986)
Three metres to the left, past a blank slab is a crack. Climb this in its entirety.

★★ **11.   Gauntlet Route** 10m E3 5c   (1985)
Originally climbed with a motorcycle glove placed over a pointed branch which
would have impaled anyone taking a fall above the groove. This has now been
pruned to discourage the wrong sort of visitors to the crag. Left again is a
deceptively-easy-looking groove; climb this and the overhanging crack above to
finish on good jugs. Strenuous.

12.   The Prayer Battery 10m E3 5c   (1984)
Climb the groove just left of Gauntlet Route, past suspect blocks (exciting).

★ **13.   The Angel of Death** 10m HVS 5a   (1979-83)
Climbs the clean groove, which is gained by an awkward start and step right.

14.   Angel Delight 10m HVS 5b   (1978)
Start as for The Angel of Death but continue direct.

15.   Mr and Mrs Liptrot Go to the Seaside 10m E4 6a   (1986)
Climb the wall and crackline just left of Angel Delight. A crucial hold has
fallen off the lower section, though the route can now be started from Angel
Delight. Very sustained.

★★★ **16.   Pigeon Toad Orange Peel** 15m E5 6b   (1985)
The best route in the quarry. Do this in one push and you are cruising. The thin
crack in the overhanging wall is climbed to the overlap by a series of
increasingly technical and strenuous moves. Finish on the left.

★★ **17.   A Thief in the Night** 12m E4 6b   (1986-87)
Another pumpy test-piece, that is both strenuous and technical. This aptly-named
route takes the crackline just left of Pigeon Toad Orange Peel. Start as for that
route and gain the crack on the left (peg) and follow it to the top.

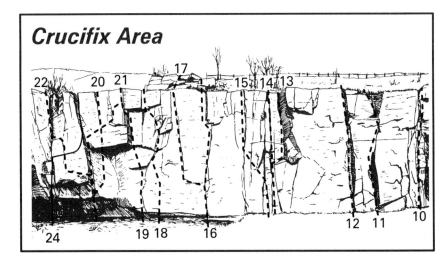

Crucifix Area

★ **18.   The Crucifix**   10m   E2 (2 pegs for aid)   5c   (1968)
This route takes the three bands of overhangs at its right side. Start four metres
to the left of Pigeon Toad Orange Peel, just right of a blank groove which leads
to the first small roof. Use two aid pegs in a faint crackline to gain a hold on
the left, then swing round on this and layback round the first roof. Make a hard
move to pass the second roof, then gain the small ledge above and finish direct.
Good thread belay.

★★ **19.   Exile and the Kingdom**   12m   E4   6b   (1986)
An inspiring line forced direct into the impressively-positioned hanging groove
in the Main Wall. Finish directly.

20.   Threshold of a Nightmare   12m   E2   5c   (1985)
Start six metres to the left at an obvious crack/groove. Surmount the initial
overlap, then climb the slab on the right to the roof. Go through this and finish
directly past peg runners.

21.   Jemima Puddleduck   17m   E2   5c   (1978)
Start as for Threshold of a Nightmare, but continue straight up the blocky
groove until above the large roof on the right a traverse right can be made
above the overhang to a flake. Go up a flake, then step right and finish up the
rib.

22.   The Last Supper   12m   HVS   5a   (Pre-1979)
Surmount the initial overlap as for Jemima Puddleduck then step left above the
large overhang on the left to gain a good hold at the base of the hanging wall.
Move left, then up this wall to reach a grassy corner on the left and follow this
to the top.

23.   The Hollow Men   27m   E3   6a   (1986)
A high left-to-right traverse of the wall, starting up Jemima Puddleduck and
finishing up Angel Delight.

24.   Knight of the Bath   15m   VS   4b   (1978)
Start six metres to the left and climb a small corner, then traverse right across
the smooth groove of The Last Supper into a block-filled groove and finish up
this.

Pool Area

*The rest of the routes start on the back wall, which is at right-angles to the
Main Wall, and is bounded on its right by an obvious steep slab and then a
grassy break. In summer it may be possible to walk to the foot of these routes,
but in wetter times it will be necessary to reach the dry land at the base of the
slab either by descending a route or by abseiling. These routes are described
from left to right, starting with:*

25.   Earwig   10m   HVS   5a   (1978)
The obvious arête left of the pond.

26.   Napoleon Solo   10m   E3   6a   (1986)
The wall and thin crack just right of Earwig; crux low down.

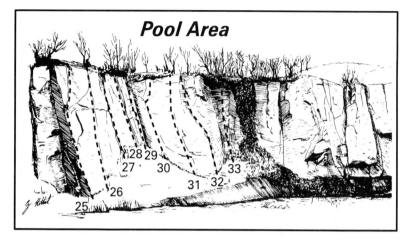

Pool Area

27. Anarchy 10m VS 4b (1978)
The crackline splitting the wall on the right, on excellent hand jams.

28. Artificial Insinuation 10m VS 4b (1978)
The cracks three metres to the right.

29. Larceny 8m S 4a (1978)
Climb the obvious corner on the right and finish up the left wall.

★★ **30. Hogmanay Slab** 9m VD (1968)
Pleasant climbing up the left-hand side of the slab on good holds.

★★ **31. Chasing Rainbows** 10m E2 5b (1985)
A solitary runner protects this pleasantly-angled slab. However, escape is possible if one's nerve goes. Climb directly up the slab just right of Hogmanay Slab with increasing difficulty.

32. Metropolis 10m VS 4b (1968)
Five metres to the right is an obvious crackline sloping from right to left. Follow this to a groove, then climb this and pull round the arête on the left to finish.

33. Flat Battery 12m VS 4c (1986-87)
A disappointing route. Six metres right of Metropolis is a loose rib, climb this and finish up the slab above.

First Ascents at Ousel's Nest
1968 Jan 1   **Hogmanay Slab** John Spencer, Steve Jones
1968 Apr 19   **Metropolis** John Spencer, Phil Bond
1968 May 9   **The Crucifix** Hank Pasquill (second did not follow)
1968   **The Angel of Death, The Last Supper** Ian Lonsdale, John Spencer
1978 Feb 13   **Anarchy** Pete Grimshaw, Mark Davis
1978 Feb 16   **Artificial Insinuation** Paul Cropper
1978 Feb 16   **Knight of the Bath**
1978 Feb 20   **Earwig** Nick Colton
1978 Mar 12   **Resurrection** Dave Kenyon, Ian Lonsdale

1978 Apr 8	**Angel Delight** Paul Cropper, Rehan Siddiqui	
1978 Apr 26	**Jemima Puddleduck**	
1978 June 12	**Sorry Sid** Nick Colton	
1978 Aug 19	**Please Ring the Plumber** Pete Grimshaw	
19789	**Larceny** Nick Colton	
1979-83	**Angel's Kiss**	
1984 Aug 8	**The Prayer Battery** Geoff Hibbert, Mick Bradshaw	
1985	**Wiggerley Worm** Geoff Hibbert, Mick Bradshaw	
1985 May 1	**Pigeon Toad Orange Peel** Geoff Hibbert, Mick Bradshaw	
1985 Sep 16	**Chasing Rainbows** Geoff Hibbert, Dave Williams	
1985	**Threshold of a Nightmare** Geoff Hibbert, Chris Hemmings	
1986 May	**Captain Hookleg** Bruce Goodwin, Clive Morton	
1986 June 8	**Lace** Bruce Goodwin, Clive Morton	
1986 July 9	**Mr and Mrs Liptrot Go to the Seaside, Exile and the Kingdom** Mark Liptrot (unseconded)	
1986 July 9	**Napoleon Solo** Mark Liptrot (solo)	
1986 July 16	**The Hollow Men** Mark Liptrot (unseconded)	
1986	**The Red Rose** Geoff Hibbert	
1986 July	**A Thief in the Night** Mark Liptrot (unseconded)	
1986-87	**Flat Battery** Geoff Hibbert	
1990 June 23	**Faith and Energy, Little Wall** Andy Griffith (solo)	

The Wilton Quarries   O.S. ref.   SD 69 13

Situation and Character

Collectively the four quarries are the biggest rock playground in the area, and the number of high-quality routes is astonishing. Indeed, there are many classic climbs hereabouts, comparable to the best of the English outcrops. There is something for everyone at Wilton, with long, serious routes in Wilton One, some interesting, technical test-pieces in Two and shorter, generally easier climbing in Three. Wilton Four is the shortest of the quarries and the surroundings are somewhat dismal, but even here, there is good climbing to be had.

History

> '*There is only one quarry at Wilton, which is about 500 yards long. The most noticeable feature of the quarry is the Prow...*'

> '*... Except for some easier routes on the Prow, and in the Graveyard. Wilton is not a place for learning to climb, and some of the harder routes should be left for experts*'.

> Les Ainsworth, 1966 in a letter to Eric Byne

It seems possible that climbers were visiting the Wilton quarries regularly by the late 1940s, as nearby Brownstones was proving popular and had a guidebook to it as early as 1947 (Lancashire Caving and Climbing Club Journal). The first recorded Wilton route, however, was by Rowland Edwards and Ray (Slim) Cook in 1959; *Belly Wedge Chimney* was climbed on their first visit to Wilton Three and was named after an incident as Ray followed – 'he weighed about sixteen stones, but he could climb as well as the next man.' During the next year, Edwards, sometimes accompanied by Cook, systematically worked his way through most of the easier routes and natural lines in the quarry. By the end of

1960 the pair of them had discovered *Forked Cracks, Parallel Cracks, The Groove, Crack and Slab, Fallout, Green Slabs* and many others.

In 1961 the classic *Rappel Wall* and *Rappel Wall Indirect* were added to Edwards' list, but attention moved to Wilton One, where The Prow beckoned. By June a guidebook had been produced by Graham Kilner and Harry Taylor which listed five of their routes on the Inside Face, including the superb *Flywalk*, the easier *Rambling Route, Bird Chimney* and a route called *Sunset Boulevard*, which was a pegged version of *Dawn*. The latter route was eventually freed by Mick Pooler in 1963, after he had soloed up to the niche and did not relish the prospect of reversing down. His friends dropped him a rope and he then went on to lead the route.

1962 started in Wilton Three with ascents of the *Eeny, Meeny, Miney, Mo* routes by Pooler, which he followed up with *Canopy* (which had been pegged the previous year), whilst *Kay* was cleaned and climbed by Edwards. At about this time, having seen Edwards attempting *Crooked Crack*, Evans soloed up afterwards to produce the right-hand variation. The direct route up the crack had to wait a short time before Edwards came back to finish it. Over in Wilton Three Edwards found a way up *Constable's Overhang* using home-made knife blades as, at that time, the crack was so thin. The route was named after a policeman who ambled into the quarry and accused the team of having stolen a motorbike which lay at the foot of the buttress. Fortunately, he was eventually convinced of their innocence. Edwards also pegged *Canine Crucifixion* (originally called *S.A.S.* and free-climbed by Les Ainsworth later).

Pooler then moved into Wilton One, where the first tentative steps were being taken away from the relatively predictable lines on the Inside of The Prow. Accompanied by Dave Brodigan, he started off with *Fingernail* and then he tackled the arête of *Christeena*, which proved that the routes were not always as improbable as they appeared from the bottom. A few weeks later Brodigan was in action again, this time with John Nuttall and the up-and-coming Evans. On a bitterly cold day, they attempted the first breach in the walls away from The Prow. During the climb Nuttall complained that he was going to blackout on the stance because of the cold, hence the route was named *Blackout*.

In 1963 most of the attention moved to Wilton One and though Evans and Ken Powell added several routes in Three, the only really significant one was Evans' *Slipshod*. During an early attempt on Western Terrace, which was repulsed by grass and heather cornices, Evans was able to study the possibilities on Grey Wall and soon he was trying a weakness that he had identified. The result was *Frightful Fred*, which covers some impressive ground for its grade. However, the main problem for the climbers on that occasion was not the difficulty of the climbing, but the time it took. They started in mid-afternoon and by the time that Evans had finished the main pitch it was getting so late that Powell had to be lowered down and dispatched to the phone to let Mum know that everyone would be home late.

As soon as the warmer, drier weather appeared, Powell and Nuttall attacked the higher walls again. Their first foray was a cautious ascent of *Dandelion Groove*. At the time it was particularly vegetated and unappealing, but it was always obvious that all the holds were there and that protection was possible, even though the risks of testing it due to slipping on the mud or vegetation were probably quite high. They then moved to the next obvious breaks, Manglewurzle

Rib and Remembrance Corner, but the time was not right and they still needed both more cleaning and more experience, so they went back to The Prow where Powell led *Spider Crack* on the Outside Face. Though some aid was used, this turned out to be a morale booster and Evans went prospecting in The Graveyard, where he uncovered *Great Slab*, sharing both the cleaning, which was extensive, and the leads with Powell. The next day Powell added *999*, but the top groove was very dirty and so the climb finished up Great Slab, until the groove was eventually cleaned by Ainsworth in late 1966. Meanwhile back at The Prow, Edwards added the amusing *Eliminate*.

By 1964 word was getting round that it was not necessary to trek all the way from mid-Lancashire to the Chew Valley or Yorkshire to climb and things started to take off at Wilton. The first break-through was a successful attempt by Evans on *Manglewurzle Rib* and this was immediately acclaimed as the hardest route at Wilton – though this accolade tended to move regularly to the most recent new addition. It is a sobering thought that whilst routes such as these can now be laced up with Friends and micronuts, in the early Sixties the leaders at Wilton often prayed for a fourth runner to supplement a jammed-in engineering nut, or a sling round a spike that needed three or four steel krabs just to keep it there.

After this, attention moved to the Outside Face of The Prow, which had previously been neglected, because many of its small, flat holds were then grassy and took some cleaning. Nevertheless, Evans soon added *Left Edge* in The Graveyard and *Flingle Bunt* on The Prow. Whilst encouraging friends on a second ascent of the latter, Evans looked down from the top of The Prow and noticed some flat holds. He abseiled down and this confirmed his view that the wall was climbable, so he set off armed with three pegs, as it was clear that there would be no other protection. It was a struggle to knock the first peg in and the second one had to be placed from an even more precarious position, so it was not driven in as well as he might have wished. Nevertheless, this was sufficient and after a couple of trying moves above the peg, he produced the brilliant *Cameo* with just two runners. Shortly afterwards one of the pegs was replaced by the infamous bicycle crank, which provided comfort for many a leader for several years. Cameo was followed up by Evans' *Patience*, which took two days, several falls and some tension to sort out, and *Horrocks' Route* by Powell. Ainsworth then decided to explore on the Bolton end of the quarry, where he created *Jean* and *Ruby*, whilst Evans opened up Chimney Buttress with the stunning *Leucocyte Left-hand*. Other notable routes to fall in Wilton One during 1964 were *Green Wall, Niche Indirect, Undertaker's Crack* and several other oddments in The Graveyard by Evans.

Meanwhile, over the road, Edwards climbed *Betty's Wall* and *Central Crack* in Wilton Three. Edwards next cast his pioneering eye over Wilton Two, ascending *Falling Crack* (as an aid route), *Throsher* and the tough *Saturday Crack*. He also soloed many of the more obvious lines. Evans and Powell also managed to grab a few of these lines, including *Wilton Wall*, which Powell pegged. This later appeared on the front cover of *The Climber*, which further popularised the quarries.

The next year was one of consolidation – all of the recent new climbs started to receive regular ascents, considerably improving them. The most significant event of the year was the completion of the *Red and White Girdle* by Evans and Allan

Brook. It took two days to sort out, but was immediately acclaimed as a major breakthrough. Evans' other successes that year were *Peanuts, Kurma* and *Tryptophane*. On Remembrance Day, Edwards and Powell at last managed to succeed with *Remembrance Corner* on the day before Powell joined the RAF. Shortly afterwards, Edwards also left the area and so this was the last contribution from both of these climbers.

1966 saw the production of the first readily available guidebook to the Wilton quarries – written by Evans with some help from Powell and distributed free by Bowden Black at his shop in Bolton. Like all good guidebooks though, it was immediately out of date with its own author adding *Wombat Chimney* almost before it was out.

In early 1967 Evans met Pasquill who was partway up a new line on Chimney Buttress. Whilst Evans watched, *Leucocyte Right-hand* was snatched from in front of him, though he then joined Pasquill on that first ascent. This was the first of a long series of hard free routes by Pasquill. Others quickly followed; *Willow Arête* – stolen from the young Ian Lonsdale who had cleaned off some holds then replaced the sods hoping to complete the route later. *Central Route* – which had stopped all-comers previously, proved easy, and routes such as *Virgin's Dilemma* and *Cheat* added further to his growing reputation. Pasquill really confirmed his arrival with a stunning, on-sight lead of *Christine Arête*. A number of years later he repeated the routes in an old pair of Mountain boots; not as an act of bravado, but because his EB's were 'shot at' and he could not afford new ones. Impressive stuff though.

Evans chipped in with *Knuckleduster* and Ainsworth added the fierce *Wipe Out* with John Mason (looking at it now it seems a good name), *Flimnap the Pirate* and a free ascent of *Ann* (with John McGonagle), but by 1968 Pasquill was really starting to motor. Three major routes followed: *Paradox*, later repeated with Evans, who was heard to remark 'You've really left me behind this time', *Max* – named after the pet dog from the Wilton Arms, and *White Slabs Bunt* which remained unrepeated by anyone other than Hank for several years. Evans had previously made four or five unsuccessful attempts at White Slabs Bunt, reaching just short of the halfway break and the 'Bunt' itself was a loose, layback flake at about five metres. Again it is worth reminding modern rock-jocks that the poor peg runners on climbs at that time were placed en route and that the sharp-edged mantelshelf ledges that are now so welcome, were often hidden under a botanist's paradise. Another of Pasquill's successes was over in Wilton Three, where he managed to lead the long-standing problem of *Shiver's Arête*. The bottom section of this had been done by Ray Evans in 1963 as *Chiver's*, a direct start to Rappel Wall Indirect, leaving less than four metres at the very top. However, although it had been top-roped several times, the route had frightened off all previous lead attempts.

The first Lancashire guidebook appeared in mid-1969, as did the annual crop of new routes. Almost inevitably it was Pasquill in the lead, with a willing and able group of seconds including Jim Fogg, Graham 'Penk' Penketh and Dave Hollows. Hollows deserves particular mention as he was a bold, gifted climber in his own right, barely less able than Pasquill himself, and the only person at the time, making repeats of Pasquill's major lines. Routes such as *In Memoriam,*

Dave Kenyon **Getting Rid of The Albatross** (E6 6c), Hoghton Quarry. *Photo: John Mason*

Nothing Fantastic, Thin Air, Roll Over (gained from the right, the independent start was added later by Lonsdale), and *Loopy* all date from this time. Whilst over in Wilton Two, Pasquill managed a free ascent of Wilton Wall. Perhaps the most technical of the climbs at that time was *Master Spy* and for its day it was clearly pushing the limits. On the first attempt Hollows managed to get across the flake and then had a trying time trying to get some protection, just before he fell on it, then Pasquill managed a few more feet, before he too fell off. The next day the pair returned and both led the route.

The pace of exploration slowed into the Seventies, although Dave Cronshaw and Ainsworth remained active, producing *Merchant Crack, La Rue, Deodand* and a host of minor routes. Pasquill was still active at this time, and added routes such as *Adidas, Puma* and *The Hacker* in Wilton One. However, his major contribution was an audacious free ascent of *Constable's Overhang*, which represented a major step up in the difficulty of the routes in the area. *Falling Crack* also lost its remaining aid points a few weeks later, but on that occasion the poor rock at the top was too much even for Pasquill without a clean-up abseil first.

Things were not to remain quiet for long though; Lonsdale, who had already been around for quite some time, began to get new route fever. Strange practices such as clearing away loose rock and soil from prospective new routes, and drying the fingers with chalk rather than on the shirt-lap, had started to become accepted. Armed with new ideas and an obsessive determination Lonsdale set about areas of unclimbed rock and old aid routes to produce a series of often good and popular climbs. *Regatta De Blanc, Tweeker* (free), *Dracula, Supercrack* (*Obituary* free) and *Vampire* (free) all proved popular, as did his free ascent of *Spike*. Other Lonsdale-creations saw less traffic, some (*Ummagumma* for instance) because of bad rock, others such as *Isle of White*, because they were obviously too bold. Other notable additions were made by Dave Knighton, including a free ascent of *Josser* and by Geoff Mann. Mann was a late convert to climbing, who produced a very hard, free version of The Shakes, renaming it *K.P.* after Pasquill's newly-born daughter Katy.

During the late Seventies and early Eighties the idea of training for climbing was gaining favour and the gifted amateur started to feel pressure from the athlete. The first of the manic trainers to make an impression were the two Johns – Hartley and Monks. Hartley used his fitness gained from weights, karate and innumerable hours spent bouldering, aided by his willingness to garden tons of overlying sods and rubble, to create a series of often excellent routes, usually of a highly technical nature. Hartley attracted some criticism because of the extent of his cleaning, and his willingness to preplace pegs (or in the odd case, bolts) near to the crux of a prospective route, but time has now shown that he was only a couple of years ahead of his time. He found this method of cleaning and preparation, followed by an unpractised ascent preferable to the 'multiple top-rope, wire-the-move' method, and his routes are all well worth doing if you are up to them; *The Devil's Alternative* takes in one of Wilton's hardest moves, whilst *Sleepwalk* and *Astradyne* have dozens of suitors each summer. *Pigs on the Wing* and *Iron Orchid* are musts for any aspiring hero.

Dave Cronshaw feeling a bit exposed on **The Complete Streaker** (VS 4c), Denham Quarry.

Photo: John Ryden

Anyone climbing with Monks was in for a hard time; always just one more route. Left to his own devices he would solo literally hundreds of feet of Extreme rock and train, train, train. Often climbing new routes with Hartley, he also produced a good few of his own: *Ego Trip* (a free version of the aid route Stet climbed with Tony Preston) being a fine hard companion to K.P.

All this activity and 'big number' routes attracted the occasional foreign visitor. New Zealander Roland Foster popped over in 1983 to add *Join the Army, get Yourself Killed, Two PVC Girls go Slap Happy* and *Shaggy Mamba* which links Cronshaw's old route Black Mamba (free-climbed earlier in the year by Dougie Hall) to one of Pasquill's come-back routes, *Shaggy Dog*, climbed the previous year. Hank turned his rekindled enthusiasm on the glaringly obvious arête between Paradox and Leucocyte on Chimney Buttress. He had partial success, climbing the upper half, and Jerry Peel managed the lower section. Hall later put the two pieces together to produce a hard and as yet unrepeated route.

Another personnel change was due at the end of 1983. Hartley signed off his string of first ascents with *Counter Intelligence*, an opposing line to the classic *Master Spy*. Hartley and Monks' purple patch came to an end, Monks took up running ($2^1/2$ hours for his first marathon!) and for the first time in years youth began to get a look in.

By the middle of the 1980s it seemed that all the major lines had been climbed, and Mark Leach's ascent of *Against All odds* in 1984 seemed to confirm that all the 'last great problems' had been ticked. This route had previously been documented as 'S-Groove, not led' and had been tried on a rope by Pasquill in the early 70s and again by Pasquill and Peel ten years later, amongst others, no-one could pass the obvious good hold under their own steam though. The line proved too good to leave, however, and 1983 saw renewed interest – Hartley placed a bolt runner and various climbers attempted to lead it. The following year Leach succeeded without the bolt runner though using side runners in adjacent routes to safeguard the crux move – he still brushed his hair on the floor more than once!

Paul Pritchard joined Phil Kelly on the occasional new route; Jimmy Mac (named after Kelly's boss on the bins) and *Plenty of Zzzzz* which continues Ray Evans' *Grey and White Girdle* for about 60 metres. Over the next two years Pritchard set about the place with a vengeance; virtually every unclimbed few feet of rock got a seeing-to, and a host of new routes appeared ranging from the appalling to the excellent. *The Soot Monkey, Eliminator* (direct), *The Pretentious Gallery, Boy Racer* and *Cleansweep* were amongst Pritchard's pick of 1985, with a long awaited futuristic free ascent of Black Pitch (*Run Wild, Run Free*) from Leach taking pride of place. The following year saw the first routes to be graded E7, Pritchard having become confident enough to string together 6b moves at a most disconcerting height above both the ground and protection (which were often the same thing). *Perimeter Walk*, climbed solo after practice, takes a thin green wall in the less popular Allotment area, with Kelly clearing away a landing strip on the ground as Pritchard climbed and *Strawberry Kiss* had only marginal protection, which ensures that neither of these two routes will become polished. Pritchard's final efforts for the 1987 guidebook focused on the overhanging wall immediately right of Scout Cleft in Wilton Two. Just before he left the area, he had nearly solved the problem of *Axe Wound*, but though he had his hands on the top of the crag, he had never actually completed the route.

However, others thought he had and so it was, inadvertently, included in the guidebook before it had a true ascent. This was rectified in 1992 when Gareth Parry made a complete ascent.

Immediately after the guidebook appeared there was a lull in new route activity, until 1990, when Parry added *Sandy* in Wilton Three. It is surprising that this line had been missed in the past, but it did show that there were still possibilities at Wilton. The other significant event during this year was Dave Pegg's completely unaided ascent of Triffid Wall to give *Gigantic*.

1992 was a busy year at Wilton, with several quality climbs being claimed. Foremost amongst the activists at this time was Matt Nuttall, who added *Under the Matt, L'Arête* and *It'll be Rude Not To*, with Parry seconding the latter, whilst Parry took the lead on *Beyond the Perimeter*. Al Holden also paid a few visits, during which he added *Press Intrusions* and *Big Al*, whilst Geoff Hibbert claimed *Rugosity Atrocity* and *Snakebite* with Chris Hemmings and *Powerage* with Mike Arnold.

After this spate of activity, it appeared that there was little left to add at WIlton. However, prayers for virgin rock were answered, when a major rockfall occurred at Wilton Two in 1996. Although this obliterated five routes, Paul Dewhurst and Alan White quickly claimed two new ones above the debris. Back in the main quarry in 1996, Parry eliminated a little aid (about eight pegs) from Adrenalin Direct and renamed the route *Chocolate Girl*.

Access

The quarries at Wilton are all owned by North West Water, which has taken a generally constructive approach to permitting climbing on its quarries. However, Wilton Two and Three are shared with Bolton's two gun clubs. There are agreed times for shooting and at these times a red flag will be flying. During these times members of *Bolton Gun Club* and *Bolton Rifle and Gun Club* have absolute preference over climbers and for safety, North West Water also insists that climbers should not be in any part of either quarry whilst there is any shooting. The shooting times are subject to alteration by agreement and for the latest information climbers should consult prominent notices at the quarries.

This is by no means a perfect agreement, though it is an amicable one, which the BMC fought hard for. However, to a large extent, the agreement depends upon climbers behaving sensibly and thoughtfully. In particular, it is important to note that the gun clubs are bound by these times and may not shoot at any other times, so **please do not climb on these days, even if there is no shooting when you arrive**, because gun club members may turn up at short notice.

Unfortunately, although this agreement generally works well, there have been some limited occasions when the gun clubs have been unable to use the quarries because of climbers. Besides this being completely unfair to the shooters, such problems could jeopardise the current good relations between North West Water and climbers which secures us access to many other quarries in Lancashire.

Currently, the agreed shooting times in both Wilton Two and Three are all day on Wednesdays, Fridays, Sundays and on Boxing Day, in **both** quarries. Climbing is permitted at all other times. If there are any changes to these arrangements in future, notices will be posted on site.

In Case of Accidents

The access gates to quarries Two and Three can be opened with keys from either Taylor's Farm (across the road from the Wilton Arms and obvious by its large green silo) or from the Wilton Arms itself.

Approach

The complex of four quarries which makes up the Wilton area lies only six kilometres North of Bolton on the A675 Bolton–Preston road. From Bolton, follow this road until the Wilton Arms pub is reached on the left, directly below the spoil heaps from Wilton One. Continue for nearly one kilometre to a sharp left turn (Scout Road) and follow this steeply to a small parking area on the right 300 metres up. Shortly before this parking space there is a green gate on the right-hand side, from where a track leads directly into Wilton Three. Wilton Two and Four are situated a little nearer to the sharp bend in the road and are also on the right. Wilton One lies about 40 metres from the sharp bend on the left-hand side of the road. It is best reached by following a faint path that leads slightly leftwards about 25 metres before the sharp bend.

For climbers approaching from Blackburn or Preston, the Wilton Quarries can be reached from Junction 3 of the M65 by following the A675 towards Bolton (past Abbey Village and Belmont) for about 12 kilometres. Scout Road forks right about three kilometres past Belmont and is the first road on the right.

The Climbs

The routes in all four quarries are described from LEFT to RIGHT.

Wilton One   O.S. ref.   SD 699 134

Wilton One is the largest of the four quarries.

The Allotment

This lies at the far south (Bolton) end of the quarry. At first this area is scrappy and unclean, though it improves as the crag increases in height farther right. The fenced off area at the far end of the quarry is on private land and no climbing must take place in that area.

1.   The Deep 8m HVS 5a   (1979)
Climb the shallow groove in the buttress immediately to the right of the fence.

2.   Barbara Ann 10m HVS 5b   (1970)
Thirty-five metres right of the fence is a narrow buttress. Follow the central crack by two hard mantels, trending left, then step right over the overhang to finish.

3.   Rhonda 10m A2   (Pre-1972)
The thin crack one metre right, just before a short rise in the quarry floor.

The next buttress lies 15 metres farther right, behind a clump of willow trees.

4.   Grassy 10m HVS 5a   (1974)
The crackline three metres from the left edge of the buttress.

★ **5.   Rugosity Atrocity** 15m E2 5b   (1992)
Start at a letter-box and climb the wall above on rugosities (side runner in
Willow Wall at eight metres).

6.   Willow Wall 17m HS 4a   (1966)
Climb the most obvious crackline in the centre of the wall, to the large ledge.
Traverse right and finish up the short wall behind.

7.   Asleep for Years 15m VS 4b   (1977)
The twin cracks two metres to the right. At the terrace step right and finish up
the short wall.

8.   Press Intrusions 14m E2 5b   (1992)
Start at a vague crack and climb to the right side of a large ledge at five metres.
Continue up the crozzly wall above using good rugosities, then finish up Asleep
for Years.

9.   Falling Wall 15m E1 5b   (1983)
A scrappy line up the vague cracks in the green wall one metre left of Willow
Arête.

★ **10.   Willow Arête** 14m E1 5b   (1968)
The right arête of the buttress. Start just left of the arête and climb up easily for
five metres as for Falling Wall, then move right to the arête and follow this to
the large ledge. Finish up the short wall behind.

★★ **11.   It'll be Rude Not To** 14m E6 6c   (1992)
Climb the thin crack just left of Kurma to a small square-cut slot (good
micronuts), then move left to an undercut (crux) and back right to the crack.
Follow this to the break, then move one metre left and climb over the overlap to
the top.

12.   Kurma 17m VS 4b   (1965)
Start in the deep corner just right of the willows. Climb the corner to the
horizontal fault, then traverse to the left arête to reach a large ledge, and finish
up the wall behind.

13.   Adidas 18m HVS 5a   (1974)
The crack which starts about four metres to the right of the deep corner is
followed to the horizontal break, then traverse left to the continuation corner
above Kurma and use an iron spike to finish up this.

★★ **14.   Puma** 14m E3 5c   (1974)
Start at twin cracks four metres farther right, where the ground level falls
slightly. Climb up to the break, step slightly left, then surmount the overhang
and continue to the top.

★ **15.   The Foot of an Oncoming Mexican** 14m E4 6b   (1967/1986)
Free climbs the old aid route Needles and Pins; three metres to the right of
Puma, with two pegs. Step right at the break and climb the headwall.

★ **16.   Zapling** 14m E3 6a   (1986)
Power up the hanging flake left of Merchant Crack, gained from that route.

The Allotment

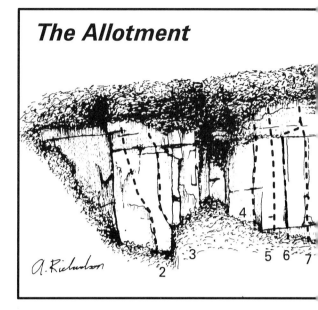

17.   Merchant Crack   10m   HVS   5a   (1971)
Start three metres to the right and climb a short, shallow corner then the
continuation crack to the horizontal break. Step right to finish.

18.   La Rue   20m   HVS   5a   (1971)
From the top of Merchant Crack, follow an obvious traverse line leftwards until
it is possible to finish up the corner of Adidas (directly above the start to
Kurma).

★ **19.   Perimeter Walk**   9m   E7   6b   (1986)
An unprotected problem taking the challenge of the narrow slab right of
Merchant Crack, with the crux high up.

★★ **20.   Beyond the Perimeter**   9m   E5   6a   (1992)
Climb the right arête on its left, with a bold crux at the top.

★ **21.   Flimnap the Pirate**   9m   VS   4c   (1966)
The slim corner groove round to the right of Beyond the Perimeter.

22.   Reeling in the Years   10m   VS   4c   (1980)
One metre right is a thin crack; climb this for six metres, move right, then step
back left to finish.

23.   Big Al   8m   E3   5c   (1992)
One metre left of Baby Arête climb the wall.

24.   Baby Arête   8m   HVS   5a   (1968)
The short arête on the right, and just left of the vegetated corner of Grotty
Muckden, is climbed on its right-hand side.

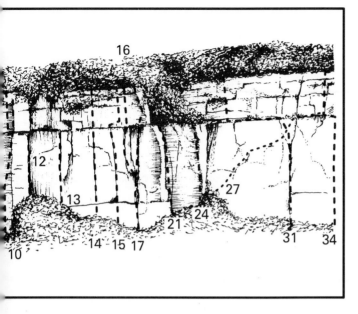

25. Rope 'n' Rubber 18m E2 5c   (1986)
The wall between Baby Arête and Grotty Muckden. Blinkers needed for this
climb.

26. Grotty Muckden 8m VD   (1964)
The second large corner past the clump of willow trees is somewhat overgrown.
Climb it to a muddy landing.

⋆ **27. Tryptophane** 24m HS 4a   (1965)
A good route involving bold climbing up the wall right of Grotty Muckden.
Start in the corner and follow an obvious line of holds up and rightwards across
the wall, culminating in a couple of thought-provoking moves to reach the
break. Go right along the break to finish up a short corner.

28. Pot-Pourri 18m VS 4c   (1982)
Start three metres to the right of Grotty Muckden and climb directly to a vague
left-facing groove and the break above. Finish direct; unprotected.

29. Under the Matt 18m E4 6a   (1992)
Climb the unprotected wall midway between Pot-Pourri and Lady Grinning Soul.

30. Lady Grinning Soul 20m HVS 5a   (1980)
From two metres left of Valine, climb up a shallow right-leading ramp to gain a
crack. Move left and go up to join Tryptophane. Finish up that route.

31. Valine 15m VS 4c   (1974)
Climb the obvious crackline nine metres right of the corner, until it is possible
to step left to gain the horizontal fault. Finish as Pot-Pourri.

32. Land 15m VS 4b (1977)
Move right on to the wall from six metres up Valine, traverse right for two
metres to a shallow depression, then finish straight up past the break.

33. Boy Racer 15m E5 6a (1978-79/1985)
Boldly and delicately attack the wall right of Valine and finish just right of
Land. The crux is low down, but it is still scary and committing.

★ **34. Proline** 15m E1 5b (1974/1980-82)
The twin cracks at the foot of an obvious grassy cone. Climb these stepping left
at the break to finish as for Boy Racer.

★ **35. First Cut** 14m HVS 5a (1977)
From the top of the grassy cone go up to the left of a pair of large pockets,
then continue up the wall above.

★ **36. Green Wall** 15m VS 4b (1964)
Start one metre right and climb up to the right-hand large pocket, then step right
and follow a shallow corner to the horizontal break. Move right along this and
finish on the left.

★★ **37. The Pretentious Gallery** 15m E5 6b (1985)
Start just right of Green Wall and climb delicately up and right to a peg. Keep
left of the peg and gain the overlap and second peg by some tricky moves.
Finish either up the centre of the upper wall or up the left arête.

38. Dinah 15m E1 5b (1968/1974)
The block-filled crack on the right.

★ **39. Eliminator** 15m E3 5c (1980)(1985)
A stiff unprotected problem direct up the wall right of Dinah, at the upper limit
of its grade. The initial crux section can be avoided by gaining the line from six
metres up Dinah (E1, 5b).

40. Ruby 17m VS 4c (1964)
Right again the main quarry floor rises, and just left of an overhang is a crack.
Climb this for eight metres, until it is possible to traverse right and finish up
Jean.

41. Insertion 15m HVS 5b (1980)
Get your leg over the roof between Ruby and Jean and continue direct to the
break, passing a doubtful block. Finish up Ruby.

★ **42. Jean** 15m VS 4c (1964)
Gain the undercut groove just to the right, either direct, or by a traverse from
the left side of the overhang. Follow the groove to the horizontal fault, then
finish up the short broken groove on the right.

43. Gravitational Experiment 15m E4 6b (1982)
Climb the steep thin cracks right of Jean, direct.

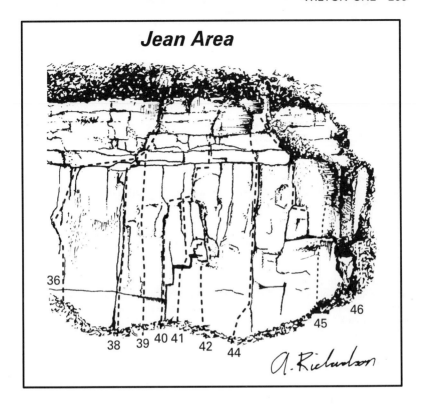

Jean Area

36 38 39 40 41 42 44 45 46

A. Richardson

44. Crow's-nest 14m E1 5b   (1974)
Right again is a pod at nine metres. Start below this and climb diagonally right
(very poor peg) to a large ledge. Step back left and enter the pod with
difficulty, then continue to the top.

45. Headbutt Wall 12m E4 6a   (1986)
Start two metres left of the arête and reach the ledge on Eccles' Escalator via a
problem wall. Pass the peg above by tricky moves (use of the arête is only for
wimps).

46. Eccles' Escalator 14m VD   (1964)
Gain the ledge on the right-hand side of the wall from the right, then follow a
series of undercut ledges on the left. Steep!

DESCENT: *the block-filled chimney on the right* (**Christmas Chimney**)
provides an excellent easy descent for the routes hereabouts.

47. Lime Street 55m S 4a   (1971)
A high-level traverse of The Allotment area along the obvious dirty horizontal
break. From the top of Eccles' Escalator, follow the break leftwards until about
four metres from Grotty Muckden. A finish can be made rightwards up a short
groove. Belay at will, but make sure that you have made it out first.

Ordinary Route (E1, 5b): an alternative traverse, starts up Jean and traverses left at half-height, along a line of holds to finish down Pot-Pourri. Good pendulum possibilities for the second!.

The Pitface

This is the area of more broken rock which stretches right to Chimney Buttress. Despite the appearance of some sections, there are a number of good routes.

48.   Is it a Cheesecake or a Meringue?   9m   HVS   5a   (1985)
Start two metres right of a large two-block pinnacle and climb a crack which turns into a groove.

★ **49.   Power of the Mekon**   9m   E1   5b   (1983)
Climb the wall one metre farther right by an exquisite series of moves on rugosities.

50.   Grovel   9m   S   4a   (1972)
The loose, grassy, block-filled groove on the right, about 25 metres past Christmas Chimney.

★★ **51.   Regatta de Blanc**   9m   VS   4c   (1980)
Reasonable and interesting climbing up an improbable-looking wall. Start just right of Grovel, climb rightwards then go up on good rugosities to a ledge. Finish leftwards easily over blocks.

52.   Streaker   9m   VS   4c   (1972)
The narrow protruding rib on the right.

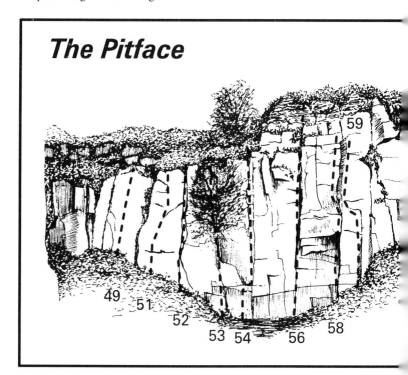

The Pitface

53.   Georgina   10m   S   4a   (1972)
The obvious left-slanting crack, past a tree.

★ **54.   Jaws**   10m   HVS   5a   (1971)
The block-filled crack from a ledge on the right.

55.   The Mouth   18m   VS   4c   (1972)
Climb Jaws for six metres until it is possible to reach a ledge on the right.
Mantel on to this, then traverse right to a large ledge and finish over an
overhang.
Variation Finish: the hanging corner above the mantelshelf.

56.   Ummagumma   15m   HVS   5b   (1980)
Right again is an undercut slab whose left edge is formed by an awesome
off-width crack; climb the crack by whatever means you see fit, to a scoop on
the left and finish easily up this.

57.   The Devil's Alternative   17m   E5   6b   (1982)
Start two metres to the right and climb to the right side of the higher overhang
guarding the undercut slab. Make an evil mantel on to the slab above (peg) and
climb the wall (peg) using two shallow grooves. Traverse right to an in-situ
belay on Silently Screaming.

★ **58.   Deodand**   14m   E1   5b   (1972/1974)
The corner at the right side of the undercut slab, passing an overhang at five
metres.

★★ **59. Silently Screaming** 14m E3 6a (1982)

A technically demanding little test-piece, which gives a well-protected little gem of a route. Climb the arête right of Deodand. Start in the short corner right of the arête and climb up to a letter-box, then traverse left to the arête. Move up to peg and continue past a second peg to an in-situ belay on the ledge.

60. Transfiguration 9m VD (1971)

The pillar and blocky groove on the right.

61. It 8m E1 5c (1985)

A boulder problem up the wall one metre right, past a bucket.

62. This 6m VS 4c (1971)

The short flake just to the right proves strenuous.

DESCENT: *from the top of the mound in the centre of The Pitface an easy scramble* (**That**) *leads diagonally leftwards and provides a convenient descent route for the climbs hereabouts.*

★★ **63. The Pit and the Pendulum** 15m E6 6c (1986)

Desperate climbing with a bold start. Start four metres right of the corner go up and climb a thin, blind flake to a sloping ledge. With feet on the ledge (peg) move right into a short, shallow groove and up this to the break (bolt above on the right). Finish up Erythrocyte.

64. Erythrocyte 14m VS 4c (1964)

Start three metres right of The Pit and the Pendulum and climb the pillar above to a loose finish over blocks (bolt on left).

★★★ **65. Sleepwalk** 15m E4 6a (1969/1982)

"*A route that I usually start cool and methodically, but always end up desperately slapping one on for the finishing break*" (Geoff Hibbert). Originally pegged as Vaccination. Climb the slab on the right to a ledge, then move right and follow the thin, slightly kinked, left-leaning crack above to the horizontal break. Lower off on Friends to avoid the loose top, then retrieve them afterwards.

★★ **66. Astradyne** 14m E5 6b (1982)

Stick insects and masochists are amongst those most likely to succeed on this gruelling test-piece of stamina. Climb the bulging crack splitting the next wall, three metres left of the corner to a ledge. Peg belay on left.

● **67. Houses of the Holy** 15m VS 4c (1977)

Climb the off-putting corner on the right for six metres then follow the crack which branches to the left.

Chimney Buttress

This is the steep imposing buttress to the left of and slightly set back from the Outside Face of The Prow. All the routes are strenuous and sustained, but well worth the effort.

★★ **68. Paradox** 21m E2 5b (1968)

Tucked away esoterically, but once viewed, this is a line that just has to be climbed. Jamming cracks don't come much better than this and the airy traverse across to the arête is also very rewarding. Climb a diagonal crack just left of the left arête of the buttress, to a niche. Take the continuation crack above to its end. Hand-traverse right to finish easily up the arête. A direct finish is possible but detracts from the route's quality.

★★ **69.   Parasite** 18m E5 6b   (1980)
Hard, thin, technical, balancy climbing may, with luck, get you to the top. A direct line up the arête to the right, utilizing the iron loop for protection. Two pegs in the break at half-height.

★★ **70.   Leucocyte Left-hand** 18m E2 5c   (1964)
Although the difficulties are short-lived, the climbing is excellent. Climb directly up to the iron loop and move right to gain a ledge. Move up left into a niche until a couple of hard moves lead to easier ground and the top.

★★ **71.   Leucocyte Right-hand** 18m VS 4c   (1967)
This was Hank Pasquill's first new route, though it was then much harder than it is now. Nevertheless, many VS leaders will be intimidated by it, until they commit themselves and find that the holds are really all there. From the large ledge on the Left-hand, move up into the short corner on the right and climb it and the crack above exiting on the right.

★ **72.   The Hacker** 18m E4 6b   (1973)
Three metres to the right of the iron loop is an obvious small ledge at four metres; gain this and pass it with difficulty to the overlap. Go over this and up

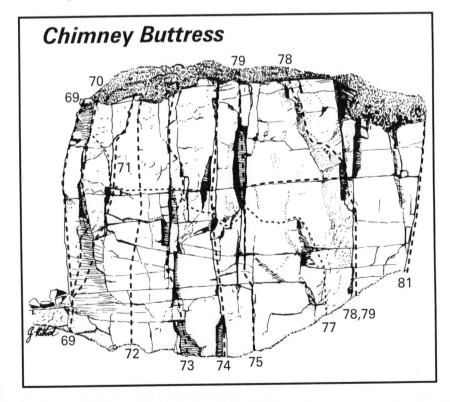

Chimney Buttress

to the break of Steeplejack. Climb the headwall boldly, trending left at the top. It is possible to traverse right to finish up Central Route, just above the overlap (E3, 6b).

★★★ **73.   Central Route**   18m E1   5b   (1967)

One of the best climbs on the buttress, never desperate, but always interesting. Five metres to the right of the iron loop is a large ledge at six metres. Gain this and climb the crack above to a peg. Move right and go up to jugs (5c if taken direct), then trend up and back left to the crack and finish up this.

★★★ **74.   Max**   18m E3   5c   (1968)

A strenuous and sustained climb with some interesting moves. Three metres to the right again, climb a thin crack to a shallow cave at nine metres. Climb into the overhanging niche above and exit from this by a hard move. Follow the continuation crack to the top.

★ **75.   Wombat Chimney**   20m E2   5b   (1966)

Two metres to the right of Max, follow a crack to the first break. Go up and leftwards to a rest below a tantalising flared chimney. Struggle up this to easy ledges on the right.

★★ **76.   The Soot Monkey**   20m E6   6c   (1985)

Start two metres to the right of Wombat Chimney and climb a hard, boulder problem wall to a peg. Move up and right through a slight bulge, then trend back left. Make a scary move up and right to the break of Cleansweep (peg). From a standing position on this break, go left to a rest on the right arête of Wombat before moving back right to a strenuous finish.

★★ **77.   Steeplejack**   50m E1   5c   (1982)

An interesting, rising girdle of Chimney Buttress, with good positions. Despite the territory that is traversed, the difficulties are relatively short. Climb the thin crack two metres to the left of Loopy to a ledge, then traverse leftwards along ledges into Wombat Chimney. Step down and move left into Max and thus into Central Route. Climb this to just over the overlap and foot-traverse left to finish up Leucocyte Left-hand.

★★★ **78.   Loopy**   14m E4   6a   (1968)(1970)

One of the original Wilton test pieces and still good value. The ground starts to rise up towards a corner bounding the right-hand end of Chimney Buttress. Midway up the slope, is a steep crack running up to a small monolith near the top of the crag. Follow the crack (peg) to a semi-rest below the monolith. There is a choice of three finishes; a) Move up left into the hanging groove but break out left onto the slab and climb it diagonally leftwards (hardest and best), b) move up left into the groove and fight up it, (more in keeping with the crack below), c) swing right into the green groove on the right of the monolith and follow it to the top; easier but a poor alternative.

★★★ **79.   Cleansweep**   27m E5   6a   (1968/1985)(1988)

Big arms are essential on this long, strenuous pitch. Free-climbs the old aided girdle traverse, Big Dipper. From the second peg on Loopy, go left around the nose and traverse the fault line past two pegs into Wombat Chimney; finish up this. Can also be done starting up The Corner and gaining Loopy at nine metres by a short traverse (peg).

80. Friends 12m HVS 4c (1980)
Climb The Corner until it is possible to step left and gain a niche. Finish
directly through this.

** **81. The Corner** 10m VS 4c (1965)
The corner which limits Chimney Buttress on its right gives good traditional
climbing on small, but adequate holds.

82. L'arête 10m E4 6a (1992)
Climb the obvious arête on the right of the corner (hidden peg on right) and
continue boldly to the top.

There is a low-level traverse of Chimney Buttress stretching from Parasite to
The Corner and if so desired the horizontal excitement can be extended by
continuing right round at the same level, to finish at Scimitar.

Outside Face of The Prow

*The Prow is the obvious centrepiece of Wilton One: a huge monolith thrusting
out from the mother rock and detached on three sides. Its outside face is about
18 metres high and tends to become green after wet weather. The Inside Face is
about 14 metres high and with perfect clean rock. In sunny weather the Inside
Face is something of a suntrap.*

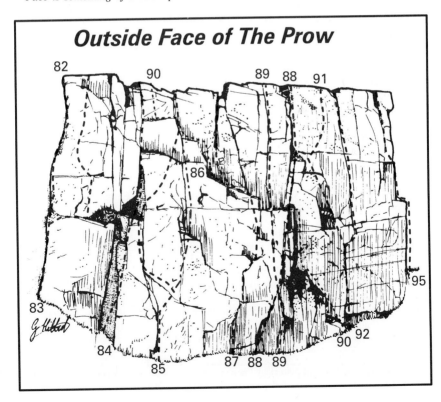

Outside Face of The Prow

★ 83. Peanuts 21m HVS 4c,5a (1964)
1. 9m. Start just right of The Corner. Climb up and right to good holds on
the arête, swing round this and make an awkward mantel on to the belay ledge
of Fingernail.
2. 12m. Step back left and go up to a ledge (peg). Attain a standing position
on this then either finish rightwards or via a ramp on the left.

84. Horrocks' Route 17m VS 4b,4a (1964)(1983)
1. 8m. Right again is an overhung corner. From the base of this move up and
right until the arête can be gained and followed to a large belay ledge.
2. 9m. Climb the short corner above the belay, then climb easily to the top.
Horrocks' Route Direct (E1, 5b): takes the overhung corner direct and finishes
up the thin cracks just left of the belay.

★★ 85. Fingernail 20m S 4a,– (1962)
A traditional climb, which crosses steep rock without too much difficulty.
1. 10m. 3 metres right of the arête is an iron hook set in the wall at five
metres. Climb up to it by the crack on its left, then continue up and leftwards to
a spacious belay ledge and an in-situ peg belay.
2. 10 m. Step right around the short arête on to a steep slab, climb diagonally
right to an obvious weakness, and follow this to the top.

86. Orange Peel 21m S 4a (1964/1971)
As for Fingernail but at the hook step right, then climb the steep wall via a
crack and finish easily.

★★ 87. Flingle Bunt 20m VS 4c (1964)
The top section of this climb is thought-provoking, but all the holds are there.
Halfway up Eastern Terrace is a shallow, wide-angled groove. Start directly
below this. Climb up slightly right into a short groove and climb ledges to gain
Eastern Terrace. Enter the shallow groove above and follow it boldly to the top.

88. Spider Crack 20m HVS 5a (1963)
Just to the right is another right-leading overhang. Layback round this and
continue straight up to the terrace, then climb the deep crack above.

89. Jubilee Climb 18m E2 5c (1977)
Start just to the right of Spider Crack and climb directly to Eastern Terrace.
Follow the thin crack left of Spider Crack to finish.

90. Eastern Terrace 25m M (1961)
The obvious line of ledges which splits the buttress diagonally from right to left.

★★ 91. Lazy Friday 18m E4 5c (1977)
A bold proposition up the blank slab left of Cameo, with the crux just where
you do not want it: at the top! Since the peg went, it is advisable to get a side
runner in Spider Crack. Climb Cameo for eight metres then move out left and
climb a shallow corner, Continue up and right to finish directly up the wall on
small holds, avoiding easier possibilities on the left.

Right: The ever fashion conscious Hank Pasquill at Wilton. *Photo: Brian Cropper*
Overleaf: A youthful Al Evans on **Pagan** (E1 5b), Lester Mill Quarry. *Photo: Brian Cropper*

★★★ **92. Cameo** 18m E1 5a   (1964)
First done with just two peg runners, one of which was an old bicycle crank!
The pegs have long since gone, but despite improvements in protection it still
feels very committing near the top. Start two metres right of Eastern Terrace
and climb past breaks to a ledge below a thin crack. Follow the crack past a
tiny groove to easier ground to finish.

★ **93. Pathetique** 18m E5 6b   (1985)
The rugositied wall right of Cameo direct, finishing up a thin crack. A runner
low down in Cameo provides protection.

94. Wedgewood 18m HVS 5a   (1975-79)
Start three metres to the right, below a shallow groove at the top of the wall
(Christeena). Climb the wall directly to a small overlap (poor nuts), go left for
two metres to a crack then exit via this.

★★ **95. Christeena** 14m VS 4c   (1962)
Gain the large ledge on the end of The Prow. Move up left to a jug (peg) and
mantel on to this. Step left into a groove and finish easily up this. Entry into the
groove can be intimidating, but it is more straightforward than it at first appears.

Inside Face of The Prow

★★ **96. Christine Arête** 14m E3 5c   (1967)
The striking left arête of the Inside Face gives very thin climbing. Most leaders
resort to side runners.

★★★ **97. Dawn** 14m HVS 5b   (1961/1963)
Two metres to the right of the arête is a wide crack; climb this to a break and
niche. Go up and right into a small alcove, then make hard moves to the top.
After an easy start, the angle of the wall starts to tell and the top section of this
route can be very strenuous.
Dawn Left-hand (E2, 5c): A harder alternative is to climb the shallow groove
on the left above the break.

★ **98. Innominate** 14m E3 6b   (1963/pre-1983)
Start just to the right, and climb a very thin blind crack using old peg holes,
then traverse right along the undercut flake to finish up the crack just left of the
corner of Ann. Side runner in Dawn.

★★ **99. Eliminate** 18m VS 4c   (1963)
Although it certainly does not live up to its name as an 'eliminate', the climbing
is nevertheless interesting. Six metres right of the arête climb the short groove
to a ledge, then traverse right along the breaks until it is possible to finish easily
up the ridge of Rambling Route.

Previous page: Eric Robinson making an early ascent of **Frightful Fred** (VS 4c), Wilton One.
Photo Ray Evans
Left: This is Nigel Bonnet, utterly **Unjust** (6a), Brownstones Quarry.   *Photo: Brian Cropper*

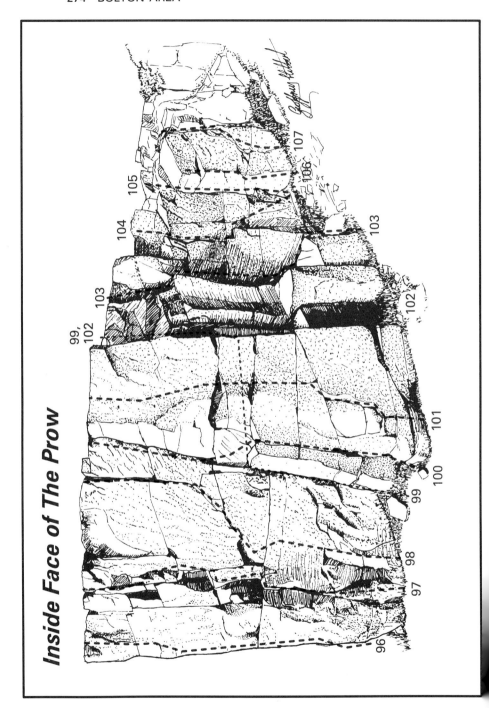

Inside Face of The Prow

★★ **100. Ann**   14m   E1   5b   (1967)

Good climbing, good protection and a sunny aspect on Wilton's most unusual feature makes this probably the most popular route of its grade in the quarry. Right of Eliminate is a short arête, climb the peg crack on its right to a ledge then follow the steep groove above using both cracks, or (harder) just layback the right crack.

★★★ **101. Cheat**   14m   E3   5b   (1967)

Start just under two metres to the right of Ann and climb a blind crack with a long stretch to reach the break of Eliminate. Step right and take the vandalised line of chipped holds up the wall above. Sadly it provides designer climbing at its best.

★★ **102. Rambling Route**   12m   VD   (1961)

Farther right is a very short chimney, followed by a groove. Climb the chimney by laybacking or bridging, then from the ledge finish up the groove or the ridge on the left. Traditional quarry climbing at its best.

★ **103. Bird Chimney**   10m   S   4a   (1961)

To the right again is a groove which turns into a wide chimney. Follow this to the top, or (more usual) finish on the left.

★★ **104. Flywalk**   12m   VS   4c   (1961)

An excellent way to get to the top of The Prow, with the added interest at the infamous rocking block. Follow the line of holds leading left across the next wall from the corner, to a rocking block. Finish up the crack and over a small overhang. A direct start is possible (5c), whilst the problem just to the left, moving right into Flywalk is 6b.

105. Flytrap   8m   HVS   5a   (Pre-1968)

The corner in which Flywalk starts, exiting right at the top.

106. Veteran Cosmic Rocker   6m   E4   6c   (1984)

The flying arête right of Flytrap, which is started on the left and finished on the right past a series of dynamic pinch moves. Slightly easier (6b) if climbed on the left side of the arête.

107. Scimitar   6m   D   (1961)

The crescent-shaped crack rising right into the corner.

DESCENT: *The gently rising gangway, known as* **Max's Dilemma**, *is the descent route.*

108. Helix   62m   E1   4c,4b,5c,4a   (1964)

A girdle of The Prow.
1.   9m.   As for Peanuts pitch 1.
2.   30m.   Traverse easily right (many variations possible) to belay on the large ledge on the end of The Prow.
3.   17m.   Swing right, around the arête and into Dawn. Place a high side runner and traverse right along the obvious break (crux) to join Ann at her ledge. Nut belay.
4.   6m.   Follow the traverse of Eliminate and finish up that route.

Opposite Wall
This is the wall directly opposite the Inside Face of The Prow.

109. Geoff's Wall   13m   E1   6a   (1992)
At the left side of the wall there is a shallow scoop at three metres. Climb the
steep wall to gain this, then finish easily over large ledges.

110. Baby's Bottom   6m   HS   4b   (1970)
Start three metres from the left side of the wall. Climb to a small overlap, then
move awkwardly right on to a ledge and finish straight up.

111. Brontosaurus   12m   S   4a   (1992)
Start at a small overhang up a thin crack to a large ledge. Finish slightly to the
left, as for Baby's Bottom.

112. Stegosaurus   12m   VD   (1969)
The blocky crack in the centre of the wall.

113. Nappy Rash   12m   E1   5b   (1975)(1986)
From the foot of Stegosaurus, follow right-leading ramps, via a hard move up to
reach a high handhold. Move right and climb direct to the top.
The **Direct Start** is E3, 6a.

114. Opposition   14m   VD   (1969)
Start in the corner on the right and follow a series of ledges to the top.

115. Spec Crack   14m   D   (1969)
The left-slanting groove directly opposite Eliminate.

Jimmy Nip Buttress
*This is a small, isolated buttress midway between The Prow and White Slabs. Its
main feature is a deep crack in its centre.*

★ **116. Powerage**   14m   E5   6b   (1992)
Start on the left and climb up trending right to a jug and runner in Jimmy Nip,
then move back left to a peg and one last strenuous pull for the break, then
traverse off. A more direct, but more artificial variation is possible at 6c.

★ **117. Jimmy Nip**   14m   E3   6a   (1975/1983)
Climb the deep crack in the centre of the buttress to the break, then step right to
finish.

118. Titanosaurus   12m   E4   6b   (1969/1982)
The thin crescent-shaped crack in the small buttress 10 metres to the right.
A grassy **DESCENT** *route is available down the slope on the right.*

White Slabs
*Above 40 metres past The Prow there is a steep section of higher rock which
continues to the top end of the quarry. The initial section, up to the long
prominent corner of Remembrance Corner, is known as White Slabs.*

119. White Crack   6m   VD   (1964)
At the start of White Slabs is a crack starting at half-height. Climb the wall beneath this, and finish up the crack.

★ **120. Goon**   15m   HVS   5a   (Pre-1965)
The next crack, with its crux at the top.

121. Crater Traitor   18m   E6   6a   (1984)
Very bold climbing up the wall right of Goon. Climb a vague groove which gets progressively harder, to a RURP at 10 metres. Wobble up and go right past this to a peg and climb the wall on the left (crux) to the break. Bolt belay above.

122. Red Flowers are Red   19m   E2   5b   (1983)
Another serious route, though at a more amenable grade. Climb the wall directly just left of Dandelion Groove, via some small pod-shaped depressions.

123. Dandelion Groove   20m   S   4a   (1963)
The first groove on White Slabs is gained easily from the left, then followed to the top.

124. Prickpocket   20m   HVS   5a   (1977)
Just right is an obvious crack in the top wall. Climb directly up the lower wall to gain and finish up this crack.

125. Snakebite   12m   E4   6a   (1992)
Climb the centre of the wall left of Manglewurzle to some easy ledges, then continue to a peg beneath an overlap. Pass this about one metre on the left of the peg to a good hold above the overlap (on right), then go back left up the headwall.

126. Manglewurzle Rib   27m   HVS   4b,5a   (1964)
1. 10m.   The crack below the rib on the right is started from the left and climbed past a peg at six metres to a small grass ledge.
2. 17m.   Go right to the rib, then take the crack on the right to the top.

★★★ **127. Isle of White**   24m   E4   6a   (1977/1978)
One of the best routes of this grade in the quarry. Adequate protection and consistently interesting climbing make this a classic route with a big feel. Follow the unprotected wall left of White Slabs Bunt to the break, then continue directly to an obvious undercut; pass this, then trend rightwards to finish over the overhang as for W.S.B.

★★★ **128. White Slabs Bunt**   25m   E3   6a   (1967/1971)(1984)
Often referred to as the best route at Wilton. It certainly is one of the most substantial climbs in the quarry. The quality of the climbing and the variety of moves make it an essential route for anyone climbing at this grade. Start six metres left of Remembrance Corner, below an overlap at eight metres. Climb to the overlap (two pegs), then move left and surmount the left side of the overhang and continue to the girdle break. At the break move right for about three metres (peg) and climb the flake crack above to two exposed mantels which give access to a shallow scoop. Pass the capping roof via a crack, then finish on the left.

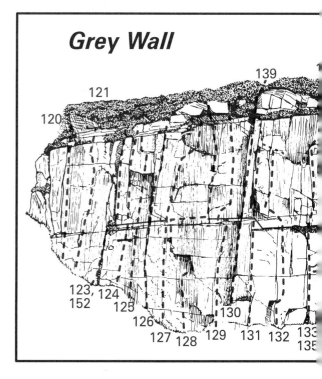

Grey Wall

★★ White Lightnin' (E5, 6b): a short variation on White Slabs Bunt. From the second peg at the right side of the overhang, climb directly to the girdle break.

★ 129. Strawberry Kiss 25m E7 6b   (1984/1986)
This route supersedes Thin White Line. Climb the thin crack just left of the corner to the break. Arrange protection in the flake of White Slabs Bunt and from the break, launch up the committing wall above past sustained fingery climbing to a move left at a thin crack, and thus relief!

130. Remembrance Corner 21m VS 4c   (1964)
The prominent corner groove running the full-height of the crag, passing a tree near the top.

Grey Wall

The next section, to the sandy cave at half-height where the wall becomes predominantly red, is perversely known as Grey Wall. It is split diagonally from right to left by Western Terrace and several routes either end on, or start from, this terrace. To the right of the Terrace is The Pit.

★★ 131. Sobeit 23m E3 5c   (Pre-1968/1977)
Just round the arête are two thin cracks. Climb the left-hand one to the break then the sentry-box above. Exit via Western Terrace.

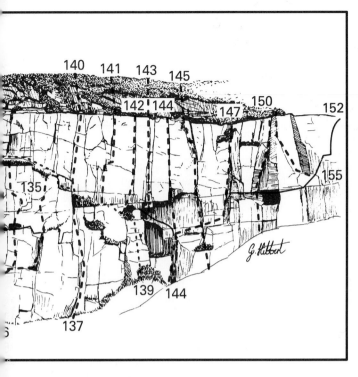

★★★ **132. Supercrack**   24m   E3   5c   (1964/1975-79)
Follow the right-hand crack to the break, step left and continue up the
continuation crack above and finish round to the left. A brilliant and sustained
route, that gives consistently high-quality climbing all the way.

133. Life in the Fast Lane   21m   E2   5c   (1977)
From the metal spike on Patience, gain the bad break above and go over the
overhangs directly to gain the Terrace. Leave the Terrace slightly rightwards to
a loose finish.

134. In Memoriam   24m   E2   5c   (1969/1978)
Climb Patience to the metal spike, and gain the bad break above. Surmount the
overhangs rightwards to a thin crack. Climb this and escape right on to Western
Terrace.

★ **135. Patience**   23m   HVS   5a,4c   (1964)
1.   14m.   Climb to a large metal spike at the left of Grey Wall, then traverse
right to a peg belay in a corner/niche.
2.   9m.   Go up to a ledge, then step left on to a ramp and finish straight up.

136. Impatience   21m   E2   5c   (1980)
Start below the centre of the traverse of Patience and climb a slim groove to the
traverse. Step right and climb twin cracks to a small overhang at the sandy
break, then gain the foot of a ramp, step left and follow a crack to the terrace.

★ 137. Dracula 12m E2 5b   (1978)
Climb the stepped, overhanging groove below the iron spike on Niche Indirect,
and continue past the spike and a peg to a niche and climb the wall on the right
to finish at the foot of Vampire.

138. Niche Indirect 20m E1 5c   (1964)
Climb the short corner four metres to the right of the niche on Patience, then
traverse left past the metal spike and finish as Patience.

139. Western Terrace 36m S   (1963)
The obvious diagonal break splitting Grey Wall from right to left. Exposed in its
upper reaches.
1.   24 m.   Climb a short ramp to gain the terrace proper, then traverse easily
leftwards and go up the small steps to a grassy bay (peg belay).
2.   12 m.   Continue leftwards at the same height, step down, then finish up the
right arête of Remembrance Corner, in a fine position.

Upper Grey Wall

The next routes start from Western Terrace and follow the walls above.

★ 140. Vampire 9m E3 6a   (1974-75/1977)
From the obvious step in Western Terrace, where Dracula ends, climb the crack
above into a small niche. Leave this to gain the top by hard moves.

★★★ 141. Spike 10m E4 6a   (1974-75/1979)
A technical climb with the crux at the top, so keep a bit in reserve! A good
introduction to the routes on this wall. Start three metres right of Vampire, at a
line leading up and right to two niches in the wall. Follow it to the first niche
(peg) and pass a second peg by hard reaches to a second niche then finish up
the crack above.

★★★ 142. Run Wild, Run Free 12m E6 6b   (1969/1985)
The steep crack above the ramp of Western Terrace, which was originally
pegged as Black Pitch. A serious start to the left of the crack, leads to the
crack, then follow this with much difficulty; bold crux at six metres.

★★★ 143. Ego Trip 12m E5 6b   (1964/1983)
The twin cracks above and slightly to the right of the initial ramp of Western
Terrace give a fine route. Steep and strenuous climbing leads past a monstrous
crux at half-height.

Grey Wall – The Pit

The next climbs start from the depression known as The Pit.

★★ 144. K.P. 17m E6 6b   (1969/1978)
If you can only just make it on London Wall, you will fail on this ferocious
finger crack. Originally pegged as The Shakes. The thin crack right of Ego Trip,
rising out of a shattered sentry-box. Initially gained by a rising traverse from the
belay of Frightful Fred.

★★ 145. Josser 17m E5 6a   (1969/1978)
A good E5 at the lower end of the grade. Strenuous and sustained with adequate
protection. From the large ledge on Frightful Fred climb a vague groove to a

small overlap on the right. Pass this and fight up the crack above (2 pegs) to a
second overlap; move left under this overlap and finish direct, or take the
overlap direct.

★ **146. Welcome to the Pleasuredome** 17m E5 6b   (1985/1986)
Bold and forceful climbing up the steep wall right of Josser. From the belay
ledge, climb direct, passing a tiny overlap (crux) and peg (not in place), and on
to the exposed wall above. Trend leftwards (peg) at the top. Significantly harder
for the short.

★★ **147. Frightful Fred** 26m VS 4c,4c   (1963)(1964)
A good introduction to the climbing in this part of Wilton, providing plenty of
variety, with nothing too difficult, but nevertheless, not for the faint-hearted!
1. 8m. Ascend the wide chimney at the left of The Pit, then move right on to
a large ledge, Peg belay.
2. 18m. From the right of the series of ledges, mantel on to the lowest of two
ledges on the left wall of a shallow groove and move up to a peg, then swing
up to a ledge on the right. Either, climb the right of a slab to a triangular ledge
and make an awkward step left to finish, or, step awkwardly round to the left
and climb the wall on the left by a series of ledges, then traverse back and
finish over several small ledges. The latter is a little harder, but is a very
artificial line.

148. Jimmy Mac, Bin Man Extraordinaire 20m E2 6a,4c   (1967/1983)
Previously known as Fearful Frank.
1. 8m. The thin crack just left of Bohemian is not very worthwhile.
2. 12m. As for Frightful Fred, then continue straight up the groove over
several small ledges to the top.

149. Bohemia 21m HVS 5b   (1977)
The crackline just right leads up through a hanging groove to the top.

★★★ **150. Adrenalin** 25m E4 6a   (1969/1981)
Good holds and good gear lure one ever farther up this impending groove. An
excellent pitch. Climb the broken crack which starts three metres left of the
large sandy cave, on poor rock to a possible belay on the left of the cave.
Continue up the obvious overhanging crack in the groove above.

★★ **151. Chocolate Girl** 28m E7 6c   (1969/1996)
A completely free version of Adrenalin Direct, taking the superb parallel line
under Gigantic, but not quite as hard. Start in the large corner below the sandy
cave and climb easily up the wall trending slightly left to the cave (possible
belay). Launch out and go up the crack (two pegs) until a wild slap gives good
holds and a Quadcam 2 placement. Excellent and pumpy moves leftwards past
two further pegs lead to Adrenalin at some undercuts, then finish up this.

★★ **152. Grey and White Girdle** 101m HVS 4c,5a,5a,4b,4b,4c,–   (1965)
A sustained and interesting traverse, with some impressive positions, which
crosses virtually all the best climbs from Dandelion Groove to Blackout.
1. 17m. Climb Dandelion Groove for nine metres to a ledge on the right, then
foot-traverse this rightwards to a peg belay, three metres left of Remembrance
Corner.

2. 15m. Gain the corner and climb round the arête to a peg. Descend slightly to the sandy belt and traverse awkwardly rightwards to a small corner. Step down into a small cave and go down again to belay on the iron spike of Patience.

3. 12m. Regain the horizontal break and follow it rightwards to join Patience at the foot of its ramp; follow this ramp to a belay on Western Terrace.

4. 20m. Reverse Western Terrace to its initial rib and climb down this until it is possible to move right, along a series of unstable flakes, to gain Frightful Fred at the top of its chimney. Follow that route to its peg belay.

5. 12m. Climb Frightful Fred to an obvious ledge on the right, overlooking Bohemian. Peg belay.

6. 15m. Descend diagonally right (peg) and enter a loose and sandy cave. Leave this cave (thankfully) by its right-hand end and hand-traverse along the horizontal break to Knuckleduster. Continue this traverse around the blunt arête to gain and climb a short groove (as Thin Air) to the huge ledge on Knuckleduster. Peg belay.

7. 10 m. Either continue as for Plenty of Zzzzs, or (4c) climb the short thin crack in the wall above the peg belay and move right to a finish up Blackout pitch two.

★★ **153. Plenty of Zzzzs** 31m E2 4c,5b   (1984)
An extension to the Grey and White Girdle, but it can also be done as a route in its own right. Some interesting climbing, but this stops abruptly at Kettle Crack, after which it is necessary either to enter 'black spot country' or to lower off. Start on Blackout at pitch seven of Grey and White.

1. 13m. As for Grey and White, but at the top of the short crack, traverse right over ledges to reverse the crux slab of Blackout and a belay under the roof of Clapped Out.

2. 18m. From the roof on Master Spy swing right into Wipe Out. Move right across the wall of Black Mamba, and on to a ledge and peg on Shaggy Dog. Go right across Kettle Crack to a final stiff move to reach a bolt belay. Either abseil off (preferable), or go right to finish up Fall Out Chimney, (lethal). Whilst the block above the bolt seems stable, it is inadvisable to hang on the rusting iron bar which appears to support it!.

Red Wall

At the end of The Pit the rock becomes very sandy, and the rock to the right of this point to the top corner of the quarry is known as Red Wall.

154. Knuckleduster 25m HVS 5a,4c   (1964/1966)(1982)
Start at the base of the arête just right of the sandy cave
1. 17m. Step left to the crack and follow it past the horizontal break and go over the overhang to a large ledge (care needed past loose blocks).
2. 8m. Starting on the arête move up delicately until the groove on the right can be gained and followed to the top.
2a. 8m. (**Fist Finish**, 5b): climb the short crack in the back wall and continue up a vague groove above.

★★ **155. Gigantic** 17m E8 6c   (1964/1990)
An awesome effort forced a free ascent of Triffid Wall to create this marathon test of endurance. The crux moves are at the top of the route and despite an

abundance of protection, they are not destined to become polished. From Knuckleduster pitch two, swing left round the arête then follow a steep left-slanting crack and finish up the groove on the left as for Adrenalin.

★ **156. Thin Air**   15m   E5   6a   (1970)

A bold pitch. Climb the smooth wall just right of the blunt arête to a peg. Pass this by a hard move to gain a short groove leading to the break and the belay ledge of Knuckleduster. A finish can then be made up Knuckleduster or Hot Air.

★ **157. Hot Air**   12m   E5   6b   (1985)

A very bold top pitch to Thin Air. Leave the belay ledge of Thin Air/Knuckleduster by its right arête and attain a hold in the bottom of a shallow groove. Enter this groove by a desperate mantel and finish direct.

★ **158. Nothing Fantastic**   21m   E3   5c   (1969)

Four metres right of the blunt arête is a rightwards-curving crack. Follow this with an awkward move rightwards above a poor peg , then climb direct to the horizontal break and the large ledges of Blackout. Climb the thin crack above the ledge to finish.

★★ **159. Blackout**   20m   VS   4b,–   (1962)

Another classic Wilton route, which is not as difficult as it might seem, though there are many capable leaders who might disagree. At the north end of the quarry, just past the final rise in the quarry floor, is a pedestal which marks the start.

1. 14m.   Ascend the pedestal, then the groove behind for a little, until a traverse left can be made to a ledge. Left again is another ledge and a peg belay.

2. 6m.   Climb up behind the belay veering right.

★ **160. Clapped Out**   14m   E4   6b   (1968/1981)

From the top of the initial groove on Blackout, surmount the overhang (poor peg) and struggle up the continuation crack above, then move left to finish and avoid loose rock.

★★★ **161. Master Spy**   20m   E4   6a   (1970)

The original Master Spy, although not direct is very impressive and utilizes the undercut flake to reach the technical crux. Follow Clapped Out to the roof then launch out tentatively right along the undercut flake (easier than it looks) for four metres to a vertical crack and a rest. The crack above holds out to the end.

★★★ **162. Counter Intelligence**   18m   E4   6b   (1982)

The hardest of the espionage trio. A powerful start leads to a hard mantel finish, that is slightly easier to do as a rock-over – but which way to face? Two metres right of the start of Blackout, an impressive vertical crack leads to the right-hand end of the Master Spy roof. Climb the crack (peg) and pass the roof, then traverse leftwards to a nasty mantel and a crack to finish.

★★★ **163. Master Spy Direct**   18m   E4   6a   (1983-86)

The obvious direct connection of the two previous routes. An excellent combination of the best climbing on the previous two routes.

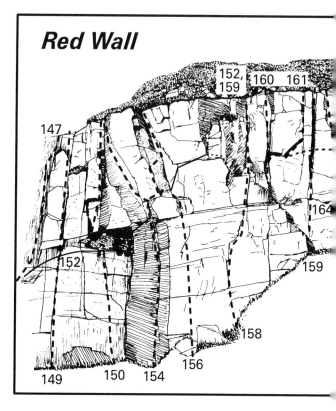

Red Wall

★★ **164. Wipe Out**   18m   E2   5b   (1966)
The awesome hanging groove three metres to the right of Blackout. Superb and
unrelentingly steep, but with well protected climbing. A classic jamming and
bridging problem that builds to a fine crescendo.

★★ **165. Black Mamba**   17m   E4   6b   (1971/1982)
Brilliant, technical and it can be well protected. Start in the centre of the steep
wall right of Wipe Out, and climb slots to a sloping ledge and peg. Move up to
gain a standing position on this ledge (bolt), then make a particularly venomous
move up and left to gain the base of an easy groove. Finish up this.

★★ **166. Shaggy Mamba**   17m   E6   6b   (1983)
Break out right from the bolt of Black Mamba, and make desperate moves to
gain good holds on Shaggy Dog. Finish as for that route.

167. Black Dog Blues   17m   E5   6b   (1985)
Climb Black Mamba to the peg and either lurch/jump or make a l..o..ng reach
up and right for a ledge and continue up the cleaned groove above (peg).

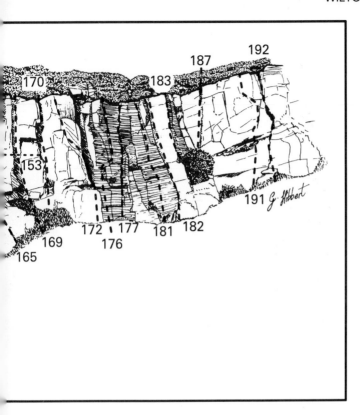

★★ **168. Shaggy Dog** 14m E4 5c   (1982)
A serious proposition that has seen some near-ground falls. From six metres up
Kettle Crack, swing left on to a ledge on the face (peg). Move left and climb
straight up the wall to a somewhat '*out there*' finish.

169. Kettle Crack 12m E2 5c   (Pre-1968/1971)
The crack to the left of a huge block supported by an iron bar.

● **170. Fall Out Chimney** 12m HS 4a   (Pre-1967)
The ugly chimney on the right; do not touch it, especially with a bargepole!

★ **171. Myrmidon** 17m E5 6b   (1985)
The thin crack in the arête to the right is climbed (crux) to a long reach
rightwards which gains ledges on Overtaker's Buttress. Join and finish up that
route.

172. Overtaker's Buttress 18m E3 5c   (1978)
Climb the groove in the narrow buttress on the right to a sloping ledge, move
left along this to the arête and finish up the arête passing a small overhang.

173. Twazack Left-hand 15m VS 4c   (1964/1975)
Farther right is a deep bay. Start in the left corner of this and climb up to a
large block which forms an overhang. Move left and go up the shallow groove
which bounds the block on its left, to a small ledge on an arête on the left.
Finish direct.

174. Twazack Right-hand 15m VS 4c   (1964)
As for Twazack Left-hand to the block, then climb the corner/groove which
bounds the block on its right.

*The following two routes centre on cracks on either side of the steep arête
which marks the right side of Twazack's bay. The stability of the upper section
of this arête gives great cause for concern, and these routes are probably best
left alone.*

175. Rebellion 15m E1 5b   (1969)
The crack on the right-hand side of the bay, (gained from the grass ledge on the
left) moving right at the overhang to the subsidiary corner.

176. Roll Over 15m E2 5b   (1969/1976)
Just right is a clean-cut S-shaped crack at the top of the crag. From the grassy
ledge on the left, swing round the arête and climb the steep crack above.

177. Dinosaur 24m HVS 4c,4b   (1969)
A long neck and a small brain are essential for pitch 1.
1. 12m. 3 metres to the right is a corner with a wide, block-filled crack in it.
Climb this to a swing right on to the belay ledge.
1a. 12m. Climb the corner for three metres to a niche, then move up and
right to a good hold which enables a swing right to be made to join Great Slab.
Follow this to the belay.
2. 12m. The crack which forms a continuation to the corner.

178. Slap Happy 18m E3 6a   (1992)
The sharp, left-slanting crack and arête right of Dinosaur, leads past a peg to a
ledge. Finish up Knock Out.

★ **179. Knock Out** 9m VS 4c   (1966)
From the belay of Great Slab, climb the crack on the right of Dinosaur.

★ **180. Great Slab** 26m VS 4b,4c   (1963/1966)
Start beneath the centre of the impressive slab at the north end of the quarry.
1. 9m. Mantel on to the slab, and climb via a rust flower, to a large grass
ledge on the left of the slab.
2. 17m. Cross the slab at its sandy weakness, then climb the groove to a
small overhang. Traverse right along a small ledge to the arête. Finish up this
on its left.

★★ **181. Virgin's Dilemma** 20m HVS 5a   (1967)
A bold problem; not quite so common nowadays! Start just left of the large
corner groove of 999, move up on to the slab and climb to the rust flower. Step
right and climb the slab above directly, passing a peg to enter a shallow
chimney.

★★★ **182. 999**   18m   HS   4c   (1963)
The open groove on the right gives a good well-protected route, with its crux at
the top.

★★ **183. Left Edge**   8m   HVS   4c   (1964)
From the grassy ledge in the corner at a higher level, climb the left arête and
finish as for Great Slab. Good, bold climbing.

The Graveyard
*Right of the grassy ledge, the rock arcs round rightwards and becomes The
Graveyard; an uninspiring piece of rock on the whole but with one or two
exceptionally good lines.*

184. Coffin Crack   6m   VS   4c   (1964)
From the wide grassy ledge in the top corner of the quarry, climb the crack in
the left wall.

185. Green Chimney   6m   D   (1964)
The aptly-named chimney starting from the angle of the large ledge.

★ **186. Chance Encounters**   9m   E3   5c   (1984)
Just to the right (peg) a direct line up the small diamond-shaped buttress.

187. Susan   6m   VS   4c   (1967)
The crack which slants right from the back of the ledge.

188. La Morte   12m   HVS   5b   (1979)
Start below a sandy cave and climb ragged cracks, passing the cave on the left,
and continue to a ledge. Finish up the wall above via a small pod.

189. Undertaker's Crack   10m   VS   4c   (1964)
Traverse right from the wide grass ledge to the base of a hand-jam crack. Climb
this to a niche below an overhang (peg). Leave the niche to the left then finish
up the short wall above.

★★ **190. Join the Army, Get Yourself Killed**   18m   E5   6a   (1983)
The impressive wall left of Soixante-neuf. Gain a ledge in the wall left of
Soixante Neuf either direct from the ground, or by a traverse in from the left
above the cave. Clip the poor peg above the ledge (hard and dangerous if you
are less than average stature) then step left and finish direct.

★ **191. Soixante-neuf**   14m   E2   5c   (1979)
Gain a niche and finger crack, then go up this to a ledge on the arête. Finish
direct or gain the ledge on the arête from the front face via a mantel.

192. Graveyard Direct   9m   S   4a   (1962)
Climb the obvious chimney in the centre of the wall to a ledge, then finish up
the hanging chimney.

193. Graveyard Ordinary   14m   M   (1962)
From the initial chimney go up ledges on the right, and finish up a narrow
chimney.

194. Bolton Buttress 10m S 4a (1969)

Just to the right is a short triangular buttress. Climb this, then step across the wall at an obvious ledge and finish up Graveyard Direct.

195. Mary 9m VD (1967)

The layback corner on the right, then finish up the short blocky corner.

196. Saturation Point 12m HVS 5a (1979)

The narrow face one and a half metres right of the corner.

197. Coffin Digger's Spade 10m S (1962)

Farther right is a V-shaped fault filled with blocks, with a tree and a sandy cave below it. Gain the cave from the left, then climb over a doubtful block to The Spade, and pass behind it to finish on its left.

198. Catalepsy 12m HS 4b (1979)

Just to the right is a thin crack. Climb this to a ledge, then continue via a sloping ledge on the wall above to the right side of The Spade. Finish over the blocks above.

199. Neddy's Walk 10m VD (1964)

Climb a short groove behind a bush to a ledge, then move up a series of ledges and finish by a mantel over the overhanging wall on the right.

200. Crash and Burn 15m HVS 5a (1979)

Four metres to the right follow the curving crack then finish up the leaning jam-crack on the left.

201. Ape 6m VD (1974-75)

Six metres right ascend the wide crack.

202. Overhanging Weetabix 6m E2 5c (1984)

On the right is a small buttress with a double overhang. Climb the crack on its left-hand side to the break, then step left and surmount the roof by a thin crack.

203. The Overhang 6m VS 4b (1962)

Follow Overhanging Weetabix to the break, then traverse right and finish up the arête.

204. Horror Arête 8m VS 5b (1975-79)

Go over the nose on the right by a gymnastic move, and finish up the arête above as for The Overhang.

205. Avoidance 8m D (1974-75)

Start three metres to the left and traverse left to finish up the arête of The Overhang.

206. Chocky 6m S (1974-75)

On the right of the buttress climb the chock-filled corner.

207. Tombstoned 39m HVS 5a (1965)

Originally known as the Girdle of the Graveyard. A traverse of The Graveyard is possible, the line is obvious but lacks any sort of appeal.

Ian Lonsdale taking time on **Ten Minute Traverse** (E3 5b,5c) on the first free ascent, but will he swing?   *Photo Brian Cropper*

First Ascents at Wilton One

1961	**Eastern Terrace** Graham Kilner, Harry Taylor
1961	**Rambling Route, Bird Chimney, Flywalk, Scimitar** Graham Kilner, Harry Taylor
	Rambling Route and Bird Chimney originally called Amen Reverse and Green Chimney respectively.
1961	**Sunset Boulevard** (A1) Graham Kilner, Harry Taylor
	First free ascent as Dawn, by Mick Pooler, Ray Evans, 1963.
1962 Mar	**Fingernail** Mick Pooler, Dave Brodigan
1962 Apr 22	**Christeena** Mick Pooler, Dave Brodigan
1962	**Graveyard Direct, Graveyard Ordinary, Coffin Digger's Spade, The Overhang** Mick Pooler, Dave Brodigan
1963 Mar 12	**Blackout** Dave Brodigan, John Nuttall, Ray Evans
1963 Apr 12	**Frightful Fred** Ray Evans, John Nuttall
	Wall Finish by Ray Evans, John Nuttall, 15 June 1964.
1963 Apr 17	**Great Slab** Ken Powell, Ray Evans (alts)
	The route originally finished up 999, until the groove finish was cleaned by Les Ainsworth, Paul Hamer, 1966.
1963	**Dawn** Mick Pooler
	First free ascent of Sunset Boulevard.
1963 Apr 18	**999** Ken Powell, John Nuttall
1963 Apr 29	**Western Terrace** Ray Evans, Ken Powell (alts)
	Surprisingly, this route had repulsed at least two previous attempts, because of it's condition.
1963 June 2	**Dandelion Groove** Ken Powell, John Nuttall
1963 July	**Eliminate** Rowland Edwards
1963 Aug 11	**Spider Crack** Ken Powell, John Nuttall, with some aid on the first pitch
1963	**Innominate** (A1)
	First free ascent by Hank Pasquill, pre-1983.
1964 Feb	**Eccles' Escalator** Ray Evans, Ken Powell
1964 Mar	**Manglewurzle Rib** Ray Evans, Ken Powell
1964 May 10	**Flingle Bunt** Ray Evans, John Nuttall, Brian Johnson
1964 May 23	**Left Edge** Ray Evans, John Nuttall
1964 May 29	**Cameo** Ray Evans, John Nuttall, Les Ainsworth
1964 June 6	**Triffid Wall** (A2) Ken Powell, Ray Evans
	First free ascent by Dave Pegg as Gigantic, 24 May 1990.
1964 June 13	**Patience** (with tension) Ray Evans, John Nuttall,
	First ascent without tension by Les Ainsworth, Ray Evans, 19 Aug 1964.
1964 June 26	**Horrocks' Route** Ken Powell, Bob Hampson, John Nuttall
	Horrocks' Route Direct by John Hartley (solo), 1983.
1964	**Diversion** Ray Evans, Ken Powell
	Reclimbed as Orange Peel after a rockfall in 1971.
1964 Aug 1	**Grotty Muckden** Les Ainsworth and party
1964 Aug 1	**Twazack Left-hand** Les Ainsworth (second did not follow)
	Originally climbed with the Right-hand finish. The left hand start was not added until about 1975.
1964 Aug	**Erythrocyte** Les Ainsworth
	A few weeks earlier, Ken Powell and Bob Hampson had climbed a similar line up the bottom section called Red Wall.
1964 Aug 8	**Jean** (1pt aid) Les Ainsworth, Ron Atkinson
	Aid peg dispensed with by Bob Hampson, Ken Powell after removal of a block when placing the peg a couple of weeks later.
1964 Aug 9	**Ruby** Les Ainsworth, Ron Atkinson
1964 Aug 16	**Helix** Ray Evans, Bob Hampson (alts)
1964 Aug 23	**Green Wall** Ray Evans, Ken Powell
1964 Aug 23	**White Crack** Ray Evans (solo)
1964 Aug 26	**Leucocyte Left-hand** Ray Evans, Ken Powell
1964 Sep 19	**Tombstoned** Ray Evans, Dave Sant (Var)

Dave Cronshaw and Les Ainsworth on the first free ascent of **Slime Corner** (HVS 5a), Hoghton Quarry, in far from ideal conditions.   *Photo: George Philips*

1964 Oct   **Niche Indirect**   Ray Evans, Bob Hampson
1964 Oct 24   **Stet**   (A2)   Ken Powell, Bob Hampson
First free ascent by John Monks, Tony Preston or John Hartley as Ego Trip, 1983.
1964   **Twazack Right-hand**   Ray Evans, Ken Powell
1964   **Obituary**   (HVS/A1)   Ken Powell, Bob Hampson
First free ascent as Supercrack by Ian Lonsdale, 1975-79
1964 Nov 8   **Remembrance Corner**   Rowland Edwards, Ken Powell, Bob Hampson
This was to be the last new route in the quarries for both Edwards and Powell.
1964 Nov 11   **Peanuts**   Ray Evans (second did not follow)
1964   **Coffin Crack, Green Chimney, Neddy's Walk**   Ray Evans
1964   **Undertaker's Crack**   Ray Evans, Bob Hampson
1965   **The Corner**   Ray Evans (second did not follow)
1965   **Grey and White Girdle**   Ray Evans, Allan Brook
Pitch 3 made independent of Patience by Ian Lonsdale, Les Ainsworth, 1975
1965   **Tryptophane**   Ray Evans, Brian Johnson
1965   **Kurma**   Ray Evans, Allan Brook
1966 Easter   **Willow Wall**   Ray Evans
1966 May 15   **Knuckleduster**   Ray Evans, Eric Robinson
Second pitch originally done as a variation finish to Blackout by Ray Evans, Ken Powell, 12 Sep 1964.
1966 Aug 8   **Wombat Chimney**   Ray Evans, Les Ainsworth
1966   **Flimnap the Pirate**   Les Ainsworth, Paul Hamer
Pre-1967   **Fallout Chimney**
1966   **Wipe Out**   Les Ainsworth, John Mason
1966   **Knock Out**   Ray Evans, Bob Hampson
1967   **Needles and Pins**   (A2)
First free ascent as The Foot of an Oncoming Mexican by Bill McKee, Chris Calow, 16 June 1986.
1967   **Leucocyte Right-hand**   Hank Pasquill, Ray Evans
1967   **Central Route, Christine Arête, Virgin's Dilemma, Cheat**   Hank Pasquill
1967   **Ann**   Les Ainsworth, John McGonagle

1967   **White Slabs Bunt**   (2pts aid)   Hank Pasquill
Aid eliminated by Hank Pasquill, 1971.
1967   **Fearful Frank**   (A1/VS)   John McGonagle, Ray Miller
This was a peg start combined with the Wall Finish of Frightful Fred to make a virtually independent line.
First free ascent as Jimmy Mac, Bin Man Extraordinaire by Phil Kelly, Paul Wood, Paul Pritchard, 5 Aug 1983.
1967   **Susan**   Les Ainsworth, Ian 'Spider' McQuirk
1967   **Mary**   Terry Wareing, Les Ainsworth
Pre-1968   **Kettle Crack**   (VS/A1)
First free ascent by Hank Pasquill, Ian Lonsdale, 1971.
Pre-1968   **Flytrap**   Hank Pasquill
Originally known as Bypass.
1968 Easter   **Willow Arête**   Hank Pasquill and party
1968 Easter   **Baby Arête**   Hank Pasquill (solo)
1968   **Dinah**   (1pt aid)
Aid eliminated by Hank Pasquill, 1974.
1968   **Paradox**   Hank Pasquill
1968   **Max**   Hank Paquill, Les Ainsworth
Originally made a detour to avoid loose rock part way up. Straightened out later by Hank Pasquill.
1968   **Loopy**   Hank Pasquill, Ian Lonsdale
Pre-1968   **Obeit**   (A1)
First free ascent by Ian Lonsdale, Dave Caine as Sobeit, 25 June 1977.
1968   **Clapped Out**   (A1)
First free ascent by John Monks, Denis Gleeson, 23 Apr 1981.

1968	**Big Dipper** (E2/A1)
	Aid substantially reduced by Hank Pasquill, Ian Lonsdale.
	First free ascent by Paul Pritchard, Mark Leach as Cleansweep, 1985.
	Corner start added by John Stringfellow, Geoff Mann, 1988.
1969	**Vaccination** (A1) Graham 'Penk' Penketh, Paul Madrid
	First free ascent by John Hartley, John Monks as Sleepwalk, 1982.
1969	**Stegosaurus, Opposition** Les Ainsworth, Dave Cronshaw
1969	**Spec Crack** John 'Spec' Spencer
1969	**Titanosaurus** (A1)
	First free ascent by Mark Leach, Paul Wood, 1982.
1969	**In Memoriam** (1pt aid) Hank Pasquill, Jim Fogg, with 1 aid pt
	Aid eliminated by Ian Lonsdale, 1978.
1969	**Black Pitch** (A1) Hank Pasquill, Jim Fogg
	First free ascent by Mark Leach, Paul Pritchard as Run Wild Run Free, 1985.
1969	**The Shakes** (A2) Hank Pasquill, Des Britt
	First free ascent by Geoff Mann as K.P., 1978.
1969	**Josser** (A2) Jim Fogg, A. Chadwick
	First free ascent by Dave Knighton, 1978.
1969	**Adrenalin** (VS/A2) Jim Fogg, Graham 'Penk' Penketh
	First free ascent by Hank Pasquill, Geoff Mann, 1981.
1969	**Adrenalin Direct** (VS/A3) Hank Pasquill, Jim Fogg
	First free ascent by Gareth Parry as Chocolate Girl, July 1996.
1969	**Nothing Fantastic** Hank Pasquill, Graham 'Penk' Penketh
1969	**Rebellion** Hank Pasquill, Jim Fogg
1969	**Dinosaur** Hank Pasquill, Dave Hollows
1969	**Roll Over** Hank Pasquill, Dave Hollows
	Originally gained from Dinosaur.
	Line made independent by Ian Lonsdale, 26 July 1976.
1969	**Bolton Buttress** Les Ainsworth (solo)
1970	**Barbara Ann** Dave Cronshaw, Roger Vickers
1970	**Loopy Left-hand** Hank Pasquill, John Grundy, Jim Fogg
1970	**Baby's Bottom** Dave Cronshaw, Les Ainsworth
1970	**Thin Air** Hank Pasquill, Dave Hollows
1970	**Master Spy** Hank Pasquill, Dave Hollows (shared leads and attempts)
1971	**Merchant Crack, This** Dave Cronshaw, Les Ainsworth
1971	**La Rue, Lime Street,** *T'other* Les Ainsworth, Dave Cronshaw
1971	**Transfiguration** Les Ainsworth, Dave Cronshaw, Bob MacMillan
1971	**Jaws** Les Ainsworth and Dave Cronshaw
1971	**Orange Peel**
	Climbed the line of Diversion after it had been destroyed by a rockfall.
1971	**White Slabs Bunt** Hank Pasquill
	Remaining aid eliminated.
1971	**Kettle Crack** Hank Pasquill, Ian Lonsdale
	First free ascent.
1971	**Black Mamba** (bolt and lassoed spike for aid) Dave Cronshaw (unseconded)
	Aid completely eliminated by Dougie Hall, 1982.
Pre-1972	**That, Rhonda** (A2)
1972	**Streaker, Georgina** Dave Cronshaw, Les Ainsworth
1972	**Grovel** Les Ainsworth, Dave Cronshaw
1972	**The Mouth** Les Ainsworth, Dave Cronshaw, Bob MacMillan
1972	**Deodand** (1pt aid) Dave Cronshaw, Les Ainsworth,
	Aid eliminated by Ian Lonsdale, 1974.
1973	**The Hacker** Hank Pasquill
	Originally traversed into Central Route. Line straightened by Roland Foster,
	Phil Parker, 1984.
1974	**Grassy, Crow's-nest**
1974	**Adidas, Puma** Hank Pasquill
1974	**Proline** (A1)
	First free ascent by Tony Preston, 1980-82.
1974-75	**Jimmy Nip** 2pts aid) John 'Spec' Spencer
	Aid completely eliminated by John Monks, 1983.

1974-75	**Goon, Ape, Avoidance, Chocky**	
1974-75	**Vampire** (A1)	

First free ascent by Ian Lonsdale, Mike Bromley, Nigel Holmes, 8 June 1977.

1974-75   **Spike** (A1)
First free ascent by Al Pearce, 1979.

1975   **Nappy Rash** John 'Spec' Spencer
Direct Start, 1986.

1977   **Jughandle Wall** Stephen Lee

1977 Mar 28   **First Cut** Ian Lonsdale

1977 Apr 16   **Asleep for Years** Dave Knighton, Nigel Holmes, Paul McKenzie

1977   **Land** Dave Johnson (solo)
Midnite Cruiser. A variation finish to Land, 1978-79.

1977 May 19   **Lazy Friday** Jerry Peel, Ian Lonsdale

1977 May 19   **Houses of the Holy** Dave Knighton, Nigel Holmes

1977 May 20   **Bohemia** Dave Knighton, Con Carey

1977 June 5   **Jubilee Climb** Ian Lonsdale, Paul Cropper

1977 June 8   **Vampire** Ian Lonsdale, Mike Bromley, Nigel Holmes
First free ascent.

1977 June 25   **Sobeit** Ian Lonsdale, Dave Caine
First free ascent of Obeit.

1977 Aug 30   **Dracula** Ian Lonsdale, Frank Roberts, Mike Blood

1977 Aug 31   **Prickpocket** Ian Lonsdale, Mike Bromley

1977   **Isle of White** Ian Lonsdale, Mike Bromley
Independent start Hank Pasquill, Ian Lonsdale.

1978   **Overtaker's Buttress** Dave Cronshaw, Dave Knighton

1978   **K.P.** (A2) Geoff Mann
First free ascent of The Shakes.

1978   **Josser** Dave Knighton
First free ascent.

1975-79   *The* Hank Pasquill
Superseded by The Pit and the Pendulum.

1975-79   **Supercrack** Ian Lonsdale
First free ascent of Obituary.

1975-79   **Wedgewood** Ian Lonsdale

1975-79   **Life in the Fast Lane** Dave Johnson, Ian Johnston

1975-79   **Horror Arête**

1979 Apr   **Saturation Point** Dave Knighton, Dave Cronshaw

1979 May   **La Morte** Dave Cronshaw, Dave Knighton, Les Ainsworth

1979 May   **Soixante-neuf** Dave Knighton, Les Ainsworth, Dave Cronshaw

1979 July 4   **Insertion** Ian Lonsdale, Dave Staton

1979   **The Deep**, *The Shark, The Fin* Dave Cronshaw, Les Ainsworth

1979   **Catalepsy** Dave Knighton, Ian Ault

1979   **Crash and Burn**

1979   **Spike** Al Pearce
First free ascent.

1980 Apr 29   **Reeling in the Years** Dave Cronshaw (solo)

1980 Apr   **Lady Grinning Soul** Ian Lonsdale, Dave Cronshaw

1980 May 1   **Regatta de Blanc** Ian Lonsdale, John Monks

1980 May   **Impatience** Dave Cronshaw, Ian Lonsdale

1980   **Ummagumma** Ian Lonsdale, Mick Bullough

1980   **Friends** Ian Lonsdale, Mick Burrow, Dave Geelan

1980   **Parasite** Top arête by Hank Pasquill, Doug Shaw, John Monks.
Bottom arête only by Jerry Peel.

1980   **Eliminator** Dave Cronshaw, Ian Machin
Originally started from Dinah. Independent start by Paul Pritchard (solo), 1985.

1981 Apr 23   **Clapped Out** John Monks, Denis Gleeson
First free ascent.

1981   **Adrenalin** Hank Pasquill, Geoff Mann
First free ascent.

1980-82   **Proline** (A1) Tony Preston
First free ascent.

1982	**Titanosaurus** Mark Leach, Paul Wood
	First free ascent.
1982	**Pot-Pourri** Dennis Gleeson
1982	**Gravitational Experiment, Astradyne** John Hartley, John Monks
1982	**The Devil's Alternative** John Hartley, Paul Clarke
1982	**Silently Screaming** John Hartley, Paul Clarke, Mark Kemball
1982	**Steeplejack** Dave Cronshaw, John Ryden, Les Ainsworth
1982	**Knuckleduster, Fist Finish** Mark Kemball, Ian Lonsdale, John Hartley
1982	**Sleepwalk** John Hartley, John Monks
	First free ascent of Vaccination.
1982	**Counter Intelligence** John Hartley
1982	**Shaggy Dog** Hank Pasquill, Paul Clarke
1982	**Black Mamba** Dougie Hall
	Aid completely eliminated.
Pre-1983	**Innominate** Hank Pasquill
	First free ascent.
1983 Aug 5	**Jimmy Mac, Bin Man Extraordinaire** Phil Kelly, Paul Wood, Paul Pritchard
	First free ascent of Fearful Frank.
1983	**Falling Wall** Tim Lowe, Dave Vose
1983	**Ego Trip** John Monks, Tony Preston or John Hartley
	First free ascent of Stet.
1983	**The Power of the Mekon** Dave Williams, Paul Heaton
1983	**Shaggy Mamba** Roland Foster
1983	**Red Flowers are Red** Dai Lampard, Nigel Holmes, Denis Gleeson
1983	**Join the Army, Get Yourself Killed** Roland Foster
1984	**Ordinary Route** Dai Lampard, Geoff Mann
1984	*The Death of Timothy Grass* Andrew Gridley, Steve Sharples
1984	**Veteran Cosmic Rocker** Mark Leach, after practising
	Had already been done on the left side by Paul Pritchard, Gary McCandlish, 1984.
1984	**Crater Traitor** Paul Pritchard, Gary McCandlish
1984 July 3	**Plenty of Zzzzs** Phil Kelly, Paul Pritchard
1984 Aug 16	**Chance Encounters** Tim Lowe, Dave Vose, Dave Kenyon
1984 Aug 16	**Thin White Line** Tim Lowe, Bernie Bradbury
	Extended from the Girdle ledge by Paul Pritchard, Phil Kelly as Strawberry Kiss, 16 Sep 1986.
1984	**Overhanging Weetabix** Geoff Hibbert, Dave Williams
1985 May 16	**Black Dog Blues** Paul Pritchard, Andrew Gridley
1985 May 17	**Myrmidon** Paul Pritchard, Phil Kelly, Andrew Gridley
1985 June 25	**Welcome to the Pleasuredome** Pitch 2: Tim Lowe, Dave Vose – Pitch 1: Paul Pritchard, 4 July 1986
1985 July 4	**Pathetique** Paul Pritchard, Dave Peace
1985 Oct 1	**The Pretentious Gallery** Paul Pritchard, Al Newby
1985 Oct 5	**Hot Air** Paul Pritchard
1985	**Is it a Cheesecake or a Meringue?** Paul Pritchard (solo)
1985	**It** Mark Leach (solo)
1985	**The Soot Monkey** Paul Pritchard
	Gained from 6 metres up Wombat.
	Direct Start added later in the year by Paul Pritchard.
1985	**Run Wild Run Free** Mark Leach
	First free ascent of Black Pitch.
1985	**White Lightinin'** Paul Pritchard
1985	**Cleansweep** Paul Pritchard, Mark Leach
	First free ascent of Big Dipper.
1985	**Boy Racer** Paul Pritchard, Al Newby
	Made Midnite Cruiser into an independent line.
1983-86	**Master Spy Direct** Paul Clarke,
1986 Apr 30	**The Pit and the Pendulum** Paul Pritchard, Phil Kelly
1986 June 16	**The Foot of an Oncoming Mexican** Bill McKee, Chris Calow
	First free ascent of Needles and Pins.

1986 July   **Zapling** Denis Gleeson, Ian Lonsdale, Sean Walsh
1986 July   **Headbutt Wall** John Hartley
1986 Sep 11   **Perimeter Walk** Paul Pritchard (solo after practice)
1986 Sep 11   **Rope 'n' Rubber** Paul Pritchard (solo)
1986 Sep 16   **Strawberry Kiss** Paul Pritchard, Phil Kelly
                Extended Thin White Line.
1990 May 24   **Gigantic** Dave Pegg, 24 May 1990
                First free ascent of Triffid Wall.
1992 June   **Rugosity Atrocity** Geoff Hibbert, Chris Hemmings
1992 June 30   **L'arête** Matt Nuttall
1992 June   **Geoff's Wall, Brontosaurus** Geoff Hibbert (solo)
1992 July 22   **Press Intrusions** Alan Holden
1992 July   **It'll be Rude Not To** Matt Nuttall, Gareth Parry
1992 July   **Beyond the Perimeter** Garry Parry, Mark Nuttall
1992 July   **Big Al** Alan Holden (solo)
1992 July   **Powerage** Geoff Hibbert, Mike Arnold
1992 July   **Snakebite** Geoff Hibbert, Chris Hemmings
1992 Aug 11   **Slap Happy** John Stringfellow
1992   **Under the Matt** Matt Nuttall
1996 July   **Chocolate Girl** Gareth Parry
                First free ascent of Adrenalin Direct.

Wilton Two   O.S. ref.   SD 696 134

There is no climbing allowed in Wilton Two or Three on Wednesdays, Friday or Sundays

The climbs are described from LEFT to RIGHT.

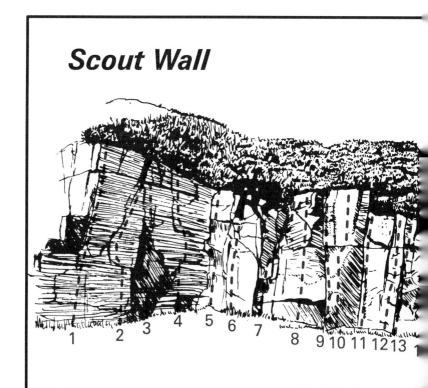

Scout Wall

Scout Wall

The section on the left when entering the quarry is known as Scout Wall. At the extreme left of this is:

1.   Arête Not   8m   HS   4a   (1963)
Follow the arête as near as possible.

★ **2.   Concrete Crack**   9m   E3   6a   (1982)
An explosive, bouldery start gains access to a fingery and sustained crack. Excellent protection. Start immediately left of Cement Mix. Pull up and move left to the obvious thin crack, then climb this to a finish up Cement Mix. A thin, fingery dash usually pays dividends on the technical start.

3.   Cement Mix   9m   E1   5b   (1971)
Six metres left of the corner climb the obvious, semi-rubble-filled groove.

★ **4.   Tosser's Wall**   10m   E4   6b   (1986)
The steep wall between Cement Mix and Short Corner.

5.   Short Corner   9m   E1   5c   (1973/1981)
Follow the corner on the right easily to a peg near the top. Pass this by a couple of hard moves.

6.   Start   8m   D   (1964)
Follow vertical drill-holes two metres to the right of the corner and finish up a short groove.

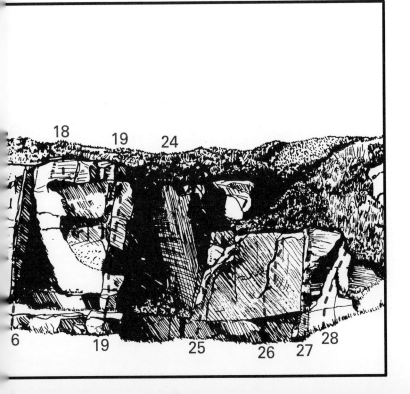

7. Boomerang 8m D (1964)
Four metres to the right of the corner is a sloping ledge at three metres. Gain
this and move up the slab above, then swing diagonally right and finish up the
niche above.

8. Puss Soldiers 9m E4 6b (1985)
A serious line up the wall to the left of Shallow Groove.

★★ **9. Shallow Groove** 9m HVS 5b (1964)
Good protection makes this high-stepping crux very enjoyable. The obvious
steep groove six metres right of the corner.

★★★ **10. Shallow Green** 9m E2 5c (1976)
Balance and concentration makes this route a delight to climb. Lose either one
of these and it could all go horribly wrong. Make committing, friction-type
moves up the slabby nose just right to an overlap and peg. Move right to gain a
good hold, then pull boldly on to the wall above and climb this.

★ **11. Shukokia** 9m E3 6a (1974-75)
Climb the shallow groove on the right, then continue up the thin crack with a
difficult move to finish.

★ **12. Kung Fu** 9m HVS 5a (1974-75)
Climb to a sentry-box just right, gain entry to this and finish straight up above
the break.

13. Misunderstandings 9m E1 5b (1984)
A steep line of scoops just right of Kung Fu.

14. Roopy Roo 8m HVS 5b (1964)
Start three metres to the right and climb a series of scoops to a grassy finish.

15. Median Crack 9m HVS 5a (1964)
Start one metre right and climb the wide crack to a ledge, then finish up the
wall above.

★ **16. The Bod** 9m E1 5b (1974-75)
Good climbing up the left-facing groove one metre to the right.

The Traverse of the Beer Drinking Gods (E4, 6a,6a) starts at Arête Not and
traverses the walls in two pitches finishing up The Bod. Obviously, there is
'crater potential' on much of the route!

★ **17. Disappearing Aces** 9m E3 6a (1967/1982)
Previously pegged as Ace of Spades. Climb the steep groove right of The Bod.
Short and sharp.

★★★ **18. Tweeker** 12m E3 5c (1974-75/1978)
A classic route of this grade, offering a pumpy little crux passing the peg.
Climb Throsher to the second large ledge, then traverse left to below a hanging
groove. Nip up this (peg), to a rest below the roof, where a quick tweek on the
nipple helps to pass the roof and so gain the top.

** **19.   Throsher**   8m   VS   4c   (1964)
Good protection and enjoyable moves make this a popular route at this grade.
The thin crack, just left of the arête which overlooks the pit.

20.   Ledge and Groove   9m   E1   5b   (1964/1973-75)
Climb to the ledge at three metres, and swing right, around an arête, into a
groove above the pit. Ascend up this boldly to the top.

*The next four routes start from the large ledge in the bay to the right. This can
be reached from Throsher by a long step right, or by an easier traverse from
lower down on the right.*

21.   Twin   8m   E2   5b   (1974-75)
The next groove, which starts from the left side of the large ledge.
Smut Ball Fungus (E4, 6a): goes right from Twin at three metres and follows
the wall above.

22.   Volper   8m   HVS   5a   (1967)
The crack and shallow groove in the centre of the left wall.

23.   Scout Cleft   8m   VD   (1964)
From the darkest recesses of the cleft, mantel on to a ledge on the left then go
back right into the cleft to finish.

* **24.   The Axe Wound**   8m   E6   7a   (1992)
The radically overhanging wall right of Scout Cleft, passing two bolts.

25.   The Spoiler   9m   VS   4c   (1964)
Climb the crack on the right arête of the bay, then steep slabs lead to the top.

*The next route starts eight metres to the right, on a gently overhanging wall just
past an unclimbed crackline.*

*** **26.   Against all Odds**   9m   E5   6c   (1984)
Once a '*Last Great Problem*' of the quarries, the S-shaped feature (previously
known as 'S' Groove) in the steep wall left of Frostbite more often than not
lulls one into a false sense of security before violent rejection just below the
top. Side runners.

* **27.   Frostbite**   8m   E2   5c   (1974-75)
The shallow corner which bounds the leaning wall on its right.

* **28.   The Curve**   8m   S   4a   (1964)
The right-slanting crack one metre farther right, which bounds the steep slab on
its left.

Main Wall
*To the right is a break containing an easy way down. Farther right is Main
Wall, a series of clean buttresses increasing in height to the magnificent Wilton
Wall on the right, behind the right-hand edge of the firing range.*

29.   The Hornet   8m   HVS   5a   (1983)
Previously known as Keep off the Grass. Start just left of the initial crack of
The Bee, at a short groove. Climb this avoiding an illegal ledge on the left, then
finish up the short wall above.

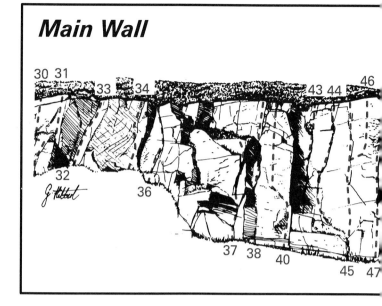

Main Wall

30 31
33 34
43 44 46
32
36
37 38 40
45 47

★★ **30.   The Bee** 9m E1 5b   (1974-75)
A justly popular route, exciting, but with not too bad a sting in the tail. At the
base of the descent route is a short diagonal crack leading to a ledge at three
metres. Climb this then step down left on to the face and climb boldly to a
break and the top.

31.   The Wasp 9m E3 6a   (1982)
Climb the short arête right of The Bee to a ledge, then climb up using the thin
crack in the rib above.

★ **32.   Laying the Ghost** 8m E2 6b   (1974-75/1982)
From a couple of metres up Slanting Slab swing left to a thin crack (peg) and
follow this to the top.

★ **33.   Slanting Slab** 8m S 4a   (1964)
Three metres past the short rib of The Hornet. Climb the narrow slab.

*Round the arête is a blank overhanging wall (unclimbed as yet) its right edge
forming the bulging corner of Direct.*

★★ **34.   Savage Stone** 8m E4 6c   (1982)
Climb Direct until it is possible to swing left into the hanging groove and climb
it desperately past one good hold and one peg .

35.   Direct 8m HVS 5a   (1964)
Layback up the corner which bounds the leaning buttress on its right.

36.   Kukri Crack 6m VD   (1964)
The clean crack, obvious by its name, in the wall right of Direct.

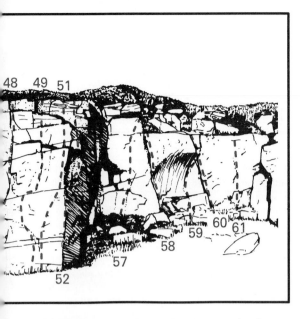

DESCENT: *from routes in this vicinity is by the stepped corners just to the right*; **Three Corner Climb** (M).

37. Spline 10m D   (1964)
Ascend a shallow corner on the left arête of Deep Groove to a large ledge, then take the corner on the left.

38. Deep Groove 9m D   (1964)
Follow the large groove to the ledge, then the corner above.

39. Meandering Molly 10m VD   (1964)
From two metres up Deep Groove traverse rightwards to the arête, then go up this and the centre of the short wall behind.

40. Cross Tie 9m S 4a   (1964)
Climb the arête for three metres then move left into the centre of the wall and finish up this.

41. I'm Cured, Bouncy Bouncy 8m E2 6a   (Pre-1982)
Start slightly left of The Rapid Rambler and climb the short wall to a ledge, finish easily.

42. I'm the Rapid Rambler; Fondle Fondle 9m VS 4c   (1985)
A tactile experience for the person who has done everything. One metre left of The Mud climb the overgrown corner groove and exit leftwards.

43. The Mud 8m VS 5a   (1974-75)
Aptly named climbing up the crack one metre left of Flake Crack.

★ **44. Flake Crack**   10m   S   (1964)
Follow the obvious flake crack; very sandy after wet weather.

★ **45. Big Dorris**   12m   E2   5b   (1977)
From the base of Flake Crack climb diagonally rightwards to a thin crack in the
centre of the wall, then follow this with increasing difficulty to the top.

★ **46. Painted Smile**   14m   E5   6c   (1986)
Climb Big Dorris for eight metres, to a no-hands rest and runners. Break out
right and gain a poor peg by desperate finger tearing moves. Finish slightly
more easily.

★★ **47. Falling Crack**   14m   E2   5b   (1964/1974)
A classic sandbag, but it is well protected. After a reasonable start, this classic
crack pitch suddenly demands special commitment. Only those with unwavering
confidence make it to the top unruffled. The prominent crack in the centre of
the wall is followed to a hard move into a niche where the crack narrows.
Finish more easily over the overhang.

★★★ **48. Wilton Wall**   14m   E3   6a   (1964/1969)
Another old peg climb that has come into its own as an unaided test-piece.
Climb Falling Crack for three metres then traverse right on a detached block to
a crack. Climb the crack, with a hard move to stand on a flat hold. Enter the
upper groove by a further hard move and gain the large ledge. Finish easily.
The direct start is 6a.

★★★ **49. Pigs on the Wing**   14m   E5   6b   (1982)
Technically absorbing climbing with some exceedingly thin pulls. Start just left
of The Swine. Climb up leftwards then go straight up on small holds to gain
good holds (nut) leading right across the wall to The Swine. Climb the thin
crack just left of The Swine to the ledge.

★★ **50. Pigs Direct**   12m   E6   6c   (1985)
Although most climbers will probably heave a sigh of relief when they reach the
good holds on the original route, gluttons for punishment can trade the easier
finish for some even thinner moves. Climb Pigs on the Wing to the good hold,
then continue very boldly up the wall above.

★★★ **51. The Swine**   14m   E3   6a   (1974-75)
Crack the crux at four metres and you can spend the rest of the day posing on
the good finishing holds. Start three metres left of Iron Orchid and climb
diagonally rightwards (crux) to gain good holds just left of the arête at six
metres. Continue to a peg and finish straight up.

★★★ **52. Iron Orchid**   15m   E4   6b   (1982)
The E points are for the excellent moves up the bold arête, but the 6b is all
saved for the sting in the tail. Climb the right arête of the Main Wall to a peg
at eight metres, move up then traverse right to another peg in an overhanging
scoop. Climb the blunt right arête of the scoop to gain the large ledge.

★★ **53. Dancers at the End of Time**   24m   E4   5c,6b   (1966/1978/1982)
Previously known as Main Wall Traverse.
1.   6m.   Start under Saturday Crack and traverse up and left to the arête. Peg
belay.

2. 18m. Continue traversing left at the same height, crossing Wilton Wall and Falling Crack to finish up Big Dorris.

54. Two PVC Girls Go Slap Happy 10m E5 6b   (1983)
The wall just left of Saturday Crack with two pegs (one missing).

★ **55. Saturday Crack** 9m HVS 5a   (1964)
Right of the Main Wall the wall falls back; climb the prominent V-groove.

56. Dirty Corner 8m VD   (1966)
Start one metre to the right and climb the wide crack to a grassy ledge, then finish up the corner itself..

57. Flight of the Condom 8m E1 5b   (1985)
Start two metres right of the corner and climb the wall above, moving right into Loose 'n' Even 'Arder to avoid a loose finish.

The massive flake on Flake Traverse fell down recently and demolished two routes and the start to Loose 'n' 'Ard.

58. Loose 'n' Even 'Arder 9m HS 4b   (1996)
This is a resurrection of Loose 'n' 'Ard. Climb the crack on the left side of the large rock scar.

59. Mad Duck's Disease 10m VS 4c   (1996)
Climb the thin, right-leading crack on the right edge of the large rock scar, then finish up Smokey.

60. Smokey 9m VD   (1964)
The wide crack on the right.

61. Ringing Wall 9m E1 5b   (1974-75)
Climb the centre of the wall on the right, using loose flakes.

★ **62. Buttocks** 9m VD   (1974-75)
The short crack in the centre of the next buttress, then move left and finish up a short, chimney groove.

63. Crack and Chimney 9m M   (1974-75)
The crack on the right of the buttress is either climbed direct, or via a crack one metre to the left.

Near the quarry exit there is a small, isolated slab with two worthwhile problems. **Camille Claudel** (5c) *takes the middle of the slab, whilst* **The Undercut** (5c) *follows the slab just right via, you guessed it 'The Undercut'.*

First Ascents at Wilton Two

1963	**Arête Not** Rowland Edwards (solo)
1964	**Start, Boomerang, Shallow Groove, Roopy Roo, Median Crack, The Curve, Direct, Kukri Crack, Spline, Deep Groove, Meandering Molly, Cross Tie** Rowland Edwards (solo)
1964	**Throsher, Scout Cleft, Flake Crack, Saturday Crack** Rowland Edwards,
1964	**Falling Crack** (VS/A2) Rowland Edwards
First free ascent by Hank Pasquill, 1974.
1964	**Slanting Slab, Dirty Corner, Smokey,** *Loose 'n' 'Ard* Ray Evans, Ken Powell

1964 **Ledge and Groove** (A1) Ray Evans, Ken Powell
  First free ascent, 1973-75.
1964 **The Spoiler** Raye Evans, Ken Powell
  Originally called The Trembler.
1964 **Wilton Wall** (A1) Ken Powell, Bob Hampson
  First free ascent by Hank Pasquill, 1969. This also eliminated the aid on the
  section shared with Main Wall Traverse.
1966 **Main Wall Traverse** (A2)
  Aid eliminated by Mick Johnson, Roger Hindle, as Sunday Premier, 1978.
  Route extended by John Hartley, John Monks as Dancers at the End of Time,
  1982.
1967 *Flake Traverse*
Early 1967 **Ace of Spades** (A1) Terry Wareing, Paul Hamer
  First free ascent by Dennis Gleeson, John Monks as Disappearing Aces, 1982.
1967 **Volper** Les Ainsworth, Terry Wareing
Pre-1969 **Kung Fu** Rowland Edwards (solo)
1969 **Wilton Wall** Hank Pasquill
  First free ascent.
1971 **Cement Mix** Dave Cronshaw, Les Ainsworth
1973 **Short Corner** (A1)
  First free ascent by Ian Lonsdale, Jonathan Fitton, 1981.
1974 **Falling Crack** Hank Pasquill
  First free ascent.
1973-75 **Ledge and Groove**
  First free ascent.
1974-75 **Shukokia**
1974-75 **The Bod, The Bee, The Swine** Hank Pasquill
1974-75 **Twin, The Mud, Ringing Wall, Buttocks, Crack and Chimney**
1974-75 **Frostbite** Hank Pasquill, Ian Lonsdale
1974-75 **Phantom** (A1)
  First free ascent by John Hartley, John Monks, as Laying the Ghost, 1982.
1974-75 **Tweeker** (A1)
  First free ascent by Ian Lonsdale, Andy Lewandowski, 1978.
1976 Mar **Shallow Green** Nigel Bonnett (solo after top-roping)
1977 Sep 6 **Big Dorris** Ian Lonsdale, Mike Bromley
1978 **Sunday Premier** Mick Johnson, Roger Hindle
  First completely free ascent of Main Wall Traverse.
  Route extended by John Hartley, John Monks as Dancers at the End of
  Time, 1982.
1978 **Tweeker** Ian Lonsdale, Andy Lewandowski
  First free ascent.
1981 **Short Corner** Ian Lonsdale, Jonathan Fitton
  First free ascent.
Pre-1982 **I'm Cured Bouncy Bouncy**
1982 Sep 5 **Concrete Crack** Ian Lonsdale, Andy Moss, Mark Leach, Phil Kelly
1982 **The Wasp** John Hartley, John Monks
1982 **Savage Stone, Pigs on the Wing** John Hartley
1982 **Iron Orchid** John Hartley, Tony Preston, Jim Burton
1982 **Disappearing Aces** Dennis Gleeson, John Monks
  First free ascent of Ace of Spades.
1982 **Laying the Ghost** John Hartley, John Monks
  First free ascent of Phantom.
1982 **Dancers at the End of Time** John Hartley, John Monks
  An extension of Sunday Premiere.
1983 Mar 22 **The Hornet** John Hartley (solo)
1983 **Two PVC Girls Go Slap Happy** Roland Foster, Mick Ryan, Greg Rimmer
1983 **Join the Army, Get Yourself Killed** Roland Foster
1984 **Misunderstandings** Ian Lonsdale (solo)
1984 **Against All odds** Mark Leach
  Previously top-roped. Led after 2 days.
1985 May 31 **I'm the Rapid Rambler; Fondle Fondle** Phil Kelly, Paul Pritchard

1985	**Puss Soldiers** Andrew Gridley
1985	**Pigs Direct** Mark Leach, Paul Pritchard
1985	**Flight of the Condom** Paul Pritchard (solo)
1986	**Tosser's Wall** Paul Pritchard, Andrew Gridley, Geoff Hibbert
1986 Apr 29	**Painted Smile** Paul Pritchard (unseconded)
1986	**The Traverse of the Beer Drinking Gods** Paul Pritchard, Andrew Gridley (alts), Geoff Hibbert
1986	**Smut Ball Fungus** Paul Pritchard, Geoff Hibbert
1992	**The Axe Wound** Gareth Parry
1995	**Camille Claudel** Geoff Hibbert
1995	**The Undercut** Geoff Hibbert
1996 Apr	*Rockfall destroyed Flake Traverse, Flying Motorcyclist and Loose 'n' 'Ard*
1996 May	**Loose 'n' Even 'Arder** Alan White, Paul Dewhurst *Takes the line of the old Loose 'n' 'Ard*
1996 May	**Mad Ducks Disease** Paul Dewhurst, Alan White

Wilton Three   O.S. ref.   SD 695 135

There is no climbing allowed in Wilton Two or Three on Wednesdays, Fridays or Sundays

Wilton Three is the first quarry on the right when approaching from the A675 up Scout Road. The quarry is one of the most popular in the whole Lancashire area, and is very well used on warm summer evenings by locals to work up a sweat and a thirst before a session in either the Wilton Arms or the Bob's Smithy.

Orange Wall

The first recorded climbs are on the clean buttress at the left side of the quarry and directly behind Wilton Two. The climbs are described from LEFT to RIGHT.

1.   Twin Cracks 6m D   (1960)
The corner left of the chimney is gained from the left, then the parallel cracks are climbed direct.

2.   Sneck 6m S 4a   (1979-83)
Gain the large ledge just to the right, then climb the blunt arête finishing on the right.

DESCENT: *a gully on the right provides the usual descent.*

3.   Al's Idea 6m E1 5c   (1984)
Climb the arête which requires a dodgy heel hook.

4.   Zee 6m S 4a   (1974-75)
Just left of Great Chimney. Layback the loose crack.

5.   Great Chimney 8m M   (1960)
The wide chimney on the left of the wall, finishing to the left at the capstone.

6.   Orange Wall 9m VS 4b   (1963)
The wall right of Great Chimney can be climbed by several ways.

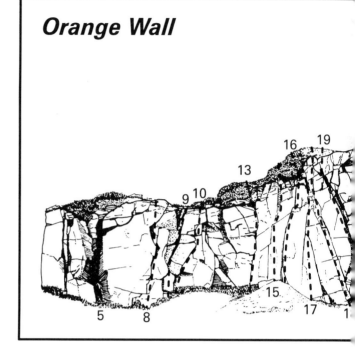

Orange Wall

7.   Orange Crack 8m HS 4a   (1963)
The jamming crack on the right side of the wall, which forms the left side of a
leaning pedestal.
Cracked Orange (HVS, 5a): takes a somewhat artificial line up the wall
immediately left of the crack.

8.   Justine 6m S 4a   (1967)
The crack which forms the right side of the pedestal.

9.   Orange Groove 9m VD   (1963)
The right-slanting chimney just right, very popular.

10.   Monolith Crack 8m VS 4b   (1963)
Just to the right is a half-ship-shaped monolith. Climb to a good hold and thus
the right crack of the monolith. Finish up the steep wall above.

★ **11.   Cedric** 8m S 4a   (Pre-1967)
Four metres left of the corner, follow the stepped groove.

12.   Orange Squash 9m E3 6a   (1981)
Start midway between Cedric and Orange Corner. A hard start gains an obvious
undercut at three metres, and the ledges of Cedric on the left. Move back right
on to the wall and climb it by a steep crack.

13.   Orange Corner 8m VD   (1960)
The corner which limits the wall on its right. Often muddy.

Constable's Overhang Area

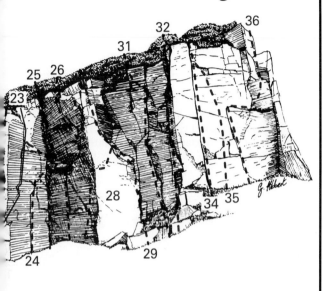

Constable's Overhang Area

The rock turns a right-angle and becomes a slabby wall split by several prominent cracks.

14.   Oak Leaf Wall 9m VS 4b   (1960)
The line of ledges four metres right of the corner.

15.   Tea Leaf 7m VS 4b   (1974-75)
From the highest point at ground level climb a thin crack to its end, then continue up the wall above and finish up a short groove.

★ **16.   Oak Leaf Crack** 9m VD   (1960)
The obvious straight crack immediately right.

★★ **17.   Forked Cracks** 9m VS 4b   (1960)
Sometimes dusty, but the moves have a real feel-good factor. Just to the right two cracks converge to form an inverted Y. Climb the right-hand one. A direct line from the bottom can be climbed at 5c.

★ **18.   Parallel Cracks** 10m S 4a   (1960)
Gain the hook then take the twin, parallel cracks on the left.

★ **19.   The Groove** 10m VD   (1960)
From the metal hook move up into a chimney/groove which is hard to enter but soon eases.

20.   No Idea   10m   VS   4b   (1997)
From the foot of The Groove climb directly up a small arête that forms the left
side of Slime Chimney.

★ **21.   Slime Chimney**   12m   VD   (1960)
The deep chimney which cuts the left wall of the recess opposite the quarry
entrance. The capstone is negotiated on the right.

22.   Get Off It!   13m   E2   5b   (1997)
Climb the right-hand side of the arête left of The Grader.

★★★ **23.   The Grader**   14m   E3   5c   (1975-79)
Finger-jamming at its best. Start from Slime Chimney, but swing right around
the arête at six metres to the base of a diagonal crack. Start the crack by a hard
move and follow it to join Lightning at its triangular block. Pass this by a
further hard move and finish as for Lightning. A direct start is possible at 5c.

★★ **24.   Lightning**   14m   E3   5c   (1966/1974-75)
Once the mid-way ledge is left, there is no going back on this racey finish.
Climb the vertical crack in the wall just right of The Grader, then step right to
join the ledge at mid-height on the back wall. Hand-traverse back left to a block
and finish up a thin crack.

25.   Thunder   14m   HVS   5a   (1962)
Climb the left corner of the recess to the ledge, then continue more awkwardly
up the corner to the top.

★★★ **26.   Constable's Overhang**   14m   E5   6b   (1962/1974)
A fantastic route with quite a reputation. Climb the peg-scarred crack (or the
wall just left; easier) in the back wall of the bay to a ledge. Step right from the
ledge and climb a steep crack to a peg (Rock 3 above). Fight up the dogleg
crack above to an entertaining exit on to the slab above.

27.   Nameless Edge   12m   HVS   5a   (1976)
The corner which limits the recess on its right.

★★ **28.   Slipshod**   14m   E1   5a   (1963)
When one quivers around the arête, it is interesting to note that this route used
to be given VS! Climb the right wall of the recess until a scary and exposed
move right round the arête leads to a finish up Green Slabs.

29.   Green Slabs   12m   VD   (1960)
The aptly-named slabs are climbed until at a large detached block it is possible
to traverse left and finish up the arête.

30.   Fallout   10m   VS   4b   (1960)
From Green Slabs climb straight up the overhanging wall above using a rocking
block.

31.   Pulley   12m   S   4a   (1966)
Climb the crack just to the left to a hard move on to a slab in the corner. A
move over some blocks is then followed by a mantel to an exit gangway leading
left.

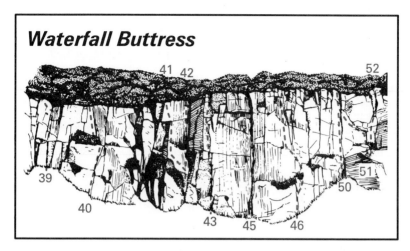

Waterfall Buttress

32.   Block and Tackle   10m   VD   (1963)
To the left of both The Arête and Central Crack climb the open blocky groove.

33.   The Arête   10m   VS   4b   (1974-75)
The arête just left of Central Crack.

★★★ **34.   Central Crack**   10m   HVS   5a   (1964)
The striking, near-perfect crack opposite the quarry entrance is one of the most
popular routes here.

35.   Mutual Peanut   9m   E1   5b   (1976)
Climb directly up the wall two metres to the right of Central Crack to a flake
crack on the right, just left of the large ledge. Continue up this flake, to an
overlap, then swing left and join Central Crack at the top.

36.   Crack and Slab Variant   9m   D   (1960)
Gain the large ledge at half-height by climbing the flake crack that leads to its
left-hand edge. From the ledge climb on to a large block and finish up the short
crack on the right. The large ledge can also be reached at a slightly harder
grade, either via the blunt arête itself, or by the first crack to the left of this.
Ascendveass (VS, 4b): finishes up the short groove above the large ledge,
immediately to the left of the normal finish.

★★ **37.   Crack and Slab**   9m   D   (1960)
An excellent beginners' route. Gain the right-hand side of the large ledge by
climbing the flake crack that starts just right of the blunt arête. Then finish over
a large block and the short crack above, as for the previous route.

38.   Chockstone Crack   6m   VD   (1964)
The short, dirty crack at the extreme right, which starts at a much higher level
and leads to the top of Crack and Slab.

Waterfall Buttress

The rock turns a right-angle and becomes Waterfall Buttress. At first this is broken and vegetated but soon becomes a solid buttress which sometimes has a waterfall.

39.   Bloomer 11m S   4a   (1974-75)
At the left side of the back wall climb the crack which forms a shallow groove at the left.

40.   Groper 12m HS   4a   (1974-75)
Six metres right, climb the shallow groove, then step left and finish on poor holds.

★ **41.   30-Foot Wall** 12m   HVS   5a   (1980-83)
Climb 40-Foot Corner on to the slab, then go diagonally left to the arête and follow this to the top.   A direct start is possible at 6a.

42.   40-Foot Corner 10m VS   4b   (1960)
The deep corner left of Waterfall Buttress proper.

★★ **43.   Canine Crucifixion** 12m E2 5c   (1962/1967)
A miniature classic. Not as grand as some of its illustrious neighbours, but nevertheless, containing technical interest aplenty and a well-protected crux. The left edge of Waterfall Buttress proper is an arête. Climb the crack just right of this to its end. Move up and right then go back left to finish easily up a short corner.

44.   Chikarna 12m E4 6b   (1988)
Start about three metres to the right and climb the the wall for about three metres, then traverse left to a small undercling and some protection. Continue directly to a peg below the top overlap, then swing left to an easy finish up Canine.

★ **45.   Brastium** 12m E1 5b   (1969)
Climb the steep crack that starts just over a metre farther to the right. This route is sometimes obscured by a waterfall and in such conditions the grade and quality may alter somewhat.

★★ **46.   Betty's Wall** 12m HVS 5a   (1964)
Rowland Edwards' last contribution at Wilton, still gives good value. From the crumbling ledge on Route Four move left and go up to the base of a shallow groove (peg), then finish up this.

47.   Cabbage Man Meets the Death Egg 12m E3 5c   (1986)
The thin crackline on the right.

48.   Hodgepig Boogie 12m E3 5c   (1986)
One metre right climb the next thin crackline.

49.   Route Four 9m S   4a   (Pre-1967)
Farther right a white streak runs down the rock; climb the loose crack which this hides.

50.   Route Three 8m VD   (Pre-1967)
Three metres right climb the delicate crack.

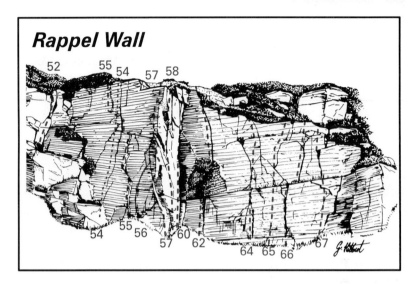

Rappel Wall

51. Route Two 8m HVS 5a (Pre-1967)
From Route One, traverse left beneath the overhanging wall to join and finish
up Route Three.

52. Route One 6m D (Pre-1967)
The short, block-filled corner on the right.

DESCENT: *an easy series of ledges in the corner gives an easy descent* (**Route a Half**).

53. Fire and Theft 30m E3 5c (1985)
A girdle of Waterfall Buttress. Follow Canine Crucifixion to the top of the
crack, then traverse right and finish up Route Two.

Rappel Wall Area
*Right of the descent route, the next continuous area of rock is called Rappel
Wall Area.*

54. Barbecue 14m S 4a (1969)
Climb directly to the ledge halfway up Rappel Wall, then finish up the poor
crack above, just right of Rappel Wall.

★★ **55. Rappel Wall** 17m VD (1961)
A good beginners' route. Follow the obvious weakness which splits the wall
from right to left, to a chockstone at two-thirds-height. Move left and exit via a
sandy scoop.

56. Peg Free 14m VS 4c (1974-75)
An enjoyable climb up the right side of the wall. Start just left of the right arête
of Rappel Wall and either climb thin crack that curve rightwards towards the
arête, or follow a line of jugs on the left side of the arête. Continue up a short
crack to a small ledge, then traverse left to finish up Rappel Wall.or Barbecue.

⋆⋆ 57.   Shivers Arête   14m   E1   5b   (1963/1968)
Climb the right-hand side of the arête on good holds to a spike runner, then
press on up the arête to a peg below the crux and pass this by a hard move, to
gain the top. The finishing move can feel quite precarious. All the difficulties
are concentrated into the last couple of moves.

⋆ 58.   Canopy   14m   HVS   5a   (1961/1962)
Start just left of the corner of Kay and climb diagonally left to the bottom of a
thin peg-scarred crack; follow this passing a small overlap.

59.   Rappel Wall Indirect   25m   VS   4c   (1961)
Climb the deep corner of Kay to a ledge at four metres, then follow a line of
ledges leftwards to the arête. Step up a little, then traverse left to finish up
Rappel Wall.

⋆⋆ 60.   Kay   14m   VS   4b   (1962)
The deep corner on the right gives good climbing and is easier than it looks.

61.   Easy to Cheat   14m   E2   5c   (1982-85)
Follow Crooked Crack to the overhang, then pull leftwards on to the wall and
finish straight up.

⋆⋆ 62.   Crooked Crack   12m   VS   4c   (1962/1963)
A popular route with variety and protection. From the deep corner gain the
ledge near the bottom and from the right of this climb the crack which splits the
overhang to a mantelshelf on the lip, then follow the crack.
Variation: from the mantelshelf on the lip, escape to a ledge on the right and
finish to the left.

63.   The Gay Dwarves and Mr Plod Go to the Tupperware Party
         10m   E2   5b   (1984)
Climb the dirty wall between Crooked Crack and Mo direct, on disposable holds.

⋆ 64.   Mo   10m   HS   4a   (1962)
To the right is an orange patch with a crack on either side. Climb the wall
below, then use both cracks until it is possible to finish, using the right one.

65.   Miney   9m   VD   (1962)
The thin, ragged crack on the right is gained by the wall on the right, and is
climbed using holds on the wall.

66.   Meeny   8m   VD   (1962)
The wide crack on the right is reached by a subsidiary crack, then climbed on
jams, or as a layback.

67.   Eeny   6m   VD   (1962)
The short crack starting halfway up the wall is reached by climbing the wall
below.

68.   North Wall   6m   VD   (1974-75)
Ascend the centre of the short buttress which stands out on the right.

The Playground
This is the more broken area on the right.

69. North Corner   6m   VD   (1974-75)
The short corner set back a little, and slightly lower.

70. Curver   6m   VD   (1974-75)
The crack just to the right.

71. Finger Distance   6m   HVS   6a   (1984)
Climb the wall immediately right of the crack via a long reach.

72. Short Chimney   6m   D   (1974-75)
At the end of the trough in the quarry floor there are two chimneys. This is the
shorter, left-hand one.

73. Belly Wedge Buttress   6m   VD   (1959)
Go straight up the narrow buttress between the two chimneys.

74. Belly Wedge Chimney   6m   D   (1959)
The right-hand chimney.

75. Belly Wedge Wall   8m   S   4a   (1959)
Climb the wall to the right of Belly Wedge Chimney.

76. The Slab   6m   D   (1974-75)
12 metres right at a slightly higher level is a small slab. Numerous variations
are possible – backwards, upside-down, no hands etc.

77. Unnamed Crack   6m   D   (1986-87)
Farther right again, above the trench in the quarry floor, is a tower. Climb the
crack on the left side.

78. Hanging Arête   6m   D   (1960)
Climb the steep arête of the tower.

★ **79. Right-hand Route**   6m   VS   4c   (1962)
The right wall of the tower is split by a peg-scarred crack. Climb these
strenuously to a break, then go left to finish up Hanging Arête.

80. Rodin's Requiem   6m   E5   6c   (1984)
Start just left of The Square, at an overhang. Surmount the overhang with the
utmost concentration then tackle the wall above.

80. The Square   6m   VS   5c   (1964)
Nine metres right of the tower is a cubic block on the hillside. Climb its
right-hand side. Alternatively, from the small overlap make a long and awkward
reach left to gain a sidepull and thus the top.

81. The Third Party   140m   E3   4c,5c,5c,4b,–,4b   (1967)
1. 21m.   Climb Twin Cracks to a small ledge on the right arête, then traverse
to Great Chimney. Continue along the upper ledge of Orange Wall and round
the arête, then descend a little and cross to Monolith Crack. Some difficult
moves past large blocks at the same level lead to the ledge halfway up Cedric.

2.   21m.   With an in-situ peg , traverse to the corner and descend this to a large ledge. From the right of this ledge continue at the same level, then move up slightly to The Groove. Move up and right, then belay below the capstone on Slime Chimney.

3.   18m.   Descend the chimney until it is possible to follow a short crack (Grader) to join Lightning, then continue into the left corner of the recess and gain the sloping ledge. Cross this to the right corner of the recess and descend very awkwardly for three metres until at a ledge a traverse can be made to join Slipshod. Follow this to Green Slabs and belay on the large block. (It is advisable to place a at the top of Slipshod to protect the second.)

4.   10m.   Cross to the ledge at the top of Pulley, then move round the arête and with hands on the obvious break traverse to Central Crack. A hard move to a high foothold enables the ledge on Crack and Slab to be reached.

5.   46 m.   Secure one end of a 45-metre rope to the block then, using a 'third party', get the rope fixed to one of the fence posts above Rappel Wall. Make a tyrolean traverse to the large ledge below Rappel Wall, climb to Rappel Wall, then descend until it is possible to traverse right on an obvious line to a belay on Shivers Arête.

6.   24m.   Go along the ledge to Kay and ascend this until it is possible to traverse to a ledge above Crooked Crack, with feet just above the peg. Descend Mo for three metres, then continue the traverse until it is possible to finish up Eeny.

An excellent low-level traverse (6a) is possible round practically the whole quarry, and boulder problems litter every spare bit of rock.

First Ascents at Wilton Three

1959	**Belly Wedge Chimney** Rowland Edwards, Ray Cook
	This was the first recorded route at Wilton.
1959	**Belly Wedge Buttress, Belly Wedge Wall** Ray Cook
1960	**Twin Cracks, Great Chimney, Orange Corner, Oak Leaf Wall, Oak Leaf Crack, Forked Cracks, Hanging Arête, 40-Foot Corner, Green Slabs** Rowland Edwards (solo)
	Orange Corner was originally known as Clay Corner.
1960	**Parallel Cracks** Ray Cook, Rowland Edwards
1960	**The Groove, Slime Chimney, Fallout** Rowland Edwards, Ray Cook
1960	**Crack and Slab, Crack and Slab Variant** Rowland Edwards
	Ascendveass Andrew Gridley, Phil Kelly, Gary McCandish, 1985
1961	**Canopy** (A1)
1961	**Rappel Wall** Rowland Edwards, Ray Cook
1961	**Rappel Wall Indirect** Rowland Edwards, Ken Bretherton
	This started up Crooked Crack, traversed across to the arête and then finished up Rappel Wall.
	Chiver's, a direct start was done by Ray Evans, 1963.
1962 Mar 11	**Eeny, Meeny, Miney, Mo** Mick Pooler
1962 May 27	**Canopy** Mick Pooler
	First free ascent.
1962	**Kay** Rowland Edwards
1962	**Crooked Crack** (Variation), **Right-hand Route** Ray Evans (solo)
1962	**Thunder** Rowland Edwards (unseconded), with 1 nut for aid
Mid-1962	**Constable's Overhang** (A2) Rowland Edwards
	First free ascent by Hank Pasquill, 25 May 1973.
1962	**SAS** (A1) Rowland Edwards (solo)
	First free ascent by Les Ainsworth, Ian Cowell, Ray Miller, as Canine Crucifixion, 1967.
1963	**Crooked Crack** Roland Edwards (solo)
	The variation finish had previously been done by Rowland Edwards.

1963 June 1	**Slipshod** Ray Evans, Ken Powell, John Nightingale, John Nuttall	
1963	**Orange Wall, Orange Crack, Orange Groove, Monolith Crack, Block and Tackle** Ken Powell, Ray Evans (varied leads)	
1964	**Central Crack, The Square** Rowland Edwards	
1964	**Betty's Wall** Rowland Edwards, Betty Edwards	
1964	**Chockstone Crack**	
1966 July 13	**Lightning** (A1) Dave Thompson, Tony Booth	

Also started from the left as Zig-Zag.
First free ascent, 1974-75.

1966	**Pulley** Les Ainsworth, Paul Hamer
Pre-1967	**Route Four, Route Three, Route Two, Route One**
1967	**The Third Party, Justine, Cedric** Les Ainsworth, Terry Wareing
1967	**Canine Crucifixion** Les Ainsworth, Ian Cowell, Ray Miller

First free ascent of SAS.

1968	**Shiver's Arête** Hank Pasquill

The bottom section of this had previously been done as Chiver's and the top arête had been top-roped.

1969	**Brastium** (2pts aid) Martin Battersby and party
1969	**Barbecue**
1974 May 25	**Constable's Overhang** Hank Pasquill

First free ascent. A major step forward.

1974-75	**Zee, Tea Leaf, The Arête, Bloomer, Groper, Peg Free, North Wall, North Corner, Curver, Short Chimney, The Slab**
1974-75	**Lightning** *First free ascent.*
1976 Apr	**Mutual Peanut** Nigel Bonnett
1976 Oct 17	**Nameless Edge** Nigel Bonnett
1975-79	**The Grader**
1981	**Orange Squash** Ian Lonsdale (unseconded)
1979-83	**Sneck**
1979-83	**30-Foot Wall** Ian Lonsdale
1984	**The Gay Dwarves and Mr Plod Go to the Tupperware Party** Paul Pritchard (solo)
1984	**Finger Distance** Geoff Hibbert
1984	**Rodin's Requiem** John Hartley (solo)
1984	**Al's Idea**
1985	**Fire and Theft** Andrew Gridley, Steve Sharples
1982-85	**Easy to Cheat** Gary McCandlish
1986	**Cabbage Man Meets the Death Egg** Paul Pritchard, Martin Mandell
1986	**Hodgepig Boogie** Paul Pritchard, Greg Rimmer, Ian Lonsdale
1986-87	**Cracked Orange, Unnamed Crack**
1988	**Chikarna** Andrew Gridley, Geoff Hibbert
1997	**No Idea, Get Off It!** Geoff Mann, Chris Fletcher

Wilton Four

O.S. ref.   SD 696 134

Over the years this quarry has become needlessly neglected by the majority of climbers. This is a pity, because it contains some excellent climbing. It is the smallest of the four quarries on this site and lies at the top of Scout Road, just before the sharp bend at the top.

Sanction Wall

The first routes are on the very steep wall on the left side, and the climbs are described from LEFT to RIGHT.

1.   Sally 6m VS 5c   (1979-83)

Climb the short, thin crack at the left side of the wall, starting partway up the banking.

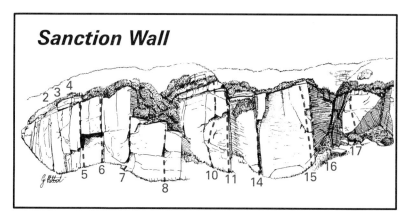

Sanction Wall

2.   Teacher's Crack   9m   E4   6c   (Pre-1972/1982)
At the base of the hollow are two obvious cracks. This is the first of these.

★★ 3.   Hell's Bells   9m   E5   6b   (Pre-1972/1985)
A demanding and very sustained test piece. Climb the second crack past a
powerful undercut move at mid-height.

4.   White Horse   8m   E4   6b   (Pre-1972/1982)
The next crack. A bold lead and with no gear until the crux has been passed!

★ 5.   Haig   7m   E2   6b   (Pre-1972/1982)
Start at the left side of the cutaway roof. Climb to the roof and pass it on its
left side to finish up a crack with one hard move.

6.   Johnnie Walker   6m   VS   5a   (1971)
The crack on the right-hand side of the square-cut overhang.

7.   Long John   6m   VS   5c   (1974-75)
The crack which lead directly to a landing below the right arête of this wall.

8.   Neat Whisky   5m   VS   6a   (1979-83)
One metre left of the obvious arête. An interesting problem up the wall via an
obvious pocket.

9.   Dimple   6m   VS   5b   (1974-75)
Start three metres to the right of the arête and go diagonally up leftwards to the
top of the arête.

10.   Mort Subite   6m   E5   6c   (1986)
Just left of the arête of Glenfiddich, climb a thin crack, passing the overlap with
extreme difficulty. RP protection.

Fridge-freezer Zawn
*To the right of the arête the ground level drops away to form an uninspiring
pit. The most striking feature of this area is a steep arête which bounds its right
side.*

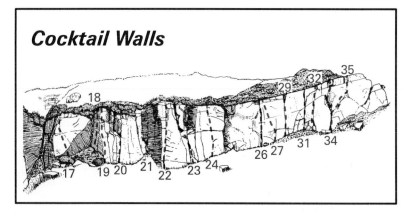

Cocktail Walls

★ **11. Glenfiddich** 10m HVS 5b   (1974-75)
Climb the right side of the left arête with a peg, finish on the right wall.

12. Suspended in Cryonics 9m E5 6c   (1986)
The wall right of Glenfiddich which is boundless in its complexities, has one
bolt leading to a bolt belay.

13. 100 Pipers 8m HS 4a   (1974)
The deep corner on the right.

14. Cutty Sark 10m HVS 5b   (1974)
Five metres to the right of the corner climb the V-shaped groove.

★ **15. Lady Ice** 10m E5 6b   (1984)
Farther right, past an impossible-looking wall, is an impressive arête, rising
menacingly out of the rubbish tip. Climb this arête on its left side (peg and bolt).

16. Cold Emotions 9m E4 5c   (1984)
Climb the impressive arête on its right side with no gear; the in-situ gear on
Lady Ice was placed tantalisingly out of reach on purpose!

Cocktail Walls – Left
*Farther right the next rock commences at an obvious triangular slab and
continues as a series of short walls to the angle at the right of the quarry.*

★ **17. Inverted Triangle** 8m HS 4a   (1970)
Start at the foot of a triangular slab and climb this trending leftwards to the top.

18. Dewar's 8m HS 4a   (1974)
Start one metre right of the corner and take a direct line to the top.

19. Vat 69 8m VS 5a   (1974)
Climb the obvious arête to an awkward finish.

20. Clan Dew 9m S 4a   (1974)
Start two metres right and climb the crack to a large ledge, then finish up the
niche above.

21.   Central Avenue   9m   HVS   5a   (1976)
Start from the foot of the corner on the right and climb the wall to gain a
shallow wall. Finish up this, with a swing right at the top.

⋆ **22.   Cossack Crack**   10m   E2   5b   (Pre-1971/1974)
Half a metre right of the next steep arête climb a vague crack.

23.   Smirnoff   12m   VS   4c   (1971)
From the gully on the right, gain the large overhang and layback round it on its
left. Finish up the flake above.

24.   Martell   10m   E2   5c   (1974)
Climb the centre of the wall between the gully and the dirty corner, via a thin
crack above a ledge.

Cocktail Walls – Right
Cocktail Walls continue past a dirty corner, which forms the angle of the quarry.

25.   Dry Cane   9m   E2   5c   (1974)
Start four metres to the right of the dirty corner at the right-hand end of the
crag, and climb the wall behind.

26.   Gordon's   8m   S   4a   (1971)
The first crack on the right wall of the dirty corner.

⋆ **27.   EKU 28**   10m   E3   5c   (1982/1985)
Two metres right, climb the thin crack then finish leftwards.

28.   Coke   11m   S   4a   (1971)
A poor route that starts from EKU 28 and then follows an obvious rising
traverse which leads to a finish up Bacardi.

29.   Bacardi   9m   S   4a   (1971)
The next, more prominent, crack.

30.   Pasty Man   8m   VS   4b   (1982)
The wall between Bacardi and Pedestal Crack.

31.   Pedestal Crack   6m   D   (Pre-1970)
The aptly-named wide crack.

32.   Daiquiri   6m   D   (1971)
One metre right again climb the crack and wall.

33.   Mild   15m   S   4a   (1971)
From three metres up Cider follow an obvious traverse line leftwards, eventually
finishing up Bacardi.

34.   Cider   8m   D   (1971)
Six metres right of the pedestal climb a groove.

35.   Bitter   9m   D   (1971)
From the start of Cider follow a right-leading line to the top.

The Lancashire Levitators (6a): an interesting low-level traverse starts from the triangular slab which faces the quarry entrance, and continues to the final route. Never more than half a metre from off the ground, protection is difficult to arrange for the second man.

First Ascents at Wilton Four

Prc-1970	**Pedestal Crack**
1970	**Inverted Triangle** Les Ainsworth, Dave Cronshaw
Pre-1971	**Cossack Crack** (A1)
	First free ascent, 1974.
1971	**Johnnie Walker, Gordon's** Dave Cronshaw, Les Ainsworth
1971	**Smirnoff** *Originally top-roped because of poor rock.*
1971	**Bacardi** Bob MacMillan, Rob Meakin
1971	**Daiquiri** Rob Meakin, Bob MacMillan
1971	**Mild, Bitter** Les Ainsworth (solo)
Pre-1972	**Teacher's Crack** (A1)
	First free ascent by John Monks, John Hartley or Rob Trevitt, 1982.
Pre-1972	**Bell's Crack** (A2)
	First free ascent by Mark Leach as Hell's Bells, 1985.
Pre-1972	**White Horse** (A1)
	First free ascent by John Monks, 1982.
Pre-1972	**Haig** (A1)
	First free ascent by John Monks, 1982.
1972	**Cider** Dave Cronshaw (solo)
1974	**100 Pipers, Dewar's, Martell, Coke** Les Ainsworth, Dave Cronshaw
1974	**Cutty Sark, Vat 69, Clan Dew, Dry Cane** Dave Cronshaw, Les Ainsworth
1974	**Cossack Crack**
	First free ascent.
1974-75	**Long John, Dimple, Glenfiddich**
1976 Apr	**Central Avenue** Nigel Bonnett
1975-79	**Pasty Man**
1982	**Teacher's Crack** John Monks, John Hartley or Rob Trevitt
	First free ascent.
1982	**White Horse, Haig** John Monks (solo)
	First free ascents.
1979-83	**Sally, Neat Whisky**
1984 Apr 5	**Cold Emotions** John Hartley (solo)
1984 June 14	**Lady Ice** John Hartley, Hank Pasquill
1985	**EKU 28** Paul Pritchard
	The top had previously been climbed as a direct finish to Coke in 1982.
1985	**Hell's Bells** Mark Leach
	First free ascent of Bell's Crack.
1986 May 16	**Mort Subite** Paul Pritchard (unseconded)
1986	**Suspended in Cryonics** Paul Pritchard (unseconded)

Minor Crags

Moor Gate Quarry   O.S. ref. SD 665 111

This quarry which lies by the side of the B6226 at the Blundell's Arms, has been noted as a possibility, but a raft would be essential.

Pilkington's Quarry   O.S. ref. SD 660 120

This quarry lies just off George's Lane in Horwich, just after the back road to Brownstones and before Montcliffe Quarry. There used to be over a dozen climbs in the quarry, which were comparable with the best at Wilton, but unfortunately it has now been re-opened and only a few of the original routes still exist. It looks likely that it will be impossible to climb in the quarry for many more years, but this note is included as a reminder to climbers for the day after quarrying ceases.

Graded List of Climbs in the Bolton Area

E8
Gigantic   6c

E7
Strawberry Kiss   6b
Perimeter Walk   6b
Chocolate Girl   6c

E6
Pigs Direct   6c
The Axe Wound   7a
The Soot Monkey   6c
K.P.   6b
The Midas Touch   6c
It'll be Rude Not To   6c
Age of Reason   6b
The Karma Mechanic   6c
King of Kings   6b
Run Wild, Run Free   6b
Shaggy Mamba   6b
The Reaper   6c
The Pit and the Pendulum   6c
Crater Traitor   6a

E5
Mort Subite   6c
Suspended in Cryonics   6c
Myrmidon   6b
Against all Odds   6c
The Pretentious Gallery   6b
Schwarzenneggar Mon Amour   6c
If You Can't Lick 'em Lick 'em   6c
Painted Smile   6c
Hot Air   6b
Thin Air   6a
Black Dog Blues   6b
Beyond the Perimeter   6a
Rodin's Requiem   6c
Ego Trip   6b
Septic Think Tank   6b
Lady Ice   6b
Don't Think   6b
Two PVC Girls Go Slap Happy   6b
Powerage   6b
Pigeon Toad Orange Peel   6b
White Lightnin'   6b
I Shot Jason King   6a
Renaissance   6a
Where is My Mind?   6c
Nobody Wept for Alec Trench   6a
Boy Racer   6a
Join the Army   6a
Parasite   6b
Pigs on the Wing   6b
Italian Job   6b
Constable's Overhang   6b
Welcome to the Pleasuredome   6b
Astradyne   6b
Hell's Bells   6b
Pathetique   6b
I'm Spartacus   6b
The Nausea   6b
The Devil's Alternative   6b

E5 (contd.)
Epidural   6b
Office Party   6a
Cleansweep   6a
Please Lock Me Away   6b
Josser   6a

E4
Savage Stone   6c
Veteran Cosmic Rocker   6c
Titanosaurus   6b
White Horse   6b
Teacher's Crack   6c
Shaggy Dog   5c
Summer Lightning   6b
Iron Orchid   6b
Walking on Glass   6b
The Foot of an Oncoming Mexican   6b
Black Mamba   6b
Dancers on the Edge of Time   5c, 6b
Smut Ball Fungus   6a
Puss Soldiers   6b
A Thief in the Night   6b
Gates of Perception   6a
The Hacker   6b
Sparrow   6b
L'Arête   6a
Chikarna   6b
The Lamb Lies Down on Broadway   6a
The Taciturn Boy   6b
Counter Intelligence   6b
Terroriffic   6a
Cold Emotions   5c
Fingertip Control   5c
Gravitational Experiment   6b
Clapped Out   6b
Sleepwalk   6a
Spike   6a
Traverse of the Beer Drinking Gods   6a,6a
Snakebite   6a
Isle of White   6a
The Lean Mean Fighting Machine   6a
Tasty   6b
Tosser's Wall   6b
Mr and Mrs Liptrot Go to the Seaside   6a
Exile and the Kingdom   6b
Traverse of the Beer Drinking Gods   6a,6a
Ice Cool Acid Test   6a
The Eleventh Hour   6a
Master Spy Direct   6a
Master Spy   6a
Adrenalin   6a
To Infinity and Chuck a Left   6a
Headbutt Wall   6a
Under the Matt   6a
Loopy   6a
Lucky Heather   5c
New Jerusalem   6a
Faith and Energy   6a
I Claudius   6a
To Infinity and Beyond   6b
The Absent Minded Professor   6a
Land   6a

E4 (contd.)
There's More to This 6b
Stolen Goods 6a
Lazy Friday 5c

E3
Innominate 6b
Each Way Nudger 6b
Shibb 6b
Orange Squash 6a
Falling off the Edge of the World 5c
Tweeker 5c
White Slabs Bunt 6a
Concrete Crack 6a
Satin Saphire 5c
Zapling 6a
Sheppey 6a
Vampire 6a
Shukokia 6a
Mumbled Prayer 6a
Agrajag 6a
The Swine 6a
Jimmy Nip 6a
Sobeit 5c
The Prayer Battery 5c
Skin Game 6a
Confusion 5c
Disappearing Aces 6a
Brightside Revisited 6a
Nothing Fantastic 5c
Chance Encounters 5c
Escharchado 5c
Pandooi 6a
Gauntlet Route 5c
One Minute to Midnight 5c
The Beast 6a
The Grader 5c
Changing of the Guards 5c
Lightning 5c
Tangerine Trip 5c
The Snurcher 6a
Fire and Theft 5c
Christine Arête 5c
Give Thanks 5c
The Wasp 6a
Silently Screaming 6a
Klondyke 6a
Long Distance Runner 5c
Puma 5c
Eliminator 5c
Hodgepig Boogie 5c
The Third Party (Wilton) 4c,5c,5c,4b,-,4b
The Friable Sausage 5b
Big Al 5c
Silent Solace 6a
Cabbage Man Meets Death Egg 5c
The Hollow Men 6a
Specific Gravity 5c
Napoleon Solo 6a
The Third Party (Anglezarke) 5c
After the Gold Rush 6a
Wilton Wall 6a

E3 (contd.)
Phantom Zone Left-hand 5c
Max 5c
Supercrack 5c
Slap Happy 6a
Aint Nothing to It 6a
Overtaker's Buttress 5c
Surfin' Bird 5b
Guillotine 5c
Third Time Lucky 5c
EKU 28 5c
Cheat 5b
Flyer 6a
Double Trip 5c

E2
Haig 6b
Laying the Ghost 6b
I'm Cured, Bouncy Bouncy 6a
Temptation 6b
Frostbite 5c
The Crucifix 5c
Leucocyte Left-hand 5c
Silk Cut 5c
Falling Crack 5b
Non-stop Screamer 5b
Aethelred 5b
The Red Nose 5b
Niff Niff the Guinea Pig 5b
Forte Dicks 5c
Kettle Crack 5b
Dicktrott II – The Movie 5c
Step Left 5c
Dracula 5b
In Memoriam 5c
Overhanging Weetabix 5c
Rope 'n' Rubber 5c
Jubilee Climb 5c
Return to Fantasy 5c
Phantom Zone 5c
Rockin' Horse 5c
Dipper 5c
Toots 5c
Jimmy Mac, Bin Man Extraordinaire 6a,4c
Rock Lobster 5c
First Finale 5b
Dancing on the Valentine 5c
Shorty 5b
Mission Impossible 5b
The Gay Dwarves and Mr Plod 5b
Lubalin 5b
Shallow Green 5c
All in the Mind 5b
Initiation 5c
Dawn Left-hand 5c
Anasazi Arête 5b
Son of Dicktrot 5c
The Golden Tower 5a,5c
Erratic Traversion 5c
Years From Now 5c
Lucky Strike 5b,4c,5a
Easy to Cheat 5c

Dave Kenyon – **Wilt the Stilt** (E2 5c), Hoghton Quarry. *Photo: Dave Cronshaw*

E2 (contd.)
Plenty of Zzzzs 4c,5b
Martell 5c
Don't Stop Believing 5c
Red Flowers are Red 5b
Wipe Out 5b
Life in the Fast Lane 5c
Blue Stilton 5c
Rugosity Atrocity 5b
Soixante Neuf 5c
Dry Cane 5c
Press Intrusions 5b
Angel's Kiss 5a
Field of Screams 5b
Step into the Groove 5c
Naff Naff The Route 5b
Fathamathon 5b
Twin 5b
Chasing Rainbows 5b
Roll Over 5b
Impatience 5c
Threshold of a Nightmare 5c
Canine Crucifixion 5c
Cossack Crack 5b
Chalk Lightning Crack 5b
Acme Surplus Overhang 5a
Mental Mantel 5b
Big Dorris 5b
Paradox 5b
Wombat Chimney 5b
Micheal Portillo 5b
Splits 5b
Kelly's 'i' 5c
Any Which Way You Can 5c
Gemime Puddleduck 5c
Get Off It! 5b

E1
Thirsty Work 6b
Cement Mix 5b
Steeplejack 5c
Power of the Mekon 5b
Evil Crystal 5b,4c
Pagan 5b
Street Legal 5c
Jane's Route 5b
Traumatic Eversion 5c,4b
Helix 4c,4b,5c,4a
Thunder 5a
The Open Book 5b
Precious Cargo 5b
Nappy Rash 5b
Ringing Wall 5b
Geoff's Wall 6a
Slipshod 5a
The Bod 5b
Proline 5b
Short Corner 5c
Deodand 5b
Horrock's Route Direct 5b
Willow Arête 5b
Al's Idea 5c

E1 (contd.)
Dizzy the Desert Snake 5b
Cotton Terror 5a
Punchline 5b
Letter-box Wall 5b
High Revver 5b,4c
Nowhere Man 5b
Falling Wall 5b
The Rapidity of Sleep 6a
Spud 5b
The Changeing 5a
Bombing Basil 5b
Ann 5b
The Bee 5b
Ledge and Groove 5b
Rebellion 5b
Brastium 5b
Niche Indirect 5c
It 5c
Heretic 5c
Misunderstandings 5b
Dicktrott 5c
Black Dog 5c
Crow's-nest 5b
Central Route 5b
Return of the Native 5c
Brittle Fingers 5b
No Screws in Skem 5b
Flight of the Condom 5b
Shivers Arête 5b
Peg Free 5b
Camembert 5b
The Beauty of Poison 5b
Dinah 5b
The 10p Giro 5b
Formula One Bribery 5c
Red Wall Direct 5b
Saffron 5b
Ordinary Route 5b
Horwich Eliminate 5b
Show us yer Topos 5b
Botch Weld Job 5b
Disappearing Chip Buttie Traverse 5b
Rhythm of the Heat 5c
Many Happy Returns 5a
Cameo 5a
Corned Beef Dictator 5a
Reservoir Camels 5b
The Eight-Legged Atomic Dustbin 5b
Mu'Azib 5b
Le Mans Finish 5b
Cad Eye the Heather 5b
Bay Horse 5b
Shudabindun 5b
Mutual Peanut, 5b

HVS
Finger Distance 6a
Minor 5c
Nameless Edge 5a
Elaine 5c
Ummagumma 5b

Mark Leach on **The Dangler** (E4 6b), Hoghton Quarry. *Photo: Paul Horan*

HVS (contd.)
Organ Grinder 5b
Double or Quits 5b
The Water Margin 5a
Betty's Wall 5a
Captain Hookleg 5a
Planet of the Apes 5a
The Angel of Death 5a
Cholera 5a
Stadium 5a
Broken Toe 5a
Rabid 5a
Cutty Sark 5b
Angel Delight 5b
Virgin's Dilemma 5a
Jaws 5a
Empty Arête 5a
Gollum 5b
Hydrophobia 5a
Grey and White Girdle 4c,5a,5a,4b,4b,4c,–
Unseasonal Weather 5a
Peanuts 4c,5a
Vulture 5a
Dribbles 5b
Terror Cotta 5a
Life During Wartime 5b
Wedgewood 5a
Spider Crack 5a
Patience 5a,4c
Feeding the Rat 5a
30-Foot Wall 5a
Canopy 5a
Saturday Crack 5a
Knuckleduster 5a,4c
Blossom 5a
Kung Fu 5a
Shallow Groove 5b
Dinosaur 4c,4b
Volper 5a
Goon 5a
The Deep 5a
Resurrection 5a
Dawn 5b
Cracker 5a
Bob Bandits 5b
Central Crack 5a
God Save the Queen 5a
Wiggerley Worm 5a
Gallows Pole 5a
Esmeralda 5a
Crash and Burn 5a
Sorry Sid 5a
Superb 5a
Flytrap 5a
Left Edge 4c
The Razor's Edge 4b
Nasty Little Lonely 4b
Neighbourhood Threat 5a
Saturation Point 5a
Lace 5a
Tombstoned 5a
Manglewurzle Rib 4b,5a
Earwig 5a

HVS (contd.)
The Creaking Fossil 4c
Friends 4c
Bag of Bones 4c
Prickpocket 5a
Letter-box 5b
The Last Supper 5a
Wormhole 4c
Ascendveass 4b
State of Awareness 5a
Needle Stick 4c
Roadrunner Pinnacle 4c
Terra Firma 5b
Tintinnabulation Direct 5b
Insertion 5b
Grond II 5a
Glenfiddich 5b
Fools Gold 5b,4c
Gilt Complex 5b
Mixed Veg 5b
Grit Salad Surgery 5b
Barbara Ann 5b
Bohemia 5b
Kaibab 5b
P.C.2 5b
Neon Shuffle 5a
Double Gloucester 5a
Stilton 5b
I See No Ships 5a
Soot Juggler 5b
Roopy Roo 5b
Blueberry Hill 5b
Gritstone Rain 5b
La Morte 5b
Ding Dong 5b
Bellringer 5b
Any Which Way But Loose 5a
Blue Tile 5a
Mirror Man 5a
The Blimp 5a
Is It a Cheesecake or a Meringue? 5a
Median Crack 5a
Zarke 5a
Lady Grinning Soul 5a
First Cut 5a
Merchant Crack 5a
Brick Thick 5a
Hunter Killer 5a
Finger Chimney 5a
Baby Arête 5a
Adidas 5a
La Rue 5a
Whiter Shade of Pale 5a
Helical Happiness 5a
Central Avenue 5a
Route Two 5a
Cracked Orange 5a
Fleabite 5a
Airbourne Attack 5a
Grassy 5a
Direct 5a
The Hornet 5a

Blackburn Area

Compiled by Les Ainsworth, Dave Cronshaw, Geoff Hibbert and Jessica Stam

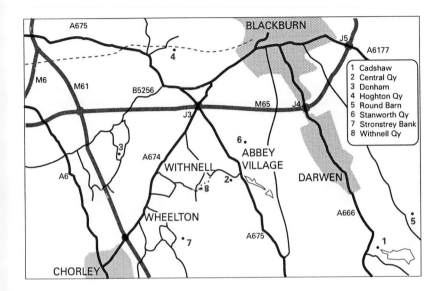

1 Cadshaw
2 Central Qy
3 Denham
4 Hoghton Qy
5 Round Barn
6 Stanworth Qy
7 Stronstrey Bank
8 Withnell Qy

Since the previous guidebook the main development in the Blackburn Area has been at Stronstrey Bank. Here, determined efforts to remove the loose skin that previously deterred most climbers, has revealed several good climbs, making the buttresses ideal for a summer evening's visit. There have also been a few interesting additions at Round Barn and Withnell, but generally developments have been limited.

The majority of the climbing around Blackburn is in traditional gritstone quarries. The most impressive of these is at Hoghton, where the Main Amphitheatre provides far more than its fair share of classics, including Mandarin, which must rate as one of the all-time gritstone greats. Unfortunately, however, access problems at Hoghton have severely restricted climbing there in the past few years and it must be hoped that these problems can be resolved satisfactorily.

The opening of the new East Lancashire motorway (M65) has improved access to the quarries near Abbey Village. In particular, Stanworth is now an excellent place for an evening's climbing. Central and Withnell Quarries are much more broken, but nevertheless, they also offer some worthwhile climbing and many of the routes should improve if they get sufficient traffic.

Denham and Round Barn remain popular, and they are especially good in the evenings, because they then get the sun. The outcrop at Cadshaw remains a popular place for novices, but unfortunately the quarries opposite are often deserted. This is a pity, because much of the climbing there is well worthwhile.

Billinge Hill Quarry

O.S. ref.   SD 658 283

Situation and Character

Situated in Billinge Woods, a country park on the north-west fringe of Blackburn, this quarry provides the closest climbing ground to the centre of the town. The rock is good quality gritstone, similar to Hoghton (in texture if not in stature), but is only between eight and nine metres high and about 30 metres long. The crag is north and east-facing and therefore, it is often wet and slimy and slow to dry out.

History

All the routes were climbed and named by Dave Cronshaw, John Ryden and Ian Vickers during guidework in 1986. However, most of them had been climbed previously, but no records were kept.

Approach

The quarry is best approached from the Billinge End Road entrance to the woods, where there is a small car park. Walk up the main track and, 100 metres beyond the bend where the track levels out, there is an old iron gate on the left. A path immediately after this gate leads through overgrown rhododendrons to the quarry beyond a pond. Circumnavigate the pond on its left to reach the rock.

The Climbs

The routes are described from LEFT to RIGHT, starting at an obvious rightward-slanting ramp.

1.   Pockets 4a   (1986)
Start at the foot of the ramp and climb the wall, using the obvious pockets.

2.   Ledgeway 4a   (Pre-1980)
Climb the ramp, moving left to follow the ledge system to the top.

3.   The Monkey's Gangway 4b   (Pre-1980)
Climb the ramp, but step up and right to climb the upper slab direct.

★ **4.   Monkey's Direct** 6b   (1986)
Climb the wall directly to join the finish of Monkey's Gangway.

5.   Roote's Arête 5a   (1986)
Climb the faint arête and slab direct.

6.   Roote's Groove 4b   (Pre-1980)
Climb the faint groove just right of Roote's Arête, and finish up the crack above.

7.   Ripper's Ramp 4b   (Pre-1980)
Start at the ramp to the right of Roote's Groove and follow it leftwards, then straight up to an overlap. Finish direct.

8.   Spider's Crack VD   (Pre-1980)
Climb the left-slanting crack right of Ripper's Ramp.

9.   Barry's Wall   5b   (1986)
Climb the wall on the right and finish up the slab above.

★ **10.   Mad Monkey's Mantel**   5c   (1986)
Start a metre right of Barry's Wall and mantel on to the large hold at two
metres. Finish direct.

11.   The Monkey's Sand Pit   VD   (Pre-1980)
Climb cracks to the left of the obvious arête to a sandy hole. Finish directly
from the hole.

12.   Paddy's Arête   HS   4a   (Pre-1980)
Climb the arête to a crack and finish up this.

13.   The Big Greenie   VS   4c   (Pre-1980)
Climb the big green corner to the overhangs, reach over to good jugs and swing
right then finish direct. As its names implies, the corner is often wet and slimy.

**14.   Squirrel Nutkin and the Park Warden went to the Three Bears'
Underwear Party**   E3   6a   (1986)
Start a metre right of the corner and climb the slab direct.

15.   Lady C's Lost Lover   E3   6b   (1988)
The slab between Squirrel Nutkin and Randy Gardener's Groove, via a very thin
hairline crack and a slight arête.

16.   The Randy Gardener's Groove   HS   4a   (Pre-1980)
Climb the groove by a series of mantelshelves, passing a niche.

17.   Where the Hell is Goldilocks?   VS   4c   (Pre-1980)
Climbs the big corner at the meeting of the two walls – desperate when wet, yet
seldom dry!

Overhanging Wall
*Several lines have been top-roped on this wall as it is seldom dry and
protection is poor. When it eventually does dry out, it should give several
desperate leads for an aspiring hard-man.*

There are many variations to the lines described, and the crag can be girdled at
several points. Little is known of the history to the quarry, so apologies must be
made for any obscure route names which are not those of the first ascensionists,
whoever they may be!

First Ascents at Billinge Hill Quarry

Pre-1980   **Pockets, Ledgeway, The Monkey's Gangway, Roote's Groove, Ripper's
Ramp, Spider's Crack, Mad Monkey's Mantel, The Monkey's Sand
Pit, Paddy's Arête, The Big Greenie, The Randy Gardener's Groove,
Where the Hell is Goldilocks?**

1986   **Monkey's Direct, Roote's Arête, Barry's Wall, Squirrel Nutkin and the
Park Warden Went to the Three Bears' Underwear Party** Ian
Vickers (solo),

1988   **Lady C's Lost Lover**

Cadshaw Quarries

O.S. ref.   SD 708 180

Situation and Character

Cadshaw lies four kilometres south of Darwen just off the A666 Darwen–Bolton road. There are several quarries on the site, with heights ranging from three metres in the Small Quarry to 23 metres in the Main Quarry. The rock is of variable quality gritstone, but on the whole it is much better than appearances might suggest and many of the routes are very rewarding.

History

Although climbers had visited the quarries in the pre-1950s, the first serious attempts on the Main Quarry was John Wareing and Tim Dowberkin's impressive *Green Slab* in the early 60s. In 1964 Les Ainsworth decided to explore the quarry whilst waiting for his partner to arrive. The result of this exploration was Ainsworth's first ever new route, *Klud*, which was only overcome after a mammoth two-hour struggle with the overhanging summit sods. Ainsworth had more success on his solos of the neighbouring routes *Ku* and *Klux* and by 1965 he had persuaded others across to the quarry. With Paul Hamer he climbed *Baboon* and the classic *Orang-Outang*, then went on to add *The Ape* with Les Houlker and John Mason. In 1968, Ainsworth turned his attention to Weasel Quarry where he did *Instant Insanity* with John Mason. Things then lay dormant until 1973 when Dave Cronshaw found an alternative finish to one of Ainsworth's earlier routes to produce *Delusion*, and also around that time more routes were added to Weasel Quarry, one of which was named *Allsopp's Arête* which was thought to be a fitting tribute to Allan who had recently died.

1976 saw Cronshaw's free ascent of the old aid route *Gorilla* with Rick Walsham, and *Rhesus Negative* with Phil Warner (one of his earlier aid routes). Dave Knighton and Dave Lyon paid a brief visit one day when lectures did not appeal and stayed long enough to add *Kashmir*.

The buttress above the mineshaft in the Main Quarry began to cause concern during 1975 and was eventually blown up professionally the following year, destroying two of Ainsworth's earlier routes (*Klukard* and *Mandrill*) and also affecting the girdle, *Little X*. Shortly afterwards, Cronshaw climbed the right corner of the recess – *Resurrection Shuffle*, and also *Salamander*. Later, in 1977, Cronshaw cleared out the rotting aid wedges then free-climbed the fine *Monkey Business*. The following year three routes were found on the previously neglected States Wall.

Ian Lonsdale paid a brief visit and added *Bombay Door*, then Mark Liptrot free-climbed the desperate *Marmoset*. Things started to hot up again in 1987 whilst guidebook work was going on. Dave Etherington started to visit the quarry with an eye for a new line and spotted some obvious gaps. The first of these gaps to be filled was *Slap Happy* which was eventually accomplished with Jeff Hope and is in effect a direct version of Hope's route *Rhesus Positive*, added the previous year. Among the other routes to fall that year were *Teddy's Boy* (Hope and Etherington) and *The O-Zone* by Cronshaw and John Ryden and *Picnic at Hanging Rock* by Cronshaw, Ryden and the up-and-coming Ian Vickers.

The quarries now appear to be reaching maturity and since the previous guide, the most significant development has been the resurrection of the old girdle, *Little X* by Cronshaw. Unfortunately, another recent phenomenon has been the appearance of bolts on Orang-Outang, which had been climbed for some thirty years without. It is hoped that this retro-bolting was just an isolated incident that will not be repeated.

During the final stages of preparation for this guidebook it was decided that it was worth providing brief descriptions of the problems in the Small Quarry. Most of these were first done in the sixties, or even before, but they had never either been named or described. Geoff Hibbert took on the task of writing all the descriptions, but though the climbing was enjoyable, he was struggling to think of over forty route names. Eventually his problem was resolved by using the titles of the books in the library at his local pub. He ran out of books before he could give the same treatment to Sunken Quarry.

Access and Approach

The quarry and rocks at Cadshaw are owned by North West Water, whose managers are happy to permit climbing.

Fifty metres north of the B6391 Turton road (Green Arms Lane) is a bus stop, and a track signposted '*Egerton*' leads through woods and past the Small Quarry, then round the shoulder of the hill into the main quarry at Yarnsdale Delf in less than 10 minutes. The Second Quarry lies a little past this and the other quarries are across the stream from the Second Quarry.

The Climbs

The climbs in all the quarries are described from LEFT to RIGHT.

Small Quarry

This is the short quarry, which lies just to the left of the track, about 400 metres from the main road. It contains some good problems on clean rock and many of these are in the easier grades. Although these are only up to about five metres in height, it is felt, nevertheless, that it is worth including short descriptions, but no heights are given. The first climbs are three cracks just left of an arête on the left side of the lower tier. Most of these problems have been climbed since the late Sixties.

1.   Folklore   VD
The left-hand crack.

2.   Myths   4c
The middle crack.

3.   Legend   4a
The right-hand crack.

4.   The Silver Falcon   5a
The wall immediately left of the arête.

5.   In Praise of Idleness   4c
The arête is climbed on its left side.

6.   Life on Earth   M
Go up large steps to a crack finish.

7.   Willy Visits the Square World   5a
Climb the short wall immediately right, using just the low undercut to the top.

8.   The Visitors   VD
The short arête on the right.

9.   This Game of Golf   4b
The wall one metre right.

10.   Success   M
The shallow groove.

11.   More Magic   4b
Start below and right of a block and climb the blunt arête on its right.

12.   Great Wall of France   5b
Climb the wall just right, with a thin pull.

13.   The Proud Sheriff   4a
Pull through the left-hand side of the overlap.

14.   John Citizen and the Law   5b
Pull through the left-hand side of the overlap and finish left of a thin crack.

15.   Living Embryos   5a
The thin crack on the right.

16.   The Atom Rush   5c
A bold problem up the wall on the right, using tiny holds.

17.   Wildlife in Britain   5a
Climb the arête.

18.   Joy of Nature   4b
The corner crack.

19.   In the Blood   4c
The arête to the right.

20.   God, Genes and Destiny   5c
Another scary problem up the wall to the right. The use of the big ledge at two-thirds-height is cheating.

21.   The Rhesus Danger   4b
The flake on the right can be laybacked.

22.   Calculus Made Easy   4c
Climb the wall two metres to the right.

23.   Essentials of School Algebra   5a
The wall just right of the crack.

24.   The Betrothed   5a
Traverse the wall leftwards from Essentials of School Algebra to Folklore.

The next routes start above a pond.

25.   Three Act Tragedy   5a
The arête above the centre of the pond.

26.   Narrow-boat Painting   VD
The crack on the right.

27.   Beers of the World   4a
The wall right again.

28.   The Ocean   D
The crack two metres to the right.

29.   S.P.Q.R   VD
The wall just right again.

30.   Mating and Whelping of Dogs   5a
The obvious mantelshelf problem.

31.   Kidnapped   5b
Make a thin pull up the wall to the right, avoiding the block on the right.

Farther right, but still at the same level is a short wall.

32.   The Secret County   4a
Climb the wall just left of a crack, past a diagonally sloping ledge.

The remaining climbs in the Small Quarry are at a higher level.

33.   Rainbow in the Sky   M
The short arête at the left side of the wall directly behind Folklore.

34.   Cut Flowers and Bulbs for Pleasure   D
The crack on the right.

35.   Leaf in the Storm   4b
The wall on the right, passing a hole at two-thirds-height.

36.   Bird of Paradise   5a
Climb the wall on the right of the hole.

37.   Things a Boy Can Make   VD
Climb the green crack at the right-hand side of the wall.

38.   Elements of Insurance   4c
A small, isolated wall 10 metres right has an awkward exit.

39.   The Cloud Above the Green   4b
The short arête 10 metres farther right.

40.   Feeding and Digestion in Animals   VD
Climb the wall 10 metres to the right.

41.   Intermediate Magnetism and Electricity   VD
The crack on the last section of rock, immediately above the right side of the pool.

42.   Insurance   4b
The wall just to the right of the crack.

43.   The Secret Country   4a
Climb the wall at its left-hand side.

Yarnsdale Delf

This is the large quarry, also known as the Main Quarry. The first routes lie on the complex wall to the left of the main amphitheatre.

1.   Ku   14m   VD   (1964)
At the left end of the complex wall are two *'eyeballs'* above a two-metre high pedestal. From the top of this pedestal, step right and go up trending slightly right to a short wall and the top.

2.   Time Out   14m   E1   5c   (1987)
Start five metres right at a small corner/groove. Climb this to flakes on the right then gain the short slab above on the left (peg). Finish directly. The flakes can also be gained by a finger-traverse from the left.

3.   Yarnsdale   14m   HVS   5b   (1976)
The next shallow groove to a ledge, step left and through a narrow chimney to easy ground.

4.   Klux   14m   S   4a   (1964)
Just right is a square-cut overhang at three metres; layback around this to a ledge and take the shallow recess above.

5.   Baptism   15m   VS   4b   (1975-79)
Start at the base of the rib at the left side of the amphitheatre. Climb up to a ledge and the flake above, turning the overhang on its right.

6.   The Mog   17m   VD   (1968)
Climb easily up a series of ledges in the left corner of the amphitheatre until it is possible to traverse left across the cracked wall near the top, to finish up the arête.

7.   Baboon   18m   VS   4b   (1966)
Start seven metres to the right and go up the corner to a ledge at three metres. From a higher ledge (peg) make an awkward move right and surmount the butterfly overhang above to reach a large ledge. Finish up the crack in the short steep wall above.

★★ **8.   The Ape**   20m   HVS   5a   (1966)
An eliminate that takes in some interesting mantels. On the right is an overhang at four metres, with a hanging groove on its left. Gain the groove and climb it to its top, then step left to a small ledge on the slab of Orang-Outang, or, from halfway up the groove go diagonally left, below a bulge, then pull up right and make an airy mantel on to the same ledge. Mantel on to the ledge above, then finish up the arête immediately right of Baboon.

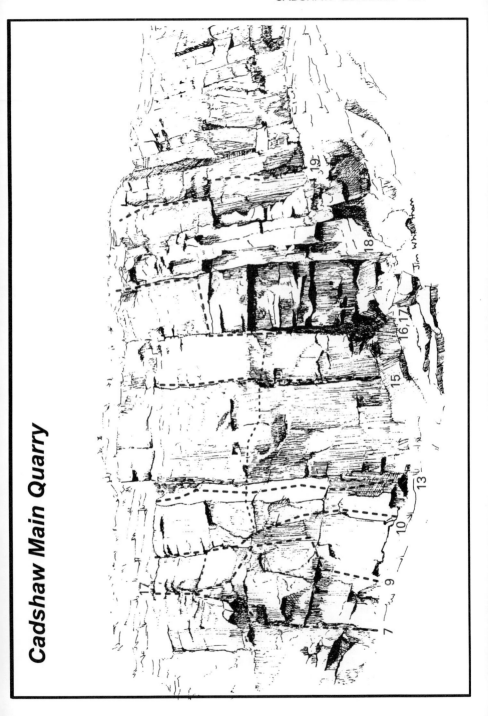

Cadshaw Main Quarry

★★ **9.   Orang-Outang**   20m   VS   4c,4b   (1966)
A classic outing on this quarry. On the original ascent a filed-down brass nut
offered the main protection and the slab above was considered airy. Sadly, the
route was recently desecrated by two bolts, but fortunately these have now been
removed, to leave the route in its original condition.
1.   12m.   Climb up to the overhang at four metres, then hand-traverse right
until a gymnastic mantel can be made on to a large ledge. Climb the wall above
on its left to a large ledge. Nut belay.
2.   8m.   Gain the large ledge on the left and make an exposed swing on to the
ledge on the skyline. Finish up the short wall as for Baboon.

★★ **10.   Green Slab**   19m   VS   4b,4c   (1958)
When the route is dry, the top pitch gives good climbing which is easier than it
looks.
1.   12m.   Start at a V-groove below a bulging arête. Climb the groove to a
ledge on the left (on Orang-Outang), then take the thin crack in the shallow
corner to the belay ledge of Orang-Outang.
2.   7m.   Climb the steep slab by its corner.

★ **11.   Slap Happy**   20m   E4   6b   (1987)
Climb the edge just left of the start of Green Slab to the ledge of
Orang-Outang. Step right and slap up the bulging arête directly to a ledge then
step right and ascend the left side of the slab.

★ **12.   Rhesus Negative**   23m   E1   5b   (1969/1976)
The leaning crack in the slab to a ledge on the arête. Stand on the flake and
move up to a small overlap (peg), move right and pull up at a short crack to
gain easier ground above.

★ **13.   O-Zone**   20m   E3   5c   (1987)
Takes a direct line up the centre of the slab. Go up to a thin dog-leg crack in
the slab left of Gibbon. Climb this and move up leftwards to gain a tiny ledge
on the horizontal break. Carry on direct up the slab (bolt on left) to a short
crack, then finish diagonally to the left.

14.   Gibbon   20m   VS   4c   (Pre-1964/1967)
The oft-damp corner which bounds the long slab on its right.

15.   Gorilla   21m   E1   5b,4c   (Pre-1964/1976)
Takes a line up the centre of the back wall of the amphitheatre, just left of the
old mineshaft.
1.   9m.   Climb the overhanging crack to a ledge. Peg and nut belay.
2.   12m.   Climb the wall behind to a small ledge near the top, then traverse off
right to finish behind a tree.

★★ **16.   Salamander**   21m   VS   4c,4a   (1977)
After a committing move to get established on to the wall, the climbing
gradually relents. Start at the left side of a square recess, behind blocks where
the mineshaft used to be.
1.   12m.   Climb the crack in the left wall of the recess to a ledge on the arête.
Continue up the corner above to a large ledge on the right. Nut belay.
2.   9m.   Finish up the corner on the right. Belay on trees well back.

17. Little X 33m VS 4c,5a,4b   (1966/1996)
A right-to-left girdle of the main part of the quarry.
1. 10m. Climb the first pitch of Salamander to a ledge on the arête, then move left along ledges to the belay on Gorilla.
2. 14m. Move easily to the corner, then cross the wall on the left using a horizontal crack (peg) and move down to a triangular block on the arête. More unprotected for the second.
3. 9m. Move up the corner of the slab to a horizontal crack, then traverse along this to the ledge on Baboon and finish up this route.

★ **18. Resurrection Shuffle** 23m E2 5b,4a   (1977)
1. 14m. The right corner of the recess, over several roofs to a large ledge. Nut belay.
2. 9 m. Up the corner behind, as for Salamander.

Farther right, past a rather unstable corner which has been climbed, the ground level rises, and the next feature is a waterfall, which sometimes flows down a series of clean rock steps.

19. Primate 15m S 4a   (1968)
Start just left of the waterfall at a corner/groove; climb this to a ledge at eight metres, then follow ledges in the corner above. Finish left at the top.
Original Start (VD) followed the waterfall until a traverse left could be made to the ledge at eight metres.

20. Waterfall 14m VD/Impossible   (1967)
Takes the series of clean rock steps by easy though often wet mantels, to a loose finish. The route is graded for dry conditions, otherwise it will be found to be an ungradable exercise in masochism.

21. Bandarlog 10m HS 4b   (1972)
At the top of the mound on the right is a deep hanging V-groove; climb this to a finish on the right.

22. Klud 12m HS 4a   (1964)
Three metres right is another groove; climb this over a bulge then go up past an overhang to exit on the left.

The next four routes have a common finish, so in order to avoid the hanging gardens above, a ring bolt abseil point has been planted near the top for those who do not possess green fingers.

★★ **23. Delusion** 15m VS 4c   (1964/1973)
The variation start to Klud has now been extended into a completely separate climb, which is interesting throughout. Go up the shallow groove a metre right to a ledge on the right (peg runner), then traverse diagonally right for three metres to finish straight up past a break.

At a lower level are three cracks splitting the bulging wall.

24. Monkey Crack 14m E2 5c   (1966/1978)
Take the left-hand crack.

★★ **25. Monkey Business** 14m E2 5b   (1967/1977)
The impressive crack just to the right gives sustained and strenuous climbing.

26. Marmoset 14m E4 6c   (1969/1985)
Follow the desperate thin crack on the right to its end, cross the blank wall and
go left to finish.

27. Chimpanzee 9m S 4a   (1967)
The right-hand corner of the wall, stepping off to the right at the top.

Second Quarry
The following routes are situated in a large bay 100 metres farther right.

★★ **28. Picnic at Hanging Rock** 14m E3 6a   (1987)
Although the Second Quarry is not the most impressive of places, the leaning
tower at the left side gives a worthwhile climb with the crux near the top. At
the left side of the bay is a wall with a niche at half-height. Scramble up to a
belay beside a large block. Climb up into the niche and take the crack above to
the horizontal handrail, traverse left for a couple of metres, then, using a small
sloping ledge, go up the wall trending slightly right.
★ **Picnic Hamper** (E2, 5b): hand-traverse the break rightwards from the horizontal
handrail to a dynamic swing-up which enables the arête to be gained. Continue
more easily to the top.

29. Teddy's Boy 9m E2 5c   (1987)
The leaning wall to the right, bounded on the left by a grassy rake. The route
takes the overhanging wall and crack to a small tree near the top. Start below
the top crack, climb up and left of a thin crack, to a horizontal break. Step right
and pull into the flake/crack to finish.

States Wall
*To the right of the Second Quarry is a long, leaning wall parallel with the
stream; this is States Wall. The first routes start in the deep corner on the left.
All the routes at present end at a long ledge upon which there is a convenient
abseil point.*

30. Utah 18m HS 4b   (1978)
From the arête left of the deep corner traverse past a pointed block to below a
small inverted triangular niche. Go up to this, then move diagonally right to a
large ledge. Gain the flake above and exit on to a sloping ledge, then go up to
the long ledge and peg belay on the right. Abseil descent.

31. Colorado 14m VS 4c   (1978)
From the base of the deep corner climb the short wall on the left to the large
ledge. Move up to an awkward sloping ledge above and continue up a short
V-groove to the long ledge.

★ **32. Blind Alley** 14m HVS 5a   (1987)
Start just right of the corner and climb the wall to a square niche. Step right and
pull through the centre of the overhangs above, finishing up a shallow corner to
the long ledge.

33. California 15m VS 4c (1978)

Climb the wide crack on the right to the overhang, then pass this on its right to a ledge above. Traverse left to the peg belay.

Weasel Quarry

This quarry lies hidden in the trees on the other side of the stream, opposite States Wall. It can be reached by crossing the stream either by a very airy walk over a natural tree bridge, or with more difficulty at the waterfall.

34. Naturalist 9m S 4a (1995)

A scrappy route up the small section of natural gritstone overlooking the stream which forms the extreme left edge of the quarry. Start below an obvious crack and climb to this, then continue using the crack or the wall just to the left.

★ **35. Instant Insanity** 15m HVS 5a (1968)(1995)

This route is somewhat unique by starting on quarried rock and finishing on natural grit. Start at the left side of the amphitheatre, at the crack nearest the arête. Climb the crack until it is possible to traverse round the arête at half-height, to a small ledge overlooking the stream, finish directly above.
Unnatural Finish (5a): after rounding the arête it is possible to avoid the natural gritstone by following the awkward right-trending crack that leads to the top of Loony Bin.

★ **36. The Loony Bin** 12m HVS 5b (1966/1987)

Start as for Instant Insanity but climb direct to the top by exciting jug pulling. However, note that one of the holds is a little wobbly, so arrange adequate protection just in case.

★ **37. Kashmir** 14m HVS 5a (1976)

Start two metres to the right at an obvious wide crack and follow this to the horizontal break, then step left to a short crack and from the top of this swing right into a niche and exit right at the top.

★ **38. Bombay Door** 14m HVS 5a (1982)

Follow Kashmir to the horizontal break, then step right to a crack. Climb this, move left to the niche, then exit to the right at the top.

39. Boogie Mamma 12m E1 5b (1975-79)

The leaning block-filled crack on the right.

On the remaining routes in the quarry, a preplaced rope hung from the top will be necessary to enable a belay to be made at the top of the routes.

★ **40. Allsopp's Arête** 9m IIVS 4c (1973)

Start just to the right of the left arête of the next buttress, by a tree close to the rock. Climb the steep crack to a ledge, then continue up just right of the arête.

41. It'll All End in Tears 10m E1 5c (1984)

The wall is climbed in the centre of the buttress starting from a ledge at two metres. Pull into a small niche then climb the thin crack above, step left and finish up a large flake.

42. Quarry Groove 10m S 4a (1965)
The groove just right to ledges on the right. Finish up a small flake.

43. Spilt Milk 10m S 4a (1984)
The weakness three metres right of Quarry Groove, to finish up that route.

44. The End 9m HS 4b (1973)
Ascend the centre of the next buttress, cut through the overhang by a V-groove.

Sunken Quarry
This small hidden quarry may be reached by following the green track for 150 metres, around the hillside to the right (towards Cadshaw Rocks), and provides some interesting problems up to eight metres high.

First Ascents at Cadshaw Quarries

1958	**Green Slab** John Wareing, Tim Dowberkin	
Pre-1964	*Lemur Up left side of mineshaft, route now blown up.*	
Pre-1964	**Gibbon** (A1)	
	First free ascent by Les Ainsworth, John Mason, 1967.	
Pre-1964	**Gorilla** (A1/VS)	
	First free ascent by Dave Cronshaw, Rick Walsham, 1976.	
1964	**Ku, Klux, Klud** Les Ainsworth (solo)	
1965	**Quarry Groove** Les Ainsworth (solo)	
1966	**Baboon, Orang-Outang** Les Ainsworth, Paul Hamer	
1966	**Little X** Les Ainsworth, Paul Hamer	
	Reclimbed after rockfall by Dave Cronshaw, 1996.	
1966	**The Ape** Les Ainsworth, Les Houlker, John Mason	
1966	*Klukard, Mandrill Les Ainsworth, Les Houlker, John Mason, Bill Stansfield*	
	These routes were destroyed when mineshaft was blown up.	
1966	**Monkey Crack** (A1/VS)	
	First free ascent by Dave Cronshaw, 1978.	
1966	**The Loony Bin** (S/A1)	
	First free ascent by Dave Cronshaw, John Ryden, Sep 1987.	
1967	**Waterfall** Les Ainsworth, Don Pinder, Paul Hamer	
1967	**Monkey Business** (A1/VS)	
	First free ascent by Dave Cronshaw, Aug 1977.	
1967	**Chimpanzee** Les Ainsworth, John Mason, Les Houlker	
1967	**Gibbon** Les Ainsworth, John Mason	
	First free ascent.	
1968	**The Mog** Les Ainsworth (solo)	
1968	**Primate** Les Ainsworth	
1968	**Instant Insanity** Les Ainsworth, John Mason	
	Unnaturatural Finish by Dave Cronshaw, Les Ainsworth, 1995.	
1969	**Rhesus Negative** (A1) Dave Cronshaw, Jim Wild, John Crompton	
	First free ascent by Dave Cronshaw, Phil Warner, 1976.	
1969	**Marmoset** (A1) Dave Cronshaw, John Crompton	
	First free ascent by Mark Liptrot, 1985.	
1972	**Bandarlog** Dave Cronshaw, Bob MacMillan, Les Ainsworth	
1973	**Delusion** Dave Cronshaw, Les Ainsworth, Bob MacMillan	
	Originally a variation start to Klud by Les Ainsworth (solo) 1964, but extended into a completely independent line.	

Right above: The photo that started Rocksport magazine. Les Ainsworth on **The Finger** (VS 4b).
Right below: A motley crew during a Lancashire meet at Brownstones in 1977. From left: Nigel Bonnet, Dennis Gray, Ian Lonsdale, Hank Pasquill, the two Moss brothers, ?, Dave Cronshaw.
Overleaf: Les Ainsworth and Les Houlker on **Orang-Outang** (VS, 4c) at Cadshaw Qy in 1965 – decades before the route was retrobolted. *Photos: George Philips, Brian Cropper, John Mason*

The CLIMBER

APRIL, 1964   The Monthly Magazine for Mountaineer and Rambler   2s

1973	**Allsopp's Arête** Dave Cronshaw, Les Ainsworth
1973	**The End** Les Ainsworth. Dave Cronshaw
1975-79	**Baptism, Boogie Mamma** Dave Knighton, Rehan Siddiqui
1976	**Yarnsdale** Dave Cronshaw (solo)
1976	**Kashmir** Dave Knighton, Dave Lyon
1976	*Mineshaft blown up because the rock had become unstable. Lemur, Klukard and Mandrill destroyed. The first half of Little X was also destroyed.*
1969	**Rhesus Negative** Dave Cronshaw, Phil Warner *First free ascent.*
1976	**Gorilla** Dave Cronshaw, Rick Walsham *First free ascent.*
1977	**Salamander** Dave Cronshaw, Geoff Crick *On new rock following NWWA blowing up the mineshaft. Previously there was a route called Mandrill up this area of rock.*
1977	**Monkey Business** Dave Cronshaw *First free ascent.*
1977	**Resurrection Shuffle** Dave Cronshaw, Rick Walsham
1978	**Monkey Crack** Dave Cronshaw *First free ascent.*
1978	**Utah** Les Ainsworth, Dave Cronshaw
1978	**Colorado** Dave Cronshaw, Les Ainsworth
1978	**California** Dave Cronshaw (solo)
1982	**Bombay Door** Ian Lonsdale, Dave Cronshaw
1984 Apr 17	**It'll All End In Tears** Dave Cronshaw, John Ryden
1984	**Spilt Milk** John Ryden, Dave Cronshaw
1985	**Marmoset** Mark Liptrot *First free ascent.*
1986 May 29	*Rhesus Positive* Jeff Hope
1987 May 6	**Picnic at Hanging Rock** Dave Cronshaw, Ian Vickers, John Ryden *Picnic Hamper by Jeff Hope, Dave Etherington, 25 May 1987.*
1987 May 27	**O-Zone** Dave Cronshaw, John Ryden
1987 May 29	**Teddy's Boy** Jeff Hope, Dave Etherington
1987 June 7	**Slap Happy** Dave Etherington, Jeff Hope
1987 Aug 29	**Time Out** Dave Cronshaw, John Ryden
1987 Sep	**Blind Alley** Dave Cronshaw, John Ryden
1987 Sep	**The Loony Bin** Dave Cronshaw, John Ryden *First free ascent.*
1995	**Naturalist** Les Ainsworth, Dave Cronshaw

Cadshaw Castle Rocks

O.S. ref. SD 708 182

Situation and Character

Cadshaw Castle Rocks or Fairy Buttery (Battery on OS maps) is a small natural outcrop of sound rock, situated on the sunny side of a pleasant valley, opposite Cadshaw Quarry. It is an ideal place for beginners.

History

In 1937, Allan Allsopp wrote a guide to Cadshaw Rocks which described about thirty routes. These included *The Niche, Pagan's Progress, The Mantelshelf, Central Buttress, Central Wall, Split Block Crack* and the *Girdle Traverse*. It is likely that most of these routes were the work of Allsopp himself and he

Previous page: Les Ainsworth on the first ascent of **End of Time** (E2 5b) Denham Quarry.

Photo: Les Houlker

Left: An amazing early pegging shot entitled 'On **Main Wall** Wilton Quarry, near Bolton' *The Climber* magazine from November 1962.

Photo: Mr F Redman

continued his developments through the war years, until by 1951 all but a few of the present routes had been climbed. Around that time a problem known as *Altar Direct* (now a part of Druid's Direct) was climbed. The execution of the problem had to be very precise, and it is thought that Jim Nightingale was the originator; he actually conquered the problem wearing a pair of leather breeches which gave his knees extra purchase on the rock – bad style but effective!

The last remaining gaps at the crag were the double overhangs (at that time) of the unled *Split Block Overhang* of which the first lead is unknown, and *Druid's Face* which was occasionally top-roped but was left to Nightingale to lead (amidst stiff competition) in 1961.

Access and Approach
North West Water, the owners of the land hereabouts, are happy for climbers to visit Cadshaw Rocks and Quarries.

The rocks are reached by following a path down from the quarry to the stream. Cross this by a footbridge and ascend a short slope to arrive at the foot of the rocks.

The Climbs
The climbs are described from RIGHT to LEFT.

1.   The Staircase   8m   M   (Pre-1937)
The short easy-angled slab at the right-hand end of the rocks.

2.   Druid's Corner   10m   VD   (Pre-1937)
Start two metres left of the right edge of the crag. Ascend to a square notch on the arête and continue up this on its right.

3.   Niche Indirect   15m   HS   4b   (Pre-1937)
From Druid's Corner make a rising traverse past a small flake to the niche in the centre of the wall, traverse right to the arête and finish up this.

★★★ **4.   Druid's Face**   12m   E2   5b   (1961)
A classic test-piece on natural gritstone. Gain the niche in the centre of the wall from directly below, and climb over the overhang above via a crack. Move up rightwards to a slight depression in the upper wall. Reach up for a hidden hold and so the top; superb.

★ **5.   Pagan's Progress**   14m   VS   4c   (Pre-1937)
Immediately to the left an overhang at two metres guards a prominent scoop (*The Altar*). Start up a short corner and turn the overhang on its right then step back left on to *The Altar*. Traverse left to a ledge and climb up into the recess above (*The Crow's Nest*). Using the block above (*The Coffin*) as a right foothold, climb the short wall above.

★★ **6.   Druid's Direct**   14m   E3   6a   (1967)
Start directly below the centre of the overhang and make a precarious mantel on to *The Altar*. Climb straight up and over the second overhang, finishing up the rippled wall. A delicate yet strenuous route.

★★ **7.   Pagan's Direct**   12m   HVS   5b   (Pre-1951)
Classic gristone climbing with a gymnastic start and an exposed finish. Climb
the nose which forms the left edge of the buttress, and go up to *The Coffin*.
Hand-traverse this to a thin crack in the wall above then finish up this.

Stonehenge (5b) is an entertaining rightwards traverse from the corner on the
right-hand side of *The Altar*, keeping below the roof until a pull out can be
made on the initial nose of Pagan's Direct.

8.   Pagan Wall   10m   S   4a   (Pre-1937)
The narrow wrinkled wall on the left-hand side of the buttress.

9.   Corner Chimney   10m   D   (Pre-1937)
The block-filled cleft in the corner.

10.   East Face Climb   10m   VD   (Pre-1937)
Start two metres left and follow a more-or-less direct line up the wall, stepping
on to a large flake, to a poor finish.

11.   Column Climb   12m   D   (Pre-1937)
Ascend the corner above the prominent rock column, gain a flat triangular ledge
and climb leftwards to the top.

12.   Crack and Wall   10m   S   4a   (Pre-1937)
The sharp-edged crack two metres left leads to a good ledge then the short wall
above, or climb diagonally rightwards from the ledge at VD.

13.   Overhang and Wall   10m   HS   4b   (Pre-1965)
The small triangular overhang just left is climbed directly to the good ledge,
finishing up the wall just to the right of the corner crack.

★ **14.   Overhang Crack**   10m   VD   (Pre-1937)
The thin crack left of the overhang leads to a good ledge, then the steep corner
crack to finish.

★ **15.   The Mantelshelf**   10m   S   4a   (Pre-1937)
Polished holds up the wall on the left lead to a difficult mantel at four metres.
Step left and follow the crack which bounds the overhang on its left.

16.   Blue Lights   10m   VS   4b   (1966)
Follow The Mantelshelf to its namesake, then go carefully over the overhang
above, the stability of which gives some climbers great cause for concern.

★ **17.   Oak Tree Chimney**   9m   VD   (Pre-1937)
The wide block-filled crack leads to the tree.

18.   Tyro's Delight   12m   M   (Pre-1965)
From four metres up Oak Tree Chimney, gain the good ledge on the left then
leave the left end of this ledge via a ridge.

19.   The Slab   9m   VD   (Pre-1937)
The steep slab and wall on the left. Numerous variations are possible, the best
being on the left.

20.   Central Chimney   9m   VD   (Pre-1937)
The chimney behind the projecting leaf of The Slab.

21.   Central Buttress   8m   VS   5a   (Pre-1937)
The narrow buttress on the left, is taken directly.

★ **22.   Central Crack**   10m   VD   (Pre-1937)
The corner crack, exiting on the right at the constriction.

★ **23.   Central Wall**   10m   HS   4b   (Pre-1937)
Just to the left is a clean slabby wall. Climb it by its centre, passing through the
Bull's Horns (a gap in the overlap which splits the wall at half-height) and the
steep wall above to a recess below the top overhang. Finish left or right through
this.

24.   The Snout   9m   D   (Pre-1937)
The polished nose on the left is gained with difficulty, then good holds lead
more easily to the top.

25.   Snout Wall   9m   VD   (Pre-1937)
The thin crack in the wall which forms the left edge of The Snout.

26.   Zig Zag   9m   VD   (Pre-1965)
Start in the short V-Groove just to the left. Pull over rightwards onto a small
ledge and continue steeply to the top.

27.   West Corner   9m   VD   (Pre-1951)
The corner just to the left, finishing up the right branch.

28.   West Chimney   9m   VD   (Pre-1937)
The block-filled left branch.

29.   West Slab   9m   VD   (Pre-1951)
Climb the steep slab on the left diagonally rightwards into Western Chimney.
West Slab Direct (VS, 4b): a more direct line up the slab.

*Left again is an overhang at four metres, bounded on each side by cracks. Care
should be taken with the rock in this vicinity.*

★ **30.   Split Block Crack**   9m   HS   4b   (Pre-1937)
The thin corner crack on the right of the overhang, with surprisingly awkward
moves through the bulges.

31.   Split Block Overhang   8m   HVS   5a   (Early 1960s)
Climbs directly over the overhang on sloping holds.

★ **32.   Split Block Climb**   8m   S   4a   (Pre-1937)
The shallow hanging groove on the left side of the overhang.

33.   West Wall   6m   S   4a   (Pre-1937)
The face climb just to the left, passing an overlap at half-height.

34.   Curving Crack   6m   D   (Pre-1937)
The prominent hand-jam crack on the left.

35. West Rib 6m VD (Pre-1937)
The rib on the left has a difficult finish on sloping holds.

36. Easy Chimney 6m M (Pre-1937)
The obvious deep cleft.

37. West Mantelshelf 8m D (Pre-1937)
The short wall leads to a broad ledge, then go up the wall just left of the
chimney passing a small ledge (the West Mantelshelf).

38. West Buttress – Ordinary 9m D (Pre-1937)
Start just right of the left arête of the crag and climb diagonally right to the top.

39. West Buttress – Direct 8m VD (Pre-1937)
From the start of West Buttress – Ordinary, take a direct line to the top.

40. The Bulges 8m VD (Pre-1965)
The bulging arête with an undercut start is climbed on the right.

41. West Face 6m VD (Pre-1937)
The short, steep end wall of the crag.

★★ **42. Girdle Traverse** 55m S 4a (Pre-1937)
There are numerous variations to this traverse, and belays are possible at many
points. Start from the notch on Druid's Corner and traverse the wall past the
niche, to the top of the nose. Move round into Corner Chimney then make an
ascending traverse to the triangular ledge on Column Climb. Go along to
Overhang Crack and climb down a couple of moves to gain the ledge of The
Mantelshelf on the left. Cross to Tyro's Delight and cross Central Wall at
roughly the same level, step down to the ledge on Zig Zag and follow this to
West Chimney. Move up then traverse left across to the top of Split Block
Overhang. Descend to a narrow ledge and go round the rib into Easy Chimney.
Gain the ledge on West Mantelshelf and descend obliquely left until an easy line
leads round the arête, crossing West Face to finish.

There is an interesting low-level traverse at 5b, which keeps no more than a
metre above the ground, from right to left.

First Ascents at Cadshaw Castle Rocks

Pre-1937   The Staircase, Druid's Corner, Niche Indirect, Pagan's Progress, Pagan
              Wall, Corner Chimney, East Face Climb, Column Climb, Crack and
              Wall, Overhang Crack, The Mantelshelf, The Slab, Central Chimney,
              Central Buttress, Central Crack, Central Wall, The Snout, Snout
              Wall, Split Block Climb, West Wall, Curving Crack, West Rib, Easy
              Chimney, West Mantelshelf, West Buttress – Ordinary, West Buttress
              – Direct, West Face, Girdle Traverse   Allan Allsopp
Pre-1951   Pagan's Direct, West Corner, West Slab   Allan Allsopp
1961   Druid's Face   Jim Nightingale
              First top-roped in the mid-fifties.
1960-64   Split Block Overhang
Pre-1965   Tyro's Delight, Zig Zag, The Bulges   Allan Allsopp
1966   Blue Lights   Possibly Harry Taylor
1967   Druid's Direct

Central Quarry

O.S. ref.   SD 641 217

Situation and Character

The quarry is situated about six kilometres south-west of Blackburn, just south of Abbey Village. North West Water, Forestry Division currently use the quarry as a storage depot, but nevertheless, still appear to permit climbing.

Most of the climbing in the quarry lies on a series of buttresses of up to 12 metres in height at the right-hand side, culminating in the much higher Main Wall. Although there is much loose rock, especially on the Main Wall, the climbing avoids these areas and most of the routes are both sound and enjoyable.

History

This rather esoteric quarry was visited in 1967 by Les Ainsworth and Paul Hamer, but after doing about a half-dozen climbs to the right of the Main Wall, they decided that there was too much loose rock and left without making any records. During the early '70s Robin Barley was doing research work in the quarry and during his drilling he noted some potential lines on the Main Wall. After work he returned with Jerry Peel and the pair excavated *Vendetta* and *Co-Axial*. Although these were on by far the highest buttress in the quarry, they were also on some of the worst rock and although they recorded their climbs, their experience of the quarry was not sufficient to tempt them to do any more exploration.

The next activity occurred in 1976 when Ainsworth returned with Dave Cronshaw and in a busy morning, they managed to clean and climb *Camina*, *Lode Star* and *Pot-Pourri*, before the rain came. This showed that there was some reasonable rock in the quarry, but the quarry saw few, if any, other climbers for about two more years. Then, in preparation for the forthcoming guide Ainsworth and Cronshaw arranged to meet Barley at the quarry. Before Barley arrived, Cronshaw had climbed *Verboten* and was partway up *The Birch*, when Barley arrived, so he joined them on the latter. However, both routes had taken a lot of cleaning and so there was no enthusiasm for further exploration. The next climbers to explore the quarry were Neil Hyde and Kev Glass, who added three routes, the best of which was *Sabre*.

The quarry was then again ignored until John Morrissey and Dave Carpenter tenuously ascended *Gibberish Crack*, a route which has since had a facelift. It was this trundling that attracted Goi Ashmore to the quarry, who soloed *Little Matchstick Owen's Route* and *A Thing of Hate*, before losing his suicidal urge and retiring to Withnell. The last route in the quarry to date was *Riding High*, memorable for the high ground-falls encountered on its first two ascents. Climbed in mid-December it was too cold to differentiate between holds and icicles. Immediately after the previous guide appeared, Ian Conway and Richard Baker decided to investigate the crag and managed to find some good rock on the right side of the Main Wall, that had previously been missed. Their route, *Kissing the Gunner's Daughter*, follows an imposing line and showed that there are still some gems to be found.

During work on this guidebook, Cronshaw climbed the left side of The Shield to give *The Sword* and added a direct finish to Lode Star. Then in 1997 Paul Dewhurst visited the quarry with Michael Jackson and during the evening they added three climbs, *Let's Do It*, *A Fist Full of Stakes* and *Pale Face Cometh*.

Approach

Leave the M65 at the Blackburn West exit, Junction 3 (as for Stanworth) and follow the A675 southwards for about two kilometres to Abbey Village. At the south end of the village, opposite the Hare and Hounds pub, turn right along Dole Lane towards Withnell then park about 300 metres farther on at a sharp right-hand bend, directly in front of the quarry entrance.

The Climbs

The routes are described from RIGHT to LEFT and they all lie on the rock at the right-hand side of the quarry.

Southworth's Bay

The first rock where climbs have been recorded can be identified by a small concrete bunker which nestles against the foot of the rock.

1.   Rubber Bullet 7m S   4a   (1986)
Start at the left side of the concrete bunker and climb a shallow groove.

2.   Spy 6m VS 4b   (1986)
Climb the wall of the next buttress, 10 metres left, with a move left at the top block.

Tree Buttress

Fifty metres farther left is an area of orange rock, which is set back slightly. The buttress can be further identified by a lone birch that grows at it top.
DESCENT *from this buttress is best made via the grassy slope about 25 metres rightwards (towards the quarry entrance) from the birch tree. At the right-hand side of this buttress there is a square-cut arête with a corner groove at its top.*

3.   Camina 10m VD   (1976)
Start three metres right of the square-cut arête and climb a left-facing corner then the flake crack above.

⋆ **4.   Lode Star** 12m VS 4c   (1976)
Start just to the left and climb past a small capped groove until it is possible to hand-traverse left at a small overlap on to the large ledge on Pot-Pourri. Finish up the arête.

⋆ **5.   Lode Star Direct** 10m VS 4b   (1996)
From the traverse on Lode Star continue up to a small ledge on the right, then cross the wall on the left to finish up the arête.

⋆ **6.   Pot-Pourri** 12m VS 5a   (1976)
Start just to the left of the square-cut arête with a corner groove at its top. Climb to the overlap (peg), then make a long reach to a good hold and continue to the ledge. Finish up the groove above.

7.   Mad Barney 12m VS 4b   (1981)
Start directly below a hanging corner at the top of the crag. Climb the wall, trending first left, then back right to a finish up the hanging corner.

A route (**Paul Can't Climb**, 5b) *has been climbed up the obvious triangular groove on the left, but the blocks over which it passes are extremely unstable and the holds are brittle. Therefore, no description is given.*

8. Bizz Energy 14m HVS 5a   (1983)
Left again is a slabby wall which is cut away at its base. Pull on to this wall below an obvious peg (the use of stacked boulders at the start is unethical). Pass the peg and follow the right side of the wall above.

9. Verboten 12m S 4a   (1978)
The large corner on the left.

★ **10. Sabre** 15m E1 5b   (1981)
Climb the sandy wall just right of The Birch to an overhang, then go boldly over this to reach a hanging flake crack, which can be followed to a grassy finish.

★★★ **11. The Birch** 17m HVS 5b   (1978)
A much better route than first appearances might suggest. Start directly below the birch and climb a crack to the overhang. Gain the inverted triangular niche above, then finish up the thin crack above, or via the groove on the left.

Pale Wall
To the left the rock is poor and about 20 metres left there is a massive square roof near the foot of the rock. The rock to the left of this is known as Pale Wall.

12. Riding High 10m S 4a   (1986)
At the right side of Pale Wall there are two large ledges. Start below the higher of these and climb the obvious short, wide crack to a ledge. Step left and finish up a thin flake crack.

13. Pale Face 10m S 4a   (1987)
The crack and groove system that splits the centre of the face.

14. Gibberish Crack 12m S 4a   (1985)
The wide crack on the left side of the undercut blunt arête.

15. Little Matchstick Owen's Route 10m HVS 5c   (1986)
Start two metres to the left and climb the wall to a good ledge, then continue up twin cracks.

The Shield Area
About 20 metres farther left there is a steep slab that can be identified by a shield-shaped scar.
16. A Thing of Hate 9m HVS 4c   (1986)
Unprotected. Climb up to *The Shield*, then follow the right edge of this and step right to finish.

17. Sword 9m VS 4c   (1996)(1986)
Follow the thin groove-like left edge of *The Shield*, then finish just right of the corner at the top.
Direct Finish (5b): a contrived piece of climbing which takes a direct line up the centre of *The Shield* between the two routes.

Chorley Walls

10 metres farther left there is a blunt, stepped arête. The rock to the left of this is known as the Chorley Walls.

18. Let's Do It 12m HS 4b (1997)
Two metres left of the nose is a crack. Climb this to a scoop, then continue directly to the top.

19. A Fist Full of Stakes 12m VS 4c (1997)
Start two metres to the left and climb easily to a crack at half height, then finish up this.

20. Pale Face Cometh 12m S 4a (1997)
Climb over obvious blocks on the left to a ledge at half-height, then follow the leftward-trending crack to the top.

★★ **21. Kissing the Gunner's Daughter** 15m E3 5c (1988)
A hard route with a subtle and poorly protected start and a strenuous, but well protected finish. Right of Main Wall is a grooved wall, with an obvious hanging crack in the right-hand arête. Climb a short corner to the base of the crack and gain the crack from the left. Follow the crack strenuously to finish.

Main Wall

This is the large gloomy buttress at the far right-hand side, generally obscured by a profusion of slime, although there is some potential here if one is equipped with industrial sand-blasting equipment. Two routes were described in an earlier guide; **Vendetta** *(VS, 4c) and* **Co-Axial** *(HVS, 5b), but these have now fallen into a state of disrepair and can only at present be recorded as unjustifiable. An aided traverse of the wall exists, using either pegs or Friends, with huge pendulums to avoid the looser sections.*

At present there are no recorded routes on the left-hand side.

First Ascents at Central Quarry

1972-73	**Vendetta, Co-Axial** Robin Barley, Jerry Peel	
1976	**Camina, Lode Star** Les Ainsworth, Dave Cronshaw	
1976	**Pot-Pourri** Dave Cronshaw, Les Ainsworth	
1978	**Verboten** Dave Cronshaw, Les Ainsworth	
1978	**The Birch** Dave Cronshaw, Robin Barley, Les Ainsworth	
1981	**Mad Barney** Neil Hyde, Kev Glass	
1981	**Sabre** Kev Glass	
1983	**Bizz Energy** Neil Hyde, Kev Glass	
1985	**Gibberish Crack** John Morrissey, Dave Carpenter	
1986	**Rubber Bullet, Spy** Goi Ashmore	
1986	**Paul Can't Climb** Kev Glass	
1986	**Riding High** John Morrissey, Dave Carpenter	
1986	**Little Matchstick Owen's Route, A Thing of Hate** Goi Ashmore (solo)	
1987	**Pale Face** Dave Cronshaw, Les Ainsworth	
1988 May 21	**Kissing the Gunner's Daughter** Ian Conway, Richard Baker	
1996	**Lode Star Direct, Sword** Dave Cronshaw, Les Ainsworth	
	Sword Direct Finish by Goi Ashmore 1986, as a variation to Thing of Hate.	
1997 Aug 7	**Let's Do It, A Fist Full of Stakes, Pale Face Cometh** Paul Dewhurst, Michael Jackson	

Denham Quarry

'Denham Quarry in Lancashire offers wide scope for rabbits (as Showell Styles would call them) the ordinary non-hard man... '

'... For the sake of the 'almost-hard man' the VSs must be mentioned. The fame of Mohammed the Mad Monk of Moorside Home for Mental Misfits has even reached the deep south and the intellectual flatlands of Cambridge!'

Peter Stone, Rocksport, Dec. 1971

Situation and Character

The quarry lies eight kilometres south-east of Preston, near the village of Brindle. Climbing here is on variable quality gritstone and being west-facing, it is ideal for an evening visit.

The quarry offers a wide variety of climbing, with something to suit most climbers and some classic gritstone quarry climbs.

History

The early history at Denham is still rather vague although it is known that various parties climbed here during the 1950s, making first ascents and at least one guidebook was written to the crag. This guide was handwritten and had a very restricted circulation. Les Ainsworth was shown a copy of the booklet but it was in the days before photocopiers and Ainsworth was unable to make a duplicate. One route stood out in his mind however, a route called *The Green Caterpillar* which is probably now the line taken by *Narrow Slab*, the caterpillar having unrolled itself in about 1963.

Ainsworth noticed the crag whilst taking a rather circuitous route back to college and with Paul Hamer soon set about climbing all the obvious lines; in many cases reclimbing lines which had been done previously and renaming them with such 'inspired' names (though some may say 'tortuous') as *Mohammed the Mad Monk of Moorside Home for Mental Misfits*, and also adding some routes of their own such as *Gnomely, Mohammed the Mediaeval Melancholic* and *Main Break*. Ainsworth and Hamer were then joined by Ian Cowell to add the prominent *Layback*, then whilst Ainsworth was cleaning *Step in the Clouds* with Cowell, Hamer joined John McGonagle on *Concave Wall*. The next weekend Cowell returned, intent on forcing a bolt route over the overhang, *Super Indirectissima*. Armed with a star drill and hammer it took about 20 minutes for each bolt in those days and when it started raining Ainsworth retreated to belay in the car. By then Cowell was right at the lip and getting very wet, so he eventually came down, whereupon the rain promptly stopped and with virtually all of the drilling done, Ainsworth led the route without any of the graft. Hank Pasquill made a fleeting visit and left having made the first free ascent of *Dry* which was one of the routes pegged by the previous generation of Denham devotees, then Ainsworth added *Our Man from Cairo* at the extreme right. The locals then believed that there was little remaining to be done in the quarry, but this illusion was shattered when Dave Knowles claimed *Mad Karoo* in the summer of 1969. No-one had attempted routes on this wall, and at first there was some scepticism about the route, and then uncertainty as to its proper line. Rereading the description showed the true line, and two more obvious gaps suddenly came to light. Dave Cronshaw and Ainsworth then turned their attention to this wall and Cronshaw clocked up *Time*, with Ainsworth in tow. The pair then switched leads for Ainsworth to complete *End of Time*; a brilliant route which unfortunately had to resort to a point of aid to reach the break. Next in line was the obvious traverse of the large horizontal fault which did not succumb without a little tussle with a large block which fell on to Ainsworth's shoulder near the top whilst he was placing his first runner. Ainsworth confessed to feeling 'a little naked in the way of protection' as a fall would have been nasty, and thus the route was named *Complete Streaker*. Soon after Ainsworth climbed *Timepiece*.

Things were then dormant at Denham for some time until Dave Knighton appeared on the scene in 1977. With Eric Dearden he converted the old aid route Sticky into a free route with just one point of aid (later eliminated by Dave Kenyon); *That's All It Takes*. Knighton then turned his attention to the right arête of the wall and soon produced the superb *Flick of The Wrist*, and the summer's activities ended with Nigel Bonnett claiming the short arête above the pool on the *Last Day But One* of his holidays.

1980 saw Tony Brindle *Going for the One*, followed closely by *Eric's Arête* by Dearden, and then in 1981 attention turned to the Overhang Area when Cronshaw forced two interesting routes through the roofs with *Chronometer* and *Chrono-Logical*, the aid route *Super Indirectissima* having been done by Ainsworth and Ian Cowell some 13 years previously.

In 1982 Cronshaw renewed his attentions to the aid route *Toreador*, and after a couple of failures he completed the route free, with John Ryden. Then 1983 saw Greg Rimmer knocking off *Jimmy Sideways*, whilst Malc Haslam retaliated with the neighbouring *Lock off Locomotion*. This latter route became derailed later, when a huge block fell from the roof, rendering it obsolete. This pair clubbed together with Mick Ryan and visiting Kiwi Roland Foster to establish *Screaming Meemies* whilst Dearden had returned to the main walls of the amphitheatre and put up *Cyclops*.

Preston ace, Andrew Gridley arrived on the scene in 1987 when he climbed the fiercely technical problem, *Fujari*, followed closely by more intimate contact on his *Private Palpate*. After small fillers-in by various climbers, the latest addition of any note was made early in 1988 when Cronshaw took a dive and nearly ended head-first into the pool when he fell from the top moves on *Acapulco*. At the other side of the Pool Area Andy Griffith squeezed in two hard routes with Mick Taylor on either side of Mohammed, which he called *They Don't Sell Bolts at Glacier Sports* and *Mick the Quilt* respectively. A few days later Griffith discovered yet another gem, *Eff Vee Tee* on the Overhang Area. Finally, it is interesting to note that an obvious V Diff arête, *Tower Ridge*, had managed to escape everyone's notice for some thirty years or so until Cronshaw soloed it in 1996, proving that there is still some scope left for even the most modest climbers.

Access and Approach

The quarry is under the ownership of Chorley Council, having been given to the borough for 'quiet public enjoyment'.

From the M6 (Junction 29) follow the A6 south for nearly two kilometres to a
small roundabout at Clayton Green. Turn left here on to the B5256 and continue
for about a kilometre to another roundabout. Follow the left turning from this
roundabout and cross the M61 almost immediately, then after a further 50
metres turn right into Holt Lane and follow the road round until it is possible to
drive into the quarry on the left a few hundred metres farther on.

If approaching from the M65 (Junction 3) turn north towards Hoghton and
Preston along the A675 and continue for about one kilometre to meet the old
Blackburn – Preston road at the Royal Oak. Turn left and after about 300
metres, at a sharp bend, turn onto the B5256, then follow the road through
Brindle and turn left after about a kilometre into Holt Lane. The Blackburn –
Leyland bus route runs along the B5256.

The Climbs

The quarry is conveniently divided up into three areas; the Pool Area on the
right, which provides the best climbing; the Overhang Area marked by the great
overhangs on the left side of the crag; and the Intermediate Area which lies
between the other two.

The routes are described from RIGHT to LEFT.

Pool Area

The first three routes are all poorly protected.

1. Ashimoto 10m D   (1966)
From the centre of the end wall follow an obvious line of ledges and a ramp to
a finishing groove.

2. Waldo 10m HS   (1972)
From the foot of the ramp on Ashimoto, mantel onto the left wall then up to a
large ledge (and the first and only runner, in a borehole) finish easily right.

★ **3. Short Circuit** 12m E1 5c   (1988)
Climb the wall between Waldo and Our Man from Cairo direct via a borehole at
half-height.

★ **4. Our Man from Cairo** 12m HVS 5b   (1973)
Climb the left-facing groove for four metres, high peg, then make an awkward
pull out right onto a small sloping ledge. Move across to another small ledge on
the right then up left, finishing past three prominent nebs.

5. Gnomely 12m HVS 5a   (1966)
From the sloping ledge on Our Man from Cairo move up and left to ledges,
then follow the weakness above.

6. Narrow Slab 12m D   (Pre-1966)
Climb the centre of the narrow slab to the left, turning the capping overhang on
the left.

★ **7. Splash Arête** 14m VD   (Pre-1966)
The top of the arête is pleasantly exposed, but the holds are all very positive.
Just above and left is a large ledge, gain this and then up to a further two

ledges and traverse left to the arête and disproportionate exposure. Finish airily up the arête.

*The bolts on the old aid route (**Splash**, A1) up the centre of the wall on the left have now virtually rusted away and the next route is:*

★ **8.   Last Day but One**   10m   E3   5c   (1977)
From the large ledge, climb the prominent right arête of the pool, on its right side to the notch, then cross over and climb the left side, to an easy finish up Splash Arête.

The next five routes have a common start in the corner recess at the left edge of the pool.

9.   Wet   25m   VD   (1966)
From the corner traverse right, moving down slightly to reach the right-hand corner, climb this over large ledges.

10.   Damp   21m   VS   4c   (1966)
Follow Wet to the centre of the wall, then reach up to a mantel ledge and climb the shallow groove above to the terrace. Finish directly up the wall behind.

★ **11.   Acapulco**   18m   E2   5b   (1988)
The shallow groove in the wall left of Damp is gained from below on creaky flakes. From the terrace take the problem wall left of Damp via two pockets.

★ **12.   Dry**   17m   E1   5b,4b   (Pre-1966/1971)
1.   9m.   Climb the corner recess without respite, to the terrace.
2.   8m.   Move up left to a ledge on the arête, then take the stepped ledges on the right to finish.

★★ **13.   Flick of the Wrist**   18m   E2   5c   (1977)
Sustained and delicate moves on steep rock lead to the horizontal break, then the climbing relents. Climb the corner for a couple of metres to a swing left around the slabby arête. Surmount the bulge above with difficulty, past an ancient bolt, to the horizontal break. Pull over the overhang to a ledge then finish up the arête.

★ **14.   That's All it Takes**   20m   E4   6b   (1973/1977/1980)
Originally pegged as Sticky. Start four metres left of the arête and gain a footledge at two metres. Use peg slots and small flakes to reach an overlap. Cross this on its left to a cave in the break. Leave the cave by a flake in the roof and climb the upper wall on widely spaced but positive holds. Actually the route takes more than most people have to give!

The following six routes start from the large ledge at the base of the wall. Protection is generally lacking, thus making these routes serious undertakings. Various problems exist on the short wall below the ledge.

★★ **15.   End of Time**   21m   E2   5b   (1973/1977)
A cool approach will pay dividends on this route. From the large ledge mantel onto a small ledge on the right at three metres, then move up rightwards to gain the break with difficulty. From the left side of the cave, climb the overhang on large but awkward holds and finish direct.

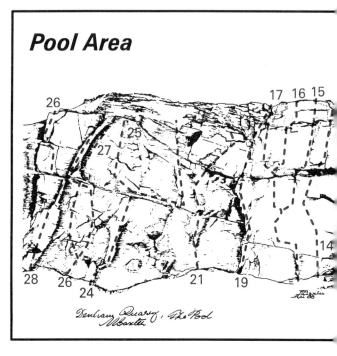

Pool Area

★ **16.   Time**   20m   E1   5a   (1973)
From the mantel at three metres on the previous route, continue direct via a
pocket to the break. Go diagonally right a couple of moves, passing another
pocket, then climb a shallow scoop and finish to the right above this.

★ **17.   Mad Karoo**   20m   HVS   4c   (1969)
Follow Time to the horizontal break, then trend left and climb the wall on
flakes, just right of the shallow corner.

★★ **18.   Complete Streaker**   29m   VS   4c   (1973)
A little naked in the way of protection. Climb Concave Wall to the obvious
horizontal break. Traverse this almost to the arête (peg), gain the ledge above
the overhang and streak up the blunt arête in a fine position.

19.   Concave Wall   18m   S   4a   (1966)
Climb easily over ledges in the angle of the wall, then finish up the shallow
groove which forms the corner.

20.   Bevel   24m   VD   (1966)
From the ledge, traverse left across ledges to where D.C. left his mark for
posterity. Go up and right to a large ledge then follow the diagonal break
leftwards, finishing over poor rock.

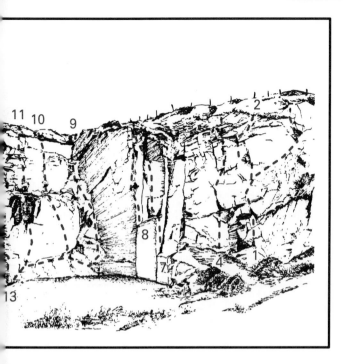

21. Monk Puzzle 18m HVS 5c,4c (1978)
1. 9m. Start six metres left of the angle of the wall, directly below the
chiselled D.C. Climb up past a curious hole to a ledge then go up right to a
large ledge and a poor tape belay.
2. 9m. Follow the flake above to a small overlap then climb straight up
passing some friable rock.

Between the angle of the wall and the first pitch of Monk Puzzle are some
interesting boulder problems. These include the slight scoop just left of the angle
of the wall (5b) and the shallow peg cracks right of Monk Puzzle (6a). There is
also a low-level traverse from the corner of Wet, to Green Finger Crack at 5b –
6a depending on which bits are missed out.

22. Brittle Nerve 17m E3 6a (1983-86)
The obvious right-slanting weakness four metres left is climbed (peg) to the
large ledge. Continue up the easier wall above.

★ **23. Timepiece** 27m HVS 5a (1973)
From a circular rock feature just to the left, climb the steep wall on slots to the
left end of a large ledge. Hand-traverse out to the left along the break, passing
an obvious groove. Traverse left round the arête to finish up a short crack.

24. Mohammed the Morbid Mogul 25m S 4a (1966)
Left again is a shallow corner; climb this to the large ledge then traverse easily
right to *D.C.'s* epitaph. Step up and left then go direct to finish up a crack in
the short wall above.

25.   Private Palpate   17m   E4   6b   (1986-87)
From where Timepiece traverses off left, climb the thin crack in the wall above
past two pegs (not in-situ).

26.   Going for the One   21m   E2   5b   (1980)
Start midway between the two Mohammed climbs, move up to a small overlap
and step right to climb the left side of the thin flake above. Traverse off left to
Mad Monk and stride across its groove to gain a thin crack. Climb this until it
is possible to swing left to finish.

27.   They Don't Sell Bolts at Glacier Sports   15m   E5   6b   (1989)
Start as for the previous route, but climb direct past the overlap and shallow
groove, then continue past a break (peg, not in-situ) and finish up the blunt
arête above.

★★ **28.   Mohammed the Mad Monk of Moorside Home for Mental Misfits**
       15m   VS   4c   (Pre-1966)
The appealing right-leaning groove at the left side of the Pool Area should not
be missed by any visiting VS climbers. At the top finish slightly right, or follow
the old peg crack.

29.   Mohammed Arête   15m   E1   5a   (1986)
From the base of the groove-proper on the Mad Monk, climb the arête on its
right-hand side.

30.   Mohammed the Mediaeval Melancholic   14m   VS   4c   (1966)
Climb the left side of the arête to finish up a short crack.

31.   Mick the Quilt   15m   E4   6a   (1990)
Start in the centre of the narrow wall on the left and climb to the obvious ledge
at three metres, then continue to the top with side runners first in Green Finger
Crack then in the Melancholic. Much of this climb is close to the vertical sandy
streak where top soil washes down the rock and so the holds may be very sandy.

32.   Green Finger Crack   10m   VS   4b   (1975-79)
The obvious loose-looking flake crack at the left side of the wall, is gained by
delicate moves to start.

33.   Cyclops   9m   VS   5b   (1983)
Just left of the Pool Area there is a small isolated buttress with a prominent
hole at half-height. Start just right of the hole and surmount the initial overhang
using a drill hole, then continue direct to the top. Stake belay.

Right Intermediate Area

*The next continuous section of rock lies about 35 metres farther left. At its right
side, it is characterized by three grooves.*

34.   Eric's Arête   9m   E1   5b   (1980)
The slightly friable right arête which limits the area.

Ron Fawcett losing his head on **Mandarin** (E2 5b), Hoghton Quarry.   *Photo: Dave Cronshaw*

35.   Den Dièdre   6m   VD   (1966)
The first groove.

36.   Tower View   6m   VD   (1966)
The middle groove.

37.   Tower Ridge   6m   VD   (1996)
The next arête on its left side.

38.   Tower Groove   8m   D   (1966)
The third groove, which is a deep V-groove.

39.   Ledgeway   6m   M   (1966)
The broken series of ledges in the corner on the left.

40.   The Clangers   6m   HS   4b   (1986-87)
The ancient peg crack just to the left.

41.   Notions of Disposability   8m   E1   5c   (1986-87)
From the left edge of the wall make awkward moves up the right side of the
arête.

42.   Albert's Arête   6m   D   (1966)
The arête on the right of the large bay, gained easily from the left.

43.   Nuts   10m   HS   4b   (Pre-1975)
The grassy corner in the centre of the bay. Carry a machete.

44.   Pop   10m   HVS   5a   (1981)
Start three metres left of the corner, below a niche. Gain this directly via a
small hole at three metres, and continue to the top.

45.   Rivet   10m   VS   4c   (1966)
To the left are twin cracks. Go up these to a ledge on the right, then exit
awkwardly up and left.

46.   Fujari   10m   E5   6c   (1986-87)
The line of small holds in the wall on the left provides a desperate sequence of
moves on undercuts, to gain a short finishing crack (two pegs, not in-situ).

47.   Janet   10m   HVS   5a   (1982)
Climb the right side of the left arête and finish up the loose top of Aviemore
Arête.

48.   Aviemore Arête   9m   S   4a   (1966)
The arête on the left with a loose finish.

There is a low-level traverse around the area with one 5c move.

Paul Cropper on the classic **Rhododendron Buttress** (E2 5c), Hoghton Quarry.

Photo: Brian Cropper

Left Intermediate Area

After a gap of about 20 metres, there is a more broken area of rock which contains generally easy climbs. Unfortunately, some of these are in danger of disappearing under a cloak of vegetation.

49. Hough 9m VD (1970)
Start as for Curving Crack but climb the short, thin groove and square niche above to a heathery finish.

50. Curving Crack 10m D (1966)
The wide curving crack, immediately to the left. Finish to the right by scrambling over heather.

51. Slanting Groove 9m D (1966)
The shallow groove snaking right, then the groove above.

52. Thin Finger Crack 10m VS 4c (Pre-1975)
The peg-scarred crack just to the left.

53. Groove and Wall 12m HS 4a (1979-83)
The groove which starts immediately on the left. Climb the groove to the top of the rib, then finish direct. Care is needed with the rock on the top wall.

★ **54. Low Rib** 12m VD (1966)
Start at the rib which projects from the lowest ground level and climb this for a few moves until forced left. Continue to the top of the rib, then climb up and left to a large ledge on the arête. Follow the arête to the top.

55. Finito 10m HVS 5a (1978)
Start two metres left at a corner with a hole on its left wall, and climb this on its left until it is possible to move right to finish.

Far Intermediate Area

The short buttress 20 metres farther left and at a slightly higher level.

56. Sprain 6m VS 4c (1979-83)
Start just left of the right arête of the buttress. After a difficult start climb over the overhang by a V-shaped groove.

57. Midget 6m VD (1979-83)
Start in the angle of the buttress, then step right on to a nose and surmount the overhang above.

58. Nosey 6m VS 5b (1986-87)
Ascend the overhanging nose on sidepulls then climb straight over the overhang above.

59. The Ceaseless Tide 6m VS 5c (1986-87)
Just left of Nosey is a blunt rib; climb this and the wall above.

60. Fingerbore 6m VS 4c (1968)
Start one metre left and climb directly to the overhang via boreholes, then finish up the groove on the left.

61.   Abrasions and Lacerations   12m   VS   5a   (1986-87)
A right-to-left traverse of the area just below the overhanging band.

Overhang Area
The next climbs are on the final section of unbroken rock, which starts from the main quarry floor. At its right, this area consists of three poorly-defined and somewhat broken buttress. Then it drops down to a lower level and the Great Overhang.

62.   The Edge   9m   VD   (1986-87)
Keep to the right side of the first buttress.

63.   Trigular   9m   M   (1966)
Ascend the centre of the buttress past several drill marks, to a ledge. Then go right to finish.

64.   Extra   12m   D   (1966)
The right corner of the next shallow bay, finish to the left.

65.   Intra   12m   VD   (1966)
Climb the centre of the bay, passing between the overhangs.

66.   Lintel   9m   S   4a   (1966)
Climb the overhang which Intra avoids, swing round the overhang on its left, then finish easily.

67.   Central Buttress   12m   D   (1966)
Climb the left side of the bay to the overhang at four metres, then traverse left and follow a line of boreholes to the top.

68.   Central Buttress Direct   14m   VD   (1966)
Climb the Central Buttress directly, starting just right of a sapling.

69.   Cuckoo's Nest   9m   HVS   5b   (1979-83)
To the left and at a higher level is a steep slab. Climb this just right of the corner, via a pocket.

70.   The Layback   9m   VS   4c   (1966)
The corner crack, with an awkward pull out left at the top.

71.   Dislocation   9m   VD   (1966)
From the base of Layback move up left and climb the corner, borehole runner.

72.   Wings   9m   E1   5c   (1987)
Below and left of the previous route is a butterfly overhang. Starting up a short rib climb the overhang by a short hanging groove, then the arête above.

73.   Butterfly   9m   S   4a   (1972)
Start just left. Climb a flaky wall and the corners above.

74.   Step in the Clouds   9m   S   4b   (1966)
From behind some large blocks on the ground climb up to a ledge (or gain the ledge by the ramp on the left, better). Gain the top of a small block above the ledge, then traverse right to a small ledge and an easy finish.

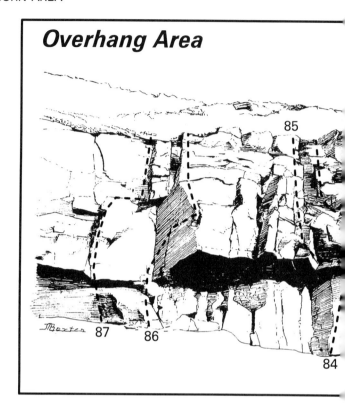

Overhang Area

85

87   86

84

75.   The Funny Farm   9m   HS   4b   (1966)
Climb the corner groove where the ground level drops, at the overhang pull out
right, then finish straight up the steep ramp.

76.   There's a Ghost in My Acid House   9m   E1   6a   (1989)
Climb the centre of the wall on the left of the corner groove.

77.   Quasimodo   10m   E1   5b   (1978)
Climb the arête on its left to a sloping ledge, then finish up the groove above.

78.   Super Indirectissima   14m   A2   (1966)
The obvious line of ancient bolts across the Great Overhang, finishing with an
awkward free move.

79.   Screaming Meemies   12m   E3   6a   (1983)
On the left the roof narrows considerably above a small yellow promontory.
Climb through the roof at this point (Friends) and continue up the short
left-slanting corner above.

★★ **80.   Toreador**   12m   E3   6a   (1968/1982)
Also known previously as Bullworker. Sustained climbing up an old peg route,
which requires strong fingers. If the peg near the top is missing, it is very tiring

to arrange alternative protection. Start six metres farther left and climb a slabby
rib to the overlap. Start the steep peg crack above and follow it to the top.

81. Eff Vee Tee 14m E4 6b   (1985)
From Toreador, move left across wall to a bolt, then make long reaches to gain
the arête (niche and undercut). RPs protect the final moves.

★ **82. Main Break** 15m HS 4a   (1966)
Left again is a steep rib leading to a break in the overhang. Start left of the rib
and climb up through the break, then step left and climb a slab.

83. Ganglion 34m VS 4a   (1975)
Climb through the overhang as for Main Break, but traverse left above the roof
for six metres. Either step up and swing left across a bottomless groove, or
move down to cross the groove (or maybe jump across it?). Continue along,
crossing a V-groove then climb a short arête and broken rock to finish. Poor
protection.

84. Chronometer 12m HVS 5a   (1981)
Farther left the overhang is broken by a hanging groove. Climb a rib to the
overhang, then from a good hold above, make a long reach rightwards to enter
the groove. Climb it then exit left to a ledge and finish easily above.

★ **85.   Crono-Logical**   14m   E2   5c   (1981)
Follow Chronometer to the good hold but make a committing swing leftwards
on to a jutting block. Make an impressive mantel on to this and finish easily.
Excellent protection is available but it needs a little thought.

*The blocks lying on the ground to the left are the remains of a rib which used
to form the start of* **Lock off Locomotion** *(E2, 6a). This route hand-traversed
the lip of the roof leftwards to finish up the next route. It has not been ascended
since the demise of the rib.*

86.   Jimmy Sideways   14m   HVS   5a   (1983)
Where the large overhang ends is an undercut slab with a sycamore beneath its
left side. Step from a boulder into the corner then gain the rib on the right and
so to the top.

87.   Rockdancer   14m   HVS   5a   (1978)
From the boulder at the start of Jimmy Sideways climb a crack in the centre of
the slab until it is possible to traverse rightwards into the corner. Finish on the
right.

88.   Rocking Horse Droppings   10m   S   4a   (1981)
Four metres left of the sycamore is a short wall. Start at the left side of this and
step up, then move right across the wall to a finish up the right side.

First Ascents at Denham Quarry

Pre-1966	**Mohammed the Mad Monk of Moorside Home for Mental Misfits**
	Originally pegged.
Pre-1966	**Narrow Slab** *Originally climbed as Green Caterpillar*
Pre-1966	**Splash** (A1)
Pre-1966	**Dry** (A1/VS)
	First free ascent by Hank Pasquill, Dave Cronshaw and others, early 1971.
1966	**Ashimoto** Les Ainsworth, Paul Hamer
1966 July	**Gnomely** Les Ainsworth, Paul Hamer
1966 July	**Splash Arête** Current line Les Ainsworth, Paul Hamer
	Originally finished up the corner and known as Amen Corner.
1966 July	**Bevel, Main Break** Les Ainsworth, Paul Hamer
1966 Aug	**Concave Wall** John McGonagle, Paul Hamer
1966 Aug	**Wet, Damp, Den Dièdre, Tower View, Tower Groove** Les Ainsworth, Paul Hamer
1966 Aug	**Mohammed the Morbid Mogul** Les Ainsworth (solo)
1966 Aug	**Aviemore Arête** Les Ainsworth, Les Houlker
1966 Aug	**The Layback** Les Ainsworth, Paul Hamer, Ian Cowell
1966 Sep	**Low Rib, Ledgeway, Mohammed the Mediaeval Melancholic, Albert's Arête, Slanting Groove, Rivet, Trigular, Extra, Central Buttress, Central Buttress Direct, Intra** Les Ainsworth, Paul Hamer
1966 Sep	**Lintel** Les Ainsworth (solo)
1966 Sep	**Dislocation** Les Ainsworth (solo)
	Originally called Hanging Corner. Line slightly changed and renamed in 1970 when a leader dislocated his shoulder on the second ascent immediately afterwards.
1966 Oct	**Super Indirectissima, Step in the Clouds** Les Ainsworth, Ian Cowell
1966 Oct	**Curving Crack** Les Ainsworth, Paul Hamer
1966 Aug	**The Funny Farm** Les Ainsworth, Paul Hamer
1968	**Fingerbore** Les Ainsworth (solo)
1968 Aug	**Toreador** (A1) F. Snalam, D. Emmerson
	First free ascent by Dave Cronshaw, John Ryden, 28 June 1982.
1969 July	**Mad Karoo** Dave Knowles

1970	**Hough** Les Ainsworth (solo)
Early 1971	**Dry** Hank Pasquill, Dave Cronshaw and others
	First free ascent.
1972 Apr	**Our Man from Cairo, Butterfly** Les Ainsworth, Dave Cronshaw
1972 Apr	**Waldo** Dave Cronshaw, Les Ainsworth
1973 Mar	**Time** Dave Cronshaw, Les Ainsworth
1973 Mar	**End of Time** (1pt aid) Les Ainsworth, Dave Cronshaw
	Aid eliminated 1977.
1973 June	**Complete Streaker** Les Ainsworth, Dave Cronshaw
1973 July	**Timepiece** Les Ainsworth, Dave Cronshaw, Bob MacMillan
1973	**Sticky** (A2) Brian Evans
	Reduced to 1 aid pt by Dave Knighton, Eric Dearden as That's All it Takes, 1977.
	Aid completely eliminated by Dave Kenyon, Malc Haslam, 1980.
Pre-1975	**Nuts**
Pre-1975	**Thin Finger Crack**
Pre-1975	**The Edge**
1975-79	**Green Finger Crack** Gordon Marsden
1975	**Ganglion** Dave Knighton, Sam Morris
1976 July 29	*Crooked Hill* Dave Knighton and Allan Whalley
	A girdle which started up Splash for 3 bolts aid then pendulumed left and continued the traverse around the amphitheatre, at A1/Hard VS.
1977 July 27	**That's All it Takes** (1 pt aid) Dave Knighton, Eric Dearden
	A major aid reduction that whittled down the aid to one peg on the route previously known as Sticky.
1977 Aug 8	**Flick of the Wrist** Dave Knighton, Eric Dearden
1978 June 14	**Quasimodo** Eric Dearden, Dave Knighton
1977 Aug 30	**Last Day but One** Nigel Bonnett
1978	**Monk Puzzle, Finito** Dave Cronshaw, Les Ainsworth
1978 July	**Rockdancer** Eric Dearden, Dave Knighton
1980	**Going for the One** Tony Brindle, Brendan Conlon, Eric Dearden
1980	**Eric's Arête** Eric Dearden, Tony Brindle
1981	**Pop** Dave Cronshaw, John Ryden
1981	**Chronometer** Dave Cronshaw, Les Ainsworth, John Ryden
1981	**Crono-Logical** Dave Cronshaw, John Ryden, Les Ainsworth
1981	**Rocking Horse Droppings** Dave Cronshaw (solo)
1982 June 28	**Toreador** Dave Cronshaw, John Ryden
	First free ascent.
1982	**Janet** Rob Trevitt
1979-83	**Groove and Wall**
1979-83	**Sprain**
1979-83	**Midget**
1979-83	**Cuckoo's Nest**
1980	**That's All it Takes** Dave Kenyon, Malc Haslam, 1980
	Aid completely eliminated.
1983	**Cyclops** Eric Dearden
1983	**Screaming Meemies** Roland Foster, Malc Haslam, Greg Rimmer, Mick Ryan,
1983	**Jimmy Sideways** Greg Rimmer, Mick Ryan, Malc Haslam
1983-86	**Brittle Nerve**
1986	**Mohammed Arête** Eric Dearden, N. Ogden
1986-87	**The Clangers**
1986-87	**Notions of Disposability** Goi Ashmore
1986-87	**Fujari** Andrew Gridley
1986-87	**Private Palpate** Andrew Gridley
1986-87	**Nosey**
1986-87	**The Ceaseless Tide** Malc Haslam
1986-87	**Abrasions and Lacerations**
1987	**Wings** Dave Cronshaw (solo)
1988 Jan 7	**Short Circuit** Dave Cronshaw (solo after top roping)
1988 Jan 31	**Acapulco** Dave Cronshaw, John Ryden, Roger Vickers, Ian Vickers
1989 Mar 17	**There's a Ghost in My Acid House** Goi Ashmore

1989 June   **They Don't Sell Bolts at Glacier Sports** Andy Griffith, Mick Taylor
1990 May 21   **Mick the Quilt** Andy Griffith, Mick Taylor
1990 June 29   **Eff Vee Tee** Andy Griffith, Mick Taylor
1996 June 25   **Tower Ridge** Dave Cronshaw (solo)

Hoghton Quarry   O.S. ref.   SD 626 265

Please read Access notes before visiting Hoghton Quarry

*'On the one hand there are many climbers who are ignorant
of the existence of Hoghton, whilst on the other hand there
are its devotees who consider it to be the finest quarry in the
country. I am not going to spend time here discussing
whether or not Hoghton IS the best quarry, but the fact still
remains that it is ONE OF the best, and as such deserves a
guide.'*

Paul Hamer, Rocksport, 1968

Situation and Character

This magnificent quarry lies below Hoghton Tower, just off the Blackburn –
Preston road (A675). In the past it was a mecca for the 'bash-and-dangle
brigade', though now it boasts an excellent free-climbing arena which provides
varied climbing in interesting positions; ranging from steep slabs and walls to an
abundance of overhangs. Because of the northerly aspect of the main walls, they
may need a short spell of dry weather before they come into condition. Liqueur
Wall, though, faces south and provides good climbing in a sunny situation. The
lack of traffic over the past couple of years also means that if access is
regranted, many of the classic lines, are likely to be overgrown and will need a
couple of ascents before they regain their previous quality.

Incidentally, carnivorous climbers may be interested to learn that sirloin of beef
originates from Hoghton Tower after a previous visitor, King James I, was so
taken by the food that was laid on, that he knighted a loin of beef. Tower
Woods were also the setting for much of Harrison Ainsworth's *'Lancashire
Witches'*.

History

As far as is known, the quarry was first used for cliff assault practice by the
armed forces during the Second World War.

In the 1950s more conventional methods were used to scale the crag: quarries
were popular as training grounds on which aid techniques could be practised in
preparation for the bigger walls in the Alps. During 1955 John 'Fritz' Sumner
pegged *Ten Minute Traverse*, using custom-made 1-inch pegs specially
manufactured for the ascent by Keith King. Sumner also went on and aided the
imposing *Rhododendron Buttress* which gained some notoriety amongst the local
climbers when Tony Crook (attempting the third ascent) fell from the lip of the
overhang when a peg foothold came out. His belayer, John Britt, only just
succeeded in preventing an impressive decking from 25 metres, all the more
impressive as no belay plates were in existence at that time! The following year
Alan Atkinson left the commonly used bivouac spot (the *Waiting Room*) by a
different route and attacked the roof-crack above using wooden wedges. On the

lip of the roof, Atkinson had the disconcerting experience of watching the wedges in the back of the roof slowly work loose and drop out as the crack widened slightly. He named the route *Scimitar Crack* for obvious reasons, though it is now known as *The Dangler*.

Towards the late 1950s Hoghton had become established as a centre for artificial climbing, attracting Joe Brown and Ron Moseley, together with other members of the Rock and Ice crew, and this group made several aided ascents though details are sketchy. By the mid-Sixties a number of free routes had been done, such as *Cave Route, Zig Zag, Partnership, Bowker's Crack, Scoop and Wall* and a free version of *Route One*. Mostly these were climbed by various combinations of John Hamer, John Wareing, John (Aussie) Parkinson and Bill Bowker. Meanwhile, aid routes continued to be put up until the late 1960s, including Terry Wareing and Ian (Spider) McQuirk's bolting extravaganzas, *Terry's Torment* and *Drupe*.

In 1965 Les Ainsworth and Paul Hamer free-climbed *Overhanging Crack*; not by design but simply because Ainsworth did not trust the rotting wooden aid wedges. At that time though, the big problem was an unfinished aid route which was set to breach some impressive territory up the huge roofs left of Hoghton Walls. Up to 1966 many teams had pegged the first pitch up to The Pasture and then John Hamer and Parkinson climbed this free, also adding a variation start called *Patella*. Within a couple of months Stan Bradshaw had finished the route on pegs. Later, John Hamer set out on a free ascent (as a peg route) but managed to keep going without using aid, and thus completed *Mandarin* – one of the best routes in the whole of the area. Hamer followed this success with an attempt at *Hope Not* which ended prematurely with both John and Aussie dangling below The Pasture. After a short rest they completed the route however.

Around the same time Bradshaw put up an impressive display by soloing the first ascent of *Wilkinson's Sword Edge*. Liqueur Wall had been spared the attentions of the new-router up until 1967, when Ainsworth began to explore the area, immediately making solo first ascents of *Kümmel* and *Kirsch*.

Also, during he summer of 1967 *The Wasp* was added: Ainsworth and Paul Hamer had both made protracted attempts at the route and had actually reached a point about four metres below the top, but progress was slow as all the mud from the main crack was being dug out whilst leading. They left it there and returned two weeks later to complete the route, only to be told that Brian Molyneux and Geoff Hamridding had aided it the week before. Ainsworth and Paul free-climbed the route soon after, though this was something of an anticlimax, again having joined the ranks of an aid route that had been free-climbed, rather than being the first major deliberate free-climb at Hoghton that Ainsworth had dreamed of. Ascents of The Wasp and Mandarin had opened up another new area of rock and *Boadicea* was soon aided by Phil Paget and Roger Grimshaw. This lucrative period ended in 1968 with Tony Makin and Terry Devaney adding yet another route to Hoghton Walls which turned out much easier than the rest of the routes in the area and so was a free climb which they called *Thespis*.

Just as the guide was going to press Geoff Fishlock and Paget completed the mammoth task of traversing the main areas of the crag, from what was then *Shake Not* (now *Lamentably Gentlemanly*), to *Ergonome's Enigma*. The resulting traverse (*Tobacco Road*) was a route of epic proportions and included many artificial sections.

During the early 1970s the main preoccupation was the clearing of vegetation from the area beyond Rhododendron Buttress and when this task was completed, some good routes were discovered by Ainsworth, Dave Cronshaw, Bob MacMillan and Rob Meakin. The most notable of these were *Chattox* (with 1 aid point), *Crème de Menthe, Goldwasser* and *Molotov Cocktail* which succumbed to Cronshaw and Ainsworth, Meakin and Ainsworth's *Book of Fate, Malkin Tower* (MacMillan) and *Demdike* (Ainsworth and party) which was probably best of all. In 1972 Cronshaw and Ainsworth returned their attentions to the Main Amphitheatre to tackle the mighty *Goliath's Groove* and to make the first free ascent of *Slime Corner* which seemed an appropriate name under the prevailing conditions! The following year *Strong's Flake* received its first lead from Dave Pyecroft, having been top-roped many years earlier by Frank Strong.

A lull followed, and things remained quiet until Dave Knighton appeared on the scene in 1976. This long, hot summer saw Knighton cleaning and free-climbing Rhododendron Buttress, which immediately heralded the start of a new wave of development at the crag. Knighton soon added to the crag's repertoire with *Fallout* (with a point of aid) which was a different proposition then because of loose blocks (cleaned off and freed by Ian Lonsdale the following year). From *Fallout*, Knighton spotted what was later to become *Highway Star* and then Knighton teamed up with Lonsdale for the latter to steal *War of Attrition*. In 1977 Knighton and friends went to work on *Boadicea* and transformed it into a brilliant free climb though retaining 1 point of aid; an indiscretion which was later eliminated by Ron Fawcett, together with the tension move on *War of Attrition*. Ian went on to free-climb *Goulash* (with Paul McKenzie) and to rid *Ten Minute Traverse* of its aid, with Nadim Siddiqui.

Knighton's onslaught continued unabated; *Lady, Visions of Jan, Sheer Heart Attack* and the particularly bold line of *Keep it Coolin'* were soon in the bag. Knighton then turned his attention to free-climbing the girdle traverse, which he renamed *When The Levee Breaks*. *Flight of the Rat* was added, though unfortunately it necessitated a peg and long sling to bypass a particularly stubborn block in the overhang. It is interesting to note that much of *Flight of the Rat* was originally pegged in 1956 by Mick Tullis, armed with materials like araldite and titanium pegs that were then being used to build the top secret TSR2 plane at British Aerospace in Preston. Knighton then climbed *Every Face Tells A Story* with Jenny Hyslop. In June the following year Cronshaw joined forces with Knighton for his free ascent of *Rhododendron Arête*, though this was not without incident as Knighton took a spectacular flier before succeeding.

A month later some new blood arrived on the scene in the shape of Dave Kenyon and Malc Haslam. This pair began to slowly work through all the crag's remaining gaps and aid routes and soon *Maraschino* had been rid of its aid and the last stubborn aid points on *The Dangler* were eliminated (the aid having been reduced to two points by Cronshaw a little earlier). Kenyon and Haslam began to make a series of technical test pieces such as *Speech Impediment* and *New Wave*. In April 1981 Lonsdale joined Kenyon to add a top pitch to Ian's earlier route *Black Pudding Team Special*, and in 1984 Kenyon free-climbed Knighton's old aid route *Candlemass* to produce a very hard and very classy route – *The Excitable Boy*.

During the summer of 1983 Gary Gibson visited the quarry to add *All Roads Lead To Rome*, a classic pitch which was soon smouldering under the smell of burning rubber and hot on Gary's heels came Haslam and Greg Rimmer with *For God's Sake Burn it Down*. Cronshaw retaliated further, and with Mick Ryan, found *Golden Delicious* more to his taste. Kiwi, Roland Foster, was also operating in the area at the time and was particularly impressed by Hoghton. Foster took an immediate shine to the steep wall to the right of The Wasp, up which Mark Leach and Ian Conway had forced a free version of the old route *Shake Not (Spider Rider)* the previous year. Foster decided that *Spider Rider* needed straightening out, thereby avoiding the escape rightwards on to the arête, and succeeded in climbing *Lamentably Gentlemanly* with John Noblett. Later, looking at the chalk marks snaking up the wall, Foster noticed the expanse between it and The Wasp, and over several days he filled the space with *Getting Rid of the Albatross*, Hoghton's first E6.

Kenyon, along with Foster, transformed Gath into Dave Pearce's dream of a '*Burning Desire*' another super-route. Foster then turned his attention to the *Keep It Coolin'* Wall, playing serious *Mind Games* and *La Lune Dans La Carniveau*. Malc Haslam returned with Ronnie Marsden to produce and direct *Greg Rimmer: The Motion Picture*, a very serious line under The Pasture.

In 1986 Cronshaw and John Ryden climbed yet another new route on Hoghton Wall, naming it *Burning the Phoenix*. Paul Pritchard started to get a look in, pulling over the roof of the top pitch of *The Knickertwister* to produce *On the Brink* (the first pitch had been free-climbed by Fawcett in the 70s) and within days his belayer, Phil Kelly, with Ann Smith, had climbed the blatantly obvious crack below the Mandarin traverse: *Let's Go Play* – a wicked trip. Pritchard then added *Void* and over two days managed the serious and stratospheric traverse *Do the Aqua Melba*, followed by Kelly on both routes.

By July, Andrew Gridley had completed *The French Lieutenant's Marrow*, a superb slab climb just left of Slime Corner's main pitch utilizing bolt runners, and it was a contender for one of the best pitches at Hoghton. Cronshaw then became attracted to a partially-cleaned line over the roofs below War of Attrition. Cronshaw succeeded though this ascent was a little tainted when he was forced into using a rest point whilst trying to gain the upper wall. Kenyon duly repeated the route, without the rest point, to give *Biodegradable Man*. In August Cronshaw and Lonsdale created *The Luddite*, a free version of an ancient aid route, then Cronshaw co-opted Kelly and the pair climbed a line aptly named *Hoghton Weaver*, followed by *Steppin' in the Slide Zone*.

In April 1987 Cronshaw turned to the much-neglected line which was to become *Flight of The Rat* and after a quick abseil to remove a sandy block, both he and Kenyon led the first pitch, then Cronshaw returned the next weekend with Ryden to add a direct finish. Kenyon free climbed *Silverside* in May. After this, apart from a brief spurt in 1991 when Tim Hatch added *Stickman* and Ian Vickers did *Black Tripe Trip* little else has been done.

Access and Approach

The land on which the quarry lies is part of the de Hoghton Estate and it is used as a breeding ground for game birds. It is their desire that these birds are not disturbed and after extensive B.M.C. negotiations an agreement was made for limited climbing access to the quarry between February 1st and May 31st each year. Recently this period has been further reduced in order to avoid disturbance to nesting ravens and peregrines. Unfortunately, the access agreement was not renegotiated for 1998 and so the future access situation is uncertain. Accordingly, climbers should check the current access situation with the BMC before visiting the quarry.

If the access situation is resolved, any climbers visiting the quarry should expect that, because the routes have seen little traffic over the past couple of years, many of the climbs may well have become overgrown.

To reach the quarry from the M65 (Junction 3) turn north towards Hoghton and Preston along the A675 and follow this for about a kilometre to meet the old Blackburn – Preston road at the Royal Oak. Turn left here and continue along the main road for about a kilometre to Chapel Lane, which leads leftwards immediately before the Boar's Head pub. After about 600 metres and just after crossing a railway bridge, park considerably out of the way on the roadside by an old chapel. From here a short track leads rightwards into a field and a foot crossing over the railway. Immediately after crossing the railway turn left and follow a cleared path for 100 metres to a muddy cutting. Continue up this small gorge into the quarry.

The Climbs
The climbs are all described from RIGHT to LEFT.

Hoghton Wall
Hoghton Wall is the large open face which rises from the end of the muddy cutting, and which is bounded on its left by the Main Amphitheatre.

★★ **1.   Lamentably Gentlemanly** 21m E5 6b   (1968/1982/1983)
Sustained climbing up an old peg route, finishing in a fine position. Start six metres right of The Wasp. Climb the short wall, with care, to the sandy break. Climb the crack above past three pegs to the stepped overhang. Pull over this (Friends in the break) then move leftwards and sprint up the short, hairy groove to finish.

★★★ **2.   Getting Rid of the Albatross** 24m E6 6c   (1983)
An atmospheric route with a superb top wall. Start between Lamentably Gentlemanly and Wasp, below a small niche. From the sandy break follow a thin crack to the niche and continue up flakes and slots on the right to the left end of a stepped overhang. Move left and fight up an intermittent peg crack (crux) to finish in a fine position.

★★ **3.   The Wasp** 24m HVS 5a   (1967)
Good exercise in bridging, but unfortunately it can be slow to dry out. The impressive corner at the quarry entrance is climbed in its entirety to a large ledge on the right.

4.   The Sting 8m HVS 5a   (1973)
The short continuation corner above The Wasp.

5.   Goulash 27m E1 5b   (1967/1977)
Originally pegged (A1). Climb the thin crack two metres left of The Wasp, then traverse right along the horizontal break and finish up the final section of Wasp.

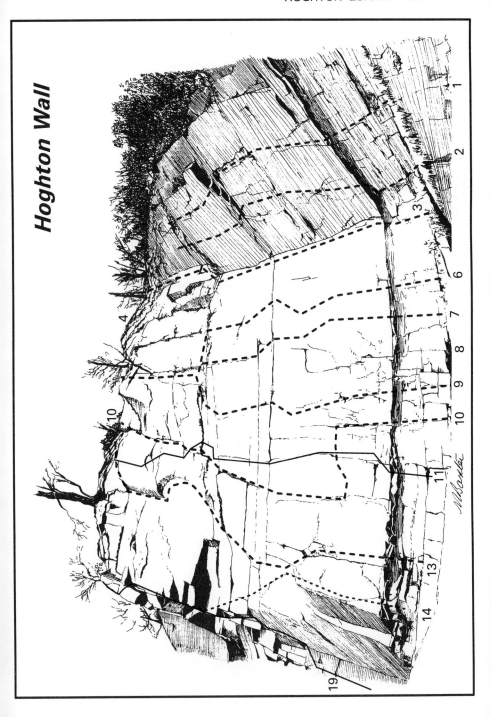

Hoghton Wall

★★★ **6.   All Roads Lead to Rome**   37m   E5   6b   (1983)
An excellent route requiring a certain amount of faith in friction and some
commitment. Start two metres right of Boadicea and climb the thin crack and
wall to a slight overlap (bolt) with increasing difficulty to a grassy ledge,
traverse left along the break on poor rock and finish up Boadicea.

★★★ **7.   Boadicea**   37m   E2   5c   (1968/1977)
Originally pegged (A1). A well-protected but sustained route with two distinct
cruxes, which gives one of the all time classic quarry climbs. Climb the obvious
crack six metres left of The Wasp, past two breaks to finish up a bulging crack,
passing a tree near the top.

★ **8.   For God's Sake Burn it Down!**   38m   E4   6b   (1983)
Climb the crack left of Boadicea, past a small overlap to a break. Step left and
go up to a peg, then make some thin moves to gain a second break. Move right
to a crack, finishing up the last few moves of Boadicea.

★★ **9.   Every Face Tells a Story**   37m   HVS   5b   (1966/1978)
Originally pegged as Hazard (A1). Start at a crack just right of Thespis. Climb
the crack past a bulge then continue to the first horizontal break. Climb the wall
above to the peg on Burn it Down. Either go left to a finish up Lady, or use the
peg for aid to gain a second horizontal break and follow this right to finish up
Boadicea. The aid peg can be omitted at E3, 6b.

★ **10.   Thespis**   37m   HVS   4c,4c   (1968)
1. 14m.   Climb the right-facing flake groove in the centre of Hoghton Wall,
then traverse left along the obvious ledge to a peg belay.
2. 23m.   Climb the wall and short corner above to a break. Step right to a peg
(possible belay), then up the shallow groove to a tree at the top.

★★ **11.   Burning the Phoenix**   37m   E4   5b,6a   (1986)
A good introduction to the harder climbs at Hoghton. Requires faith in Friends.
1. 23m.   Climb the crack two metres left of Thespis to a ledge at 10 metres,
continue in the same line to the grassy break. Step right to a peg belay.
2. 14m.   Traverse left for three metres and climb the wall (pegs) to an overlap
(Friend). Over this on the left and up a short awkward wall to a ledge. Belay on
the right at the tree.

★ **12.   Lady**   37m   HVS   4c,5a   (1977)
1. 10m.   The crack a metre left of Burning the Phoenix to belay as for Thespis.
2. 27m.   Traverse right to the end of a narrow ledge, then climb straight up
the wall above to the first horizontal break. Follow cracks above to the second
horizontal break (peg), then foot traverse this right for three metres to the final
peg-scarred crack of Boadicea and finish up this.

★★ **13.   Route One**   35m   VS   4b,4c   (1950s/early 1960s)
The classic peg route of the Fifties has now become the trade route of this wall.
1. 14m.   Start about two metres right of the arête which forms the right
boundary of the Main Amphitheatre. Climb up the obvious crack, then up the
wall diagonally left to a large ledge and bolt belay.
2. 12 m.   Up the corner to a mantel, then follow a line of ledges right to a
peg below an obvious square overhang. Climb the overhang on its left.

★★★ **14. Golden Delicious** 39m E3 5c,5c (1981/1983)(1985)
Steady climbing with gradually increasing exposure. The moves out of Mandarin
are particularly memorable.
1. 12m. Climb the thin crack (peg), just right of the arête, to the large ledge.
Bolt belay.
Variation Start (6a): the slanting crack on the left that joins the parent route at
the peg.
2. 27m. From the left of the ledge climb to the roof. Pass this on the left and
gain the traverse ledge of Mandarin (in-situ peg) go up to the overhang and
move left onto the exposed arête. Climb up to a small triangular overhang and
step left (crux) to finish up a crack. Trend right to the tree belay on Mandarin.

★★ **15. The Knickertwister** 36m E5 6a,6b (1969/1978/1986)
A hard version of Golden Delicious.
1. 15m. Start as for the alternative start to Golden Delicious, but climb the
corner, then bear left to a vertical crack which leads to the large ledge and bolt
belay.
1a. 14m (**Direct Start**, 5c). Start up the corner, but instead of bearing left,
continue up the wall to the belay ledge.
2. 21m (**On the Brink**). Climb the crack above the belay, to the roof and
move right under this. Make a long reach to a slanting hold on the lip (bolt)
and make a dynamic move on to the wall above. Go up this and trend leftwards
to finish up the easier top section of Mandarin.

The next five routes have a common start at the easy-angled corner on the left.

★ **16. Blind Eye** 17m E5 6c (1987)
Takes the diagonal overlap on the right, starting up Let's Go Play and finishing
up Knickertwister (bolt). Serious towards the top.

★ **17. Let's Go Play** 17m E5 6a (1986)
From a metre up the corner, gain the thin crack in the yellow wall on the right.
Up this to a poor peg and up to another peg. Finger-traverse right along the
break to the large ledge and a bolt belay. Abseil off.

★★ **18. Ten Minute Traverse** 36m E3 5b,5c (1955/1966/1977)
The traverse which was originally pegged at A1 proves every bit as good as it
looks.
1. 18m. Climb the corner to an iron spike then up and move right to gain a
large flake; foot-traverse the horizontal break right until it is possible to step
round onto the belay ledge of Let's Go Play. It is also possible to hand-traverse
the break (harder but better protected).
2. 18m. Climb the corner at the right end of the ledge to the roof, then
straight up the crack above (pegs).

★★★ **19. Mandarin** 37m E2 5b,5b (1960/1967)(1967)
A superb climb, that defies all superlatives. The climbing is maintained at an
even grade with adequate protection and some really impressive positions. Few
climbers will forget an ascent of Mandarin and most will consider it one of the
best quarry climbs in the country.
The route is described as it was originally climbed, but it is probably best
climbed as one pitch by avoiding the traverse to *The Pasture*.

1.   20m.   Follow Ten Minute Traverse to the large flake, then climb up this and the square-cut overhang above. Continue up a short wall to the roof, then traverse left onto the large grassy ledge (*The Pasture*) and a bolt belay.
Patella (5b): instead of crossing Ten Minute Traverse to reach the flake, climb straight up a short chimney and over another overhang to reach the square-cut overhang.
2.   17m.   Traverse back under the roof to gain an obvious traverse ledge. From the end of this bridge up to the overhang and pass this on the right then continue to a niche. Exit left round an arête to an exposed finish up easy rock to a tree belay.

Waiting Room Area

The Waiting Room is the name given to a conspicuous ledge at the right side of the Main Amphitheatre, at about six metres, just left of some large blocks on the quarry floor. The first four routes to be described lead to the ledge itself from which it is possible to descend easily by an abseil from an excellent belay.

20.   Twin Spikes   9m   VD   (1955)
Climb the ledges on the left side of an easy-angled corner to a ledge on the left, then climb up past the remaining quarry spike and traverse left to *The Waiting Room*.

21.   Groove and Ledge   8m   S   4a   (1958-61)
The groove on the left.

22.   Blunt Arête   8m   E1   5b   (1961-63)
The blunt arête between Groove and Ledge and Slanting Crack, with a long reach to finish.

★ **23.   Slanting Crack**   8m   E1   5b   (1956)
The crack which goes diagonally left across the orange wall on the left. At the overlap step right and make an awkward mantel into *The Waiting Room*.

★ **24.   Greg Rimmer: The Motion Picture**   18m   E4   6a   (1983-86)
Start as for Slanting Crack and follow the continuation flake to the break, traverse left to a hanging groove. Up this to a ledge, move left and up to *The Pasture*.

★★ **25.   Dangler, The**   15m   E4   6b   (1956/1977/1979)
An old A3 aid route, which requires very gymnastic contortions to surmount some of the roofs. From *The Waiting Room* climb the short corner which starts below a roof with an obvious circular crack, surmount this (crux) and up to a large roof, which is avoided by a traverse to the left. Finish up a short wall to reach *The Pasture*.

★ **26.   Sheer Heart Attack**   12m   E2   5c   (1967/1977
From the left side of *The Waiting Room*, make a move round the arête to a good hold (peg), then climb the arête to a small ledge. Continue up the flake crack above. then make a difficult mantelshelf onto the horizontal break, then step right and up another crack to *The Pasture*.

The Pasture

The large ledge at mid-height on the right of the amphitheatre is known as The Pasture. It can be reached by abseil, or by various routes. Also it can be left by any of 10 routes.

The first five routes to be described climb rock which is sometimes friable and due to difficulties in arranging good protection these routes are all serious undertakings.

★★ **27. Do the Aqua Melba** 21m E6 6b (1986)
Serious climbing in a sensationally exposed position, starting from a bolt belay at the right end of *The Pasture*. Climb delicately right along the lip of the roof to the good hold below the small overhang on Golden Delicious, then follow this to finish.

★★ **28. Void** 17m E5 6b (1986)
A slightly less sustained version of Aqua Melba, but nevertheless, it can feel very serious. From the start of Aqua Melba, climb up past a small sloping ledge on the right at three metres, to a peg. Step left to a large hold and finish straight up.

★ **29. La Lune Dans La Carniveau** 17m E5 6b (1983)
From the bolt climb direct to a peg, move right and finish straight up.

★★ **30. Keep it Coolin'** 17m E3 5b (1977)
The name says it all. Start at the large block behind the tree. Climb straight up for three metres to a small ledge, then make a rising traverse right into the centre of the wall, and up to a peg. Continue direct to the top.

31. Mind Games 14m E5 6a (1984)
Start as for Keep it Coolin' but climb direct up the wall.

32. Disowned 14m VS 5a (1979-83)
A poor route. Start just right of Partnership and take a direct line up the corner.

33. Partnership 17m VS 4c (1963)
A line of mantelshelves in the corner above *The Pasture*, starting and finishing on the left.

34. Claymore 12m S 4a (1977)
From the start of Partnership, continue straight up to a large ledge, and then finish up the left-slanting ramp.

★ **35. Hope Not** 15m HVS 5a (1967)
The steep crack four metres left. Strenuous at 12 metres. Exit to easier ground past a sloping ledge on the right.

36. Spazzm E1 5c (1983)
A direct finish to Hope Not.

★★ **37. Silverside** 15m E6 6c (1969/1987)
Free-climbs the bolt route in the wall left of Hope Not in an impressive situation. A desperate sequence of moves leads past some ancient bolts and a

bolt runner (new) to a short peg-scarred crack which slants leftwards to a large ledge. Easier climbing leads to the top.

Main Amphitheatre

This is the name give to the distinctive main area, which contains much excellent climbing.

38.   Burning a Nun   18m   E5   6b   (1987)
The counter line to Greg Rimmer. Start in the shallow corner nine metres left of Slanting Crack. From a ledge at two metres, traverse diagonally right, past a thin curving crack, to gain a hanging groove. Up this to a ledge then cross to join Sheer Heart Attack. Follow this to the horizontal break, step left and over the overlap to finish.

39.   Sirloin   15m   VS   4b   (1969)
Originally A2. Climb the shallow corner past a flake to a ledge, then move easily right until it is possible to climb up through an obvious gap in the overhang to *The Pasture*.

★ **40.   Slime Corner**   39m   HVS   5a,5a,4b   (1961-63/1972)
An old A1 which has since become a classic Hoghton route.
1.   15m.   The broken wall in the centre of the amphitheatre, just left of Sirloin, leads to a large ledge just left of *The Pasture*.
2.   9m.   Ascend the corner to a ledge and small tree on the right.
3.   15m.   Up the ledges to a large ledge from which it is possible to walk off to the right. Move left along this, then up the wall using old chiselled holds, and finish up the short wall above.
3a.   9m.   **Original Finish**. Continue up the groove over ledges to the top (easier and not in keeping with the rest of the route).

41.   Five Minute Traverse   9m   S   4a   (1967)
From Slime Corner pitch two, traverse up and right on to *The Pasture*.

★ **42.   Spleen Road**   40m   VS   4b,4c   (1976)
A high-level girdle of the left side of the Main Amphitheatre.
1.   25m.   Start from the walk-off ledge near the top of Slime Corner. Stride across the corner then step down to gain an obvious line of ledges which lead to a blunt arête on Highway Star. Continue along the break to join Goliath's Groove below the final flake. Nut belay.
2.   15m.   Traverse the ledge to the arête, then step onto the front face and continue left along the bad belt (peg in Rhododendron Buttress) to a ledge on the left side of the buttress. Finish easily to a tree belay at the top.

43.   Baron of Beef   32m   A2/E4   A2,6b,–   (1974/1981)
1.   14m.   Start midway between Slime Corner and Fallout, below a short hanging groove and use skyhooks in bolt holes, until it is possible to peg up the wall above to the belay on Slime Corner.
2.   10m. (**Cannibalistic Incantations**)   Climb the shallow corner on the right and pull over the overhang to a good pocket, then layback the groove above to a ledge and tree belay.
3.   8 m.   The short wall by a crack in its centre.

Main Amphitheatre

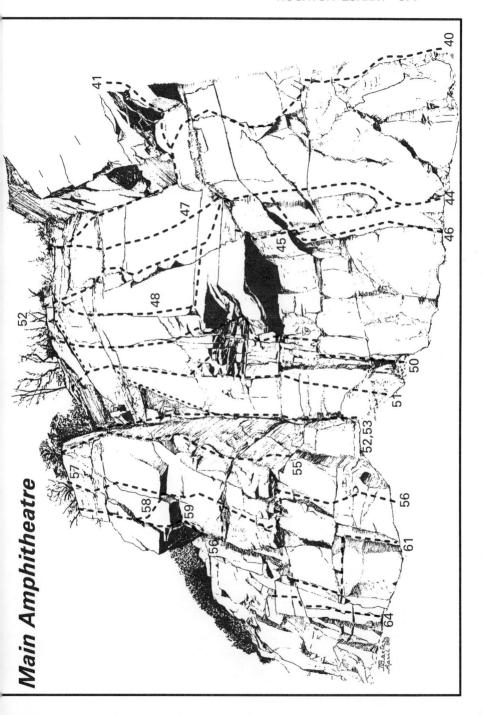

44.   New Wave   14m   E4   6b   (1980)
Starting up the thin crack just left, gain the hanging groove on the right (peg).
Continue up the flake above to the large ledge.

45.   Fallout – Direct Start   14m   E2   5c   (1983)
Start up initial crack of New Wave and swing left into a flake/groove. Go up
this to the roof, move right and go up to the large ledge.

⋆ **46.   Fallout**   42m   E2   5b,5b   (1967/1976/1977)
1.   17m.   Climb the corner below the right side of the Main Overhang to a
ledge (originally pegged at A1), then traverse right to the good ledge on New
Wave. Go up this to *The Pasture*.
2.   25m.   From the left side of the ledge climb up to an indefinite groove and
follow this to a large ledge at its top. Ascend the short corner then finish up the
break on the left.

⋆⋆ **47.   The French Lieutenant's Marrow**   24m   E6   6b,4b   (1986)
A strenuously thin and serious climb.
1.   15m.   Start at Slime Corner pitch two and climb the steep slab between that
route and Fallout to a grassy ledge and a bolt belay. Either walk off home or
continue up.
2.   9m.   The old chiselled holds of Slime Corner to finish.

⋆ **48.   Highway Star**   30m   HVS   5b,5a   (1976/1982)
1.   9m.   Start as for Fallout pitch two, make a rising traverse beneath the
groove of Fallout, to a bolt belay above the Main Overhang.
2.   21m.   The obvious crack in the blunt arête above the belay to a break. Step
right and continue to the top.

49.   Main Overhang   17m   A1   (1967)
The obvious line of bolts over the large overhang, finishing on the belay ledge
of Highway Star.

⋆⋆ **50.   Flight of the Rat**   41m   E4   5c,6a   (1956/1977/1987)(1987)
Two contrasting, but equally interesting pitches.
1.   17m.   Start at the obvious easy chimney beneath the left side of the Main
Overhang. Ascend this to a ledge on the right and climb a steep friable rib until
it is possible to move right on to the left side of an undercut slab. Go up and
right (Friend) over the overhang to the belay of Main Overhang.
2.   24m.   Step back left to regain the crackline and follow this with increasing
difficulty to the top.

⋆⋆⋆ **51.   Burning Desire**   27m   E5   6b   (1971/1983)
This very strenuous route takes the crack two metres left. From a ledge, gain the
crack and follow this until level with the lip of the overhangs. Finger-traverse
right and move up to a borehole. Move left to regain the crackline and follow
this to finish.

⋆ **52.   Deaf School**   30m   E2   5b   (1978)
Follow Goliath's Groove for nine metres to a sloping ledge on the left of an
overhanging scoop. Layback right past a peg on the lip, to a break. Traverse
right for a couple of moves, and then up the top of Burning Desire to a break,
which can be hand-traversed right to a rhododendron. Finish direct.

★ **53.   Goliath's Groove**   27m   HVS   5a   (1967/1972)
The deep corner groove at the left of the amphitheatre. At the top layback the
flake on the left.

★★ **54.   When the Levee Breaks**   148m   E2   4c,5b,5b,5b,4c,5a,4a   (1969/1977/1982)
Originally pegged in a similar line as Tobacco Road. A girdle of Hoghton Wall
and the Main Amphitheatre, starting at The Wasp. A very worthwhile
expedition, providing that the conditions are right.
1.   38m.   Climb The Wasp for 18 metres, to the horizontal break, then
hand-traverse left past a small bush until beneath the short corner on Thespis.
Move up to stand on the break and continue along to the belay ledge of Route
One.
2.   10m.   From the left-hand edge of the ledge foot-traverse the sandy break
across to the flake on Mandarin. Climb down and across left to *The Waiting
Room* (part of Ten Minute Traverse in reverse).
3.   21m.   From the left-hand side of *The Waiting Room*, pull up and round the
arête to a good hold (peg) and traverse across to reach Sirloin. Climb the crack
on the left to gain the large ledge on Slime Corner, Peg belay.
4.   37m.   Traverse left as for Highway Star to the hanging ledge above the
Main Overhang. Step left into a crackline and follow this to the horizontal break
and traverse left into Goliath's Groove below its final flake. Nut Belay.
5.   18m.   Cross the ledge on the left to the arête, then step on to the front face
and cross at the bad belt (peg in Rhododendron Buttress) to a ledge on the left
side of the buttress. Traverse left across the top of the corner on Visions of Jan
to gain another small corner, tree and nut belay.
6.   12m.   Reverse mantel down to a break, then make an awkward move left to
where the ledge widens (pegs) and traverse left to a bolt belay below the groove
on Zig Zag.
7.   12m.   Climb the corner on the left to a muddy ledge then take the crack in
the steep slab above, as for Cave Route, to finish.

Rhododendron Buttress

*Rhododendron Buttress is the impressive buttress which is situated at the left
side of the Main Amphitheatre. To the left of the buttress itself the rock becomes
more broken, and the area is bounded on its left by an impressive leaning wall.*

★★★ **55.   Rhododendron Arête**   29m   E3   6a   (1967/1979)
Originally aided at A2. Although the arête looks very blank, there are actually
plenty of good holds. However, although most of the route is well protected, the
top section can feel a little bold. Follow the left arête of the amphitheatre,
starting up a crack slightly right of the arête, to a ledge, then continue past a
small overlap to a very small ledge below impending rock. Go up and right to
another ledge, then step left and finish up the arête.

★★ **56.   Cave Route**   42m   HS   4b,4a,–   (Early 1950s)
A must for easier-grade visitors.
1.   15m.   Climb the short steep slab at the left of the amphitheatre, then go up
a corner groove to a small overhang. Move left to the cave, then climb direct to
a large ledge (peg belay).
2.   15 m.   Traverse left over poor rock, then continue the traverse at a slightly
higher ledge until it is possible to step around an arête to Wobbling Groove. Go

up for a move, then move left and up easily to a large ledge on pitch three of Zig Zag.

3. 12 m.   Ascend the corner as Easy Route to a muddy ledge on the right, then either go up the crack in the steep slab which overhangs the corner, or climb the crack on its right.

★★★ **57.   Rhododendron Buttress**   18m   E2   5c   (1955/1976)
A classic route, originally an A1, which takes a dramatic line directly up the front face of the buttress. From the right end of the first belay ledge on Cave Route, then cross the wall up left to a good ledge below the overhang. Surmount this by a crack and continue to the sandy break, step left then follow the thin crack (crux) to the top.

★★ **58.   War of Attrition**   20m   E2   5c   (1976)
A fine climb, which is basically a variation of Rhododendron Buttress. From the good foothold over the roof on Rhododendron Buttress, traverse left with difficulty to below a right-slanting overlap. Surmount the overlap via a thin crack, then climb the groove and short wall above to finish up a finger crack on the left of Rhododendron Buttress.

★★ **59.   Biodegradable Man**   20m   E5   6b   (1986)
An impressive roof climb. From the second pitch of Cave Route climb up to the roof (old bolts), then swing right (peg) and make some exhilarating moves over the roof to gain the slanting overlap of War of Attrition. Continue up this to finish.

*The bolts on the aid route over the left side of the roof (**Terry's Torment**, A2) have thankfully now virtually rusted away and so the next tenable route is:*

★ **60.   Strong's Flake**   14m   E2   5b   (1973)
From the belay ledge of Cave Route, climb the massive flake on the left, which rises from the left side of the buttress. Friable rock to start.

61.   Finger Traverse   14m   VS   5b   (1965)
Climb the short layback crack just left of the start of Cave Route, then finger-traverse left with increasing difficulty until the ledge widens. Climb the corner on the left, then either step round to Bowker's Crack, or finish on the right.

62.   Pandora's Box   15m   E1   6a   (1980)
A rather artificial route, but interesting and varied. Start below the left end of the Finger Traverse ledge, and gain the ledge by a technical mantel up a scoop on the arête, or more easily by using a chipped hold on the right. Move right, and climb the thin crack until it is possible to swing right and up into the cave of Cave Route. Hand-traverse left to the top of Finger Traverse, then step back right and climb to the large ledge on Cave Route.

★ **63.   Bowker's Crack**   8m   VS   4c   (1960-61)
Just left is a short wall. Climb the right corner of this.

64.   Speech Impediment   8m   E2   6b   (1979)
Takes the zig-zag crack between Bowker's Crack and Cyclops, finishing up a blank-looking wall.

65.   Cyclops 8m   VS   4c   (1964)
The crack at the left side of the wall.

★ **66.   Visions of Jan**   32m   E2   4a,5b,4c   (1977)
1.   9m.   Ascend the corner immediately left of Cyclops to a ledge, then go up
to the large ledge above. Finish at a larger ledge on the right. Nut belay.
2.   14m.   Scramble rightwards easily then go up to the base of the shallow
overhanging corner. Ascend this past a peg on the left wall to a ledge at the
top. Tree and nut belays on the left.
3.   9m.   Follow the left-slanting groove to a ledge, then surmount the overhang
which is split by a wide crack, and scramble through rhododendrons to finish.

67.   Crack 'A' Jack   21m   E2   5b   (1991)
From the nut belay at the top of Visions of Jan (pitch 1) climb the cracked wall
above to a ledge and a sandy break on Choice Exit. Continue up the left side of
a shield and from its top traverse right to a tree on the arête. Easy ground above
leads to a finish up Visions of Jan.

68.   Wobbling Groove   24m   HVS   5b   (1976)
Start as for Visions of Jan pitch two. Climb up and left to a ledge on the right
of a blunt arête (junction with Cave Route), then follow a thin crack into a
shallow scoop. Pull out of this on to a ledge at the start of the traverse on
Choice Exit, (peg on right), then move left and go up into a groove and follow
this past two pegs. Finish up a groove on the right.

★ **69.   Choice Exit**   31m   VS   4a,5a   (1967)
1.   8m.   Climb the corner as for Visions of Jan to a ledge, then move up and
left to another ledge and belay below a groove.
2.   23m.   Climb the groove to a small ledge, then go up to a sandy break and
traverse right along this past a small ledge (peg) to a tree belay on the right.

70.   Easy Route   36m   D   (Early 1950s)
1.   15m.   Start six metres to the left, at a short, easy-angled slab. Gain a ledge
on the left, step right, then reach the large ledge above, either direct, or (easier)
by traversing right and then mantelshelving back left.
2.   21m.   Proceed up a series of ledges in the centre of the bay. At the top of
the corner make a muddy landing on the right, then step back left across the
corner and finish through undergrowth.

71.   Easier Route   36m   D   (Early 1950s)
1.   9m.   The obvious weakness four metres left of Easy Route.
2.   27m.   As for Easy Route to the muddy ledge, then walk right along this
finish up an obvious short break.

★ **72.   Zig Zag**   35m   HVS   4b,4c,5a,–   (1965/1966)
Start below the short corner which marks the junction between Rhododendron
Buttress and Overhanging Crack areas.
1.   10m.   From a small ledge at two metres, traverse right on small ledges until
an awkward move round the arête makes it easy to gain the ledge above. Belay
as for Easy Route pitch two.
2.   9m.   On the right of the ledge is a corner, (hook belay). Climb the corner
then go easily up to a large ledge on the left. Bolt belay.
3.   6m.   The hanging groove on the right leads to a tree.

4. 10 m. The stepped wall behind.

★ 73. Steppin' in the Slide Zone 14m E2 5c (1986)
Start at Easy Route's first belay. On the left is a borehole in a blunt arête; climb this (tape) and make an interesting move on to the sloping ledge above. Climb ledges then continue up the thin crack in the wall above to a large pocket. Leap for the top.

Overhanging Crack Area
Past the Main Amphitheatre the rock becomes a little more broken until the impressive leaning wall of Overhanging Crack is reached. This area extends from the right side of the leaning wall to a deep corner round the arête.

★ 74. Che 24m HVS 4c,5b (1971/1979)
1. 9m. Climb the corner made with the large leaning wall on the left, to a large ledge. Nut belay.
2. 15m. Step left on to the leaning wall, then gain the hanging groove on the right, and climb this to a ledge. Go up to the obvious inverted triangular niche then finish straight up.

★ 75. Overhanging Crack 20m HVS 5b,5a (1964/1965)
1. 10m. The deep crack up the left side of the leaning wall leads to a large ledge and tree belay on the left. Awkward to start.
2. 10m. Scramble up and left to a higher ledge then climb the T-shaped crack making an exit to the left.

★★ 76. Poo 12m E7 6c (1988)
The obvious hanging groove on the left gives some of the best and most technical climbing in the quarry. Start slightly left of the groove at a small ledge, pad (crawl) across the hanging slab below the overhang (bolt on lip), then make a hard move to reach a small hold over the lip. Palm up the arête (dynamically) to a hold at mid-height (bolt). A bewildering sequence palming the groove leads to a good edge and scary, but easier climbing to finish.

77. The Black Tripe Trip 20m E4 6b,6a (1991)
1. 13m. Climb the centre of the scooped wall on the left to a ledge, then go up and right to the tree on Overhanging Crack. Climb easily to the ledge above, bolt belay on the left.
2. 7m. Climb up to an obvious V-slot at the top.

★★ 78. Black Pudding Team Special 23m E2 5c,5c (1977/1981)
This route gives good climbing throughout its length.
1. 14m. The peg-scarred arête on the left. Climb the arête, exiting on the right to a large ledge and tree on Overhanging Crack. Climb easily to the ledge above, bolt belay on left.
2. 9m. Make a delicate traverse left to the arête and go up this past pegs.

79. Drupe 21m E1/A1 5c (1967/1983)
Round the left arête of the leaning wall is a crack, climb this to the break, then continue up the wall and over the overhang on bolts.

80. Ergonome's Enigma 21m A2 (1969)

Ascend the thin crack two metres left into a niche above the overlap. Leave the niche by a crack on the left and follow this to the roof. Traverse right under the roof for two metres, to a thin crack splitting it, go over this then the overhang above to finish up the scooped wall.

81. Suicidal Tendency 17m E1 5b (1968/1970)

The route follows the rising break which cuts across the face below the initial overlap of Drupe. Start on the left and finish at Overhanging Crack.

82. Device Dièdre 14m VS 4c (1971)

The corner which limits the wall on its left. Finish to the right.

83. Preston Guild 40m VS/A2 4c/A2,A1 (1967/1969)

An uninspiring peg route which girdles the Overhanging Wall Area.
1. 22m. From the left side of the first belay ledge on Zig Zag, step left on to the leaning wall as for Che and continue leftwards until pegs have to be resorted to in a faint crack. Belay at the top of Overhanging Crack, pitch 1.
2. 18m. Climb easily up a large flake to a slightly higher ledge, then go under the overhang of Drupe and follow a line past Ergonome's Enigma to an obvious exit through the overhangs.

Lookout Area

The area from Device Dièdre to the break at the far end of the quarry is known as the Lookout Area. Until the early 1970s much of the rock hereabouts was cloaked with vegetation, but its removal has revealed a wide variety of climbs, including several in the easier grades. Although many of the climbs in this area are excellent when they are free of vegetation, the very nature of the rock means that these climbs will always be in danger of being lost under a veil of rhododendrons. To maintain the routes in good condition requires only a modest effort on every ascent, but if this is neglected only a major gardening effort will save them. Visiting climbers are therefore asked to assist with maintaining this area.

★★ **84. The Luddite** 18m E3 5c (Late 60s/1986)

A dastardly solution to this section of wall. Start in the centre of the wall on the left. Climb to an overlap (bolt), then move right and up a short crack to a horizontal break. Ascend the wall above to a peg, step left and finish direct.

★ **85. Hoghton Weaver** 23m E2 6a (1986)

Start as for The Luddite but at the bolt gain the short break up and to the left, then go up to a second break. Move right to a very thin diagonal crack and follow this to an overlap and a peg – junction with The Excitable Boy. Traverse left to a crack and finish up this.

★★ **86. The Excitable Boy** 17m E4 6b (1975/1984)

This previously mediocre peg route (Candlemass) now gives fine free climbing, Start in the corner on the left. Climb this (bold) to a ledge. Step right to gain the main crack and follow this to an overlap and a peg. Make some baffling moves on to a small ledge then make a long reach to the top.

87. Assheton Arête 18m S   4a   (1967)(1970)
Climb the arête just left of The Excitable Boy for a few moves then pull round
into an easy-angled groove. Climb this to a ledge and move up to a block. Pass
this on its left to gain a ledge and finish up the short break behind.
Direct Finish (VS, 4c): from the groove on the parent route, climb the obvious
crack above, and finish as for Hoghton Weaver.

88. Royal Declaration 20m HS 4a   (1971)
Start at a lower level, three metres right of an overhung corner. Climb a short
crack and the groove above, until it is possible to ascend the shallow corner to a
ledge on the right. Finish easily.

★ **89. Book of Fate**   21m HVS 5a   (1972)
From the first ledge on The Motorway gain a higher ledge on the right, then a
triangular niche. Move up, then go diagonally right to a shallow corner and up
to a large ledge on the right. Traverse back across the face to some obvious
large holds and an easier finish. Poorly protected.

90. Hermit of Tower Wood 18m VD   (1972)
From the triangular niche on Book of Fate continue up the shallow corner to the
top.

91. The Motorway 37m M   (1971)
Probably the best easy way down from most of the routes, and because of this
the route is marked with red paint. Start six metres left of the overhung corner
and follow a sloping ledge left to a large ledge (*The Hard Shoulder*). Scramble
up to another ledge complex (*The Central Reservation*), then continue left across
this to reach the top.

92. Sliproad 20m VD   (1972)
Starting two metres left, gain the ledge above and move to the *The Hard
Shoulder*. From the right of this follow small holds to the ledge above, then
continue past two ledges to a vertical crack. From the base of this go diagonally
right for four metres until the top can be reached easily.

93. Lookout Ridge 27m D   (1971)
The left wall of the bay ends at a long arête, which starts at a much lower level.
Follow this to the top (*The Hard Shoulder*), then go up slightly and finish easily
up the final blunt arête to reach *Lookout Point*.

94. Lookout Gully 29m D   (1971)
The gully bounding Lookout Ridge on its left. Finish as for that route.

95. Trunk Road 18m VD   (1971)
The series of short corners on the left of Lookout Gully to *The Hard Shoulder*.

96. Malkin Tower 22m S   4a   (1971)
1. 17m. Where Lookout Gully and Trunk Road split there is a vertical crack.
Follow this to a large ledge, then continue up the groove behind, which is best
entered from the left (peg – not in place). Belay on *The Central Reservation*.
2. 5m. The wall behind, to reach *Lookout Point*.

97. The Trial 18m HVS 5b   (1984)

Start three metres left of Malkin Tower at a lower level. Climb the crack (awkward to start) to a large sloping ledge, then go up the short wall behind to easier ground, finishing up the groove above to *The Central Reservation.*

★ **98. Chattox** 24m HVS 5b   (1972/1984)

Takes the break through the large overhang which stretches across the top of the quarry at the Blackburn end.

From the corner on the left, climb a weakness two metres right until it is possible to move back to the corner at a drill hole (spike). Move up this, then move right and up to the obvious break which splits the overhang. Surmount the overhang (peg) to gain the hanging corner above. Step left to a good pocket and continue to a small niche. Finish straight up. Variations on the bottom section are possible on the right.

★★ **99. Demdike** 31m HVS 5a,4c   (1972)

Despite first appearances, this is an excellent route, especially if the top slab is clean.

1.   14m.   Climb the cracks just left of the corner to a peg at nine metres, then step left to gain a line of flakes leading diagonally right to a large niche. Nut belay. It is possible to start this pitch by starting up Scoop and Wall, to gain the flakes on the right.

2.   17m.   Climb to the overhang, then traverse left to an arête. Step up to a ledge then from this move up on small holds to a wide crack on the right. Either finish straight up, or, keeping low, move across to a small niche and make a rising traverse right to finish at the top of the hanging corner of Chattox.

100. Scoop and Wall 22m HS 4a,4b   (1963)

Start at the far end of the quarry, 10 metres right of an obvious easy way up the short end wall.

1.   8m.   Climb the crack to a small ledge. From the left of this gain the massive ledge and tree belay.

2.   14m.   Climb the crack in the corner until it is possible to traverse right to the arête on a sloping ledge. Move up to a ledge, then finish up a short slab.

101. Scoop and Wall Direct 10m VS 4c   (1966)

Start at Scoop and Wall pitch two and follow it to the sloping ledge, then continue straight up over a large block, step left and finish direct.

★ **102. Suspended Animation** 18m S –,4a   (1973)

1.   6m.   The crack three metres to the left.

2.   12m.   The flake crack behind the tree leads to a ledge on the left. Gain the next ledge, then finish easily up the arête.

★ **103. Wilkinson's Sword Edge** 9m E1 5b   (1966)

Start from the large belay ledge of Suspended Animation and climb the vertical razor-edged arête just to the left.

104. The Minihang 8m D   (1972)

Set back from Wilkinson's Sword Edge is a large overhang. Climb the V-groove to the overhang, then step right and climb the wide crack which splits it.

Liqueur Wall

To the left the quarry curves round and back towards the main area past a stretch of rock known as Liqueur Wall. At the extreme right end it is very short and the following two routes start here:

105. Ouzo 12m D   (1972)
Start three metres left of the easy way down the short end wall, and follow an easy line of ledges left to finish up Strega.

106. Strega 9m VD   (1972)
Start in the corner on the left which contains two overhangs, and climb the wall just right of this corner.

The next routes start at a lower level, at a deep corner which bounds the main sweep of Liqueur Wall on its right.

107. Drunk for a Penny 9m HS 4b   (1991)
Start up a thin crack three metres right of the corner and climb the wall directly to the terrace.

108. Advocaat 18m S 4a   (1970)
Climb the corner to the terrace at nine metres, then move right for two metres and climb to the top via a series of three strenuous mantels.

109. Chartreuse 18m S 4a   (1970)
Climb the corner of Advocaat to the terrace, then step left and continue to a higher ledge on the right. Finish more easily.

110. Grand Marnier 20m HS 4a   (1972)
Climb the corner of Advocaat to the terrace, then traverse left to the arête and climb this.

111. Wilt the Stilt 15m E2 5c   (1986)
Climb the arête left of the corner and finish up Grand Marnier.

★★ **112. Crème de Menthe** 15m VS 4b   (1972)
A fine line up the next corner, passing four overhangs.

★ **113. Curaçao** 17m HVS 5b   (1972)
Climb the groove two metres left, to a peg below the capping overhang. Move up and right to a small ledge, and from the right of this continue with difficulty, until at nine metres a good flake handhold ends the difficulties. Finish more easily, passing the final overhang on the left.

★ **114. Artichoke** 17m E5 6a   (1986)
Gain an obvious slot at three metres, then continue with difficulty past a peg to gain the final flake crack on The Effect of Alcohol and finish up this.

★ **115. The Effect of Alcohol** 18m E2 5c   (1975)
Climb the deep corner, with a fallen pedestal below it, to the roof. Move right under the roof and finish up the thin layback crack.

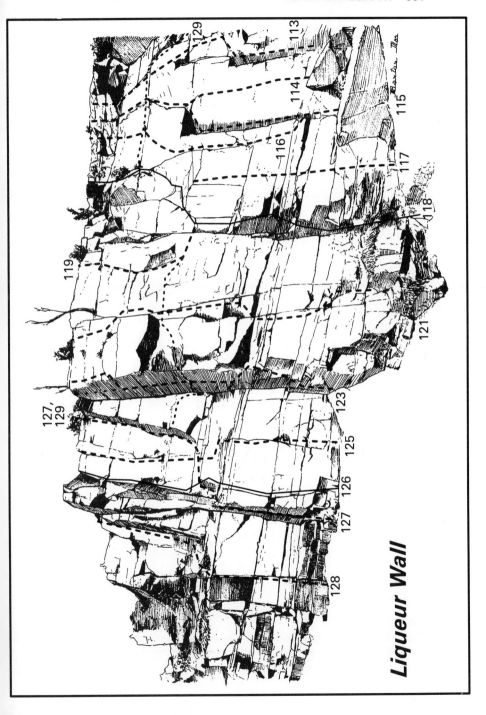

Liqueur Wall

116. Winston Groovy 17m E4 6a   (1984)
From the foot of Effects of Alcohol, move awkwardly left round the arête, then
climb the wall on sloping holds and a thin crack above (peg) to a small ledge.
Move right and finish up the centre of the wall above the roof.

117. Stickman 19m E6 6c   (1991)
A direct line up the central wall. Climb past a detached-looking block to the
obvious horizontal break at two-thirds-height (peg). Make a hard move from
this, using an undercut and thin edges, to reach an obvious jug below the large
ledge. Finish up Kümmel.

118. Kümmel 20m S 4a   (1967)
In the centre of Liqueur Wall is a deep corner; climb this past a large ledge to
an even larger ledge at its top. From the right of this ledge climb up a
prominent flake then finish easily.

★ **119. Trappistine Finish** 17m HS 4b   (1987)
From the second large ledge on Kümmel, step back left across the corner and
finish up a slim corner above.

120. Kirsch 20m S 4a   (1987)
From the second large ledge on Kümmel, step back left across the corner and
continue leftwards until it is possible to finish up the left-hand corner.

★ **121. Benedictine** 17m E1 5c   (1968/1978)
Start three metres to the left and climb cracks to a ledge, then step right and
climb the crack which bounds the overhang on its right, until a step left can be
made on to the wall above the overhang. Finish direct.

122. Intoxicated E6 6b   (1984)
A serious undertaking. The striking arête on the left, with a peg in Maraschino.

★★ **123. Maraschino** 15m E3 6a   (1972/1979)(1987)
A good-looking line, which lives up to expectations. The thin crack which splits
the narrow wall on the left. At three-quarters-height move right, then finish up
the arête.
Direct Finish (6a): from the top of the crack, continue up a series of breaks to
the top. A worthy alternative to the normal finish.

124. Tia Maria 15m VS 4c   (1972)
The deep, orange corner on the left of Liqueur Wall.

★ **125. In the Pink** 15m E1 5c   (1984)
Takes the crack between Tia Maria and Cirrhosis. Start up the crack three
metres left of Tia Maria to the right side of a large ledge and climb the crack in
the leaning wall above.

126. Cirrhosis 15m E1 5b   (1979)
Farther left is a short arête leading to a large ledge. Climb the crack on the right
of this to the ledge, just below a groove which forms the right side of a pointed
tower. Climb this groove to the top (in-situ peg).

★ **127. Goldwasser** 18m VS 4b (1972)
Climb the short, thin groove on the left of the arête to the ledge. From the right-hand side of this ledge, follow a right-leaning ramp to the top.

128. Sloe Gin 15m VS 4c (1968)
Start at the extreme left, below a large square-cut recess. Gain the recess and exit on the right to a large ledge. Traverse right then climb the obvious corner.
Pastis (HVS, 5a): from the recess, exit left to the ledge. Ascend a groove and go diagonally rightwards to the top section of Sloe Gin.

129. Molotov Cocktail 51m VS 4b,4c (1973)
A girdle of Liqueur Wall.
1. 27m. Ascend Strega for a couple of metres, then traverse left under the second overhang, and continue at this level to Crème de Menthe. Surmount the overhang above, then go diagonally left to a small ledge just left of the top of The Effect of Alcohol. Traverse along this until it is possible to drop down to a large ledge on Kümmel. Step left on to another ledge and belay on the left side of this.
2. 24m. Tension left to the arête, then go round this to the deep corner. Ascend the corner to a horizontal crack which leads to the base of the ramp of Goldwasser, then finish up this.

Long Wall
This is the broken wall directly facing Liqueur Wall, which ends at the central path through the quarry. Half a dozen climbs have been done several years ago, but these have now become overgrown.

First Ascents at Hoghton Quarry

Early 1950s	**Easy Route, Easier Route** Geoff Leach	
1950s	**Cave Route** Pitch 1 (1pt aid) Steve Ripley, Dave Johnson	
Early 1950s	**Route One** (A1)	
	The first pitch was often avoided by climbing the tree.	
	Aid reduced to 2 pts by John Hamer, John Wareing, 1961-63.	
1955	**Rhododendron Buttress** Pegged by John 'Fritz' Sumner	
1955	**Ten Minute Traverse** (A1) John 'Fritz' Sumner	
	At that time the route finished after the traverse. It was extended to the top in 1966 by Paul Hamer, Don Pinder.	
	First free ascent by Ian Lonsdale, Nadim Siddiqui, 1 May 1977.	
1955	**Twin Spikes** Alan Atkinson	
1956	**Slanting Crack** Alan Atkinson	
1956	**The Dangler** (A3) Alan Atkinson as Scimitar Crack	
	Reduced to 2pts aid by Dave Cronshaw, 1977.	
	Aid completely eliminated by Dave Kenyon, Malc Haslam, 7 July 1979.	
1956	**Flight of the Rat** (A2) Mick Tullis	
	Reduced to 2 pts of aid by Dave Knighton, 1977.	
	Aid completely eliminated by Dave Cronshaw, Dave Kenyon, Mar 1987.	
	New Direct Finish by Dave Cronshaw, John Ryden, Mar 1987.	
1958-61	**Groove and Ledge**	
1960	**Mandarin** (A2) Originally finished at The Pasture	
	First free ascent to The Pasture by John Hamer, John 'Aussie' Parkinson, 1967.	
1960-62	**Bowker's Crack** Bill Bowker	
1961-63	**Blunt Arête**	
1961-63	**Slime Corner** (A1)	
	First free ascent by Dave Cronshaw, Les Ainsworth, July 1972.	

In the mid-sixties it became traditional to climb the route by pulling on the pegs with the occasional sling, rather than using etriers.

1961-63   **Route One**   (2pts aid) John Hamer, John Wareing, 1961-63.
A major aid reduction.
Aid completely eliminated, 1980-82.

1963   **Scoop and Wall**   John Wareing, John Hamer

1963   **Partnership**   John Hamer, John 'Aussie' Parkinson

1964 Mar   **Overhanging Crack**   (A1)   Tony Makin
First free ascent by Les Ainsworth, Paul Hamer, Mar 1965.
Second pitch added by Les Ainsworth, 1969.

1964   **Cyclops**   Bill Bowker

1965   **Overhanging Crack**   Les Ainsworth, Paul Hamer
First free ascent.

1965 June   **Finger Traverse**   Les Ainsworth

1965 June   **Zig Zag**   John Hamer, John McGonagle
The present 3rd pitch was added by John Wareing, John 'Aussie' Parkinson in 1966.

1966   *Terry's Torment*   Terry Wareing, Ian 'Spider' McQuirk

1966   **Hazard**   (A1)   Paul Hamer
Aid reduced by Dave Knighton, Jenny Hyslop as Every Face Tells a Story, 17 June 1978.
Aid completely eliminated by Malc Haslam, Greg Rimmer, 1978.

1966   **Scoop and Wall Direct**   Paul Hamer, Les Ainsworth

1966   **Wilkinson's Sword Edge**   Stan Bradshaw (solo)

1967 Jan   **Goliath's Groove**   (A1)   Paul Hamer, Tony Makin
First free ascent by Dave Cronshaw, Les Ainsworth, Apr 1972.

1967 Feb   **Mandarin**   (to The Pasture)   John Hamer, John 'Aussie' Parkinson
Patella was done the following weekend by John Hamer, John Parkinson.

1967 Mar   **Mandarin**   (A1)   Stan Bradshaw, Ian 'Spider' McQuirk
Route completed to the top of the crag.

1967 Apr   **Goulash**   (A1)   Tony Makin, John McGonagle
First free ascent by Ian Lonsdale, Paul McKenzie, 19 Apr 1977.

1967 May   **Ducked**   (with tension and 3 pts aid)   John Hamer, John Wareing
First free ascent by Dave Knighton as Sheer Heart Attack, 9 July 1977.

1967 May   **Mandarin**   John Hamer, John 'Aussie' Parkinson
First free ascent. This route more than any other put Lancashire on the climbing map.

1967 May   **The Wasp**   (A1)   Geoff Hamridding, Brian Molyneux

1967 July   **The Wasp**   Les Ainsworth, Paul Hamer, Ian 'Spider' McQuirk
Originally attempted by Les Ainsworth and Paul Hamer as a free route, cleaning mud out of the cracks whilst leading. They almost reached the first horizontal break, but the route was pegged the next weekend.

1967 June   **Hope Not, Choice Exit**   John Hamer, John 'Aussie' Parkinson

1967 June   **Main Overhang**   Terry Wareing, Ian 'Spider' McQuirk

1967 July   **Rhododendron Arête**   (A2/VS)   Ray Miller, Ian Cowell
First free ascent by Dave Knighton, Dave Cronshaw, 17 June 1979.

1967 July   **Assheton Arête**   Paul Hamer, Don Pinder
Direct Finish by Dave Cronshaw, Les Ainsworth, 1970.

1967 Aug   *Grasper*   (A2/VS)   John McGonagle, Ian McGonagle
This route started on poor pegs, then reversed most of the first pitch of Preston Guild.

1967 Sep   **Fallout**   (A1)   John McGonagle, Ray Miller
Aid reduced to 1pt by Dave Knighton, John Tout, 25 Aug 1976.
Aid completely eliminated by Ian Lonsdale, Dave Walsh, 26 May 1977.
Direct Start by Dave Cronshaw, Malc Haslam, 9 Aug 1983.

1967 Sep   **Five Minute Traverse**   Ian Cowell, Ray Miller

1967 Oct   **Kümmel, Kirsch**   Les Ainsworth (solo)

Dave Cronshaw likes a **Maraschino** (E3 6a), Hoghton Quarry.   *Photo: John Ryden*

1967 Nov	**Drupe** (A2) Ian Cowell, Ray Miller

Drupe   (A2)   Ian Cowell, Ray Miller
Initial crack climbed free by Malc Haslam, Chris Riley, Greg Rimmer, 1983.

1968 Apr 10   **Thespis**   (HVS/A1)   Tony Makin, Terry Devanney
Aid completely eliminated Les Ainsworth, Ian Cowell a few weeks later.

1968 Sep 1   **Boadicea**   (A2)   Phil Paget, Roger Grimshaw
Aid reduced to 1pt by Dave Knighton, Duncan Sperry, Ian Lonsdale,
Nigel Bonnett, 5 Apr 1977.
Aid completely eliminated by Ron Fawcett, Iain Edwards, a few weeks later.

1968 Sep 7   **Shake Not**   (A2)   Phil Paget, Roger Grimshaw
First free ascent by Mark Leach, Ian Conway as Lamentably Gentlemanly,
1982.
Straightened out to its present line by Roland Foster and John Noblett, 1983.

1968   **Suicidal Tendency**   Les Ainsworth, Paul Hamer

1968   **Benedictine**   (A1/VS)   Ian Cowell, Ray Miller
First free ascent by Dave Knighton, Eric Dearden, 1978.

1968   **Sloe Gin**   Les Ainsworth (solo)

1969 Sep   **The Knickertwister**   (A2)   Phil Paget, Geoff Fishlock
First free ascent of Pitch 1 by Ron Fawcett, S.T. Brooks, 1978.
First free ascent of Pitch 2 by Paul Pritchard as On the Brink, 23 June 1986.

1969   **Sirloin** (VS/A2)   Geoff Fishlock
Later the two pitches were split into separate routes, Sirloin and Silverside.

1969 Nov   **Tobacco Road**   (A2/HVS)   Geoff Fishlock, Phil Paget
Done over a couple of weekends. Pitch 12 reversed much of Grasper and
then continued to Overhanging Crack.
Deadline (A2/VS) by Bill Cheverst, C Dickinson, March 1972, followed a
similar line to much of the central section in reverse.
Aid reduced to 1 pt and line of first 11 pitches slightly altered by Dave
Knighton, Eric Dearden, Steve Bradley as When the Levee Breaks, 1977.
The last two pitches were then renamed Preston Guild.
Remaining aid eliminated in a continuous ascent by Dave Kenyon, Malc
Haslam, 5 May 1982.

1969   **Ergonome's Enigma**   (A2)   P. Fletcher, J. Thompson

Late 1960s   **The Luddite**   (A1)
First free ascent by Dave Cronshaw, Ian Lonsdale. 13 Aug 1986.

1970 May   **Advocaat, Chartreuse**   Les Ainsworth (solo)

1971   **Gath**   (A2)
Reduced to 1 rest pt by Dave Kenyon, Malc Haslam, as Burning Desire, 1983.
First free ascent by Roland Foster, 1983.

1971   **Che**   (1pt aid)
Aid eliminated by Andy Lewandowski, Dave Knighton, 9 July 1979.

1971 Dec   **Device Dièdre**   Les Ainsworth, Dave Cronshaw

1971 Dec   **Royal Declaration**   Dave Cronshaw, Les Ainsworth

1971 Dec   **The Motorway, Lookout Ridge, Lookout Gully, Trunk Road**   (Cleaned
and described)   Les Ainsworth, Dave Cronshaw, Bob MacMillan, Rob
Meakin (all solo)

1971 Dec   **Malkin Tower**   Bob MacMillan, Rob Meakin

1972 Jan 15   **Chattox: Variation, Demdike**   Les Ainsworth, Dave Cronshaw

1972 Jan 15   **Chattox**   (1pt aid)   Dave Cronshaw, Les Ainsworth
Aid eliminated by Dave Cronshaw, John Ryden, Greg Rimmer, 1984.

1972 Jan   **Book of Fate**   Rob Meakin, Les Ainsworth

1972 Jan   **Hermit of Tower Wood, Sliproad**   Les Ainsworth, Dave Cronshaw,
Bob MacMillan, Rob Meakin (all solo)

1972 Jan   **The Minihang**   Les Ainsworth (solo)

1972 Feb   **Ouzo, Strega, Grand Marnier**   Les Ainsworth, Dave Cronshaw

1972 Feb   **Crème de Menthe, Goldwasser**   Dave Cronshaw, Les Ainsworth

1972 Feb   **Maraschino**   (A1)   George Phillips, Dave Cronshaw, Les Ainsworth
First free ascent by Dave Kenyon, Malc Haslam, 3 July 1979.

1972 Feb   **Curaçao**   Dave Cronshaw, Les Ainsworth, Rob Meakin,

---

Rob O'Hara is the **African Queen** (HS 4b) at Stanworth Quarry.   *Photo: Geoff Hibbert*

1972 Mar   *Drambuie*   Dave Cronshaw, Les Ainsworth
            Route destroyed by rockfall, 1974 and superseded by The Effects of Alcohol.
1972 Mar   *Glayva*   George Phillips, Dave Cronshaw, Les Ainsworth
            Route destroyed by rockfall, 1974 and superseded by The Effects of Alcohol.
1972 Apr   **Goliath's Groove**   Dave Cronshaw, Les Ainsworth
            First free ascent.
1972 July   **Slime Corner**   Dave Cronshaw, Les Ainsworth
            First free ascent. This ascent was done in the rain a day after the route had been cleaned and there was a thin veneer of mud oozing over the holds.
1972   **Tia Maria**   Dave Kenyon, Malc Haslam
1973   **The Sting**   Al Evans, Dave Parker
1973   **Strong's Flake**   First lead by Dave Pycroft
            Originally top-roped by Frank Strong in 1967.
1973   **Suspended Animation**   Rob Meakin, Les Ainsworth (alts)
1973   **Molotov Cocktail**   Les Ainsworth, Dave Cronshaw (alts)
1974   **Baron of Beef**   (A2)   Dave Cronshaw, George Phillips
            First free ascent of Pitch 2 by Dave Kenyon (unseconded) as Cannibalistic Incantations, 1981.
1974 Mar   *Short Rib, Engineer's Groove, Dave's Route, Dave's Route, Trapeze Artist, The Threader*   Various combinations of Les Ainsworth, Dave Cronshaw, Bob MacMillan, Rob Meakin
            These routes are all on the poor wall directly facing Liqueur Wall
1975   **Candlemass**   (A1)   Dave Knighton, Sam Morris
            First free ascent by Dave Kenyon, Malc Haslam as The Excitable Boy, 1984.
1975   **The Effect of Alcohol**   Ron Fawcett, Iain Edwards, 1975
            Superseded Drambuie and Glayva after they had been destroyed by a rockfall.
1976 July 13   **Wobbling Groove**   Dave Knighton, Nigel Holmes
1976 Aug 25   **Fallout**   Dave Knighton, John Tout
            Aid reduced to 1pt.
            Aid completely eliminated by Ian Lonsdale, Dave Walsh, 26 May 1977.
1976 Sep 15   **Highway Star**   Dave Knighton, Ian Lonsdale
1976 Sep 19   **Spleen Road**   Dave Knighton, Andy Lewandowski
1976 Oct 17   **War of Attrition**   Ian Lonsdale, Dave Knighton
            Some tension was needed to traverse onto the line. Ron Fawcett did the first ascent without this tension a few weeks later.
1977 Apr 5   **Black Pudding Team Special**   (Pitch 1)   Ian Lonsdale, Nigel Bonnett
            Pitch 2 was added by Dave Kenyon, Ian Lonsdale, 4 Apr 1981.
1977 Apr 5   **Boadicea**   (1pt aid)   Dave Knighton, Duncan Sperry, Ian Lonsdale, Nigel Bonnett
            Aid eliminated by Ron Fawcett, Iain Edwards, a few weeks later.
1977 Apr 19   **Goulash**   Ian Lonsdale, Paul McKenzie
            First free ascent.
1977 May 1   **Ten Minute Traverse**   Ian Lonsdale, Nadim Siddiqui
            First free ascent. This was another landmark route.
1977 May 30   **Visions of Jan**   Dave Knighton, Pete Herridge
1977 June 9   **Lady**   Dave Knighton, Mick Dempsey
1977 June 29   **Keep it Coolin'**   Dave Knighton, Sam Morris
1977 July 9   **Sheer Heart Attack**   Dave Knighton
            First free ascent of Ducked.
1977   **When the Levee Breaks**   (1pt aid)   Dave Knighton, Eric Dearden, Steve Bradley.
            Aid reduced on first 11 pitches of Tobacco Road.
            Remaining aid eliminated in a continuous ascent by Dave Kenyon, Malc Haslam, 5 May 1982.
1977   **Dangler**   Dave Cronshaw.
            Reduced to 2pts aid.
1977   **Claymore**   Les Ainsworth, Dave Cronshaw
1977   **Flight of the Rat**   Dave Knighton
            Reduced to 2 pts aid.
1978   **Benedictine**   Dave Knighton, Eric Dearden
            First free ascent.

1978 June 17   **Every Face Tells a Story**   Dave Knighton, Jenny Hyslop
      A reduced aid ascent of Hazard.
      Aid completely eliminated by Malc Haslam, Greg Rimmer, 1978.
1978 June 20   **Deaf School**   Dave Knighton, Jenny Hyslop
1978   **The Knickertwister**   Ron Fawcett, S.T. Brooks
      First free ascent of Pitch 1.
1979 Apr 7   **Cirrhosis**   Dave Cronshaw, Malc Haslam, Dave Kenyon
1979 June 17   **Rhododendron Arête**   Dave Knighton, Dave Cronshaw
      First free ascent.
1979 July 3   **Maraschino**   Dave Kenyon, Malc Haslam
      First free ascent.
      Direct Finish by Dave Kenyon (unseconded), 1987.
1979 July 7   **Dangler**   Dave Kenyon, Malc Haslam
      Aid completely eliminated.
1979 Aug   **Speech Impediment**   Dave Kenyon, Malc Haslam
1980 May 21   **New Wave**   Dave Kenyon, Malc Haslam
1980   **Pandora's Box**   Les Ainsworth, Dave Cronshaw
      The start was a long-established problem, first done by John Wareing in the early 1960s.
1981 Apr 4   **Black Pudding Team Special**   (Pitch 2)   Dave Kenyon, Ian Lonsdale
1981   **Gleb Nerzhin**   Dave Knighton, Eric Dearden
      Extended to the top by Dave Cronshaw, Mick Ryan as Golden Delicious, Aug 1983.
1981   **Cannibalistic Incantations**   Dave Kenyon (unseconded)
      First free ascent of Pitch 2, Baron of Beef.
1979-83   **Disowned**
1982   **Lamentably Gentlemanly**   Mark Leach, Ian Conway
      First free ascent by Shake Not.
      Straightened out to its present line by Roland Foster and John Noblett, 1983.
1983 June 30   **All Roads Lead to Rome**   Gary Gibson, Adam Hudson
      Previously climbed to the break by Dave Kenyon, Malc Haslam, 1979.
1983 Aug   **Golden Delicious**   Dave Cronshaw, Mick Ryan
      An extension of Gleb Nerzhin.
1983   **For God's Sake Burn it Down!**   Malc Haslam, Greg Rimmer
1983   **Burning Desire**   (1 rest pt)   Dave Kenyon, Malc Haslam
      A virtually free ascent of Gath.
      Remaining aid eliminated by Roland Foster, 1983.
1983   **Getting Rid of the Albatross**   Roland Foster
1983   **La Lune Dans La Carniveau**   Roland Foster, Mick Ryan, Malc Haslam
1983   **Spazzm**   Malc Haslam, Mick Ryan
1984 June 7   **In the Pink**   Dave Cronshaw, John Ryden
1984   **Mind Games**   Roland Foster – After top-rope practice
1984   **The Excitable Boy**   Dave Kenyon, Malc Haslam
      First free ascent of Candlemass.
1984   **The Trial**   Dave Cronshaw, John Ryden
1984   **Winston Groovy**   Roland Foster
1984   **Intoxicated**   Dave Kenyon (unseconded)
1983-86   **Greg Rimmer: The Motion Picture**   Malc Haslam, Ronnie Marsden
1986   **Artichoke**   Dave Kenyon (unseconded)
1986 May 6   **Burning the Phoenix**   Dave Cronshaw, John Ryden
1986 June 23   **The Knickertwister**   Paul Pritchard
      First free ascent of Pitch 2 as, On the Brink, 23 June 1986.
1986 June 26   **Let's Go Play**   Phil Kelly, Ann Smith
1986 July   **The French Lieutenant's Marrow**   Andrew Gridley
1986 July   **Biodegradable Man**   (1pt aid)   Dave Cronshaw, John Ryden
      Aid eliminated by Dave Kenyon (unseconded), 1986.
1986 Aug 5   **Do the Aqua Melba, Void**   Paul Pritchard, Phil Kelly
1986 Aug 13   **The Luddite**   Dave Cronshaw, Ian Lonsdale
      First free ascent.
1986 Sep 7   **Steppin' in the Slide Zone, Hoghton Weaver**   Dave Cronshaw, Phil Kelly
1986   **Wilt the Stilt**

1987	**Blind Eye** Dave Kenyon (unseconded)
1987 Mar	**Flight of the Rat** Dave Cronshaw, Dave Kenyon
	Aid completely eliminated.
1987 Mar 29	**Trappistine Finish, Pastis** Dave Cronshaw, John Ryden
1987 May 28	**Burning a Nun** Nick Wilkinson (unseconded)
1987 May	**Silverside** Dave Kenyon (unseconded)
	First free ascent of Sirloin, Pitch 2.
1988	**Poo** Dave Kenyon
1991	**The Black Tripe Trip** Ian Vickers, Dave Cronshaw
1991 May	**Crack 'A' Jack** Dave Cronshaw, John Ryden
1991 June 4	**Drunk for a Penny** Penny Johnson, Tim Hatch
1991 July 4	*Dead Drunk for Two Pence* Tim Hatch, Penny Johnson
1991 June 29	**Stickman** Tim Hatch

Round Barn Quarry   O.S. ref.   SD 728 191

Situation and Character

The quarry is located about 900 metres south-east of the southern entrance to the Sough tunnel on the railway from Bolton to Darwen. It overlooks a back road between Darwen and Bolton, a little over two kilometres north of Edgworth.

For the most part the quarry is composed of two tiers and all the climbing (as yet) is on the more stable upper tier. The rock on this tier is generally solid, though it would be advisable to clean any intended new route before leading. The shaly lower tier does deter some climbers from climbing at Round Barn, but as there are no climbs on it, this impression is unfounded and some of the climbs here are very worthwhile.

There is an abundance of belay stakes available for most climbs, but some are rather feeble.

History

Numerous parties had undoubtedly visited and dismissed Round Barn Quarry, including John Spencer and the rest of the Wilton 'crew' whose main explorations centred on a vast 100-metre route around the walls, roofs and doorways of one of the buildings in the quarry floor. They named this route the *Big Wet*, but, as happens to most routes in this part of the quarry, it was demolished/fell down.

The first real wave of development began in the early Seventies when Dave Cronshaw, Bob MacMillan and Les Ainsworth started to clean and record the routes in 1974. On the first visit MacMillan climbed *Sough*, whilst Ainsworth claimed *Lancashire Lad* and *July Wakes*. Shortly afterwards, ascents were made of *Last Straw, Blackburn Buttress, Red Rose Rib, Lancashire Lass, Black Pudding* and *Barnacle*. These were followed in 1975 by more routes on Lancashire Wall, including *Mudlark* and *Vixen* by Cronshaw and *Foxhead* by Ainsworth. However, Nigel Bonnet and Steve Marsden stole a real gem in the shape of *The Pross*, which subsequently saw off a good few attempts at a repeat. The old '*Crags*' magazine chronicled these developments, unwittingly spurring Ryden to visit the crag, and the result was 'simultaneous' ascents of many routes. Certainly *Black Pudding* and *Gulag Archipelago*, were the work of Ainsworth, but the two Johns (Ryden and Grundy) claimed a number of separate lines, including *Barn Owl, Red Rose Wall* and the ever-interesting *Railroad Groove*. At this time, Cronshaw also began his protracted campaign on the

Lancashire Wall, adding *East Lancs, Yorkshire Queer* and *Psychlops*. Later, in 1979, Ryden spiced up Black Pudding and took the true line to produce *Mustard*. In the same year Cronshaw managed to dispense with the aid nut at the start of the Gulag Archipelago.

Ryden dug out many of the dodgier Eiger Sanction areas, and his patience was rewarded with such classics as *One Flew Out* and *Armagideon Times*. In more recent years, a series of shorter and cleaner buttresses have been the focus of Cronshaw's attention with ascents of *Forbidden Fruit, Hold In The Wall* and *Gay Deceiver* in 1984 and *Burgess, Third Man* and *MacLean* in 1985.

The 90s have seen a few additions, the best being Cronshaw's *Lancastrian* and *Decree Nisi* and Tim Greenhalgh's *Baldy's Delight*.

Approach
Eight kilometres south of Blackburn on the Edgworth road is the Crown and Thistle pub. From the southern end of the next group of houses on the left, a well-marked footpath leads directly into the quarry in 200 metres. Limited parking is possible just to the north of the houses, but the space at the start of the track into the quarry should be left clear.

The Climbs
The routes are described from LEFT to RIGHT.

The Pit Area
At the remains of the ruined building on the left of the quarry entrance, the quarry narrows and appears to end. However, there is still a little climbing on isolated buttresses. The first climbs are located on a short wall capped by an overhang, which is situated just to the right of a deep, forbidding pit. This wall can be further identified by an obvious corner groove at its right-hand end.

1.   Burgess 8m HVS 5a   (1985)
Four metres to the left of the corner/groove, follow a series of widely spaced holds which lead to a break in the overhang.

2.   Third Man 8m E2 6a   (1985)
Climb the wall one metre left of the arête, then step left to a blind crack and finish directly over the roof.

3.   MacLean 8m S 4a   (1985)
Climb the corner/groove to the roof, then step right to an easy finish. A direct finish is possible, but the rock quality is poor and a long reach is necessary.

4.   Fisherman's Friend 8m VS 4c   (1996)
Eight metres to the right is a buttress with an overlap near its top. Start at a short corner, then climb the narrow wall, taking the overlap at its centre and finishing with a committing mantel.

5.   Fishface 6m VD   (1996)
A little farther right above a jumble of blocks is a fishhead feature. Climb into the eye, then finish easily up the arête. Often wet.

The next three climbs are on the buttress just to the right of the jumble of blocks.

★ 6.   Gay Deceiver 9m HS 4b   (1984)
The blunt arête on the left-hand side of the buttress.

★ 7.   Hold in the Wall 9m HVS 5b   (1984)
From a small inverted triangular niche pull up right into the centre of the wall
then climb this via *'The Hold'* (peg near the top).

8.   Forbidden Fruit 8m E1 5c   (1984)
The twin cracks just to the right.

Scarey Buttress
*This is the buttress with a large cave beneath it, which lies directly behind
ruined buildings about 60 metres left of the quarry entrance. The rock is
unstable and some previous routes now lie on the quarry floor, so beware.*

9.   Thundercrap 8m S 4a   (1979-83)
The obvious jamming crack two metres left of the recently-formed corner
groove on the left of the cave. A top-rope may be advisable.

★ 10.   Blackfoot Sue 10m VS 4b   (1979-83)
A much better climb than initial appearances might suggest. Climb over doubtful
blocks at the right of the cave until it is possible to traverse left to a triangular
niche. Ascend the flake crack to the roof, then traverse right to finish just left of
the Scarey Monster's Eyes.

North Walls
*About 30 metres to the right of Scarey Buttress there are three small buttresses
directly above a good path that leads from the top of Scarey Buttress.*

★ 11.   Lancastrian 8m HVS 5b   (1996)
Start in the centre of the front face of the first buttress and climb this to a peg,
then step left to finish on widely spaced holds.

12.   Lost Arrow 8m HVS 5a   (1981)
Surmount the overhang at the right-hand side of the front face and continue up
the crack to the left of the arête.

13.   Limbo 8m S 4a   (1981)
Takes the crack up the right-hand side of the inside wall, traversing left along
the horizontal break to finish.

14.   Downward Bound 8m VD   (1983)
The arête of the small buttress immediately to the right.

15.   Star Sailor 14m VS 4c   (1984)
Climb the corner to the left of The Pross to the overhang then hand-traverse
right to finish up that route.

★★ 16.   The Pross 14m E1 5b   (1975)
The original hard route of the quarry. Though it is now easier since a block fell
off it is ,nevertheless, still strenuous and sustained. The third buttress is
characterized by a curious hole beneath a neb. Ascend a crack on the right of

North Walls

the arête, then traverse round and go up to the hole. Move right below the roof then finish up the crack directly above the arête.

17. Ghost Dancer 12m E1 5c   (1984)
Start a little to the right. Climb the wall direct via a flake and a small sandy pocket.

★ **18. Ho** 12m VS 4b   (1978)
On the right there is a groove capped by an overhang. Climb this and the crack above.

Entrance Walls
Immediately to the right of the third buttress is a more continuous section of rock that directly faces the quarry entrance.

19. Gogo 8m VS 4b   (1975)
Starting by large fallen blocks, climb the left side of the arête until it is possible to pull over to gain a sandy ledge and the top.

★ **20. Polo** 8m S 4a   (1975)
The corner two metres to the right.

21. Sough Direct 8m S 4a (1974)
Start at an obvious sandy, disc-shaped depression and climb the wall
immediately to the left via mantelshelves.

★ **22. Sough** 8m VD (1974)
Start on the front of the buttress. Make a high mantel, then trend left and go up
to finish.

★ **23. Tunnel Vision** 9m S 4a (1996)
Climb the slight rib on the right past two overlaps, then finish up a short
chimney which is in common with the next route.

24. Fo 9m VD (1975)
Climb the block-filled crack one metre right. The wall on the right has a ledge
at its base with a quarry spike protruding from it.

★ **25. Manque de Ville** 9m VS 4c (1978)
Start just left of the quarry spike, move up, trending right to the arête via a
sandy pocket, then move back left and go through the overhang on good holds.

★ **26. Lonesome Traveller** 9m VS 4c (1979)
Climb the arête on its right, using the thin crack.

27. Spanish Stroll 9m VD (1979)
Climb directly up the corner on the right.

28. Barn Owl 9m D (1975)
From the base of the corner trend right up the wall to finish up the arête.

29. Barnstormer 9m S 4a (1974)
The groove on the right. Climb directly to the top.

★ **30. Last Straw** 9m HVS 5a (1974)
A good climb on well spaced holds. Start two metres to the right and climb
directly to a small sandy cave near the top (peg). Continue directly, or step right
from the cave and finish up a crack.

★ **31. Decree Nisi** 9m E1 5c (1996)
Climb the blunt rib immediately to the right, with an awkward move to gain a
hidden finger slot just above the overhang, then continue up the crack above.

32. Wop 9m S 4a (1977)
The obvious groove to the right.

33. Pencil 9m VD (1975)
Climb the right rib of the groove to a ledge, then step right and continue to the
top.

★ **34. Trevor's Answer** 9m VS 4c (1978)
Just to the right there is a cave-like recess. Climb the right side of this and
continue just right of the arête.

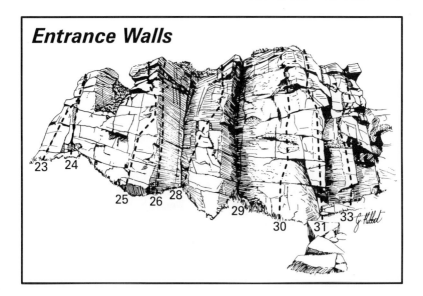

Entrance Walls

---

35. Ron's Dilemma 8m VS 4b   (1978)
From the foot of the descent route, climb the wall to an excavated ledge at the
top.

DESCENT: from the routes hereabouts is immediately to the right of Ron's
Dilemma.

Terrace Walls
*Immediately to the right of the descent route there is a steep slab with a
conspicuous crack splitting it. At this point there is a wide terrace below the
climbing and above a shaly pit. The Terrace Walls range from this slab to a
point about nine metres from the end of the terrace, where it starts to narrow,
just past Black Pudding Slab.*

36. Flake Out 6m VD   (1976)
Start two metres left of the crack at a sandy pocket, and climb to the top via
twin sandy pockets.

37. Crackling 8m VD   (1975)
Climb the conspicuous crack directly to the top.

★ **38. Barnacle** 9m S 4a   (1974)
Start at the lowest point of the slab, one metre to the right of Crackling. Make a
difficult move to the horizontal break and continue direct to a sandy pocket,
then trend right to finish.

39. Clog and Billycock 6m D   (1976)
Two metres to the right follow the cracks.

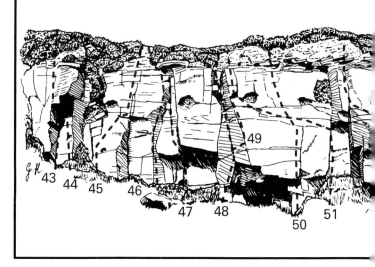

Terrace Walls

40.   Barnraker 6m D   (1977)
Climb flakes to finish at a curious sandy '*cave*'.

★★ **41.   Red Rose Rib** 9m S   4a   (1974)
A good, varied climb. The arête right of the slab. Start on the left, then mantel
on to the arête and finish on the left.

42.   Red Rose Wall 6m HS   4b   (1977)
The crack just round the arête.

43.   Shear Brow 6m HS   4a   (1977)
Farther right is a groove capped by a prominent square-cut roof. Climb this,
then exit left.

44.   Killing Floor 8m HS   4a   (1977)
Climb the right edge of the groove to an overhang and finish up a short corner
on the right.

★ **45.   Stubby Pinnacle** 6m D   (1976)
Right again is a pedestal. Step right from the top of this to cracks on the slab
and follow these to the top.

★ **46.   Railroad Groove** 8m S   4a   (1977)
Just to the right is a right-slanting groove with an overhang at the bottom.
Climb this, finishing left at the top.

47.   Right Track 8m VS   4c   (1980)
From the left side of the alcove on the right, climb the hanging crack with an
awkward start.

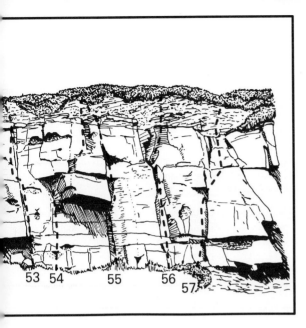

53 54   55   56
                        57

★ **48. Flake and Groove** 9m VS 4b   (1977)
Gain the flake crack on the right of the corner. Go up this, then move back into
the corner groove to finish.

49. Baldy's Delight 11m E2 5c   (1995)
Climb Flake and Groove for about three metres until it is possible to swing right
using obvious holds to gain the left edge of Black Pudding Slab (peg). Finish up
the arête.

To the right is an obvious undercut slab – Black Pudding Slab.

★★ **50. Mustard** 10m VS 4c   (1979)
A bold start leads to pleasant slab climbing above. Ascend directly up the centre
of the slab, starting by a thin finger-crack on the right edge of the overhang.

★ **51. Black Pudding** 12m HS 4b   (1974)
Start at a shallow chimney on the right of the slab and take a diagonal line from
the extreme bottom right of the slab to the top left.

The obvious dirty corner that starts at this point (**Offal Corner**) *is not
worthwhile.*

No Future Wall
*Right of Black Pudding Slab the rock steepens and the terrace extends another
nine metres before falling away to the shale beds below.*

52. Gardeners' Question-Time 8m S 4a   (1980)
Immediately right is a square-cut niche guarded by an overhang below. Climb
the wall to enter this, then finish up the left edge of the slab above.

53.   Ah-Med-It   8m   S   4a   (1979)
The hanging crackline three metres to the right, starting from a fallen block.

54.   Blackburn Buttress   14m   VS   5a   (1974)
Immediately to the right is a large block-overhang. Climb the short wall on the
left of this, then make a sensational mantel right on to a ledge above the
overhang and follow ledges to the top. It should be mentioned that doubts have
been expressed about the stability of the block-overhang in the past, but it
continues to defy gravity.

★ **55.   The First Third**   12m   HVS   5a   (1980)
Start beneath the right-hand end of the block-overhang. Climb directly up the
arête then go up the corner crack through two overhangs to a final groove.
Finish on the left as for Blackburn Buttress.

*To the right the access ledge terminates above shaly walls. The upper wall has
previously been dedicatedly trundled, gardened, dismantled, reassembled and a
top ledge excavated. From this ledge a couple of terminal moves up
consolidated moor lead to a belay stake. However, in recent years, the wall has
reverted to it previous overgrown and shaly nature.*

56.   Rising Dread   12m   HS   4b   (1979)
At the end of the access ledge twin cracks/grooves lead up to a ledge at eight
metres. Sandy moves rightwards lead to the top ledge and a grovel finish.

57.   Helter Skelter   12m   VD   (1979)
From the end of the access ledge step right to an obvious green groove. Climb
this till forced out on the right wall, then go up to the top via two ledges.

The Void
*Above the centre of The Void is a recess and ledge with a peg belay (The
Cuckoo's Nest). This is the start for the routes between* **Sometimes a Great
Notion** *and* **Complete Control**, *inclusive. It can be reached by the following
route*:

58.   Cuckoo Waltz   6m   S   4a   (1979)
This route only leads to the Cuckoo's Nest and so to reach the top it is then
necessary to climb one of the other routes in The Void. From the end of the
access ledge ascend the first three metres of Helter Skelter then descend
diagonally right along an obvious ledge.

59.   Sometimes a Great Notion   9m   VD   (1979)
Step left up sandy ledges from the Nest, then follow the left-slanting ramp.

★ **60.   One Flew Out**   9m   HS   4a   (1980)
The corner/groove immediately above The Nest, finishing up parallel cracks
above the overhang.

★★ **61.   Armagideon Times**   9m   HVS   5b   (1980)
Although it is difficult to get to the foot of this route, the climbing is worth the
effort. Climb the wall immediately to the right of the arête on thin, awkwardly
spaced holds. Peg low down on right.

★ 62. Complete Control 12m VS 4c (1980)

Traverse right from *The Nest* past a peg and step down to a corner niche. Climb directly up to a ledge on the right, then step back left above an overhang to finish up a thin crack.

Isolation Ward

This is the large, heather-covered, sloping area at the right side of The Void which can be reached by an awkward **DESCENT** *via the broken heathery corner to the south, or by abseil. The next two   utes start from the base of the slope.*

63. Equaliser 9m S 4a (1980)

Climb diagonally left from the foot of the desc t rake to join a crackline above the niche on Complete Control.

64. Suspect Device 12m HS 4a (1980)

From the bottom of the rake climb directly up to an obvious corner/groove finish.

Lancashire Wall

The remaining routes lie at the southern end of the quarry on Lancashire Wall, the steepest and cleanest area of rock in the quarry. This wall starts at half-height above a shale band and is best gained from the top via a grassy slope on the left.

65. July Wakes 10m VD (1974)

Start in the centre of the first wall and climb this, veering right and finishing up the arête which bounds the left side of the Lancashire Wall recess.

★ 66. Dawn Chorus 10m E2 5c (1987)

The arête right of July Wakes on its left-hand side, with two pegs.

★ 67. Milton Friedman ate my Lunch 10m E2 5c (1991)

Climb the arête of Dawn Chorus on its right side and watch out for the barn door.

★ 68. Rave On! Boris Yeltsin 12m E1 5c (1991)

Follow the very thin horizontal crack in the wall left of Mudlark, until it is possible to finish up Milton Friedman.

69. Mudlark 6m S 4a (1975)

The short corner on the left side of Lancashire Wall. Move left at half-height then regain the corner above.

★ 70. Vixen 9m S 4a (1975)

Right of the deep corner some cracks split the wall. Climb the left of these.

71. Foxhead 9m HS 4b (1975)

The right-hand crack leads to the horizontal break, just left of the '*Fox's Head*', then finish up the wall above as for Vixen.

Lancashire Wall

★★ 72. Gulag Archipelago 14m E1 5b (1976/1979)
A surprisingly exposed route for its length, even though the crux is low down.
Farther right is a conspicuous hanging groove above a shale band. Traverse right
along the band (peg above overhang) to the groove. Gain this with interest and
continue to the top.

The final routes start from the large grassy ledge at the right of Lancashire
Wall. This can be gained by an airy step down from the right.

★★ 73. East Lancs 10m VS 4c (1976)
Steady and well protected VS climbing. From the left of the grassy ledge climb
a groove to a small overhang at four metres, then traverse left below this to a
hanging groove on the left of a rib. Finish up this (crux). A direct finish has
been top-roped, but it has little merit.

★★ 74. Legendary Lancashire Heroes 27m HVS 5a (1980)
An exposed traverse of the suspended section of Lancs Wall going from right to
left. Start up East Lancs and continue along the obvious horizontal crackline
from the overhang at four metres into Gulag Archipelago. Awkward moves left
then lead to better holds and the finishing crack of Vixen.

★ 75. Lancashire Lad 9m HS 4b (1974)
The obvious groove which starts just to the right.

76. Yorkshire Queer 8m HVS 5a (1978)
Two metres right of the next corner ascend the leaning crack.

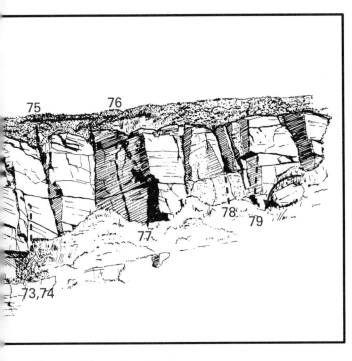

★ **77. Psychlops** 8m E3   5c   (1982)
Takes the curving crack immediately left of the large '*eye*'. Gain the crack and
continue strenuously on awkward holds.

78. Lancashire Lass 8m S   4a   (1974)
The corner/groove on the left of the airy step.

★ **79. Los Endos** 8m HS   4a   (1996)
Start just right, below an overhang at half-height. Gain the overhang and pass it
on its right, then finish up the arête.

First Ascents at Round Barn Quarry

1974 July   **Sough** Bob MacMillan, Les Ainsworth, Dave Cronshaw
1974 July   **Sough Direct** Les Ainsworth, Bob MacMillan, Dave Cronshaw
1974 July   **Lancashire Lad** Les Ainsworth, Bob MacMillan, Dave Cronshaw
1974 July   **July Wakes** Les Ainsworth, Dave Cronshaw, Bob MacMillan
1974 Aug   **Barnstormer, Lancashire Lass** Bob MacMillan, Dave Cronshaw, Les
                     Ainsworth
1974 Aug   **Last Straw, Blackburn Buttress** Dave Cronshaw, Les Ainsworth,
                     Bob MacMillan
1974 Aug   **Red Rose Rib** Les Ainsworth, Dave Cronshaw, Bob MacMillan
1974 Aug   **Black Pudding, Barnacle** Les Ainsworth, Dave Cronshaw
1975   **Mudlark, Vixen** Dave Cronshaw, Les Ainsworth, Bob MacMillan
1975   **Foxhead** Les Ainsworth, Dave Cronshaw, Bob MacMillan
1975   **Pencil, Barn Owl**, *Limpet*, **Crackling** John Ryden
1975   **Gogo, Fo** John Ryden, Dave Melling
1975   **Polo** Dave Melling, John Ryden

1975	**The Pross** (1pt aid) Nigel Bonnett, Steve Marsden
	First free ascent by Nigel Bonnet (unseconded), 1975.
1975	**Offal Corner** John Ryden, Dave Cronshaw
1976 July 13	**Wobbling Groove** Dave Knighton, Nigel Holmes
1976	**Flake Out, Clog and Billycock, Stubby Pinnacle** John Ryden
1976	**Gulag Archipelago** (1pt aid) Les Ainsworth, Dave Cronshaw
	Aid eliminated by Dave Cronshaw, John Ryden, 1979.
1976	**East Lancs** Dave Cronshaw, Les Ainsworth, Bob MacMillan
1977	**Barnraker, Red Rose Wall** John Ryden, John Grundy
1977	**Shear Brow, Killing Floor, Railroad Groove** John Ryden
1977	**Flake and Groove** John Ryden, Dave Cronshaw
1977	**Wop** Andy Moss, Steve Moss
1978 Aug	*Biro,* **Trevor's Answer** John Ryden, Roger Vickers
1978 Aug	**Ron's Dilemma** Roger Vickers, John Ryden
1978 Sep	**Manque de Ville** Roger Vickers, John Ryden
1978	**Ho** John Ryden, Steve Weaver
1978	**Yorkshire Queer** Dave Cronshaw, Les Ainsworth
1979 May	**Mustard** John Ryden, John Grundy
1979 May	**Ah-Med-It** Yunus Ahmed, Roger Vickers, John Ryden, John Grundy
1979	**Lonesome Traveller** Dave Cronshaw, John Ryden
1979 July	**Rising Dread** Roger Vickers, John Ryden
1979	**Spanish Stroll** John Ryden, Roger Vickers
1979	**Helter Skelter** John Ryden, Yvonne 'Trifle' Ryden
1979	**Cuckoo Waltz, Sometimes a Great Notion** John Ryden
1980 Apr	**Suspect Device** John Ryden, John Grundy
1980 May	**The First Third** John Ryden, John Grundy
1980	**Right Track** Dave Cronshaw, John Ryden
1980	**Gardeners' Question-Time** John Ryden, Tim Fairless, John Grundy
1980	**One Flew Out, Equaliser** John Ryden, John Grundy
1980	**Armagideon Times** John Ryden, Dave Cronshaw
1980	**Complete Control** Dave Cronshaw, John Ryden
1980	**Legendary Lancashire Heroes** John Ryden, Dave Cronshaw (alts)
1981 Mar	**Lost Arrow** Dave Cronshaw, John Ryden
1981 Mar	**Limbo** Dave Cronshaw, John Ryden, John Grundy
1982	**Psychlops** Dave Cronshaw, John Ryden
1979-83	**Thundercrap, Blackfoot Sue** John Ryden, John Grundy
1983	**Downward Bound** John Ryden
1984 Apr 4	**Gay Deceiver, Hold in the Wall, Forbidden Fruit** Dave Cronshaw, John Ryden
1984	**Star Sailer, Ghost Dancer** Dave Cronshaw, John Ryden
1985	**Burgess, Third Man, MacLean** Dave Cronshaw, John Ryden
1987 May 7	**Dawn Chorus** Dave Cronshaw, John Ryden
1991 Aug 16	**Rave On! Boris Yeltsin** Goi Ashmore, Marc Bellingall
1991 Aug 16	**Milton Friedman Ate My Lunch** Goi Ashmore (solo)
1995 May 1	**Baldy's Delight** Tim Greenhalgh
1996 May 26	**Fishface** Les Ainsworth (solo)
1996 July 23	**Fisherman's Friend, Lancastrian, Decree Nisi** Dave Cronshaw, Les Ainsworth
1996	**Tunnel Vision, Los Endos** Dave Cronshaw (solo)

Stanworth Quarry   O.S. ref.   SD 638 241

Situation and Character

Stanworth quarry lies about one kilometre north of Abbey Village, and to the east of the A675 Bolton – Preston road. Several years ago the original quarry was filled in, but although some routes were lost, the majority of the good climbing was left. The remaining rock provides varied climbing on generally good gritstone in small sheltered bays faced by steep grassy slopes.

More recently, the owners, Biffa Waste, have re-excavated some spoil within the quarry in order to resurrect some of the original climbing. This has greatly improved the climbing on South Pole Buttress and climbers are most grateful for all their efforts.

History

It was not until the mid-Sixties that climbing began at Stanworth; Ray Evans and Ken Powell climbed around 20 routes here during 1965 but unfortunately made no records. A year later, in 1966, Les Ainsworth and Paul Hamer also found the quarry and climbed eight routes which were later to be lost under a pile of rubble. Both Les and Paul were so enamoured with the place that they immediately forgot all about it, and it was not climbed on for the next ten years.

Then in 1977, whilst working on a forthcoming supplement, Ainsworth managed to coax a small team out for a look on a snowy December day. This visit turned out to be extremely productive and within a fortnight, members of the team had ascended over thirty routes, including such climbs as *Praying Manteler* and *Alexander the Great* by Dave Cronshaw, *Eskimo Nell, North West Passage* and *African Queen* by Al Evans, *Euphrates* by Ian Horrocks, *Columbus* and *Peary* by Ainsworth on the first visit. The next weekend Cronshaw and Ainsworth added five routes on Space Buttress (now lost) then they respectively claimed *Scott* and *Antarctic Arête*. On the Sunday they turned their attention to warmer climes with *Amazon* falling to Ainsworth whilst Cronshaw added *Ganges* and the two *Nile* routes. Unfortunately, some of these routes have since been covered with infill.

A few fillers-in followed then Cronshaw cleaned and climbed *Meridian* and *Brasilia*, though an aid nut was needed on the latter. The Seventies exploration ended with Cronshaw's imaginative *Fuchs Across the Pole*. Unfortunately, the interesting traverse start to this has now been lost, hence a slight name change. In 1982 Dave Kenyon and Malc Haslam contributed *Floodgate, Stranded Passenger* and free ascents of both *Brasilia* and *Raleigh*.

1985 saw a year of dramatic change when it was proposed to fill in the quarry with spoil from the adjacent slate quarry. However, these plans were modified by careful BMC negotiations, led by Ian Lonsdale, to ensure that much of the best climbing was saved.

When the dust had settled several routes were claimed but some doubt arose as to whether or not they had been led. Kenyon set about re-establishing his crown, by repeating all these routes; many succumbed fairly quickly but the most stubborn of them (*Mount Vinson*) needed many visits to complete.

More recently, the main developments at the quarry have, perhaps surprisingly, not been on the new routes front. During discussions on site between the BMC and the quarry owners, Biffa Waste, Fred Edwards, the Site Manager offered to scoop some of the infill from two parts of the quarry to try to recover some of the lost climbing. Unfortunately, the attempt to recover Space Buttress did not succeed, but the climbing at South Pole Buttress was greatly improved. This imaginative approach from Biffa has been most appreciated by local climbers.

Access and Approach
The quarry at Stanworth is owned by Biffa Waste, whose managers have been very proactive in their approach to climbing at the quarry (see previous paragraph). Biffa owners are happy to permit climbing at Stanworth.

From the Junction 3 on the M65, the quarry can be reached by travelling towards Bolton on the A675 and taking the first track on the left (signposted to Stanworth Farm) after the restaurant. After a couple of hundred bumpy metres there is a stile on the right behind some trees and cars can be parked just beyond this, about 50 metres from a transformer on a pole at the washing plant (**N.B. It is not safe to park beneath this transformer**). Cross the stile and a metalled road to a second stile. Undercut Buttress rises straight ahead in about 60 metres.

The Climbs
The first routes to be described lie on Undercut Buttress, which lies about 100 metres south of the washing plant entrance. From this point the routes are described from RIGHT to LEFT.

Undercut Buttress
This is the small undercut buttress immediately before North Pole Buttress.

1.   Dynamo 5m E2 5c   (1987)
Takes the overhanging wall via a hole.

2.   Toit Groove 6m HVS 5a   (1986)
Climb the overhanging groove on the left side of the wall.

North Pole Buttress
This buttress was originally named as a telegraph pole used to stand directly above it. However, this has now been removed and the buttress is now identified by a large overhang at the top of its right-hand side.

3.   North West Passage 8m S 4a   (1977)
Start at the right side of North Pole Buttress, behind the trees, and climb the deep groove stepping right near the top to a ledge and exit.

★ **4.   Rust Never Sleeps** 10m HS 4a   (1984)
Start left of the trees, below a sentry-box at four metres. Gain this via a ledge on the right, then climb the groove above until it is possible to step left on to the wall above the overhang. Finish up the right edge of this.

★ **5.   Rust Never Sleeps Direct**   10m   VS   4c   (1993)
Start at the short arête on the left and climb up to the sentry-box. Step left on to
a higher ledge and climb the overhang above to finish up the wall.

★ **6.   Vega**   10m   HS   4a   (1978)
Start in the deep corner just to the left and finish up the V-groove which cuts
through the overhangs.

7.   Arctic Circle   5m   E1   5c   (1986)
Three metres to the left, ascend the blunt arête to the break.

8.   Shale Surprise   6m   E2   6a   (1987)
The wall just to the left again to the break.

★ **9.   Eskimo Nell**   12m   HS   4b   (1977)
The wide crack to the roof. Move left through the roof to finish.

★ **10.   Spitting Image**   12m   E5   6a   (1986)
The wall on the left, moving left into the centre at the crux. Continue to the
roof and a peg, then follow the flake above leftwards to the lip and finish above.

★ **11.   Subzero**   12m   E6   6b   (1983)
Climb the wall on the left, directly to a hole below the break, and finish directly
over the roof above.

★ **12.   Peary**   12m   VS   4c   (1977)
Start at an obvious curving crack and either climb the crack, or the groove on
its left to the overhang (peg). Climb the overhang directly by exciting moves.

★ **13.   Energy Vampire**   12m   E1   5c   (1981)
Climb the thin crack to a peg, then move diagonally right to the large ledge and
finish up the wall above on good holds.

14.   Nansen   10m   VS   4b   (1977)(1977)
From a ledge at one metre climb the wall on the right, eventually gaining the
blunt arête on the left just below the large ledge, then continue to a drill hole on
the large ledge. Ascend the overlap one metre right of the corner crack (peg) on
good holds.
Hudson (VD): a variation start to Nansen. On the left is a glacis (scoop); gain
this from the left and continue to the drill hole.

15.   Bering Strait   9m   S   4a   (1977)
Climb the chimney crack to the top of the '*Icicle*', then take the wide corner
crack above to finish.

★ **16.   Abruzzi**   10m   VS   4c   (1979)
Climb the rib on the left, then the crack above.

★ **17.   Aurora**   10m   HVS   5b   (1996)
Follow the faint right-slanting weakness which leads to the top of the rib. At the
large ledge, step slightly left and climb the short wall above via four small
overlaps.

North Pole Buttress

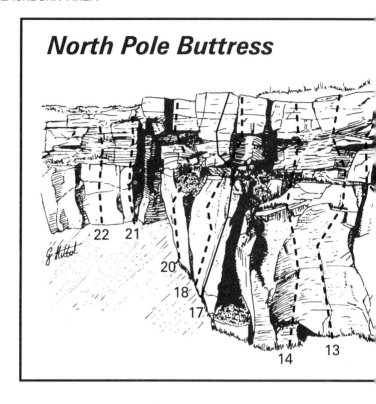

★ **18.   Baffin**   10m   HVS   5a   (1977)
From a slot in the centre of the wall, follow the very shallow depression to the
large ledge, then finish up the crack of Abruzzi.

19.   Ross   9m   VS   5a   (1977)
Climb the wide crack at the left of the wall, then move up left to finish easily
up a short corner.

20.   Barents   8m   VS   4c   (1977)
Starting one metre to the left, climb up the centre of the wall and continue up
the short corner above.

★ **21.   Scorched Earth**   8m   E1   6a   (1996)
Climb the right side of the wall on the left, which contains some bore holes.

22.   Blacky Woo Woo Bon Bon Pipkins   8m   HVS   5c   (1983)
Climb the centre of the wall trying not to be distracted by the route name!

23.   Pack-ice   8m   VD   (1978)
The flake crack just to the left.

24.   Melt   8m   S   4a   (1987)
The wall on the left. Gain a sloping ledge at three metres then finish up a short
corner.

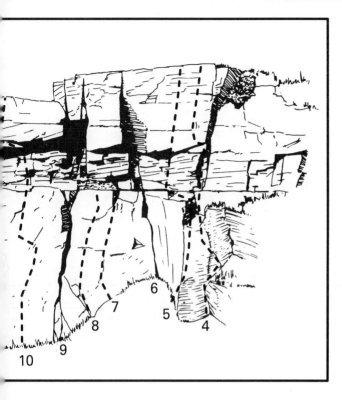

25. Spitsbergen 9m VS 4c (1981)
Start down to the left and take the shallow groove and corner.

The Tropics
To the left is a grassy banking which gives an easy way down. The rock
between this and the end wall of the quarry (The Equator) is known as The
Tropics. The first climb lies just to the right of an obvious left-facing corner.

26. Edge Game 8m E2 6b (1987)
The problem arête to the right of the corner.

27. Mason Master 8m HS 4b (1986)
The left-facing corner and a short wall above.

28. Jack the Lad 8m D (1986)
The wide crack with a pedestal at its base leads to a step left near the top.

29. Haymarket 8m HVS 6a (1986)
The problem wall between the previous route and Thorn Hill, without recourse
to the edges.

30. Thorn Hill 8m D (1986)
The ragged crack on the left.

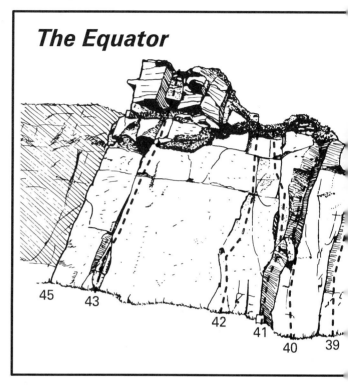

31. Beano 8m HVS 5c   (1985)
The steep slab starting at two finger slots. Move up and left then go straight up
to finish.

32. Cancer 6m S 4a   (1977)
The thin crack via a mantel at half-height.

33. Goll's Wall 6m VS 4b   (1984)
The slab between Cancer and Tropical Corner.

The Equator
*At the end of the quarry the rock increases in height, and this end wall is
known as The Equator.*

34. Tropical Corner 6m D   (1977)
The chimney at the right-hand corner of The Equator.

35. Monsoon 6m VS 5a   (1983-86)
Start one metre left of Tropical Corner. Gain an obvious high jug and gain a
flake on the left to finish.

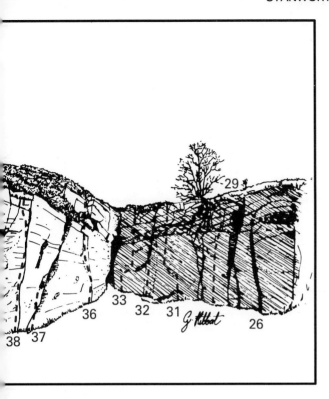

36. Too Hard for Greg Rimmer 6m E1 6a   (1984)
Start about four metres left of the corner, directly below an arête at the top of a crag. Use a small finger slot to reach a faint flake, then finish above.

37. Edge of Extinction 8m E3 6b   (1985)
To the left is a right-leading flake/crack; take this and the short groove to finish (peg).

38. Floodgate 8m E1 5c   (1981)
The crack one metre to the left.

39. Blue Nile 9m E2 5c   (1977)
Left again is a ledge at two metres. From this climb the converging cracks to an awkward finish.

The flaky line between Blue Nile and Luxor has been climbed at 6b, but it is rather artificial.

40. Luxor 9m HVS 5a   (1979)
On the left is a protruding column of rock at half-height, pierced by a borehole. Gain the niche on the right of this then keep to the right and finish up a short hanging groove.

★ 41. White Nile 9m HVS 5a   (1977)
Pleasant, well protected climbing, with some unusual holds. Start in the corner and
climb the left side of the column, then continue past the borehole runner on Luxor.

★ 42. Stranded Passenger 10m E4 6c   (1981)
Just left is a letter-box at three metres. Gain this, then move right and follow a
thin crack and the wall above to the top.

★★ 43. African Queen 15m HS 4b   (1977)
A good introduction to jamming techniques. Four metres right of the obvious
arête is a crack which forms an inverted Y. Climb this to a ledge and cave, then
continue in the same line to the top.

44. Tigris 14m HVS 5b   (1978)
Gain a curving flake from African Queen, or go direct, and finish up the arête
and a corner above.

★★ 45. Euphrates 14m E2 5b   (1978)
Climb the arête to large ledges near the top, then finish up the corner above.
The holds on the arête are small and there is no protection until the break is
reached.

★★ 46. Ganges 15m VS 4c   (1978)
An out-of-balance move relatively high up, makes this a thought-provoking
exercise. Two metres left of the arête a line of small ledges leads to a large neb.
Follow these (peg) to the break, then step right and continue up a corner to the
top.

From the foot of Amazon a rather artificial eliminate can be made just right of
the crack at 6b.

★ 47. Amazon 15m S 4a   (1977)
Follow the wide crack which leads left from the Ganges Delta. At the top step
right, then exit left. Belay stakes well above.

*The deep crack at the left side of the corner contains some very unstable blocks
and should be avoided.*

★ 48. Brasilia 17m E3 6a   (1978/1981)
The crack system which splits the centre of the steep wall on the left of the
deep corner. Climb cracks to reach a small groove which can be followed to a
sandy cave. Scramble off to the left.

The Lovely Charlotte (E7, 6b †) starts at an arete on the left and climbs via a
peg and a groove to a monster jug. Finish over the overlap past an old nest.

49. Machu Picchu 10m VS 4b   (1981)
The blocky, unappealing groove that slants leftwards on the left side of the steep
wall.

South Pole Buttress
*This is the small buttress directly opposite North Pole Buttress. At the time of
writing this buttress still retains its telegraph pole, but this has been
decapitated. Recent re-excavation by the quarry owners has enabled some of the
earlier climbs to be resurrected.*

★ **50. Fuchs up the Pole** 7m VS 5b (1978)
From a ledge at the right side of the buttress, use a sloping ledge to gain then climb the shallow, right-facing groove in the leaning wall.

51. Weddell 6m D (1977)
The chimney on the left.

The deep groove on the left has not been climbed, because of concerns about the stability of some blocks near the top.

★★ **52. Mount Vinson** 10m E7 6c (1986)
Start at a line of hanging flakes just over one metre left of the unclimbed groove. Power up the flakes passing several overlaps to the crux just under the top (sky hook runner).

★ **53. Meridian** 10m HVS 5a (1978)
The conspicuous, steep crack three metres to the left is climbed to a difficult finish.

54. Antarctic Arête 10m VS 4b (1977)
Start up the left side of the jutting rib and finish up the corner on the left, as for Oates.

55. Oates 10m HS 4b (1979)
Climb the corner on the left.

56. Death Before Dishonour 9m E3 6a (1991)
This route has not yet been re-ascended since the bottom was re-excavated. Climb Amundsen for three metres, then step right and climb the wall above by a thin crack.

★ **57. Amundsen** 9m E1 5b (1977)
The classic jamming crack on the left. A typical strenuous gritstone crack, which at no point seems to be the right width.

58. Scott 7m VS 4b (1977)
The shallow groove on the left.

*Two metres farther left at a slightly higher level, an interesting problem (**Abrasions**, 5c) takes the wall via a sloping ledge.*

Navigator's Buttress
This is the overhanging buttress about 20 metres farther left. Only one of the previous routes now remains.

★ **59. Raleigh** 6m E4 6b (1978/1982)
The brutal, thin crack which splits the leaning wall.

First Ascents at Stanworth Quarry

Routes in italics have been (temporarily?) lost due to infilling.

1977	*Magnetic North*	
1977	*Billy the Kid, Butt, Marco Polo, Quito* Dave Cronshaw	

1977	*Praying Manteler, Cousteau*, Drake, **Peary, Hudson, Barents** Les Ainsworth, Dave Cronshaw
1977	*Caper del Montis* Dave Cronshaw, Bob MacMillan
1977	*Alexander the Great, Columbus*, **Ross, Cancer** Dave Cronshaw, Les Ainsworth, Bob MacMillan
1977	**North West Passage, Eskimo Nell** Al Evans, Brian Cropper
1977	**Nansen, Bering Strait, Ganges, Blue Nile, White Nile, Amundsen, Scott,** *Frobisher* Dave Cronshaw, Les Ainsworth
1977	**Baffin** Les Ainsworth, Dave Cronshaw, Bob MacMillan
1977	**Tropical Corner** Les Ainsworth (solo)
1977	**African Queen** Al Evans, Brian Cropper
1977	**Euphrates** Ian Horrocks, Phil Warner
1977	**Amazon, Antarctic Arête**, *Tasman* Les Ainsworth, Dave Cronshaw
1977	*Flinders, Pitcairn, Magellan, Bass Strait, Cook* Dave Cronshaw, Les Ainsworth
1977	**Weddell** Bob MacMillan, Les Ainsworth, Dave Cronshaw
1978	*Kid Gloves, Humboldt* Dave Cronshaw, Brian Tucker
1978	**Vega** Dave Cronshaw, Les Ainsworth, Bob MacMillan
1978	**Pack-ice** John Ryden, Dave Cronshaw
1978	**Tigris** Dave Cronshaw, Les Ainsworth
1978	**Brasilia** (1pt aid) Dave Cronshaw, Phil Warner *Aid eliminated by Dave Kenyon, Mick Ryan, 1981.*
1978	**Fuchs up the Pole** Dave Cronshaw, John Ryden, Les Ainsworth *Originally involved a serious traverse, but foreshortened due to infilling and renamed from Fuchs Across the Pole.*
1978	**Raleigh** (A1) *First free ascent by Dave Kenyon, Greg Rimmer, 1982.*
1978	**Meridian**, *Mercury, Apollo* Dave Cronshaw, Les Ainsworth
1978	*Gemini* Dave Cronshaw, Bob MacMillan, Les Ainsworth
1978	*Yuri* Les Ainsworth, Dave Cronshaw
1978	*Columbia* Les Ainsworth, Dave Cronshaw (solo)
1979	**Abruzzi, Luxor** Dave Cronshaw, Phil Warner
1979	**Oates** Dave Cronshaw, Les Ainsworth
1980	*Vasco de Gama* Dave Cronshaw
1980-81	*Yellow Peril* John Noblett, Greg Rimmer
1980-81	*Strawberry Blonde* Mick Ryan
1980-81	*Danuta's Right Hand* Chris Riley
1980-81	*Hogmanyay Hangover* Bob Whittaker, Geoff Hamridding
1980-81	*Arm Strong* Malc Haslam, Mick Ryan, Greg Rimmer
1980-81	*Moonraker* Malc Haslam, Mike Haslam,
1981	*Strawberry Blonde* Mick Ryan (solo)
1981	*The Minor* Greg Rimmer, Malc Haslam, Mick Ryan, John Noblett
1981	**Energy Vampire** John Noblett, Mick Ryan
1981	**Spitsbergen** Dave Cronshaw, John Ryden
1981	**Floodgate** Dave Kenyon, Malc Haslam
1981	**White Nile Direct** Dave Cronshaw, Malc Haslam
1981	**Stranded Passenger** Dave Kenyon (solo)
1981	**Machu Picchu**, *Sandanista, Matto Grosso, Polynesia* Dave Cronshaw
1981	*Gravity Well* Dave Kenyon
1982	**Raleigh** Dave Kenyon, Greg Rimmer *First free ascent.*
1979-83	*Pat Garrett* Dave Cronshaw
1979-83	*Wesley Powell*
1979-83	*Spazz Energy* Dave Kenyon, Malc Haslam
1983	**Blacky Woo Woo Bon Bon Pipkins** Dave Kenyon (solo)
1983	*Armstrong Variation* Dave Kenyon (solo)
1983	*Voyager* Dave Cronshaw (solo)
1983	**Subzero** Dave Kenyon, Greg Rimmer
1984	*Splash Down* Dave Cronshaw, Greg Rimmer
1984	**Rust Never Sleeps** Dave Cronshaw, John Ryden
1984	**Goll's Wall** Dave Pearce (solo)

1984	**Too Hard for Greg Rimmer** Dave Kenyon, Malc Haslam
1984	*Pocket Wall* A. Stevenson
1985 May 30	**Edge of Extinction** Dave Cronshaw, Bob MacMillan
1985 May 31	**Beano** Dave Cronshaw (solo)
1983-86	**Monsoon** Malc Haslam, Chris Riley
1986 May 20	**Spitting Image** Phil Garlick
1986 Aug 17	**Arctic Circle** Phil Garlick (solo)
1986	**Toit Groove, Mason Master, Jack the Lad, Haymarket, Thorn Hill** Dave Cronshaw, John Ryden
1986	**Mount Vinson** Ian McDonald
1986 Sep	**Shale Surprise** Phil Garlick (solo)
1987 July 1	**Melt** John Ryden, Dave Cronshaw
1987	**Dynamo** Dave Cronshaw (solo)
1987	**Edge Game** Dave Kenyon (solo)
1990	**Abrasions** Dave Cronshaw, Bob MacMillan
1991	**Death Before Dishonour** Ian MacDonald
1993	**Rust Never Sleeps Direct**
1996	**Aurora** Dave Cronshaw, Les Ainsworth
1996	**Scorched Earth** Dave Cronshaw (solo)

Stronstrey Bank Quarry   O.S. ref. SD 619 186

Situation and Character
Stronstrey Bank Quarry is a sandy gritstone quarry situated high on the west edge of Anglezarke Moor, above the hamlet of White Coppice. There are actually three distinct areas, which each offer pleasant climbing up to 11 metres high.

Since the previous guidebook, extensive cleaning has greatly improved most of the existing climbs and has also revealed several good new climbs. As a result of this, the Stronstrey Bank area should be much more pleasant for climbers, especially for summer evening visits. Nevertheless care must still be taken, as some of the tops still contain loose rock. Some of the climbs can become very green after wet weather, but others dry quickly, especially those on Black Brook Buttress.

History
The quarry was mainly developed by Colin Dickinson with John Cottingham, Frank Menzies and Bob Scoltock, between 1972 and 1974. In 1977 Karl Lunt added *Screaming Abdabs* then in 1980 he uncovered the outlying buttresses with *Anthem* and *S-Bend* on the Bank itself and *Bastille Day* and *Bomber* on Black Brook. During guide work, in 1981, Kev Glass added a half-dozen more climbs, the best of which were *The Max Factor* and *Stacked Hand*.

Nothing more was added until 1993, when Goi Ashmore made a short foray to Black Brook to add the *Sad Mads*.

Two years later during another bout of guidebook work Dave Cronshaw and Les Ainsworth turned their attention to the quarry. They rapidly concluded that there was too much doubtful rock and set about removing this with a vengeance. Thin cracks became deep, V-grooves and the thin loose skin in other parts turned into much more appealing wall climbs. Over half the routes probably changed to some extent and some new ones were added. The activities were typified by *Hidden Groove* and *Stopgap* which completely transformed and replaced Mam and Stopgap Swinger respectively. The most notable of these new routes were

Synergy, Green Toothbrush, Cat's-eyes, White Groove and *Clockwork Orange* by Cronshaw and *Dog Lead Ramp* by Ainsworth. Finally, Cronshaw visited Black Brook, where he added *Wisden* and *Stumped.*

Approach

The best approach is from White Coppice cricket ground. There are signs to White Coppice from Wheelton, just over one kilometre towards Blackburn on the A674 from Junction 8 of the M61, where the dual carriageway ends. Alternatively, from Anglezarke, continue up the hill between the quarries for about three kilometres, then follow the White Coppice signs into the village. Cars can be parked at the cricket ground except on match days, when it is best to park on the rough track by the reservoirs. The quarry can be reached in slightly less than ten minutes from the cricket ground and Black Brook Buttress takes a little less time.

To reach the quarry, cross the bridge directly above the cricket ground, then turn immediately right over two more bridges. About 50 metres past the third bridge an obvious track leads diagonally right up the moorside. After about 150 metres a grassy bowl is reached. The isolated buttress at the top of this is the Bank itself, but to reach the main climbing, continue past the grassy bowl, then follow an obvious path into the quarry. The easiest way to reach the Bank is by contouring back left from the quarry.

Black Brook Buttress can be reached by following the track directly ahead after crossing the first bridge. It is the obvious solid buttress at the far end of a quarry on the left of the stream

Access

All the climbing areas at Stronstrey Bank are owned by North West Water. The managers are willing to permit climbing on these crags, but they stress that there have been concerns about the stability of some of the rock.

The Climbs

The numbers included in brackets after some route descriptions refer to the numbers painted on the rock and as a result of recent developments the same number is sometimes shown for two routes. The climbs are described from LEFT to RIGHT.

Entrance Wall

On the left of the entrance to the quarry is a short wall with a large ledge at its foot.

1.   Sam 7m S 4a   (1980)

From the extreme left end of the large ledge, make a surprisingly difficult move up to gain the arête, then step left and go up the slab on small holds to the top. The arête can be gained much more easily from the right.

2.   Entry Crack 6m VD   (1995)

The crack directly above the left side of a large block on the ledge.

3. Wam 5m S 4a (1980)
Take a line up the highest part of the front face on good holds to a solid
chockstone, then finish up the jamming crack.

4. Reunion Wilderness 5m HVS 5a (1981)
Climb the left side of the arête right of Wam.

Tower Wall

*The next climbs lie on relatively featureless rock at a higher level, about 25
metres farther right.*

5. Radio Gnome Invisible 6m VS 4c (32) (1979)
At the left of the wall, cracks form a faint Y. Climb up the left side of the Y
and finish slightly to the right up the wall above.

6. Hidden Groove 7m VD (31) (1995)
The deep groove is more obvious than its name suggests.

7. Thwinger 7m S 4a (31) (1973-74)
Climb the wall immediately right of the deep groove and at the top, step left
and finish as for Hidden Groove.

8. Thinger 7m VD (30) (1973-74)
Mantel on to the top of the slabby ledge one metre right then continue up small
ledges to finish just left of a small tower.

9. Swinging Brick 8m VD (29) (1973-74)
Start at the toe of a small protruding buttress. Climb over the capstone and
finish just left of Decadent.

10. Decadent 6m D (28) (1972)
The shallow corner then the broken groove immediately right of the protruding
buttress.

★ **11. Orange Pod** 9m HVS 5a (1995)
The thin crack one metre right to the ledge on top of the large block, then climb
directly up the centre of the orange wall using horizontal breaks (peg) via an
obvious small pod near the top.

★ **12. Sportos** 8m VS 4c (27) (1973-74)
The fine, curved crack just to the right.

13. Pathos 7m VD (26) (1973-74)
Two metres right there is block-filled crack-cum-groove. Climb the left edge of
this.

14. Chevalier 7m D (25) (1973-74)
The wall finishes on the right at an indefinite arête. Follow this, starting from a
flat-topped triangular block.

Main Buttress

After a short break, the rock continues with another buttress, which extends to the back of the quarry. Past the shallow corner in the middle of this section, the rock increases in height to give the longest and most serious routes. However, although the climbing is good, some of the blocks on the higher section are suspect and top-roping may be advisable for climbs to the right of Synergy.

Extensive cleaning has completely altered the old route called **Dog Lead** *and this has now been superseded by the following two climbs.*

15.   Dog Lead Crack   7m   S   4a   (24)   (1995)
The wide crack at the left side of a clean wall.

16.   Dog Lead Ramp   9m   VD   (24)   (1995)
The obvious right-leading ramp, starting at the same point as Dog Lead Crack. Protection is poor.

17.   Rampant Digit   7m   S   4a   (23)   (1992)
The V-shaped groove at the right side of the clean wall.

18.   Greyhound Track   7m   S   4a   (22)   (1972)
The next groove.

19.   Green Toothbrush   7m   HS   4b   (1995)
The thin crack up the centre of the wall between Greyhound Track and Finger Five.

20.   Finger Five   7m   VS   4b   (21)   (1973-74)
To the right are two cracks which form the left corner of the higher section. Climb these.

Extensive cleaning has completely altered **Stopgap Swinger** *to give*:

21.   Stopgap   10m   VD   (20)   (1995)
The obvious deep V-groove. Exit on the left.

★★ **22.   Synergy**   11m   E1   5b   (19)   (1995)
An easy start, but the finish is steeper than it looks. At the centre of the wall is a large cave at two levels. From the lower cave, hand-traverse left then move up to a jamming crack and follow this to the top.

23.   Coppice Cave   11m   HVS   5b   (19)   (1975)
Gain the higher cave and exit by the left crack.

24.   Stron   11m   HVS   5b   (18)   (1975)
As for Coppice Cave, but exit via the right-hand crack.

25.   Panic Attack   10m   E2   5c   (17)   (1995)
Starting four metres right of the cave, and climb twin cracks to two overlaps at half-height. Step left and finish up the thin, left-slanting crack above.

26.   Screaming Abdabs   9m   VS   4b   (17)   (1977)
From the twin cracks on Panic Attack, follow the deep crack that trends right through the roof, taking care not to dislodge the whole rockface.

Main Buttress

The Roadworks

The next routes lie at the other side of the quarry on rock which has been extensively cleaned at the top to provide easy exits. However, until the earth at the top stabilizes, the tops can get muddy after wet weather.

27.   Layby 6m S 4a   (1995)
The obvious right-leaning chimney crack.

★ **28.   Cat's-eyes** 7m VS 5a   (1995)
From blocks at the left side of the leaning wall, pull up right to a thin crack, then make a surprisingly awkward move to gain the ledge and finish easily up the corner groove.

★ **29.   Canine Crawl** 8m E1 5b (16)   (1973-74/1995)
From the right side of the leaning wall follow a curving flake and move up to a handhold on a block on the arête at half-height. Step right and finish up the obvious jamming crack. Strenuous.

30.   Stronstrey Corner 7m S 4a   (1995)
The corner that bounds the overhanging wall on its right. Exit to the right at the top.

31.   Boredom 14m S 4a   (1981)
Climb Stronstrey Corner to the horizontal break at half-height and follow this rightwards to a pedestal just past Max Factor. Finish up the corner on the left.

32.   Flake Crack 7m VD (15)   (1975)
The deep crack three metres to the right, which forms the right side of a large flake.

33.   Muddy 7m VS 4b (14)   (1981)
The crack one metre right, which can be muddy.

34. The Max Factor 7m VS 4c (13) (1981)
Cracks in the blunt arête just to the right.

Green Wall
The steep wall on the right, which can get very green after damp weather.

35. Pinchblock 5m S 4a (10) (1973-74)
The crack three metres to the right of the corner. farther identified by the
'pinchblock' at about two metres.

36. Feeble Finger 6m S 4a (9) (1972)
The curving crack two metres to the right.

37. Edge of Sanity 7m HVS 5a (1995)
To the right a short crack leads to the first horizontal break. Climb the crack
and finish up the arête above on its left side.

38. Coppice Crumble 7m D (8) (1972)
The ill-defined corner cracks.

39. Lay Off 8m S 4a (7) (1973-74)
The cracks on the right of the slab.

40. Notch 6m E1 5c (6) (1981)
A boulder problem up the arête on a separate piece of rock 12 metres right. An
obvious notch at the top of the arête helps to identify it.

Playing Card Wall
*This is the last continuous area of rock on the right side of the quarry. At its
left side it forms two very short tiers and the right side is more broken.*

41. Trumped Ace 7m 4a S (1973-74)
From the short corner at the left end of the wall, climb up and right to enter an
obvious groove.

★ **42. Stacked Hand** 7m HVS 5b (5) (1981)
Climb the centre of the steep wall to the right of the corner, with a long reach
from the first break.

★ **43. White Groove** 7m VS 4c (4) (1995)
The shallow, light-coloured corner-groove from the recess in the centre of the
wall. The first couple of moves are awkward, but it soon relents.

44. Deck of Cards 8m VD (4) (1973-74)
From the back of the recess, move up right on to a pedestal, then step back into
a groove and continue to the top.

Adam Richardson spurts **Mustard** (VS 4c) on Black Pudding Slab, Round Barn Quarry.
Photo: Geoff Hibbert

45. Butch 8m HS 4b (3)   1981)
Three metres to the right ascend parallel cracks. At the square recess step left, then finish direct.

46. Clockwork Orange 8m HS 4b   (1995)
Immediately right of the square recess, climb a direct line up the cracks.

47. First Night 7m VD (2)   (1975)
The obvious right-slanting groove above a very small cave.

48. Gong 6m S 4a   (1981)
Gain large ledge at two metres at the right side of the wall, then finish up cracks in the wall above.

49. Small Wall D   (1981)
The isolated block on the right at a lower level.

Stronstrey Bank   O.S. ref. SD 620 187

The Bank itself is on the route to the quarry, but is nearer to the village. Most of the climbs are on the obvious buttress above the centre of the grassy bowl and at the left side of a bay of broken rocks.

50. Beyond the Realms of Death 10m HS 4b   (1980)
Start at a short corner capped by a square-cut overhang. From the overhang, move left on to a sloping ledge and follow a crack to a ledge on the arête. Move up and right to another ledge and a short wall to finish past a bolt at the top.

51. Banker 8m VD   (1995)
Start as for Beyond the Realms and take a direct line past the right side of the overhang to a pedestal. Step left on to the ledge above and climb on to the top at a bolt.

52. Anthem 6m D   (1980)
Start four metres to the right and gain a triangular ledge at two metres. Finish up the crack directly above the right side of the ledge.

53. The S-Bend 6m D   (1980)
The chimney on the right.

54. Bleak Outlook 6m HVS 5b   (1981)
The arête at the far end of the bay, on its left-hand side.

Black Brook Buttress   O.S. ref. SD 623 189

This is the small crag on the left bank of Black Brook, above the cricket ground at White Coppice. The routes are on the solid buttress farther right.

55. Wisden 7m E1 5b   (1995)
Start at the extreme left side of the solid buttress, directly below a faint crack and climb the wall just to the right side of this to the top.

Dave Cronshaw splits the screen on **Split Screen** (HVS 5a), Stanworth Quarry.

Photo: Geoff Hibbert

56. More Mad than Sad 8m HVS 5a   (1993)
Start as for Wisden and move diagonally right past blocky holds to the
horizontal break at five metres. Follow this rightwards then aim for the top just
over a metre before the arête.

57. More Sad than Mad 8m E1 5b   (1993)
Climb the left side of the arête to a groove capped by an overhang. Step right at
the overhang to finish on the right side of the arête.

★ **58. Bastille Day** 7m VS 4b   (1980)
The obvious shallow chimney near the left edge.

59. Bomber 6m HS 4b   (1980)
Mantel on to a sloping ledge $1^1/_2$ metres farther right, then follow the corner
crack to the top.

60. Stumped 6m HS 4c   (1995)
The shallow depression in the wall one metre right of the corner is climbed to a
ledge on the arête. Finish up a short wall.

First Ascents at Stronstrey Bank Quarry

1972	**Decadent, Rampant Digit, Greyhound Track, Feeble Finger, Coppice Crumble** Colin Dickinson, Bob Scoltock, John Cunningham
1973 Apr	**Thwinger, Thinger, Swinging Brick, Sportos, Pathos, Chevalier, Finger Five, Canine Crawl**, *The Mole*, *Grapevine* Colin Dickinson, Frank Menzies
1974 Apr	**Pinchblock, Lay Off, Trumped Ace, Deck of Cards** Colin Dickinson, Frank Menzies
1974 Apr	*Dog Lead* Colin Dickinson, Frank Menzies *Superseded after rockfall by Dog Lead Crack and Ramp*
1974 Apr	*Stopgap Swinger* Colin Dickinson, Frank Menzies *Superseded after rockfall by Stopgap*
1975	**Coppice Cave**
1975	**Stron** Dave Cronshaw, Les Ainsworth
1975	**Flake Crack**
1975	**First Night**
1977	**Screaming Abdabs** Karl Lunt, Steven Lee
1979	**Radio Gnome Invisible** Kev Glass
1980	**Sam, Wam, Beyond the Realms of Death, Anthem, The S-Bend, Bastille Day, Bomber** Karl Lunt, Steven Lee
1981	**Reunion Wilderness, Boredom, Muddy, The Max Factor, Notch, Stacked Hand, Butch, Gong, Small Wall, Bleak Outlook** Kev Glass
1993	**More Mad than Sad, More Sad than Mad** Goi Ashmore
1995 Oct	**Entry Crack, Wisden, Banker** Les Ainsworth, Dave Cronshaw
1995 Oct	**Hidden Groove** Dave Cronshaw, Les Ainsworth
1995 Nov	**Orange Pod, Dog Lead Crack** Dave Cronshaw
1995 Nov	**Dog Lead Ramp** Les Ainsworth, Dave Cronshaw
1995 Nov	**Green Toothbrush, Synergy, Edge of Sanity, Clockwork Orange** Dave Cronshaw, Les Ainsworth
1995 Nov	**Stopgap** Dave Cronshaw (solo)
1995 Dec	**Panic Attack, Cat's-eyes, White Groove** Dave Cronshaw, Les Ainsworth
1995 Dec	**Layby** Les Ainsworth, Dave Cronshaw
1995 Dec	**Canine Crawl** Dave Cronshaw, Les Ainsworth *Extensively cleaned and new line climbed.*
1995 Dec	**Stronstrey Corner** Dave Cronshaw (solo)
1995	**Stumped** Dave Cronshaw, Les Ainsworth

Withnell Quarry

O.S. ref.   SD 633 217

Situation and Character

The quarry lies on the hillside immediately south of Withnell and slightly east of Brinscall. It is also known as Brinscall Quarry.

The quarry has been re-opened as a working quarry, with the loss of some poor routes. However, there is still some climbing on the walls at either edge of the quarry and these are generally sound and of good quality. Furthermore, the climbs that remain, lie well away from the active workings.

History

This huge quarry saw its first climbing activity in 1977 when two unknown climbers put up a now deceased route in the Subsidiary Workings. The first really major wave of development however, occurred in 1978 when Dave Cronshaw and Les Ainsworth discovered Brick Buttress and ascended five routes before encountering access difficulties caused by the local water bailiff.

The crag lay dormant until the late Kev Glass solved most of the other obvious gaps on the buttress during guidebook work in 1981. The best of these was undoubtedly the undergraded *Marie, Marie*.

The first climbs away from Brick Buttress came in 1986 when Cronshaw remembered the hidden New Walls and returned with John Ryden to create *Split Screen* and the crag's hardest route, *Emotional Paralysis* which had previously been attempted on sight without much success by Goi Ashmore, who turned his attention to the remaining lines on Brick Buttress, producing some good pitches such as *The Factory Syndicate* and the direct finish to *Blinkers*.

1987 was a busy year which saw a huge trundling effort to unearth routes in the previously neglected Main Quarry. Unfortunately, these have all either been lost, or are under immediate threat of being lost, due to further quarrying.

Fortunately, these losses have more than been made up for by two routes on the Yellow Wall Area by Cronshaw and Ryden and by more sustained development of the New Wall. Ashmore drew attention back to the New Wall with *Counter Insurgency*, but then it was left to Cronshaw to clean up the remaining lines, in all senses of the term, by adding *Crack 'n' Up* in 1995, followed by *Withnell Arête* and *Crossover* the following year.

Access and Approach

As part of the quarry is still being worked, the best time to visit is on Sundays. However, most of the climbing lies well away from any quarrying activity and no difficulties have been encountered.

To reach the quarry from the M65, leave the motorway at Junction 3 (as for Stanworth) and follow the A675 south for nearly two kilometres to Abbey Village. At the south end of the village, opposite the Hare and Hounds pub, turn right along Dole Lane towards Withnell. Follow this past Central Quarry to a surfaced track which forks left about 500 metres from the A675. This track starts off as Twistmoor Lane, but farther on it becomes Butterworth Brow. The quarry is obvious and there is plenty of parking in the various lay-bys.

The Climbs

Since quarrying operations recommenced, the climbing is restricted to two areas at the extreme left and right sides respectively. The routes on both areas are described as they would normally be encountered. Thus, the climbs on Brick Buttress are described from left to right, whilst the remaining climbs are described from RIGHT to LEFT.

Brick Buttress

This is the area of rock at the left side of the quarry, that directly overlooks a small square pool. It is reached by scrambling through the trees, starting about 150 metres to the left of the quarry entrance.

1.   Hookworm 8m   HS   4b   (1978)
The left side of the wall is marked by a detached pedestal with an old drill embedded at its base. The route takes this crack.

2.   Strangle 8m   HS   4b   (1986)
One and a half metres right. The series of irregular cracks.

3.   Tangle 8m   HVS   5a   (1986)
On the right there is an obvious overlap at three metres. Mantel over this, then continue up the wall above.

4.   Wangle 9m   HS   4b   (1978)
The obvious wide crack.

★ **5.   Criminal Neglect** 21m   HVS   5a   (1986)
An interesting traverse of the buttress. Climb Wangle until the crack widens, then traverse the thin horizontal crack until it is possible to finish up Arête-Toi.

6.   Dangle 11m   E1   5c   (1986)
Just to the left of the lowest point on the wall is a crack with a triangular hole below the break. Climb to the break, then go up the thin crack system above.

★ **7.   Mangle** 12m   HVS   5a   (1981)
Starting at the lowest point on the wall, climb a very thin crack to the break, then continue parallel to Dangle up indefinite cracks.

8.   Gaffer 11m   VS   4c   (1978)
Start two metres to the right at twin cracks, then climb the crack/groove above.

★★ **9.   Marie, Marie** 10m   E1   5b   (1981)
Fine climbing up the thin crack just left of the arête (peg).

★ **10.   Arête-Toi** 9m   S   4a   (1978)
The arête direct (peg).

11.   Weezy Wonk 9m   VD   (1978)
Start just right of Arête-Toi, and follow stepped ledges to the top.

12.   Scrabble 9m   VD   (1978)
Four metres right of the arête is a groove. Climb the right edge of this.

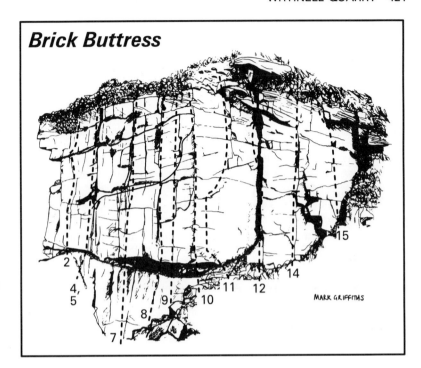

Brick Buttress

MARK GRIFFITHS

★ **13.   Blinkers** 9m HVS 5a   (1979-83)
The centre of the wall just to the right, finishing over the bulge on hidden holds.

14.   Old Granny Glass 9m S 4a   (1979-83)
The thin crack just to the right.

15.   The Evil Fencepost 8m VS 4c   (1986-87)
Start directly below a triangular overhang at the top of the crag and climb the wall, finishing to the left of the top overhang.

There is a short break in the rock followed by a short steep wall.

16.   Withnell Arête 10m D   (1996)
Start slightly right and at a lower level, immediately below a stepped arête at the left side of a smooth wall. Climb the wall directly to the arête, then finish easily.

17.   Factory Gate 8m E1 5b   (1987)
Start farther right at a higher level and climb the wall on its left past a finger-slot and finish through a small overlap.

18.   The Factory Syndicate 7m E1 5c   (1987)
Climb the centre of the wall, crossing the left-hand end of a ledge.

19.   Lock Out 7m VS 4c   (1996)
Start just to the right and climb a thin crack and the overhang above.

20.   Exercise One 9m S   4a   (1987)
Start up the corner and hand-traverse left across the break and ledge to finish up Withnell Arête.

There is also a low-level traverse from The Factory Syndicate back to the first route with some 5b climbing.

New Wall
The remaining climbs are situated at the right side of the quarry and are described from right to left. The New Wall is the hidden wall almost directly opposite Brick Buttress and about 100 metres into the quarry. It can be reached by scrambling through trees, starting about 20 metres right of the quarry entrance. The wall overhangs by about 5°, and has a discontinuous ledge running its length.

21.   Novelty 8m E2   5c   (1997)
Start five metres right of the lowest point of the wall, directly below an overhang at the top. Climb a very thin crack and the wall to a peg below the overhang, then move left to a bolt belay.

22.   Crack 'n' Up 9m HVS   5b   (1995)
Climb the next crack directly to the bolt belay.

23.   Counter Insurgency 12m HVS   5a   (1988)
Climb the wide crack which rises from the lowest point on the wall, with surprisingly awkward moves at the start. At the break step right and go up cracks to a square chimney above, then traverse left to finish.

★ **24.   Crossover** 15m HVS   5b   (1996)
Gain and climb the thin crack which starts one metre farther left, to reach the break. Traverse to the twin crack, then take a diagonal line leftwards to finish at the top of the arête.

★★ **25.   Split Screen** 12m HVS   5a   (1986)
Sustained climbing up the steep wall. Just left are twin cracks, climb these to the break and continue up the cracks above.

★★ **26.   Emotional Paralysis** 14m E3   5c   (1986)
A good, strenuous route, which is sustained throughout. At the left-hand side of the wall is a thin crack, follow this to the break (peg). Swing right then climb the exposed wall above on good slots.

27.   Slab Dab 10m S   4a   (1986)
At the top of the left-hand banking is a short chimney, climb this until it is possible to step right to finish up the obvious flake above.

Yellow Wall Area

Yellow Wall is situated about 60 metres farther left. It is identified by a large overlap, split by a curving crack. It is approached across stepping stones over the waterlogged ground directly below. To reach the climbs, scramble up to the prominent ledge at 10 metres. Belay stake well back.

28. Yellow Niche 14m E1 5b   (1992)
From the right end of the ledge, climb up to the right end of the overhang of Yellow Wall and swing right to a small triangular niche, then make a hard move up to an exit crack. Belay stake well back.

★ **29. Yellow Wall** 15m HVS 5a   (1992)
From the left end of the ledge follow a curving crack up and through the overhang. Belay stake well back.

First Ascents at Withnell Quarry

1978	**Hookworm, Wangle, Gaffer, Arête-Toi** Dave Cronshaw, Les Ainsworth
1978	**Weezy Wonk, Scrabble** Les Ainsworth, Dave Cronshaw
1981	**Mangle, Marie, Marie** Kev Glass, Marie Howie
1979-83	**Blinkers** Goi Ashmore
1979-83	**Old Granny Glass** Kev Glass
1986 May 19	**Split Screen, Emotional Paralysis** Dave Cronshaw, John Ryden
1986 June 26	**Slab Dab** Dave Cronshaw, John Ryden
1986	**Strangle, Tangle** Dave Cronshaw, Ian Vickers
1986	**Criminal Neglect, Dangle** Goi Ashmore
1986-87	**The Evil Fencepost** Goi Ashmore
1987	**Factory Gate, The Factory Syndicate, Exercise One** Goi Ashmore
1988 Easter	*Stolypin* Goi Ashmore (solo)
1988 Easter	**Counter Insurgency** Goi Ashmore, Rob Scott
1991 Apr 10	*Banana Republic, Gorilla Monsoon* John Stringfellow, Geoff Dawson
1991 May 14	*Down to Earth* John Stringfellow, Geoff Dawson
1991 Aug 3	*British Foreign Policy* Goi Ashmore, Adam Senior
1992	**Yellow Niche, Yellow Wall** Dave Cronshaw, John Ryden
1995	**Crack 'n' Up** Dave Cronshaw (unseconded)
1996	**Withnell Arête** Dave Cronshaw (solo)
1996	**Lock Out, Crossover** Dave Cronshaw, Les Ainsworth
1997	**Novelty**

Minor Crags

Flying Shed Quarry   O.S. ref. SD 583 217

The quarry lies across the M61 from Denham, but unfortunately, the best climbing, namely the rock to the left of Optrex Slab, has been destroyed since the previous guidebook. However, about twelve climbs of between nine and twelve metres still remain. These are mostly between VD and VS, with one HVS.

From the small roundabout on the B5256 by the bridge over the M61 about 200 metres on the Leyland side of the Denham turning, take the first exit after the road from Denham, and continue for about 100 metres to the Lord Nelson. Turn left and continue to the Duke of York, then take a small turning on the left about 150 metres farther on. Car parking is possible below the miraculous *'flying shed'*, provided that care is taken not to block access.

Hoghton Bottoms
O.S. ref. SD 628 263

A short and somewhat dusty natural grit crag, below the viaduct on the Blackburn–Preston railway line, just past Hoghton Quarry.

Kemp Delf
O.S. ref. SD 723 277

A small quarry about 100 metres south of the B6234 at Stanhill. From the bend on the Blackburn side of the village a track below some transmission lines leads directly into the quarry. Some climbing has been done including some good bouldering, and there are possibilities for about a dozen climbs of up to nine metres. As it is so conveniently located it certainly appears worth further development.

Knowle Heights Quarry
O.S. ref. SD 684 222

A small quarry 800 metres west of Darwen centre contains some problems including an obvious off-width crack: **Flash** (5c).

From Manor Road, alongside Bold Venture Park turn right into Westland Avenue and park here. From the top of the avenue follow a track which leads off right and take the right-hand fork just past some cottages. The quarry is on the left before some trees.

Star Delf
O.S. ref. SD 717 317

A small quarry consisting of three clean slabs just off the Rishton – New Inns road. Climbing has obviously taken place here in the past as an 'unnatural' line of polished holds follows the central slab. Farther across the fields lies Rabbit Delf which has potential for an eight-metre roof climb.

Pendle and Bowland Area

Compiled by Les Ainsworth, Dave Cronshaw, Paul Horan, John Proud and Rob Smitton

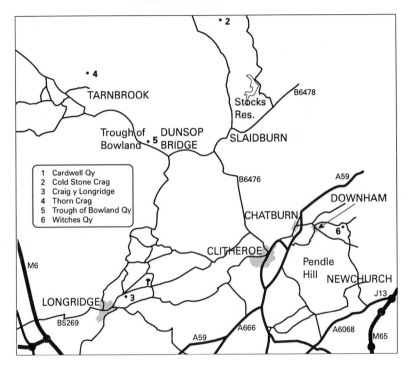

The area which surrounds Pendle Hill is one of great beauty, within which are four crags, each with its own distinct character. The limestone of Witches' Quarry, near Downham, offers excellent climbing at all grades, on good sound rock in pleasant situations. Another limestone crag is the Trough of Bowland Quarry, which though not very extensive, has a number of good climbs.

On gritstone, Craig y Longridge has become renowned for excellent bouldering, and attracts many climbers who wish to improve their stamina. The far end of the crag also provides a few longer, traditional routes.

Farther north and in complete contrast are Cold Stone and Thorn Crags. These are both small, natural gritstone crags set high on the wild moors of the Forest of Bowland. Neither crag is very extensive, but on a summer day they are both well worth the walk needed to reach them and to enjoy some superb climbing in a pleasant, quiet setting.

Cardwell Quarry

O.S. ref.   SD 637 402

Situation and Character

Cardwell is a small gritstone quarry that faces north on Jeffrey Hill, about four kilometres north-east of Longridge. It is sandy gritstone up to nine metres high and is slow to dry out, but it is in a beautiful situation for a summer's evening. It is a complete contrast to the hard-core bouldering atmosphere at Craig y Longridge, but will appeal to lower-grade climbers seeking peace and quiet.

History

The quarry was discovered by John Proud, whilst he was walking in 1983. Shortly afterwards he visited the crag with Mike Rayner and Rayner led the first route, *Bite the Dust*. This involved a frightening mantelshelf on to an earthy ledge and the experience taught them that it was wise to clean any potential routes before attempting to lead them. This view was confirmed when Proud led *Brush Up* on the same visit. Over the next few weeks Proud started the cleaning process and returned with various partners to add *Columniation, Spring Clean* and *Kleeneze*.

After this initial burst, the quarry lay neglected again, apart from a quick visit in April 1984 with Dave Smalley, when Proud added only two routes, including *Hernia Wall*. Over the next couple of years Proud continued to clean the crag, place belay stakes and then claim most of the best climbs at the crag, such as *What the Eye Doesn't See, Owling, Hodder Wall, Drought Line* and *Evening Crack*.

In 1989, Proud prepared a typescript guide to Cardwell and, during work for this, he soloed several of the remaining gaps, including *Shrew Rib, Shrewd Rib*, and *Mitton Mantel*. This marked the end of the main development at the quarry, though Proud was still able to find *Midsummer Madness* and *Rama's Lamb* in 1990 and 1991 respectively.

In 1997 Proud's one-man reign at the crag appeared to come to an end, when a new line was described in the notes that were being prepared for this guidebook. He promptly soloed the route, *Batty,* to check it, only to discover afterwards that it had not actually been done before. Thus, to date, Proud retains his record of having been involved in every first ascent at Cardwell and there are not many gaps left, if anyone else wants to get a look in.

Approach

From the centre of Longridge follow the Jeffrey Hill signs, forking left at the White Bull then taking another left turn about one kilometre farther on, just past Beacon Fell View Caravan Park. Continue past the Golf Course to a gate on the left just about 100 metres after the brow of a hill and 200 metres short of the road junction at the top of Jeffrey Hill. Park thoughtfully near this point. The quarry lies about 100 metres down a reed-covered quarry track that leads from this gate. No dogs, please, if there are sheep in the field.

Metal belay stakes are in place at the top of a heather bank. Do not cross the fence.

The Climbs

The routes are described from LEFT to RIGHT.

1.   Chimney Sweep 8m D   (1983)
The short, wide, overhanging chimney between two noses at the left side of the quarry.

2.   Midsummer Madness 8m HVS 5a   (1990)
Climb directly to the nose, then move right.

3.   Trowel Corner 8m D   (1983)
Pull into an undercut recess on the right of the second nose, then climb the stepped corner and pull out left above the nose.

4.   Block Out 9m HVS 5a   (1986)
Start a metre to the right. Climb into a triangular niche, then pull on to a large ledge and finish up the wall above.

5.   Batty 9m HVS 5a   (1997)
Climb on to the left side of a sandy block (loose), then continue up the crack through the left side of the overhangs above.

6.   Bats in the Belfry 9m HVS 5a   (1986)
Climb on to the right side of the sandy block, then follow the cracks that split the overhangs above on their right.

★ **7.   What the Eye Doesn't See** 9m VS 4c   (1986)
Start at the left end of an overhung recess at three metres. Gain the blunt rib on the left, pull on to the ledge right of the previous climb and climb the wall above.

★ **8.   Owling** 10m HVS 5a   (1986)
Start below the centre of the large recess and climb straight up, through overhangs, passing a borehole in the top overhang.

9.   Rama's Lamb 10m VS 4c   (1991)
Climb the groove directly to the left side of the nose, then climb this by the crack to its left.

★ **10.   Bite the Dust** 10m VD   (1983)
Climb the wall two metres right, below a prominent rock nose at the top of the crag. Swing right below the nose to an awkward landing on a ledge, then finish up the wall. A direct finish over the nose would be much harder!

11.   November Ember 10m HS 4b   (1985)
Gain the triangular sentry-box on the right, then surmount the overhang above, finishing just right of Bite the Dust.

★ **12.   Hernia Wall** 10m S 4a   (1984)
Start below the centre of overlapping slabs two metres to the right. Trend left to the top slab.

13. Groin Right 10m HS 4b (1984)
Follow the right edge of the slabs, straight up to the top slab, but avoiding the next climb.

14. Columniation 10m VD (1983)
Start just to the right below a square recess and continue up the overlapping column.

15. Spring Clean 10m VD (1983)
Start one metre right. Climb up the lower wall past a small letter-box, then gain the upper recess by a mantel.

16. Brush Up 10m D (1983)
Start at the right-hand end of an undercut wall one metre to the right. Climb left of the nose to a pleasant top wall.

17. Dirty Trick 10m VS 4c (1989)
Boulder directly up an overhanging nose, then climb the wall above.

18. Come Clean 10m S 4a (1985)
Climb immediately right of the overhanging nose, then continue through overlaps to a vertical borehole line in the top wall.

19. Shrew Rib 10m VS 5a (1989)
Start one metre right at the centre of an overlap and pull on to a large ledge directly above. Continue up the wall just left of a blunt rib.

20. Shrewd Rib 10m VS 4c (1989)
Climb through the overlap at its right-hand end without using the block on Kleeneze. Continue up the blunt rib above.

21. Kleeneze 10m VD (1983)
Start just to the right and use a triangular block to gain the ledge, then follow the steep groove to the top.

22. Dust Bowl 10m D (1983)
Start just below the 'butterfly' with a central bore hole, then climb past the large ledge and upper recess.

23. Mitton Mantel 10m VS 4c (1989)
Make a difficult mantelshelf on to a large ledge, then step right and follow the steep front face to overcome a small overhang on the right.

24. Loud Arête 10m VD (1985)
Start two metres to the right below a hole in the rock. Climb the rib, then step left into a recess and follow the steep corner to the top.

★ **25. Hodder Wall** 10m S 4a (1985)
Start two metres to the right at a small, sloping niche. Climb the smooth slab above to the top.

26. Ace of Spades 10m VD (1985)
Climb the right-angled corner to large ledges then bridge up loose rock. Exit left.

27. Drought Line 9m VS 4c   (1986)
Gain a nose from its right side, then follow an S-shaped crack up the top wall.

★ **28. Evening Crack** 8m HVS 5a   (1985)
Climb the centre of the lower wall, to gain the obvious, deep crack in the
overhang.

29. Last Crack 8m E1 5b   (1989)
Climb the curving crack to the overlap, reach up to a slot, then go straight up
and exit on the right.

30. Windy Arête 7m VS 4c   (1988)
From the ledge on the right reach up to a pocket, then make committing moves
on to a ledge. Finish easily.

31. Mr Sheen 45m 4a S   (1988)
Start up Trowel Corner, then traverse right below a large ledge. Step up into the
recess of Owling, cross below the overhang, then move down to a sentry-box of
November Ember and hand-traverse across the slab. Step up and traverse the
ledge round Brush Up buttress; continue across Hodder Wall to the corner.
Horizontal ledges then lead past Evening Crack to a finish round the top nose of
Last Crack.

First Ascents at Cardwell Quarry

1983	**Chimney Sweep, Trowel Corner**	John Proud, Dave Smalley
1983 Aug	**Bite the Dust**	Mike Rayner, John Proud
1983 Aug	**Brush Up**	John Proud, Mike Rayner
1983 Aug	**Dust Bowl**	John Proud (solo)
1983 Sep	**Columniation**	John Proud, Mike Rayner
1983 Sep	**Spring Clean**	John Proud, Dave Smalley
1983 Sep	**Kleeneze**	John Proud, Mike Rayner, Doreen Rayner
1984 Apr	**Hernia Wall, Groin Right**	John Proud, Dave Smalley
1985 May	**Loud Arête**	John Proud, Dave Smalley
1985 May	**Hodder Wall, Ace of Spades**	John Proud, Mike Rayner, Doreen Rayner
1985 Sep	**Come Clean**	John Proud, Doreen Rayner
1985 Sep	**Evening Crack**	John Proud, Mike Rayner
1985 Nov	**November Ember**	John Proud, Doreen Rayner
1986 Aug	**Drought Line**	John Proud (solo)
1986 Sep	**Bats in the Belfry, What the Eye Doesn't See**	John Proud, Mike Rayner
1986 Oct	**Block Out, Owling**	John Proud, Dave Smalley
1988 Sep	**Mr Sheen**	John Proud, Pete Dobson, Doreen Rayner
1988 Oct	**Windy Arête**	John Proud, Martin Jones
1989 June	**Dirty Trick, Shrew Rib, Shrewd Rib, Mitton Mantel**	John Proud (solo)
1989 June	**Last Crack**	John Proud, Pete Dobson
1990 June	**Midsummer Madness**	John Proud (solo)
1991 July	**Rama's Lamb**	John Proud (solo)
1997 Sep	**Batty**	John Proud (solo)

Cold Stone Crag
O.S. ref.   SD 712 607

Situation and Character
Cold Stone is a small gritstone crag on the Lancashire/Yorkshire border almost exactly at the centre of a line drawn from Clapham to Slaidburn and about $1^1/_2$ kilometres west of the Slaidburn to Clapham road.

Although the crag is relatively small, it gives quite a good variety of climbing from steep wall and roof climbs to the more laid back style of slab climbing. This variety makes up for its small size and makes it a pleasant place to visit. Due to its exposed southerly aspect it dries very quickly.

History
It is not clear when climbers first visited the crag. Certainly members of the Gritstone Club visited the crag in 1982 and 1983 and reported doing ten climbs up to HVS, but unfortunately nothing was recorded. The first recorded routes were not done until 1994, when John Ryden and Dave Cronshaw made a visit. The first route was *Jack the Lad* by Ryden, whilst Cronshaw was responsible for *Kerouac, Jolly Jack Tar* and *Jack the Ripper*. It was rumoured that the names were influenced by Ryden's new son Jack.

Cronshaw soon returned to meet the main challenge of the crag and, with Pete Black, he forced *The Jackdaw* and *The Jackal* up the impressive right-hand buttress. A year later he returned with Les Ainsworth and together they climbed the remaining routes.

Access and Approach
The crag is owned by North West Water, whose managers have no objection to climbing at the crag.

From Slaidburn follow the B6478 towards Long Preston for nearly five kilometres to a crossroads, then turn left (northwards) towards Clapham and continue along a twisting road for seven kilometres to a point where the road crosses into Yorkshire at a cattle grid. This point is about eight kilometres south of Clapham Station.

The crag is just over one kilometre to the west of this point and its top is just south of the boundary wall. It can be reached in about twenty minutes by using the wall as a guide and keeping to the north of it, then cross the wall with care at the crag. However, take care to avoid the boggy sections after wet weather.

The Climbs
The climbs are described from RIGHT to LEFT, starting at the imposing face nearest the boundary wall.

1.   The Jackdaw 7m E1   5b   (1994)
Starting at the very edge of the wall, gain and climb a flake crack to an awkward exit.

2.   The Jackal 9m E2   5b   (1994)
Start one metre left and climb the wall to a slanting break (peg), then go left through bulges to finish at a runnel.

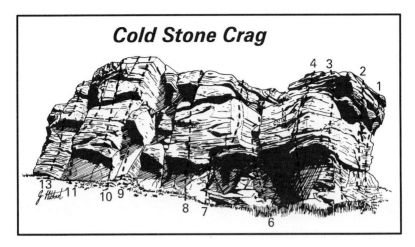

Cold Stone Crag

3. Kerouac 7m HVS 5a   (1994)
From the left end of the initial wall climb up left to a ramp, then finish up the short ramp above.

★ **4. Jackanory** 7m E1 5b   (1995)
Around on the front face there is a large overhang. Surmount this with a long reach to reach the crack above, then either finish up the crack or the wall on its left.

5. Jumping Jack Flash 6m HS 4a   (1994)
Named after the obvious rolling stone. Climb the chimney on the inside of the chockstone.

6. Jack It Up 6m S 4a   (1995)
Climb the chimney on the outside.

7. Jolly Jack Tar 8m HVS 5b   (1994)
Start at the left side of the overhang at a small beak of rock and climb rightwards to gain a ramp. Finish up this, or climb the blunt arête direct.

8. Jack the Ripper 7m HVS 5b   (1994)
Start just left using sloping holds to reach a good hold in the break, then make some committing moves up into a niche and pull out right to finish.

9. Donkey Jacket 10m VS 4c   (1995)
Farther left there is a deep square recess with an overhang on its left wall. Layback around this to a ledge and finish up the arête.

10. Jacksonville 10m HS 4b   (1994)
From the right edge of the nose, gain the slab and continue up the cracks above.

11. Jack the Lad 10m VD   (1994)
On the other side of the nose is a flake crack. From the base of this make a rising traverse across the right wall to finish up the arête.

12.   Jack Frost   8m   VD   (1995)
The flake crack on the left is climbed past several overhangs.

13.   Uncle Jack's Blue and White Army   8m   D   (1995)
Climb the front of the next projecting buttress.

First Ascents at Cold Stone Crag

1982-83	**Kerouac, Jack It Up, Jolly Jack Tar, Jack the Ripper, Donkey Jacket, Jacksonville, Jack the Lad, Jack Frost, Uncle Jack's Blue and White Army** Probably Gritstone Club members
1994	**Jumping Jack Flash** Dave Cronshaw, John Ryden
1994	**The Jackdaw, The Jackal** Dave Cronshaw, Pete Black
1995	**Jackanory** Dave Cronshaw, Les Ainsworth

Craig y Longridge   O.S. ref.   SD 619 384

Situation and Character

Craig y Longridge is located about two kilometres north-east of the centre of Longridge, facing south-east towards the Ribble Valley.

Most of the quarry is composed of a short, overhanging gritstone wall, which gives fierce problems. The top metre of the wall is often loose and so the practice on most climbs is to reverse back down, or jump off. Although most of the climbs are short, their overhanging nature makes them very strenuous. Newcomers to the crag can become demoralised by their failure on some of the pumpy problems, but persistence will soon bring its rewards and the crag is an excellent place to develop strength.

At the far end of the quarry the height increases and there are some interesting longer climbs. Unfortunately, these often suffer from seepage but, given the right conditions, they can be most worthwhile and it is a pity that so few climbers are willing to explore them.

History

Andrew Gridley discovered the crag early in 1983 and climbed *Jacob's Ladder*, which was the only route he thought was climbable at the time. He returned 14 months later with Steve Sharples who added the open corner of *New Stone Age*, whilst Gridley ascended *Neolithic Technology, Dyno ... Bucket* and *Company of Wolves* and also introduced Paul Pritchard, who soon claimed some interesting problems, such as *Central Icefall Direct* (covered in verglas at the time!) *Slug The Thug* and *The Howling*.

The crag remained a closely-guarded secret until Gridley's tongue was loosened in the pub. The next day, Phil Kelly turned up and climbed the poor *Semen Scream*, whilst Prichard claimed *Wobblebottom*. However, pride of place went jointly to Pritchard who traversed the obvious horizontal break in duvet and gloves to create *Ascent of Man* and to Gridley who fell slapping for the top on what was later to become *Thirty Feet of Pain*, during a solo attempt. This problem was solved a few months later by Pritchard, though he had to resort to the safety of a rope and an in-situ peg runner!

Gridley continued his developments during 1985 with *Spah's Daehniks* and *Descent of Man*, whilst Tim Gridley climbed *Timothy's Route*. Then, the brothers' attention turned to The Pit, where they started somewhat tentatively with two shorter routes at the left side and followed this by *Red Animals*, which attacked the highest part of the wall.

As news of the crag spread, Rob Smitton began visiting and soon usurped Gridley's crown. Smitton began by adding *Black Jake* and *Babylon Blitz* late in 1985, just as the supplement was going to press. Mark Leach got a short look-in and put up *Imitation Arapiles* and *Like A Slug But Sucks* which were all named by Pritchard. Kelly returned to climb *Muscles in their Imagination*, but not before Will Steel had completed *Waiting in the Wings* just to its left whilst waiting for Kelly to complete his line. Muscles ... was later improved by Smitton, when he lined the back of some of the deeper pockets with waterproof cement to stop seepage!

In 1986 Pritchard added *Renal Failure* and Simon Nevett started exploring the right side of The Pit, where he uncovered *Never Mind the Bullocks* and *Mother Earth*, whilst Leach claimed F*ertile Data*. However, Smitton formed the main impetus and climbed a series of excellent traverses including *Bend of the Rainbow*. Smitton's other efforts from 1986 included *Grow Wings* and *Still Raining, Still Dreaming*. Another interesting traverse was *Tarot Plane* by Kelly, which was originally named *Horizontal Heavyweight*. Pete Black climbed *The Gauntlet* and Mick Lovatt added *Big Marine* in the same year. By 1987 many of the gems had gone, but Malc Haslam managed to find the difficult *Eat 'em and Smile*. There were also two new traverses, *Unnatural Selection* by Gridley and Smitton's *Mr. Skin*.

The big prize at Longridge was the continuous ascent of the traverse. First done by Dave Kenyon in the late 1980s, it has still had no more than a handful of crossings. With no single move any harder than 6b, one could be forgiven for thinking that by modern standards it cannot really be that hard. However, whilst there are no moves harder than that, there are few that are much easier. Add to this the total length of around a hundred metres with only one shake-out at three-quarters distance and you have the kind of stamina pump that the French and Spanish could only dream of (not to mention Yorkshiremen – but then their dreams are all of the wet variety!).

During 1989 and 1990 some attention once more focused on the higher rock at the far right of the quarry, where there were some obvious lines that had, surprisingly, been completely ignored. The first line to go was *Puppeteer* by Pete Thursfield and this was followed by Tim Gridley's *J.F.P.* in September 1989. Both of these were seconded by John Proud and over the next couple of weeks Proud returned with Doreen Rayner to attack the obvious groove at the left side of the wall to create *Out of Step* and the neighbouring steep wall of *Pinnochio*. Over the next few months, Proud, together with various seconds, systematically claimed most of the other lines in this area, the best of which were *The Puppet, Mother's Day, Punch* and the high girdle, *After Eight*, on which leads were shared with Pete Dobson. The only other climbers who got a look in at that time were Sharples, who added the impressive *Top Out* and Dobson, who claimed the short, but interesting *Easy Club*.

Access and Approach

The crag is best approached from Longridge by heading north-east from the town centre along the road signposted '*Jeffrey Hill*'. Where the road forks, bear right following the sign to the golf course and continue for another 500 metres, passing a large caravan site on the right. Shortly after this a gravel pull-in and iron gate will be seen on the right. Park, go over the stile and left over the fence into the field where the crag will be seen. No access problems have arisen, but please respect the farmer's fences and livestock.

The Climbs

Most of the climbs are only problems and so heights are only given for the longer routes at the right side of the quarry. The numbers in brackets after some climbs correspond to the numbers painted on the rock.

The climbs are described from LEFT to RIGHT, starting from a drill mark at the left side of a small cave.

Problem Wall

This is the overhanging wall that gradually increases in height from the left end of the quarry. For much of its length there is a horizontal break near the top, but at some points the rock is set back slightly above this break, so that this is effectively the top of the climbs. These points, known as the Set Backs, provide convenient landmarks.

1.   Session's End   5a   (1985)
Traverse rightwards from the left side of the crag to The Race.

2.   Pudding   4a   (4)   (1986-87)
Climb directly from the drill mark at the left of a cave.

3.   Pie   4b   (5)   (1986-87)
Climb up via the right side of the cave.

4.   Gorse Bush   4a   (6)   (1985)
Climb the wall one metre to the right via a small niche.

5.   Absolute Beginners   4a   (7)   (1986-87)
Climb up via a drill mark at two metres.

6.   Bramble Ramble   4a   (8)   (1985)
Start one metre to the right and climb just left of the obvious vertical weakness.

7.   The Race   4c   (9)   (1985)
Climb the wall one metre to the right, immediately right of a vertical weakness, via a good ledge at three metres.

8.   Escalator   4b   (10)   (1985)
Start at a drill mark three metres to the right.

9.   Snail Trail   4c   (11)   (1985)
The wall one metre right of the drill mark.

10.   Paul Pritchard's Jacket   5a   (12)   (1985)
Faint cracks one metre to the right.

11.   Stoning a Leper   5b   (13)   (1986-87)
Exit leftward out of the sandy cave.

★★ **12.   Kiss the Razor's Edge**   6c   (1995/1997)
A 'last great problem', the ultra-low counter traverse to Tarot Plane. Best done
out of the nettle season. From a low jug on Stoning a Leper, traverse rightwards
with feet just above soil level and hands avoiding Tarot Plane, until a junction
can be made with Central Icefall Direct.

13.   Pay the Witch   5c   (14)   (1986-87)
Exit rightwards from the centre of the sandy cave and pull quite boldly up the
headwall.

14.   Late Pickings   5c   (14a)   (1986-87)
Climb up the right side of the cave, starting at a crack.

15.   Rifted Victim   5b   (16)   (1986-87)
Surmount the protruding blocks on their right and pull leftwards into the groove.

16.   Naked Lunch   4c   (17)   (1986-87)
Start one metre to the right and climb a faint overhanging crack and the wall
above.

17.   Black Jake   5b   (18)   (1985)
Climb past a slot at two metres, then continue up the obvious weakness.

★ **18.   Timothy's Route**   5c   (19)   (1985)
Start one metre farther right. Unusual in that it is possible to top out in relative
safety. Only 5a to touch the top.

★ **19.   Wobblebottom**   5c   (20)   (1985)
One of the few problems at Longridge to top out. An early breakthrough that
opened the floodgates. Start at the left side of the *First Set Back* and snatch up
to the break, step left and surmount the short juggy arête above.

★ **20.   Seven-A**   6a   (21)   (1985)
Gain the top of the *First Set Back* by undercutting an unfriendly horizontal slot.
Feels dangerous on first acquaintance.

★★ **21.   Tarot Plane**   6a   (22)   (1986)
The first of the excellent traverses. Traverse left from Central Icefall Direct to
link up with Session's End and so reach the end of the crag. A hard, low
variation when crossing Snail Trail and P.P's Jacket makes it particularly good
value.

★ **22.   Central Icefall Direct**   5a   (23)   (1984)
The juggy break at the right side of the *First Set Back*.

23.   Hitting the Wall   6a   (24)   (1985)
A low traverse right from Central Icefall Direct to Pump 'til you Jump. Can be
very greasy.

24.   Babylon Blitz   5b   (25)   (1985)
Climb the wall using footholds in Central Icefall Direct and top out using the
short, leaning arête and hanging garden to the left.

★ **25.   Thirty Feet of Pain**   6b   (26)   (1985)
An excellent route for which it is advisable to rope up. The overhanging wall
two metres to the right.

26.   Haardvark   6a   (27)   (1985)
Climb the sandy, overhanging wall three metres farther right

★★ **27.   Cruel Country**   6b   (28)   (1986)
A high-level leftwards traverse above Hitting the Wall, from Pump 'til you
Jump to Central Icefall Direct. Avoids the greasiness that affects the lower part
of this wall and provides the best line hereabouts for the full traverse.

28.   Pump 'til you Jump   5c   (29)   (1985)
Climb the slightly right-leading weakness past interesting ledges.

29.   Twelve Dreams   6b   (30)   (1986-87)
A very low-level traverse from Pump 'til you Jump to Mad Aardvark's Tea
Party.

★ **30.   Still Raining, Still Dreaming**   6b   (31)   (1986)
A big route, rarely soloed, but with adequate protection where it really matters.
Climb the wall immediately right of Pump 'til you Jump (Friend protection high
up).

31.   Grow Wings   6b   (32)   (1986)
The overhanging wall one metre farther right. The lower half is the crux, but
above the peg a degree of optimism is needed. A crucial low hold has recently
snapped off this route, since when there has been no record of it being climbed.
It will certainly now be a lot harder.

★ **32.   Imitation Arapiles**   6a   (33)   (1986)
Good, committing climbing into and beyond the shallow cave at the top.

★ **33.   Going Deaf for a Living**   6a   (34)   (1986)
Traverse leftwards from Mad Aardvark at about four metres, then move up
slightly and continue to Pump 'til You Jump. Embarrassingly difficult for the
short-legged.

34.   Mad Aardvark's Tea Party   6a   (35)   (1985)
The faint, dog-leg crack with a good jug at four metres.

★★ **35.   Gruts**   6a   (36)   (1986-87)
Traverse tenaciously from Mad Aardvark's Tea Party to Muddy Wobble Block;
a bit like doing pull-ups sideways.

36.   Pop Tart   6b   (37)   (1995)
Climb the overhanging wall on the right, starting at a loose block.

★ **37. Like a Slug but Sucks** 6b (38) (1985)
Climb the wall one metre left of the *Second Set Back*. Different starts are
possible.

38. Slug the Thug 5c (40) (1984)
A direct line to the left side of a recess at the *Second Set Back*.

39. Added Incentive 5c (41) (1986)
The overhanging wall up the centre of the *Second Set Back*.

40. Muddy Wobble Block 5a (42) (1985)
The obvious, blocky weakness.

★★ **41. Mr. Skin** 6b (43) (1987)
A brilliant low sequence. Getting to the sandy cave is hard, leaving it is even
harder. Traverse rightwards from Muddy Wobble Block to Semen Scream with
the crux passing Blatantly Slimy Slug. Jump off where the good holds end or
continue as far as Bend of the Rainbow for 1st prize.

42. Waiting in the Wings 5c (44) (1985)
Climb the wall immediately left of a thin crack to a loose wall at the right side
of the *Second Set Back*.

43. Muscles in their Imagination 6a (45) (1985)
Climb to the left side of a small cave. Finish on the left.

44. Weir Aardvark 5c (46) (1985)
Gain the cave at its highest point.

★ **45. Blatantly Slimy Slug** 5b (47) (1985)
The thin crackline on the right.

46. Company of Wolves 5b (48) (1984)
Climb the wall one metre to the right.

47. The Howling 5c (49) (1984)
Climb the wall from the right side of a cave at the foot of the crag.

48. Dyno ... Bucket 5b (1984)
Climb the wall on the right, just right of a faint crack, past a 'bucket' at three
metres.

49. Semen Scream 5c (51) (1985)
Climb the steep wall at the left side of the *Third Set Back* via an obvious cave.

★ **50. Smeg City** 5c (52) (1985)
The steep wall two metres to the right gives a satisfying problem on excellent
rock. Jumping for the first good jug reduces the grade.

51. The Gauntlet 6b (53) (1986)
Climb the faint right-leading crack.

★ **52. Big Marine** 6b (54) (1986)
The wall one metre to the right. There is also a low start on two crimps at 6c.

★★ **53. Renal Failure** 6c (55) (1987)
Climb the wall one metre farther right. Similar, but harder than Big Marine.

★★ **54. The Motion Vector** 6b (1996)
Powerful crimping on tinies. From a hanging start in a niche, climb up the wall,
avoiding the undercut on Push to Prolapse.

★ **55. Push to Prolapse** 6b (56) (1986)
Short, but power-packed. This one involves slapping for the top from that
Longridge rarity – a good undercut. A direct line one metre left of the right side
of the *Third Set Back.*

★★★ **56. Bend of the Rainbow** 6b (57) (1986)
Longridge's best traverse and possibly its best route of any kind. Traverse right
from a lonely jug to the right of Push to Prolapse, until bridged smugly across
New Stone Age.

★ **57. Eat 'em and Smile** 6c (57) (1987)
A direct line immediately to the right of the lonely jug.

★★ **58. Rug Thug** 6a (58) (1986-87)
Climb the vague right-leading crackline. Hard and unrelenting.

★★★ **59. In Excess** 6a (59) (1986-87)
Hard and surprising climbing one metre farther right.

★★ **60. Fertile Delta** 6c (60a) (1986)
Essentially a direct start to Porridge Gun, but containing one of the crag's most
finger-searing pulls. Two metres to the right is an excellent jug. Use this and
continue up the wall above. A hanging start can be made from a square-cut
pocket.

★★ **61. Porridge Gun** 6a (60) (1986)
Brilliant climbing, both technical and strenuous and on perfect rock. It eases off
slightly towards the top, but it is still a long way down! Start one metre right
and climb up and left until it is possible to finish up Fertile Delta.

★ **62. Anal Cave-In** 6b (61) (1985)
Start one metre right and climb directly to the top of the crag via a shallow cave.

★ **63. Scorched August** 6a (62) (1985)
An under-rated route that does not get the attention it deserves.

★ **64. New Stone Age** 5c (63) (1984)
Awkward moves up the obvious big groove line.

65. Unnatural Selection 6c (1986)
Traverse rightwards near the foot of the crag from New Stone Age to Jacob's
Ladder.

66. Unknown Arête 5b (64) (1986)
Climb the right-hand arête of the groove, mainly on the outside.

⋆ **67.   Missing Link**   6c   (66)   (1986-87)
A very rarely repeated problem. Climb the wall two metres right of the groove.

68.   Chocolate Popsicle   6c   (1991)
Climb the wall one metre farther right, with a massive reach from an undercut.

⋆ **69.   Moschops**   6a   (67)   (1986-87)
Climb the wall one metre to the right. Committing and exciting.

⋆⋆ **70.   Ascent of Man**   5c   (68)   (1985)
Traverse leftwards along the high break from Jacob's Ladder to New Stone Age;
brilliant. Never desperate, but a test of strength, stamina and nimble-footedness –
like ballet sideways.

71.   Jacob's Ladder   5b   (69)   (1983)
Climb twin cracks to a concrete post.

72.   Spah's Daehniks   6a   (70)   (1985)
The boldest route on this wall, with an uninviting landing. Traverse right along
the high break from Jacob's Ladder to Runaway.

⋆ **73.   Orifice of Faeces**   6a   (71)   (1985)
A direct line to a gorse bush near a concrete post.

⋆ **74.   Neolithic Technology**   6a   (72)   (1984)
Climb the wall at two faint parallel cracks.

75.   From Ape to Aardvark   6a   (73)   (1985)
A direct line starting at an obvious horizontal finger-slot.

⋆⋆ **76.   Descent of Man**   5c   (74)   (1985)
Unusually vertical for Longridge, but what it lacks in steepness, it makes up for
in technicality. An intricate and satisfying sequence. Traverse left at a low level
from Runaway to Jacob's Ladder. An on-sight link-up with Ascent of Man is
still impressive.

77.   Runaway   4a   (75)   (1985)
The juggy wall.

78.   And She Was   5a   (76)   (1986-87)
Climb the steep wall via ledges on the right.

79.   Some Friend   5a   (77)   (1985)
Start between two trees and climb directly to the top.

80.   Thug   5a   (78)   (1985)
Three metres right of the trees climb a blunt rib.

81.   Headline   5a   (79)   (1986)
Start three metres to the right and climb via ledges to finish just right of a large
tree at the top of the crag.

82.   Unnamed   5a   (80)   (1986)
Climb the wall directly to an in-situ sling.

83.   Year of the Rabbit   4a   (1986-87)
The prominent jutting prow at the right-hand end of the wall. Exit up loose rock.

84.   Way Out   VD   (1990)
Farther right, and at a slightly higher level, there is a square-cut recess. Climb
this and exit left at the top.

The Pit Area

*After a short break, the ground level drops to form a pit which often has some
seepage at its base. Here the routes are higher and so heights are given. It is
important to note that the last metres or so of some of these climbs is currently
very loose. Hopefully, this will soon be rectified, but until they have been
properly cleaned, climbers may wish to consider leaving a rope at the top of
some routes.*

The first climbs start from a higher ledge on the left.

85.   Bwink Bwink Bonk   8m   HVS   5c   (81)   (1985)
From the short chimney at the left side of The Pit, climb the right-hand side of
the right arête.

86.   Shap's Master Flasher   10m   E2   6a   (82)   (1985)
Climb up and rightwards behind the large tree on the ledge at the left side of
The Pit.

★ **87.   Out of Step**   12m   HVS   5a   (1989)
Start at a lower level, just left of the obvious groove that splits The Pit at its
left side. Climb ledges to reach the top of the broken groove and finish up this,
just left of a finger of rock.

★★ **88.   Pinnochio**   12m   E1   5b   (1989)
Steep and varied wall climbing giving an excellent introduction to this area of
the crag – get the rope and runners out. Start immediately right of the base of
the groove at the left side of The Pit. Climb straight up to a recess right of the
finger, step on to the nose and finish direct.

★ **89.   J.F.P.**   12m   E1   5b   (1989)
Start two metres right of the groove and climb the wall, then continue up a
short, left-leaning groove (peg at top). Finish up the wall above.

★ **90.   Top Out**   12m   E2   5c   (1989)
Start two metres to the right and climb the wall past a stump to a peg just
above the horizontal break. Gain the niche above, then move left to a sling,
continue to small niche above and finish up the top wall. Care is needed at the
very top.

91.   Red Animals   12m   E2   5b   (84)   (1985)
Start one metre right at a niche and climb straight up to a bolt, then continue
past two shallow caves.

★ **92. Puppeteer** 12m E2 5c   (1989)
Start one metre to the right, where the ground begins to fall away. Climb the
steep wall to broken horizontal ledges at five metres, then continue right of a
borehole to the top.

93. Never Mind the Bullocks 12m HVS 5a   (1987)
Start directly below the top of the groove that bounds The Pit on its right.
Climb the awkward wall to a peg below an overlap, then continue to a footledge
and finish up the groove itself.

94. Mother Earth 12m E2 5b   (1987)
Where the ground level begins to rise, climb into a sandy corner, then follow
the leftward-slanting corner crack (dirty) to the top.

The Vaults
*At the right-hand side of The Pit, the bank rises and the height decreases. The
remainder of the crag right of this is known as The Vaults.*

★ **95. The Puppet** 12m VS 4c   (1989)
From the right-hand side of the pit at a slightly higher level where the bank
starts to rise, climb large ledges to a shelf and traverse left to the arête. Finish
up a prominent, short, V-groove. Exposed.

96. Marionette 10m HS 4b   (1989)
Start just to the right. Climb via a slot to the ledge and go straight up steep
broken wall.

97. No Strings 9m S 4a   (1989)
Follow the left-leading, open groove at the top of the bank via several ledges.
Exit left at the top.

★ **98. Punch** 10m HS 4b   (1989)
Three metres to the right is a short, inverted, triangular slab. Climb the left edge
of this to a large ledge on the arête. Finish up a short groove.

99. Judy 9m VS 4c   (1989)
Climb the centre of the slab, then straight over the overhang to the top.

100. Sandy 9m VS 4c   (1989)
Start three metres farther right and climb a short wall to a sandy ledge, then
escape leftwards and finish up Judy.

*The next few routes are on excellent rock, but they all finish on a large cleaned
ledge from which escape is difficult. Therefore, it is wise to hang a belay rope
down to the ledge before climbing any of them.*

101. Good Friday 9m VS 4b   (1990)
Bridge up the obvious corner at the left end of the wall and exit right on to the
belay ledge.

★ **102. Mother's Day** 6m HVS 5a   (1990)
Start at the left end of the wall and climb to a peg on the arête. Continue to an
interesting mantel on to the ledge.

⋆ **103. Easy Club** 6m HVS 5c   (1990)
Start two metres to the right and climb bulging ledges. Continue past a peg
using a finger-flake to the top.

104. Peggy Day 6m HVS 5b   (1990)
Start two metres to the right, behind a tree stump. Climb the lower wall to a
jutting triangular ledge, then go straight up past a peg on the right.

105. Strangeways 6m VS 5a   (1990)
Climb the open corner, then step right at the top to finish.

The next climbs start on the front face at a lower level.

106. Flat as a Fluke 8m HVS 5a   (1990)
Boulder over rounded ledges at the left end of the wall to a large ledge and
finish up the left side of an arête.

107. Has Pete Had His Supper? 8m VS 4c   (1990)
Start one metre to the right. Climb large ledges to below a steeper crack, which
is climbed moving right.

*Some more climbs have been done to the right, but they would need much more
cleaning and are possibly unstable.*

⋆ **108. After Eight** 50m HVS 5a,5a   (1990)
A right-to-left, high-level girdle of The Vaults and The Pit, giving good
climbing and exciting situations, especially in the dark as on the first ascent.
1. 35m. Follow Flat as a Fluke to a ledge at three metres, then traverse to the
corner and cross the wall at the level of the pegs to the arête. Move round and
traverse to the ledge and niche on Punch (thread). Committing moves around the
arête and overhanging wall lead to a belay on No Strings.
2. 15m. Traverse left to the V-groove of Puppet, move round the arête to
gain the corner and an obvious ledge (peg on left). Continue at the same height
past a threaded peg, then make an ascending hand-traverse to reach Pinnochio's
nose. Finish up that route.

⋆ **109. From Here to There to You** 50m 5a   (1990)
A low-level traverse from the start of Pinnochio rightwards across The Pit. At
the right end (Mother Earth) move up and climb the first two metres of The
Puppet, then continue round The Vaults, going low at the arête of Punch, then
follow a lower traverse line on the front wall into Strangeways. Finish at the
next arête, continue into brambles, or better still reverse Pinnochio.

*There is also some easier bouldering on two other buttresses in the field directly
in front of The Pit:*

Curry Slabs – *sunny, west-facing slabs down to the right of the main crag –
about eight problems up to 5a.*
Pool Buttress – *hidden east-facing buttress and flanking slabs opposite Curry
Slabs towards the pool from the main crag – about sixteen problems up to 5a.*

First Ascents at Craig y Longridge

1983 Feb	**Jacob's Ladder** Andrew Gridley	
1984 Apr	**New Stone Age** Steve Sharples	
1984 Apr	**Neolithic Technology, Dyno ... Bucket, Company of Wolves** Andrew Gridley	
1984 Apr	**Central Icefall Direct, Slug the Thug, The Howling** Paul Pritchard	
1985 Feb 17	**Wobblebottom** Paul Pritchard	
1985 Feb 17	**Semen Scream** Phil Kelly	
1985 Feb	**Anal Cave-In, Ascent of Man** Paul Pritchard	
1985 Feb	**Spah's Daehniks** Andrew Gridley	
1985 Mar	**Bwink Bwink Bonk, Shap's Master Flasher, Red Animals** Andrew Gridley, Tim Gridley	
1985 Mar	**Descent of Man** Andrew Gridley	
1985 May	**Thug** John Marsden	
1985 May	**Timothy's Route** Tim Gridley	
1985 June 23	**Waiting in the Wings** Will Steel	
1985 June 23	**Muscles in their Imagination** Phil Kelly	
1985 June	**Muddy Wobbleblock** Andrew Gridley	
1985 July	**Smeg City** Greg Rimmer	
1985 July	**Snail Trail**	
1985 July	**Hitting the Wall, Mad Aardvark's Tea Party** Andrew Gridley	
1985 July	**Haardvark, Pump 'til you Jump**	
1985 Aug	**Session's End, Blatantly Slimy Slug, Gorse Bush, Weir Aardvark, Bramble Ramble, Escalator, Orifice of Faeces** Andrew Gridley	
1985 Aug	**Scorched August** Rob Smitton	
1985	**The Race, Paul Pritchard's Jacket, Thirty Feet of Pain, Runaway** Paul Pritchard	
1985 Aug	*Dissenting*, **From Ape to Aardvark**	
1985 Sep	**Seven-A** Steve Sharples	
1985 Sep	*Bomb Squad* Andrew Gridley	
1985 Oct 22	**Black Jake** Rob Smitton	
1985 Oct 23	**Babylon Blitz** Rob Smitton	
1985	**Some Friend**	
1986	**Tarot Plane** Phil Kelly	
1986	**Cruel Country, Still Raining, Still Dreaming, Grow Wings, Bend of the Rainbow** Rob Smitton	
1986 May	**Imitation Arapiles, Like a Slug but Sucks, Fertile Delta** Mark Leach	
1986 May	**Going Deaf for a Living, Added Incentive** Steve Sharples	
1986 July	**Push to Prolapse, Porridge Gun** Paul Pritchard	
1986 July	**Unknown Arête, Headline** Steve Sharples	
1986 Aug	**Unnamed** Steve Sharples	
1986 Aug	**The Gauntlet** Pete Black	
1986	**Big Marine** Mick Lovatt	
1986 Nov	**Unnatural Selection** Andrew Gridley	
1986-87	**Missing Link** Pete Black	
1986-87	**Pudding, Pie, Late Pickings, Year of the Rabbit** John Proud	
1986-87	**Absolute Beginners** Graeme Railton	
1986-87	**Stoning a Leper, Pay the Witch** Nick Wilkinson	
1986-87	**Rifted Victim** Nick Beard	
1986-87	**Gruts, In Excess, Naked Lunch, Twelve Dreams, Rug Thug, And She Was** Rob Smitton	
1986-87	**Moschops** Paul Pritchard	
1987 May	**Mr. Skin** Rob Smitton	
1987 June	**Never Mind the Bullocks, Mother Earth** Simon Nevett	
1987 June	**Renal Failure** Paul Pritchard	
1987 June	**Eat 'em and Smile** Malc Haslam	
1989 Mar	**Puppeteer** Pete Thursfield, John Proud	
1989 Mar	**The Puppet** John Proud, Doreen Rayner	
1989 Sep	**Pinnochio** John Proud, Doreen Rayner, Mike Hodson	
1989 Sep	**J.F.P.** Tim Gridley, John Proud	

1989 Sep	**Marionette** John Proud, Pete Dobson	
1989 Sep	**No Strings** John Proud, Doreen Rayner	
1989 Sep	**Sandy** John Proud, Martin Jones	
1989 Oct	**Out of Step** John Proud, Doreen Rayner	
1989 Oct	**Punch, Judy** John Proud, Martin Jones	
1989 Oct	**Top Out** Steve Sharples, Tim Gridley	
1990 Mar	**Mother's Day** John Proud, Simon Nevett	
1990 Mar	**Flat as a Fluke, Has Pete Had His Supper?** John Proud, Martin Jones	
1990 May	**Easy Club** Pete Dobson, John Proud	
1990 May	**Peggy Day** John Proud, Martin Jones	
1990 May	**Strangeways** John Proud, Mike Hodson	
1990 Sep	**After Eight** Pete Dobson, John Proud (alts)	
1990	**Way Out, From Here to There to You** John Proud	
1990	**Good Friday** John Proud, Martin Jones	
1991	**Chocolate Popsicle** Andrew Griffith	
1995	**Kiss the Razor's Edge** Olly Ellsworth	
1995 July 3	**Pop Tart** Andrew Griffith	
1996	**The Motion Vector** Pete Black	
1997	**Kiss the Razor's Edge** Extended by Ian Thorns	

Thorn Crag
O.S. ref.   SD 596 571

Please read the Access section before visiting Thorn Crag

Situation and Character

This pleasant little esoteric crag is situated in some of Lancashire's most inspiring yet bleak landscape, above the village of Tarnbrook, to the east of the Trough of Bowland road. It lies about five kilometres north-west of the summit of the Trough road and 12 kilometres west-south-west of Lancaster.

The crag offers some first-class bouldering and some longer climbs of all grades – all on excellent rock.

History

The first climbers to visit the crag were probably Alan Atkinson and his friends from Blackpool in the 1950s, who would tramp the surrounding moors on most weekends, often walking up the Trough of Bowland with huge rucksacks full to the brim with beer, to doss in the shooting hut below the crag. It was Thorn Crag that introduced Atkinson and his friends to climbing and they would happily swarm all over the crag in blissful ignorance of climbing in other areas, and in fact when they did widen their horizons, it soon became apparent that they had been climbing routes that were a good match, in terms of difficulty, to routes in other areas. The friends still continued to trek the moors together though they soon began to realize that it was easier on both body and soul on a Sunday morning to go climbing on the crag than to trudge the moors all day with a thick head.

The modern wave of developments began in 1985 when Andrew Gridley and Paul Pritchard discovered a small boulder-field on the side of the moor. On closer examination, it turned out to be two tiers of perfect natural gritstone attaining a maximum height which initial appearances from the road could not suggest. Both climbers were surprised to discover an ancient and rusting peg in the route now known as *Prior Visit*, and they realized that they were not the first to discover the crag.

Honours between Pritchard and Gridley were even, though most routes were bound to have been done before. Two of Pritchard's routes (*Epée Edge* and *Kissing the Pink*) were undoubtedly first ascents, as was Gridley's ascent of the off-width roof crack *Air Aardvark*.

As news of the crag spread, Owain Jones and Steve Edmondson paid a visit, and stayed the weekend, sleeping under the crag. Jones made the second ascent of *Kissing the Pink* and went on to claim a route that Pritchard and Gridley had managed to evade; the awesome-looking off-width crack on the right-hand side of the upper tier – *Grimly Fiendish* was billed as 'like Goliath but with runners' and looks excellent, as does the crack to its left, *New Rose*, which Jones climbed and Edmondson repeated immediately after.

Dave Cronshaw and John Ryden made the effort one winter's day and trudged up to the crag to see what all the fuss was about. They were pleasantly surprised at what they found, but even more surprised when Gridley appeared through the mist and rain to 'keep an eye on' the raiders. The two sides joined together for Cronshaw to lead *The Fireman's Slippery Pole,* before a swift retreat to the pub.

As well as Martin Dale's bold solo ascent of *Raging Horn* in 1991, the crag was further shocked to receive Dave Pegg four years later, who couldn't resist *The Last Temptation*, to give the boldest lead in Bowland.

Approach

Thorn Crag lies at the crest of the fell which can be seen east of the Trough to the right of the Trough of Bowland road. To reach it by car when travelling from Dunsop Bridge, follow the road towards Lancaster which passes the Trough of Bowland Quarry and continue along it for a further five or six kilometres until, on a sharp left-hand bend it is possible to turn right into a cul-de-sac leading to the sleepy hamlet of Tarnbrook. Follow this road to the hamlet, and park on its fringes with consideration for the small community.

The crag can be seen on the left skyline, but a direct approach is amazingly difficult and so the approach gains height more easily by heading well past the crag and then turning back. From the entrance gate to the access land at the edge of the hamlet, follow the track for about three kilometres to a small shooters' parking space. From this point, an old pony track leads back westwards towards the crag. Keep as high as possible and then scramble directly up to the foot of the Lower Crag. Allow about at least an hour.

Access

The crag is on the Grosvenor Estate, through which there are access paths, but no general access. However, climbing is permitted outside of the nesting season (April 1st to June 15th), provided that there are no general access restrictions in force, either because of shooting in the area, or because there is a high fire risk. In either event, this will be indicated clearly at the entrance gate to the access area.

During the permitted climbing period, the Estate's only two requirements are that dogs should under no circumstances be taken on to the access land and, if you know in advance that you intend to climb at the crag, they would be grateful if you could phone them at 01524 791339.

The Climbs

The routes are described from LEFT to RIGHT.

Upper Tier

The Upper Tier comprises two fine buttress separated by a short wall.

1. Pelvic Thrust 10m S 4a (1986-87)
Start three metres to the left of the central crack of the first buttress. Climb up trending leftwards then finish direct.

2. Raging Horn 10m E4 6a (1991)
From the foot of Pelvic Thrust step up and right on to the wall and climb directly up the shallow depression above. Side runners in Pelvic Thrust would reduce the grade to E3.

★★ **3. The Fireman's Slippery Pole** 11m HVS 5a (1986)
Climb the central crack direct. A deceptive climb, which is more strenuous and sustained than it appears.

★ **4. Kissing the Pink** 9m E4 5c (1986-87)
Probably the best natural gritstone arête in Lancashire. The moves are not particularly hard, but are unprotected and slightly overhanging, with a long reach to the square-cut top reserved for the moment that you least appreciate it. Couple this with a slight grittiness which tends to make for sudden foot slippage and you have a compact little adventure, be careful but enjoy. Start at a higher level and climb the right arête of the first buttress on its right side.

5. Toro Toro Aardvark 8m HVS 5a (1986-87)
The small wall between the two main buttresses is split by two flake cracks. The left-hand one has not been climbed. This route follows the right-hand crack direct.

★★ **6. The Last Temptation** 11m E6 6c (1995)
The impressive leaning crack that splits the left wall of the second buttress. It would become a classic gritstone test-piece if it were on Froggatt.

★★ **7. Grimly Fiendish** 10m E2 5c (1986-87)
The wide overhanging crack that splits the front face of the right-hand buttress proves an unforgettable experience.

★ **8. New Rose** 10m E1 5c (1986-87)
Climb the crack right of Grimly Fiendish to the capping roof, then pull left over this to gain the top.

Boulder Valley

Farther right is a mass of boulders within which are some good problems. Walking into the boulders by the obvious path finds a crescent crack with some 'buttonholes' above, which gives **Button Moon** *(5c). Immediately left of this is* **Pinch 'n' Pull** *(5a), whilst the small overhang opposite is taken by* **Flying Pleb** *(5a).*

Lower Tier

The Lower Tier is more broken but it has some good climbs. It starts almost directly below the left-hand buttress of the Upper Tier.

★ **9.   The Fallen Madonna with the Big Boobies** 9m E1   5b   (1986-87)
Climb the left arête of the first solid buttress.

10.   Prior Visit 9m VS   4c   (1985)
Two metres right of The Fallen Madonna is a right-slanting crackline containing an ancient peg below an overlap. Take this direct.

★ **11.   Long Shore Drift** 9m E2   5c   (1986-87)
Climb the short wall immediately to the right and finish at Termination.

12.   Termination 9m S   4b   (1986-87)
Climb the next groove on the right by a pleasant crack.

13.   Left of Centre 9m E2   5c   (1993)
Start at the bottom right of the next buttress and step left using a pocket (crux) to a downward-pointing flake. Follow this to the top.

Lower Slab

The next three climbs lie on the slab directly below Termination.

14.   Look No Hands 6m S   4c   (1986-87)
The obvious crack up the front of the buttress.

15.   Lower Slab Direct 6m HVS   5b   (1987)
Climb the centre of the buttress.

16.   Banana Land 6m D   (1985)
Climb the easy right arête.

Thin Buttress

This is the slim buttress that lies about 10 metres farther right and at the same level as the rest of the Lower Tier.

★★ **17.   Epée Edge** 8m E4   5c   (1985)
Start in the centre of the wall and gain a shallow depression, then finish up the left arête past small overlaps.

★ **18.   Aardvarks don't Dyno** 8m E1   5b   (1985)
The right arête proves harder than it looks.

Overhang Buttress

*About 20 metres farther right at a higher level, the crag gives its last fling at an obvious overhang. The crack in the roof gives an interesting problem, **Air Aardvark** (6a), and farther right the buttress increases in height to provide one last route.*

★ **19. Ride a Wild Aardvark** 8m HVS 5a (1985)
Start up a stepped groove, then either move left and finish up the arête, or finish up the shallow corner above.

First Ascents at Thorn Crag

1985	**Prior Visit** Named by Paul Pritchard and Andrew Gridley
1985	**Banana Land** Sheila Elliott (solo)
1985	**Epée Edge, Aardvarks don't Dyno** Paul Pritchard (solo)
1985	**Air Aardvark** Andrew Gridley, Paul Pritchard
1985	**Ride a Wild Aardvark** Andrew Gridley
1986 Oct 26	**The Fireman's Slippery Pole** Dave Cronshaw, John Ryden, Andrew Gridley
1986-87	**Pelvic Thrust** Paul Pritchard
1986-87	**Kissing the Pink, The Fallen Madonna with the Big Boobies, Long Shore Drift** Paul Pritchard (solo)
1986-87	**Toro Toro Aardvark, Termination** Andrew Gridley (solo)
1986-87	**Grimly Fiendish, New Rose** Owain Jones
1986-87	**Pinch 'n' Pull, Flying Pleb, Look No Hands** Andrew Gridley
1986-87	**Button Moon**
1987	**Lower Slab Direct**
1991 May 29	**Raging Horn** Martin Dale (solo)
1993 Apr 28	**Left of Centre** Brian Davison, Rick Richardson
1995	**The Last Temptation** Dave Pegg

Trough of Bowland Quarry   O.S. ref.   SD 628 519

Situation and Character

The quarry faces roughly south-west and gets plenty of sun, so most of the rock dries quickly apart from one or two seepage lines and after prolonged rain there is some drainage from the hillside above. The right side of the crag has a large number of trees and the routes are generally dirtier and slower to dry. The crag is limestone of quite a compact nature, but with a number of detached blocks. Good protection is often hard to find. The climbing is generally of a balancy nature, with a predominance of sloping holds; the routes are often steeper than they appear from below, which can be quite disconcerting at first.

History

Though easily accessible, the quarry is only briefly seen from the road which may explain its relatively slow development. The initial lines, including *Bowland Wall, Owl Wall* and the *Girdle* were climbed by Jim Ingham Riley and friends during a couple of visits in 1966. Riley recalls coming face to face with an owl near the top of Owl Wall. Whilst checking the routes for the first Lancashire guide, Ian Cowell missed the line of *Bowland Wall* and found himself on what is now *Guillotine*, the name resulting from a potentially nasty rockfall which sliced his rope in two. The route was then completed by Les Ainsworth. That was the state of play until 1977 when Roger and Glenn Brookes added *Owl Stretching Time* and *Deceptive Bends* (then described in two pitches with a belay on Owl Ledge). In 1980 Roger added *Captain Beaky.*

Above: Johnathan Westaway bouldering at Hutton Roof.   *Photo: Jon Sparks*
Below: Adam Richardson micro-crimps **The Atom Rush** (5c), Cadshaw Small Quarry.
Photo: Geoff Hibbert

Access and Approach

The quarry belongs to North West Water, whose managers are willing to permit climbing at the crag, provided that climbers respect the site for its high botanical interest and also that they leave no litter.

The quarry lies above the road through the Trough of Bowland from Dunsop Bridge, one kilometre north of Sykes Farm. There is good parking by the small waterworks directly below the crag, though the crag is actually hidden from view here. The simplest approach is to walk a short way up the road to where it crosses the stream. A gate gives access to an obvious track which leads directly to the crag in only a few minutes.

The Climbs

The climbs are described from LEFT to RIGHT.

1.   Left Edge 10m   VD   (1966)
Several lines are possible, all of which lead to a finish entirely composed of loose blocks. If undeterred, the best start is probably by the left-facing slab starting below a large tree.

Just past this is a small but very steep diamond-shaped wall which gives an interesting but somewhat fragile problem.

★ **2.   Owl Stretching Time** 18m   VS   4c   (1977)
Follow the rib right of the steep wall to a large ledge on the left (belay possible, but rather pointless). Move up awkwardly just left of a large projecting block and then go straight up the wall above on good jugs to twin trees. Pleasant but over all too soon.

★ **3.   Bowland Wall** 24m   HS   4b   (1966)
Start just right again. Climb up and slightly left, then move left to the large grass ledge. The large ramp on the right is both awkward and bold to start; follow it to broken ledges and finish diagonally up the fine wall to the leftmost of the large trees.

★ **4.   The Guillotine** 21m   VS   4b   (1967)
Start as for Bowland Wall but move awkwardly right just before the large ledge, past blocks to gain the lower parallel ramp. Follow this boldly to its end then move up to the broken ledges on Bowland Wall. Continue straight up the wall using a right-slanting crack.

★ **5.   Captain Beaky** 20m   E1   5a   (1980)
A very direct line up the highest part of the crag. Start just right of Bowland Wall at a short left-facing corner; climb this and continue up the steep black wall (bold) to finish as for Guillotine.

6.   Owl Wall 23m   HS   4b   (1966)
Climb the short corner as for Captain Beaky then follow the narrow slab/ramp to a ledge with several trees (Owl's Nest Ledge). Climb the wall behind and move slightly right to another tree. Or, (easier and often drier) move right and

Ian Vickers is The Milky Bar Kid on **Bend of The Rainbow** (6b), Craig y Longridge.
Photo: Dave Cronshaw

climb an obvious break to the tree, as for Owl's Nest Direct. Finish leftwards to the large trees, the last couple of metres being quite loose.

★★ 7. Deceptive Bends 21m HVS 5a (1977)
Start a little to the right below a white crystalline wall. Move up on to this and climb diagonally right to cross Owl Wall, just left of Owl's Nest Ledge. Climb the wall above, trending slightly left then go straight up to the trees; the best route on the crag.

8. Owlet 9m HS 4b (1975-79)
Climb directly up to Owl's Nest Ledge.

9. Owl's Nest Direct 20m HS 4b (1967)
A wide and rather dirty crack runs up to the right end of Owl's Nest Ledge. Follow this then step right and go up an obvious break to the higher tree, and finish as for Owl Wall.

10. Primrose Route 18m VD (1966)
Very dirty and not recommended. The original first pitch took the large easy-angled slab (or hanging garden!) to the large tree, but a more direct approach is probably better. From the tree, climb up to a ledge and swing left to a deep groove. Go up this and finish up the left edge of a broken slab.

11. Original Route 9m M (1966)
High up the slope on the right, climb the right side of a block left of the last area of rock, then go up the centre of the wall above, passing a small tree.

12. Girdle Traverse 46m S 4a,4a (1966)
1. 21 m. Climb Original Route to the top of the block, then descend the left side of the block to a tree. Up easily as for Primrose Route for a couple of metres until a traverse can be made to Owl's Nest Ledge.
2. 25 m. Descend Owl Wall until just above the foot of the ramp. A traverse can then be made to join Bowland Wall; follow this to the large grass ledge then continue leftwards to finish up Left Edge (after reading the warning in that route's description).
★ 2a. 17 m. **Variation** (VS, 4c): from Owl's Nest Ledge step up then diagonally left to gain the ledges on Bowland Wall. Reverse this until just above the large protruding block. Step left onto the block and finish as for Owl Stretching Time. There is hardly any independent climbing and the girdle is less complete, but it is higher, better and safer.

First Ascents at Trough of Bowland Quarry

1966   **Left Edge, Bowland Wall, Owl Wall, Primrose Route, Original Route, Girdle Traverse**   Jim Ingham Riley, Don Hopkin, Tom Meredith
1967   **The Guillotine, Owl's Nest Direct**   Les Ainsworth, Paul Hamer
1977 May 27   **Deceptive Bends**   Roger Brookes
1977 May 27   **Owl Stretching Time**   Roger Brookes, Glenn Brookes
1975-79   **Owlet**
1980 Aug   **Captain Beaky**   Roger Brookes, Paul Clarke

Witches' Quarry

Please read the Access section before visiting Witches' Quarry

Situation and Character

The quarry is situated at Lower Gate, about seven kilometres north-east of Clitheroe and nearly three kilometres past the village of Downham. It is generally of reasonable quality limestone, with very little loose rock, though in some short sections low down, it can have a crumbly skin. The climbs give a good variety of routes, but most of them lie between about Severe and E2. It should be noted that whilst most of the climbs are gradually becoming cleaner, there is still a little loose rock and some of the pegs are very old.

Belays at the top are on special belay stakes and it is important that climbers should avoid trampling the meadow at the top, by keeping close to the edge of the quarry and descending via one of the stiles at either end.

The crag gets its name from climbers who suggested that it was the quarry referred to in '*The Lancashire Witches*' by Harrison Ainsworth. In this book a witch who was chased over the quarry, saved herself by turning into a cat. However, climbers are still advised to put more faith in their runners.

History

Climbing at Witches' Quarry probably began around the early 1960s, but the early history is very vague. Certainly, *Beelzebub, Broomstick, Thrutch* and several other of the easier routes had been climbed by the mid-Sixties by Geoff Fishlock, as had *Peel Off,* though this route used an aid peg which was eliminated in 1970 by Malc Haslam. Malc's brother Mike also climbed *Witch Bane,* though he originally called it *Central Wall.*

Next on the scene were Les Ainsworth and Dave Cronshaw who added *Hemlock, Cauldron Crack, Coven Crack* and *Halloween Outing* during their first visit in 1971. On the same day Fishlock led *Alice, Elizabeth* and *Jennet.* On their next visit Ainsworth and Cronshaw started up the then mossy wall left of *Beelzebub* and were finding it rather hard to remove the moss whilst climbing until they found the key hold, previously hidden by a dead shrew. A few minutes later a new *Shrew* appeared at Witches'. Ainsworth followed this up with *Abbot Paslew* and then it started to rain and so Ainsworth consoled himself with a slippery ascent of *Nance.* However, before that, Fishlock managed to snatch *Cracklap* and *Witches' Brew,* whilst Rob Meakin and Bob MacMillan did *Familiar's Fall* and got part way along the second pitch of the traverse of the Central Wall. Next weekend the weather was kinder to Meakin and MacMillan and they made further headway on their traverse. However, after three falls at the same point, Rob threw in the towel and let Cronshaw finish *Sorcerer's Apprentice.* Meakin then made up for his failure by doing the second ascent of Sorcerer's Apprentice and leading *The Spell.* Ainsworth then added *Black Mass* and the day ended with some soloed routes on the Downham Walls.

The Lancashire guide of 1975 contained all the routes known at the time, and helped to give the crag the attention that it deserved. Ron Fawcett paid a visit and free-climbed *The Reeve* and *Prayer To Absent Friends* then Al Evans discovered the popular free version to *Witchcraft.* Evans also repeated Fawcett's climbs thinking them to be first ascents. In 1975/76 Gordon Fishlock, Pete

Black and Ronnie Marsden climbed *Witch Way* and *Black's Magic*, as well as *Witch Arête* and *Witchcraft Crack* with John Wilmott and Ron Valovin respectively.

Nothing further was done until 1978 when Dave Kenyon took over the explorations, starting with *Tarot Wall* and working through the obvious lines and not so obvious eliminates, to add almost thirty routes including *Witchfire at Lammas, Waxen Doll, Brimstone, The Dark One, Ducking Chair* and *Black Orchid*. The only other people to get any sort of a look in over this period were Dave Cronshaw who discovered *Satan's Slave*, Gordon Lancaster who climbed *First Impressions,* and Jerry Peel with *The Nameless One*.

After the loss of access to the quarry in the early eighties, all further developments at the quarry ceased and the next significant event in the quarry's climbing history was the successful outcome of access negotiations between the BMC, led by Ainsworth and John Belbin, and the owners. Local climbers then rallied round and undertook the hard work that was necessary to regain access, such as the erection of stiles and surfacing of the entry track. Prominent in this work were members of the Clitheroe and the Craven Mountaineering Clubs and other locals, spearheaded by Ainsworth, Belbin, Cronshaw, Paul Horan, Godfrey Metcalf, Rob Smitton and Shaun Stephens. During these clean-up operations and the subsequent guidebook checking, a few remaining gaps were identified. The first of these was *Any Witch Way but Lucifer* by Horan, in early 1998. Soon afterwards, Cronshaw straightened out and improved The Spell to give *Spellbound*, which was repeated within minutes by Smitton. It was repeated again three days later, by Horan who was later told that it had already been done. However, the day was not wasted, as Horan went on to climb the intriguingly named *It Started with a Kiss*. Finally, on the last day of the extended deadline for this guide, Paul Smitton noticed another gap, whilst he was climbing Cracklap and squeezed in the surprisingly independent *Hell Hounds on My Trail*.

Approach

This quarry lies east of Downham and just north of Pendle Hill. To reach the quarry from Downham, (when coming from Chatburn), take the road which bears left immediately after the Assheton Arms, and follow this for about three kilometres. At the top of a steep hill the quarry can be seen on the right, a few metres from the road. Cars should be driven into the field below the quarry, through the gate just above an old lime kiln. For drivers approaching or departing via Downham, it will first be necessary to drive to the top of the hill and then turn round.

Access

Many climbers will remember that climbing has not been permitted at Witches' Quarry for several years. This was not due to either the intransigence of the owner, or bad behaviour from climbers, but merely reflects some rather unique local factors. The present landowners and tenant have a very positive attitude towards climbers but, nevertheless, they wish to ensure that climbing does not introduce additional problems for them. This is a very reasonable concern and so all climbers who visit the crag are asked to ensure that our sport and enjoyment is conducted in a way that takes proper account of their concerns.

The main objective of the access arrangements is to ensure that climbing can take place as a background activity that does not attract non-climbers into the quarry. Previously, problems have been caused by motorists picnicking in the quarry and by roadside parking causing traffic jams. Much of this can be avoided if climbers drive into the quarry and leave their cars where they are not visible from the road. In addition to the normal requirements for climbers to leave no litter and to behave with full consideration for others, climbers are asked to keep to the following five guidelines:

(1)   Cars should be driven into the quarry, out of sight from the road (it is essential to close the gate afterwards) and there should be absolutely no parking on the lane. If the track into the quarry is not drivable, it is essential that climbers either go elsewhere, or park at the layby at the foot of the hill.

(2)   Parking is limited to six cars. If there are more when you arrive, please accept this and go elsewhere for the day. This is important, because whilst the owners recognize the importance of the quarry to climbers they do not want the quarry to become a picnic site. If necessary, please show any non-climbers these notes and politely ask them to leave.

(3)   The meadow directly above the quarry is an important ecological and economic asset. Therefore, please use the belay stakes that are provided and keep close to the quarry edge when descending. It is particularly important that the grass away from the quarry edge should not be trampled between May and the end of July.

(4)   Dogs must not be taken to the quarry.

(5)   No fires should be lit in the quarry.

The Climbs
The climbs are described from LEFT to RIGHT, starting at a short, detached buttress at the extreme left. **DESCENTS** are via stiles at either end of the quarry.

1.   Hrothgar 8m VS 4c   (1979-83)
From the foot of the right arête, climb up to and follow an obvious line of holds leading left for two metres, then finish direct.

2.   Avenging Angel of Death 8m HVS 5b   (1978)
Follow the right arête.

Twiston Walls
The first part of the main quarry wall stretches rightwards, gradually increasing in height to the right side of an obvious long, horizontal overhang near the top of the crag. The most prominent feature of the wall is the deep, overhung, corner crack of **Beelzebub***, which is about halfway along the Twiston Walls.*

3.   Belladonna 9m VD   (1979-83)
Climb a curving crack at the left side of the main crag, to a large ledge. Finish up the right-hand of the two cracks above.

4.   Farrak   9m   HVS   5a   (1979-83)
Climb the wall just to the right, using a short, deep crack at four metres to gain
a ledge. Climb the wall above via a thin crack, moving right to a stump at the
top.

★★ **5.   Broomstick**   9m   VS   5a   (1968)
A classic, lower-grade limestone crack climb, but beware of the reachy last
move. Four metres from the left end of the main wall is an obvious wide crack
that trends slightly rightwards. Follow this to its top.

6.   Problem Child   10m   E1   5b   (1998)
A direct line up the pocketed, bulging wall between Broomstick and The Omen.
A long reach is helpful.

7.   The Omen   10m   HVS   5a   (1978)
Climb the centre of the wall two metres to the right of Broomstick to a shallow
groove. Follow this to a ledge on the right, step back left and climb the wall
above directly to the top (runner in Broomstick).

8.   Alice   9m   S   4a   (1971)
The wide crack right of Broomstick, behind a protecting leaf of rock.

9.   Elizabeth   10m   VD   (1971)
Just right is another flake; climb this, then finish as for Alice.

10.   Seven Years After   10m   HVS   5b   (1980)
Climb the bulge immediately to the right, then continue directly up the wall
above.

11.   Jennet   12m   S   4a   (1971)
Climb the wall and short flake crack on the right, then finish direct.

12.   Coven Crack   12m   HS   4b   (1971)
Two metres to the right is a shallow cave at ground level. Climb the flake crack
above this, then step left and finish as for Jennet.

13.   Hemlock   15m   S   4a   (1971)
A direct line from the right side of the cave. Avoid the large overhang by the
flake crack on its left, then finish direct. The overhang can also be taken direct
at 5b.

14.   Cauldron Crack   14m   S   4a   (1971)
Follow an obvious weakness one metre right, passing the large overhang on its
right.

15.   Sixth Finger   14m   VD   (1998)
Climb the groove one metre right then continue up and left to a tree belay.

★ **16.   The Shrew**   14m   VS   4b   (1971)
A good wall climb on holds that are not always obvious. Climb the blunt arête
two metres to the right, then move right to a ledge directly below an overlap.
Climb this by the flake crack at its right side and finish direct.

★ **17.   Warlock Wall**   14m   HVS   5b   (1973)
Climb the thin overhanging crack two metres to the right, to a ledge on The
Shrew. Move on to blocks on the right of the overhang and finish direct.

18.   Mist Over Witches'   14m   E2   5c   (1981)
Start one metre right and use undercuts to reach round the bulge to a short
crack, which can be used to reach a second crack. Step left above the bulge and
move up (bolt) then step right and reach round the overhang to better holds.
Surmount the overhang and finish as for Warlock Wall.

★ **19.   Beelzebub**   14m   VS   5a   (1968)
The obvious deep, overhung corner crack about 25 metres right of the left end
of the crag. It is best climbed facing left.

★ **20.   Witchfire at Lammas**   14m   HVS   5b   (1975-79)
Start just to the right and surmount the square-cut overhang to gain a small
ledge below a second roof. Climb this via a good flake hold, and continue up
the short wall above to a junction with Beelzebub.

21.   Abbot Paslew   14m   VS   4c   (1971)
Starting one metre right, climb to a small ledge at five metres, beneath a small
overhang. Go over this overhang and the one above to an easier finish.

22.   Halloween Outing   14m   S   4a   (1971)
On the right is a cracked wall. Climb the left-hand crack.

23.   Witches' Favourite   14m   HVS   5a   (1971)
Climb the cracks one metre right and continue in a direct line through the bulge
at the top.

24.   Witches' Brew   14m   HS   4b   (1979-83)
Climb the cracks of Witches' Favourite until it is possible to step right above an
overhang and finish up the wall above.

25.   The Flying Magician   14m   HVS   5b   (1979)
Climb the corner just right, to below an overhang. Surmount this to gain a ledge
on Witches' Brew and finish up that route.

★ **26.   Hell Hounds on My Trail**   14m   VS   4c   (1998)
Climb the blunt arête between Flying Magician and Cracklap without stepping
into either route. At the overhang step right across Cracklap and surmount the
overhang at its widest point. Finish boldly up the headwall, aiming for a
distinctive arch-shaped hold.

★ **27.   Cracklap**   14m   HS   4b   (1971)
Three metres to the right is a system of wide cracks trending left. Climb these.

28.   Darkness   15m   E2   5b   (1979-81)
Immediately to the right, a thin crack leads up to a bulge at two-thirds-height.
Follow this with difficult moves round the bulge to reach a small ledge (peg).
Continue direct.

★ 29.   Familiar's Fall   15m   HVS   5a   (1971)
The next obvious feature is a shallow corner leading to the left side of a large
overhang. Climb this corner, then layback the overhang to an easier finish.

30.   Satan's Slave   15m   E1   5b   (1978)
Starting three metres to the right, climb up to the centre of a long ledge. Gain
good holds below an overhang (peg), then make long reaches to climb the
overhang and the wall above to a ledge and short finishing groove.

★ 31.   It Started with a Kiss   15m   HVS   5b   (1998)
Start about one metre left of the memorial plaque. Make a difficult move round
the overlap and climb directly to a ledge. Continue up the groove to a fine open
finish up the crack on the left of Thrutch.

32.   Thrutch   15m   VS   4b   (1968)
Start directly above the memorial plaque and below the right side of the long
ledge and climb up to it. Continue up a groove and step right to finish up an
obvious clean, wide crack at the top.

Central Wall

*This is the steep continuation wall, where the crag is at its highest, which
continues to a vegetated gully (Central Gully) on its right. It is further identified
by the large, pointed boulder (The Magician's Hat) at its foot and provides
some of the best middle-grade climbing on the crag.*

★ 33.   The Spell   17m   HVS   5a   (1971)
A somewhat wandering line, but nevertheless, a worthwhile route. Climb the
steep wall two metres to the right of the memorial plaque to a small ledge on
the left. Move up, then step right in an exposed position, to gain a horizontal
break (peg on right). Finish direct.

★★ 34.   Spellbound   17m   HVS   5b   (1998)
Straightens out The Spell and gives more sustained climbing. Climb the cracked
wall to a ledge on the right, then continue up a thin crack to a small overlap.
Follow a short groove up left to the horizontal break (peg, out of sight) and
finish up the wall above on spaced holds.

★★ 35.   Waxen Doll   20m   E3   6a   (1979)
A well-protected climb with some surprising holds in hidden pockets. Start just
before a large pointed boulder on the ground (*The Magician's Hat*) and follow a
right-sloping ledge to the foot of an obvious groove. Ascend to a peg, then
move left and up past a second peg to a horizontal break (peg) and finish direct.

36.   Resurgent Spirit   17m   E4   6a   (1980)
From the first peg on Waxen Doll take a direct line to the top.

★★ 37.   Witch Bane   20m   HVS   5a   (1969)
At the bottom, the groove gives sustained and technical bridging and this is
followed by an entertaining flake finish that is easier than it looks. Follow the
right-sloping ledge as for Waxen Doll to the groove. Climb the groove to a
ledge on the right (*Malkin Ledge*), then step left and climb a flake crack,
finishing directly.

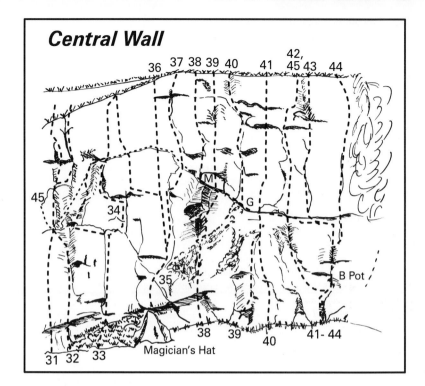

Central Wall

Magician's Hat

38.   Devil Worshipper   17m   E4   6a   (1980)
Starting two metres to the right of *The Magician's Hat,* climb easy, cleaned rock
to a short, capped groove immediately right of the groove on Witch Bane.
Climb this groove and the overhang above to a gangway on the right, then
follow this easily leftwards to *Malkin Ledge.* Climb the steep wall at the back of
this ledge by some intricate moves to a sapling at the top.

*Four metres to the right of The Magician's Hat is a wide crack. This has been
climbed, but is scrappy and not recommended.*

★★ **39.   Black Mass**   20m   HVS   5a,5b   (1971)
A satisfying climb on excellent rock. The difficulties increase with height,
although the final groove is not as hard as it first appears.
1.   11m.   Start five metres to the right of *The Magician's Hat,* immediately
right of the wide crack. Gain thin cracks in the arête, directly or from either
side, then follow these and the wall above to a peg belay on the ledge (*The
Gallery*). A much easier start is also possible on the left.
2.   9m.   Follow an easy gangway leftwards to *Malkin Ledge,* then finish up the
short, overhanging groove on the right.

★★ **40. Brimstone** 18m HVS 5a,5b (1978)
1. 10m. Two metres to the right of the arête there is a shallow, hanging groove. Climb the fine crack on the left side of this to a peg belay on the ledges above (*The Gallery*).
2. 8m. Step left and climb the wall above, surmounting a small overhang on good holds to finish direct.

41. Dark Secrets 18m E1 5b,5c (1980-81)
1. 10m. From a point three metres up Peel Off, step left into a groove, and follow this to *The Gallery* (peg belay).
2. 8m. A serious pitch. Continue up the blunt rib, immediately right of the peg, to below an obvious small roof. Pull over this roof then continue up the wall to finish. From the small roof an easier finish is possible by moving left then finishing up Brimstone.

★★ **42. Peel Off** 18m VS 4c (1970)
1. 10m. Start two metres to the left of the gully which limits Central Wall on the right. Gain a ledge at four metres (*The Boiling Pot*), then step up and hand-traverse left to *The Gallery* (peg belay).
2. 8m. Move back right past a rib and climb the flake crack, which proves easier than it looks, but is nevertheless very worthwhile.

★★ **43. Crucible** 18m E1 5b (1979-83)
Follow Peel Off to *The Boiling Pot*, then continue in a direct line to a ledge below a shallow groove. Climb the groove, using holds on the right wall, to a large ledge and an easy finish.

★★ **44. Cloven Hoof** 18m E1 5b (1978/1998)
A route of considerable character, with steep, sustained climbing and good protection where it matters. There is also a direct start up the fingery wall to the right. From *The Boiling Pot*, step right and follow an obvious line of pockets and cracks up the wall, to gain a slab and easier climbing to the top.
Direct Start (5b): climbs the pink wall on the right of Peel Off.

★★ **45. Sorcerer's Apprentice** 74m HVS 4a,5a,5a,4c (1971)
An entertaining traverse of the Twiston and Central Walls, with an interesting hand traverse on the third pitch.
1. 18m. Climb Broomstick until it is possible to traverse at mid-height to Alice. Continue in the same line to Cauldron Crack, move down and belay on the ledge below the overhang on Shrew.
2. 27m. Traverse awkwardly above the corner of Beelzebub, step down and follow the horizontal break across Cracklap and Familiar's Fall, to a belay at the right of the long ledge (on Thrutch).
3. 20m. From the ledge move up and right to the horizontal break. Hand-traverse right (peg) on good holds to *Malkin Ledge* and reverse the easy gangway of Black Mass to a peg belay on *The Gallery*.
4. 9m. Step right and finish up Peel Off.
Alternative Finish (5b): Continue the traverse to Cloven Hoof and then to finish up that route.

Sweet Dreams Buttress
This is the section of rock which stretches right from the Central Gully, and ends in a lower, dome-shaped, overhanging wall.

46.   Witch Arête   17m   VS   4c   (1975)
Just right of Central Gully is a short wall, capped by a bulge, at the left side of which is a thin crack. Climb this crack to gain the arête and after a short detour into the gully, follow this to a twin bolt belay on a large ledge at the top of the crag.
Alternative Start (4c): Climb the first crack right of the gully.

47.   The Necromancer   17m   HVS   5c   (1978)
Two metres to the right is a shallow scoop at three metres. Gain this directly and climb it to a ledge above. Surmount the bulge via a thin crack and a long reach to a good hold, and either finish direct, or (better) move left on to the arête and follow this to a twin-bolt belay on a ledge at the top of the crag.

★ **48.   Witch Way**   20m   VS   4c   (1976)
Separating the short wall and the overhanging face on the right is a slabby wall. Climb this to the right side of a slab, then traverse left in a good position to join Witch Arête and finish up this.

49.   Satanic Rite   9m   VS   5a   (1975-79)
At the left side of the small, dome-shaped buttress is an undercut groove capped by an overhang. Climb this groove, stepping left to surmount the overhang at the top.

50.   Sweet Dreams Left-Hand   10m   HVS   5c   (1980-81)
Starting at the centre of the dome-shaped buttress, climb directly to the top and a difficult finish.

★ **51.   Sweet Dreams**   10m   HVS   5b   (1972/1975-79)
This route takes the groove at the right side of the wall, with a deep niche near its foot. Follow the groove and continue directly up bulging rock to a good hold. Move right to finish.

52.   The Nameless One   8m   VS   5b   (1980-81)
Start two metres to the right and ascend the steep wall between Sweet Dreams and the edge of the buttress.

53.   Any Witch Way but Lucifer   18m   HS   5a   (1998)
Climb the wall and arête immediately right to the slab. Continue more easily up the right-hand groove system above to an exposed finish on the right above the left side of Witchcraft Buttress.
Variation Finish (5c): from the large niche near the top, follow a curving weakness rightwards in an exposed position to finish at the same place.

54.   Crossing the Line   11m   S   4a   (1998)
Climb the slab two metres farther right and follow the left-hand groove. Either step left and continue to the higher tree, or move right to finish up Lucifer.

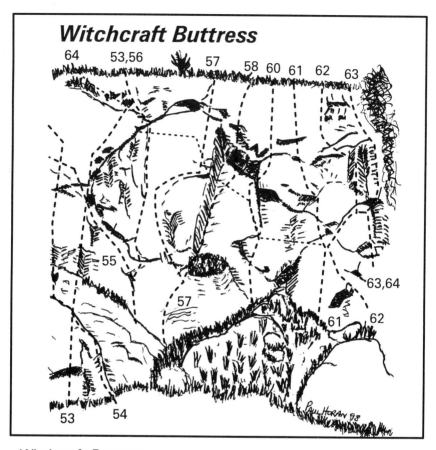

Witchcraft Buttress

Witchcraft Buttress

A fine steep buttress, offering some excellent climbing. It is identified by the large overhang which spans the top of the wall. The climbs are reached by short, easy scrambles.

55.   Witchcraft Crack   14m   HS   4b   (1976)
A poor climb which takes the obvious shattered crack at the left-hand side of Witchcraft Buttress.

56.   Witchcraft Left-Hand   14m   E1   5b   (1981)
An indifferent start leads to a short, but interesting finish. In the steep wall on the right is a thin crack. Gain the base of this crack from the left, then climb it and move up right to gain a good flake. Continue up the wall on good holds to finish.

★★ **57.   Witchcraft**   15m   E2   5b   (1972/1975)
Excellent wall climbing, with an awkward, but well-protected, traverse. Start two metres to the right and climb a short, bulging wall to a large square ledge on the right. Continue up the groove above the left side of the ledge, until it is possible to move up and right over a slight bulge. Step left to arrange some

nuts, then traverse back right on small holds to gain an arête and follow this to the top.

★★ 58. The Dark One 15m E3 5c   (1981)
Quite intimidating. After a bold start, protection improves for the more strenuous upper section. The big groove which runs from the right side of the ledge on Witchcraft to the left side of the large overhang. Climb the groove to a good hold at six metres (peg on left), move up (peg), then step right and follow a thin crack up to the overhang. Using undercuts, make a long reach and a bold move round to better holds and the top.

★ 59. Spelling 16m E3 6a   (1998)
An eliminate. Climb the arête to the right of The Dark One to a roof, then swing left on to Witchraft below a smaller roof. Reverse the traverse of Witchcraft, then finish up a steep, block-filled crack.

60. Prayer to Absent Friends 15m E1 5b   (1971/1975)
Bridge up the wide-angled corner four metres right of The Dark One to the roof. Pull up left into a short bottomless corner below a second roof and make a long reach right to a hidden jug, which enables a swing to be made on to the front face. Finish up a line of flake holds which are not always above suspicion.

★★ 61. The Ducking Chair 15m E3 6a   (1981)
The wall on the right has a niche at five metres containing a peg. Gain this directly (crux), and climb through the apex of the niche to a crack in the roof above. From the crack, reach up and left to small holds and use these to get established on the headwall, then make an easier finish.

★★ 62. Black Orchid 17m E2 5b   (1978)
Good technical climbing on steep rock. Well-protected at the bottom, but there is a poorly protected, thought-provoking finish. Using thin left-slanting cracks (peg), gain the niche on The Ducking Chair from the right (poor peg), then follow another crack back right to a ledge on the arête at the foot of a white groove. Climb this, then finish by moving up and left to gain a ledge just below the top. Serious in its latter stages.

63. Return of the Incubus 14m HVS 5a   (1979-83)
Climb the narrow wall to the right of the arête on the right edge of Witchcraft Buttress. Continue directly over an overhang, then finish up and slightly to the left.

★ 64. Hubble, Bubble, Toil and Trouble 30m E1 5b   (1981)
A right-to-left traverse across Witchcraft Buttress. Start as for Return of the Incubus and climb up to a ledge on the arête. Reverse the thin crack of Black Orchid into the niche (peg), and continue to the corner of Prayer to Absent Friends. Climb the corner to the second roof, then traverse left under it to gain a short arête by an awkward move. Step up and continue leftwards along the obvious line to finish.

Downham Walls

The remainder of the quarry, after a grassy break.

65. Baalbreth 10m HS 4a   (1981)
Climb up the extreme left edge of the wall.

★ **66. The Reeve** 9m VS 4c   (1969-71/1975)
The system of narrow cracks splitting the face to the right.

67. Satan 9m VS 5a   (1975-79)
Just right is a groove in the centre of the wall at its top. Climb a short wall to
gain the groove, then follow it to the top.

68. Walpurgis Eve 9m S 4a   (1974-75)(1998)
Climb the wall one metre right to a mantel, then continue direct.
Alternative Start (VS, 4c): climb the left side of the right arête all the way.

★★ **69. Serenity** 10m S 4a   (1971)
A worthwhile excursion for anyone climbing at this grade. From the mantel on
Walpurgis Eve, step right and move up to the higher of two ledges. Turn the
arête on its right and finish up the left edge of the slab. Twin-bolt belay.

70. Tibb 9m S 4a   (1971)
Just right, two grooves meet at half-height to form a Y. Climb the scrappy
left-hand groove to a twin-bolt belay.

71. Pendle Groove 10m HS 4a   (1971)
The right-hand groove.

72. Downham Racer 10m E2 5c   (1979)
Climb the steep wall just to the right, to a sloping shelf, and continue up a short
groove to a good ledge. The slabby wall just left of the arête provides a good
finish, taken more or less up its centre.

★ **73. Tarot Wall** 10m HVS 5a   (1978)
From a ledge at two metres on Mouldheels, move up slightly, then swing left
using a drillhole in a small, inverted triangular niche. Make a long reach up,
then finish via the obvious flakeline in the wall above. The niche can be gained
more directly, with difficulty, but the holds are brittle and a long reach is helpful.

74. Mouldheels 12m VD   (1971)
The poor, right-slanting groove on the right.

75. Black's Magic 15m HVS 5a   (1976)
Just right is a low dome-shaped buttress flanked on its right by slabs. Climb the
centre of the dome to gain the slab above, then step right and climb a shallow
scoop with difficulty to a ledge on the right. Finish up a short wall on the left.

76. Nance 12m VD   (1971)
Climb the slabs on the right of the low dome to the foot of a deep groove
which starts at mid-height. Follow this to the top.

77. Witch Trial 9m HVS 5c   (1979)
Climb the thin, right-leaning crack which used to be pegged, passing one peg to
finish up a fin of rock.

78   Diabolos Vobiscum 9m VD   (1975-79)
Climb the wall between Witch Trial and the arête on the right, past a small tree
to a ledge. Finish up the rib above

79. Wicca 9m VD   (1975-79)
Just round the arête are two cracks. Climb the left crack, then step right to
finish up the slab.

80. First Impressions 9m HS 4b   (1978)
The right crack, finishing up the slab.

First Ascents at Witches' Quarry

1968	**Broomstick, Thrutch** Geoff Fishlock
1968	**Beelzebub** Geoff Fishlock, Mike Haslam
1969	**Witch Bane** Mike Haslam
1970	**Peel Off** (1pt aid) Malc Haslam, Dave Kenyon
	Aid eliminated by Dave Kenyon, Malc Haslam a few weeks later.
1971	**Alice, Elizabeth, Jennet, Witches' Brew, Cracklap** Geoff Fishlock
1971	**Coven Crack, Cauldron Crack, The Shrew, Halloween Outing, Black Mass, Nance** Les Ainsworth, Dave Cronshaw
1971	**Hemlock, Sorcerer's Apprentice** Dave Cronshaw, Les Ainsworth
1971	**Abbot Paslew** Les Ainsworth
1971	**Familiar's Fall, The Spell** Rob Meakin, Bob MacMillan
1971	**Prayer to Absent Friends** (A1)
	First free ascent by Ron Fawcett, 1975.
1971	**The Reeve** (A1)
	First free ascent by Ron Fawcett, 1975.
1971	**Serenity** Geoff Fishlock (solo)
1971	**Tibb, Pendle Groove** Les Ainsworth (solo)
1971	**Mouldheels** Dave Cronshaw (solo)
1972	**Sweet Dreams** (A2)
	First free ascent, 1975-79.
1972	**Witchcraft** (A1)
	First free ascent by Al Evans, 1975.
1973	**Warlock Wall** Les Ainsworth, Dave Cronshaw
1974-75	**Walpurgis Eve**
	Alternative Start by Paul Horan, Dave Herd, Mar 31, 1998.
1975	**Prayer to Absent Friends, The Reeve** Ron Fawcett
	First free ascents.
1975	**Witchcraft** Al Evans
	First free ascent.
1975 summer	**Witch Arête** Geoff Fishlock, John Wilmott
1976 summer	**Witch Way** Geoff Fishlock, Pete Black, Ronnie Marsden
1976 summer	**Witchcraft Crack** Geoff Fishlock, Ron Valovin
1976 summer	**Black's Magic** Geoff Fishlock, Pete Black, Ronnie Marsden
1978 summer	**First Impressions** Gordon Lancaster
1978	**Avenging Angel of Death, The Omen, Brimstone, Black Orchid** Dave Kenyon, Malc Haslam
1978	**Cloven Hoof** Dave Kenyon, Malc Haslam
	Direct Start by Mark Halstead, 21 Apr 1998.
1978	**Satan's Slave** Dave Cronshaw, Malc Haslam
1978	**The Necromancer** Malc Haslam
1978	**Tarot Wall** Dave Kenyon, Malc Haslam
1975-79	**Witchfire at Lammas** Dave Kenyon, Malc Haslam

1975-79	**Wicca** Ron Heald
1975-79	**Satanic Rite, Satan, Diabolos Vobiscum**
1975-79	**Sweet Dreams**
	First free ascent.
1979	**The Flying Magician** Dave Kenyon, Malc Haslam
1979	**Waxen Doll, Downham Racer, Witch Trials** Dave Kenyon, Malc Haslam, Andy Smith
1980	**Seven Years After** Dave Kenyon (solo)
1980	**Resurgent Spirit, Devil Worshipper** Dave Kenyon, Malc Haslam
1979-81	**Darkness**
1980-81	**Dark Secrets** Dave Kenyon
1980-81	**Sweet Dreams Left-Hand** Dave Kenyon (solo)
1980-81	**The Nameless One** Jerry Peel
1981 Oct	**Hrothgar, Crucible**
1981 Oct	**Witchcraft Left-Hand** Dave Kenyon, Malc Haslam
1981 Oct	**The Ducking Chair** Dave Kenyon
1981 Oct	**Hubble, Bubble, Toil and Trouble**
1981	**Baalbreth**
1981	**Mist Over Witches'** Dave Kenyon
1981	**The Dark One** Dave Kenyon, Malc Haslam
	Direct Finish by Dave Kenyon, Malc Haslam, 1981.
1979-83	**Belladonna, Farrak, Witches' Favourite, Return of the Incubus**
1998 Feb 2	**Any Witch Way but Lucifer** Paul Horan, Ian Tapley
1998 Mar 15	**Spellbound** Dave Cronshaw, Les Ainsworth
1998 Mar 18	**It Started with a Kiss** Paul Horan (unseconded)
1998 Mar 23	**Crossing the Line** Paul Horan, Phil Gooby, Michael Boyes, Ken Daykin
1998 Apr 19	**Hell Hounds on My Trail** Paul Smitton, Ian Tapley, Rob Smitton
1998 Apr 28	**Sixth Finger** Paul Horan (unseconded)
1998 June	**Spelling** Roy Healey, Derek Hargreaves
1998 Aug 31	**Problem Child** Peter Johnson, Alasdair Shaw

Minor Crags

Baines Crag   O.S. ref. SD 543 617

Very close to the car-parking space at the top of the Quernmore – Littledale road. This crag is really only a collection of boulders but it has some pleasant problems on excellent gritstone; rough, sound and very clean. Called Quernmore Crag in previous editions.

Dunnow Crag   O.S. ref. SD 708 515

This is a small, natural limestone crag on a wooded knoll just over one kilometre south of Slaidburn. The rock is good limestone, up to 12 metres high, which is steep or overhanging, giving generally sustained climbing in the higher grades. It is reached by walking down the River Hodder from the main car park in Slaidburn, to a sewage works, then strike out right to a good track immediately below the crag. The foot of the rock can then be reached by scrambling up the hillside from the left side of the crag.

At present only two climbs have been reported. **Hodder** (VS, 4c) which takes an obvious short weakness at the right-hand side of the crag and **Slaid** (E2, 5c), up the steep wall starting about two metres left, then trend left near the top to an obvious hole.

Little Bowland Quarry

O.S. ref. SD 649 472

This is a small quarry of excellent limestone about five kilometres north east of Chipping and one kilometre west of Whitewell. The quarry lies about 80 metres east of the road at a public footpath. A shallow cave with a scoop above it provides some interesting, short problems on good limestone.

Newchurch-in-Pendle Quarry

O.S. ref. SD 820 392

A small gritstone quarry on the south side of Pendle Hill, just off the Sabden Hall road about one kilometre west of Newchurch. Some climbs have been done, but the climbing is limited and some of the routes currently need recleaning.

Nogarth

O.S. ref. SD 845 394

Several interesting slabs up to 18 metres long, about two kilometres north-west of the centre of Nelson. Just a pity that it is not a few degrees steeper.

Windy Clough

O.S. ref. SD 536 606

Reached from the Birks Bank car park on Rigg Lane (O.S. ref. SD 526 604): where the track forks, go right and follow the obvious path until the crag appears after about 15 minutes. There are outcrops all over the land north-west of the ridge of Clougha Pike but the main concentration is on the western rim of the Clough, giving problems and short routes on gritstone which is a joy to handle. The setting and the views compare with any crag in the area.

Further problems can be found over the top, west from the main edge; most notably an undercut wall providing several fiendish mantelshelves. There is more rock at Little Windy Clough, and close to the summit of Clougha, but they are only worth the walk if you enjoy it for its own sake. There is also a small quarry of some interest, just beyond the aqueduct, found by taking the left-hand fork of the track.

Wiswell Quarry

O.S. ref. SD 753 370

This small quarry consists of an overhanging face 12 metres high with a couple of old bolt routes and a traverse, **The Maze** (A2). On the easier-angled wall on its left is **Sideline** (HS).

Park in the lane 50 metres before Wiswell Moor Farm, then from a gate opposite follow a winding track to the crag which is situated below the radio mast.

Carnforth Area

Compiled by Les Ainsworth, Ian Conway, Dave Cronshaw,
John Gaskins, Karl Lunt and Stew Wilson

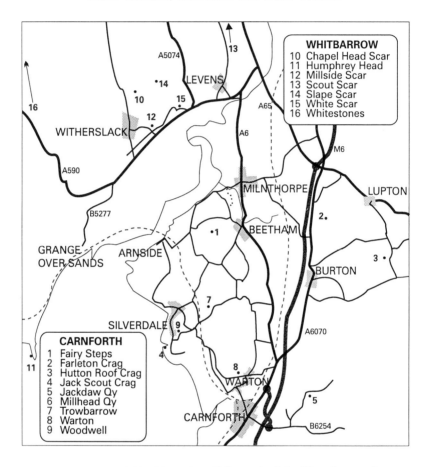

WHITBARROW
10 Chapel Head Scar
11 Humphrey Head
12 Millside Scar
13 Scout Scar
14 Slape Scar
15 White Scar
16 Whitestones

CARNFORTH
1 Fairy Steps
2 Farleton Crag
3 Hutton Roof Crag
4 Jack Scout Crag
5 Jackdaw Qy
6 Millhead Qy
7 Trowbarrow
8 Warton
9 Woodwell

The crags described within this section all lie north of the River Lune and most of them also within the Arnside/Silverdale Area of Outstanding Natural Beauty. This is a charming limestone area and though the scenery is never dramatic, it is generally very picturesque, with the climbing interspersed on a variety of crags in fine woodland and more open areas. Apart from the red squirrel, whose numbers are unfortunately rapidly dwindling, wildlife in the area is thriving. This is largely due to sensitive land management and an active Countryside Management Service in the area, but climbers have also made some small contributions to improving the environment in full co-operation with the landowners, conservationists and local authorities. It is to be hoped that we can all continue to work together in this most effective way.

The area also enjoys a relatively benign micro-climate; low-lying, mild and relatively low in rainfall, often dry when it is raining in the Lakes. Virtually all the crags face west or south and dry quickly. Some, such as Woodwell, deep in the trees, are slower to get wet at the onset of rain, but these are also slower to dry afterwards. Two crags in particular stand out as drying almost instantaneously – Warton Upper Crag and most of Trowbarrow – and on these two, all year-round climbing is certainly possible. All this makes the Carnforth area an ideal one to escape to when the weather is bad elsewhere.

Most of the climbing lies on a number of small, mostly natural, crags. Each of these has its own character, though perhaps the most distinctive is the part-time sea cliff at Jack Scout. However, all of them are characterized by relatively short, but nevertheless worthwhile climbs on excellent rock, with their shortness being more than made up for by their quantity and quality. This makes it an ideal place to get a lot of climbing done relatively quickly.

Some of the crags, such as Crag Foot, only support a handful of climbs, whilst others are much more extensive. The biggest collection of climbs is on Warton Hill, and there have been many additions since the previous guidebook, with more than double the number of routes at Warton Pinnacle. Since the previous guidebook, tree thinning at Fairy Steps, in co-operation with Forest Enterprise, has enabled the rock to dry out much quicker and has greatly improved the climbing. Therefore, a full description to Fairy Steps is now included.

There are also two big limestone quarries, which provide a complete contrast. Trowbarrow, the most varied of these, has recently become a Nature Reserve in which climbers are welcomed. The Main Wall at Trowbarrow is certainly one of the most dramatic pieces of rock in Lancashire, whilst Red Wall now provides a unique collection of harder climbs that have so far resisted the attentions of the bolters. Elsewhere at Trowbarrow there is a good selection of climbs throughout the grades.

The other large quarry, Warton Main, remains a daunting place to many climbers. However, whilst it is undeniable that there is a lot of loose rock, much of the climbing is very worthwhile and the worst sections can generally be avoided. Those who make the effort to come to terms with the crag usually feel well rewarded and many believe its better routes to be amongst the finest in the county.

On the eastern side of the M6 and just within the Cumbria boundary, lie Farleton and Hutton Roof. Both of these are generally short, limestone crags with excellent rock and pleasant surroundings, which makes them ideal for a summer evening visit. Since the previous guidebook the Upper Crag at Farleton has been extensively developed. Though this is a somewhat esoteric crag, the routes should improve with traffic and climbers who venture there will be rewarded by many exposed finishes on good, juggy, Farleton rock.

Crag Foot Area   O.S. ref.   SD 481 731

Situation and Character
Just over one kilometre west of Warton village there are three small crags hidden in the trees immediately above the lower road to Silverdale. The largest of these is Crag Foot, which, despite initial appearances is relatively tall. It is

also extremely sheltered from most winds and often stays dry even when it is raining. The other two crags in this area, Barrow Scout Cove and Scout Crag Quarry, are smaller, but they are nevertheless worth a short visit.

History

Crag Foot is extremely secretive in nature and was first unearthed, literally, by Al Evans and John Girdley, in 1974. Evans and Girdley rapidly claimed the best lines, including *Left* and *Right Foot Eliminates, Pseudopod* and the excellent *Plimsoll Line*, which usually stays dry in the rain. However, they narrowly missed the 1975 guidebook with *Achilles' Heel* and *Toe and Heel*. Later in that year Dave Knighton added the thought-provoking *Stiletto* and *Footsie*. Since then the only additions have been two rather strenuous and gymnastic finishes, *Footloose* and *Big Toe*, by Steve Blackwell and Brian Davison respectively.

Approach

Crag Foot lies above the lower road from Warton to Silverdale, about one kilometre before the level-crossing. Cars can be parked immediately below the crag in the second lay-by on the right after the Scout Crag Caravan Park.

The Climbs

The climbs are described from left to right and **DESCENTS** are possible at either end of the crag by slightly awkward scrambling, or by abseil. The routes are described from LEFT to RIGHT.

1.   Achilles' Heel   10m   VS   4c   (1975)
Start at a shallow groove below the obvious roof at the left of the crag. Climb up and left to a pedestal/ledge, then step left and go over the bulge. Ascend the left edge of the slab to finish up a ragged flake crack.

2.   Footloose   10m   E2   5b   (1991)
Go straight up to the main overhang on its left-hand side. Reach a hold on the right of the short corner above, then swing on this and finish using flakes. A long reach is an advantage.

3.   Big Toe   14m   E2   5c   (1992)
Follow Left Foot Eliminate to the overlap, then step left and surmount the roof at its widest point using an ear of rock on the left. Protection is in Left Foot Eliminate.

★★ **4.   Left Foot Eliminate**   15m   HVS   5b   (1974)
The striking roof crack above the start of Achilles' Heel is as good as it looks, but unfortunately it is often dirty. Climb the groove to the overlap and bridge uncomfortably over it then move right to below the crack and power up it.

★ **5.   Footsie**   15m   VS   4c   (1975)
Climb the steep wall behind the obvious large tree and make awkward moves to gain a niche below the crack of Left Foot Eliminate. Move right as for the girdle and finish up an obvious short crack.

The large overhang between Footsie and Stiletto can be climbed direct at 5c.

★ 6.   Stiletto   15m   HVS   5a   (1975)
Start about three metres right of the tree. Climb the wall to the overhang, step
right and climb a short groove on to the hanging slab (this section is hard, but
can be avoided on the right). The hanging crack above is *'easy when you know
how'*.

★ 7.   Right Foot Eliminate   15m   HS   4b   (1974)
Start a little farther to the right and find the line of least resistance up the wall,
moving right to a projecting tree. Climb the right-hand side of the large flake
then make some exciting moves to the right, around the overhang, to easy
ground.

★ 8.   Toe and Heel   14m   HVS   5b   (1975)
A direct line below the finish of Right Foot Eliminate, using a short groove on
the lower wall and hidden holds on the bulbous overhang above. Good climbing
throughout.

9.   Nonopod   14m   HVS   5b   (1974)
The rock and the protection are rather dubious. Climb the bulging wall just right
of Toe and Heel to the girdle break, then climb the shattered right side of the
bulbous overhangs via a sort of groove.

10.   Athlete's Foot   12m   VD   (1974)
The obvious set-back break three metres right of Nonopod.

★ 11.   Pseudopod   14m   VS   4b   (1974)
A surprising route where the rock improves at the right-hand end of the crag.
There is a large overhang, almost a shallow cave; this can be climbed direct
(about 5b) or, more easily, by its left edge. Climb the slab to an amenable
overlap and continue to the large overhang, split by an obvious crack, which
sooner or later reveals its secret.

★★★ 12.   The Plimsoll Line   39m   VS   4c,4b   (1974)
An entertaining little girdle, which is full of character.
1.   24m.   The first of the hanging slabs is gained as for Achilles' Heel.
Traverse delicately rightwards then awkwardly go round to below the crack of
Left Foot Eliminate. Move round resolutely on to the second hanging slab,
behind the large tree and cross pleasantly rightwards to belay on the large flake
of Right Foot Eliminate. Thoughtful ropework pays dividends on this pitch.
2.   15m.   Step down to the tree and traverse below the overhang. Continue at
much the same level and grapple briefly with the tree on Athlete's Foot to gain
the slab below the large overhang of Pseudopod. Purists and masochists will
continue rightwards to finish up a vile cleft, but the final crack of Pseudopod is
altogether a better alternative.

First Ascents at Crag Foot

1974	**Left Foot Eliminate, Right Foot Eliminate, Athlete's Foot, Pseudopod, The Plimsoll Line** Al Evans, John Girdley	
1974	**Nonopod** Al Evans (solo)	
1975	**Achilles' Heel** Al Evans, John Girdley	
1975	**Toe and Heel** John Girdley, Al Evans	
1975 Dec 26	**Footsie, Stiletto** Dave Knighton, Andy Lewandowski	
1991	**Footloose** Steve Blackwell	
1992 Aug 28	**Big Toe** Brian Davison (unseconded)	

Barrow Scout Cove

O.S. ref.   SD 482 728

This is a small crag in the woods about 15 metres above the road, just south of Crag Foot. Although it is short, it is ideal for a summer evening visit and the views from the top can be particularly rewarding after the enclosure of the woods. Park in the first lay-by on the right about 300 metres north of the entrance to Scout Crag Caravan Park. From the north side of this lay-by, follow a very overgrown track for about 50 metres, then head diagonally right up the hillside to the left end of the crag. A path along the foot of the crag leads to a cave at its right end.

The Climbs

These are described from LEFT to RIGHT.

1.   Johnno 8m VS 4c   (1985)
Start at the left-hand end of the crag where the first weakness cuts through the roof. Climb up and left through this weakness to a large yew tree near the top.

★ **2.   Serial Thrilla** 8m E5 6c (*F7b*)   (1998)
Start five metres to the right and climb the roof direct passing three bolts.

★ **3.   Whitewood** 12m E1 5c   (1985)
On the right is an obvious break in the overhang. Start just to the right of this immediately before a step up on the path and climb a slight rib to the overhang (peg then a small nut on left). Move up left through the roof to gain a small ledge, then either continue left or finish up the corner flake above.

★ **4.   Like a Dick Only Smaller** 10m HVS 5b (*F6a*)   (1998)
A surprising climb, with the difficulty not where it is expected. Start four metres to the right at the second of two short shallow groove. From the base of this move left to a bolt above the initial bulge, then use an undercut to reach a jug (a poor intermediate hold may be necessary for shorter climbers), power across the roof past another bolt to a bolt just above the roof and a tree belay just above this.

★ **5.   Sleeping Sickness** 10m E2 5c (*F6a*)   (1985/1990)
Start immediately to the right and climb the overhang past two bolts to a finish on good jugs. At the time of writing the bolts are in a poor state.

The next climbs are situated just left of the cave at the right end of the crag.

6.   Scouse 8m HS 4b   (1985)
Four metres to the left of the cave is a triangular niche at three metres. Climb into this then go up the wall above, finishing to the left of a small overhang.

7.   Pincher 8m VS 4c   (1996)
Climb up to the top of a tiny left-facing corner, level with the niche on Scouse, then step right and finish directly up the wall.

8.   Caveman 8m HVS 5a   (1996)
From the left side of the cave gain and climb a V-groove and cracks to the top.

First Ascents at Barrow Scout Cove

1985	**Johnno**, **Whitewood**, **Scouse** Roger Grimshaw, Carl Hodge	
1985	**Sleeping Sickness** (A1)	
	First free ascent by Dave Cronshaw, Ian Vickers, 1990.	
1990	**Sleeping Sickness** Dave Cronshaw, Ian Vickers	
	First free ascent.	
1996	**Pincher** Les Ainsworth, Dave Cronshaw	
1996	**Caveman** Dave Cronshaw, Les Ainsworth	
1998 Mar 28	**Like a Dick Only Smaller** (3 bolts) Nadim 'Sid' Siddiqui, John Gaskins (both led)	
1998 Mar 31	**Serial Thrilla** (3 bolts) John Gaskins	

Scout Crag Quarry

O.S. ref. SD 483 726

This small quarry lies between Barrow Scout Cove and Scout Crag Caravan Site. To reach it, park in the lay-by as for Barrow Scout Cove, then walk back along the road for about 150 metres to a footpath on the left, immediately after a limekiln. Walk up this footpath for about 20 metres, then scramble up left to the old quarry track and follow this into the quarry itself.

The Climbs

These are described from RIGHT to LEFT.

1. Botany 8m VS 4c (1996)

There is some loose rock on this route. From the lowest point on the main face of the quarry, move up and right, then finish up a blocky groove that forms the right-hand edge of the crag.

2. Reliant 8m VS 4c (1996)

Start immediately to the left and climb up to the obvious diagonal crack which leads leftwards. Follow this to its end, then climb directly to the top.

3. Shardik 7m HVS 5b (1996)

Start at a tree where the ground just starts to rise and climb straight up.

4. Old Nog 6m VS 4c (1996)

From a stump at the foot of the rock, climb to a small triangular niche at four metres using good, but hidden holds, then either continue directly to the top, or step right then finish direct.

First Ascents at Scout Crag Quarry

1996 Mar   **Botany, Reliant, Shardik, Old Nog** Cliff Brown, Derek Jewell

Fairy Steps

Please read the Access section before visiting Whin Scar

Situation and Character

These crags are at a local beauty spot, located about one kilometre south-west of Beetham, which is a small village just off the A6, about two kilometres south of Milnthorpe. They are marked as Whin Scar on the 1:25,000 O.S. maps.

The Steps themselves lead through a narrow cleft that splits the limestone escarpment and it is reputed that anyone passing through the cleft without touching the sides will be granted a wish.

The climbing at Fairy Steps is situated on two parallel escarpments, the Upper and Lower Crags. These are both several hundred metres long and they consist of climbable rock of up to a maximum of 10 metres high, interspersed with many broken sections.

It is a pity that this area has been ignored and written off by climbers in the past, because this has only resulted in paths becoming lost, an increase of lichen growth and an overuse of the other documented crags in the area. The crags face west and as a result of recent tree thinning many of the buttresses now enjoy afternoon sunshine, which has greatly improved the climbing. This makes Fairy Steps a pleasant little crag that is well worth an evening visit.

History

Fairy Steps has certainly been climbed on since the late Fifties, but it never really attracted serious attention from rock-climbers prior to 1967, due to its limited height and scattered nature. In the winter of 1967/68 Stewart Wilson with a variety of partners from St Martin's College in Lancaster, notably Brian Beeker, Tom Farrell, Wilf Parkinson and Bob Haywood, made several visits to the crag when they cleaned and named many routes. They were not submitted for the first Lancashire guidebook (the Rocksport Guidebook), for fear of seeming inconsequential and trivial. Most of the routes on the Upper Crag originated from that time: *Taliesin* and *The Druid* being the best.

In the intervening years between the 1969 and 1975 guidebooks, Bill Lounds paid numerous visits, concentrating on the areas of rock on the Right-hand Section of the Lower Crag. The best routes of this period were *Neetabulb*, climbed with Wilson and *Gloom*, with Pete Lucas. Lounds was also responsible for the first routes on the Left-hand Section of the Lower Crag, of which *White Africa Flake* and *Black Africa Flake* were probably the most notable. In the third edition of the guidebook, published in 1983, it was again decided to 'demote' Fairy Steps to minor crag status, and this policy continued with the fourth edition.

In 1990 the North of England guidebook (published by Cordee) included the crag as it is geographically in Cumbria rather than Lancashire. In preparation for this, the crag was revisited by Karl Lunt, Matt Ellis, Maggie Wilson and Stew Wilson and new routes were discovered on both sections of the Lower Crag. The best of these were *Betel*, *The Shadow* and *Gothic Wall*, which was top-roped. The latter was eventually led in 1995 by John Gaskins.

After the publication of the North of England guidebook, Lunt returned to seek out many new lines. He soled *Cullinan, The Dark Side, Browned Off* and *Coppertone* and added *Je ne Sais Quoi, Going Underground, Missionary Position* and *White Man's Burden* with Alison Sharman.

In 1996 Dave Cronshaw, mainly with Les Ainsworth, added six routes on the Right-hand Section of the Lower Crag, the best being *Sun Seeker* (with Ainsworth leading) and *Seen the Light, Nebula* and *Zulu* by Cronshaw. During other cleaning visits, Cronshaw climbed *La Luna, Dark Continent* and *Darkening* and he also soloed most of the climbs at Whin Scar. Gaskins also made many additions at this time, including *Feel the Darkness, Black Moon* and *Holidays in the Sun*. During the past year, the most significant event has probably been the thinning of trees near the foot of the rock, which should ensure that the crag gets much more sun and dries out quickly. This was the work of several youths from the Merseyside area organized by Eric Grindle with co-operation from Martin Colledge of Forest Enterprise. These improvements to the crag environment were, in many respects, as important as the new routes themselves.

Access and Approaches

All the crags at Fairy Steps are in a limestone pavement area and so no bolts must be placed. The Upper and Lower Crags are leased by Forest Enterprises whose managers are happy to permit climbing at all times. Whin Scar is owned by Dallam Tower Estate whose managers are willing to permit climbers to visit these crags at their own risk provided that there are no dogs and that the number of visitors to Whin Scar at any one time is kept to a maximum of six. Whin Scar lies within an area where shooting is permitted and no climbing is permitted at Whin Scar on shooting days. Therefore, climbers should avoid Whin Scar between October and January, except on Sundays.

From Milnthorpe follow the A6 south and immediately after crossing the bridge over the River Bela, turn right into Beetham at a sign for the Heron Corn Mill, then turn right again just before the Wheatsheaf Inn. Follow a narrow minor road to a junction and take the left turn, signposted to Storth and Arnside

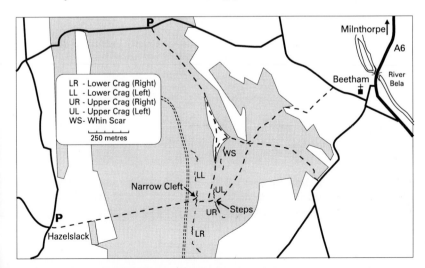

eventually trending uphill until the brow of the hill is reached. There is a lay-by on the right and over the road a locked gate with a stile to its right gives access to the track leading to Fairy Steps in about ten minutes of easy walking.

Follow the track for nearly eight-hundred metres to a clearing and a cairn with a marker disc at a fork. Follow the right fork and re-enter woodland after about one hundred metres. The climbs at the left end of Whin Scar can be reached by striking out left for about thirty metres through the woods at a yellow waymarker post about 200 metres after the woods have been re-entered. However, to reach the climbs on the other crags, it is best to continue along the track through the woods for a further 200 metres to a signpost at a junction with the Hazelslack path. Just over one hundred metres down from this signpost the path splits through the Lower Crag at the Narrow Cleft, whilst the Steps themselves cut through the Upper Crag about 30 metres above the signpost. All the climbs are then best reached by walking along the foot of the appropriate crag.

Alternatively, the Steps themselves can be reached in a little over 10 minutes, by following a good path from Hazelslack (O.S. ref. SD 477 787) via the Narrow Cleft.

The Climbs

The focal points of the Lower and Upper Crags are where the path cuts through them at the Narrow Cleft and the Fairy Steps respectively. Climbs on the Right-hand Sections of the Lower and the Upper Crags are described from left to right, facing the rock, from these points, whilst all the other climbs are described from right to left. The crags are further split into individual buttresses.

Whin Scar can be reached by walking along the foot of the rock from the Steps, but it is much easier to return to the signpost and reach them as described in the Approaches.

Lower Crag (Right-hand Section)

These climbs are described from LEFT to RIGHT, starting right of the steps in the Narrow Cleft (as one faces the crag).

Gaslight Area

An attractive face twenty-five metres right of the wide cleft. The face is about twenty metres long and has three yew trees growing out of the rock.

1.   Limelight 6m VS 4c   (1996)
Climb the right-trending groove at the left-hand side of the wall, midway between the two trees.

2.   Fire Starter 6m VS 5a   (1996)
Climb the right-facing groove on the right of the second tree and finish up the wall above.

3.   Gaslight 6m VS 5a   (Pre-1975)
Climb the obvious crack four metres to the right of the second, big yew. At the top bulge, move left and climb the good continuation crack.

4.   Incandescent 6m HVS 5b   (1996)
On the right is a niche at four metres. Gain this with difficulty using a short crack and finish at a small tree.

5.   Lanterns 6m HVS 5b   (1996)
Start one metre right at two undercuts and climb the wall direct.

Nightshade Wall
A rather gloomy, small wall about 25 metres farther right, with two shorter walls on its left and right.

6.   Feel the Darkness 6m HVS 5c   (1996)
The thin crack just to the left of the first tree.

7.   Nightshade 6m VS 4a   (Pre-1975)
Climb the wall at its highest point between the two trees which grow out of the crag.

Moonlight Area
The crag continues as a line of shorter walls up to four metres high. After 40 metres the height increases and gives a wall between a sheaf of hazels and a big yew.

8.   La Luna 6m HVS 5a   (1995)
The thin crack just to the right of the hazels.

Twilight Buttress
This is the very attractive buttress with a prominent overhang, about 30 metres farther right. Sunny and open now due to felling.

9.   Twilight 7m HVS 5a   (Pre-1975)
To the left of the prominent overhang climb the winding crack on the left of the buttress passing through two bulges.

★ **10.   Neetabulb** 8m E2 5c   (1970)
Start two metres to the right of Twilight at a short crack. Climb the wall above the crack to a break below the overhang. Climb this using a thin crack.

★ **11.   Friday the 13th** 8m E4 6a   (1993)
Climb Neetabulb to the break, then from a good handhold just left of the crack, move up left to a slot and finish direct.

12.   Talcum 6m HVS 4c   (1996)
Climb the thin, left-slanting diagonal crack, then the wall above. Often damp.

Farther right is a detached face with an easy gully behind it.

13.   Parasol 6m S   (Pre-1975)
Climb the obvious wide crackline in the front face of the detached block. Step right at the top.

Shadow Wall

Six metres right, beyond a block-filled chimney is Shadow Wall. This is an extensive area with a fine wall at the left end and a higher but more broken right-hand end. This area ends at a corner which has been dry-stone walled.

★ 14. The Shadow 8m VS 5a   (Pre-1975)
Climb the centre of the left-hand wall on fine rock starting with a layaway on a small nose of rock.

15. Black Moon 8m HVS 5c   (1996)
Start six metres to the right, below an overlap. Gain the large ledge via a horizontal slot, then finish easily.

★ 16. The Dark Side 8m HVS 5a   (1992)
Climb the corner groove and continuation crack through a small overhang at the top.

Flat Wall

Five metres farther right there is a flat wall with a holly at its left side and a yew in the centre near the top.

17. Shady Deal 7m VS 4c   (1997)
Climb the left-slanting crack to a dead stump and finish on the left of this.

18. Solstice 7m VS 5a   (1997)
Climb through the overlap direct to a short crack at the top of the wall.

19. Roamin' in the Gloamin' 7m HS 4b   (1997)
Start from a pedestal just to the right and climb the wall directly through a small overlap at the top.

Ambre Solaire Area

Fifty metres to the right a large yew marks the left side of a clean wall.

20. Ambre Solaire 7m VS 4c   (Pre-1975)
Climb the wall one metre to the right of the big yew moving up rightwards to finish up doubtful rock right of a stump.

21. Coppertone 7m VS 5a   (1992)
Start two metres to the right and climb the wall up and to the left, step right to a tree, then finish direct.

22. Goleu 7m E2 5c   (1970)
Start eight metres to the right, at the large, square block on the ground. Climb the curving, small corner above the block to the overhang. The overhang is difficult.

★ 23. Ultra Violet 7m E1 5c   (1994)
Three metres to the right is a blunt rib. Ascend this to a bulge, surmount this and a farther bulge to finish.

★ **24.   Sun Seeker**   7m   VS   5a   (1996)
Just to the right is a short corner groove. Climb this, or the bulging wall on its
right, to a ledge. From the overhang climb up and to the left with increasing
difficulty until a high flake handhold enables the ledge on the left to be gained.
Either step left and finish, or finish direct.

★★ **25.   Browned Off**   7m   HS   4b   (1992)
A short but entertaining route. Just to the right is an overhang at head-height.
Start on its right and step left into a shallow depression. Finish straight above.

Bronzed Adonis (5c): the severely undercut arête on the right gives an
interesting problem.

Gloom Area
*Ninety metres farther right the path opens out into a pleasant clearing
containing a pleasant open face of excellent rock eight metres high. The main
feature is a shallow corner in the centre whilst at the left side is a short, pink
wall bounded on the right by an impressive face. The rock continues around to
the right and ends beyond an impressive small buttress of clean rock with a fine
overhang. The route names reflect the area's former condition before the wood
was thinned.*

26.   Seen the Light   7m   S   (1996)
Climb the crack at the left side of the wall, then instead of finishing over easy
blocks, step right and climb the edge of the wall.

27.   Dusk   8m   HVS   5b   (Pre-1992)
Start directly below the bulge at the left end of the crag to the right of the short
pink wall and a slanting crack. Climb strenuously over the bulge on poor holds
to a good flake. Move right at the top to finish.

★★ **28.   Gothic Wall**   9m   E4   6a   (1995)
A fingery climb. Start two metres to the right at a short, shallow depression and
climb up, then transfer to another slim vertical crack on the right. A hard move
up leads up to better holds and a less difficult finish at a small ash tree.

★★ **29.   The Dark Ages**   8m   E1   5c   (Pre-1975)
An interesting route, but the crux move is easier for those with a long reach.
Start just to the left of the central corner crack. Climb the wall leftwards on
sketchy holds to a prominent block hold just left of the overlap. The steep wall
leads on gradually improving holds to the top.

★★ **30.   Gloom**   8m   VS   5a   (1972)
A really good route up the obvious groove. At the top it is usual to finish either
right or left of the overhang, but it can also be climbed directly on good holds.

31.   Umbra   9m   E1   5c   (Pre-1975)
Climb the rounded arête just right of Gloom. A very hard rock-over is followed
by a thin crack. Swarm up the face to the left of the yew.

32.   Underworld   9m   E3   6b   (1996)
Start on the right just before some blocks on the floor and climb bulging rock to
a short crack at the top.

The final three climbs are located at an obvious neb about thirty metres farther to the right.

33.   Going Underground   8m   E1   5c   (1994)
From the centre of the slim wall left of Troglodyte, climb up left to a small ledge beneath a yew, then pull out right over the bulge to finish.

★ **34.   The Troglodyte**   8m   S   4a   (1992)
The flaky, corner groove just left of the neb.

35.   Nebula   9m   S   (1996)
Start one metre right and climb the bulging wall to a shallow depression. Traverse right with hands on the obvious horizontal break to reach a tree belay directly above the neb.

Lower Crag (Left-hand Section)

This section of Lower Crag extends leftwards from the Narrow Cleft and so the climbs are described from RIGHT to LEFT.

Cassius Area

After about twenty metres the rock increases in height at a slightly concave wall of fine rock, with a big yew tree growing from its foot at the left end.

1.   Pernambuco   6m   HS   4b   (Pre-1975)
Climb the wide crack in the centre of the wall to a small overhang, then the leftwards-trending crack.

2.   Recife   6m   HS   4b   (1992)
Climb the shallow groove on the left until it is possible to finish up Pernambuco.

3.   Cassius   6m   S   4a   (Pre-1975)
Just left of the big yew climb the fine slab.

4.   Morocco Crack   6m   VD   (Pre-1975)
At the left edge of the slab climb the slim layback crack.

5.   Mohammed   6m   VD   (1995)
The corner behind a group of three trees.

★ **6.   Je ne Sais Quoi**   6m   HVS   5b   (1994)
Start three metres farther left, just left of the blunt arête at an obvious foothold and climb easily to a ledge. Step right and finish up the blunt arête to an awkward finish over the overlap.

7.   Short Flake   6m   VD   (1996)
The flake crack on the left, just before an obvious right-leading rake.

8.   Travail   7m   HVS   5c   (1994)
Start on the easy, right-leading rake. Climb the wall past a hollow flake to a twin-stemmed tree.

★ 9.   Inconnu Flake 7m E1   5c   (1993)
A poorly protected climb. From a standing flake on the left, climb a wall to
reach a short, thin crack to the left of the twin-stemmed tree. Finish on good
holds.

10.   Calcaire 6m E1   5c   (1994)
Follow the vague crack two metres to the left, behind a birch tree.

Cape Horn Area
*The rock on the left becomes more broken and about a hundred-and-twenty
metres farther left there is a prominent right-facing cave/corner. This is Cape
Horn Area. About 30 metres before this there are interesting problems on a
short wall with a roof at hip level.*

11.   Horn A Plenty 6m S   4a   (Pre-1975)
To the right of the cave/corner climb the undercut groove.

12.   Paine 6m E2   6a   (1992)
The flat wall on the left.

13.   Cape Horn 6m VS   4c   (Pre-1975)
Climb the cave/corner.

Africa Flake Wall
*Forty metres farther left is Africa Flake Wall. This is a fine, steep wall of
excellent rock, which is named after a prominent down-pointing flake in the
centre of the right-hand wall, that is shaped like Africa.*

14.   Pygmy Warrior 7m E1   5b   (1994)
Start by a large block at the right-hand end of the wall. Climb the wall directly
through the overlap.

★ 15.   The Missionary Position 7m HVS 5a   (1994)
Start directly below a yew tree at the top of the crag. Finish on the left past the
short top crack.

★ 16.   White Man's Burden 7m E1   5c   (1994)
Start one metre right of Africa Flake. Climb the wall past a flake/jug near the
bottom, then continue past a thin break to the top.

17.   Black Africa Flake 7m E1   5c   (1972)
An awkward and surprisingly strenuous climb up the right-hand side of the
Africa Flake.

★ 18.   White Africa Flake 7m VS   4b   (1972)
Climb the left-hand side of the Africa Flake past a holly.

19.   Holidays in the Sun 8m E3   5c   (1996)
Start at a slightly lower level and climb a short vague crack then the wall above.

20.   Apartheid 8m VS   4c   (1972)
Climb the crack at the left side of the wall, two metres to the right of Kudu. At
the top, keep to the right.

● **21. Kudu** 8m HS 4a   (1972)
A poor route, which follows the right-slanting edge of the huge detached blade
of rock forming the left end of Africa Flake Wall. The holds are generally good,
but care should be taken to avoid suspect rock on the left.

22. Zulu 6m VS 4c   (1996)
12 metres to the left is a block leaning against the face. From the top of this,
move left to gain better holds and finish direct.

Zambia Face
*Fifty metres farther left is a clean face with a large gnarled ash growing on a
ledge on its left at half-height.*

23. Zambia 6m HS 4b   (1994)
At the right-hand end of the wall is an obvious flake crack. Climb this and the
wall above, finishing on the right of a small overhang.

Zimbabwe Area
*This is a steep clean buttress about twenty-five metres farther left. It can be
further identified by a slim, single-stemmed yew growing beside it and a deep
chimney on its right. Currently there are no recorded climbs.*

Unconquerable Area
*Thirty metres farther left is a tall buttress with an unmistakable right-slanting
flake crack.*

24. Unconquerable Arête 6m VS 4b   (1995)
At the right-hand side of the wall there is a wide curving crack. Climb this, then
surmount the overlap to a good hold and finish just right of the arête.

★ **25. Right Unconquerable** 7m VS 4c   (Pre-1975)
Start three metres to the left, at a big block below the flake. Climb the V-crack
and the right-slanting flake to the top.

*About 20 metres farther along is a wall above some large blocks, with a corner
on its right containing a large, dubious, undercut block.*

26. Insuperable 6m HVS 5b   (1992)
Start on the left where the ground rises. Pull over the left end of an overlap and
make a long reach to a flake, then up right to finish.

South Africa Area
About 30 metres farther left is the next continuous area of rock.

27. Vorster's Groove 6m HS 4b   (Pre-1975)
Start two metres left of the short arête below a cracked corner. Climb the corner
and exit rightwards.

Dave Pegg on the first ascent of **The Last Temptation** (E6 6c), Thorn Crag.

Photo Jon Sparks

28.   Game Reserve 6m HVS 5b   (Pre-1975)
Climb the long, slim crack two metres left of the corner. Very awkward and
deceptively steep.

★ **29.   South African Lawn Tennis Association** 6m HS 4b   (Pre-1975)
Start below the cracked wall to the left of the arête. Climb the thin cracks to a
gnarled stump. Move back up and go right to finish at the arête.

30.   Preston's of Bolton 6m S 4a   (Pre-1975)
Start one metre farther left at a wide crack in a corner. Climb this and the
undercut rib above.

31.   Springbok 6m VS 4c   (1992)
Just two metres to the left is a thin crack. Climb this and the short hanging
groove above.

32.   Tutu 6m S 4a   (1995)
Climb the crackline just to the left of a high yew on the rock.

★ **33.   Cullinan** 6m E2 6a   (1992)
A gem of a route. Just to the left is a blunt arête on the right end of a smooth
wall. Take a line up the right edge of this wall via a small pocket at half-height
(crux). The grade can be reduced to 5c by taking the arête on its right side.

34.   Cultural Elite Sign-up Sheet 6m E2 6a   (1997)
Start directly below an obvious right-facing hold at three metres. Gain this
direct, then finish rightwards past a tree.

35.   Sharpeville 6m HVS 5c   (1992)
The left-slanting crack and a bulge on the left.

36.   Simonstown 6m VS 4c   (Pre-1975)
The deep-cracked corner with a bulge at the top.

37.   Democracy 10 m 6b   (1997)
A low-level traverse of the wall from Simonstown to Tutu.

38.   Wildebeest 6m VS 4c   (1995)
Gain a scoop two metres to the left by some awkward moves, then finish up
easier rock.

★ **39.   Dark Continent** 7m S 4a   (1995)
The short, wide crack on the left is climbed to a ledge, then finish up the
shallow, stepped corners on the left.

★ **40.   Betel** 6m HVS 5b   (1989)
Start about 10 metres farther left, at a shallow groove three metres left of a
gnarled oak tree in the centre of the crag. Climb the groove, to a good
handhold, then easier rock leads to the top.

Dave Cronshaw and Les Ainsworth, two roughnecks on **Roughneck** (HVS 5b), Farleton Crag.
Photo: George Philips

41. Pepul 6m VS 4c   (1989)
Start at the foot of the second groove left of the big oak. Climb the left-trending
groove towards the bleached, dead yew. Move up and right over the overlap on
good holds. Finish up the cracked rib to the left of a tree-filled groove.

42. Two-timer 6m S 4a   (Pre-1975)
Start at the front face of the huge block. Climb this to a ledge and crevasse.
Step across this and climb the fine cracked slab above.

*Two metres left of the huge block is a massive yew in front of an easier-angled
face, split at mid-height by a long ledge which has a yew growing on the left
end and a slim holly to the right.*

43. Yew Tree Drive 8m S 4a   (1995)
Start directly behind the large yew tree and climb to an obvious ledge either by
a flaky wall, or the short groove on its left. Continue up short walls above and
to the left of a yew.

44. Final Score 7m S 4a   (Pre-1975)
A pleasant climb. Start two metres to the left, below the shallow obvious groove
in the upper slab above the ledge. Climb the steep wall via flakes to the holly.
Climb the easy groove above.

45. Stranded in the Jungle 8m HS 4c   (1996)
Start two metres to the left, below the yew tree at the left-hand end of the long
ledge. Climb up and rightwards to a ramp and short crack, then gain the ledge
and finish up Final Score.

Eight metres left past a broken gully is a wall with a tree at its foot.

46. Evil Primevil 6m E1 5b   (1996)
Climb the wall a metre left of the tree to the break. Above this the rock is poor
and it is best to escape down the tree, though the top has been climbed.

47. Anybody Out There 6m HVS 5c   (1996)
Climb the wall three metres left of the tree to a break and a good hold.
Continue up the wall above on good rock.

48. Darkening 6m S 4a   (1996)
The flake crack and blocky groove just to the left.

Isolated Walls
*About 30 metres farther left, just after a cracked block standing forward from
the crag is a small bay.*

★ **49. Isolation** 7m HS 4b   (1997)
Climb the centre of the wall on the right-hand side of the bay via a hand-rail
then a ledge.

*A further 10 metres left is an obvious short, leaning wall, just past a tree. This
gives an interesting boulder problem (**The Trick,** 7a), which takes a line
between the slot and the break on the right side of the block. Easier for the tall.*

Upper Crag (Right-hand Section)

These climbs are described as one faces the crag, working RIGHTWARDS from the Steps.

Steps Area

The short, easy-looking wall of good quality rock immediately right of the Steps has many pleasant problems, including a traditional Severe up the right wall of the Steps on flakes from the point that The Steps level out. It is pleasant to scramble all over this rock, but only the four traditional climbs are described.

1.   Puck 6m M   (1967)
Start at the right of the foot of the steps at a big block. Surmount the block and follow the obvious crackline to the right of a small bush.

2.   Robin 6m M   (1967)
Start one metre right below a jammed block. Climb the right wall of the groove and climb the crack above and right (or finish direct from the block).

3.   Merryweather 6m D   (1967)
Climb the wall direct from the central 'doorstep' at its foot.

4.   Sourmilk 6m D   (1967)
Climb the wall above three parallel, short, vertical cracks and finish up the crack above.

Medusa Area

About twelve metres farther right is the Medusa Area. This extends for twelve metres and ends at two large blocks below an open cleft at the top. A large yew which grows out of the face is a point of reference.

5.   Medusa 6m D   (1967)
Start at the stump just left of the big yew. Climb the easy steps to a steeper finish at a little corner.

6.   Stoneface 6m S 4a   (1967)
Immediately to the right of the yew. Climb the steep face.

7.   The Sword 6m S 4a   (1967)
Directly above a pointed block climb the steep crack.

8.   The Shield 6m S 4a   (1967)
Start just to the right of The Sword. Climb on to the top of the block. Finish up the short face above.

Druids' Area

The Druids' Area consists of two fine steep faces separated by a steep crack which widens to become a chimney. Both faces have a more-or-less continuous bulge at mid-height. The climbing is both steep and interesting on surprising holds.

DESCENT: *fallen blocks 10 metres farther to the right form a deep recess, that provides a useful descent route.*

★ **9. Cormach** 6m HS 4b (1968)
Start two metres to the left of the central crack, behind a slim tree. Climb
leftwards and turn the overhang on the left. Continue up leftwards to a short
vertical runnel and the top.

★ **10. Cernunnos** 6m VS 5a (1968)
An excellent steep climb on good holds. Reach the bulge as for Cormach, then
move right on jugs. A long reach leads to a pocket and the top.

★★ **11. The Druid** 6m HVS 5a (1968)
Poor holds and a poor landing combined with a technical start, make this a hard
route. Start on top of the large block below a V-shaped vertical slot in the
bulge. Climb up to the bulge on undercuts and gain poor holds in the first
horizontal break. A hard pull reaches a good vertical edge high up on the right.
Finish more easily.

12. Gofannon 6m S 4a (1967)
Climb the crack/chimney which separates the two steep walls.

★ **13. Epona** 6m S 4a (1967)
Climb the blunt rib one metre right of the chimney moving slightly right to
finish. Surprising holds.

★★ **14. Mabon** 6m S 4b (1967)
A great climb on superbly sculpted rock. Just right of the crack is a cluster of
hazel trees. Climb up to the bulge just right of the hazel trees. A pull over the
bulge on twin, vertical runnels leads to fantastic holds and the top.

★ **15. Taranis** 6m S 4a (1967)
A good route. Start from a block two metres to the right. Climb up to and
through the next break in the bulge.

The Tower
About fifteen metres farther right, just past a cave of blocks, is a tower of
excellent, steep rock. It presents two faces separated by a fine cracked arête.

16. Tower Wall 6m VS 4c (1994)
The wall just to the left of the central crack.

17. Tower Crack 6m HVS 5b (1994)
From a crack in the centre of the front face of the tower, climb up, then move
slightly right and finish direct.

18. Tower Arête 6m S 4a (1994)
The crack on the right-hand arête.

Rune Area
An inscription on the rock face just to the right of the corner on the right
identifies the Rune Area. Other inscriptions of some antiquity are to be found
hereabouts.

19. Scrawl 6m VD (1992)
The wall beside the inscription is climbed between two trees.

Fantasy Area

An interesting area with superb steep rock and some fine lines about twelve metres farther right. It is identified by a block on the ground with a shallow cave on the right. The wall continues to two large yews, between which there are several easier climbs.

20. Celtica 6m VS 5a   (1992)
Climb the left-slanting flake which rises from the right side of the block.

★★ **21. Taliesin** 6m VS 4c   (1968)
Great climbing with steep moves, but a good landing. Start one metre right of the large block in front of the recess, at the left side of a finger-flake at chest-height. Pull strenuously on to the flake and climb the steep wall direct on flat holds to finish at a good flake.

22. Merlin 6m VS 4c   (1992)
Climb the right side of the flake, then finish up the wall above.

23. Rheaed 6m VS 5a   (1992)
The blunt arête left of the corner is harder than it looks.

24. Woodbind 6m D   (1994)
Ascend the corner.

25. The Mote of Mark 6m HVS 5b   (1992)
The very thin crack one metre right of the corner.

★ **26. Caerliol** 6m VS 5a   (1992)
Start one metre farther right and by using a flake at head-height, gain then climb the crack or the flake on the right.

★ **27. Celyddon** 6m VD   (1967)
Start immediately to the left of the first big yew. Climb the flake edge and a recess above.

28. The Dark Stair 6m M   (1967)
Climb the easy groove behind the big yew. Useful as a **DESCENT**.

29. Goddeu 6m D   (1967)
Start at a tall upstanding flake to the right of the first yew. Climb the wall on good holds.

★ **30. Et tu Brute** 18m 6a   (1996)
Start as for Stranger Than Fiction and traverse rightwards below the break to the first yew. A higher variation with hands on the break is possible at 5b.

Upper Crag (Left-hand Section)

From the fine easy arête above, that bounds the Steps on their left, this section of the Upper Crag extends to an overhanging buttress some metres farther left. The rock then becomes much more broken. The climbs are described from RIGHT to LEFT.

★ 1.   Fantasia 8m   D   (1967)
Climb the arête that guards the left side of the Steps.

2.   Mr. T 8m   S   4c   (1967)
Climb the corner left of the arête and finish up the slab direct without using
holds to the right.

3.   Cruella 8m   S   4b   (1967)
Climb the very blunt rib left of the corner and finish up the slab on initially
poor holds.

4.   Silveste 7m   VD   (1967)
Climb the corner below the yew. Step to the right of the tree to finish.

5.   Felix 7m   S   4a   (1967)
Start directly below the tree and trend slightly left up the wall to the top.

6.   Popeye 7m   S   4a   (1967)
Climb the thin flaky crack in the wall just to the right of the chimney.

7.   Olive 7m   D   (1967)
Climb the chimney.

*The next eight metres left consists of ivy-covered rock. Some large blocks mark
the starts of the next climbs.*

8.   Tom 6m   VD   (1967)
Start on the right of the blocks and climb the leftwards-leading cracks then the
shallow left-facing corner above.

9.   Jerry 6m   S   4a   (1967)
Start at ground level directly behind the blocks and climb the wall on good
flake holds.

10.   Fairy Tales 6m   D   (1967)
From a flat block on the left, climb the wall on rounded flakes.

*To the left the rock is generally lower and more broken. Some short isolated
problems have been done, but nothing is recorded until Whin Scar.*

Whin Scar

Although this crag is the natural continuation of the Left-hand Section of the
Upper Crag, it is best approached by following the Beetham Fell track for about
200 metres from the signpost between the Steps and the Narrow Cleft, to a
marker post with a yellow arrow on it. From that point, head directly through
the trees for about 30 metres to reach the rock. The first identifiable feature of
the crag is a wall with a shallow, left-facing corner in its centre and a small
'flying' buttress on its right. It is further identified by a thin, inverted-crucifix
crack.

The climbs are described from RIGHT to LEFT.

Crucifix Area
This is the wall with a shallow, left-facing corner in its centre.

1.   Sepulchre 6m D   (1996)
The wide, block-filled crack on the right-hand side of the wall.

2.   Crucifixion 6m E1   6a   (1996)
Midway between the left-facing corner and Sepulchre is an inverted-crucifix crack. Climb this to a yew at the top.

3.   Barabbas 6m HVS 5b   (1996)
From a good flake hold on the arête, cross a scoop to gain a flake at the top of Crucifixion. A direct entry to the scoop is possible at 6b.

4.   Landmark Corner 6m HS 4b   (1996)
The shallow, left-facing corner leads to the break, then finish diagonally to the right.

Deep Bay Area
This is the deep bay twenty-five metres farther left.

5.   Chockstone Chimney 6m D   (1996)
The obvious shallow chimney at the back of the bay, with a chockstone near its top.

★ **6.   Pillar Front** 6m HS 4b   (1996)
Climb the centre of the rounded pillar on the left side of the bay.

7.   Bay Watch 6m S 4a   (1996)
Left again is a corner and twin cracks. Climb these.

8.   Home and Away 6m VD   (1996)
Climb the wall on the left using a crack to reach a ledge. Then finish up the wall above.

Final Collection
The remaining climbs at Whin Scar lie on a collection of small buttresses approximately 80 metres farther left. This point can be further identified by a short bifurcated pinnacle that bounds on its right, though this is most prominent when looking back rightwards.

9.   Crozzly Wall 6m S 4a   (1996)
The crozzly wall about eight metres left of the pinnacle.

★ **10.   Whin Crack** 6m VS 4c   (1996)
A steep wall split by a fine crack.

11.   Rigg Up 6m S 4a   (1996)
Gain the footledge at chest-height on the wall to the left of the crack, then finish up the wall above via a couple of flakes.

12.   Rigg Crack 6m S 4a   (1996)
The cracked wall 12 metres to the left is climbed to a slight scoop at its top.

13. Rigger 6m S 4a (1996)
Climb the deep groove capped by a large overhang six metres to the left.

★ **14. Intellect** 6m E2 6b (1996)
Just right of the arête on the left side of the wall climb the crack.

15. Send You No Flowers 6m HVS 5b (1996)
The arête is climbed on its left.

16. Whindow Dressing 5m HVS 5a (1996)
Start round the arête and climb the leaning flake crack and the wall above. The landing is poor.

17. Last Fling 6m HS 4b (1996)
Start six metres to the left and climb the crack up the centre of the final wall.

First Ascents at Fairy Steps

1967	**Puck, Robin, Merryweather, Sourmilk, Medusa, Stoneface, The Sword, The Shield, Gofannon, Epona, Mabon, Taranis, Celyddon, The Dark Stair, Goddeu** Stew Wilson
1967	**Fantasia, Mr. T, Cruella, Silveste, Felix, Popeye, Olive, Tom, Jerry** Stew Wilson, Tom Farrell, Brian Beeker, Bob Haywood
1968	**The Druid** Stew Wilson, Brian Beeker, Tom Farrell
1968	**Cormach, Cernunnos, Taliesin** Stew Wilson
1970	**Neetabulb, Goleu** Bill Lounds, Stew Wilson
1972	**Gloom** Bill Lounds, Pete Lucas
1972	**Black Africa Flake, White Africa Flake, Apartheid, Kudu** Bill Lounds
Pre-1975	**Gaslight, Nightshade, Parasol, The Shadow, The Dark Ages, Pernambuco, Cassius, Morocco Crack, Horn a Plenty, Cape Horn, Right Unconquerable, Vorster's Groove, Game Reserve, South African Lawn Tennis Association, Preston's of Bolton, Simonstown, Two-timer, Final Score**
Pre-1975	**Twilight, Ambre Solaire, Umbra** Bill Lounds
1982 Apr	**Celtica** Stew Wilson (solo)
1989	**Betel** Karl Lunt, Stew Wilson, Maggie Wilson
1989	**Pepul** Stew Wilson, Maggie Wilson, Karl Lunt
Pre-1990	**Woodbind**
1990	**Intellect** John Gaskins (solo)
Pre-1992	**Dusk**
1992 Apr	**Merlin, Rheaed, The Mote of Mark, Caerliol** Stew Wilson (solo)
1992 Sep 4	**The Dark Side, Coppertone, Browned Off, The Troglodyte,** *Nemesis* Karl Lunt (solo)
1992 Sep 8	**Insuperable, Cullinan, Sharpeville** Karl Lunt (solo)
1992 Sep 10	**Recife, Paine** Karl Lunt (solo)
1992 Sep 29	**Springbok** Karl Lunt (solo)
1992	**Scrawl**
1993 Dec 13	**Inconnu Flake** Dave Cronshaw, Ian Vickers
1993 Dec 13	**Friday the 13th** Ian Vickers, Dave Cronshaw
1994 July 7	**Ultra Violet, Going Underground** Karl Lunt, Alison Sharman
1994 July 16	**Je ne Sais Quoi, Travail, Calcaire** Karl Lunt, Alison Sharman
1994 Sep 3	**Pygmy Warrior, The Missionary Position, White Man's Burden** Karl Lunt, Alison Sharman
1994	**Zambia, Tower Wall, Tower Crack, Tower Arête** Dave Cronshaw (solo)
1995 Feb	**La Luna** Dave Cronshaw, Les Ainsworth
1995 June	**Mohammed, Tutu, Wildebeest, Dark Continent, Yew Tree Drive** Dave Cronshaw (solo)
1995 Aug	**Unconquerable Arête** Les Ainsworth, Dave Cronshaw
1995 Nov 6	**Gothic Wall** John Gaskins

1996 Jan	**Limelight, Sepulchre, Crucifixion, Barabbas, Landmark Corner, Chockstone Chimney, Pillar Front, Bay Watch, Home and Away, Crozzly Wall, Whin Crack, Rigger** Dave Cronshaw (solo)
1996 Jan	**Fairy Tales** Dave Cronshaw, Les Ainsworth (both solo)
1996 Feb 1	**Send You No Flowers, Last Fling** John Gaskins (solo)
1996 Mar 3	**Incandescent, Rigg Up, Rigg Crack, Whindow Dressing** Dave Cronshaw (solo)
1996 Mar 10	**Talcum, Seen the Light, Zulu** Dave Cronshaw, Les Ainsworth
1996 Mar 10	**Sun Seeker, Nebula** Les Ainsworth, Dave Cronshaw
1996 Mar 10	**Short Flake** Les Ainsworth (solo)
1996 Mar 21	**Holidays in the Sun** John Gaskins, Tim Chapman
1996 Apr 22	**Et tu Brute** John Gaskins
1996 May 8	**Black Moon** John Gaskins (solo)
1996 May 16	**Fire Starter, Lanterns, Feel the Darkness, Underworld** John Gaskins (solo)
1996 Sep 20	**Evil Primevil** John Gaskins (solo)
1996 Sep 20	**Anybody Out There** John Gaskins, Philip Warner
1996 Oct	**Darkening** Dave Cronshaw
1996 Nov 26	**Cultural Elite Sign-up Sheet, Stranded in the Jungle** John Gaskins (solo)
1996 Dec 21	**Isolation** John Gaskins (solo)
1997 Jan 4	**The Trick** John Gaskins (solo)
1997 June 21	**Bronzed Adonis, Shady Deal, Solstice, Roamin' in the Gloamin'** Karl Lunt (solo)
1997 Aug 17	**Democracy** John Gaskins

Farleton Crag

O.S. ref.   SD 539 796

Situation and Character

The crag (which is not actually in the county of Lancashire) is located about eight kilometres north-east of Carnforth and is very obvious from the M6 as the obvious limestone hill immediately east of the motorway about two kilometres south of the Kendal and South Lakes exit.

The rock is sound on the whole, although some large and useful reference features have fallen down recently. The crag dries relatively quickly, but some parts are screened by trees in summer.

History

The earliest climbers to visit Farleton were probably Ian Dobson and Roger Gott, who discovered the main crag in 1966. During their early visits they climbed most of the easier lines, including *Farleton Crack, Appleton Crack, Earwig Two, Idleness* and *Doodlebug*. Dobson introduced Stew Wilson to the crag in early 1967 and this group added a further batch of climbs, including *Deb's Crack*. However, the most notable route was *The Shriek of Baghdad* by Wilson, which still stands as the classic of the crag (as its polished state testifies!). Later that year Wilson introduced Bill Lounds and Chris Eilbeck to the crag, and Lounds immediately went for the impressive wall immediately to the right of The Shriek, where he produced *Agrippa* and *Herod*, two powerful climbs that were ripe for Lounds' powerful approach. Lounds also started to explore the far right end of the main crag, which he opened up with *Enyoka*, a short, but nevertheless demanding route.

Word of the new crag was soon out and the following year Allan Austin sneaked past the frontier guards from Yorkshire, to add the technical gems of *Roughneck* and *The Gent*, whilst Ian (Sherpa) Roper led *The Family Way*. As work on the first Lancashire guidebook was nearing completion, Lounds and Wilson discovered Farleton Quarry, which was even more hidden than the main crag, and there they climbed *Yoruba, Ebo* and the pumpy *Uhuru*.

In early 1971 Les Ainsworth spent a day soloing at the main crag after which he walked up to the top of the fell, where he was immediately attracted to the large roof. However, he could not commit himself to the last two moves and so he retreated and finished up *Avoidance*, a scrappy route, but at least it was a first foothold on the Upper Crag. The next weekend Ainsworth returned with Dave Cronshaw to add *Rose Amongst Thorns* and *Pudding Club* on the main crag. Shortly afterwards the pair returned with Bob MacMillan and Cronshaw led the finger-traverse of *G Squared*.

During 1973 and 1974 Al Evans and Dave Parker made a systematic attempt to fill in many of the gaps at the main crag, particularly at the right-hand side of the crag, where they added *Instant Whip, Pork Chop* and the interesting *Green Machine*. They also visited the quarry, which they girdled with one rope move to create *The Pit and the Pendulum*. However, they found out shortly afterwards that someone else had already climbed a strenuous, but completely free, girdle in the opposite direction, called *Mister Universe*. At about the same time, Evans visited the Upper Crag where, much to everyone's surprise, he uncovered *California Dreaming*.

Development during the late 1970s was limited and the new routes were mostly fillers-in. However, notable exceptions to this were *The Pill* and *Watching the Motorway Flow* by Evans and John Girdley respectively. Another interesting climb was Evans's Direct Finish to The Shriek, which is still a much underestimated route. There were also three new routes pioneered on the Upper Crag, the most notable of which was *Buckshot*. The next additions of any significance were the long-standing problem of a *Direct Finish* to The Shriek, which was solved by Evans in 1983 and Cronshaw's *Dimple, Dimple*, then Wilf Williamson produced *The Coil*, a short, but desperate problem.

John Gaskins became a regular visitor to the crag in 1991, when he led *Cheyenne*, though it was some years before he discovered that his was actually the first lead and that it had only been top-roped before. Over the next few years he went on to add some hard problems on the main crag, such as *Pandemonium, Mathematics of Change* and *Chemical Warfare*, an eliminate near The Shriek. Also in 1995 Walkington turned his attention to the previously neglected right-hand side of Upper Crag, where with *Farleton Prow* and *Arthritic Crack*, he showed that there was some reasonable climbing to be had. This inspired Cronshaw and Ainsworth to revisit the Upper Crag the following year and after a sustained campaign, they uncovered sixteen new climbs. The best of these were the 'wind' routes, so named because the wind during a couple of their earlier visits was so strong that small stones that they dislodged whilst climbing were reaching the top before the climbers! On one of these visits they were accompanied by a group from Bury, who added *Bury Route* on the Upper Crag. During another of their visits they met Walkington and Gaskins (probably the first time that there had been two independent teams on the crag at the same time), who were trying an extremely improbable crack that split the overhang above Rose Amongst Thorns. On that occasion their attempt was in vain, but a couple of months later Gaskins forced the incredible *Look Mum There's Vikings on the Tundra Again*.

Approaches

From the south, the best approach by car is to leave the M6 at the Carnforth exit (Junction 35), then follow the motorway spur to the A6. and turn right. About one kilometre along the A6, at another roundabout, turn on to the A6070 and follow this for a little over five kilometres through Burton-in-Kendal, past the large working quarry at Holme Park, to Holme Park Farm. Cars should be parked out of the way at a turning just past some houses on the left.

From Kendal, the parking spot can be reached by turning south down the A6070 at a roundabout on the A65 a couple of hundred metres after crossing the M6. Holme Park Farm is on the left about two kilometres south of the roundabout.

The crag is about 15 to 20 minutes walk from this point. To reach the crag, follow the public bridleway just south of the farm (signposted '*Limestone Link, Clawthorpe Fell*') through the farmyard and up a straight track for 600 metres to a 'roofed' sign which reads '*253*'. Go through the gate immediately after this sign and about 50 metres farther on, follow a track leftwards, which soon becomes grassy. After about 100 metres bear slightly right to a grass track and continue along this for a further 200 metres or so. At this point the woody area on the right becomes a little more dense and there is a cairn about 30 metres to the right of the track. From this cairn turn right and follow a path up the scree. At the top of the scree head up to the left side of a short rock pillar and scramble up the side of this until the crag can be seen a few metres above.

The Climbs

The routes are described from RIGHT to LEFT.

Eggyoka Buttress

This is the short buttress directly above the pillar on the approach route. It can be further identified by the shallow corner of Eggyoka, which rises between two trees at the foot of the crag.

1.　Lumumba 6m HS 4a (Pre-1975)

Climb the right-hand part of the wall using fingery edges and finish up a split above the horizontal break.

★ **2.　Enyoka** 6m HVS 5b (1967)

Start one metre to the left behind an ash tree and climb to the horizontal break via a slim corner. Finish up the bulging wall above using a very high slot.

3.　Eggyoka 6m VD (Pre-1975)

The open corner that identifies this buttress.

4.　Monkey Wrench 6m VD (Pre-1987)

Climb the bulging buttress on the left, which is split by a wide crack, then finish up the wide cracks above the break.

5.　Rock Ivy Line 6m VD (Pre-1987)

The shallow, blocky groove on the left.

★ **6.　Anaconda** 6m S 4a (Pre-1987)

The smooth finger-crack two metres left of Rock Ivy Line.

7. Primrose Path 20m S 4a (Pre-1987)
Pleasant horizontal gymnastics. Start up Lumumba then girdle steadily leftwards, to finish just before a flourish of yew antlers, by climbing Anaconda. The route originally continued past this, but has been shortened to avoid some very doubtful blocks.

Family Planning Centre
40 metres farther left is a pock-marked wall split by an obvious horizontal break near its top.

8. The Coil 6c (1984)
A desperate problem up the thin, right-slanting, intermittent crack in the centre of the wall. Finish up The Pill.

★ **9. The Pill** 10m HVS 5b (1976)
Follow The Family Way to the break, then hand-traverse right for two metres until it is possible to pull over the bulge at an area of crozzly rock.

10. The Family Way 6m VS 5a (1968)
The left side of the wall is split by an obvious flake crack. Climb this and the cracks above.

11. Chastity 6m HS 4c (1990)
Start just right of and below a conspicuous stump on the face one metre to the left of Family Way. Climb the bulging wall on good, but small, holds past the sapling to reach a good ledge. Continue up the V-groove above.

Pudding Area
15 metres left of The Family Way, past some broken buttresses, the wall steepens again.

12. Pudding Flake 7m VD (1996)
Climb the wide flake crack that marks the right-hand limit of the wall, then step left and finish up the crack above.

13. Green Machine 9m HVS 5b (1973)
Start three metres left of the flake crack and climb flake cracks to the break, then continue rightwards up the very thin diagonal crack in the wall above.

★ **14. Pudding Club** 7m S 4a (1971)
The open, blocky groove just left of Green Machine.

15. Dimple, Dimple 7m HVS 5b (1984)
One metre to the left there is a line of dimples directly below a crack at the top. Follow these past the bulge, then finish up the top crack.

16. Klayfire 7m VS 4c (1976)
The thin finger-crack in the wall left of Dimple, Dimple.

17. Flaykier 6m VS 4c (1975)
Two metres left of the tree-choked grooves, climb the wall on obvious flaky holds.

18. Pandemonium 6m 7a (1994)
The undercut wall between Flaykier and Cracker.

19. Cracker 6m VS 5b (Pre-1979)
The small corner on the left, with a very hard, undercut start.

20. Prowler 6m VS 5a (Pre-1979)
Start just to the left and climb the nose of the wedge-shaped prow.

21. Caliban 6m HS 4b (1967)
Climb the centre of the strangely wrinkled wall just left of Prowler.

Main Wall
*Four metres to the left is an ash at the foot of the crag and past this the rock
increases in height.*

★ **22. G Squared** 10m HVS 5a (1971)
Climb the thin crack behind the ash to the break, traverse left and follow a
second crack to the top.

★ **23. Mathematics of Chaos** 8m E5 6c (1995)
Start one metre to the left and follow a direct line through G Squared via two
undercuts. Jam up the breaks at the top.

★ **24. Pork Chop** 9m E1 5b (1973)(1974)
Start at the left arête of the wall and pull over the first overhang on the blunt
rib, then climb directly to the top.
Louis Wall (5b): the initial overhang can be avoided by easier climbing up the
obvious scoop on the right.

★ **25. Doodlebug** 9m HS 4a (1966)
The square-cut chimney at the right side of a recess.

26. Instant Whip 9m VS 4c (1974)
Climb directly up the groove in the centre of the recess, and finish over a bulge.

★ **27. Idleness** 10m VS 4c (1966)
Climb the flake crack at the left side of the recess and step left to a good
foothold just below the overhangs. Finish via the wide crack that splits the
overhangs.

28. Man of Straw 9m VS 5b (1989)
Three metres to the left is a vague crack at head height. Climb this to the ledge,
then continue up the wall above.

29. Feet of Clay 10m HS 4b (Pre-1987)
Climb the square-cut groove beneath and just right of, a hefty ash, then finish
behind the tree or (harder) by the dimpled scoop on the right.

30. Fat Good Crack 9m VS 5a (1976)
Start just to the left of the large ash. Climb the fine layback flake and dimpled
bulges above.

31. Doggo 9m HS 4b (1976)
Start four metres left of the large ash. Climb a blocky crack to a ledge, then finish up the scoop on the right.

32. Earwig Two 10m VS 4c (1966)
Climb the deep flake crack to an obvious jagged beak, then semi-hand-traverse right to a chimney and climb it on the outside.
Earwigo (S) the line on the inside of the chockstone.

33. Earwig One 9m HVS 5a (1970)
Climb to the beak (as for Earwig Two) then gain an awkward hanging groove which leads to the top.

34. Cheyenne 11m E5 6c (1991)
Climb Earwig Two to the beak, then move left for about two metres to the middle of the overlap and make a very hard move over this to an easy finish.

★ **35. Agrippa** 9m E2 5b (1967)
Four metres left of the beak, a crack runs through the centre of a small roof. Climb up to the roof, then surmount it by a painful jam.

★ **36. Herod** 10m HVS 5a (1967)
One metre left of Agrippa, climb the thin groove to a stepped-break in the overhangs and continue via a crack.

★★ **37. The Shriek of Baghdad** 11m HVS 5a (1967)(1976)
The classic of the crag, but the polished start may deter some climbers. However, it is worth persevering and the traverse is particularly worthwhile. Two metres left of Herod, layback up a smooth flake/crack, hand-traverse left at the top to gain a niche and exit from this by a crack.
★ **Direct Finish** (5c): continue through the roof above the initial flake crack.

38. Chemical Warfare 10m E2 6a (Pre-1996)
Take a direct line up the undercut rib to finish up The Shriek!

★ **39. Watching the Motorway Flow** 10m E1 5b (1978)
Start three metres left of The Shriek and just past an arête. Climb the crack with an ash near its top in the right wall.

40. Slime Gut 9m HS 4c (1966)
The corner to the left of The Shriek!

★ **41. Appleton Crack** 10m HS 4b (1966)
Climb the polished V-shaped groove a little to the left of Slime Gut, step right under the overlap and finish up the slab above.

42. Hazy Daze 8m HS 4b (1976)
Three metres to the left, follow the deep, twisting crack.

43. The Easy Way 7m D (Pre-1979)
The cracked corner left of Hazy Daze.

44. The Black Pig 9m VS 4b (1992)
Climb the dark, crozzly wall on the left.

★ **45. Girdle Traverse** 26m HVS 4c,5a   (Pre-1975)
A strenuous route stretching leftwards from Idleness to Slime Gut.
1. 8m Climb Idleness to the good foothold and hand-traverse left using the
break to reach a belay on a ledge with a tree.
2. 18m Continue at the same level to the wall of Agrippa. Trend down
leftwards slightly to the first crack on Agrippa and climb this to the roof.
Hand-traverse left to The Shriek, step round the arête on the left, and finish up
Slime Gut.

Debutante's Area
This is the area on the left of a large ash that grows from the crag.

46. Farleton Crack 8m VD   (1966)
The wide, steep crack that forms the left side of a pillar immediately left of the
ash.

47. Deb's Wall 8m E4 6b   (Pre-1987)
The centre of the wall on the left.

★ **48. Deb's Crack** 8m VS 5a   (1967)
A slippery struggle up the slim groove/crack.

★ **49. Super Dick** 9m HVS 5a   (Pre-1975)
On the left there is a prow. Climb this, starting on its left and using the edge of
Pleb's Chimney. Move up and out on to the prow at half-height.

50. Pleb's Chimney 8m VD   (1968)
The polished chimney on the left.

51. Heatwave 8m VS 5a   (1967)
Climb the centre of the next wall.

★ **52. Shower Crack** 8m VD   (1967)
The shallow groove at the left side of the wall.

53. Avalanche Route 7m VD   (1966)
The deep fissure one metre farther left.

★ **54. Mon Cadastre** 7m VD   (1990)
Start at the foot of the prow just to the left. A hard move gains better holds,
then these are followed directly up the arête.

The Dummy Wall
*15 metres left, past an easy way down, a large fallen slab, or 'dummy wall',
leans against the crag.*

55. Pleasant Wall Variant 6m S 4a   (1996)
Climb the short wall on the right of the dummy wall itself, keeping about one
metre left of the deep crack on the right.

56. Pleasant Wall 6m S 4a   (1967)
Climb on to a block at the right side of the dummy wall, then step right and
climb a rough wall to the top.

57. Scraper 7m S 4a   (Pre-1979)
The crack immediately left of the *'dummy wall'*.

58. The Gent 7m E1 5c   (1968)
The wall on the left is characterised by three pockets at head height. Start with hands on the two right-hand pockets and climb the wall using tiny flakes (much harder variations are possible about one metre to the right).

★ **59. Roughneck** 7m HVS 5b   (1968)
Start two metres to the left and climb directly to a short vertical runnel at the top.

60. Rough Crack 6m S 4a   (1967)
Layback up the next crack.

61. The Spoon 6m VD   (1967)
Three metres to the left is an obvious smooth scoop. Gain this by a traverse from the right or direct (harder), then finish up a left-slanting crack.

62. Paddy's Penance 6m S 4b   (1967)
Start three metres to the left on the right wall of an undercut arête. Surmount the bulge by laybacking and continue on side pulls up the steep wall to the top.

63. Woodpecker 6m VS 5a   (1998)
Start three metres farther left and gain, then climb, the crack that splits the upper half of the wall,

64. Slip Stitch 6m S 4b   (1967)
Start at the obvious wide crack about 35 metres farther left, about five metres past a large block lying below the path. Climb the crack to the horizontal break, then follow the fluted front of the block above to the top.

The edge now loses height but continues to offer excellent bouldering possibilities, as does the stratum above, with superb vistas across to the Lakeland mountains. About 200 metres past Slip Stitch and on a tier behind the Main Crag, a compact, slightly overhanging wall about five metres tall is of particular note. The centre of the block provides an intricate problem, **New Rose** *(6c), whilst the shallow groove on the right gives* **21st Century Digital Boy** *(5c).*

First Ascents at Farleton Crag

1966	**Doodlebug, Idleness, Appleton Crack, Farleton Crack, Earwig Two, Slime Gut, Avalanche Route** Ian Dobson, Roger Gott
1966	*Flake and Scoop* Ian Dobson, Roger Gott
	This route was superseded by Fat Good Crack, which followed its lower half, and Doggo, which took its top half.
1967	**The Shriek of Baghdad** Stew Wilson, Ian Dobson, Roger Gott
	Direct Finish by Al Evans, John Horsfall, 1976
1967	**Deb's Crack** Stew Wilson, Ian Dobson
1967	**Pleasant Wall, Rough Crack, The Spoon, Paddy's Penance, Slip Stitch** Stew Wilson, Tom Farrell

1967	**Shower Crack**	Stew Wilson, Tom Farrell, Wilf Partington
1967	**Caliban**	Stew Wilson, Rick Stallwood
1967	**Enyoka**	Bill Lounds, Chris Eilbeck
1967	**Agrippa, Herod**	Bill Lounds, Chris Eilbeck
1967	**Heatwave**	Stew Wilson, Ian 'Sherpa' Roper
1968	**The Family Way**	Ian 'Sherpa' Roper, Allan Austin
1968	**The Gent, Roughneck**	Allan Austin, Ian 'Sherpa' Roper
1970	**Earwig One**	Al Evans, Dave Parker
1971	**G Squared**	Dave Cronshaw, Bob MacMillan, Les Ainsworth
1971	**Pudding Club**	Les Ainsworth, Dave Cronshaw, Bob MacMillan
1973	**Pork Chop**	Al Evans, Dave Parker
	Louis Wall, 1974.	
1973	**Green Machine**	Dave Parker, Al Evans
1974	**Instant Whip**	Al Evans
Pre-1975	**Lumumba, Eggyoka, Girdle Traverse, Super Dick**	
1975	**Flaykier**	
1976	**The Pill, Klayfire, Doggo, Hazy Daze**	Al Evans, Dave Parker
1977	**Fat Good Crack**	Dave Parker, Al Evans
1978	**Watching the Motorway Flow**	John Girdley
Pre-1979	**Cracker, Prowler, The Easy Way, Scraper**	
1984	**Dimple, Dimple**	Dave Cronshaw, John Ryden
1984	**The Coil**	Wilf Williamson (solo)
Pre-1987	**Monkey Wrench, Rock Ivy Line, Anaconda, Primrose Path, Feet of Clay, Deb's Wall**	
1989	**Man of Straw**	Dave Cronshaw, John Ryden
1990	**Chastity, Mon Cadastre**	Stew Wilson, Maggie Wilson
1991 July 30	**Cheyenne**	John Gaskins (unseconded)
1992 Apr	**The Black Pig**	Karl Lunt (solo)
1994 July 25	**Pandemonium**	John Gaskins (top-roped)
1995 Aug 25	**Mathematics of Chaos**	John Gaskins (unseconded)
1995 Aug 31	**Chemical Warfare**	John Gaskins, Steven Micklethwaite, Tim Chapman
1996	**Pudding Flake, Pleasant Wall Variant**	Les Ainsworth, Dave Cronshaw
1998 July 4	**Woodpecker**	Dave Cronshaw, Les Ainsworth

Farleton Upper Crag   O.S. ref.   SD 541 802

Situation and Character

The Upper Crag is the escarpment of rock near the summit of the fell, that can
be seen from both the A6070 and M6 and which lies about 500 metres north of
the main crag. Although it is known as the Upper Crag, it is actually the lower
tier, whilst the main crag, which is at a lower elevation, is on the upper tier.

The crag is longer than the rest of the rock at Farleton, but is rather broken and
much of it is split by several small grassy ledges. The crag is very deceptive,
because it is dominated by a fairly nondescript lower section, that guards some
excellent rock at the top. However, it is well worth climbing the often lineless
and ledgy bottom sections to be rewarded with some classic finishes, mostly at
around Severe to VS. Many of the routes are very recent and they should
generally improve with traffic.

Approaches

The Upper Crag can be reached in a little over ten minutes from the cairn on the grassy track, where the path to the main crag strikes for the scree. Instead of leaving the grassy track at this point, continue in the same line along the grassy track until the Upper Crag comes into view above the track. When close to the crag, it is advisable to move on to the path that runs parallel to the track about 25 metres closer to the crag.

Alternatively, from the end of the main crag continue north (leftwards) until it is possible to descend through the broken lower tier, then continue northwards up a path.

The Climbs

The most obvious feature of the crag is the prominent prow of Rose Amongst Thorns, which lies about 20 metres short of a stone wall at the foot of the crag. The climbs are described from RIGHT to LEFT starting about 100 metres before this wall. Large boulders on the path at this point, and farther up, provide useful cues for locating the climbs.

Cubic Block Area

About 100 metres before the wall there is a large cube of rock just to the left of the path. The first route is located a little before this, just to the right of a large tree that grows part way up the crag.

1.   Arthritic Crack   9m   E2   5c   (1995)
Start just down the fell from the cube of limestone about eight metres right of the tree at a left-leaning pillar. Climb the pillar using the crack on its right. Sustained and well protected, but there is some loose rock.

2.   Rheumatic Crack   8m   VS   4b   (1996)
The deep crack which forms the left side of the pillar is more awkward than first appearances might suggest.

3.   Square Route   9m   HS   4b   (1996)
Start just left of the trees growing from the crag, below a square neb. Climb the crack on the right side, then step left on to the top of the neb to finish.

4.   Cube Route   9m   S   4a   (1996)
Climb easily into the large recess on the left of the neb, then move out right and make an interesting move to finish on the neb.

20 metres left of the trees and just up the hill from the cube of rock on the path, there is a hawthorn bush growing at about three metres.

5.   Hawthorn Flakes   8m   S   4a   (1996)
Start just left of the hawthorn bush and climb directly over a bulge to a flake crack. Use this flake to step up, then move slightly right to excellent holds and finish direct.

★ **6.   Dave's Scoop**   9m   HVS   5a   (1996)
Start two metres left of the hawthorn bush and climb up to the ledge, then enter the scoop above, exit awkwardly to the left and finish up easier rock.

7.   Trivial Pursuits   8m   HVS   5b   (1996)
Start four metres left of the hawthorn and climb a shallow groove to the break,
then the flake crack above.

8.   Hawthorn Wall   8m   S   4a   (1996)
Start one metre to the left and climb the wall to the horizontal break, step left,
then finish up the hanging corner above.

Midway Boulders Area

To the left the crag is broken by a large ledge and the next climbs are located
about 20 metres farther left at an area which is characterized by a clean-cut
groove near the top, capped by a prominent triangular overhang. This area is
known as the Midway Boulders Area, because it starts just right of some more
large boulders that lie by the path midway between Cubic Block and the wall.

9.   Little Triangle   10m   VS   4c   (1996)
Start two metres right of the prominent triangular overhang and climb the wall
to the break, then finish up the shallow groove above.

10.   Big Triangle   11m   HS   4a   (1996)
Start just left of the triangular overhang and gain the break using a small
'pinnacle'. Step right, then climb the deep groove and the triangular overhang at
its top.

11.   Midway Route   9m   VD   (1996)
Climb the obvious weakness one metre left of the small 'pinnacle' and finish up
the wide corner above the ledge.

★ **12.   Bury Route**   9m   VD   (1996)
Start two metres left of the small 'pinnacle' and climb the shallow depression
and stepped corners on the left.

13.   Prow Corner   8m   VD   (1994)
Just beyond the Midway Boulders on the path there is a prominent square-cut
roof low down. Climb the corner on the right of this to a ledge, then step left
and finish on good holds up the wall above. A rather pointless route that offers
little new climbing.

★★ **14.   Farleton Prow**   12m   E4   6b   (1994)(1995)
The impressive undercut prow demands powerful moves in an exposed position.
On the first ascent a micronut was preplaced at the base of the prow itself and
even with this, the climbing feels very serious. Climb Prow Corner for a couple
of metres until it is possible to traverse left with feet on the break beneath the
overhang, using pockets at the lip of the overhang. Ascend the arête to a good
block, then finish more easily.
Scattergun (6c): a direct start past the preplaced wire.

★ **15.   Buckshot**   14m   HS   4b   (Pre-1977)
A good climb, better than it looks. Start at a deep corner directly below the
blunt rib of Farleton Prow. Climb the corner to the square-cut roof, then traverse
left and go up to a large block. Step back right and finish up the short crack.

Windy Walls

This is the final section of the crag and it is easily recognized by the prominent prow and roof of Rose Amongst Thorns. This is the prominent nick close to the summit of the fell, which can be seen from the road. The first climbs start about 25 metres to the right of this roof and 10 metres left of the previous climbs. They can be further identified by a smooth wall at the top of the crag which is bounded by a crack on its left.

⋆ **16. Wild Wind** 14m HS 4b (1996)
Start to the left of a small hawthorn bush that lies directly below the crack at the top of the crag. Climb the wall to a ledge at the foot of the top crack. Use a hidden jug to pull up right, then either step back left and finish up the crack, or finish direct.

⋆ **17. Hurricane** 14m VD (1996)
Start eight metres to the left, below an obvious roof just above half height. Climb the wall directly to the left side of the roof, then swing left onto a projecting ledge and finish direct.

⋆ **18. Typhoon** 14m VD (1996)
Start one metre to the left, directly below a short V-groove capped by a roof near the top of the crag. Climb the crack on the right to a ledge, then step left and enter the V-groove. Exit directly over the roof.

⋆ **19. Head Wind** 14m S 4a (1996)
Start directly below the bleached tree and take a direct line to the top, finishing up twin cracks. Currently a little dirty at the bottom, but this should soon improve with traffic.

⋆ **20. Whirlwind** 14m VS 4c (1996)
Start about one metre to the left and climb up and right to a small ledge, then continue upwards avoiding a faint yellow scoop on its right. With hands on the horizontal break move left, then finish up the crack above.

21. Tornado 14m HS 4b (1996)
Start about two metres to the left, directly below the right end of the distinct square-cut neb and climb the wall and the broken groove to finish at the right side of the neb.

⋆ **22. Avoidance** 20m HS 4a (1971)
From the sentry-box at the foot of the crag below the distinct neb, climb the groove on the right side of the initial roof to reach the headwall below the roof of the neb. Traverse right, then finish up a short corner and crack.

⋆⋆ **23. Look Mum There's Vikings on the Tundra Again** 20m E5 6c (1996)
The protection is good but is awkward to place and the climbing is excellent, with a spectacular pull over the roof to a typically Farleton, finishing jug. Climb Avoidance, then climb the large roof via the thin right-hand crack.

⋆⋆ **24. Rose Amongst Thorns** 17m VS 4b (1971)
Straightforward climbing to the roof is more than compensated for by an exciting finish in a wonderfully exposed position. From the start of Avoidance climb the left side of the initial roof and the groove above to a ledge under the

roof. Move into the corner, climb to the roof then swing left on to the arête and an airy finish.

★ **25. California Dreaming** 18m HVS 5b (1974)
The next neb is composed of three blocks. Start below the central block and climb the loose wall to a small overhang and a shallow groove above (peg) to a more prominent triangular overhang. Move right around this and finish up the crack above.

26. Blood on the Tracks 18m HVS 5b (1977)
Start two metres to the left and climb through the roof to a hanging groove that leads to the left side of the three-block neb. Pass this on its right and finish up a groove.

27. Silent Jim 15m HS 4a (Pre-1979)
Two metres to the left there is a jutting rock fin. Climb the left side of this, then move diagonally right across the wall to finish up the short, deep, top corner which bounds the neb on its left.

28. Les's Arête 10m S 4a (1996)
10 metres left of the stone wall there is a large, square overhang. Avoid this on its right, then step back left and climb up the rounded rib above.

First Ascents at Farleton Upper Crag

1971 June **Avoidance** Les Ainsworth {solo}
1971 July **Rose Amongst Thorns** Les Ainsworth, Dave Cronshaw
1974 **California Dreaming** Al Evans, John Girdley,
Pre-1977 **Buckshot**
1977 **Blood on the Tracks** John Girdley
Pre-1979 **Silent Jim**
1994 May 2 **Prow Corner** Tom Walkington (solo)
1994 May 8 **Farleton Prow** Tom Walkington (unseconded)
Scattergun by John Gaskins, 8 July 1995.
1994 May 8 **Arthritic Crack** Tom Walkington, Keith Birkett, Eric Barnes
1996 Apr 13 **Square Route** Les Ainsworth, Dave Cronshaw
1996 Apr 13 **Cube Route** Dave Cronshaw, Les Ainsworth
1996 Apr 20 **Little Triangle, Trivial Pursuits, Big Triangle** Dave Cronshaw, Les Ainsworth
1996 Apr 27 **Bury Route** Paul Dewhurst, Gareth Parry, Alan White, Adam Dewhurst, Tom Moore
1996 May 31 **Tornado, Hurricane** Dave Cronshaw, Les Ainsworth
1996 July 6 **Rheumatic Crack, Dave's Scoop, Midway Route** Dave Cronshaw, Les Ainsworth
1996 July 6 **Hawthorn Flakes, Hawthorn Wall, Wild Wind, Typhoon** Les Ainsworth, Dave Cronshaw
1996 July 10 **Les's Arête** Les Ainsworth, Aly Ainsworth
1996 July 12 **Head Wind** Les Ainsworth, Dave Cronshaw
1996 July 12 **Whirlwind** Dave Cronshaw, Les Ainsworth
1996 Sep 15 **Look Mum There's Vikings on the Tundra Again** John Gaskins (unseconded)

Farleton Quarry
O.S. ref.   SD 536 809

The quarry lies on the fellside directly behind the village of Farleton, just above an old lime kiln. However, it should not be approached direct. The quarry is small and an abundance of trees nearby means that it is often slow to dry.

To reach the quarry, park thoughtfully in Farleton village and walk to the sharp bend on the road that enters the village from the A6070. From here a footpath that is signed to *Farleton Fell* leads along the left side of a field to a small gate. Go through this gate and turn left to a left fork after about 80 metres. Take this, then bear back round below the top of an old quarry and go through a curious wicket between two trees. Then strike slightly right and downwards to the foot of the quarry.

The Climbs
The climbs are described from LEFT to RIGHT.

1.   Yoruba   9m   S   4a   (1968)
The right-leaning crack with a tree part way up it at the left side of the wall.

2.   Hark to Bounty   9m   VS   4c   (1973)
Start at the centre of the wall between Yoruba and Ebo, then at the top bear slightly left to the large tree.

3.   Ebo   10m   HS   4b   (1968)
The deep crack in the centre of the wall.

4.   Uhuru   14m   E1   5b   (1968)
Farther right is a block at the foot of the wall. Climb the steep wall above this, then a thin crack to a bulge. Continue on small holds to the final bulging wall which is climbed strenuously to the top.

5.   The Pit   13m   VD   (1973)
From the corner at the foot of the quarry, climb up the large ledge, then finish up the short corner behind a tree.

⋆ **6.   Mister Universe**   37m   HVS   5a   (1973)(1973)
A right-to-left traverse of the wall, the first moves being the hardest. Climb the first three metres of The Pit to a good flake, then use this to move on to the wall above. Hard moves then lead to a niche, where a break can be followed to a finish up Yoruba.
The Pit and the Pendulum (VS 4c 1pt aid): the wall can be girdled from left to right, with a rope move from the peg on Uhuru to cross the difficult rock.

First Ascents at Farleton Quarry
1968   **Uhuru, Ebo, Yoruba**   Bill Lounds, Stew Wilson
1973   **Hark to Bounty**   Dave Parker, Al Evans
1973   **Mister Universe**
            The Pit and the Pendulum (1pt aid) by Al Evans, Dave Parker, 1973.
1973   **The Pit**

Hutton Roof Crags   O.S. ref.   SD 565 782

Situation and Character

The Hutton Roof Crags is a collection of small limestone outcrops on the side
of the hill, about three kilometres due east of Farleton Crag. In previous editions
of the Lancashire guidebook, Hutton Roof has been briefly described in the
Minor Crags section. This has led to its being neglected, except by local
climbers who are in the know. This is a great pity, because although the climbs
are short, the quality of the rock and the location makes it a very pleasant spot
for a middle-grade climber to spend a summer evening.

The best climbing is at The Rakes, which gives climbs of up to nine metres on
excellent limestone, generally ranging from VD to VS. However, the bottom
couple of moves on some climbs can be particularly hard for their grade.

There is also some climbing at Uberash Breast (O.S. ref. SD 554 781). This has
more extensive views but the climbing is not as good.

History

While on a Christmas walk in 1973 from the village of Lupton, where John
Parker lived, he and Arthur Holdsworth paused to have a look at Hutton Roof
Crags. They soloed what was to be the first recorded climb, *Original Route*
(now known as *West Coast*). Parker then returned to the crag in early 1974 and
together with Holdsworth and Peter Randall, he climbed and recorded nearly
thirty climbs. Next they discovered the impressive line of *Wings* and the
pleasant *Ronson Kirkby*. Then they worked through the problems on Ape
Buttress, including *Chimp, Gorilla Berengii* and the two *Pithecanthropus* routes.
Finally, they attacked the steeper lines on South America Wall, where they
climbed *San Antonio* and *Sandinista*. The latter was eventually solved on the
evening after a funeral and so it was named *Funereal Way*. Unfortunately, notes
of these climbs were only distributed to a few members of Kendal MC and
subsequently the original names were forgotten. Surprisingly, following the
production of this typescript guide to the crag, there was no great rush to fill in
any of the gaps and the only other route to be recorded during that period was a
traverse rightwards from Wings to a finish past the 'cyclops' eye, which was
reported in 1975 by members of Kendal Mountain Rescue Team. This route,
which they named *Cornflake*, was basically *Winged Traverse*, starting from
Wings instead of Pegasus.

Although Hutton Roof soon became a popular evening venue with locals, it was
only reported in the Lancashire guidebooks from 1975 onwards as a 'Minor
Crag' and so further developments did not tend to be reported, though it does
appear that in 1987 Nick Conway was the first person to complete the problem
traverse that bears his name.

In 1991 Stew Wilson decided that Hutton Roof deserved more recognition and
so together with Karl Lunt, Matt Ellis and his wife Maggie, he systematically
worked along the crag and recorded all the climbs. Although most of the climbs
that were recorded had probably been done many times before, it is likely that
some were new. Nevertheless, because of the lack of information, all the climbs
that were listed in the guidebook were renamed and because these have now
become established, these have been used in the current guidebook.

Approaches

The crags can be approached from either the west or the east side of the fell.

The eastern approach, from the village of Hutton Roof, is the shortest way to The Rakes (5 to 10 minutes). Park at the south end of the village in a lay-by near a phone box, then walk back up the hill to a track on the left, immediately before the turn to Kirkby Lonsdale. Follow this for 100 metres, then go through a gate and follow a path by the wall round to the left. After about 20 metres fork right, then left and head for an obvious large perched block on the skyline. Pass just to the right of this block then continue straight up the hill. At the top of the steep section the angle eases and a path bears left to South America Wall.

The western approach is via the *Limestone Link* footpath. This can be reached by following a minor road north east from the village of Clawthorpe for about two kilometres to a parking space on the wide verge just before the footpath signs, about 100 metres before another road forks right (This point can also be reached by following the approach to Farleton Crag to the third gate, then, instead of turning right across the fellside, continue straight on). Follow the *Limestone Link* eastwards passing above a house known as Kelker Well and continue through dwarf hazels until after the highest point the path drops into a small, sheltered valley containing The Rakes. To reach Uberash Breast it is necessary to strike rightwards at the start of the *Limestone Link* heading uphill in a southerly direction. The top of the hill is marked by three cairns and the rocks face west below these.

The Climbs

All of the climbs that are described are at The Rakes and these are described from LEFT to RIGHT starting at South America Wall.

South America Wall

This is situated at the extreme left end of the crag and is characterised by a steep prow which is shaped like the continent of South America. To the right of this are two very steep grooves above a steep wall.

1.   Hanging Crack D   (1991)
The hanging crack in a scoop about four metres to the left of the tip of South America!

2.   Straight Crack VD   (1991)
The obvious wide crack immediately to the right.

3.   Galapagos D   (1973)
Start one metre to the right and gain a shallow niche, then finish up the crack above.

★ **4.   West Coast** D   (1973)
Start at the tip of South America and climb the left edge of the continent to finish up an easy crack.

★ **5.   Sendero Luminoso** HS 4b   (Pre-1991)
Start as for West Coast. Climb into the niche, then move up right and follow a thin crack in the centre of the face. A long reach gains a good break and good holds lead directly to the top.

6. Argentina VS 5a (Pre-1995)
Start as for West Coast and climb the right-slanting crack to the first break, then continue up the centre of the 'continent' above.

★ **7. Belize** VS 5a (Pre-1991)
A great little climb both technical and strenuous. Start just left of the obvious vertical crack three metres right of the tip of South America. Climb the thin, left-trending crack to gain good footholds, then finish up the overhanging flake on good holds.

★ **8. Sandinista** VS 5a (1974)
Very sustained and fine in the lower half. Start at the foot of the very thin vertical crack immediately right of Belize. Climb this crack by an awkward layback from the right. The steep corner above is easier than it looks.

American Dream (6b): an interesting problem up the centre of the smooth wall between Sandinista and San Miguel.

★ **9. San Miguel** VS 5a (Pre-1991)
Start three metres to the right at the foot of another thin vertical crack. Climb this crack, moving left to a good flake on the underside of the bulge. Climb directly over the bulge and finish direct.

★ **10. San Antonio** VS 5a (1974)
One metre to the right of San Miguel a faint vertical crack leads to the obvious V-corner above. Climb the crack to the horizontal break and finish up the very steep corner above.

11. Pablo S (Pre-1991)
Climb the wide crack in the steep corner to a jammed block. Pull over the bulge rightwards and finish on excellent sculpted holds.

12. Crack Climb VD (1974)
The flaky crack two metres farther to the right.

The jumbled blocks to the right provide numerous pitches of moderate difficulty.

Cave Area
Right of jumbled blocks there is smooth slab bounded on its right by a chimney corner with overhangs above it. To the right, the crag extends as a long wall with a barrier of overhangs at two metres forming a shallow cave at the left end.

★ **13. Wrinkled Slab** VD (Pre-1991)
Start below the steep corner at the left end of the wall. Climb the corner until it is possible to step rightwards on to the wrinkled slab. Move right and go up the edge of this.

14. The Flake VD (Pre-1991)
One metre to the right is a jammed block at ground level below a flake. Climb up to and past the flake.

15.   Pot Belly   S   4b   (Pre-1991)
One metre right, climb the rounded buttress via a bulge to a vegetated crack finish.

16.   The Barrier Roof   S   4a   (1974)
Start immediately left of the barrier roof. Climb a left-facing flake and the wall above just right of an ash.

17.   Roof Route Left   VS   5a   (Pre-1991)
Climb the roof at its left side to a good jug above the lip.

18.   Roof Route One   HVS   5b   (Pre-1991)
From an undercut at the back of the cave, surmount the roof past a short crack and a jug on its lip.

19.   Roof Route Two   VS   5a   (1974)
Climb through the roof via the next crack, which forms a block at the lip.

20.   Roof Route Three   E1   5c   (Pre-1991)
Start from an obvious undercut at the back of the roof, then climb over the roof using a pocket on the lip.

21.   Roof Route Four   VS   5a   (Pre-1991)
Climb the roof at its right side, using a large flake jug on its lip.

There are two interesting problems in this area. **Roof Traverse** *(5b) traverses in either direction below the lower roof, and* **Upper Traverse**, *also 5b, hand traverses from right to left, mainly using jugs on the lip of the lower overhang.*

22.   Sinister Crack   VS   5a   (Pre-1991)
Start one metre right of the long roof, below another roof at a slightly higher level that has a left-trending diagonal crack above it. Climb the cracked wall to the upper roof, then gain the diagonal crack with difficulty and continue to the top.

23.   Dexter Wall   HS   4c   (1974)
Start at a short, left-curving crack one metre left of the right-hand end of the wall. Climb the crack and the wall on its right, then make long reaches between horizontal breaks to finish.

Sycamore Buttress
This is the taller, bow-fronted buttress a little farther right, behind a large sycamore tree.

24.   Sylvie   S   4b   (Pre-1991)
A pleasant climb. Start just right of a shallow corner at a steep arête. Climb the arête and the face above.

25.   Daphne   S   4a   (1974)
Start one metre to the right at a right-trending flake below a five-stemmed ash tree. Climb the flake and wall just left of the ash.

26.   Hebe   VD   (Pre-1991)
Four metres to the right, climb the groove, then step right on to the slab and climb this to the top.

A wide, left leading groove, **Groove Line** *(M), at the left-hand side of this buttress, provides a useful* **DESCENT**.

Sunny Wall
After 25 metres of more broken, easy-angled rock, the crag increases in height at a bowl surrounded by trees. This is Sunny Wall. At the left end of the wall a three-metre high block stands at the foot of the crag and a large ash grows up against the face.

27. Hedera Wall D   (Pre-1991)
Climb the wall two metres past the block.

28. Sunny Groove D   (1974)
Start one metre to the right and climb a shallow groove directly above large blocks.

Just before the ground level drops away, there is a one-metre high flake at the base of the crag.

⋆ **29. T' Owd Man VD**   (Pre-1991)
From the flake, climb the wall direct. A good steep route.

30. T' Owd Trout VD   (Pre-1991)
An attractive climb. One metre to the right, ascend the obvious shallow cracked groove.

The Hollow
Past some blocks the ground level falls slightly at a small, wooded hollow.

31. Hollow Slab VD   (1998)
Start at the left side of the hollow and climb a small bulge to reach a large ledge. Continue up the centre of the wall above.

32. Hollow Route VD   (1998)
Follow the next crack to a higher ledge. From the left side of this ledge step left and finish up a shallow groove.

33. Holloween VD   (1998)
Climb the bulge on the right to reach the higher ledge, then finish up the centre of the wall above.

⋆ **34. The Crooked Man S 4a**   (1974)
Start at the foot of a steep layback crack which trends right. Climb this and move rightwards in the shade of a big ash to a shallow groove in the steep wall above. Climb this on excellent rock.

Ash Tree Wall
A rather nondescript area of wall and easy-cracked slabs which extends rightwards from the big ash in the hollow to the fine crack of Wings.

35. Ash Tree Slab VD   (Pre-1991)
Start immediately to the right of the ash. Climb the slab and shallow depression up to the left, finishing directly above the tree.

36.   The Chopping Block   VD   (Pre-1991)
Start two metres to the right and take a direct line over steep rock to the
obvious block at the top.

37.   Cracked Groove   VD   (1974)
Start two metres to the right at a shallow depression. Climb this and the wall
above to finish.

38.   Speedy Recovery   S   4a   (Pre-1991)
Start on the right at a slightly lower level immediately right of some blocks.
Climb the steep wall to a bulge and follow the short ragged crack to the top.

39.   The Ashes   D   (Pre-1991)
Start one metre to the right below twin saplings. Climb the wall and crack
above on good holds.

40.   Ash Gully   M   (Pre-1991)
Climb the gully containing an ash.

Ronson Kirkby Area

*Towards the right end of the escarpment and beyond the cloak of ashes in front
of the crag is a fine clean face having an obvious bulge at half-height and a
straight crack running the height of the face on the left of the bulge.*

41.   Left Wall   VD   (Pre-1991)
Start just right of the gully below a left-facing flake at head height. Climb on to
a ledge, then climb the flake and slab to the top.

★ **42.   The Rib**   HS   4b   (Pre-1991)
Start at a faint rib just left of the obvious crack of Wings. Climb the rib via a
nice step up using a runnel.

★ **43.   Wings**   VD   (1974)
A very pleasant climb. Climb the groove/crack immediately left of the overhang,
with an interesting move at the overhang.

★ **44.   Pegasus**   VS   5a   (1975/Pre-1991)
Start two metres to the right, directly below a horizontal slot on the lip of the
overhang. Climb up to some blocks below the bulge. Climb to the overhang,
then pull over on the horizontal slot and reach good holds to gain the upper wall.

45.   Winged Traverse   VS   5a   (1975)
Start up Pegasus and traverse right below the roof past the 'eye' and finish
direct where the break widens. A finish can also be made via the 'eye' at a
similar grade.

★★ **46.   Cyclops**   HVS   6a   (Pre-1991)
The first moves are very problematic, but the roof itself is relatively easy. Start
below the small 'eye' pocket above the lip at the right-hand end of the bulge.
Climb the wall below and slightly right of the 'eye' on poor holds to reach the
horizontal break. Gain the eye and swarm up the easy face above.

★ **47. Serpent** S 4a (Pre-1991)

Start just right of the right end of the mid-height bulge below a little, waterworn crack. Climb the crack steeply and gain the sloping crack above the bulge. Foot-traverse left with ease and finish up the centre of the top wall.

48. Ronson Kirkby VD (1974)

One metre right of Serpent there is a good flake. Climb this to a ledge on the right. Climb directly to the next horizontal break and move left along this to the top.

49. Little Corner VD (Pre-1991)

Start two metres right of the good flake. Climb steeply to the good ledge, then ascend the little corner above finishing up the wall on good holds.

50. Concave Wall VD (Pre-1991)

Start one metre left of the descent gully. Climb easy cracks to a diagonal crack slanting left. Follow this to the top horizontal break and move left to finish as for Little Corner.

Four Walls

Just right of the descent gully are four walls ending 15 metres farther right at a vegetated mass of hazel and ivy.

★ **51. First Wall Rib** VD (Pre-1991)

Climb the rounded rib of the first wall.

52. Crackling D (Pre-1991)

Excellent climbing on superb holds. Climb the crack between first wall and second wall.

★ **53. Smooth Rib** S 4a (Pre-1991)

Climb the smooth rib immediately right of Crackling.

54. Second Wall VD (Pre-1991)

Start immediately below a short flake at the top and take a direct line.

55. Crazy Paving D (Pre-1991)

Start a metre right and climb the well-cracked slab and wall above.

56. Pedestal Crack D (Pre-1991)

Climb the crack between the second and third walls via a pedestal.

57. Third Wall Central VD (Pre-1991)

Climb the centre of the third wall using prominent pockets.

The fourth wall is to the right of a small ash tree and has a precarious block at its left side.

★ **58. The Runnel** D (1974)

Start below and right of a brown water-stain. Climb the crozzly runnel above on excellent rock. There are variations at a similar grade on either side of the runnel.

Ape Buttress

This is the long undercut wall 25 metres right, which gains height and becomes a fine buttress of excellent rock. The upper wall is pure jug-pulling pleasure, but to reach it, some hard work on the bulge at chest-height is necessary.

★ **59.   Primate**   VS   5a   (1974)
Start two metres right of the left end of the wall at a slim groove at head-height. Reach up to good holds on a ledge and pull strenuously up the bulge to finish above on parallel, vertical cracks.

60.   Swamp Fever   HVS   5b   (Pre-1991)
Start one metre right, below an obvious right-facing flake hold above the roof. Climb direct to this and the wall above.

61.   Malaria   HVS   5b   (Pre-1991)
Start a metre right below a vertical crack. Reach this with difficulty and continue more easily.

★ **62.   The Lemur's Tail**   HS   4c   (Pre-1991)
Start at the foot of the obvious, thin crack a metre left of a deep groove. Climb the crack and finish up its continuation.

63.   Gibbon Take   5a   (Pre-1991)
Start five metres right of The Lemur's Tail. Climb the left-hand of the two parallel cracks which are a metre apart.

64.   No More Monkey Business   5a   (Pre-1991)
Climb the right-hand crack. Purists can increase the grade to 6b by starting right at the back of the overhang.

★ **65.   Chimp**   HS   4c   (1974)
Start at the same point and pull over the bulge at the right slanting crack using good holds, then finish up the face.

★ **66.   Gorilla Berengii**   HS   4c   (1974)
Just right and growing from the face is a slim tree. Start a metre left of this tree and pull over the bulge on an excellent flake hold. Easier climbing leads to the final crack.

★★ **67.   Gorilla, Gorilla**   VS   4c   (Pre-1991)
Start below the slim tree in the centre of the wall. Climb the bulge and pass the tree to reach the horizontal break. Climb directly up the front of the buttress just right of a curving nut-crack. More sustained and finer than its neighbours.
The Cause (6c): start at the back of the roof.

★ **68.   Pithecanthropus Indirectus**   VS   4c   (1974)
Start at the base of the obvious left-slanting crack and surmount the overhang, then step right into cracks and finish direct.

69.   Pithecanthropus Erectus   HS   4b   (1974)
Start at the extreme right-hand end of the overhang. Climb direct up the wall immediately right of the blunt arête.

★★ **70.   Nick's Traverse**   6c   (1987)
A must for all boulderers. Traverse the wall at low-level, left or right using only
the red-spotted handholds.

*Past this buttress there are a few short problems, but the only one that is
worthy of note is* **Lay Back** *(VD), which climbs the obvious corner 25 metres
farther to the right.*

First Ascents at Hutton Roof

The original names (where known) are given in brackets after the current names.

1973 Dec	**West Coast** (Original Route), **Galapagos** (Eastern Promise) John Parker, Arthur Holdsworth (both solo)
1974	**San Antonio** (Masterfoot), **Crack Climb** (Crack Climb), **The Barrier Roof** (Ivy's Agony), **Roof Route Two** (Roof), **Dexter Wall** (Peeler), **Daphne** (Rambling Route), **Sunny Groove** (Wide Rungs), **The Crooked Man** (Scoop One), **Cracked Groove** (Scoop Two), **Wings** (Gangway Crack), **Ronson Kirkby** (Gangway), **The Runnel** (Face Climb), **Primate** (Weak End), **Chimp** (Sheep Shank), **Gorilla Berengii** (Sheep Shelter), **Pithecanthropus Indirectus** (Neck End), **Pithecanthropus Erectus** (Neck End, variant), **Lay Back** John Parker, Arthur Holdsworth, Peter Randall (varied leads)
1974 Apr	**Sandinista** (Funereal Way) John Parker, Arthur Holdsworth
1975	**Winged Traverse** (Cornflake) Members of Kendal Mountain Rescue Team *Originally started up Wings, but it is more in-keeping to start up Pegasus.*
1987	**Nick's Traverse** Nick Conway
1991	**Hanging Crack, Straight Crack, Sendero Luminoso, Belize, San Miguel, Pablo, Wrinkled Slab, The Flake, Pot Belly, Roof Route One, Roof Route Three, Roof Route Four, Sinister Crack,** *Imitation Verdon,* **Sylvie, Hebe, Hedera Wall, T' Owd Man, T' Owd Trout, Ash Tree Slab, The Chopping Block, Speedy Recovery, The Ashes, Ash Gully, Left Wall, The Rib, Pegasus, Cyclops, Serpent, Little Corner, Concave Wall, First Wall Rib, Crackling, Smooth Rib, Second Wall, Crazy Paving, Pedestal Route, Third Wall Central, Swamp Fever, Malaria, The Lemur's Tail, Gibbon Take, No More Monkey Business, Gorilla Gorilla** Karl Lunt, Matt Ellis, Maggie Wilson, Stew Wilson (varied leads)
Pre-1995	**Argentina**
1998 June 12	**Hollow Slab, Hollow Route, Holloween** Les Ainsworth, Dave Cronshaw (both solo)

Jack Scout Crag   O.S. ref.   SD 459 736

Please read the Access section before visiting Jack Scout Crag

Situation and Character

The crag is just north of Jenny Brown's Point near Silverdale and is the nearest
thing in the Lancashire guidebook area to a sea-cliff, though the routes
(especially at the left side) are only sea-washed at high spring tides. More often
the outlook is over extensive sand and mud flats, laced with glittering channels
and a variety of birds. The crag gets all available sun from just after mid-day
until the very last moment, which makes it a pleasant spot.

The rock is variable, but rarely poses major problems. The routes are longer
than on most of the neighbouring crags, with some very good lines: the
strongest of which is the gently rising break of The Onedin Line. Generally the

holds are good and the angle is just off vertical, giving some good Severes and even more VSs.

The crag forms part of a Site of Special Scientific Interest (SSSI); owned by the National Trust. A number of nationally-rare tree species grow on the crag and in order to avoid damage to them and the other vegetation it is often necessary to use bolt runners and to make abseil descents (see Access section for more information).

History

The first known routes were done in 1969, including the line now known as *Cave Route*, which was originally led by Carl Dawson and named *Contraband*. Also climbed at that period, and also under a different name, was the classic route of *The Onedin Line*; led by a young lady called Sheila. Other visitors included Bill Lounds, Chris Eilbeck, Dave Thompson, Charlie Vigano and various Kendal climbers, but systematic development and recording had to wait until 1978 when John Girdley, Al Evans and various members of Lancaster University M.C. systematically climbed and recorded the most obvious lines. Most of the route names date from that period, even if the routes themselves had been done before.

The Eighties opened with Ed Robinson's ascent of the fierce *Sexless Wench*, but the most significant event was probably the weather. A combination of westerly gales and high tides, which caused some serious erosion, including the disappearance of the fine carpet of turf that used to lie at the foot of most of the climbs, leaving a much less pleasant jumble of seaweed-covered boulders. Nevertheless, in 1981 Owain Jones and his father managed to add *The Bermuda Triangle* whilst Martin Elliott climbed the pleasant *Armada*.

The next significant developments had to wait for over 12 years, when Les Ainsworth and Dave Cronshaw added *White Groove, Whitebeam* and *Sandfly* during conservation work at the crag. At the same time, Roger Bunyan, with Graham Bradley and others, added six routes in the easier grades at the far right-hand side.

Approach

From Warton follow the road towards Silverdale and turn left after the level-crossing, then first left again (signposted to Jenny Brown's Point) and continue for just over one kilometre to a junction at Wolf House Gallery, where the main road bears right into the village and towards Woodwell. Turn left and after about 500 metres there is limited parking in front of Ridgway Park. Go through the gate on the seaward side and walk towards the sea bearing slightly left at a rounded boulder and passing a limestone bench (slightly hidden) on the right. At the fence overlooking the sea, go over a stile and scramble down to the foreshore, taking care on the slippy rocks. Turn right to reach the seaward end of the cove in about 50 metres. At high tide it may be necessary to make a short traverse in.

Andy Caple on the second pitch of **Sluice** (HVS 5a), Trowbarrow.   *Photo: Jon Sparks*

Access

The crag belongs to the National Trust, which is happy to permit climbing, provided that this does not damage the rare and fragile plant environment. If climbers take a sensitive approach to climbing at Jack Scout, both the plants and the climbers can easily co-exist, but it is necessary for us to accept some limited restrictions. However, these are not very onerous, as the best climbing tends to be in the areas that are relatively free of vegetation.

Jack Scout is ecologically very unusual and the high importance of conserving this unique area has been recognized in its SSSI status. Three species of rare tree, the Lancaster whitebeam, rock whitebeam and wild service tree all grow on the crag, together with clifftop heath and grassland of special interest for its flora and fauna. It is certainly an environment that is well worth preserving, both for the climber and for other visitors. In order to avoid unreasonable ecological damage to the crag, climbers should keep to the following four guidelines:

(1)   **There should be no climbing on routes or areas of the crag that are described as being particularly sensitive.**

(2)   **No vegetation should be removed.** The ecological balance is so fragile and species are so interdependent, that even the removal of ivy can be damaging.

(3)   **Avoid using the trees or bushes for runners.**

(4)   **Avoid abseil descents**, except where these are specifically described to avoid vegetation.

The Climbs

The climbs are described from LEFT to RIGHT, starting about seven metres from the stone wall. The better climbing is generally situated towards the centre of the crag. **DESCENT** is possible at either end and is usually more pleasant at the seaward end, though this may not be practical if the tide is in.

Erect Pedestal Area

The first climbs are located on the rock just right of the stone wall at the start of the crag. This part of the crag is further identified by a large erect pedestal which rises from the ground about 10 metres to the right of the stone wall.

1.   Shooting Star   12m   VS   4b   (1978)
Previously, incorrectly named Superstar. Seven metres to the right of the stone wall is a corner split by a deep crack. Climb the centre of the wall on its left, to a shattered bulge, then step left to avoid this and finish to the right of the twisted yew tree.

2.   Whitebeam   12m   VD   (1995)
The deep crack in the corner.

The tide is out for a climber on **Coral Sea** (VS 4c), Trowbarrow.   *Photo: Dave Cronshaw*

3.   Lemming's Ville   15m   VS   4c   (Pre-1979)
Between the corner and the erect pedestal on the right is a right-leaning crack
which leads to a bottomless groove. Climb the crack, or the enjoyable slab on
its right, into the groove. The upper reaches are yew-shadowed, but surprisingly
clean and pleasant.

4.   Holly Throttled Groove   15m   D   (Pre-1979)
A poor route in the back wall of the bay behind the erect pedestal and obvious
by its name.

5.   The Bermuda Triangle   9m   HVS   5b   (1981)
Climb the bottomless corner and the hanging crack in the grooved arête on the
right of the pedestal, then step right at the top to a bolt belay. Abseil descent to
avoid damage to vegetation.

★ **6.   Armada**   9m   S   4a   (1981)
Start three metres farther right and climb the centre of the white wall to hanging
flakes. Then climb these to a bolt belay. Abseil descent to avoid damage to
vegetation.

7.   Sandfly   15m   VD   (1995)
Climb the wide crack and groove in the angle to a ledge on top of the block on
the left.

*Routes have been made between Sandfly and Question Mark. However, much of
this area is ecologically very sensitive and where there is no vegetation some of
the rock is in a dangerous state. Therefore climbers have agreed to avoid this
area.*

Stubby Pedestal Area
*After a short section of relatively uninteresting rock, the next section is marked
by a three-metre high pedestal at ground level. The short bottomless chimney
about five metres left of the pinnacle has been climbed, but has seen at least
three recent rockfalls and is poised for more and so it should be avoided.*

8.   Question Mark   17m   VD   (Pre-1979)
Directly behind the stubby pedestal, step up to a right-leaning, block-filled crack
and climb it to a ledge at six metres. Traverse right (loose) to the crack of
Unreal City, go up to the girdle break and back left to the yew tree stance.
Finish behind this.

9.   Unreal City   15m   VS   4c   (Pre-1979)
Just beyond the stubby pedestal there is a rock-fall scar at half-height beneath a
prominent roof. Climb to the roof then continue up a deep crack to the girdle
break. Pass the overhang with a long reach for a good jug.

10.   Nomad   15m   VS   4c   (Pre-1979)
Start just to the right of the rock-fall scar; pass the small, lower overhang with
difficulty. Continue directly to the girdle and step right into a finishing a groove.

⋆ **11. Celebration Day** 15m VS 4c (Pre-1979)
Three metres farther right and about eight metres before the cave there are two opposing flakes just below the girdle break. Climb up to these and move left to finish up groove of Nomad.

⋆ **12. Curlew Calling** 15m S 4a (Pre-1979)
Start immediately to the right and climb an obvious groove and the wall above to the roof. Step right across Elusive Valentine and finish up a short, easy groove.

⋆ **13. Elusive Valentine** 14m VS 4c (Pre-1979)
Climb the thin, right-leaning crack in the wall on the other side of the arête with difficulty, and continue straight up the wall. Pull over the jutting rib above the girdle break on large holds and finish up the rib over poor rock.

14. In the Wake of Poseidon 15m E3 5c (Pre-1979)
A large rock-fall, of which the scars can still be seen, has completely changed the upper part of this route; the upper wall is still friable.
Climb a shallow flake/groove two metres to the left of the cave, then the wall above, a little to the left of the cave. From the girdle break, finish up the groove above as for Curlew.

Cave Area
The deep cave at the centre of the crag is one of its most prominent features.

⋆ **15. Contraband (Cave Route)** 16m HVS 5a (1969)
Bridge up out of the cave on its left and continue up the deep pink groove to the overlap. Move left to a finish up the groove of Curlew.

16. Sexless Wench 9m HVS 5b (1980)
The overhanging rib on the right demands forceful climbing. Abseil descent from the yew, or finish up Brant's.

⋆⋆ **17. Brant's Little Brother** 18m VS 4c (Pre-1979)
The obvious V-shaped groove has several chockstones, which rattle cheerfully but seem to be going nowhere. At the top of the groove traverse right along the horizontal break past two bolts, then move up slightly to a grassy ledge and a twin-bolt belay below a short, but prominent, corner groove in the headwall. Step right into the next groove and climb this to its top.

18. Masochism Tango 16m HVS 5b (Pre-1979)
The blunt rib right of Brant's Little Brother is climbed directly to reach the horizontal break (bolt). Move up to the grassy ledge and a twin-bolt belay. Finish as for Brant's or Jackal.

⋆ **19. Jackal** 15m HS 4b (Pre-1979)
Just right again is a fine deep crack. Climb this to the girdle break, move right then go up to a small tree. Move rightwards again to the twin-bolt belay of Brant's below a short, prominent, corner groove. Climb the groove itself and finish up the wall on its left.

⋆ **20. Victim of Life** 15m HS 4b (Pre-1979)
Just to the right are two pairs of parallel thin cracks: climb these to the girdle break, then continue to a twin-bolt belay and follow Jackal to finish.

★ 21.   Spring Tide 15m S   4a   (Pre-1979)
Just to the right, an obvious series of crazy jugs leads to a breach in the
overhang. Above this step right to a twin-bolt belay, then finish up the same
groove as Brant's.

★ 22.   Crying Crocodile 15m HVS 5a   (Pre-1979)
About three metres to the right there is a dog-leg crack which leads to the
centre of the roof. Climb this to the overhang and take this directly with
difficulty (there is sometimes a peg). Cross the slab easily to reach the twin-bolt
belay on Brant's, then finish as for Brant's or Jackal.

★ 23.   Laughing Hyena 15m VS 4b   (Pre-1979)
Climb the flaky groove on the right to the overhang and over this on good
holds, then move slightly leftwards to the twin-bolt belay on Brant's and finish
up Brant's or Jackal. A direct finish has been reported at E1, but has not been
repeated since a hold came off.

24.   Vietnam Defoliation Squad 21m VS 4c   (Pre-1979)
On the right there is a deep, left-leading groove. Climb this, crossing the
overhang above the girdle to gain the slab, then wander leftwards to the
twin-bolt belay on Brant's. Finish up Brant's or Jackal.

★ 25.   Morecambe Bay Eliminate 18m VS 4c   (Pre-1979)
Start two metres to the right, directly below a service tree with a hanging
groove on its left. Climb to the break, then continue up the hanging groove to
the tree (to avoid damage to the tree use the bolt above). Move up, then go left
to a peg, then finish up the clean groove above.

26.   Sad-Eyed Lady 18m VS 4c   (Pre-1979)
Just to the right is a large white groove: start up this and escape left, to the tree
on Morecambe Bay Eliminate (to avoid damage to the tree it is 'wise' to use
the bolt above). Finish up that route.

27.   White Groove 18m VS 4c   (1994)
Climb Sad-Eyed Lady to the white groove, then step right above a bulge to gain
the obvious tree-filled bay. Finish past two small overhangs above.

Seaward Area

*The crag now deteriorates, but after about 20 metres it improves, just before the
obvious, jutting, cracked rib of Scout Rock. It has been agreed that, for
ecological reasons, there will be no climbing between White Groove and Father
Ted.*

28.   Father Ted 14m VD   (1996)
Start in the angle about five metres to the left of Bird of Prey and climb up and
left to a grass ledge. Climb a short wall to the top.

29.   Natalie 14m S   4a   (1996)
This is the blunt arête just right of the angle.

★ **30. Pocket Spider** 14m HVS 5a (1989)
Immediately left of Bird of Prey there is an obvious pocket low down, directly below a small sapling at the top of the crag. Climb the wall on various finger pockets to join Bird of Prey.

★ **31. Bird of Prey** 14m VS 4b (Pre-1979)
Two metres to the left of the Scout Rock, there is an obvious clean V-shaped groove. Follow this to a bulge near the top, then move left and finish up a shallow groove past the sapling.

32. Cornish Raider 12m VS 4c (Pre-1979)
Climb the thin groove and continuation rib that is squeezed in between Bird of Prey and Scout Rock.

33. Scout Rock 14m HS 4b (Pre-1979)
The crack in the arête looks precarious but feels sound – so far!

34. The Kitchen Sink 10m VD (Pre-1979)
Four metres to the right is a low ledge with a short, square corner at its right side. Climb this to an obvious flake with a wide crack behind it, move left (treating the flake with respect) then go back right to finish by a short crack and slab.

Both The Kitchen Sink and the next route are open to innumerable variations, though rarely hard.

35. Fern Amina 9m VD (1994)
Midway between Kitchen Sink and Great Gonzo, climb the wall to a ledge, then climb a bulge to another ledge on good holds. Finish by climbing rocks above, trending left using a crack.

36. The Great Gonzo 9m D (Pre-1979)
About nine metres to the right of Scout Rock, at red-stained rock, there is a blank slab above a small recess. Climb this on good holds to a ledge then continue to a further ledge and finish rightwards via an easy, grassy ramp.

37. Jackie 9m VD (1994)
Start about three metres to the right, below a small pedestal at three metres. Climb on easy holds to the bulge, then harder climbing leads directly to the top.

38. Nordic Skiing 9m VD (1995)
Start three metres to the right and follow a left-leading weakness over three steps to a bulge, then surmount this direct.

39. Mr Moussalli 9m VD (1996)
From the start of Nordic Skiing, take a direct line up the wall, finishing over blocks.

40. Scamp 9m D (1996)
Start two metres to the right, where the easy rocks at the foot of the crag start to rise. Climb up the wall via a hidden crack, then finish over blocks.

Traverses
There are two traverses of the crag that are of interest.

41.   Sea-Level Girdle   90m   5b   (Pre-1979)
Does not always live up to its name! Though not sustained it has some good
sections. Right of Spring Tide it is relatively easy, a fact which is sometimes
very useful to know.

★★ **42.   The Onedin Line**   45m   VS   4b,4c   (1969)
A superb outing, especially at high tide. Start at the right-hand end of the
obvious rising break on a choice of ledges (not so much choice at high tide!), as
for Morecambe Bay Eliminate.
1.   18m.   Gain the break and follow it leftwards to a stance in the trees above
Brant's Little Brother.
2.   27m.   Move awkwardly left across the groove and the top of the cave then
continue along the break to another prickly stance. It is advisable to stay roped
together for the scramble off above.

First Ascents at Jack Scout Crag

1969	**Contraband** Carl Dawson
	Also known as Cave Route.
1969	**The Onedin Line** Sheila ?
1978	**Shooting Star** John Shanklin, Russ Willmot
Pre-1979	**Lemming's Ville, Question Mark, Unreal City, Nomad, Celebration Day,** **Elusive Valentine, In the Wake of Poseidon, Masochism Tango,** **Jackal, Spring Tide, Laughing Hyena, Vietnam Defoliation Squad,** **Morecambe Bay Eliminate, Sad-Eyed Lady, Bird of Prey, Cornish** **Raider, Scout Rock**
Pre-1979	**Holly Throttled Groove, Curlew Calling, Brant's Little Brother** John Girdley
Pre-1979	**Victim of Life** John Girdley, Al Evans
Pre-1979	**Crying Crocodile, The Kitchen Sink** Al Evans, John Horsfall
Pre-1979	**The Great Gonzo** John Horsfall (solo)
Pre-1979	**Sea-Level Girdle** Al Evans, John Girdley (both solo)
1980	**Sexless Wench** Ed Robinson, Mike Wilson
1981	**Bermuda Triangle** Owain Jones, Peter Jones
1981	**Armada** Martin Elliot, Simon Cardy
1989	**Pocket Spider**
1994 Apr	**White Groove** Dave Cronshaw, Les Ainsworth
1994	**Fern Amina** Roger Bunyan, N Bunyan
1994	**Jackie** Roger Bunyan, S Duffy
1994 June	**Whitebeam, Sandfly** Les Ainsworth, Dave Cronshaw
1995	**Nordic Skiing** Roger Bunyan, Graeme Bradley
1996	**Father Ted, Mr Moussalli** Roger Bunyan, Graeme Bradley
1996	**Natalie, Scamp** Graeme Bradley, Roger Bunyan

Jackdaw Quarry   O.S. ref.   SD 529 715

Jackdaw Quarry is a flooded quarry at Capernwray, about two kilometres
north-east of the Over Kellet junction (J35) on the M6. It is used for scuba
diving and the owners are not currently prepared to permit climbing. If climbing
is permitted in future, it will be necessary to ask at the Dive Shop on site before
climbing.

To reach the quarry from the motorway, turn towards Over Kellet, then turn left at the centre of the village and keep right at a nearby fork. The quarry is on the right, immediately before a sharp bend into Capernwray.

All the climbing is on a small buttress, which can be seen at the far right end of the quarry, from the entrance taken by the divers. The routes are reached by descending a small gully on the right (facing the pool) then following a right-descending ramp to a platform about three metres above the water. A narrow, white, impending wall, unclimbed to date, is the major feature and to the right of this is a bolt belay.

1. Vixen 23m VS 4b   (1989)
To the left of the narrow, white wall is a grooveline through the blocky buttress. Finish up the groove and slab.

2. Congestion o' t' Lung 21m E2 5b   (1989)
A bold route. The climbing is superb, but some of the rock is suspect. Climb above the bolt belay and move left over the bulge. Continue up a bulging wall to a ledge, then finish on the right.

3. Consumptives Return 21m E1 5b   (1989)
Less steep and not so bold as Congestion. Start as for Congestion, then move right into a scoop and continue to a ledge. Follow a crack and flutings to the top.

4. Mazatla 23m E1 5b   (1989)
The route has a sea cliff feel about it and an air of seriousness. From a ledge at the base of the white wall, traverse right past a bolt and descend to the base of the buttress. Climb up to the foot of a hanging flake crack, then finish up a crack/groove.

★ **5. Acapulco** 24m E2 5b   (1989)
Finger jamming in a fine position above water. So named, because youngsters were jumping off the top of the crag past the climbers during the hot summer when the first ascent was made. Start as for Mazatla, but continue traversing to a block on the right, then climb up to undercut, twin cracks and follow these to the top.

First Ascents at Jackdaw Quarry
1989 May 3 **Vixen** Ian Conway, Dick Baker
1989 May 14 **Mazatla** Ian Conway, Dick Baker, Dave Nicol
1989 May 14 **Acapulco** Dave Nicol, Ian Conway, Dick Baker
1989 May 28 **Congestion o' t' Lung, Consumptive's Return** Andy McCord, Dick Baker

Millhead Quarry   O.S. ref. SD 498715

This is a small and rather lineless limestone quarry directly above a football ground in Millhead, about one kilometre south of Warton village. To reach the quarry from Warton, follow the road towards Carnforth and about 50 metres past a humpback bridge over the River Kear, turn right at a footpath. This leads past some cottages to the football ground. The climbing lies at the extreme right of this.

The routes are described from RIGHT to LEFT.

1.   Goalpost Groove   9m   VD   (1974)
The clean-cut groove on the right of the main smooth slab.

★ **2.   Main Attraction**   9m   HVS   5a   (1974)
A serious route with poor protection and some suspect rock. Climb the smooth
slab, starting just right of centre and finishing directly up the centre.

3.   Garibaldi   8m   VS   4b   (1968)
The steep rib on the left.

4.   Stormbringer   13m   VS   4b   (1974)
Start six metres left, below the highest section of the quarry. Climb easily up
easy-angled rock, then gain a ledge on the left. Make an awkward move on to a
second ledge, then traverse right to an undercut ledge below the top. Move right
to a tree to finish.

Farther left are broken rocks in the trees.

5.   Tooty Fruity   9m   VS   4b   (1974)
Climb a narrow slab on the right of a deep, sinuous crack. The crux is the exit
over the top bulge, which can be taken either on its left or right. Finish on the
terrace and descend to the right.

6.   Gimcrack   9m   S   4a   (1968)
Climb the steep crack that starts on the left.

First Ascents at Millhead Quarry
1968   **Garibaldi, Gimcrack**   Stew Wilson
1974   **Goalpost Groove, Main Attraction**   Al Evans (unseconded)
1974   **Stormbringer, Tooty Fruity**   Al Evans, John Horsfall

Trowbarrow   O.S. ref.   SD 481 758

'*The main feature is a 120-foot wall which has yielded one
artificial route which follows the line of bolts, with some
pegging near the top.*

*On the other side of the quarry opposite the bolted wall is an
impressive red-coloured natural wall which as yielded two
high standard routes, Essence of Giraffe and Izzy the Push.
There is still some scope on this wall but the routes will be
very hard. Other lines have been attempted, but soggy arms
and lack of protection have forced people off. Even with a
top-rope no-one has yet managed to breach the other lines.*'

Bill Lounds. Rocksport, 1969

Situation and Character
Trowbarrow is a large and varied limestone quarry just under one kilometre
north-east of Silverdale station. It has recently been designated as a Local
Nature Reserve and is a very pleasant place for climbers and other visitors.

Most of the quarry walls face west, catch plenty of sun and dry quickly, but there the generalisations end. Few crags or quarries can offer such diversity; the rock varies enormously in character and its reliability runs the gamut from very good to diabolical. Some of the climbs are also dreadful, but a good number are outstanding, with something of real quality at almost every grade from V Diff upwards.

Main Wall is so eye-catching that on a first visit the other attractions can easily be overlooked, but Assagai Wall is a very rewarding piece of rock, while Asylum Wall and Red Wall offer contrasting styles of desperation. The areas of rock in between, whilst being less obviously attractive, also have some very worthwhile routes.

History

The early history to the quarry is obscure but the first explorers were probably Stew Wilson, Rick Stallwood and other members of St Martin's College MC, who climbed *Original Route* and *Jomo* in 1967. In 1968 Bill Lounds made his first visit and opened up the steeper climbing in the quarry with *Rumal*, Chris Eilbeck, Lounds, Pete Lucas and Wilson added the excellent *Assagai*, whilst Wilson and Miles Martin found *Coral Sea*. Those who know the latter route today may be surprised to know that it only succumbed after a heavy cleaning session.

Lounds soon added *Izzy the Push*, the first venture on to Red Wall, with a couple of aid points, whilst *Essence of Giraffe* fell to sustained efforts by Lounds, Wilson, Martin and Stuart Butler. On the latter route, the team sieged the crag for the day, resorting to aid pegs to clean mud-choked cracks, but then, in line with the 'ground up' ethic of the day, they made a final unaided push from the bottom. Both of these ascents were impressive for their day and many subsequent attempt used more aid.

It may seem strange that the stunningly obvious lines on Main Wall were not attempted first, but in the early days they were not as obvious as they are today. In fact they did not exist at all until about 1970, when the quarry owners blasted an area indicated now by a huge cone of debris. Fortunately for climbers, the charges were fired from the right and the latter charges just failed to remove the last part of the base of wall and so we were left with the impressive Main Wall. It was also fortunate that the potential purchasers of the large blocks from the wall found an alternative source. The first climbers to visit Trowbarrow after the blast were amazed to see this overnight transformation, but also doubted whether the wall would remain standing for long. Some still find this hard to believe. Al Evans grasped the nettle and top-roped the left-hand crack in the wall (later to become *Aladdinsane*, though it was horrifically loose at that time) then cleaned and led the classic *Jean Jeanie*, which has lost all its loose holds in the intervening years and is now substantially easier; the cracks have widened over the years and intense debate goes on as to whether this is due to mechanical shifts or merely to the removal of loose linings of the cracks (surely a bit of both). Shortly after these first forays a young up-and-coming waif by the name of Ron Fawcett led the aptly-named *Aladdinsane*, while Ben Campbell-Kelly added *Touch of Class*, which has recently become harder owing to the loss of holds from its pod.

The 1975 guidebook brought the crag under scrutiny from many more climbers: *Major Tom* (Andy Hyslop) and *Harijan* (Bill Lounds) soon succumbed and Al Evans claimed a major coup with the first free ascent of the now-classic *Cracked Actor*. In 1976, Yorkshireman Pete Livesey climbed the 'blank' wall of *Javelin*, possibly without encroaching on to *Assagai* as much as everyone now does. The fine *Sleeping Sickness* fell to Dave Hilton and Phil Garner and this is another route which has increased in difficulty since the first ascent. The following year Lounds achieved completely free leads of *Nova Express, Heavy Metal Kid* (formerly Green Tony) and *Izzy the Push*, but several of the Red Wall routes were still described as 'not led' in the 1979 guidebook supplement, even some in the 1983 guidebook. In 1978 Lounds and Keith Bliss cleaned Yellow Wall (a job which is never quite finished) and climbed *Earth Eater* and *Street Boy Blues*. Lounds had earlier caught Al Evans cleaning a line on the Main Wall, obliging him to lead the pitch, which he did with initial reluctance, though ultimately with success, creating *Hollow Earth* and thereby clinching his hat-trick of what are probably the three finest routes on the wall.

Dave Knighton added two characteristically fine, hard and bold routes; *Makin' Magic*, between *Cracked Actor* and *Aladdinsane*, was for some reason omitted from the 1983 guidebook which led to a very confusing situation recently when Mark Liptrot claimed the same line (calling it *Pacific Ocean*) and at a similar time Mark Danson climbed the wall left of *Cracked Actor* and quite coincidentally called it *Making Magic*. The situation was resolved by Danson altering his route's name to *Magic Making*. The second of Knighton's contributions was *A Sense of Doubt,* a rarely repeated route up the blankest part of Assagai Wall.

Knighton was sometimes a controversial figure, frequently criticized for top-rope practice and preplacing protection, but when *A Sense of Doubt* finally received companions in 1984, similar tactics were employed. Owain Jones and Steve Edmondson added *Scary Monsters,* followed at the end of the year by the brilliant *Doubting Thomas* by Dave Bates. However, 1985 saw several first free leads on Red Wall, including *Willy the Fink* by Ron Fawcett and *Wrongo Sal* by Owain Jones who also added (after a good deal of practice) the very hard and serious *Exequy* though not without a couple of falls. Tom Walkington and Dave Bates signed the year off by girdling the wall, something which is often seen as a sign of maturity (for the wall, not necessarily for the climbers!).

Across the quarry, the wall below Original Route, with its countless micro-holds had long held a single route, its provisional name, *The Great Unled*, throwing down a gauntlet. Several teams had designs on the pitch, and it came in for a good deal of top-rope practice. There was nearly a nasty accident when a block being used as an anchor pulled out; luckily it missed the three climbers but it succeeded in destroying most of their gear! The Great Unled even suffered the placing of two bolts, but before the route could be attempted, Paul Carling declared before witnesses that he could do it without. Forced to put his money where his mouth was, he duly chopped the bolts and led the line with marginal skyhook and micro-wire protection to give *The Asylum*. Dave Bates and Tom Walkington added a neighbour, *The Nut House*, a similarly serious adventure, though subsequent routes have not followed the fine ethical example, and whilst the slab has acquired four more routes, two of these are protected by bolts.

Back on Red Wall Mark Liptrot disposed of the penultimate 'not led' when he led *Burrough's Blues*. Various gap-fillers and variations have been added, most of them by the indefatigable Dave Bates, though Liptrot claimed *Blow Out*. Perhaps the most significant addition of 1987 was Tony Mitchell's solo ascent of *Twisted Sister*. The next year Duncan Parker had a busy summer with Dave Wilcock, filling in some of the last gaps on Red Wall, to give *American Express*, and *Access Bill*. In 1989 Parker turned his attention to an obvious omission on Yellow Wall and claimed *Teardrop*. It is interesting to note that at least three other parties were also attracted to the same rock and claimed later 'first ascents' of more or less the same line. However, Karl Lunt and John Stringfellow were a little more successful and though they were beaten to Teardrop, their companion route, *Steal Your Fire*, is still credited to them. Later in the year attention turned to Red Wall, where Andy Griffith climbed *Homophobia*. By 1990 the theory had developed that every inch of Red Wall was potentially climbable and this was soon tested by Jon Allison and Tim Hatch, who managed to squeeze in two hard lines immediately left of Limestone John, with *Red Dwarf* and *Clear and Present Danger*, respectively.

The most notable additions in 1991 were *Michelin Man* by Jim Robertson and *Diary of a Sane Man* by Dave Bates. 1992 saw the talented Brian Davison add *Helden Right-hand*, his first route at the crag. *No More Heroes, Ashes to Ashes, Helden Arête* and the serious *Blow Out* followed later. During a busy few days in August 1993 T Conger filled in several of the gaps to the right of Yellow Wall, but the only other significant addition at the time was *Eek* by Luke Steer in 1994. Finally, in July 1997 Lunt surprised everyone by finding a gap on Assagai Wall, which gave *Clotted Cream*, whilst a few days later John Gaskins created one of those problems for which he is notorious, *Shallow Grave*, a variation start to Essence Direct.

Approach

Just south of Silverdale station (accessible by bus as well as by rail), a road branches east, over the railway. About a kilometre on, it bears left through dense woodland on both sides. There are several parking spaces, just before the road turns back right out of these woods. However, clubs visiting Trowbarrow are asked to car share, if possible, to reduce pressure on the parking.

Go up steps by the *Red Bridge* footpath sign to a kissing gate about 25 metres farther on. Then bear rightwards and upwards through the woods for a couple of minutes to the southern entrance to the crag.

Access

Trowbarrow has recently been acquired by Lancaster City Council (LCC) and, with the help of some financial donations from climbers and others, it is to be run as a Local Nature Reserve, in which the importance of the climbing is fully recognized. Climbers also contribute by undertaking conservation work when requested. Previously, climbing was never actually permitted and at times it was actively discouraged, and so this is a great step forward for climbing.

Because of the prominence afforded to climbing under the new arrangements, climbers themselves have a central role in ensuring the success of Trowbarrow as a Local Nature Reserve. Besides the obvious requirement for us to act sensibly and with thought for other visitors, there are three specific guidelines that LCC insist we must comply with:

(1)   There should be **no abseiling or roping down/lowering from the Main Wall** and climbers should walk down after completing their climbs. This is to protect the rock, both for climbers and because of its geological importance.

(2)   There should be **no group use of the quarry for climbing**. Indeed, the nature of the quarry and the mix of routes make it relatively unsuitable for such use.

(3)   **No more bolts should be placed**.

The Climbs

The routes are described from RIGHT to LEFT, starting at a small rise in the quarry floor, which is in turn about 50 metres past the first dip in the floor (where one of the 'long hike' descent routes comes down into the quarry). Routes have been recorded on the rock which rises above the lowest section of the quarry floor, including Shell Shock and Body Abuse on Fossil Wall, the obvious upper tier at the centre of this section. However, all these routes are loose, poorly protected and nondescript and so they have been omitted from this guidebook.

Diamond Wall

Immediately before the first small rise in the quarry floor, a small diamond-shaped buttress provides the first routes.

1.   Diamonds 14m HS 4b   (1996)
Follow the right-curving ramp on the right side of the buttress, then gain ledges on the left and continue left under the overhang to a bold, but easy landing.

★ **2.   Arc** 15m HVS 5a   (Pre-1991)
From the foot of the right-curving ramp gain a shallow left-facing corner. From the top of this traverse right, then step up to the overhang and finish as for Diamonds.

★ **3.   Lonely Wall** 12m E1 5a   (1978)
A surprisingly good route, but a serious lead since the loss of the peg. Start behind the rightmost of three small trees growing very close to the wall and climb up to a ledge, then go up and left to the horizontal break (Friend strongly advised) about one metre right of a drill mark. Go straight up to the bulge and cross it diagonally rightwards. Tree belays. The upper tier is very loose and it is best to descend the grassy ramp.

★ **4.   Little Lil** 10m E3 6a   (1991)
The short, slim, hanging corner left of the three trees.

15 metres left of the first small rise is another buttress.

5.   Boulderdash 15m HVS 5b   (1977)
Climb the centre of the lower wall with difficulty (an easier alternative exists on the left); finish by the easier blocky crack on the left.

Suspension Wall

To the left again and set back in the trees is a white wall bristling with
overhangs. A considerable amount of rock from this wall now lies at its foot
and so it is scarcely necessary to warn climbers to take care when climbing
hereabouts.

6.   PPC Madness   15m   VS   4c   (1993)
Climb to the cave at the right side of the wall, then hand-traverse left on the lip
to gain ledges on the left. Continue up short corners to finish through the break
in the top roofs.

7.   Dry Throat   15m   HS   4a   (1977/1996)
From the start of Deep Throat climb diagonally right over small overlaps to a
small ledge, then go straight up to a larger ledge above. Climb up easily on the
left and at the top finish on the right.

8.   Deep Throat   12m   S   4a   (1977)
Climb the deep flake crack which forms a corner on the left of the wall to a
ledge on the left. Continue to the top.

Washday Wall

Washday Wall can be identified by a large tree which grows above its
right-hand side, about four metres from the true top of the quarry.

9.   Blue Daz   12m   S   4a   (1977)
Start at the top of the mound on the right and climb leftwards below large
blocks to a ledge. Climb the rib above to finish.

10.   Square Deal Surf   12m   VS   4c   (1978)
A worthwhile route and better than it looks. Start at the lowest point of the
wall. Leave the low ledge from its right-hand side, then move up awkwardly to
a square recess (interesting thread). Gain the sloping ledge on the left, then step
back left and finish direct up pleasant twin cracks.

★ **11.   Facial Gymnastics**   15m   E2   5b   (1993)
From the lowest point of the wall, take a direct line up the thin crack to the
horizontal break. Move slightly left, then go back right and finish up the centre
of the wall, past a poor peg.

★ **12.   Biological Agent K9**   10m   HVS   5b   (Pre-1972)
The thin crack in the upper wall, above a drill mark and about three metres to
the left of the finish of Square Deal Surf, is fine and well-protected, but the
lower wall to reach it requires care.

13.   Tark's Traverse   18m   VS   4b   (1993)
From the deep groove at the left side of the wall, climb diagonally rightwards to
gain the horizontal break of Bio Agent, then continue along the break to its end.

Lower Wall

This is the section of rock that lies slightly below and right of Yellow Wall.

14.   Half a Pound of Cabbage 8m   S   4c   (1993)
Ascend twin cracks in the square-cut block at the right of the wall

15.   Quick Nick 9m   VS   4c   (1993)
Start two metres to the left and traverse left under a prominent overhang, then
climb directly to the top.

16.   First Cut 9m   D   (1975-79)
The deep flake crack in the corner which bounds Yellow Wall on its right,
above shot-hole mark '*156+*'.

Yellow Wall

*To the left again, above the debris cone, is the steeper and more appealing
Yellow Wall. This gives very good climbing when clean, but unfortunately the
cracks tend to ooze mud if conditions are at all damp.*

17.   Steal Your Fire 30m   E1   5c   (1993)
Climb the very right edge of Yellow Wall, then move up and left to gain a
left-slanting crack. Traverse the breaks leftwards, then move up to gain the
prominent crescent-shaped crack. Pull over a small overlap above, move left of
this, then finish direct up easy ground.

★ **18.   Teardrop** 13m   E2   5c   (1989)
Midway between shot mark '*155.05*' and the right arête of Yellow Wall is a
light teardrop stain directly below a tree at the top of the crag. Start at the right
side of the teardrop and climb between the horizontal cracks on widely spaced
holds, passing the foot of a left-slanting crack near the top.

19.   Willy the Dish 13m   HVS   5a   (1978)
Start two metres to the right of shot mark '*155.05*' and climb directly up cracks
to the top.

20.   Earth Eater 15m   VS   4c   (1978)
Start at the shot mark and climb as directly as possible, moving right near the
top.

★ **21.   Street Boy Blues** 18m   E2   5c   (1978)
Start four metres to the left of the shot mark and move up to two, parallel thin
cracks. Climb to the bulge and pass this using the obvious diagonal crack. The
final wall is easier.

22.   Sleeping Balls 15m   VS   4c   (1978)
A semi-girdle. Follow Street Boy Blues to the rising crack at three metres, then
follow this and finish on the right.

● **23.   Owl Surprise** 21m   VD   (1988)
Climbs the corner between Yellow Wall and Main Wall, starting up the pedestal
and dangerous-looking flake. Finish pleasantly on Yellow Wall.

Main Wall

*This imperious wall dominates the quarry. Its solidity is often called into
question, but it has remained substantially unaltered for some time now. Fossil
holds on the face require careful handling but the cracks are generally sound
and clean. The top couple of metres of some routes can be loose and earthy.*

24. Pale Groove 27m HVS 5a   (1998)
Climb the arête and groove to the right of Helden until an overhang is reached,
then swing right in to another crack system and follow it to the top.

★ **25. Helden Arête** 30m E1 5b   (1997)
Follow the arête right of Helden to an overlap, then swing right into a groove
and finish up this.

★ **26. Helden** 27m E1 5b   (1986)(1992)
Climb the deep groove on the very edge of Main Wall to an overhang on the
right. Break out left along a horizontal crack to the corner on Warspite. Move
up to the roof and pull round this on its left, finishing up the short headwall.
Helden Right-hand (30m, E1, 5b): a variation finish to Helden. From the top
roof use the roof crack to move right around the roof for about five metres, then
finish up easier ground.

★ **27. Warspite** 27m HVS 5a   (1974/1975)
An adventurous route starting up the big corner at the right-hand side of the
wall. About three metres below the roof a horizontal break leads left to the
arête. Move up, then go left along the first horizontal crack until a wide crack
can be taken to finish.

28. Ashes to Ashes 25m E4 5c   (1988)
A direct start to Heroes. Start at the foot of Warspite and climb the wall just
left of a small arête to reach the right-hand side of the large roof. Surmount this
using pockets, then continue up the arête and wall above as for Helden.

★ **29. Heroes** 27m E3 5c   (1978/1998)(1994)
Follow Warspite Direct until above the roof then, at a prominent rust-coloured
stain, move right to the arête using a thin horizontal crack (where the flake used
to be). Climb the arête (crux) to a small overhang, level with the traverse of
Warspite, then folow the superb, thin, left-trending crack to the top.
No More Heroes (28m, E2, 5b): at the point where Heroes and Warspite Direct
diverge, climb the wall just to the left of the rust-coloured stain to the roof, then
continue past two overlaps until it is possible to finish up Heroes.

★★ **30. Warspite Direct** 25m E2 5b   (1977)(1998)
The next corner runs up to a roof at half-height. Gain the corner from the right
and climb to the roof. Move right and climb the crack splitting the roof –
strenuous and spectacular. The widening crack above is a bit of an anticlimax.
The Man Who Fell to Earth (26m, E4, 5c): Thin climbing to link Harijan and
Warspite. Follow Harijan on to the face, then make awkward moves up the arête
to Hollow Earth and continue rightwards to the crack on Warspite Direct. Finish
up this, or, more sustained via Ashes to Ashes.

★★ **31.** **Hollow Earth** 27m HVS 5a (1977)(1978)
Sustained and strenuous, but well-protected. A climb that would be a classic on most crags, but on the Main Wall at Trowbarrow it plays second fiddle to its neighbours. Nevertheless, it is more than worthwhile and a good reason to return to the crag from far afield, even if you've done everything else. Start as for Warspite Direct, but move out left just below the roof to gain the superb, sustained diagonal crack, joining Harijan near the top.
Rock and Roll Suicide (E2, 5b): a bold alternative finish to the previous route. About two metres short of the junction with Harijan the crack widens to hand-jam size. Step up and then go right on small holds, and continue up with some anxiety until better holds arrive.

★★ **32.** **Harijan** 29m VS 4c (1977)
Although this route crosses some impressive rock, surprisingly, the climbing never exceeds VS. A must for any visiting VS leader. Start up the corner until a horizontal crack leads awkwardly left on to the face. Follow it leftwards and then up the obvious jamming crack to the top. Care is needed to avoid rope drag.

★★ **33.** **A Touch of Class** 29m E2 5c (1973)(1978)
An excellent climb, but the rock is becoming highly polished and this can be very intimidating. To the left an obvious left-slanting pod/crack splits the overhang. Move left beneath this and climb it with difficulty (well-protected with Friends). The fine jamming crack above leads to a junction with Harijan. Finish as for that route.
Alternative Start (HVS, 5a): a poor but much easier variation starts just right of Jean Jeanie and follows the wall until a horizontal crack leads rightwards to the base of the jamming crack.

★ **34.** **Moondance** 27m E5 6a (1988)
Ascend the arête just right of Touch of Class variation start and climb to the break on that route. Move right and climb to a second break and continue to Major Tom. Follow this left until it is possible to enter a depression from the left and leave it rightwards (Rocks 2 and 3). Gain the crack of Space Oddity and follow it left to climb the left-hand of two faint cracks (just right of Jean Jeanie) moving rightwards near the top.

★ **35.** **Major Tom** 32m E2 5c (1977)
An unsatisfactory line redeemed by some fine climbing. Start as for Touch of Class but after the crux take a gently rising thin crack leftwards to join Jean Jeanie, follow this until it dog-legs right, then move out left to finish up a fine diagonal crack.

36. **Eek** 30m E4 5c (1994)
Climb the arête right of Jean Jeanie, then step right above the roof and climb directly past a scoop to the diagonal crack of Major Tom, just above. Finish up this.

★★ **37.** **Jean Jeanie** 30m VS 4c (1973)
The central crackline is a classic of its grade; sustained and quite strenuous but with good protection and resting places. Climb the blocky wall to gain the crack proper and follow it to the top.

Main Wall Area

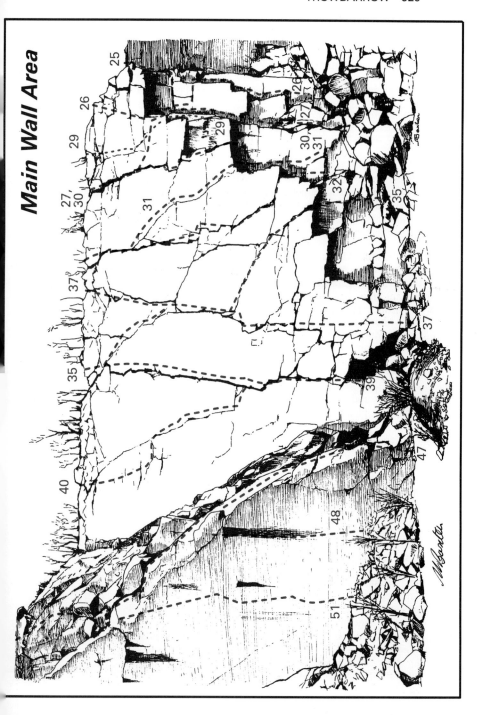

★ **38.   Blow Out**   30m   E6   6a   (1986/1997)
Top section previously known as Blow Job. Start just to the left of Jean Jeanie
and climb past several horizontal breaks and a vertical crack (thread) to the thin
crack which starts just left of the dog-leg on Jean Jeanie. Continue up this to a
small niche (peg – hard to clip). Continue direct, with much trepidation to a
second peg, then go up to meet a good crack (Major Tom) and so to the top.

★★ **39.   Aladdinsane**   29m   E1   5a   (1973)
The wide left-hand crack above the cave has a bold and awkward middle
section, which is difficult to protect.

★★★ **40.   Cracked Actor**   30m   E2   5b   (1976)
This is an established test-piece for climbers moving up the grades. However, it
is becoming ever more polished, so take care. Follow Aladdinsane to the base of
the straight section of the crack then move out left to the thin diagonal crack.
Follow this crack; the first six metres are very sustained but can be
well-protected. Finish via the horizontal breaks on the left.

★ **41.   Makin' Magic**   29m   E3   5c   (1979)
Climb Oniscus for three metres then follow the thin crack in the Main Wall to a
move right to gain Cracked Actor. Follow this for a couple of metres then move
right on to the face and climb this direct via a peg.

42.   Magic Making   29m   E1   5b   (1978)
Follow Makin' Magic until it moves right to join Cracked Actor. At this point
move left and follow a thin crack until an awkward move gains the horizontal
breaks and the finish of Cracked Actor.

43.   Space Oddity   55m   E1   5a   (1978)
A devious and unsatisfactory attempt at a girdle; it finishes in a fine position but
apart from this there is every reason to think a right-to-left girdle would be
better. Follow Oniscus for nine metres to a horizontal crack which leads to the
junction of Aladdinsane and Cracked Actor, then move down slightly and go
right along a horizontal break to join Jean Jeannie. Ascend this until it is
possible to step right to Hollow Earth, and traverse right to the base of the wide
crack of Warspite Direct. Move right along the second horizontal crack to
Heroes, then step up and continue the traverse above the large roof until it is
possible to finish past large blocks on the arête.

44.   Oniscus   32m   S   4a   (1975-79)
The corner between Main Wall and Red Slab gives a poor, loose and vegetated
route. It might improve with traffic – if it ever gets any!

45.   Main Wall Girdle   58m   E1   5a,5b   (1988)
An interesting right-to-left traverse, which proves easier than it may at first
appear, but nevertheless, the position of some of the moves may give some
pause for thought.
1.   20m.   Follow Helden until it is possible to belay on a pedestal below the
large roof.
2.   38m.   Follow Helden to the roof, then move out on to the front face and
traverse left with hands on the thin horizontal break, until it is possible to finish
up Major Tom.

Red Slab Area

The next two routes lie on the slabs at right-angles to the Main Wall.

46.   Red Slab   37m   VS   4b   (1968)

The expanse of slabs left of Main Wall can be climbed almost anywhere. The easiest line starts roughly in the centre, with a rightwards detour at the steeper section. A couple of narrow crystalline slabs on the left give the best finish. The thin right-facing corner just right of Original Route also leads quite nicely to this finish at 4c.

⋆ **47.   Original Route**   37m   VD   (1967)

The slabby rib on the left is technically easy but quite serious; what protection there is being behind perched flakes. Move right after 18 metres then finish up the back of the bay behind. A better but harder finish (S) is to move right from the ledges to the narrow crystalline slabs, and finish over the nose.

Asylum Wall

This is the steep crozzly wall round the front of the slabs.

48.   Mémoires of a Lunatic   9m   E5   6b   (1986)

Follow the obvious streak at the right side of the wall, with one bolt.

49.   Diary of a Sane Man   27m   E7   6b   (1991)

Start up Mémoires and make a diagonal traverse up and left to finish up Diaries of a Madman. A skyhook may be useful.

50.   The Idiot   10m   E5   6a   (1986)

A bold line up the lesser streak just left.

51.   The Asylum   12m   E5   6a   (1985)

Takes a line just to the left again. Climb three metres to a peg then go up to a good nut placement. Step right and climb directly to the top.

52.   The Nut House   14m   E5   6a   (1985)

Start directly below a tree at the top of the wall and follow a direct line up the wall, with one peg of its own; the peg on The Asylum is also clipped.

53.   Diaries of a Madman   12m   E5   6b   (1986)

Follow Ramp Ant to a small elder tree, climb up to a bolt then step left to a vague crack and climb up to the apex of the slab.

Ramps Area

To the left of Asylum Wall the rock becomes broken by a series of ramps and grooves.

⋆ **54.   Ramp Ant**   34m   S   4a   (1974)

The red ramp bounding Asylum Wall on its left leads very pleasantly to broken ledges and a choice of finishes. There now follows a very broken section with no climbs and no appeal. A few metres farther left the quarry wall stands forward again.

55.   Crematorium   34m   HVS   5a   (1974)
Climb the steep, shattered and often wet, groove in the angle at shot mark '*125*'
about three metres right of an ash tree at the foot of the rock. At a bulge move
left on to a slab then continue to a belay at 15 metres. Move back right and
climb right of a crack, past an overhanging block, then go left and up a crack to
a groove and wall finish.

56.   Pig in a Poke   18m   HVS   4c   (1986)(1992)
Start as for Jomo and follow Pigfall to the foot of the arête. Then step right
(block and sapling – possible belay) below a steep clean slab and climb it with
scant protection.
Direct Start (E1, 5b): the steep blank wall directly below Pig in a Poke. Start
right of the tree by the 125 mark and climb the wall, then easier ground to Pig
in a Poke.

★ **57.   Pigfall**   30m   S   4a   (1974)
Start as for Jomo, but when the easy slabs are reached move up to the foot of a
fine arête. This is exposed and poorly protected but never very hard.

58   One of these Days   21m   E4   6a   (1985)
The fine narrow wall between the upper part of Jomo and Pigfall, starting at the
top of the diagonal crack on Jomo.

★★★ **59.   Jomo**   37m   VD   (1967)
A fine varied outing, marred only by the terrace at half-height. The start feels
both hard and bold but the angle soon eases. Start below the rounded
light-coloured rib behind some saplings. Climb this to easy slabs and bear left to
a diagonal crack. Climb this to the terrace and block belays. Follow the steep
gangway behind to the small roof, which is passed (easier than it looks). Step
right onto the fluted wall to finish.

60.   Very Ordinary Route   37m   M   (1967)
Climb the cracked groove left of Jomo (often used as a cheating start to that
route) to large ledges and block belays. From the upper left end of the terraces
finish up cracks and blocks. A poor climb, but a useful **DESCENT** route – with
care!

The Front
*This is the short, rather lineless buttress that is set slightly forward from the
grooves and ramps of Jomo and the Assagai Wall.*

61.   Crinoid   34m   VD   (1970)
Round to the left is an obvious deep chimney. Reach this by any of several
possible lines and climb it to the terraces. Finish by the groove at the left side
of the upper wall (left of Night Flight).

62.   The Pate   15m   E2   6a   (1978)
Start as for Sluice, but continue directly up the bold arête right of that route's
jamming crack.

★ **63.   Sluice**   31m   HVS   5a,5a   (1974)
A bold wall and surprising finish make this climb much better than it looks.

1. 17m. Climb the wall left of the chimney at a brown streak, to horizontal cracks and welcome runners. Climb the diagonal jamming crack to the terraces.
2. 14m. Climb the centre of the upper wall via a thin right-facing corner, to the crack in the overhangs for a pleasing finale.

64. Shady Blade 27m E2 5b,5c (1986)
1. 13m. Start three metres to the left and gain a ledge at two metres. From the right side of this, climb up and slightly right to the centre of the overlap on the left of the jamming crack of Sluice, then follow the lesser crack on the left of Sluice, to the top of the wall.
2. 14m. Climb the narrow wall to the left of Jomo, without using holds in Sluice, then finish direct around the roof.

65. Incantations 15m E1 5a (1980)
From the left of the ledge at the start of Shady Blade, step up left then climb the wall just right of a thin crackline, through a small overlap. Finish leftwards up the top wall and belay on the terrace.

66. Night Flight 32m VS 4c,4c (1977)
1. 18m. From the ledge at the start of Shady Blade climb diagonally leftwards by a series of small ramps/ledges (poorly protected) and go up into a recess below cracked roofs. Climb back right through the overhangs, past an obvious borehole.
Variation (4a): climb horizontally rightwards to escape the roofs and up to belay on the terrace.
2. 14m. Climb the wall left of Sluice, to a short final crack.

A scrappy route has been claimed up the system of grooves to the recess below the roofs on pitch one, making a risky direct exit.

67. Frontage 27m HS 4a,4b (1978)
1. 15m. Start at the far left side of the wall and climb a broken groove and slab to gain a deep corner and continue to the roof. Continue through the blocks to the terrace.
2. 12m. Climb the crack immediately left of the arête above and finish easily over blocks.

Assagai Wall
This elegant wall is set back slightly and gives some of the finest climbing in the quarry. The upper part, with its striking fluted grooves, is naturally weathered.

68. Boundary Groove 15m D (1968)
Climb the blocky groove that bounds Assagai Wall on its right, then from the terrace at the top of this climb diagonally right to the top.

★★ **69. Assagai** 21m HVS 5a (1968)
One of the original routes in the quarry and still one of the best. Start from the left end of the terrace above Boundary Groove. Step down easily for about two metres, then traverse left along the obvious line (white rock) then step up and left again to a small ledge. Climb up to the horizontal break, step right and finish up the amazing fluted groove: a splendid pitch.

70.   Grave Doubts 33m E5 6b   (1998)
A right-to-left traverse of Assagai Wall, starting from a belay in the blocky
groove at the start of Sleeping Sickness. Cross the thin crack at the start of
Sleeping Sickness and move left along a faint depression until it is possible to
move up to a good flat hold. Make a long reach left to gain a small ledge and
then a step down to the niche on Doubting Thomas. Move left to a peg and the
good hold on Sense of Doubt, which is followed past another peg and a very
long reach to a positive, flat hold. Move left along a crack system which joins
the traverse of Rumal at its junction with Sour Milk Groove. Move left and
climb the wall above about two metres left of Sour Milk Groove, as for Day of
the Beanpoles.

★★ **71.   Sleeping Sickness** 21m E2 5c   (1976)
Technical and balancy to start, strenuous and committing to finish. This superb
pitch is marred only by the junction with Assagai at half-height. Start up the
blocky groove to gain a very thin crack. Follow this, thin wires, and the wall on
its right to the traverse of Assagai (this section also makes an excellent bold
start to Assagai at 5a). A Friend is helpful below the overhang, which is taken
by the small groove; difficult and blind. Follow the crackline to meet Assagai
near the top or continue straight up the tapering pillar.

★★ **72.   Javelin** 27m E1 5b   (1976)
A contrived line but offering continuously enjoyable climbing. Follow Sleeping
Sickness to the traverse of Assagai, follow this but continue left to a hidden
ledge in the centre of the wall. Move up with difficulty to the break and finish
up the central fluted groove.

★ **73.   Scary Monsters** 18m E5 6a   (1984)
Start at the lowest point of the wall and climb up to a faint seam at six metres
(two pegs may not be in place). Move up (crux) and right, then go back
leftwards to a shallow corner which meets the end of the Assagai traverse.
Finish up that route.

★★ **74.   Doubting Thomas** 23m E5 6b   (1984)
More sustained and possibly more serious than Scary Monsters. Up to the break
it relies upon peg runners and is graded on the assumption that these are in
place. Start at the foot of the ramp on the left, at the scar left by a trundled
pedestal. Climb directly to two incut holds, make an awkward move to gain a
niche and pass the bulge above by a wild leap. Finish up the wall to the right of
Javelin.

★ **75.   A Sense of Doubt** 20m E4 6b   (1978)
Easier than the two preceding routes but still serious. Start on the ramp above
the remains of the pedestal. Step right on to the wall and go up for three metres
to a break. Move left to a good hold and go up to a horizontal crease. Continue
to the traverse line of Rumal, and finish up the flutings of Javelin. Three pegs
in place.

76.   Day of the Beanpoles 17m E3 6b   (1984)
Technically the hardest route on the wall, but well-protected. Start three metres
left of A Sense of Doubt, directly below Sour Milk Groove. Climb directly up
the wall (peg, may not be in place) then finish up the wall to the left of Sour
Milk Groove.

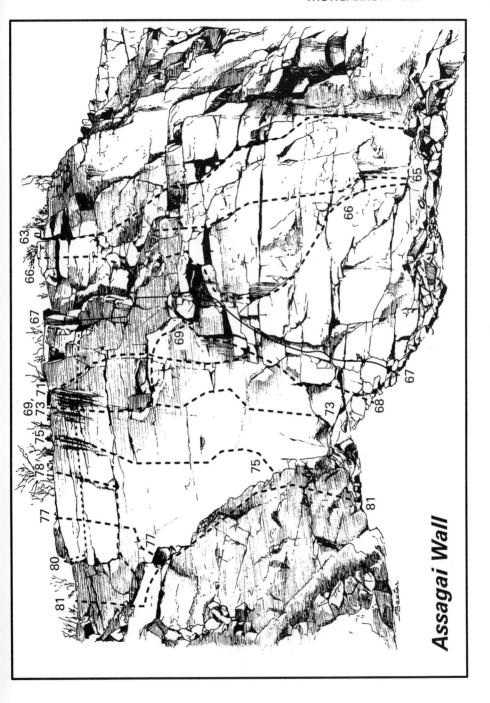

Assagai Wall

★ **77.   Clotted Cream**   12m   E1   5b   (1997)
An unlikely line that packs a lot into a short distance. Start from the right-hand
end of the sloping ledge at the top of Schizoid Man, immediately below and
right of the start of Rumal. Ascend the short wall to the break, pull through into
a faint scoop (crux), then continue up the wall above on excellent rock.

★ **78.   Sour Milk Groove**   18m   HVS   5a   (1976)
Start at the top of the ramp. Step right on to the wall and follow the horizontal
break (Rumal) to an awkward move into the left-hand of the three fluted
grooves; follow this to the top.

*There are two excellent traverses across Assagai Wall, which can be easily
combined to give a memorable outing.*

★★ **79.   Rumal**   23m   HVS   5a   (1968)
The obvious horizontal break gives some good climbing with fine positions,
after a short crux at the left-hand end. It is possible to climb it in both
directions, but it is traditionally done from left to right, starting at the top of the
ramp.

★★ **80.   Truffle**   23m   HS   4c   (1977)
The top traverse is easier than it appears, but nevertheless, the positions make it
very worthwhile. It is best done from right to left. From a small ledge about
three metres below the top of the crag and just left of Very Ordinary Route,
step awkwardly left on to the front of the wall. Continue with plentiful holds
and runners and at the end, step round to belay in the corner.

81.   Twentieth Century Schizoid Man   27m   D   (1967)
The slabby ramp up the left side of Assagai Wall is easy but not well-protected.
Finish up the short wall at the back of the bay on good holds.

End Walls
*The more broken area from this point to the left end of the quarry is known as
the End Walls.*

82.   Perseverance   29m   VD   (1970)
Take a variable line up the slab left of Schizoid Man (poorly protected) to the
sapling ledge near the top of the crag. Finish up the short wall at the back of
the bay.

*The next few routes tackle the chaotic area to the left, starting at a lower level
and working left from the short wall that rises behind some small trees to the
slab of Perseverance. Loose blocks are common!*

83.   Quisquillae   30m   HS   4a   (1977)
Immediately to the left of the wall is a short left-slanting slab/groove. Climb
this, then swing right below a broken white wall. Continue up and right past a
short corner to the left edge of a red groove. Follow this to the saplings and
finish up the back of the bay.

84. Aborigine Wall 31m VS –,4c   (1977)
1. 17m. To the right there are two obvious slablines slanting left. Follow the
rightmost of these and at the top move left to belay on a ledge below a steep
and relatively clean wall.
2. 14m. Climb the centre of the wall to a bulge, surmount this and finish
direct (better and more solid than the original finish which went right below the
bulge).

85. Boomerang 34m VD   (1967)(1979-83)
A devious excursion.
1. 17m. Take the larger, left-slanting slab to a large ledge and block belays.
2. 9m. From the right end of the ledge step on to the wall and move
awkwardly round below a large block, then go up to the sapling ledges.
Amphetamine Variation (VS, 4b): from the block, a bold alternative is to
traverse delicately right across the black slab and go up the rib.
3. 8m. Finish up the back wall of the bay.

86. Ask Les 21m S 4a   (1976)
Take an interesting short corner left of Boomerang, then the distressing corner
left of Aborigine Wall pitch two. Not recommended!

Set forward and starting slightly lower is a fine tapering wall.

87. Barrier Reef 20m S 4a   (1979-83)
Pleasant climbing up the groove in the right rib of the wall with one or two
loose blocks.

★★ **88. Coral Sea** 20m VS 4c   (1968)
Very popular, a test-piece at its grade and becoming very shiny because of this.
Pull on to the rib from the left and follow it for a couple of metres, then step
left on to the face and traverse into its centre, then ascend on improving holds,
to the top.

89. Coral Sea Direct E1 5c   (1984)(1986-87)
A desperately '*eliminate*' line taking thin cracks just left of the rib then going
left at the first opportunity to climb cracks just left of the parent route.

90. Barnacle 15m S 4a   (1977)
Ten metres left at a broken rib there is a slabby wall. Start at the lowest point
and trend left up the initial wall. Above this, several variations are possible.

*Climbs have been reported on the rock between this point and Red Wall, but
much of the rock is very poor and the routes themselves are without real merit
and so no descriptions are given.*

DESCENT: *the short, deep chimney gully immediately left of Barnacle.*

Red Wall
*Left again, in the trees directly opposite Main Wall is a slightly overhanging
wall of reddish rock, characterized by rounded holds and large depressions.
This unique wall owes its colour to haematite contamination, which sometimes
gives it a greasy feel, which is not helped by the fact that chalk never washes
off. In fact the wall is so steep and sheltered that it probably never gets wet*

directly from rain, but there is some seepage and the cracks can get muddy. The climbing, needless to say, is very strenuous and as pegs never seem to stay for very long, top-roping is the norm.

The absence of obvious natural lines means that route identification is often difficult. Particularly useful features for climbers to focus on are slightly deeper depressions, which are known as 'caves'. Three trees near the foot of the wall also serve as useful landmarks.

● **91.   Drop Acid**   14m   HVS   5a   (1988)
Above the mound at the right-hand end of the wall some hanging grooves lead to a cornice of tree roots. Climb directly to the overhang which forms a small cave, then enter the groove above its right side and continue to the '*cornice*' and the top. Looser than it looks (and it looks loose!)

● **92.   Acid Drop**   15m   HVS   4c   (1988)
The shattered groove where the mound starts to drop down – loose in places.

● **93.   Sepia Typhoid Witness**   15m   Not led   6a   (1975-79)
Start at the foot of the mound and climb the steep, blunt rib which forms the left side of the shattered groove.

★★ **94.   Izzy the Push**   15m   E2   5c   (1968/1972/1977)
The route name which we all wish we'd thought of (but only if we're fans of William Burroughs) and it is just perfect for this, or possibly for any route with a definite crux. Start directly behind the first tree and climb diagonally right to a shallow scoop, then move up into a small cave at three-quarters-height. Step left from the cave, then climb straight to the top.

95.   Michelin Man   15m   E2   5c   (1991)
Takes a direct line between Heavy Metal Kid and Izzy the Push, which is only just independent of these routes. Start just right of block and climb through horizontal breaks, making a long reach for a sharp flake in the centre of the wall. Use this to reach flat holds leading directly to the top. Strenuous.

★ **96.   Heavy Metal Kid**   15m   E3   5c   (1972/1975-79)
Originally pegged as Green Tony. Start at a block just left of the first tree and follow the obvious line of holds more or less direct, passing a small cave near the top.

★ **97.   Twisted Sister**   18m   E5   6b   (1987)
Climb the wall one metre left of the block, using a pocket to gain good finger holds, then at five metres traverse right for about two metres to gain Heavy Metal Kid. Continue up this route to the cave, then traverse left and finish as for Exequy.

98.   Homophobia   15m   E6   6b   (1989)
A direct on Twisted Sister. After the crux on Twisted Sister make a hard and long move upwards (unprotected). Continue straight up the wall using very spaced horizontal cracks.

★★ **99.   Exequy**   18m   E6   6b   (1985)
A Red Wall classic, taking a direct line to the right of Nova Express. A long reach comes in useful on the crux and a long neck is helpful if you lead this

one on-sight. Despite the name this is no funeral procession! Start two metres left of the block at a small, deep depression virtually at floor level and take a direct line to a serious crux at between five and six metres. Above this, move right to a good hold in the wall (a Friend will protect against a certain crater from higher up) and race up the wall to the top.

★★ **100. Nova Express**   15m   E3   6a   (1968/1977)
The most obvious line on Red Wall, but more searching is required to find the easiest way to climb it. Start behind the second tree and climb up for a short way, then follow the obvious line of right-leading depressions.

101. Willy the Fink   15m   E5   6b   (1975-79)
Start as for Nova Express, but climb directly up via a series of smaller depressions.

★ **102. Fluoroscopic Kid**   15m   E4   6a   (1975-79)
Start directly behind the second block and climb to a small triangular recess, then continue directly up the wall to a fine finish.

★★ **103. American Express**   17m   E2   5b   (1988)
An easier route up this section of the crag, which relies heavily upon other routes. Start three metres to the left of the block on the left of the second tree at a thin right-slanting crack. Climb this to attain a standing position in the obvious triangular niche, then traverse right for two metres into Willy the Fink. Follow this for three metres to the big jug, then traverse right, past Nova Express to finish up Exequy.

★ **104. Access Bill**   15m   E4   6a   (1988)
Although only the top section of this climb is independent, it is, nevertheless, worthwhile. Follow American Express until, just past the small triangular recess, it is possible to traverse left across a small pillar to the big jug on Essence of Giraffe. Move right into another obvious hole and finish directly up the wall above.

★★ **105. Essence of a Giraffe**   18m   E3   6a   (1968)
Start one metre farther left and three metres right of the small pit, at a depression which marks the foot of a right-leading weakness. Climb this on good holds, then step left to reach the cave directly below a large yew at the top of the crag. From the left side of the cave, move up, then go rightwards to another depression and finish up the wall above at the yew tree.

★ **106. Essence Direct**   15m   E3   5c   (1975-79)
This route is now essentially independent of Essence. Start one metre to the left, at a thin, slightly slanting crack. Climb the crack and the wall above to some black rock about two metres left of the cave. Move up and left past the Girdle stance (two pegs), then make a hard move to a cave near the top. Exit on the left side.
Shallow Grave (6c): a variation start, which can be done as a boulder problem in its own right. Start from the right edge of the pit and climb the wall (white streak) to an obvious hole at about 5 metres.

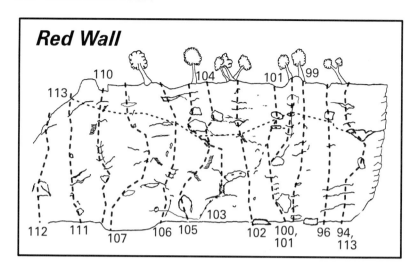

Red Wall

★ **107. Limestone John** 15m E3 5c   (1977)
From the left side of the pit climb rightwards to a shallow cave at five metres,
then continue for a further three metres until it is possible to climb up and
slightly left using widely-spaced pockets. Continue up and left to a shallow
depression directly below the left side of a tree at the top and finish up the wall
above.
Direct Finish (6a): climb the bulging wall direct instead of moving left to the
shallow depression.

108. Red Dwarf 15m E3 6b   (1990)
Follow Limestone John to an undercut pocket at four metres, then make a
couple of fingery moves up and left to reach horizontal breaks. Step right and
go up via an obvious pinch to join Limestone John, then follow this to the top.

109. Clear and Present Danger E5 6b   (1990)
Take a direct line up the wall starting just left of Limestone John. Climb direct
to cracks and make a hard move up to a horizontal break. Further hard moves
lead to a standing position in the break. Grovel up the depressions above to
finish on good holds up the headwall.

★ **110. Mugwump** 15m E3 6a   (1974/1988)
Start about one metre to the left at prominent white streaks. Climb the wall
immediately left of the streaks, bearing slightly left to a small cave at five
metres. Pull up right to a good hold in another depression, then make a hard
move up and continue directly to the top.
Big Jim Blueter (E3, 6a): keeps to the right just before the small cave, then
rejoins the original route at the good in hold in a shallow depression.

★ **111. Wrongo Sal** 15m E5 6a   (1975-79)
Start just to the left at a shallow cave at head-height. Bold, sustained climbing
leads directly up the wall via a deep hole and a spike runner.

112. Burrough's Blues   12m   E3   6a   (1975-79)

Ascend the left edge of the wall starting by an obvious birch tree at the foot of the crag.

★★ **113. Red Wall Girdle**   54m   E3   5c,5b,6a   (1985)

One of the best climbs in the area: sustained and well-protected climbing with peg belays (often not in place).

1.   21m.   Follow Izzy the Push to the large depression then traverse left at this level to the large upper depression of Nova Express and a peg belay.

2.   18m.   Move left and go down to a traverse-line which leads past the bird-limed hole on Essence of Giraffe to a peg belay.

3.   15m.   Move up slightly then follow a line of holds to the left, to an awkward move which leads to buckets and the end of the crag.

*A final, **Beetle Wall**, gives some easy routes (VD to HS) on rather featureless rock. It is most easily found from near the start of the track running westwards out of the quarry. Cross the wasteland and the wall lies below some tall pines.*

The large boulder in the middle of the quarry floor has some good problems, the slabby south face contrasting with the overhangs on the other sides.

First Ascents at Trowbarrow

1967	**Original Route, Jomo** Stew Wilson, Rick Stallwood, members of St Martin's College MC
1967	**Twentieth Century Schizoid Man**
1967	**Very Ordinary Route**
1967	**Boomerang**
1968 Apr	**Coral Sea** Stew Wilson, Miles Martin
1968	**Red Slab** Stew Wilson, Miles Martin
1968	**Boundary Groove**
1968	**Assagai** Chris Eilbeck, Pete Lucas, Bill Lounds, Stew Wilson
1968	**Rumal** Bill Lounds, Alan Greig
1968	**Izzy the Push** (2pts aid) Bill Lounds, Stew Wilson, Robin Whitham *Aid reduced to one pt by Bill Lounds in 1972.* *Aid eliminated by Bill Lounds, 1972.*
1968	**Nova Express** (1pt aid) Bill Lounds with 1 pt aid *Aid eliminated by Bill Lounds, 1977.*
1968	**Essence of a Giraffe** Bill Lounds, Stew Wilson, Miles Martin, Stuart Butler (various leads for cleaning)
1970 May	**Crinoid, Perseverance** Stuart Charlton, Kay Charlton
1972	**Biological Agent K9**
1973 Mar 11	**Jean Jeanie** Al Evans, John Horsfall
1973	**Aladdinsane** Ron Fawcett, John Heseltine *Top-roped and loose rock removed earlier by Al Evans.*
1973 Oct 28	**Touch of Class** Ben Campbell-Kelly, Roger Treglown
1974 June 2	**Crematorium** Geoff Crick, John Entwistle
1974	**Warspite** (2pts aid) Dave Thompson, Phil Garner *Aid completely eliminated by Bill Lounds, Paul Sansom, 1975.*
1974	**Ramp Ant, Pigfall** Al Evans, Jean Horsfall
1974	**Sluice** Bill Lounds, Pete Lucas
1974	**Mugwump** Bill Lounds *Big Jim Blueter by Duncan Parker, Dave Wilcock, 3 Sep 1988*
1976	**Cracked Actor** Al Evans, Dave Parker *Climbed a few weeks earlier with 3 pts aid.*
1976	**Sleeping Sickness** Dave Hilton, Phil Garner
1976	**Javelin** Pete Livesey
1976	**Sour Milk Groove** Dave Cronshaw, Les Ainsworth, Bob MacMillan

1976	**Ask Les** Les Ainsworth (solo)	
1977 May	**Hollow Earth** Al Evans, Bill Lounds	
1977	**Dry Throat, Deep Throat** Jim Cooper	
	Dry Throat was subsequently redesigned and reclimbed by Dave Cronshaw, Les Ainsworth, 1 Dec, 1996.	
1977	**Warspite Direct** Bill Lounds, Paul Sansom	
	The Man Who Fell to Earth by Keith McGregor, Derek Hargreaves, 22 June 1998.	
1977	**Harijan, Truffle, Limestone John** Bill Lounds, Paul Sansom	
1977	**Night Flight** Al Evans, Dave Parker	
1977	**Blue Daz**	
1977	**Major Tom** Andy Hyslop	
1977	**Quisquillae** Jim Cooper	
1977	**Aborigine Wall, Barnacle** Phil Garner, Dave Hilton	
1977	*Hara Kiri,* **Boulderdash** Al Evans	
1978 Feb 8	**Heroes** Dave Knighton	
	Reclimbed after the flake fell off by Brian Davison, Nick Hewitt, 27 Apr 1988. No More Heroes by Brian Davison, Nick Green, 13 Apr 1994	
1978 Mar	**Lonely Wall** Al Evans	
1978 June 18	**Space Oddity** Mark Danson, Ian Cooksey	
1978 Sep 2	**Rock and Roll Suicide** Dave Knighton, Dave Kenyon	
1978	**Square Deal Surf** Paul Cropper, Brian Cropper, Al Evans, Dave Knighton	
1978	**Willy the Dish, Sleeping Balls** Bill Lounds, Tony Charlton, John Woodhead	
1978	**Earth Eater, Street Boy Blues** Bill Lounds, Keith Bliss	
1978	**Touch of Class: Variation** Dave Knighton	
1978	**Magic Making** Mark Danson, Ian Cooksey	
1978	**Frontage**	
1978	**A Sense of Doubt** Dave Knighton, Jim Arnold, John Girdley	
1979 Apr 1	**Makin' Magic** Dave Knighton, Ed Gridley	
1975-79	**First Cut**	
1975-79	**Oniscus**	
1975-79	**Sepia Typhoid Witness**	
1975-79	**Heavy Metal Kid** Originally pegged by Bill Lounds	
1975-79	**Essence Direct**	
1978	**The Pate** Bill Lounds, Pete Lucas	
1980	**Incantations** Mark Danson, Ian Cooksey	
1979-83	**Amphetamine Variation**	
1979-83	**Barrier Reef**	
1984 Aug 7	**Scary Monsters** Owain Jones, Steve Edmondson – After top-roping	
1984	**Day of the Beanpoles** Dave Bates, Tom Walkington – After top-roping	
1984	**Coral Sea Direct** Tom Walkington, Dave Bates	
1984 Dec 4	**Doubting Thomas** Dave Bates – After top-roping	
1985 Jan 12	**The Asylum** Paul Carling, Tom Walkington	
	Previously top-roped 1975-79.	
1985 June 19	**Wrongo Sal** Owain Jones, Steve Edmondson	
	Previously top-roped 1975-79.	
1985 June 28	**Exequy** Owain Jones (unseconded)	
	Previously top-roped 1975-79.	
1985	**The Nut-House** Dave Bates, Tom Walkington	
1985	**One of these Days** Dave Bates, Giles Phillips	
1985	**Willy the Fink** Ron Fawcett	
	Previously top-roped 1975-79.	
1985	**Red Wall Girdle** Dave Bates, Tom Walkington (alts)	
1983-86	**Fluoroscopic Kid**	
	Previously top-roped 1975-79.	
1986 May 2	**Pig in a Poke** Jon Sparks, Nick Russell	
	Direct Start by Brian Davison (solo), 19 July 1992.	
1986 Aug	**Mémoires of a Lunatic, Diaries of a Madman** Mark Liptrot (unseconded)	
1986 Oct	**The Idiot** Mark Liptrot (unseconded)	
1986 Oct	**Burrough's Blues** Mark Liptrot (unseconded)	
	Previously top-roped 1975-79.	

1986 Nov	**Helden** Dave Cronshaw, John Ryden
1986	**Blow Out** Mark Liptrot
	Made into an independent line by Brian Davison, Nick Green, 28 May 1997.
1986	**Shady Blade** Pitch 1: Phil Stone, R Sagar as Stoned Free and Tatty
	Pitch 2: Dave Bates
	Originally done as separate routes.
1987	**Twisted Sister** Tony Mitchell (solo)
1988 Apr 10	**Acid Drop** Brian Davison, Andy Leanie
1988 Apr 13	**Drop Acid**, *Shell Shock* Brian Davison, Andy Leanie
1988 Apr 13	*Body Abuse*, **Owl Surprise** Brian Davison (solo)
1988 May 18	**Ashes to Ashes** Brian Davison, Colby Coombs
1988 June	**Main Wall Girdle** Brian Davison, Colby Coombs
1988 July 18	**Moondance** Brian Davison, Dave Smith
1988 Aug 17	**American Express** Duncan Parker, Dave Wilcock
1988 Aug 31	**Access Bill** Duncan Parker, Dave Wilcock
1989 Mar 5	**Teardrop** Duncan Parker, Dave Wilcock
1989	**Homophobia** Andy Griffith (unseconded)
1990	**Red Dwarf** Jon Allison
1990	**Clear and Present Danger** Tim Hatch
1991 July 6	**Arc** Dave Nicol, Dick Baker, Ian Conway
1991 July 6	**Little Lil** Ian Conway, Dick Baker, Dave Nicol
1991 Oct 27	**Michelin Man** Jim Robertson, Geoff Coverdale
1991	**Diary of a Sane Man** Dave Bates
1992 July 19	**Helden Right-hand** Brian Davison, Penny Clay
1993 Aug 3	**Steal Your Fire** Karl Lunt, John Stringfellow
1993 Aug	**PPC Madness, Facial Gymnastics, Tark's Traverse, Half a Pound of Cabbage, Quick Nick** T Conger
1994	**Eek** Luke Steer
1996 Sep	**Diamonds** Les Ainsworth, Dave Cronshaw
1997 June 3	**Helden Arête** Brian Davison (unseconded)
1997 July 14	**Clotted Cream** Karl Lunt, Alison Sharman
1997 July 18	**Shallow Grave** John Gaskins
1998	**Pale Groove** Brian Davison (unseconded)
1998 Sep 29	**Grave Doubts** Brian Davison, Nick Green

Warton

Warton village is located about two kilometres north-west of Carnforth, near
Junction 35a of the M6 (A601M). The hillside directly above the village

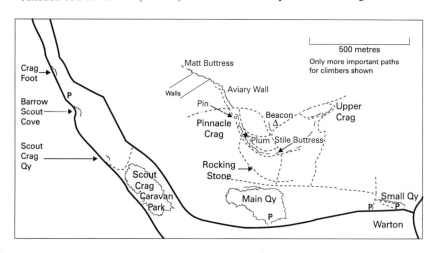

provides a variety of climbing on natural limestone buttresses and quarries, which are described in the following sections.

Warton Main Quarry   O.S. ref.   SD 492 144

Please read the Access section before visiting Warton Main Quarry

'Warton Quarry is reached by turning right at the traffic lights in Carnforth when travelling south on the A6. About two miles along this road is Warton Village; turn left at the Black Bull Hotel (where good liquid refreshment can be obtained after a hard evening's work-out...'

'... the big quarry is farther along the road, but it has not yet been cleaned up sufficiently to be described here.'

Bill Lounds, Rocksport, 1969

Situation and Character

The Main Quarry at Warton is the huge limestone quarry that dominates the view of the hillside from the M6. There is much loose rock in places and so the quarry can seem daunting on first acquaintance. However, the climbing generally manages to avoid the loosest sections and those who do take the effort to get to know the quarry will be rewarded with some of the best routes in Lancashire, especially if the sun is shining. Having said this, there are also some of the worst routes, with many being amazingly loose. These routes will be pointed out in order that they can be avoided (or appreciated by those who enjoy that sort of adventure!).

History

Apart from one or two aided forays, now lost in the mists of time and legend, the first attack on the quarry came in 1970 with the ascent of the striking line of *Plastic Iceberg*. The first pitch – hardly immaculate even now – was so loose that, in John Sheard's words *"what we needed was a disposable non-climber with a disregard for instability and no need of conventional protection"* in other words Pete Livesey, then better known in other sports, who made the first ascent with Sheard.

Dave Knighton was next on the scene in 1976 with John Wilding a young lad who was to become, in turn, the quarry's main activist in the future. Routes really started to fall in 1977; Dave Cronshaw adding *Vespers for the Dead* on which his second, Les Ainsworth, was rained off. Ainsworth consoled himself with *Limestone Rain* and *The Real World*, the latter finding the easiest way up the impressive left-hand side of the central wall. 'Big' Jim Cooper added the adventurous *Rock Folly*, and later *Dream World* with Alan Atkinson, but the best lines were snatched by Knighton; despite being decried for his top-rope practices, he created the superb *Deceptive Bends* and *Third World*, but regrettably had to resort to aid on *Killer Queen*, a soaring line up the steep wall right of *Plastic Iceberg*, though only after taking an eight-metre fall when two

A leader high on **Assagai** (HVS 5a), Trowbarrow.   *Photo: Jon Sparks*

holds snapped whilst attempting a lead. Knighton then led it by a slightly different line, with two pegs for aid. The aid was finally eliminated in 1982 when a Lakes team led by Ed Cleasby managed a clean ascent to produce a very fine, airy wall climb.

The following year, Knighton forged a line up the arête left of *Plastic Iceberg* giving *Fall of the House of Usher*, and Andy Hyslop led Knighton and Marcus Tierney up *Just Like a Woman*. The fine line of *Cosmic Debris* fell (literally?) to alternate leads by Phil Martin and Ian Welsh. As well as being involved in several first ascents, Dave Bates was later to leave his mark in quite a different way: it was his preference for a lie-in that is commemorated by the route name *Ich Bleib Im Bett*. Later, Neil Foster added *Saruman* with Andy Wiggans, whilst Steve Parr made a bold solo ascent of *The Year of the Cat*, an alternative start to his own *Modern Times*.

1980 saw Knighton completing the hardest of his Warton routes with ascents of *Terminal Trajectory* and *Up the Neck*, and then things lay quiet for some time until the ugly spectre of questionable tactics arose again. This time though it was Iain Greenwood and Mark Danson who first top-roped and then led *Comes a Time* using preplaced runners. There was no question though of the superb quality of the route and it has recently been straightened out and improved upon even further by the addition of a direct finish by Bates.

The next few years saw nothing of any real note, only a series of indifferent routes by Bates and Jonty Wilson, the best of which were *Galactic Timebreaker* and *The New World*. Then in 1984, Tom Walkington and Barry Rodgers breached the large white wall left of Wartberg to give the sustained *Oddballs*. Shortly after Bates climbed a more direct line, *Mighty Fly*, up the wall, thinking it to be a second ascent due to the old bolt and peg runners. Bates added a number of major new lines that winter, including the bold *Brainstrain* and the easier *Flash Imp*, which manages to wend a surprisingly easy way through the huge overhangs left of Third World. With Walkington, Bates made a frozen, two-day epic traverse of the left-hand side of the quarry, creating *Birdbrain Meets Clothears*.

Through the years, Jim Cooper has soloed a few routes on the Upper Tier, most of which are on rather loose rock. Two routes though (*Walking on Sunshine* and *Riding on Air*) are of much better quality than their predecessors. However, 1986 saw *Celestial Cyclone* by Bates, a Malham-style route on the Year of the Cat slab. Then 1987 saw the introduction of the E6 grade in the quarry and possibly the area's hardest route with Bates' route *The Torture Garden*, a very forceful, very direct line up the Mighty Fly wall: the name possibly refers to the excruciating bridging position Walkington managed to get into whilst seconding the route.

During the early part of September 1988, by one of those amazing coincidences, two teams, quite independently of each other, attempted to girdle the quarry. Unfortunately, although they traversed in opposite directions, the results were the same and the name of one of these girdles, *What a Waste of a Day*, says it all. Since then, little of special note has been added.

Ian Vickers has **Mémoires of a Lunatic** (E5 6b), Trowbarrow.   *Photo: Roger Vickers*

Approach

The quarry entrance is about one kilometre past the George Washington pub (alias the Black Bull Inn) at Warton, on the upper road (Crag Road) to Silverdale.

Access

The quarry is a Local Nature Reserve and a Site of Special Scientific Interest (SSSI) and so there are some minimal restrictions on climbing in order to protect the wildlife.

Between the end of February and the end of June peregrines usually try to nest in this quarry. Therefore, there are temporary climbing restrictions on parts of the crag to protect the birds during that period. Notices in the quarry provide the latest information on any climbing restrictions and the Lancashire County Council Ranger Services monitor the situation very closely so that these restrictions do not remain any longer than is necessary. In the past, this has worked well and climbing restrictions have always been fully honoured. Please keep it that way.

The quarry floor below the wall immediately opposite the Main Wall provides an excellent habitat for many small orchids, which can be easily damaged underfoot. Therefore, climbers are asked to keep away from this area from early April to the end of June and to watch where you walk at other times.

Climbers are also asked to **refrain from placing bolts**, except where this is absolutely necessary to protect long, otherwise unprotectable runouts.

The Climbs

The routes are described from RIGHT to LEFT from the quarry entrance.

End Walls

The End Walls start from the right-hand side of the car park and the top rises rapidly to the broken corner at the top of Slack Alice in the angle of the quarry. A prominent feature of this wall is the cave of Gouffle Connection above the top of a mound in the centre of the wall. Excavations on the right of the mound have increased both the height and the difficulty of some of the previous routes.

1.   Moon Ribber   15m   VD   (1976)
From the point where the second fence meets the rock, follow the left edge of a left-slanting ramp to the top.

2.   Moonshine   22m   E2   5c   (1974/1997)
Start at a fluting at the lowest point on the wall. From the top of this make delicate moves up past a bolt to a small ledge. Continue over ledges to another bolt, then step left slightly and continue to the top.

3.   Pipedream   21m   HVS   5a   (1974/1997)
Start five metres farther left at the right-hand side of low ledges and climb the faint weakness that slants left to just below a small overlap at five metres. Move right, then go up to the base of a shallow depression and follow this to its top.

4.   Paper Plane 21m E1 5a   (1981/1997)
Halfway up the mound a slanting weakness leads to ledges and the right-hand
side of the large cave. From four metres up this, climb rightwards then up, to
large ledges below the right side of a shallow depression. Climb the blocky
crackline above, keeping mainly to the wall on the left.

⋆ **5.   Papermoon** 20m VS 4c   (1974)
Follow the slanting weakness to the first ledge, then traverse horizontally right
at a small overlap, to the foot of a left-leaning crackline at the left side of a
shallow depression. Follow this to the top.

**Climbers are warned that doubts have been expressed about the stability of
the rock that currently forms the roof of the cave on the left of Gouffle
Connection. This area is currently being monitored by Lancashire Council and
climbers are asked to take care to avoid damaging the rock-movement
indicators that are in place to measure any slippage. If the rock is shown to
be moving dangerously, it will be demolished and if this is done, some of these
routes, notably Raising the Blade, Karlyn Returns and Come Here Katherine,
are likely to be completely destroyed.**

6.   Home James 22m VS 4b   (1983)
Follow the slanting weakness to ledges at the top of it, then climb the wall and
finish up the top crack.

7.   Don't Spare the Horses 25m VS 4c   (1983)
Start at the top of the mound and climb the wall and roofs on the right.

8.   Raising the Blade 25m E3 5c   (1988)
The left-leading overhanging groove/crackline that forms the right side of the
cave, starting over large, but precarious-looking blocks.

9.   Karlyn Returns 25m E4 6b   (1988)
Start as for Raising the Blade and climb directly to the roof, then surmount this
at its widest point.

10.   Come Here Katherine 25m E1 6a   (1988)
A resurrection of the collapsed route Karlyn Went Shopping Instead, starting
just left of a stepped roof, with a small groove at its lowest point. Climb this
and the wall above, moving slightly left to finish.

⋆ **11.   The Gouffle Connection** 37m VS 4b   (1975)
Start below the large cave at the top of the mound. Climb the slabs to the left
side of the overhang, then follow a short crack at the left side of the overhang
to reach the wide horizontal break near the top. Traverse left along this for five
metres until an exit upwards (careful) can be made.

⋆⋆ **12.   Vespers for the Dead** 29m HVS 5a   (1977)
One of the classics of the crag, offering pleasant wall climbing without having
to venture too deeply into the lost world of Warton Main. Climb the steep wall
directly below the left edge of the large roofs to the top of a small dome-shaped
buttress. Continue directly up the wall above (bold) to gain an obvious
leftward-curving crack. Follow this until a thought-provoking mantel can be
made to join the traverse of Gouffle Connection, finish up this.

13.   Wart Berg   30m   VS   4b,–   (1974)
1.   12m.   Start four metres to the left and climb the obvious crack to the
right-hand side of the good belay ledge.
2.   18m.   Continue past large flakes, then finish up an easy corner.

★ **14.   Dog Years**   37m   E2   5c   (1981)
Start six metres to the left of Wart Berg. Climb the shallow corner to the
left-hand side of the large ledge on Wart Berg. Continue up Wart Berg to the
top flake, then follow a thin left-leading break (No. 1 rocks) to a pull on sloping
holds which lead to a resting position (peg). Easier climbing leads rightwards to
finish.

★★ **15.   Mighty Fly**   30m   E5   6b   (1984)
Strenuous climbing with good protection where it matters; as the holds get
smaller the gear gets better. Follow Dog Years to the ledge, then just above this,
break out left on large holds to a bolt. Balance up and right (crux) past two
pegs to an overlap. A delicate move rightwards gains the break of Dog Years.
Continue straight up to large holds and easier ground leading right to the top.

★★ **16.   The Torture Garden**   27m   E6   6b   (1987)
A direct line up the white wall left of Wart Berg with some precarious and
sustained climbing. The hard moves are well protected, but the easier top section
is a long way above good gear and it can feel very intimidating. Climb to a
shallow niche, then leave this (peg) and climb the wall above to another peg
below an overlap and use an undercut jam to gain the bolt on Mighty Fly. Gain
the overlap above by a puzzling move (crux) before bold climbing leads to the
sloping jugs on Dog Years. Step left to a thin crack and follow this to the break
(peg) then go direct up to a bolt belay. Abseil descent.

17.   Oddballs   30m   E4   5c   (1984)
Sustained, but easily protected. Start at a right-facing flake crack four metres left
of The Torture Garden. Climb a thin crack/groove to an awkward step right to a
large overlap. Sustained climbing past small wires leads to another peg. A
delicate move left (peg) leads to an easier finish. It is advisable to hang a rope
down the top loose band of rock to use as a belay.

18.   Tight Sally   48m   HVS   4a,5a   (1981)
The first pitch is loose.
1.   21m.   Start five metres right of the corner of Slack Alice, and climb up to
a roof. Pass this on the right, then go up slabs to a small ledge and peg belay.
2.   27m.   Move up and right past a horizontal break on to a slab (peg on
right). Step left and follow the slab to the top, nut belay.

19.   Slack Alice   48m   HVS   4c,4b   (1974)
A frightening route; the first loose pitch leads to an even looser second pitch.
1.   21m.   Start at the large corner in the angle of the quarry. Climb the corner
to nut belays in the cave.
2.   27m.   Continue up the corner (care with the perched block!) to nut belays.

Modern Wall

About 30 metres from the corner of Slack Alice, the back wall forms a shallow bay with a small rubble cone, to the right of a large shattered block. The area between this bay and Slack Alice is known as Modern Wall. All but one of these climbs finishes on the large ledge partway up the crag, from which it is necessary either to make an abseil **DESCENT** *from twin bolts, or to finish up Modern Times Continuation.*

★ **20. Modern Times** 26m HVS 5a (1975)
A bold pitch. Start six metres to the left of the corner and climb straight up the slab past a bolt on the left at 10 metres to a small ledge with a peg just above on the left. Move diagonally left to the right side of the long narrow ledge. There is a two-bolt belay towards the left side of this ledge.

21. Modern Times Continuation 33m E1 5a,4a (1975)
From the belay ledge on Modern Times, two pitches continue to the top. However, there is some loose rock, particularly on the first pitch.
1. 18m. Climb rightwards across the wall above to a small niche. Enter the groove above from the left, then climb to an exit on the right; iron spike and peg belay.
2. 15m. Climb the wall and groove above to a loose finish on the left; tree belay.

22. Zero Tolerance 26m E2 5c (1998)
A worrying start on poor rock leads to good, steep, slab climbing. Start at the centre of the Modern Wall, directly below a prominent triangular neb on the skyline. Climb a slight rib past three bolts to a shallow scoop at 10 metres, above the poor rock. Continue up the steep slab past bolts to an obvious overhang, then step round this on its right to a good finish at the bolt belay on Modern Times.

23. Celestial Cyclone 25m E3 5c (1986)
Start 12 metres farther left at a very shallow groove on the wall just right of the foot of a rubble cone. Climb the groove (bolt) to gain the slab (bolt). Step left then go up to a bolt and peg below an overlap, then climb diagonally rightwards to the bolt belay on the ledge on Modern Times.

24. The Year of the Cat 34m E2 5a (1976)
A loose and poorly protected route, starting in the bay, to the right of the shattered block. Traverse up and right on an obvious band of good rock. Go up the slab above to the peg and bolt on Celestial Cyclone, then climb diagonally rightwards to the bolt belay on the ledge on Modern Times.

★ **25. Galactic Timebreaker** 51m E2 4c,5c (1981)(1981)
1. 21m. Climb the right-leaning flake crack five metres to the left of the shattered block to a ledge. From the left-hand end of this go up for six metres then traverse left across a slab to a ledge. Nut belays well back.
2. 30m. Move back right and go up a slab, then over an overlap to a resting place under the roof. Surmount this (peg on lip) and gain a slab which is followed to an overlap (peg). Climb up under the roof then traverse right for six metres and finish up a short groove.

2a.   **Left-hand Finish** (4c): pass the large roof on the left then go up via blocks to the top.

Main Wall

The rest of the high back wall of the quarry is known as the Main Wall. There is loose rock on some of the routes, especially those at the right-hand side, but despite appearances, there are also many limestone classics. The left side of this area is marked by a depression, where the quarry floor rises slightly, about 35 metres left of the previous route. At the right-hand side of this depression it is possible to scramble between an embedded boulder and the rock. This point is further marked by a bush at the very top of the crag.

26.   Rock Folly   93m   VS   4a,4b,4a,–,–   (1978)
1.   18m.   From the depression, climb the groove (some loose rock) or scramble up from the right, then step left on to an easy-angled slab, and move up to a belay.
2.   24m.   Climb over doubtful blocks to the pink and grey wall, then move up and right to broken ledges, and continue to the large ledge, peg belay.
3.   21m.   Walk six metres to the left, then cross a steep slab (peg) and move up to a small niche. Swing left round a block, then ascend the corner above to a belay on the left.
4.   12m.   Traverse left using doubtful blocks, then go up a short corner to a large ledge and peg belay.
5.   18m.   Walk along the ledge to a broken corner near the left end, and climb this over poor rock, finishing on the left. After the first pitch of the route there are several variations which would be possible, but all need extensive cleaning.

27.   Blinded by the Light   44m   HVS   5a   (1992)
About 35 metres farther left there is a groove, which is guarded by an undercut block and overhang at the foot of the crag. Start at the right side of the overhang and immediately above it, traverse left to climb the right side of the block into the groove. Exit the groove to easy ground (possible belay), then move up to a corner leading to an overhang just left of an arête near the top of the crag. There is still loose rock on the route.

28.   Crunchy   24m   HVS   4c   (1981)
Follow the clean slab capped with small overhangs between Rock Folly and White Fright. No start has yet been climbed so the approach is by an abseil from the terrace to a ledge at half-height. Climb the slab above this to overhangs, then move left and climb direct to the top.

29.   White Fright   44m   HVS   5a,4a   (1976)
Very loose and not recommended. Halfway along the main wall is a large cone of debris with a large ledge on the left. Take the groove on the left of this.
1.   38m.   Follow the right-slanting ramp over doubtful blocks to below a small overhang, then step right and swing right on to a ledge (no belay). Move left on to the wall (peg) and go up for three metres, then move left and up on to a steep slab (peg). From the peg step up and traverse right into the groove-line and follow this with increasing difficulty (two pegs) to a sloping ledge. Ring peg belay.
2.   6m.   Bridge up the corner at the back of the ledge to the terrace, peg belay.

30. Devil's Nightmare 46m E1 5b (1981)
Climb Limestone Rain but continue the traverse for nine metres to below a ramp
(possible belay). Climb this to a roof (peg), which is turned on the right.
Continue up to a large loose flake and go round this to enter a scoop. Climb up
and right (peg) into a slim groove (crux) which leads to the top. Belays well
back.

★★ **31. Limestone Rain** 62m E1 5a,5b (1976)
A good route, though ascents often take on an epic quality.
1.   24m.   Ascend the groove at the foot of Plastic Iceberg until it is possible to
step up and right onto a slab. Cross this to a short corner (peg), then climb the
steep wall on the right (care should be taken to protect the second for these
moves), and go across to the right side of an easy ledge system. Peg belay.
2.   38m.   Go up the shallow groove on the right to the roof, then traverse left
to the end of the overhang and go straight up (peg) to another roof. Surmount
this on the right using some doubtful blocks, then continue up an obvious
layback crack towards the next overhang. At a small ledge on the left either,
continue up to the roof then surmount it on its left, or climb straight up from
the ledge. Above the overhang follow the obvious groove to the top, then walk
well back to a belay.
32. Dance on a Volcano 25m E2 5b (1983)
A frightening climb on less than perfect rock. From the belay on Plastic Iceberg,
traverse six metres right then follow the right-trending crack/ramp line (peg) to a
pleasant finish.

★★ **33. Killer Queen** 29m E4 6a (1977/1980)(1980)
An excellent and airy route. Start from the belay on Plastic Iceberg. Traverse
right to the arête, then climb the left-hand side of this until just below the
overlap; step left and go up to a peg. Pass this to a second overlap and another
peg. Step right and climb up to a horizontal break, then go straight up the slab
above, just left of the arête, to finish.
Variation (E3, 6a): after clipping the first peg, step down and go right to the
arête. Climb the shallow groove just right of the arête, stretching left to clip the
second peg, then finish as for the parent route.

★★ **34. Brainstrain** 32m E5 6a (1985)
An exhilarating route with a bold finish. Follow Killer Queen to the first peg,
step down and traverse left for four metres then make awkward moves (crux) up
past a peg to the horizontal break. Step right then make a mind-bending runout
past a pod-shaped hole to the top.

★★★ **35. Plastic Iceberg** 50m E1 5a,5b (1970)
This was the first and arguably the best route on the Main Wall, despite the fact
that it took a Yorkshireman to discover it. It takes the prominent, deep groove
that splits the Main Wall towards its left-hand side.
1.   24m.   Climb the lower, slabby groove to an overhang which is passed on
the left. At a second overhang, move left to the arête, make an awkward mantel
and continue to the base of the left-hand groove. Step into the right-hand groove
and climb this to a belay ledge and an iron spike belay. From the second
overhang it is also possible to move right and follow grooves to the belay. This
is only just 4c, but the bottom couple of blocks appear somewhat unstable.

2.   26m.   Sustained climbing up the groove leads past a small overlap to a peg. Continue to a small overlap near the top, then pass this on its right to reach the top.

36.   Arête Variations   27m   E1   5b   (1981)
Follow the second pitch of Plastic Iceberg to an overlap (peg on left) then move down to a small footledge on the left. Traverse left along this to the arête and climb up to a jammed block on House of Usher. Climb the steep crack on the right and pull on to a small ledge, then finish on the left as for House of Usher.

★★ **37.   Fall of the House of Usher**   29m   HVS   5a   (1978)
An airy pitch with a worrying pull on to a '*way out there*' block. From the belay of Plastic Iceberg swing round the rib on the left onto a short slab. Cross this to the foot of a ramp/groove, (possible belay): follow this past two pegs to below the block which guards entry into the upper groove. Make a mind-blowing heave on to the block and continue up the groove with a swing left to finish.

● **38.   The Demise of Lady Madeline**   23m   HVS   5a   (1981)
A recent rockfall has occurred near the bottom of this route which is now in a dangerous state. Follow Plastic Iceberg pitch one for three metres, then move left to gain a steep crack: climb this through overhangs, moving left to another crack. Move right and climb over suspect rock (care) to a ledge.

39.   Future Now   15m   HVS   5a   (1978)
Follow the second pitch of House of Usher to the arête then climb leftwards and break through the overhang on the left. Finish up the wall above.

★★ **40.   Comes a Time**   35m   E5   6a   (1980)(1987)
Another excellent route: when combined with the direct finish it makes a superb outing. It takes a direct line up the slab left of Fall of the House of Usher. From the belay of Demise of Lady Madeline, follow Cosmic Debris for six metres (large Hex) then traverse right and go up to a thin crack in the slab. Sustained but well-protected climbing leads to a horizontal break. Move right, then finish as for Future Now.
Direct Finish (5c): climb direct to the top from the horizontal break. Bold.

★ **41.   Cosmic Debris**   51m   E1   5a,5b,5b   (1979-80)
This occasionally loose but otherwise good route takes the corner line left of Plastic Iceberg to give three interesting pitches.
1.   15m.   From the foot of the corner climb a shattered groove past a peg then an easy curving flake to a small stance. Good nut belay. Alternative stance six metres up the corner on a ledge on the right.
2.   18m.   Climb the corner above with increasing difficulty to gain the groove above and a nut belay.
3.   18m.   Continue up the corner to a small roof; layback this and climb to the top.

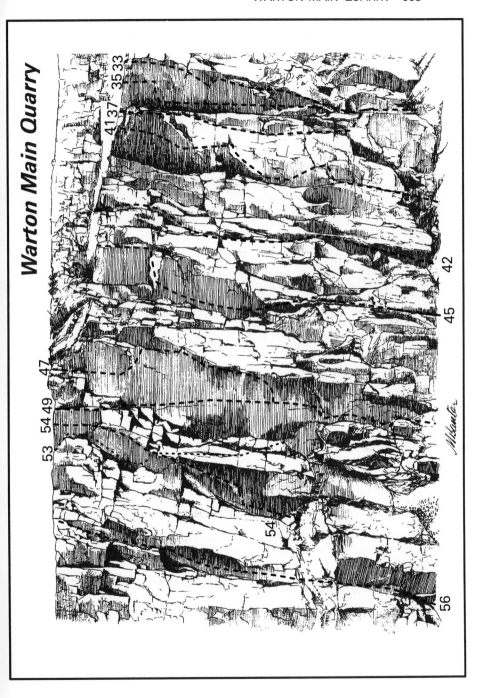

Warton Main Quarry

★ **42.   Saruman**   51m   E2   5a,5b,5a   (1980)
Takes the right-slanting ramp system to the left.
1.   15m.   Climb the right-trending slab/ramp (which forms a short chimney at
the bottom) to a sitting block belay.
2.   21m.   Climb the wall behind for a couple of metres, then move left into the
slender right-trending ramp. Follow this to ledges at its top.
3.   15m.   Climb the prominent corner behind (on the left) by a layback, then
continue over an overhang to easier ground.

43.   Ich Bleib Im Bett   51m   E2   5b,5b   (1983-86)
A good but rather bold route. Start six metres left of Saruman.
1.   27m.   Follow broken but easy ground up to a large flake at the base of a
slim groove. Climb the groove stepping right at the top to a peg belay below a
small roof.
2.   24m.   Step right and go up to boldly gain a shallow groove on the left.
Follow this to the roof and traverse left under this on good jams to exit on to
easier ground to the top.

★★ **44.   Up the Neck**   24m   E3   5c   (1980)
The rock is at its best on the slab, which gives technical moves on solid rock
and a choice of holds on the less demanding sections. From pitch one of Real
World move up below the overlap then pull over on to the slab (peg). After
another step up traverse right (crux) to a foot ledge on the arête. Climb straight
up past a second peg to a sloping ledge then continue more easily to the long
traversing ledge on Real World. Climb the wall above via a vague crackline to
its highest point.

★★ **45.   The Real World**   51m   VS   –,4b   (1977)
The easiest way up the left-hand side of the main wall. A rather broken first
pitch leads to good groove/slab climbing on the second pitch. It takes the next
big corner left of Cosmic Debris.
1.   21m.   Start below and go left of the corner at a short wall of more stable
rock. Climb the wall then scramble up and right to arrive at a small ledge, nut
belays.
2.   30m.   Climb the corner, making a delicate move right at 12 metres (crux).
Then either traverse the break to the arête and follow this to the top, or continue
up the corner for six metres then traverse/walk to the arête and so to the top.

46.   The Warton Blues   24m   E1   5a   (1983)
From the Real World belay, traverse three metres left into a steep groove/crack.
Follow this on less-than-perfect rock to the top.

★★★ **47.   Deceptive Bends**   50m   E1   5b   (1977)(1983)
A classic and justly popular climb. Start as for Third World. Follow the
crackline (peg) for nine metres until a line of holds leads out to the arête on the
right. Balance up this with much trepidation to a welcome peg (do not look too
closely!). Continue to some superb quartzy pockets and a tape. Move thinly up
and left, then go back right to a good resting place above the gorse bush. Go up
and over the bulge to a peg; step left to a crack then back right to finish. nine
metres of earthy scrambling leads to the top. A rope may need to be pulled
through to belay.
Direct Start (4c): climb the arête direct to join the original route.

★★ **48.   Terminal Trajectory** 50m E3 5c   (1980)
Although this route has some fine climbing, it is now more serious since a peg
has disappeared. Follow Third World for 12 metres, move right on to the slab
and wander up this to the bulge of Deceptive Bends. Pull over this then traverse
right for three metres to the arête and finish up a groove.

★★★ **49.   The Third World** 46m HVS 5a   (1977)
Another deservedly popular climb, taking the crackline up the centre of the huge
pink slab at the left end of the quarry. Scramble easily up to the base of the
crackline to start, then follow the crack and make an awkward move over the
overlap (peg). Pleasant climbing leads to a large groove in the overhangs
(possible belay). After a couple of bridging moves a juicy jamming crack on the
left wall is followed to the top. If 45-metre ropes are used it is necessary to pull
one through in order to belay.

★★ **50.   Flash Imp** 48m E4 5c,5a   (1985)
An intimidating route requiring a cool head. It takes a direct line up the slab left
of Third World, then wends its way through the massive roofs. Scramble up to
the large sloping ledge below the slab to start.
1.   27m.   Delicate climbing leads to a crux at nine metres (nut used six metres
up Third World). Belay at the groove.
2.   21m.   Move three metres left until it is possible to gain a short groove in
the overhangs. Ascend this then break out left to join Just Like a Woman: finish
up this.

51.   Truly Scrumptious 52m E1 5a   (1980)
Take the broken groove on the left side of Third World slab until it is possible
to traverse left across the white wall to join Just Like a Woman at the crux.

52.   Dream World 50m HVS 5a   (1983-86)
Follow the groove on the left-hand side of the slab to the roof. Traverse right to
the groove of Third World, possible belay. Continue up and traverse right.
Finish up Deceptive Bends.

★ **53.   The New World** 46m E1 5c   (1981)
Climb the white wall left of Dream World's groove, to a peg level with the
overlap on Just Like a Woman. Move left to the rib then climb a short crack,
moving left slightly to climb the wall above to a peg. Pass this (crux) to an
easier finish up a groove. A good if slightly contrived line.

★ **54.   Just Like a Woman** 38m E1 5a   (1978)
A worthwhile route best approached either by abseil or a hairy scramble in from
the left. Climb the corner crack for six metres before trending right to a small
ledge and peg. The next moves form the crux; palm the arête and if you do not
'*barn door*' off you will reach the overlap. Go over this and up a short groove
(possible belay on the left). Make an exposed traverse right to the arête then go
up and over a small overhang to finish up a friable wall.

55.   Shake, Rattle and Roll 38m E1 5b   (1983)
Start as for Just Like a Woman but continue up the groove to a hard swing left
(peg). Continue up a groove to a broken ledge, possible belay. Step left to gain
a thin groove which is followed to the top; care needed with suspect rock.

56.   Too Old to Rock 'n' Roll, Too Young to Die   38m   E2   5a   (1983)
A truly horrendous route, taking a line up the next obvious groove/slab left of
Just Like a Woman.
Start at a shallow groove/crack nine metres left of Just Like a Woman;
heart-stopping moves on disintegrating rock gain a delightful slab which is
followed with much horripilation (mad loud manic laughter an advantage) to
finish up a delectable groove.

⋆ **57.   Birdbrain Meets Clothears**   109m   E2   5a,5b,5a,5c,5c   (1985)
A magnificent expedition, girdling the left-hand side of the quarry from left to
right.
1.   37m.   Follow Just Like a Woman to the overlap, traverse right (peg) down
across the white wall into the groove of Dream World, then go delicately across
the Third World slab to a peg belay above the gorse bush on Deceptive Bends.
2.   18m.   After a fight with the gorse bush, traverse right at the same height as
the bush to gain Real World, nut belay.
3.   24m.   Walk across the slab then go round the corner to make an awkward
move across the Saruman groove. Continue at the same level until a wild swing
leads into the final steep corner of Cosmic Debris. Nut belay.
4.   12m.   Make some thin moves across the horizontal break, crossing Comes a
Time and swing round the rib to belay on Fall of the House of Usher.
5.   18m.   Step down to make an exasperating move (crux) into the groove of
Plastic Iceberg (peg). Continue along the horizontal break to finish up the
groove just right of Killer Queen.

Washington Area

*Most of the rock directly opposite the Main Wall is very poor. However, at the
far left end, closest to the quarry entrance, some climbs have been recorded on
two leaning walls. The right-hand of these walls can be easily identified by a
large L-shaped iron bar at its foot.*

The tops of all of the climbs in this area should be treated with much respect.

58.   Venator   8m   E5   6b   (1989)
Climb the overhanging wall two metres right of the iron bar, via two bolts and
a peg to reach a bolt belay.

59.   Beware of the Dentist   8m   E2   5b   (1988)
Climb the groove that starts two metres left of the iron bar. The crux is just
above a peg.

60.   Washington   24m   HS   4a   (1974)
A scrappy route with poor protection. Follow the right-leading rampline which
runs between the two leaning walls, keeping directly above the right-hand wall.

Two bolt-protected climbs **Lazy Days in Calella** *and* **Little Baby Nothing** *have
been reported on the overhanging left wall. However, the bolt hangers have all
been destroyed and so no descriptions are included in this guidebook.*

Terrace Wall

The remaining climbs in the quarry start from the large terrace which splits the Main Wall above Plastic Iceberg. Access to this ledge is from the left by a short, stepped corner. Two worthwhile routes have been climbed on the right end of the Terrace, the rest are of indifferent quality.

★ **61.   Walking on Sunshine**   24m   VS   4c   (1986)
Take the clean and solid (!) wall right of Polo direct via a thin crack near the top.

★ **62.   Riding on Air**   24m   VS   4c   (1986)
Gain the block on Polo and make a rising traverse right to the top of Walking on Sunshine.

63.   Three Steps to Heaven   27m   S   4a   (1975-79)
From the right end of the Terrace, climb the wall to a ledge at six metres. From the right of this ledge climb straight up to the top, climbing the left side of a rib nine metres from the top. Very loose finish.

64.   Polo   21m   HS   4a   (1975-79)
Farther left is a block stuck to the rock with a shot-hole in its centre. Ascend left of the block and step on to its top, then climb thin cracks to a mantel on a large earthy ledge. Continue to the top of the crag.

65.   Star Wars   24m   HS   4a   (1975-79)
Start ten metres right of Sneck. Climb diagonally right for six metres, then go horizontally right for a further six metres to beneath broken rocks at the top. Continue horizontally right for a further six metres, then climb straight to the top.

66.   Sneck   15m   VD   (1975-79)
Towards the left side of the Terrace is a block-shaped nose. Climb the corner on the right of this, passing an overhang at six metres. At the top move left and finish over doubtful rock.

67.   Rubber Band   14m   S   4a   (Pre-1982)
The corner left of the nose, moving right at six metres, then moving left to finish as Sneck.

68.   Plastic Band   12m   VD   (Pre-1982)
The corner just to the right of the top of Plastic Iceberg.

Two complete traverses of the quarry have been done. From left to right is **The Fragmented Tormentor** *and from right to left is* **What a Waste of a Day**. *These are major expeditions over much poor rock, with indefinite lines and little merit, which have not been repeated. Therefore, no descriptions are given.*

First Ascents at Warton Main Quarry

1970	**Plastic Iceberg** Pete Livesey, John Sheard	
1974 Oct	**Wart Berg** Originally climbed as Trespasser Crack by John Girdley, D. Ullerenshaw, Jill Lawrence	
1974	**Moonshine, Pipedream, Papermoon, Slack Alice, Washington** Leicester MC party	

During landscaping of the quarry, a considerable amount of spoil was excavated from the area to the right of Gouffle Connection. The extended line of Pipedream was climbed by Dave Cronshaw and Les Ainsworth in Aug 1997 and the extended version of Moonshine was climbed by Brian Davison, Dave Cronshaw, Les Ainsworth, 18 Oct, 1997.

1975 Jan 4	**The Gouffle Connection** John Girdley, Al Evans (alts)
1975 Oct 3	**Modern Times, Modern Times Continuation** Steve Parr, Steve Lund
1976 Apr 16	**The Year of the Cat** Steve Parr (solo)
1976	**White Fright** Dave Knighton, Ian Wilding (alts)
1976	**Moon Ribber**
1976 Nov	**Limestone Rain** Les Ainsworth, Dave Cronshaw (alts)
1977 Apr	**Vespers for the Dead** Dave Cronshaw, Les Ainsworth
1977 July	**The Real World** Dave Cronshaw, Les Ainsworth (alts)
1977 Nov 26	**Killer Queen** (2pts aid) Dave Knighton (unseconded)

Aid completely eliminated by Ed Cleasby, Jim Arnold, 1980.

1977 Dec 4	**The Third World** Dave Knighton (unseconded)
1977 Dec 20	**Deceptive Bends** Dave Knighton, Andy Hyslop

Direct Start by Dave Bates (solo).

1978 Jan 15	**Fall of the House of Usher** Dave Knighton, Dave Cronshaw
1978	**Future Now** Andy Hyslop, Iain Greenwood
1978	**Just Like a Woman** Andy Hyslop, Dave Knighton, Marcus Tierney
1978	**Rock Folly** Jim Cooper
1975-79	**Three Steps to Heaven, Polo, Star Wars, Sneck** Jim Cooper (solo)
1979-80	**Cosmic Debris** Phil Martin, Ian Welsh (alts)
1980 Mar	**Saruman** Neil Foster, Andy Wiggans
1980 July 11	**Up the Neck** Dave Knighton, Iain Greenwood
1980 July 12	**Truly Scrumptious** Dave Knighton, Phil Martin
1980	**Terminal Trajectory** Dave Knighton, John Girdley, Phil Martin
1980-81	**Comes a Time** Iain Greenwood, Mark Danson (after top-roping)

Direct Finish by Dave Bates, Mark Liptrot, Jim Cooper, 27 Apr 1987.

1981	**Paper Plane** Graham Aveyard, Michael Hoff

Line extended by Dave Cronshaw, Les Ainsworth, Aug, 1997.

1981	**Dog Years** Simon Cardy, Martin Elliott
1981	**Tight Sally, Crunchy, Devil's Nightmare, Arête Variations, The New World** Dave Bates, Jonty Wilson
1981	**Galactic Timebreaker** Dave Bates, Jonty Wilson

Left-hand Finish by Dave Bates, 1987.

1981	**The Demise of Lady Madeline** Pete Leaming, Justin Lucas
Pre-1982	**Rubber Band, Plastic Band** Jim Cooper (solo)
1983	**Home James, Don't Spare the Horses** Scott Umps, Giles Philips
1983	**Dance on a Volcano, The Warton Blues, Shake, Rattle and Roll, Too Old to Rock 'n' Roll, Too Young to Die** Dave Bates, Jonty Wilson
1984	**Oddballs** Tom Walkington, Barry Rogers (after top-roping)
1984	**Mighty Fly** Dave Bates, Tom Walkington
1985	**Brainstrain, Flash Imp, Birdbrain Meets Clothears** Dave Bates, Tom Walkington
1986 June 7	**Celestial Cyclone** Dave Bates (unseconded)
1983-86	**Ich Bleib Im Bett** Dave Bates, A. Lee
1983-86	**Dream World** Jim Cooper, Alan Atkinson
1986	**Walking on Sunshine, Riding on Air** Jim Cooper (solo)
1987 Apr 24	**The Torture Garden** Dave Bates, Tom Walkington
1988 July 27	**Come Here Katherine** Brian Davison, Dave Smith

Resurrection of Karlyn Went Shopping Instead, after it fell down. Original route 1981.

1988 July 30   **Beware of the Dentist**   Brian Davison, John Vlasto, Dave Smith
1988 Sep 4   **Karlyn Returns**   Dave Bates, Russell Baxter
1988 Sep 4, 11**The Fragmented Tormentor**   Dave Bates, Jim Cooper
1988 Sep 11   **Raising the Blade**   Dave Bates, Russell Baxter
1988 Sep 17   **What a Waste of a Day**   Brian Davison, John Vlasto
1989 Feb 1   **Venator**   Dave Bates, Russell Baxter
1990 Oct 8   *Lazy Days in Calella*   Dave Bates
1992 Sep 16   *Little Baby Nothing*   John Gaskins
1992 Aug 14   **Blinded by the Light**   Brian Davison (unseconded)
1998 Aug 8   **Zero Tolerance**   Nadim Siddiqui, Rehan Siddiqui

Warton Pinnacle Crag   O.S. ref.   SD 491 727

Group users please read Access notes

Situation and Character

The Pinnacle Crag is an extensive collection of limestone buttresses on the hillside above Warton, which extend north-west for about one kilometre from a point about 250 metres due south of the beacon at the top of the hill.

The area directly below the crag is lightly wooded, which means that the crag gets less sun than the Upper Crag, especially in the morning, but on the other hand, the trees also provide some shelter when a cold wind blows. The height of the crag never exceeds ten metres, but this is more than compensated for by the rock quality which is generally very solid, with some very interesting features, such as many incut pockets that can be particularly satisfying to discover.

Although the crag is known as Pinnacle Crag, the pinnacle itself is relatively small and is slightly isolated from the best climbing, which lies on the continuous area of rock known as Plum Buttress. There are also some other isolated buttresses that provide worthwhile climbing towards the extremities of the crag.

In May when the bluebells are in flower and the sun is shining, the climbing can be positively idyllic.

History

Most of the routes were first done by Stew Wilson and Rod Smallwood, though Dave Thompson did the very enjoyable *Flake and Wall*, and Robin Witham shook up *The Morning After* (so called because it was!). Bill Lounds and Chris Eilbeck added the surprisingly substantial *Plum Buttress Girdle* and Lounds used two nuts for aid to start the notorious *Plumbline*, though he managed to dispense with both of these shortly after the final manuscript had been submitted for the 1969 guidebook. Much more recently Dave Bates solved a long-standing problem with *The Crank* and opened up the climbing to the left of The Pinnacle, by climbing most of the lines on Black Buttress. Meanwhile, Phil Stone cleaned the pleasant *Bish's Tipple*, as well as claiming several lesser – and less certainly new, routes.

Many new sections of the crag have been developed since 1987. Charlie Vigano claimed the lovely *Free Style* in 1992. Les Ainsworth and Dave Cronshaw followed with their usual avalanche of new routes and new buttresses at either end of the crag, beginning in 1995 with Cronshaw's *The Monkey's Paw. Beacon Lighter, Bird Watcher, Cutting Edge, Quarantine* and *Whymper* were amongst the best of their later offerings. John Gaskins concluded explorations before the guidebook was finalised, with two good technical climbs, *Voodoo People* and *Labyrinth.*

Approach

The normal starting point for both the Pinnacle and the Upper Crags is the parking area in the Small Quarry. If this is full, there are more spaces a short way up Crag Road, just past a footpath (signposted). From either point the crag can be reached in a little over ten minutes. This footpath and the path through the Small Quarry meet near a gap in the wall at the upper end of the quarry. On emerging from the trees a few metres beyond this, turn left on to the open ground of the scarp and continue for about 500 metres to a stile directly above the start of the Main Quarry.

Past this point there is a network of paths and many ways to get to Pinnacle Crag, but the route that is described is one of the shortest and is probably the easiest to follow.

About forty metres past the stile, turn right and continue for a little over 200 metres, ignoring a path which crosses near the start, to a small stile. The small outcrop to the left of this is Stile Buttress, which marks the far right extremity of the crag. Turn left immediately before the stile and follow the line of the outcrop for a good 200 metres to reach Plum Buttress. It is a little easier under foot to avoid the path which skirts the foot of the crag, but do not stray too far from this, or you may miss the crag altogether. The isolated buttress with a double overhang about 120 metres from Stile Buttress is Mounting Buttress and Plum Buttress is the next, more continuous section.

To reach the Upper Crag from Plum Buttress, turn right (facing the crag) and follow the path at the foot of the crag.

Access

The RSPB, which owns this crag wishes to discourage the use of the crag by educational establishments or large organized groups, such as Outdoor Centres, for commercial gain. Therefore, such users are asked to avoid both this and Warton Upper Crag.

The access situation on the four buttresses to the left of the Pinnacle is not known. Climbers have not encountered any problems, but nevertheless, a low profile is advised.

The Climbs

The first climbs to be described lie on Stile Buttress and all the routes are described LEFTWARDS from this point. This buttress is isolated from the main area and lies about 200 metres to the right of Plum Buttress.

Right: Dave Cronshaw in evening light on **Sour Milk Groove** (HVS 5a), Trowbarrow.

Photo: John Ryden

Overleaf: Les Ainsworth on **Rumal** (HVS 5a), Trowbarrow.　　*Photo: Dave Cronshaw*

Stile Buttress

The small buttress immediately left of the stile where the path to the beacon crosses the path from Plum Buttress is known as Stile Buttress.

★ **1.   Free Stile** 6m HS 4b   (1992)
Climb the wall immediately left of the first arête to the break and finish over the bulge on superb pockets.

2.   Beacon Lighter 6m HVS 5a   (1996)
Start two metres to the left at a pointed block and climb a short crack to the overlap. Continue on better holds.

3.   Stile Ted Groove 6m VD   (1996)
The broken groove on the left.

4.   Simian 6m VD   (1996)
From the base of the broken groove, climb up and left to gain flakes at the top of the wall.

5.   Stile-ish Arête 5m S 4a   (1996)
The blunt arête on the left is awkward to start.

6.   Which Way 5m VD   (1996)
The wide crack which forms the right corner of a deep recess.

7.   Ming 5m S 4a   (1996)
The stepped crack in the centre of the recess to a runnel at the top.

8.   Wedgewood 5m VD   (1996)
The deep, easy-angled V-groove at the left side of the recess.

Mounting Buttress

120 metres farther left there is a taller buttress, which is guarded by an overhang on its right. At present, the buttress can be further identified by an old tree stump at its base.

★ **9.   Mounting Block** 6m S 4a   (1968)
At the right-hand side of the buttress there is a large embedded boulder below a sizable overhang. From the top of the boulder tall climbers can reach excellent holds; the moves thereafter are strenuous but surprisingly straightforward. Shorter climbers may have to jump, or use a point of aid!

10.   Supination 6m VS 4c   (1968)
Above the tree stump is a steep, clean hand-jam crack in the back of a shallow groove. Climb the crack with some difficulty.

11.   Fading Light 7m HVS 5b   (1992)
The steep, thin crack one metre to the left is climbed to a rounded finish.

Previous page: Dave Wilcock negotiation an **Access Bill** (E4 6a), Trowbarrow.
Photo: Joanna Wilcock
Left: Looking up the classic **Third World** (HVS 5a), Warton Main Quarry.   *Photo: Jon Sparks*

12. Inspired 6m S 4b   (1986)
Climb the left edge of the lower slab then the obvious curving crack above.

Parson's Buttress
Poor climbs have been done on the undistinguished rock to the left, but the next climbs described are about 10 metres farther left on an easier-angled section, split by a horizontal break at mid-height and limited on its left by an ivy-covered corner.

13. The Verger 8m VD   (1996)
Gain the base of a shallow flaky groove in the centre of the buttress, then finish up the wall above.

14. The Parson's Nose 8m VD   (1986)
Start just right of the nose itself, at an obvious flake which allows a strenuous pull on to easier-angled rock. Finish up the flake crack above.

★ **15. Bish's Tipple** 8m S 4a   (1986)
To the left is a mass of ivy and a deep corner. Climb the right wall of the corner and the left edge of the narrow upper wall.

Plum Buttress
This is the fine buttress that is guarded near its base by a large overhang.

★ **16. The Vine Line** 9m HS 5b   (1968)
The fine undercut slab at the right-hand side of the buttress is gained by a desperate mantel on to the obvious polished little shelf at head-height. Or, more often and at a more reasonable grade, the first move can be avoided by using the rib on the right. The holds above are almost too good to be true!

17. Dihedral 8m VS 5a   (1968)
The undercut groove, just before the overhang becomes much more pronounced. Hard to start, but an easier finish.

18. Yosemite Rib 9m VS 5a   (1968)
Pull into the corner groove of Dihedral and step left onto the rib. Follow it direct. **Direct Start** (6c).

★★ **19. The Plumbline** 9m E3 6a   (1968/1969)
Getting off the ground is definitely the crux, but the groove above is not without interest. Two metres to the left and directly behind a tree near the foot of the crag there is a shallow groove. Climb this to gain the horizontal break (runners on left), then continue by thin, sustained bridging.

★ **20. The Big Plum** 9m HVS 5c   (1968)(1968)
Two metres to the left there is another weakness in the overhang with a steep corner above. Difficulties at the start are proportionate to the climber's height and many people bring the route down to VS by cairn-building, or combined tactics just to leave the ground.
Peach Finish (5a): a much better finish starts at the horizontal break. Use a pocket just above the left side of the overhang, then climb the wall above using widely-spaced pockets.

** **21. Voodoo People** 9m E3 6b   (1996)
A highly gymnastic problem. Climb the roof and wall left of the Big Plum
starting from the obvious slot at the back of the roof, then struggle round the lip
to stand up and gain holds to the right of Lone Tree Variation. Then finish up
that route.

* **22. Lone Tree Variation** 9m S 4b   (1974-75)
From the foot of Lone Tree Groove make a hard starting move up and right,
then venture out right on to the wall, to find some surprising holds leading
upwards. At the tree, climb the pleasant wall directly behind its left side.

* **23. Lone Tree Groove** 9m S 4a   (1968)
At the left-hand end of the overhang is an attractive open groove with a tree
near its top. Enter the groove by a difficult move, then continue steeply on
adequate holds to the tree and an easier finish behind it. Harder for the short.

* **24. Plum Buttress Girdle** 21m HVS 4b,5a   (1969)
1. 9m. Start as for Lone Tree Variation, but continue rightwards to belay on
the tree of The Big Plum.
2. 12m. Follow the rounded horizontal break rightwards, getting a runner in
while you still can. As the break runs out completely, make a long reach up and
right to a good hold on Yosemite Rib (crux). Finish up that route.

Deadwood Area

*To the left of the overhang of Plum Buttress, the rock becomes set back slightly
and provides a series of interesting climbs up to an obvious* **DESCENT** *route.*

25. Deadwood Crack 9m VS 5a   (1968)
The obvious line three metres to the left, past a dead tree (little of which now
remains). Hard at the start, especially if the crack is climbed direct instead of
resorting to bridging on Flake and Wall.

* **26. Flake and Wall** 9m S 4a   (1968)
A satisfying little route. Climb the recess on the left, either via the flake crack
or by bridging, to reach the jammed block, then surmount this and finish direct.

27. Wart 8m VD   (1969)
Climb the centre of the narrow wall on the left to reach a faint scoop, then
finish up the groove above.

28. Thrutch 8m VD   (1967)
Previously incorrectly known as Clare's Crack. Just left again. The enjoyable
flake crack.

29. The Morning After 6m VS 4c   (1968)
Climb the overlap in the centre of the wall via an obvious undercut to reach a
large ledge, then finish to the right.

30. Fine White Line 6m VS 4c   (1975-79)
The thin flake crack at the left side of the overlap.

31.   Herbert's Horror   6m   HS   4a   (Pre-1969)
The wide crack which forms the angle with the next wall, proves surprisingly
strenuous.

32.   The Mushroom   9m   D   (1968)
The route is obvious from its name from directly below. Climb the buttress right
of the descent gully to the perched block. A good alternative **DESCENT**, as it
is nowhere-near as polished as the gully.

Left Walls
*The next section to be described starts from the front face of the buttress that
lies about eight metres left of the **DESCENT** gully.*

33.   The Gremp   7m   S   4a   (1969)
Climb the right side of the slab which can be varied by using the arête.

34.   Skutch   7m   VD   (1968)
Climb the broken flakeline in the centre of the slab to finish by the obvious
flakes.

35.   The Grump   7m   S   4a   (1980)
Climb the wall between Skutch and Dollard.

36.   Dollard   7m   D   (1968)
The wide crack on the left can be a struggle.

*18 metres farther left there is an isolated buttress which gives the following two
routes.*

37.   Orbit   6m   VS   4c   (1996)
The face right of Triplanetary. From a block gain a short crack (thread) then
climb the wall above.

38.   Triplanetary   6m   HS   4b   (1975-79)
Take a direct line up the twin cracks at the left side of the buttress.

The Pinnacle
*There now follows a long expanse of broken and often overgrown rocks, though
some good problems can be found. After about fifty metres The Pinnacle can be
found. The next route starts at the right-hand corner on the front face of the
Pinnacle, just at the point where the ground drops away.*

39.   Weakling's Wall   9m   HS   4b   (1974-75)
Swing in from the extreme right to gain a good hold on the overhanging wall.
Move up strenuously to a ledge and finish more easily.

★ **40.   The Crank**   9m   6b   (1982)
A good steep problem up the wall right of The Graunch. Start from a block on
the ground and climb the bulging wall above.

★ 41. The Graunch 9m VS 4c   (1968)
This is the clean, deep crack, with a surprisingly awkward start. The upper part
can be climbed quite elegantly, or as befits the rather odd but fairly clear name,
it's up to you!

42. Muscles Crack 6m HS 4b   (1968)
The sharp, bulging crack three metres left. The top block is an optional extra!

★ 43. The Monkey's Paw 6m HVS 5b   (1995)
The undercut arête immediately to the left is climbed directly from the cave.

44. Bumble Bee 6m S 4a   (1974-75)
A decidedly strange route from the cave at the left side of the pinnacle. Climb
the wide left-slanting crack and make an awkward bridging move out on to the
face. Finish more normally.

Aviary Walls
*The rest of the climbs lie on isolated buttresses, but despite the walk they are
very worthwhile and worth the effort. About twenty-five metres past the Pinnacle
a path cuts through the edge, and a short distance farther on there is a wire
fence. The Aviary Walls are located about 50 metres past this fence and can be
identified by a large tree that grows at the foot of the rock on the right-hand
side.*

45. Scoop Surprise 7m VD   (1996)
Climb the wall midway between the stepped crack and the tree. At the tree on
top, step left to finish

46. Head Whip 7m VD   (1996)
The fine stepped crack two metres to the left of the tree.

★ 47. Bird Watcher 7m VS 5a   (1996)
Gain the shallow scoop one metre farther left, then step left and surmount the
small overhang.

48. The Ribulator 6m HS 4c   (1996)
The wall is bounded on its left by a flat-topped pedestal. Climb the centre of
this, starting either directly, or by a swing in from the unattractive crack.

★ 49. Cutting Edge 8m VS 4c   (1996)
Start at the unattractive crack which bounds the flat-topped pedestal on its left.
Climb the flake which leads leftwards from the crack, then step right and go up
to some overlaps. Cross diagonally left through these to an excellent finishing
jug.

50. Antler Wall 6m VD   (1996)
Climb the centre of the next wall to a small tree at the top of the crag.

51. Sheilgh's Wall 7m S 4a   (1996)
A couple of metres farther left, just past a vegetated crack, climb the wall to
finish to the right of a tree.

Black Buttress
30 metres farther left is a steep black buttress.

★ **52.   Black Russian** 6m E2 6a   (1982)
Start at the right-hand end of the wall, about two metres right of Black Sheep and take a wandering line up the wall.

53.   Black Sheep 6m HVS 5b   (1982)
The central crack. Often damp.

★ **54.   Black Magic** 6m E3 6a   (1982)
Start one metre to the left and climb the wall directly on pockets.

55.   Black Jack 6m E2 5c   (1982)
Start one metre farther left, just to the right of some obvious, rounded horizontal breaks and climb up, using a handhold at the extreme right edge of the lowest break.

56.   Black Edge 6m HS 4b   (1982)
Start at a short crack five metres to the left of Black Sheep. Climb up for a couple of metres until it is possible to traverse right and finish as for Black Jack.

★★ **57.   Labyrinth** 10m E3 6a   (1997)
A left-to-right traverse, based on the vague, but obvious, break/crease that crosses the buttress. Start on a shelf at the left side of the wall below a scratched arrow, then move rightwards to gain the continuation break/crease and follow this past the central crack to finish right of Black Russian.

Isolated Wall
About 40 metres farther on is a stone wall and a further 20 metres past this lies a small buttress above open fields.

★ **58.   Quarantine** 6m HVS 5a   (1996)
Awkwardly enter the hanging groove at the right-hand side of the buttress then finish direct.

59.   Seclusion 6m HVS 5a   (1996)
Two metres to the left climb the obvious overhanging crack to an exit on a ledge and an easier finish. The holds in the crack are often wet.

60.   Hermitage 7m VD   (1996)
Climb the left side of the buttress via large flakes.

Matterhorn Wall
From Isolated Wall there are several very short buttresses up to the wall at the end of the field about a hundred metres farther on. About forty metres past this wall, the final routes are located on a buttress directly behind a very large pointed boulder. Past this the outcrop decreases in height and soon peters out after some good bouldering.

61.   Hörnli 6m VD   (1996)
The blunt rib directly behind the boulder.

62. Carrel 6m VD   (1996)
The flaky break up the centre of the buttress.

★ **63. Whymper** 6m VS 5a   (1996)
Start two metres to the left, directly below a small block. Climb the wall via a
pocket and a sharp hold.

First Ascents at Warton Pinnacle Crag

1967	**Thrutch** Stew Wilson (solo)
1968	**Mounting Block, Supination, The Vine Line, Dihedral, Yosemite Rib** Stew Wilson, Rod Smallwood
1968	**Plumbline** (2pts aid) Bill Lounds, Chris Eilbeck *Aid eliminated by Bill Lounds, 1969.*
1968	**The Big Plum, Peach Finish** Stew Wilson, Vernon Unsworth
1968	**Lone Tree Groove** Dave Thomson
1968	**Deadwood Crack, The Mushroom, The Gremp, Skutch, Dollard, The Dome, Muscles Crack, The Gremp** Stew Wilson (solo)
1968	**Flake and Wall** Dave Thompson
1968	**The Morning After** Robin Whitham
1968	**The Graunch** Bill Lounds
Pre-1969	**Herbert's Horror**
1969	**Plum Buttress Girdle** Bill Lounds, Chris Eilbeck
1969	**Wart** 1969
1974-75	**Lone Tree Variation**
1974-75	**Weakling's Wall** Al Evans (solo)
1974-75	**Bumble Bee**
1975-79	**Fine White Line**
1975-79	**Triplanetary**
1980	**The Grump** P.B. Checkland
1982	**The Crank, Black Russian, Black Sheep, Black Magic, Black Jack, Black Edge** Dave Bates
1986	**Inspired, The Parson's Nose, Bish's Tipple** Phil Stone
1992 Mar	**Free Stile** Charlie Vigano
1992 Sep 14	**Fading Light** Brian Davison, Penny Clay
1995	**The Monkey's Paw** *Recorded by Dave Cronshaw, but done before.*
1996 Jan	**Beacon Lighter, Bird Watcher, Cutting Edge** Dave Cronshaw, Les Ainsworth
1996 Feb 11	**The Verger** Les Ainsworth, Dave Cronshaw (both solo)
1996 Feb 11	**Scoop Surprise, Head Whip, The Ribulator, Antler Wall** Les Ainsworth, Dave Cronshaw
1996 Feb 18	**Stile Ted Groove, Ming, Wedgewood** Dave Cronshaw, (solo)
1996 Feb 18	**Simian** Dave Cronshaw, Les Ainsworth
1996 Mar 3	**Stile-ish Arête** Les Ainsworth (solo)
1996 Mar 3	**Which Way** Dave Cronshaw, Les Ainsworth (solo)
1996 Mar 3	**Orbit, Hermitage, Hörnli, Carrel** Les Ainsworth, Dave Cronshaw
1996 Mar 3	**Quarantine, Whymper** Dave Cronshaw, Les Ainsworth
1996 Mar 3	**Seclusion** Dave Cronshaw
1996 Apr	**Sheilgh's Wall** Sheilgh Vigano, John Mason
1996 Nov 30	**Voodoo People** John Gaskins (solo)
1997 Aug 14	**Labyrinth** John Gaskins

Warton Small Quarry
O.S. ref.   SD 498 724

Situation and Character
The quarry lies virtually in the centre of Warton Village. It is hard to imagine a more convenient crag: you can step from the car straight on to the rock, and the pub is only metres away. The rock and the routes are quite variable. Some routes are extremely polished, but others have become overgrown which seems to indicate a consensus of opinion about their quality. An attraction of the quarry is the fine low-level traverse; an excellent way to round off a day's climbing on this or the other nearby crags.

The crag is very popular with organized groups and so it is not unusual to find all the easier routes occupied. It also manages to be both sheltered and sunny, but when it does get wet, some parts are slow to dry.

History
The quarry has undoubtedly been climbed on for many years and its easier lines were probably ascended by local youngsters before the 'proper' climbers discovered the crag. The first recorded routes were by Bill Lounds, Chris Eilbeck, Stew Wilson, Pete Lucas and Stuart Butler. The best of these early routes were *Delectable Traverse* and *The Leaning Tower* by Wilson and Lounds' *Quasimodo* and *Low Level Girdle*.

Al Evans made several routes over the years, the best of which were *Movie Maker, Triceps Wall* and *Igor*. Another regular visitor was Charlie Vigano and though much of his climbing was unrecorded, he was certainly responsible for *Vigano's Variation* in 1970 and together with Les Ainsworth and John Mason, was still adding routes in 1997, including the imaginatively named *Charlie's, Les's* and *John's Routes*.

Access and Approach
The quarry is owned by the local village council, which is willing to permit climbing, providing that all litter is removed.

Warton Small Quarry lies a few metres up Crag Road, immediately north of the George Washington pub (alias the Black Bull). There is parking in part of the quarry itself but if spaces are full there is more room farther up the lane, where a footpath leads through the trees to the top of the quarry.

The Climbs
The climbs are described from RIGHT to LEFT. At the extreme right, where it abuts a stone wall, the quarry is very low, and this area is often used as a **DESCENT**. Alternatively abseil or walk round from the top end. The low cave has some good problem exits. A little to the left is a large overhang about three metres up.
Some of the first few routes should be avoided when cars (particularly your own!) are parked beneath!

1.   Sporting Eagle 6m   4b   (1975-79)
Climb up to the right-hand side of the overhang and move leftwards above it.

2.   Black Bull 6m   5c   (1975-79)
Climb the overhang, just left of centre at a thin crack.

3. The Overhang 6m 4b (Pre-1969)
Start at the left-hand side of the overhang and climb the rib until it is possible to move out left to polished jugs on its left side. Pull up to higher jugs to finish on the right.

4. Gelignite 7m 5a (1975-79)
Start one metre to the left and pull over the overhang using undercuts to make a long reach and gain dirty holds. Move right and exit as for The Overhang.

5. Blaster's Groove 6m VD (1968)
The shallow groove with drill marks, below a cluster of trees: very popular and polished.

6. Blaster's Wall 6m 4a (1968)
The wall to the left gives subtle climbing.

7. Bonnie's Wall 6m 4c (1975-79)
The wall and small roof on the left is taken on its right side.

8. Fool's Gold 6m 5a (1974-75)
The wall with a small overhang on the left.

9. Genius Silver 8m VD (1975-79)
To the left is a small cave at four metres. Gain this, then exit on the right.

10. Panhandle 9m S 4a (1968)
The wall on the left, containing a rusted spike.

11. Manhandle 9m VD (1974-75)
Start four metres to the left, below a stump at two metres. Climb the wall either left or right of the stump.

★ **12. Gunboot Rib** 9m S 4a (1977)
Three metres to the left is a blunt rib with a small niche at half-height. Climb this direct.

13. Gunboot Groove 9m S 4a (1977)
A metre to the left climb the steep corner.

★ **14. Delectable Traverse** 14m S 4a (1967)
Start just past the rib bounding the overhanging wall. Climb the rib, or the wall on the left, to an easing of the angle just below the capping overhang. Traverse left to Movie Maker and finish up the rib. It is also possible to finish direct past the capping overhang at the start of the traverse, but this misses the best climbing.

15. Townie 9m VS 4c (1975-79)
Climb the V-shaped groove in the angle, left of the start of Delectable Traverse, or climb its left rib. Surmount the overhang and finish directly past a hole in the capping overhang.

★ **16. Movie Maker** 9m HS 4b (1975-79)
The rib and roof directly below the finish of Delectable Traverse.

17. Country Boy 9m HS 4a (1968)
Start just left, directly below the left side of the large overhang. Climb up to this overhang go through it, then continue directly to the top.

18. Connie's Groove 8m HS 4a (1975-79)
The overhanging groove on the left.

19. Cracked Corner 6m VD (1967)
There is now an obvious recess, reached by a three-metre scramble. This route follows the corner above the right side of the recess.

★ **20. Groove and Slab** 8m VD (1967)
From the left side of the recess move awkwardly up a steep groove. Step out left on to a slab then back right to finish up the steep wall.

21. Burlesque 9m HVS 5b (1974-75)
Climb the overhanging nose direct up its centre.

22. Ivy Way Variant 9m VS 4b (1975)
Climb Burlesque to the first overhang, then move left and go up over blocks to reach the normal route. Cross this and finish up the overlap above.

23. Ivy Way 9m D (1967)
Start below the highest part of the quarry wall and move up with some difficulty to gain the rightward-leading diagonal break; follow this to the top.

★★ **24. The Leaning Tower** 10m VS 4c (1968)
Start up Ivy Way then move left into a shallow groove. Move up slightly, then go left again on to the face, where good holds lead to the top. One of the best routes in the quarry.

★★ **25. Quasimodo** 10m E2 5c (1968)
Usually top-roped; because protection is virtually impossible to arrange before the crux, and the landing is unfriendly. Start two metres left of Ivy Way below an overhang. Climb the blunt rib to the left side of the overhang, then pull rightwards on to the front face. Make a tricky move up then continue more easily, joining Leaning Tower to finish.

26. Igor 8m E1 5b (1975-79)
Climb the groove just to the left and the bulge above on blocky holds, and finish up the left side of the tower.

27. Original Route 10m VD (1967)
Two metres to the left is a steep groove containing a movable block. Climb the groove quite strenuously and move up rightwards towards a tree. Finish via a short crack and go leftwards up the final wall.

★ **28. Vigano's Variant** 9m VS 4c (1970)
Start two metres left of Original Route and climb over a roof, then follow a groove to a large, square-cut overhang. Take this by a crack on its left and finish straight up.

● **29. Wailing Wall** 9m HVS 5a (1968)
Climb the steep, loose wall to the right of Autumn Leaves.

● **30. Autumn Leaves** 9m VS 4a   (1968)
Climb the projecting rib to a scoop beneath an overhang. Using a good undercut, make a delicate move up to reach better holds on the left (loose) then finish trending leftwards.

31. The Red Groove 9m HVS 5b   (1975-79)
The groove on the left proves harder than it looks.

★ **32. Great Flake** 11m VS 4c   (1968)
Just to the left is a series of long slanting overhangs rising leftwards, with an obvious horizontal crack below. Climb to the right-hand end of the overhangs and move up and left using undercuts, until an awkward move leads into a groove, which provides an easier finish.

★ **33. Great Flake Direct** 9m HVS 5b   (1979-83)
Climb the overhang above the centre of the traverse.

★ **34. Bogie's Groove** 8m VS 4c   (1968)
Just left of the finish of Great Flake is a shallow groove. Climb this, using the rib on the right, to join Great Flake to finish.

★ **35. Biceps Wall** 9m VS 4c   (1968)
Climb the steep, smooth-looking wall on the left, via a shallow, left-facing corner at six metres. Then make a tricky mantelshelf to reach easier ground.

36. Triceps Wall 9m VS 4c   (1974-75)
Climb the wall on the left which is initially steep.

★ **37. Pete's Route** 10m VD   (1968)
Start to the left of this wall beneath an obvious projecting block at four metres. Climb past this, step up and right then continue up the wall to the top, on good holds. From the block a **Direct Finish** is possible at HS.

38. Ed's Route 10m HS 4b   (1975-79)
From the projecting block on Pete's Route, follow a shallow groove diagonally left, then step back right and finish direct.

39. Les's Route 9m HVS 5b   (1991)
Start three metres left, beneath an overhang at three metres. Climb a short blunt rib, then move slightly left through the overhang and go back right to a ledge. Finish easily.

The next climbs are about 12 metres farther left, just past a large boulder on the path.

40. Rampline 10m VD   (1997)
Just past the boulder the rock is split by a small overlap. Climb to the rightmost of two niches, then continue through the overlap and follow the right-leading ramp.

41. Charlie's Route 9m VS 4b   (1997)
Start three metres farther left and climb to the right side of a higher roof. Then use flake cracks on the right to enable a finish to be made up the short headwall.

42. John's Route 9m VS 4c   (1997)
Climb to the overhang via a deep groove and flake crack in its centre, then
move left round the roof to good finishing holds.

43. Ron's Route 8m HS 4a   (1973)
Climb the next groove easily to the roof, reach over then pull through on good
holds.

44. Gibbon 8m S 4a   (1997)
Climb the groove on the left, finishing at the obvious flake.

45. Finale Wall 6m S 4a   (1974-75)
The short, clean wall about three metres farther left gives a pleasant climb.

★ **46. Low-level Girdle** 26m 5b   (1968)
A classic of the genre, with well-defined breaks indicating the line for most of
the way. The feet should never be more than $1^1/_2$ metres from the ground. The
steep wall left of Gunboot Groove is the crux (a hold has recently disappeared,
making it harder and the projecting block is becoming a little rickety). Rounding
the rib at the start of Autumn Leaves is also very tricky on first acquaintance,
but virtually all of the leftward half of the traverse is good. The whole affair is
now becoming more entertaining as it becomes ever more highly polished. If the
car-park section is too easy try it one handed – seriously!

First Ascents at Warton Small Quarry

1967	**Cracked Corner, Groove and Slab** Stew Wilson
1967	**Delectable Traverse, Original Route** Stew Wilson, Tom Farrell
1967	**Ivy Way, Blaster's Groove, Blaster's Wall** Stew Wilson
1968	**Panhandle** M Birkhill
1968	**Country Boy** Stew Wilson, Rick Stallwood
1968	**The Leaning Tower** Stew Wilson, S Bradford
1968	**Quasimodo, Wailing Wall** Bill Lounds, Stew Wilson
1968	**Autumn Leaves** Stew Wilson, Bill Lounds
1968	**Great Flake** Dave Thomson
	Direct Finish, 1979-83.
1968	**Bogie's Groove, Biceps Wall** Stew Wilson
1968	**Pete's Route** Pete Lucas
1968	**Low-level Girdle** Bill Lounds
Pre-1969	**The Overhang**
1969	**Townie** Chris Eilbeck
1970	**Vigano's Variation** Charlie Vigano, Sheilgh Vigano
1973	**Ron's Route** Ron Fawcett, Al Evans, Dave Parker (all solo)
1974-75	**Fool's Gold, Finale Wall**
1974-75	**Manhandle, Burlesque, Triceps Wall** Al Evans (solo)
1974-75	**Finale Wall**
1975	**Ivy Way Variant**
1977	**Gunboot Rib, Gunboot Groove**
1975-79	**Sporting Eagle, Black Bull, Gelignite, Bonnie's Wall, Connie's Groove,** **The Red Groove, Ed's Route,** *Deg's Route, Mark's Route*
1975-79	**Genius Silver,** *Out of Townie,* **Movie Maker, Igor** Al Evans (solo)
1979-83	**Great Flake: Direct Finish**
1991	**Les's Route** Les Ainsworth, Dave Cronshaw
1997 Sep	**Rampline, Gibbon** Les Ainsworth, Charlie Vigano, John Mason
1997 Sep	**Charlie's Route** Charlie Vigano, Les Ainsworth, John Mason
1997 Sep	**John's Route** John Mason, Les Ainsworth, Charlie Vigano

Warton Upper Crag

Group users please read Access notes

Situation and Character

The Upper Crag lies in a commanding position at the top of Warton Hill and can be clearly seen from the M6. Although the crag is relatively short, its position at the top of a scree slope often gives a sense of exposure on the climbs that is out of proportion to their height. The rock is good quality limestone, with some excellent flakes and pockets and it has the further advantage that it dries out rapidly. It is a great place for the middle grade climber who just wishes to climb and enjoy the views.

However, whilst the crag catches the sun for much of the day, it comes into the shade later on and so it can be cold in the evening. Fortunately, it is only five minutes walk to Pinnacle Crag and the combination of starting at Warton Upper and then moving to Warton Pinnacle can make an excellent day.

History

The crag probably saw an initial wave of exploration by the occupants of the nearby iron-age hill fort, but unfortunately – not yet having invented writing – no records were kept. The recorded history of the crag begins with Robin Witham, Stew Wilson and friends, who worked over the crag for the first Lancashire guidebook of 1969. *Yellow Wall* and the two *Lictor* routes were probably the best of these, but the formations on *Finger of Fun* also made that a memorable ascent. It was interesting to note that after the guidebook, visitors apparently decided that Wilson's *Abomination* was before its time and started to climb a different line. This situation become so endemic that the original route was virtually ignored for several years and eventually had to be renamed *Original Abomination* in an attempt to clarify the situation.

Many of the remaining routes have not been claimed, including *Space Walk*, which contains arguably the best move on the crag. Brian Davison added *Space Flight* in 1992. However a few gaps remained and in 1996, *Black's Route* by Phil Black, Gary Smith and John Woodward, which was done during guidework, proves that some plums still await picking.

Approach

The crag can be reached in just over ten minutes. Park at either the Small Quarry or the parking area on Crag Road and follow the same approach as for the Pinnacle Crag to the gap in the wall above the Small Quarry. On emerging from the trees, turn left in the direction of Pinnacle Crag and continue for nearly 250 metres to an obvious rock step where there is a substantial amount of exposed limestone pavement (well before the stile above the Main Quarry). Immediately above this, turn right from the route to Pinnacle Crag and follow a path into trees. After about 200 metres the path levels out at a bracken-covered area and the Upper Crag can be seen slightly to the left. Follow the path straight across and into some more trees, then at a T-junction turn left, virtually parallel with the crag for about 50 metres to a white tongue of scree. Go up this, then follow a grassy path diagonally right to the foot of the crag, about three metres to the right of the descent gully. **Please do not stray on to the scree itself, as** this provides a very fragile habitat for some rare species including snails and a delicate fern known as the limestone polypody.

To reach Pinnacle Crag from the Upper Crag, follow a good path from the left end of the top of the crag to the beacon and trig. point on top of the hill. 30 metres on is a small outcrop where the view opens out and three paths fan out. To reach Stile Buttress follow the left-hand path for about 100 metres. To reach the top of Plum Buttress, follow the central path, avoiding a very faint path which branches left and passing well to the right of a pointed boulder. The **DESCENT** route lies about five metres to the right of the point at which the crag top is reached.

Access

Lancaster City Council owns this crag, and its councillors wish to discourage the use of the crag by educational establishments or large organized groups, such as Outdoor Centres, for commercial gain. Therefore, such users are asked to avoid both this and Warton Pinnacle Crag.

The Climbs

The first climb to be described is located just left of a stubby pedestal about 20 metres to the left of the descent gully. All the climbs are described RIGHTWARDS from this point.

Rock Island

This is the first area of rock on which climbs have been described, though short problems are possible farther left. The main feature of the area is a stubby pedestal about 20 metres to the left of the descent gully.

1.   Cracked Overhang   6m   VD   (1967)
The arête immediately to the left of the stubby pedestal. Start on the right and make an interesting pull round, then finish past some interesting threads. An easier start can be made on the left.

2.   Dogfish   6m   S   4a   (1975-79)
The pleasant steep wall just right of the stubby pedestal is climbed on good holds.

3.   Calcarb Arête   8m   VS   4c   (1975-79)
Follow the obvious arête at the right side of the wall, as directly as possible.

4.   Red Mist   8m   VD   (1986-87)
Climb the short corner then swing left below a bush and finish up the wide crack or the rib on its left.

★ **5.   Triple Wall**   6m   VS   4c   (1991)
The short wall on the right.

★ **6.   Twin Cracks**   6m   VS   4c   (1967)
Start below the rib on the right of the corner. Move up and left around the bulge to reach the cracks with difficulty. Finish up the all-too-brief arête. A direct pull over the bulge is harder.

7. Bop Route 6m S 4b (1967)
Start just round the rib, beneath a spreading yew. Climb the broken wall to enter a deep groove, then move left across the clean white wall to finish up the rib.

Grooves Area
To the right the rock becomes lower and more broken for about eight metres, then there is a short section of continuous rock containing two deep grooves, which ends at the descent gully.

★ **8. Black's Route** 8m VS 4c (1996)
Climb directly over the bulge to the left of the first groove on hidden, but excellent holds. Finish to the left of the bush.

9. The Gash 8m VD (1967)
Climb the first, deep V-shaped groove.

10. Grooves Eliminate 8m VS 4c (1967)
Start one metre to the right and climb the steep front face of the buttress, with an awkward bulge guarding the flaky upper groove.

11. Freebird 8m HVS 5c (1975-79)
The left wall of the next groove contains a micro-groove; start slightly to its left and gain the groove using small pockets, and continue with difficulty to the jugs on Sedgewick Wall, the temptation to cheat being ever-present.

12. Sedgewick Wall 8m VD (1968)
Climb the second deep groove, moving left when suitable holds appear. It is also possible to climb the groove directly at the same standard, or to exit rightwards through the bulges, with only a slight increase in difficulty.

★★ **13. Yellow Wall** 8m VD (1967)
An exposed route for its grade, but the rock is Warton at its very best. Start just over a metre to the right and climb the right wall until it is possible to move out rightwards between the overhangs, on to the nose. Finish straight up.

★ **14. Yellow Edge** 8m VS 4c (1967)
Start below the large nose on the right wall of the groove. Climb rightwards to a good, but not obvious, hold at the base of a small scoop. Move up and go slightly right to finish. It is also possible to start more direct by climbing over the small overhang farther right (5a).

15. The Plumb 8m S 4c (1967)
Between the nose and the descent gully is a short hanging crack. Climb this to the left-hand end of an obvious ledge, then finish more easily, direct.

Frontal Area
This is the area to the right of the descent gully, which directly overlooks the scree and which contains some very pleasant climbs.

16. Inverted Stairway 8m HS 4b (1975-79)
A series of overhangs immediately to the right of the gully; good finishing holds.

17.   Finger of Fun 8m   VD   (1967)
The obvious flakes on the left wall of a deep V-shaped groove. Awkward to
start and to finish.

★ **18.   Judith** 8m   VS   4b   (1979-83)
Go straight up the groove and out over the surprising roof.

19.   Benghazi Groove 8m   S   4a   (1967)
Start up the groove, but avoid the roof by a tricky move out right.

20.   Sabre Tooth 8m   S   4a   (1975-79)
Climb the shallow groove/crack which bounds the right wall of the groove.

21.   Ivy Way 8m   VD   (1975-79)
An obvious line on the left wall of the next groove.

22.   Ivy League 8m   S   4a   (1975-79)
Climb the back of the groove and exit rightwards.

★★ **23.   Space Walk** 8m   HVS   5b   (1975-79)
The name is not quite as ludicrous as it first seems! The very prominent jutting
arête is climbed on its left side; there is really only one hard move, but it's an
exquisite one.

24.   Space Flight 7m   HVS   5b   (1992)
The arête of Space Walk on its right side.

25.   Brainwasher 8m   VS   4c   (1967)
The wall round to the right, via a thin crack just left of the main one.

★ **26.   Brainchild** 8m   S   4a   (1969)
An awkward bulge guards the enjoyable crack.

★ **27.   Braincell** HS   4b   (1984)
Climb directly over the bulge on to a vague rib and finish over the fine, juggy
overhang.

28.   Seventh Heaven 8m   S   4a   (1967)
Climb the next deep groove, with an awkward move right to a steep crack at
the overhang: easier for the short.

29.   Soft Man's Saunter 6m   D   (1975-79)
The obvious blocky corner.

30.   Whippet Wall 6m   VS   5a   (1967)
The clean, square wall just to the right, has a couple of good moves on small
pockets which lead to a flake crack.

Above: Paul Smitton punk rocks on **Waxen Doll** (E3 6a), Witches' Quarry. *Photo: Rob Smitton*
Below: Dave Cronshaw on **Great Flake** (VS 4c), Warton Small Quarry. *Photo: Les Ainsworth*

★ **31. Lictor Left-hand** 8m VS 5a   (1967)
Just beyond the rib is an undercut wall split by two cracks. This route takes the
left-hand crack.

32. Lictor Right-hand 8m S 4c   (1967)
Climb the right-hand crack.

★ **33. Fasces** 6m VS 4c   (1967)
The wall right of the cracks has more holds than are immediately apparent.

34. V Groove 6m VD   (1996)
Climb the obvious twin cracks in a groove.

35. Deception 7m S 4c   (1967)
(Incorrectly named Description in recent guidebooks.) The next wall, set back
slightly, is steep and tricky until the thin vertical crack in its centre is gained.

Abomination Area
*Beyond Lictor the crag turns back into the hillside and its open aspect soon
changes as the trees grow close to the rock.*

36. Easy Corner 6m D   (Pre-1969)
The easy corner on the right.

37. Abominable Arête 6m VS 4c   (1975)
Two metres left of the obvious beak. Climb the blunt rib.

38. The Abomination 6m HS 4b   (1970)
Mount the beak from its left, then move slightly left and climb the layback crack.

39. The Original Abomination 8m E2 6a   (1967)
The name originally belonged to this route, but years of use have transferred it
to the easier line on the left. Mount the beak awkwardly, then climb the bulging
rib directly above to better holds.

40. The Layback 7m HS 4a   (1967)
The obvious flaky-looking crack up the centre of the wall on the right.

41. Wart Horn 8m HS 4b   (1985)
Climb the right-leading crack to the obvious rock horn.

42. Ledgeway Left 6m VD   (1985)
Start just to the right and climb direct to the top via the left side of an obvious
ledge.

43. Ledgeway 6m HS 4b   (1985)
The wall on the right is climbed, passing just to the right of the obvious ledge.

44. Flakes 6m VD   (1967)
The short right-leading flake cracks.

45. End Flake 6m VD   (1985)
The deeper flake crack on the right. At the top step right to avoid brambles.

Ed Cleasby on the first ascent of **Android** (E4 5c), Chapel Head Scar.   *Photo: Al Phizacklea*

46.   Simian Way   7m   S   4a   (1980)
15 metres farther right is a short wall with an overhang. Surmount this and the
flake wall above.

*There is also another short, but interesting, buttress nearby. This lies below the
Upper Crag about 40 metres farther right and is best located from the
right-hand side of the clearing below the crag. It lies about 25 metres above
this, immediately right of some scree and can be identified by a deep, left-facing
groove.*

First Ascents at Warton Upper Crag

1967	**Cracked Overhang, Twin Cracks, Bop Route, The Gash, Grooves Eliminate, Yellow Wall, Yellow Edge, The Plumb, Benghazi Groove, Deception, The Layback, Flakes** Stew Wilson (solo)
1967	**Brainwasher, Brainchild** Stew Wilson, Rick Stallwood
1967	**Seventh Heaven** Stew Wilson (solo)
1967	**Finger of Fun** Stew Wilson, Rick Stallwood, Tony Rice
1968	**Sedgewick Wall** Robin Whitham (solo)
1967	**Whippet Wall, Lictor Right-hand, Fasces** Stew Wilson, Rick Stallwood
1967	**Lictor Left-hand** Rick Stallwood, Stew Wilson
1967	**The Original Abomination** Stew Wilson, Tony Rice, Rick Stallwood
Pre-1969	**Easy Corner**
1970	**The Abomination** 1970
	Done by several parties who mistakenly thought that this was The Original Abomination.
1975	**Abominable Arête**
1975-79	**Dogfish, Calcarb Arête, Freebird, Inverted Stairway, Ivy Way, Ivy League, Space Walk, Soft Man's Saunter, Sabre Tooth**
1980	**Simian Way** P.B. Checkland
1979-83	**Judith**
1984	**Braincell** J. Bloe, D. Rush, 1984 as Tertium Organum
	Later made into a more independent line.
1985	**Wart Horn, Ledgeway Left, Ledgeway, End Flake**
1986-87	**Red Mist**
1991	**Triple Wall** Les Ainsworth (solo)
1992	**Space Flight** Brian Davison (solo)
1996 May	**V-Groove** Gary Smith, Phil Black, John Woodward
1996 May	**Black's Route** Phil Black, Gary Smith, John Woodward

Woodwell   O.S. ref.   SD 465 743

Situation and Character
Woodwell is a local beauty spot in Silverdale village. However, for the climber,
the wooded setting means that the crag does not have quite the same charm as
many of the others in this area.

Many of the routes at the right-hand end of the crag are unpleasantly polished,
and if conditions are at all damp, the whole crag can be abominable. The
relatively neglected areas north of the Well certainly deserve more attention.

History
Woodwell has been used for years by devotees to the Silverdale Area, such as
Stew Wilson, Bill Lounds and Charlie Vigano, who regularly climbed there, but
kept no records. Perhaps the first systematic attempt to record the routes was by
Tom Walkington, and in the absence of better information, it is best to suppose

that Walkington was responsible for most of the lines as they are now recorded, with the exception of a few late Ainsworth/Cronshaw additions in 1995. Walkington was certainly responsible for the technical problems around Tom's Traverse.

Approach

The crag is very close to Silverdale Village and is a popular local beauty spot. Therefore, climbers must take special care not to upset the local people with unnecessary noise or litter.

From Warton follow the road towards Silverdale and turn left after the level-crossing, then first left again (signposted to Jenny Brown's Point) and continue for just over one kilometre to a junction at Wolf House Gallery, where the main road bears right into the village (the road to the left leads to Jack Scout and is signposted to Jenny Brown's Point). Turn right a couple of hundred metres past the first houses in the village at the first road (Woodwell Lane), which leads to a car park. The Well itself and Well Buttress lie directly behind the fenced pool.

Climbers are asked not to stray beyond the areas described, as other crags in the area all lie on private land.

The Climbs

The routes are described from RIGHT to LEFT, as they are encountered using the first approach described above. Apart from the routes that are described, there are also many variations and lesser routes, as well as several traverses. All those routes described are between six and nine metres high, but by tradition only technical grades are given.

Tree Buttress

The first climbs lie on a buttress about 150 metres to the right of the well, just before the second single telegraph pole in the field. The most obvious feature of this buttress is a large tree that touches the crag at the top. There are two other trees that grow close to the foot of the crag.

1.   Jess VD   (1995)
Start about 10 metres to the right of the tree at a slightly higher level and climb obvious left-leading grooves.

2.   Back Breaker 5c   (1995)
Just before the ground rises, there is a shallow hanging scoop. Climb up into this and continue to the top

3.   Clap 5a   (1974-75)
About two metres right of the tree. Climb the strenuous crack above a fallen block.

4.   Tree Root 4a   (1974-75)
A very unusual chimney-like route between the crag and the tree. At the top, move right on to the rock completely for the last couple of moves.

5.   Griddle Groove 5a   (1974-75)
The groove just to the left of the tree; hard to start.

6. The Cad 5c (1986-87)

The wall between Griddle Groove and Creative Urge leads to the tree at the top.

7. Creative Urge 5c (1974-75)

The straight, strenuous crackline, starting from blocks.

8. Cannon Crack 5b (1974-75)

Just on the left. The crack which splits the overhang.

9. Long Crack 4a (1974-75)

The obvious, slightly left-leaning crack.

10. Long Crack Groove 4a (1974-75)

The open groove on the left.

11. Pussyfoot 5c (1974-75)

Three metres to the left is a big flake in the overhang; the main problem is reaching it.

12. Paws for Thought 6a (1974-75)

The bulbous arête on the left.

13. Deryn Groove 5b (1974-75)

The obvious left-facing rounded corner is gained direct, and gives a slippery struggle.

14. Flake Crack VD (1974-75)

The obvious crack just right of a yew tree which grows high on the crag.

15. Middle Tree Climb VD (1995)

Start two metres right of the next tree which grows close to the crag at a shallow groove. Climb up towards the tree at the top, then exit rightwards.

16. Battenburg 4b (1974-75)

The thin crack in the centre of the upper slab, just right of the tree.

17. Tree Arête 4c (1974-75)

The arête behind the tree is climbed without using the tree to a potentially dirty finish.

18. Rosie 5c (1974-75)

The thin crack splitting the wall on the left.

19. Pussycat 4b (1974-75)

The next crack, one metre right of Tree Corner.

20. Tree Corner 4a (1974-75)

The thin corner directly behind.the third tree which grows close to the rock.

21. Cold Comfort 4b (1974-75)

The wall two metres to the left of the corner to a poor finish.

There now follows a more broken and generally lower section, where some good problems can be found. The next route is about 50 metres farther left, on the front face of an undercut buttress standing well forward from the main line of the crag.

★ **22. The Claw** 6b   (1974-75)
Start just to the right of the arête, by a hard pull, and continue with difficulty up the arête.

Well Pinnacle
About 35 metres farther left and about 20 metres to the right of Well Buttress is a thin isolated buttress/pinnacle, which can be further identified by an obvious hanging corner at its centre.

23. The Groove 4a   (1974-75)
The groove to the right of The Nose.

24. The Nose 4c   (1974-75)
Pull into the hanging corner crack and climb it to the bulge. Step right to a good foothold and swing back left immediately to a spectacular finish on suspect flakes.

25. The Nose Left-hand 4c   (1995)
Take a line up the left face of the pinnacle, starting from its extreme left side. Move up until hands are on the obvious ledge, then move right and use incut holds to reach the short crack at the top, directly below a sapling.

Well Buttress
The long wall with the well at its left-hand side.

26. Well Worn 4c   (1974-75)
The wall behind the right-hand tree.

27. All's Well 4c   (1974-75)
A line of flakes starting left of the twin trees.

28. End's Well 4c   (1974-75)
Climb awkwardly up the thin groove two metres to the left, and finish up the loose break on the right.

29. Well What? 5a   (1974-75)
Climb the wall one metre left of the groove.

30. Well Done 5a   (1995)
Five metres to the left is a yew tree at four metres. From a large block just right of this, climb up on good holds to an overlap. The rock above is terminal, so move left to finish up the corner above the yew.

31. Wish Yew Well 5b   (1995)
Start below the yew. Climb up the rock to the left-hand side of the yew.

★ **32. Shake Well** 5c   (1974-75)
About two metres farther left is a corner. Climb this direct.

33.   Well Held   5a   (1995)
Climb the bulge three metres to the left and the wall above via an obvious jug.

34.   Get Well Groove   4b   (1974-75)
The groove above the right-hand side of the trough needs a drought to bring it
into condition.

35.   Wet Wall   4b   (1974-75)
An accurately-named route up the wall above the trough.

Isolated Buttress
Twenty metres to the left is a wall with a vague left-slanting ramp.

36.   Rampant   4c   (1974-75)
Follow the ramp and finish either up the crack on the left, or direct.

37.   Bromide   VD   (1974-75)
The groove on the left is entered using an excellent jug. At present the top is
still dirty.

Pylon Buttress
*The next section of worthwhile rock lies some way left. It can be identified
conclusively by a wooden pole a few metres away, at the edge of the field.*

38.   Pylon Crack   4a   (1974-75)
The thin crack at the right extremity of the wall.

39.   Dek's Crack   5a   (1974-75)
The wider and less attractive crack one metre to the left.

Just to the left is an obvious overhang at head-height.

40.   The Teaser   5a   (1974-75)
The right-hand crack through the overhangs, then the wall above to a tree.

41.   Mango   5b   (1974-75)
Less than one metre to the left. Climb the slightly longer crack.

42.   Okra   5b   (1974-75)
Surmount the bulge just to the left, then climb up and finish up the crack above.

43.   Leechee   4c   (1974-75)
The more prominent flake crack on the left.

★ **44.   Highlight**   4b   (1974-75)
The flaky wall on the left gives the best of the easier routes at Woodwell.

45.   Limelight   4c   (1974-75)
About a metre right of a blunt arête climb the crack on the left.

46.   Argent   5c   (1974-75)
The blunt arête just right of the gully containing a tree. A thin crack on the left
makes the initial moves more amenable.

47. Bed of Nails 5b   (1974-75)
Climb immediately left of the gully, using holds very close to the gully bed at
one point, to gain a spike and an easier finish.

48. Bed of Knives 6a   (1986-87)
The smooth-looking wall one metre farther left.

⋆ **49. Bed of Thorns** 5b   (1974-75)
Connects the two small niches in the wall by a series of agile moves.

Low Wall
*20 metres farther left, a long, low wall soon appears, its lines of overhangs
giving many enjoyable problems; some surprisingly easy – and some not!*

50. Nothing to Say 5c   (1986-87)
A direct line up the middle of the wall, to finish at a large yew tree.

51. Tom's Traverse 6b   (1985)
From a prow in the middle of the wall, take a descending line rightwards,
starting along a thin horizontal crack. Very sustained.

⋆ **52. The Hand-Traverse** 15m 6a   (1996)(1995)
Start at an embedded block at the far left of the overhangs and traverse right
with hands at about three metres or slightly less to the slanting tree at the far
right. A classic fitness test, providing that the feet are not used at all.
Low-level Start (6b): take a slightly lower line than the parent route to join it
at a good horizontal slot just under the lip of the overhang.

53. Any Questions 4c   (1974-75)
The wall immediately to the left of the overhangs is taken direct.

Pinnacle Wall
*25 metres farther left is a steep clean wall with an obvious small pinnacle on its
left. There are several possible routes up the pinnacle, but first, work out how
to get off it!*

54. The Enigma 5c   (1986-87)
The short wall immediately to the right of The Answer.

55. The Answer 6a   (1974-75)
The smooth shallow groove leads to a bulge, and finishes via a crack.

56. The Question 6a   (1986-87)
The wall between The Answer and Slanting Crack.

57. Slanting Crack 5b   (1974-75)
The slanting crackline left of The Answer. Often wet.

58. The Paradox 6b   (1986-87)
The wall just left again.

Undercut Buttress

This buttress, which is obvious from its name, lies a further 40 metres to the left, past a wire fence.

59.   Cracker VD   (1974-75)
The wall and flake crack at the right-hand side of the wall.

60.   Jack's Wall S   (1995)
Climb about two metres left above a large hawthorn tree. Good holds above the break.

61.   Bramble Jelly 5a   (1974-75)
The wide break above the small tree is easy; reaching it is a little more difficult.

62.   Edgehog 5b   (1995)
Start on the left and climb the shallow depression using holds on its right edge.

63.   Ambrosia 5b   (1974-75)
At the left of the wall a pair of cracks become more distinct near the top. Climb the wall and finish up these.

64.   Nectar 5b   (1974-75)
The next, thin crack.

65.   Twinkletoes 5a   (1995)
Traverse the buttress from left to right with feet just above the initial overhang. After the first few feet the grade eases to about 4c.

First Ascents at Woodwell

1974-75	**Clap, Tree Root, Griddle Groove, Creative Urge, Cannon Crack, Long Crack, Long Crack Groove, Pussyfoot, Paws for Thought, Deryn Groove, Flake Crack, Battenburg, Tree Arête, Rosie, Pussycat, Tree Corner, Cold Comfort, The Claw, The Groove, The Nose, Well Worn, All's Well, End's Well, Well What?, Shake Well, Get Well Groove, Wet Wall, Rampant, Bromide, Pylon Crack, Dek's Crack, The Teaser, Mango, Okra, Leechee, Highlight, Limelight, Argent, Bed of Nails, Bed of Thorns, Any Questions, The Answer, Slanting Crack, Cracker, Bramble Jelly, Ambrosia, Nectar**
1985	**Tom's Traverse** Tom Walkington
1986-87	**The Cad, Bed of Knives, Nothing to Say, The Enigma, The Question, The Paradox**
1995 Oct	**Jess** Les Ainsworth, Aly Ainsworth, Dave Cronshaw
1995 Oct	**Back Breaker, Middle Tree Climb, The Nose Left-hand, Well Done, Wish Yew Well** Dave Cronshaw, Les Ainsworth
1995	**Well Held, Jack's Wall, Edgehog, Twinkletoes** Dave Cronshaw (solo)
1996 May 7	**The Hand-Traverse** Tom Walkington
	Low level start by Tom Walkington.

Minor Crags

Heysham Head   O.S. ref.   SD 407 617

The cliffs behind Half Moon Bay (sadly no longer a 'full moon' nudist beach)
and on the headland to the north, have quite a collection of problems on
sandstones of very variable quality. The best rock is on the seaward face of the
headland, just above high water level, while the higher buttresses just below the
old chapel are also quite good, with one or two finishing holds of 'grave'
interest.

Silverdale Sea Cliffs   O.S. ref.   SD 45 75

The coastline immediately north of Silverdale comprises a series of short
limestone sea cliffs, which vary in height from about four to eight metres.
Although some climbing has been done on these crags, they are generally
broken and the climbable sections are both limited and spread out. Furthermore,
many of the crags provide important habitats for a relatively rare flora.
Therefore, in view of the abundance of other crags in the area, climbers are
asked to avoid these crags.

Whitbarrow Area

Compiled by Les Ainsworth, Dave Cronshaw and Al Phizacklea

The Whitbarrow Area is wholly within the county of Cumbria. Most of the crags are limestone and lie just north of the A590 between Kendal and Newby Bridge, just within the Lake District National Park.

Although bolts are only seen relatively infrequently in the rest of the area covered by this guidebook, within the Whitbarrow Area they provide virtually the only means of protection on crags such as Chapel Head Scar, Humphrey Head, Millside Scar and Scout Scar. On these crags, even some routes that were originally put up without bolts have now been liberally supplied with them. Needless to say, whilst some the routes on these may not generally be psychologically demanding, the climbing itself is hard and sustained, with many modern classics. However, sport climbers should be warned that many of the bolts are very spaced out and other forms of protection are also necessary.

For those lesser mortals who feel unable to cope with these harder routes, the area provides some interesting low and middle-grade climbing at Whitestones and Slape Scar. The latter is a relatively recent find, and although small, the excellent character of the rock more than makes up for this. Climbers on both of these crags will also find that, unlike some of the other crags, these actually have a top.

Whitbarrow and Witherslack Woods are designated as both 'Special Areas of Conservation' (SACs) and 'Sites of Special Scientific Interest' (SSSIs) and much of the climbing in the area lies within nature reserves managed by the Cumbria Wildlife Trust or the Lake District National Parks Authority. The limestone screes at most of the crags in the area provide important habitat for rare molluscs and snails and so climbers must keep to designated paths across all screes in order to minimize our impact on them. The limestone cliffs themselves provide relatively dry and unstable conditions and the flora is dominated by herb-rich species, which exist in isolated pockets on most of the crags within the area. Perhaps the most notable species in the area is the hoary rock-rose, which is found on isolated ledges at Chapel Head, Scout Scar, Humphrey Head and Arnside Knott. Some of the crags also provide important nesting sites for peregrine and other birds. Needless to say, climbers can both enjoy the beauty of all this wildlife and play an important role in protecting the environment by continuing to confine themselves to the accepted climbing areas and by maintaining our record of respecting climbing restrictions during the peregrine nesting season.

Chapel Head Scar

O.S. ref.   SD 443 862

Please read the Access section before visiting
Chapel Head Scar

Situation and Character

Chapel Head lies on the Witherslack Escarpment, facing south-west above
Witherslack Hall School, about 10 kilometres south-west of Kendal. It is often
in condition when the Lakeland crags are under a watery deluge.

The crag is split into five main buttresses, though because of the access
agreement, access is currently restricted only to the three on the right.

On most of the routes protection is usually completely free from bolts and it is
often necessary to make an abseil descent to avoid a loose top and to avoid
damage to the crag-top ecosystem. On the routes with a 'top out', care should
be taken on the loose band of rock that abounds on the summit. Descent from
these routes is by a way-marked path leading down the southern side of the crag.

History

Most of the early routes at Chapel Head Scar were put up on the Lower Crag
which has now been relinquished, from a climbing point of view, under the new
access agreement. In 1972, or even earlier, several of the routes were ascended
during fleeting visits by various climbers, the earliest of these that has been
identified was *Unknown Groove*, which was reputed to have been the work of
Ian Roper. The first concerted exploration of the crag however, was started by
Al Evans, who climbed *Passion Play* and *Dandelion Wine*, which could easily
have become classics. These were soon followed by more routes on the Lower
Crag by various combinations of Evans, Parker, Ainsworth and Cronshaw.
Unfortunately, although many of these were very good climbs, they are not now
accessible.

Exploration of the main crag started with a couple of poor routes. The first good
ones came in 1974, when Cronshaw and Ainsworth climbed *The Veil, Starshine*
and *Sungod*. The crag received immediate acclaim in the national climbing press
and Evans, then news editor for '*Crags*' magazine, introduced many climbers to
the delights of local climbing. One such person was Ron Fawcett, whom Evans
and Parker pointed at a line that they had been trying unsuccessfully. Fawcett
was soon past their high point and notched up his first route on the crag with
Moonchild. Word of this ascent travelled fast and Pete Livesey turned up with
John Sheard and went away with the first ascent of *Lunatic*, a fine sister route
to Moonchild.

It is also necessary to set the record straight about these early explorations,
which have been grossly misreported and embellished on subsequent retelling.
One account mentions "*trees being felled ...* " and of "*... the crag being
systematically raped, sod the wild life, get your name in the history books.*"
However, the reality was much different – a large swathe of ivy was,
regrettably, removed from Moonchild Buttress, but apart from that the gardening
was limited to the removal of a couple of small patches of ivy and two saplings
on the path.

Cyborg was the 1975 work of Ed Cleasby and Mike Lynch then in 1977 Cleasby top-roped *Half Life* before claiming it. Dave Knighton made what he thought to be the second ascent (in fact it was the first lead) and thought it necessary to place a peg. Cleasby, then more legitimately, made the first ascent of *Atomic Bong* with Andy Parkin in 1977.

Fawcett re-appeared at the crag in 1978 and succeeded in climbing the wandering, though excellent, *War of the Worlds.* Development continued with devotees Cronshaw and Knighton (one of the stronger teams operating on rock at the time) traversing the Great Buttress from right to left to produce *Cygnus X-1.* Cleasby, meanwhile, started work on the line above the swaying tree in the centre of the buttress, which was soon to become *Android* though it was to employ a little aid. Around the same time Knighton cleaned and geared up a prospective traverse, only to have Cleasby nick it whilst he was away. Knighton and Cronshaw made the second ascent of this traverse (*Fast Breeder*) and made a connection with what was *Crab Nebulae* to give the aptly-named *Chain Reaction*, showing the rate of developments at the crag at that time.

Cronshaw took the lead to attempt the hanging groove in the upper wall right of *Sun God* but had to resort to using a rest point to succeed and create *Interstellar Overdrive.* Even so, without any bolt protection, it was a bold lead. Knighton retaliated by making the first free ascent of *Android.*

Development ceased for three years, until 1983 when big George Smith and Al Phizacklea hit the headlines with the first ascent of *The Route of All Evil*, an excellent climb on superb rock. This route immediately received classic status with the help of the climbing press, and it inspired a young Martin 'Basher' Atkinson to attempt a repeat ascent even though Smith had told him that he would be too short to make the necessary reaches. Suitably peeved, Basher did the right thing and flashed the route, downgrading it in the process. As a final poke in the eye for Smith, Basher also added a direct finish and called it *The True Path.*

Phizacklea returned in 1984 to start a saga which was to last 15 months, his objective being a line up the severely overhanging rock to the left of the Android tree. In the meantime Gary Gibson made a flying visit and added *Up Town.* Winter of '85 saw Tom Walkington and friends climbing some of the smaller routes to the right of Central Gully: *Winter Pincher, Gully Wall Direct Start, Oddbods, Comedy Show* and *Veil Direct Start* kept them happy for a couple of days. After the summer ban, Phizacklea finally succeeded on his long-standing problem near Android, initially with one rest, then shortly afterwards (after sandbagging would-be second ascensionists) dispensing with it. This route became *Wargames* and because of its type of protection (drilled threads) became a crucial turning point in the crag's history. *The Perverse Pépère* followed in the same mode by Paul Cornforth and Pat McVey, but instead of drilled threads, it utilized a bolt to protect the crux jump. Steve Hubbard and Tony Mitchell added the slim groove of *Bleep and Booster* then Mitchell climbed the impressive headwall above *Great Gully* (passing two appalling bolts) to give *Darth Vadar.*

The floodgates opened and the sounds of the green woodpecker were drowned out by the sound of hammer on bolt driver. Paul Ingham with Cornforth put up the taxing *Driller Killer* then Corny completed the stunning *Super Dupont.* Steve Hubbard had been attempting a line above Android for quite some time but without success. One day during a warm spell of weather just before the annual ban, he offered Cornforth 'a go', and a few minutes later *La Mangoustine Scatouflange* was born much to Hubbard's consternation! On the last day before the summer ban, a gripped-up Cornforth made the long-awaited second ascent of Fawcett's War of the Worlds which had lain unrepeated for nearly a decade, and forty minutes later it saw a gripped-up Ingham making the third ascent.

When the crag re-opened in August 1986, competition was hot for new routes. Cornforth succeeded in climbing the curving overlap right of Super Dupont, starting up that route to give *Super Duper Dupont*. Ingham replied with *Phantom Zone* and Mark Greenbank added a diminutive *Warm Push*. Steve Hubbard broke out rightwards from the start of Phantom Zone and thus created *Stan Pulsar*, a real 'heart throbber'. Two other 'throbbers' were done by Phizacklea when he created *The Heinous Penis* and *Le Flange en Decomposition*. Attention returned to Great Buttress where Tony 'Rubber Man' Mitchell swarmed up the flutings left of Wargames to give the shocking *Electric Warrior*.

Ingham, after numerous falls, finally succeeded in redpointing his much-tried line to the left of Phantom Zone to give *Zantom Phone*. On the same day, Ingham, Mitchell and Cornforth girdled Great Buttress from Electric Warrior to Super Dupont which became the classic *Cosmic Dancer*.

Ingham then made a powerful direct start to The Perverse Pépère and Mitchell put up a route by mistake. While attempting The True Path, he wandered off route and climbed the headwall just to the right of that route and later called it *Flight Path*.

Cornforth spent quite a lot of time, firstly equipping and secondly fighting to complete the first ascent of the ridiculously overhanging, fluted area of rock rising out of Great Gully. He finally reached the top on the last dry day and *Maboulisme Merveilleux* was created.

In 1987 Ingham produced *Videodrome* and Cornforth put up *Stretchy Perineum* and *Witherslack Flange*. Meanwhile, Mitchell extended his Electric Warrior to give *Agent Provocateur*.

1988 saw Mitchell's *Prime Evil II* and Cornforth's *Tricky Pricky Ears*. In the next year Cornforth produced *Song for Europe* whilst Jim Bird added *Cement Head*. In 1991 Bird straightened out Route of All Evil and True Path to create *Eraser Head* then he went on to add *Jelly Head*. Andy Hyslop had a *Mid-Air Collision* incorporating Flight Path, Cornforth produced *Guloot Kalagna* and Dave Birkett *Unrighteous Doctors*.

1992 saw John Gaskins' *Surfing with the Alien*, Stuart Wood's *Shades of Mediocrity* and Keith Phizacklea's *Gilbert Cardigan*. Birkett did direct starts which he named *For When the Tree Falls* and *More Games*. Meanwhile Tony Burnell did *Tufa King Hard*. Then in 1993 Stuart Halford climbed *Cool Your Jets Mum*.

Finally, in 1997 the area immediately right of Moonchild, received some attention, with Keith Phizacklea adding *62 West Wallaby Street*, then shortly afterwards Steven Whittall created *War Hero*.

Approach and Access

Climbing is banned completely in the area north (left) of Central Gully. It is also banned on the rest of the crag between March 1st and July 31st, though this period may be revised and a notice at Witherslack will indicate the current situation. Up-to-date information can also be sought from the British Mountaineering Council offices in Manchester.

Chapel Head Scar lies within the Whitbarrow Local Nature Reserve, which has important semi-natural woodland, butterfly populations and limestone grassland along the cliff top. The statutory site is managed by the Lake District National Park Authority and is wardened on a regular basis. The Park Authority requests that climbers take particular note of the following good practice requirements:

(1)   Use of the marked paths to and from the crag is imperative. Access to the crags to the north (left) of Central Gully is not permitted for any reason whatsoever. In particular, this area should not be used for toilet purposes.

(2)   No ivy removal or other gardening is permitted at the crag. Also the trees and foliage surrounding the crag should not be damaged.

(3)   No litter must be left. Even small amounts of litter can cause annoyance, so please remove any litter that you may find – even if you did not leave it yourself.

(4)   No new bolts should be placed.

(5)   In the past there have been problems due to people toileting near the path. This is clearly not acceptable. Please follow the country code.

These few rules are a small price to pay to ensure that climbing can continue on this superb crag; the future rests with you.

From the A590 (Levens–Barrow road) turn off at the Witherslack signs and follow signs to the village. Continue past the village for about two kilometres to reach Witherslack Hall. Park with consideration for the locals and follow the short dirt track on the right, down to fields. A public footpath bears left across the field and into woodland. From the stile and gate, follow the track rightwards for 200 metres to a clearing where the crag can be seen. A permitted path then climbs up leftwards, passing a notice-board at the base of a scree slope. A posted path then runs diagonally rightwards up the scree then swings back left to arrive steeply at the base of Moonchild Buttress.

The Climbs

The climbs are described from LEFT to RIGHT, starting from the dirty gully 80 metres to the left from the point where the path meets the crag. This is the left-hand limit of current climbing.

Central Gully Area

This is the area of shorter climbs at the point where the path meets the crag beside the impressively steep Moonchild Buttress. The rock immediately left of Central Gully contains some quality climbs, but climbing is currently banned. It is hoped that this short section will eventually be opened up again for climbing, but meanwhile, climbers are asked to fully respect the climbing ban and to comply with on-site notices.

1.   Central Gully   27m   VS   4a   (1973)
The gully itself gives a poor route which is best avoided.

2.   Cool Your Jets Mum   12m   E3   6a   *(F6c)*   (1993)
One metre right of the gully. Climb a line passing four staples then trend
rightwards to a bolt belay.

3.   Le Flange en Decomposition   16m   E2   5c   *(F6a)*   (1986)
Three metres right of the gully. Climb the shallow groove to its top, then step
left, move up to a small overlap and continue straight up past bolts to a yew
tree.

4.   Gully Wall   16m   E1   5b   (1977)(1985)
Retrobolted! Climb the groove of Le Flange for five metres, then move right
past a stump to a shallow groove and climb this past bolts to a tree.
Variation Start (6m, E2, 5c): the tricky groove one metre right of the normal
start.

5.   Winter Pincher   15m   E3   6b   (1985)
Retrobolted! Six metres right of Le Flange. Climb the shallow, hanging groove
(bolts) to a tree. Abseil descent. Short and fierce.

6.   Oddbods   15m   E3   6a   (1985)
Retrobolted! Two metres right of Winter Pincher. A little groove (bolts).

7.   Strongbow   15m   E2   5c   (1979)
Retrobolted! Start just over one metre to the right and climb a hanging groove
to a yew. Abseil descent.

8.   Comedy Show   15m   E2   5c   (1985)
Retrobolted! The fourth little groove, which is two metres farther right. Abseil
descent from the tree.

9.   The Veil   21m   VS   4b   (1974)
Start behind a small tree that is situated about 10 metres to the right and three
metres past an horrendous hanging gully. Go up left along a shallow ramp to a
ledge, then traverse right to a blocky ledge and tree. Move up to a bush,
traverse right to the rib and finish at a yew above. Climb the flake above to
finish at the top.
Direct Start (6m, HVS, 5b): the rather pointless thin crack that leads direct to
the blocky ledge.

10.   Yashmak   21m   E3   6a   *(F6c)*   (1996)
Three metres farther right. Climb a line past three bolts.

11.   The Heinous Penis   21m   E2   6a   (1986)
Retrobolted! Two metres right at a white patch, climb past four bolts to a bolt
belay. Abseil descent. Pretty stiff, technically, for the grade.

12.   Starshine   24m   E1   5b   (1974)
Three metres to the right climb the shallow groove to a ledge, then the
disposable groove above leads to a yew. Abseil descent.

Moonchild Buttress

The tall, impressive buttress directly above the point where the path meets the crag is known as Moonchild Buttress. However, the first routes described on this buttress actually start on a small wall that leads to a ledge, with a prominent dead tree, halfway up the left edge of the buttress.

13. Jelly Head 21m E4 6b *(F7a)*   (1991)
Climb Interstellar to the roof, then pull out to the left and climb the wall past bolts, avoiding the temptation to use holds on Sun God at the top.

★★ **14. Interstellar Overdrive** 27m E3 6a   (1979/1981)
Retrobolted! Although it was originally climbed traditionally, this route has now become probably the best of the lower-grade sport climbs. The difficulties increase with height and the final groove should never be under-estimated. Start at a vague groove midway between Starshine and Sun God and climb this (bolts) to the dead, rickety tree on the ledge. Use this to step right on to the wall and climb up to the roof, then move out right to the hanging groove (bolt) which leads to the top. Abseil descent.

★ **15. Cement Head** 21m E5 6b *(F7a+)*   (1989)
Connects Interstellar and Phantom Zone. Climb Interstellar to the ledge below the tree, then step right and climb rightwards to join Phantom Zone. Follow this to the left end of the roof above then surmount this. Pull rightwards into a smooth hanging groove and follow this to a bolt belay on the right.

★ **16. Sun God** 21m HVS 5b   (1974)
Good climbing up the prominent flake-line which forms the left edge of Moonchild Buttress proper. Ascend the flake strenuously to a dead tree, then continue up the bulging flake behind to the yew. Abseil descent.

★★ **17. Zantom Phone** 27m E6 6c *(F7c+)*   (1986)
An impressive route which starts two metres right of Sun God. Follow a line of bolts, then finish up Cement Head.

★★ **18. Phantom Zone** 27m E6 6b *(F7c)*   (1986)
A superb, sustained, fingery climb. Start two metres left of the point where the path meets the lowest point of the crag and make an awkward start, then continue with increasing difficulty past bolts until it is possible to step left and finish up Cement Head.

★ **19. Stan Pulsar** 27m E5 6b   (1986)
A fine route with a puzzling start. Make awkward moves to the sidepull on Phantom Zone, then swing right to a bolt and stand on the ledge above. Climb the groove above to a rest on War of the Worlds. Pull rightwards into the hanging groove above (nut) and finish up the superb crack to a bolt belay on Zantom Phone.

Right: Charlie Vigano on **White Africa Flake** (VS 4b), Fairy Steps.   *Photo: John Mason*
Overleaf: Paul Carnforth on first ascent of **Super Duper Dupont** (E6 6c), Chapel Head Scar.
Photo: Al Phizacklea

★ **20.   Surfing with the Alien**   12m   E6   6c   (*F8a*)   (1992)
Start immediately above the point where the path meets the crag. Climb up to
an excellent sidepull, then follow the right-hand fork up a blunt arête to a bolt
belay. Abseil descent.

★ **21.   Bleep and Booster**   27m   E4   6a   (*F7a+*)   (1985)
The shallow grooveline left of Moonchild gives sustained climbing. Start directly
below the grooveline of Moonchild and climb past two bolts to a ledge.
Continue up the shallow groove and over an overlap, then climb another groove
to a short flake. Climb this to a tree and either belay or, preferably, on a bolt
three metres to the left. Abseil descent.

★ **22.   War of the Worlds**   38m   E5   6a   (1978)
Climb Moonchild to the peg, then traverse left for six metres to a groove, and
go up to a resting place and a peg, Traverse left for six metres to a hollow
flake, then go up to the roof, pulling right into the smooth groove to finish. Bolt
belay up to the right.

★★ **23.   Moonchild**   24m   E4   5c   (1974)
Start just right of a steep polished groove three metres right of the point where
the path meets the crag. Climb the wall until it is possible to move awkwardly
left into the groove, then move up awkwardly to a peg (bold) and rock over
right to a scoop. Pull out left on superb holds, then go up right and climb the
flake above to several saplings. Finish left at a yew. Abseil descent.

★★ **24.   The Moon/Loon Connection**   37m   E4   5c   (1974)(1974)
A brilliant way to combine some of the best traditional climbing on the crag.
Climb Moonchild to the bunch of saplings, then traverse right to a tree belay –
junction with Lunatic. Finish like a lunatic.

★ **25.   Dune**   60m   E4   5b,5c,4b,5c   (1976-78/1986)
A left-to-right traverse of the Moonchild Buttress that gives a scary pitch for
both leader and second. Start up Starshine.
1.   12m.   Climb the groove to the ledge, move right to a belay at the dead tree.
2.   30m.   Move down and dash right across the wall to good holds, bolt and
pegs, then go up and right to a rest and peg on War of the Worlds. Traverse
delicately right to below the black bulge on Bleep and Booster. Step down and
swing right to a good jug on Moonchild (peg). Move up rightwards to a tree,
and climb the flake above to saplings. Belay on the yew out left to give some
sort of protection for your poor second.
3.   6m.   Move out rightwards to the tree belay on Lunatic.
4.   12m.   Climb the open groove on Lunatic.

★ **26.   62 West Wallaby Street**   23m   E5   6a   (*F7a+*)   (1997)
Start three metres right of Moonchild and just left of a tree. Climb a short wall
to a staple beneath a tiny bulge, then make difficult moves straight up past bolts
to gain a good ledge. Continue straight up, then go right to a junction with
Moonchild. Either finish up this (wires) or move right and finish up War Hero.

Previous page: Dave Kells awash with fear being **Shot by Both Sides** (E3 6b) Humphrey Head
Point.   *Photo: Al Phizacklea*
Left: Pat McVey on the first ascent of **The Perverse Pépère** (E6 6a), Chapel Head Scar.
                                             Photo: Al Phizacklea

** **27.   War Hero**   23m   E5   6a   *(F7a)*   (1997)
An excellent pitch on mostly superb rock. The best of the 'easier' bolt routes.
Start eight metres right of Moonchild, where a tree grows close to the base of
the crag. Climb straight up from the tree past three bolts to a bulge (bolt). Pass
this directly (slightly easier to swing left), then go up for a couple of moves
until it is possible to step rightwards to gain a small ledge on Lunatic. Follow
this to its belay, then continue straight up the wall left of Lunatic.

Great Gully Area
The next routes start around the vegetated Great Gully.

** **28.   Tricky Pricky Ears**   23m   E5   6a   (1988)
An unusual route for the crag, being fairly bold in places. Start about three
metres higher up at a shallow groove. Climb this and the wall just left of the
overhang, then continue to the flaky ledge on Lunatic. Climb the wall above,
trending slightly right to reach a hanging groove (Darth Vadar) and finish up
this.

* **29.   Lunatic**   27m   E3   5c,5c   (1974)
The upper groove is a fine contrast to the lower wall. Start below a flake some
six metres up Great Gully.
1.   15m.   Climb to a sapling, then go up the flake above to gain a ledge.
Climb up to a big flaky ledge and tree belay.
2.   12m.   Gain the superb open groove on the right which leads to the top.

30.   Darth Vadar   15m   E5   6a   (1985)
From the tree belay at the top of the first pitch of Lunatic, move right past the
groove and continue to the hollow flake on the right, (poor bolt). Go up to a
small flake, then step right across the obvious niche. Climb the wall above to
the break (peg), and finish out rightwards up a loose groove. A harder variation
is to gain the niche from below.

** **31.   Maboulisme Merveilleux**   17m   E6   6c   *(F7c)*   (1986)
A stunning route and a much sought after prize that takes in some improbable
territory through the very steep bulge at the top of the gully to the right of
Moonchild. Unfortunately the route is very slow to dry. Start nine metres up
Great Gully at a small ledge and bolt belay. Traverse across the gully and attack
the very steep bulge on good, but well spaced, holds to a gymnastic crux at the
lip. Continue up the slab to a bolt, then finish direct. Well-protected by bolts.

● **32.   Great Gully**   18m   VD   (1974)
The tapering vegetated gully that leads to a yew in a cave. The best line is on
the left. Abseil descent.

● **33.   Captain's Crack**   18m   HS   4a   (1972)
The broken crack up the right-hand side of the gully that leads to the cave and
an abseil descent.

● **34.   Apollo's Exit**   8m   E2   5c   (1980)
The short, awkward crack through the cave roof (peg on lip). Belay well back.
Currently overgrown.

Right Wall

The smooth white wall right of Central Gully gives some excellent climbing.

★★ **35.   The Route of All Evil**   30m   E5   6a   (1983)
Retrobolted! Superb open climbing, taking the line of least resistance up the
wall right of Great Gully. Start at a short, right-facing flake at the left side of
the next wall. Climb the flake then continue to the top of the shallow groove in
the middle of the wall. Move left and go up to a good horizontal break. Step
right and go up flakes to a second break. Traverse left to a good rest (bolt) and
pull up right on good holds to a flake, then finish out right to the top. There is
an easier finish on the left.

★ **36.   Eraser Head**   25m   E5   6b   (*F7b*)   (1983/1991)
A stunning, direct line up the clean white wall; a limestone classic. Climb past
the first overhang on Route of All Evil, then at 10 metres move left and
continue up the wall to a tape in the second break (junction with Route of All
Evil). Step up and leftwards to a good nut then make wild moves on a
one-finger undercut to finish up the headwall. The top part of this route was
originally called True Path.

★ **37.   Cyborg**   30m   E2   5c,5a   (1975)
Some very good climbing in the lower half. Start as for The Route of All Evil.
1.   21m.   Ascend the corner to the flake, then traverse right for six metres to
the middle of the wall. Go straight up to a small ledge and sapling then move
out right past a peg (possible lower-off), then across disposable holds and up to
a yew tree.
2.   9m.   The rib and crack out to the left; brittle rock.

★★ **38.   Mid-Air Collision**   25m   E5   6b   (*F7b*)   (1986/1991)
A superb route with a perplexing crux – right at the end, but well-protected by
bolts. Start three metres to the right and take a direct line crossing Cyborg to
meet Route of All Evil at the first break. Continue as for this route to the
second break, move slightly rightwards, then climb straight up the headwall
passing a bolt. The top part of this route was originally called Flight Path.

39.   The Omega Factor   30m   E3   6a,5c   (1979)
First pitch retrobolted! Start eight metres right of Cyborg, below a niche
containing a holly tree.
1.   18m.   Climb awkwardly past bolts to the niche and, after a fight with the
holly, escape left (bolt) to gain a good flake then go up to Cyborg. Move right,
climb to an overlap and up the groove out right, finishing at a yew as for
Cyborg.
2.   12m.   Move right to beneath a shallow depression in the steep wall and
climb this to the top.

● **40.   Garden of Eden**   30m   VS   4b   (Pre-1979)
Jungle bashing, which starts 15 metres right, behind a clump of small trees.
Climb a shallow groove past a tree to a ledge at six metres, then move across
left to a crack. Bushwhack up this and struggle through bushes to a tree. Finish
up fairly clean rock.

Great Buttress

This is the next, steep buttress of clean rock, with a very undercut base.

41. Sad But True 27m E4 6a *(F6c+)* (1996)
A route based around Half Life in its lower half and which finishes up the hanging groove that bounds the left side of the wall. Start at a short, clean flake three metres farther right, which forms the left side of Great Buttress and climb this until it is possible to step left to a ledge and a bolt. Tricky moves then lead to steadier climbing up the wall, leading leftwards to the hanging corner high on the wall. Follow this to the top.

42. The Rocinante 27m HS 4b (1979)
Start as for Sad But True and climb the short, clean flake to a large yew. Move left into the steep, right-facing corner; go up this through a holly to a dead tree, then finish up the groove behind.

43. Half Life 27m E2 5c (1977)
Ascend to the large yew as for Rocinante, then climb a short wall to gain the horizontal break. Step left and move into a wide scoop. Climb this until it steepens then traverse right to gain an open groove which leads to the top. Bolt belay.

★ 44. Up Town 24m E3 5c (1984)
Retrobolted! A direct version of Half Life, which gives a fine, open climb, far better than the view from below suggests. Instead of stepping left at the horizontal break, step right and gain a stalactite (bolts). Go up this past more bolts, to join Half Life then finish up this. A slightly harder finish is possible at 6a, by following a line of bolts on the left.

★ 45. Atomic Bong 36m E1 5a,5b (1977)
1. 24m. From the break on Half Life, traverse eight metres right to a tree-strewn ledge, then straight up to belay in a round niche above.
2. 12m. Traverse right for six metres to a flake. Go up this, then tiptoe back left to a loose flake which leads to the top. Bolt belay. Abseil descent.

★★ 46. Chain Reaction 58m E3 5a,5c (1979)
A superb, delicate traverse of Great Buttress which has a strenuous finish.
1. 21m. Follow Atomic Bong to belay on the tree strewn ledge.
2. 37m. A sustained pitch. Traverse right along the break to a flake on Wargames, step down and move across rightwards to a rest on Android. Move delicately right and go up to gain a rest and obtain runners on the hanging flake above. Traverse strenuously past several bolts under the roof to a hanging belay at the far right end. Abseil descent.

*The original route on the buttress – **Fast Breeder** – followed Chain Reaction to the hanging flake then finished direct.*

★ 47. Shades of Mediocrity 21m E4 6a *(F7a)* (1992)
Start six metres to the right. Stand on a tufa, then climb up to a bolt. Move left at a small overlap, then continue on clean rock to a bolt belay. Care is needed with holds at the top. Abseil descent.

★ **48.   Gilbert Cardigan**   21m   E4   6b   (*F7a+*)   (1992)
Start two metres to the right at another tufa and climb up past bolts. Finish as
for the previous route. Abseil descent.

★★ **49.   Guloot Kalagna**   21m   E5   6c   (*F7c*)   (1991)
A short, sharp crux requires strong fingers and a tough skin. Four metres right
climb the forked tree then step on to the rock below a bolt and continue to a
flaky tufa. Move left at the top then go back right over the bulge. Continue to a
bolt belay. Abseil descent.

★ **50.   Electric Warrior**   12m   E5   6b   (*F7b*)   (1986)(1987)
Grasp the tufas and go, hopefully gaining the chain belay below the bulge. If
you are still going well, finish over the bulge of Agent Provacateur via a
razor-edged pocket. Start three metres right of the forked tree and climb the
'rice crispie' flutings past two bolts then step right to a bolt belay under the
shattered roof. Short, but powerful; classic tufa. Either lower off at this point, or
continue up:
★ **Agent Provocateur** (9m E6, 6c, *F7c*): the continuation line of Electric Warrior,
climbing directly through the bulge via a painful one-finger pocket.

★★ **51.   Cosmic Dancer**   38m   E5   6b,5a   (1986)
An entertaining low traverse of Great Buttress.
1.   24m.   Start up Electric Warrior to the belay, then traverse right past a tape
on Wargames and reverse part of Android to a bolt belay on La Mangoustine
Scatouflange.
2.   14m.   Climb to the second bolt on La Mangoustine Scatouflange and slide
across right to Super Dupont. Ascend this to its bolt belay then go right along
the roof to a bolt belay at its right-hand end.

★ **52.   Calling Mr Hall**   21m   E6   6c   (*F8a*)   (1990)
Start behind a holly and gain a curious fluting, then continue past six bolts to
the awkward finishing bulge. Bolt belay on left. Abseil descent.

★★★ **53.   Wargames**   24m   E5   6b   (1985)(1992)
Retrobolted! A steep and pumpy start up tufas, then easier, but still sustained,
wall climbing on excellent rock, makes this one of the best pitches of its grade
anywhere in the UK. Start immediately to the right, below a tiny yew eight
metres left of Android. Go up to the yew and crank up past bolts, then move
right into the hanging groove to gain a rest above. Climb just right of the very
shallow groove above to a good hold and move out left to a corner that leads
up to the roof. Just over this is a line of jugs, swing right along these to a
niche. Pull up to a hanging belay. Abseil descent.
More Games (E5, 6b, *F7b+*): a slightly harder direct start to reach the hanging
groove of Wargames, taking a direct line four metres right of the tiny yew.

★ **54.   Stretchy Perineum**   10m   E6   6b   (*F7b+*)   (1987)
Start six metres left of Android and climb boldly to the first bolt above a
prominent tufa at five metres. Move leftwards on undercuts to gain a
squashed-up position beneath the roof (bolt). Pull over this, slapping wildly, and
climb the wall above to a junction with Android. Traverse right and finish up
The Perverse Pépère.

★ **55.   Perverted Start**   21m   E5   6c   (*F7b+*)   (1986)
Climb to the first bolt on Stretchy Perineum, then move right and go up to a
bulge. Surmount this and continue to the junction with Android.

★★★ **56.   Android**   29m   E4   5c   (1979)(1992)
A great trad route, that finds the easiest way up this impressive buttress.
Unfortunately, it is a little neglected in this age of clip-ups. Start up the ash tree
at the centre of the foot of Great Buttress and climb it to just above the overlap,
then move left along a branch, clip a low bolt on the left and pull into the small
scoop above (bolt). Continue to a peg, then step down and across left to a larger
scoop and a peg. Climb the steep thin flake above until it eases – junction with
Chain Reaction. Move delicately right and go up to gain a rest below the
hanging flake; climb this to its top, and traverse off rightwards to a hanging
belay (this avoids the loose top wall). Abseil descent.
For When the Tree Falls (E6, 6c, *F7c*): a direct start to Android is possible
without using the tree, by starting at a tufa immediately left of the tree.

★ **57.   Android Original Finish**   46m   E3   5c,5b   (1979)
A poor finish, but the route is still worthwhile.
1.   32m.   Follow Android to the junction with Chain Reaction then traverse left
along the break to belay on a tree-strewn ledge – part of Chain Reaction in
reverse.
2.   14m.   Move back right along the break for six metres, pull directly over the
bulge past two tree stumps, then go up to a flake – junction with Atomic Bong.
Move left to another flake to finish.

★★ **58.   The Perverse Pépère**   25m   E4   6a   (1985)
Retrobolted! A fine direct on Android, requires a dynamic approach. Follow
Android past the first peg to a bolt, then crank up and dyno for a jug (bolt).
Climb delicately up to the top flake on Android, and ascend this to belay on the
right.

★★★ **59.   A Song for Europe**   23m   E6   6b   (*F7b+*)   (1989)
Excellent tufa climbing, and even better when combined with For When the
Tree Falls. From the bolt above the large scoop on Android, use tufas to climb
an obvious boltline to the left of a corner.

★★★ **60.   La Mangoustine Scatouflange**   23m   E4   6b   (*F7a+*)   (1986)(1987)
Quality climbing that takes a direct line up the wall above the tree. A few
thought-provoking moves test on-sight skills. Climb Android to the scoop on the
left, then go up and right past a bolt and make a hard move past a second bolt
for a good hold. Pump up the fluting above (bolt), to the bolt belay at the
left-hand end of the long roof. Awesome territory.
★ **Witherslack Flange Finish** (8m E4, 6a): from the tape belay on La Mangoustine,
pull over the roof above and climb the wall to a bolt belay. Exciting!

★★ **61.   Super Dupont**   21m   E5   6c   (*F7b*)   (1985)
A Lakeland limestone classic. Boulder problem moves above a small tree require
tenacity. Then contrasting climbing through the bulges leads to a Grand Finalé
on the upper wall. Start at a holly three metres right of Android and climb this
to gain the rock at a bolt. A difficult sequence past two more bolts gains a rest

in the scoop. Move out left through bulges (bolt) to a ledge. Climb the shallow groove above past a fourth bolt to a bolt belay on Chain Reaction.

★★★ **62. Super Duper Dupont** 23m E6 6c (*F7b+*) (1986)
A world-class route. The line of the wall, with climbing to match. Follow Super Dupont to the scoop then climb the exhausting right-curving undercling to make a desperate lunge past a bolt to gain a ledge; standing on this brings an end to the difficulties, a peg and a belay suspended from this.

★★ **63. Prime Evil II** 21m E6 6c (*F7c+*) (1988)
Slightly overshadowed by its neighbours, but you've still got to do a route that is 'merely' excellent. From the first bolt on Super Dupont, climb the right side of an overlap, then continue in a slightly rightward line to a larger overlap. Surmount this, then continue straight up to the bolt belay on Super Duper Dupont. Abseil descent.

★★★ **64. Unrighteous Doctors** 21m E6 6c (*F7c+*) (1991)
Probably the best route on a wall of brilliant routes. Start two metres left of the large yew growing out of the rock and climb the wall above, trending steadily leftwards to the roof at the top. Surmount this and move left to the bolt belay on Mangoustine. Abseil descent.

★ **65. Tufa King Hard** 11m E3 6a (*F6c*) (1992)
Start up parallel tufas two metres right of the yew and follow a right-leading weakness past four bolts. Pull left through the bulge above to a bolt belay. Abseil descent. Good route; awful pun.

★ **66. Driller Killer** 30m E5 6b (*F7a+*) (1985)(1987)
A little wandering in line, but still well worth doing. Start five metres right of the yew and climb directly up to some tufas to a bolt below an overlap. Traverse left, across Tufa King Hard, past another bolt to a ledge behind the yew (bolt), then go up left to a dubious bolt. Power through the bulges above to easy ground. Either traverse left to belay or climb the rotten wall above.
★ **Videodrome** (E5, 6c, *F7b+*): a variation finish to Driller Killer. Hard and a little scary. From the overlap, move up and left to a ledge, then traverse back right (bolt) to small undercuts. Continue to gain a flat hold and a bolt, then make more moves up on undercuts to enter a faint groove. Bolt belay on the left. Abseil descent.

67. Warm Push 8m E2 6a (*F6b+*) (1986)
A short problem four metres right of Driller Killer. Stand on the big hold at three metres then continue past bolts to the overlap. Bolt belay. Abseil descent.

68. Reefer Madness 10m E3 6b (1991)
Retrobolted! Start two metres to the right and use small tufas, then follow vague cracks past three bolts to reach the overlap. Move left through the overlap and continue for three metres to two bolts. Abseil descent.

69. Doctor's Dilemma 7m E3 6b (*F6c*) (1993)
Start behind the tree at the right end of the wall and climb past three bolts to a peg at the overlap. Abseil descent.

★ 70.   Cygnus X-1   65m   E2   5b,5c,5c,4a   (1979)

A high right-to-left traverse of Great Buttress. A horrible approach – walk along the base of the crag to the right-hand end, find and climb a network of yew roots on the steep ground to a second yew. Climb this tree for three metres until a traverse left along a painfully thorny ledge can be made to a peg and a rotting hanging rope belay.

1.   21m.   Follow the ledge leftwards to a short corner and a tree. Move round a detached rib and reverse layback down to a traverse line at foot level (peg). An awkward move leads to a hanging belay.

2.   21m.   Go left to the top of the flake on Android and continue under a narrow roof past a hanging belay on Wargames and descend to a good footledge. Move left to a junction with Atomic Bong and reverse the traverse to belay in the niche.

3.   15m.   From the left of the ledge step down and traverse the superb horizontal break (two old tape runners) to the corner. Dead tree belay on The Rocinante.

4.   8m.   Finish up the groove above.

Lower Crag

Although this crag once provided some good middle-grade climbing, access is currently banned for environmental reasons. From a climbing perspective this arrangement is clearly not ideal but, nevertheless, all climbers are asked to honour the existing agreement by avoiding the Lower Crag completely in order to safeguard access to the rest of the crag.

First Ascents at Chapel Head Scar

Routes in the area where climbing is not currently permitted are shown in italics.

Pre-1972	*Unknown Groove* Bob Dearman or Ian Roper	
1971 Oct	*October Country* Keith Myhill, Al Evans	
1972 Mar	*Prime Evil, Spiny Norman, Hothouse, Hothouse Direct, Passion Play* Al Evans, Dave Parker	
1972 Apr	*Dandelion Wine, Earth Abides* Al Evans, Dave Parker, Zbignew (Fred) Dyslewicz	
1972 May	*Pink Panther, Sunny Saturday* Les Ainsworth, Dave Cronshaw	
1972 May	*Wet Weekend* Les Ainsworth, Dave Cronshaw (both solo)	
1972 June	*Sun Machine* Dave Cronshaw, Les Ainsworth	
1972 June	*Passion Wine, Via Dolorosa* Dave Parker, Al Evans	
1972 June	*59th St. Bridge, Fahrenheit 451* Al Evans, Dave Parker	
1972 June	**Captain's Crack** Al Evans	
1973	**Central Gully** Al Evans	
1974	**The Veil, Starshine** Les Ainsworth, Dave Cronshaw	
1974	**Sun God** Dave Cronshaw, Les Ainsworth	
1974	**Moonchild** Ron Fawcett, Al Evans, Dave Parker	
1974	**Lunatic** Pete Livesey, John Sheard	
1974	**Great Gully** Keith Myhill, Al Evans	
1975 Mar 25	**Cyborg** Ed Cleasby, Mike Lynch	
1977 Feb 25	**Fast Breeder** Andy Parkin, Ed Cleasby (alts)	
1977 Apr	**Half Life** Ed Cleasby, Ian Postlethwaite	
1977 Apr 30	*Unknown Country* Paul Sansom, Bill Lounds	
1977 Apr 30	**Gully Wall** Bill Lounds, Paul Sanson	
	Retrobolted: 3 bolts added.	
1977	**Atomic Bong** Ed Cleasby, Andy Parkin	
1978	**War of the Worlds** Ron Fawcett	
1976-78	**Dune** (1pt aid) Ed Cleasby	
	Aid eliminated by Al Phizacklea, John Topping, 30 Aug 1986.	

Pre-1979   **Garden of Eden**   Ted Rogers
Pre-1979   *The Rib*
Pre-1979   *Tool Buttress*
1979 Jan 21   *Warchild*   Dave Knighton, Dave Cronshaw
1979 Feb 25   **Cygnus X-1**   Dave Knighton, Dave Cronshaw (alts)
1979 Feb 25   *Ganymede*   Dave Cronshaw, Dave Knighton
1979 Feb   *Ursa Major*   Dave Cronshaw, Les Ainsworth
1979 Apr 13   **Android**   (1 pt aid)   Ed Cleasby, Pat McVey
              Climbed to the tree on Atomic Bong.
              Completed with the Original Finish by Ed Cleasby, Al Phizacklea, Iain
              Greenwood, 14 Apr 1979.
              First free ascent by Dave Knighton, 1979.
1979 July 29 **Interstellar Overdrive**   Dave Cronshaw, Dave Knighton
              Retrobolted: 6 bolts added.
1979 Aug 4   **The Rocinante**   Dave Cronshaw, Dave Knighton
1979 Aug 15   **Chain Reaction**   Dave Knighton, Dave Cronshaw
1979 Aug 18   **The Omega Factor**   Dave Knighton, Dave Cronshaw
              First pitch retrobolted: 4 bolts added.
1979 Oct 7   **Strongbow**   Iain Greenwood, Al Phizacklea
              Retrobolted: 3 bolts added.
1979   *Pipistrelle*   Pat McVey, Mark Danson
1979   *Thunderchild*   Jim Arnold, Derek Firze, John Girdley
1979   *Running Blind*   Iain Greenwood, Al Phizacklea, Ian Cooksey
1980   *Pillar Front*   Iain Greenwood, Steve Hubbard
              Superseded by The Heinous Penis.
1980   **Apollo's Exit**   Mark Danson, Iain (Wilf) Williamson
1983 Sep 11   **The Route of all Evil**   George Smith, Al Phizacklea
              Retrobolted: 5 bolts added.
1983 Oct 29   **The True Path**   Martin Atkinson, Mark Danson
              Originally a direct finish to Route of all Evil, but superseded by Eraser Head.
1984   **Up Town**   Gary Gibson
              Retrobolted: 5 bolts added.
1985 Jan 5   **Comedy Show**   Dave Bates, Tom Walkington
              Retrobolted: 4 bolts added.
1985 Jan 6   **Oddbods**   Dave Bates, Tom Walkington
              Retrobolted: 3 bolts added.
1985 Jan 11   **Gully Wall: Variation Start**   Dave Bates (solo)
              Retrobolted: 3 bolts added.
1985 Jan 11   **Winter Pincher**   Tom Walkington, Dave Bates
              Retrobolted: 3 bolts added.
1985   **Veil: Direct Start**   Tom Walkington, Dave Bates, Barry Rogers
1985 Oct   **Bleep and Booster**   (4 bolts)   Steve Hubbard, Tony Mitchell
              Unethically retrobolted with a new start in 1996 much to the surprise of the
              first ascensionists.
1985 Oct 25   **Wargames**   Al Phizacklea (unseconded)
              Retrobolted: 6 bolts added.
              More Games (3 bolts) by Dave Birkett, 1992.
1985 Oct 27   **The Perverse Pépère**   Paul Cornforth, Pat McVey, Al Phizacklea1
              Originally climbed with 1 bolt runner. 2 more added later.
              Notable for being the first modern route to 'suffer' the placing of a bolt
              runner.
1985 Nov 20   **Super Dupont**   (5 bolts)   Paul Cornforth
1985 Nov 21   **Darth Vadar**   Tony Mitchell (unseconded)
1985 Nov 24   **Driller Killer**   (5 bolts)   Paul Ingham, Paul Cornforth
              Videodrome (3 bols) by Paul Ingham, 24 Feb, 1987.
1986 Feb 27   **La Mangoustine Scatouflange**   (4 bolts)   Paul Cornforth (unseconded)
              Witherslack Flange Finish by Paul Cornforth, 1987.
1986 June   **Flight Path**   Tony Mitchell (unseconded)
              Originally a right-hand finish to Route of all Evil, but superseded by Mid-air
              Collision.
1986 Aug 3   **Warm Push**   (2 bolts)   Mark Greenbank (unseconded)

1986 Aug 5   **Super Duper Dupont** (7 bolts) Paul Cornforth (unseconded)
1986 Aug 15   **Phantom Zone** (6 bolts) Paul Ingham (unseconded)
1986 Aug 23   **Le Flange en Decomposition** Al Phizacklea, Steve Hubbard
1986 Sep 3   **Stan Pulsar** Steve Hubbard (unseconded)
1986 Sep 13   **Electric Warrior** (6 bolts) Tony Mitchell (unseconded)
              Extended as Agent Provocateur (2 bolts) by Tony Mitchell, Paul Cornforth,
              21 June 1987.
1986 Sep 20   **The Heinous Penis** Al Phizacklea, Paul Ingham
              Retrobolted: 4 bolts added.
1986 Oct 4   **Maboulisme Merveilleux** (5 bolts) Paul Cornforth (unseconded)
1986 Oct 11   **Zantom Phone** (7 bolts) Paul Ingham (unseconded)
              Started up Sun God, but the line was straightened out by John Gaskins,
              21 July 1991.
1986 Oct 11   **Cosmic Dancer** Tony Mitchell, Paul Ingham, Paul Cornforth
1986 Oct 16   **The Perverted Start** (2 bolts) Paul Ingham (unseconded)
1987 June 16 **Stretchy Perineum** (2 bolts) Paul Cornforth
1988 June 28 **Prime Evil II** (5 bolts) Tony Mitchell (unseconded)
              This route should not be confused with the original Prime Evil on the Lower
              Crag.
1988 Sep 17   **Tricky Pricky Ears** Paul Cornforth
1989 Aug 31   **A Song for Europe** (6 bolts) Paul Cornforth
1990   **Cement Head** (6 bolts) Jim Bird
1990 June 29 **Calling Mr Hall** (6 bolts) Paul Cornforth
1991 Feb   **Reefer Madness** Ian Vickers, Dave Cronshaw
              Retrobolted: 3 bolts added.
1991 July 16 **Eraser Head** (5 bolts) Jim Bird
              A new lower section linked to The True Path to create an independent route.
1991 July 16 **Guloot Kalagna** (6 bolts) Paul Cornforth
1991 July 20 **Mid-air Collision** (7 bolts) Andy Hyslop
              A new lower section linked to Flight Path to create an independent route.
1991 July 21 **Zantom Phone** (7 bolts) John Gaskins
              Route made independent of Sun God.
1991 Aug   **Jelly Head** (2 bolts) Jim Bird, Andy Tilney
1991 Sep 1   **Unrighteous Doctors** (9 bolts) Dave Birkett
1992 June 10 **Surfing with the Alien** (4 bolts) John Gaskins
1992   **Shades of Mediocrity** (4 bolts) Stuart Wood
1992   **Gilbert Cardigan** (4 bolts) Keith Phizacklea
1992   **For When the Tree Falls** (2 bolts) Dave Birkett
1992   **Tufa King Hard** (4 bolts) Tony Burnell
1993   **Cool Your Jets Mum** (4 bolts) Stuart Halford
1993   **Doctor's Dilemma** (2 bolts) Jim Bird
1996 June 5   **Sad But True** (5 bolts) Stevie Whittall, Keith Phizacklea
1996   **Yashmak** (3 bolts)
1997   **62 West Wallaby Street** (5 bolts) Keith Phizacklea (unseconded)
1997 Feb 8   **War Hero** (10 bolts) Steven Whittall, Keith Phizacklea, Al Phizacklea

Humphrey Head Point   O.S. ref. SD 390 740

Situation and Character

Humphrey Head is a low, isolated headland jutting out into Morecambe Bay,
five kilometres south-east of Grange-over-Sands. It is the largest seacliff
between St Bees Head and The Little Orme, but it is entirely non-tidal.
Incidentally, this is also the place where the last wild wolf was shot in England
back in the 16th century, when Sir Edgar Harrington offered his daughter
Adela's hand to whomsoever could rid the county of the beast.

The crag has a very poor top and in order to conserve both the ecological
environment and visiting climbers, bolt belays have been established at the top

of many of the climbs, so that abseil descents are the norm. Bolts have also been used extensively and so most of the climbs can be very well-protected. However, some climbs, especially those on the Forgotten Walls still rely upon more natural protection and climbers are asked to respect this and not to retrobolt these established routes.

Although Humphrey Head came to prominence as a sport climbing venue, many of the more traditional climbs are also very worthwhile.

History

The early development of the crag was largely the work of Mick Goff who, with various partners, added numerous routes during 1966-67. Al Evans visited the crag in 1976 and cleaned a few new routes, all but one of which (*The Decent Thing*) have been reclaimed by vegetation. 1978 saw Pat McVey and Mark Danson put up the excellent *Triggerfinger*. During the ascent, Mark was scrambling up the horrible grass slope above the route, when the block on which he was pulling parted company with mother earth. Mark plummeted the full length of the crag, but was lucky to be stopped in the branches of a friendly tree. The block, however, after destroying Ed Cleasby's sack (containing watch, Helly jacket and a new pair of Hush Puppies) went on to seek its fortune on the beach. Other routes added that year (albeit in not quite so dramatic a fashion) were *Back into the Future* by Andy and Jenny Hyslop and *The Left Hand of Darkness* by Danson and friends.

Iain Greenwood and Angie Widowson visited here in January of 1981 and added the unimaginatively named *January*, then the crag seemed to have little to offer whilst the ethical views prevalent in Cumbria at that time remained. Al Phizacklea and Rob Knight, complete with bolt driver, paid a visit in 1984 and *The Firing Squad* was both the route name they used and the result of the slagging off Phizacklea received from the climbing press. The Firing Squad was quite bold to finish before it was retrobolted.

Paul Pritchard and Phil Kelly ventured up into Edgar's Arch one day in 1986 with a view to looking at the aid route across its arch. Pritchard ended up by leading the crack above the start of the aid route, on-sight, to give *The Job*.

Phizacklea with John Topping, a generator and a huge drill, placed solid belay bolts atop the routes on the Main Crag, and when this useful task was complete, Al put the drill to further use with the first ascent of *Sniffin' the Saddle* a free ascent of *Fusion*, then followed John up *Shot by Both Sides*. Paul Cornforth came over and after accompanying the other pair on *Humphrey Cushion*, he borrowed the drill and proceeded to bolt the overhanging area of rock just to the right, which soon became *Humphrey Hymen (Met a Slyman)*. In 1988 Tony Brindle and Adrian Moore freed the old aid route *Hammerlock*.

1989 was a big year with Ted Roger's *3-2-1*; Rick Graham's *Live Rounds;* Luke Steer's *Shooting the Load* and Mark Radtke's *Hollow Lands*. 1991 saw Rick Graham's *Stymen, Pork Pie* and *Sniffin' the Saddle Direct*; plus Ken Forsythe's *Humphrey Bogart* and Andy Hyslop's *Slightly Shoddy*. In the same month, John Dunne freed *Back to the Future* – an intriguing route across Edgar's Arch. In 1994 Iain Greenwood discovered new rock between The Main Crag and Edgar's Arch, with *Humphrey Dumphrey*.

During work for this guidebook, Dave Cronshaw and Les Ainsworth turned their attention to the seaward end of the crag, where they were surprised to find that there was much good rock that had been ignored in the past. *Oktoberfest* was the first climb to be discovered and this was soon followed by *Where Bolters Fear to Tread* and *Sir Edgar's Crack*. This exploration culminated with Cronshaw's bold lead of *Adela*, which then had no bolts and was a very necky proposition. During the final stages of guidework Cronshaw and Ainsworth rediscovered the lines of *Earthworm* and *Roobarb's Corner* and uncovered three other pleasant routes up this previously neglected section of crag.

Approach
From Grange-over-Sands follow the B5277 through Allithwaite, and turn left 500 metres past the village. After crossing the railway turn left down a track which leads to parking on the beach. It is also signposted from The Square in the centre of Flookburgh.

The Climbs
The climbs are described from LEFT to RIGHT. Abseil descents are advisable on many of the climbs in order to avoid loose rock and vegetation.

Landward Buttress
The first route lies on an isolated buttress 180 metres left of Main Crag and is best reached from the top. The buttress lies about 30 metres past a substantial square-cut fence post, which is itself about 150 metres left of the top of the descent gully. There are two good threads above and, although it is possible to scramble down steep grass to the buttress, it is perhaps easier to abseil in.

1.   The Left Hand of Darkness   10m   HVS   5a   (1978)
Climb the prominent right-leading flake to the overlap, then finish using jugs on the right. A slightly harder finish is possible by moving left beneath the overlap then pulling over the left edge.

2.   Right-hand Man   10m   HVS   5b   (1997)
Make awkward moves to gain the left-leaning flake, step up, then use holds on the right wall and finish up a short groove.

Descent Gully Area
The next routes lie on a clean, steep slabby area about 30 metres left of the main descent gully, which is further identified by two small trees growing from a flake near its base. The wall is characterized by amazing pockets and juggy flakes. On all of these routes, the top couple of moves constitute the crux. Climbers should also note that belays are usually well back and so allow about 10 metres of extra rope.

3.   Roobarb's Corner   18m   S   (1976)
The area is bounded on its left by a set of three staggered corners at the point where the path along the foot of the crag drops slightly. Surmount the bulge, then continue up the second corner, or the wall on its right. At the top move left and climb the top corner by a wide crack.

4.   Pocketman   20m   HS   4b   (1998)
Start between the two trees on the flake. Take a direct line on good pockets to
the right-hand side of a yew-covered ledge. Good sharp pockets provide the key
to the bulging wall above, then finish direct.

5.   Headwall Crack   20m   VS   4c   (1998)
Start at the right side of the flake and take a direct line to a ledge below a short
corner in the headwall. Climb this, then finish immediately left of the thin
continuation crack. The route can also be started behind the second tree on the
flake.

6.   Earthworm   21m   HS   4b   (1976)
About two metres right of the flake surmount the bulge and continue up the slab
above to a ledge below the short corner of Headwall Crack. Climb this for a
couple of moves, then escape left along a line of flakes.

7.   Boneless Beef   24m   HVS   5a   (1998)
Start behind the next tree, that grows from the foot of the crag. Climb
diagonally right on to the slab, then continue up the right side of the slab to a
shallow scoop below a small overlap. Traverse right across the slab, just below
the overlap, then at the end of the overlap, flake holds lead left to the top.

★ **8.   The Decent Thing**   12m   S   (1976)
The clean swathe that cuts up the vegetated slab near the top of the descent
gully, gives a pleasant pitch. Finish directly, on the left, or on the right.

Main Crag

*The Main Crag lies about 50 metres to the seaward side of the car parking
area. At its centre are two ash trees, from which a short terrace leads leftwards
at the foot of the crag.*

9.   Sniffin' the Saddle Direct   21m   E2   5c   (1991)
Start four metres left of the trees and climb the bulging wall past a bolt.
Continue up and slightly right to a good flake on Sniffin' (bolt), then finish up
the parent route.

10.   3-2-1   20m   E2   5b   (1989)
Start two metres left of the trees below a short left-facing corner. Climb this and
the corner above, then exit leftwards, crossing Sniffin' Direct, and follow a
shallow groove to a bolt belay. Abseil descent.

★ **11.   Sniffin' the Saddle**   18m   E2   5c   (1986)
Start at the same point as 3-2-1, then pull out right at a peg, to a shallow niche,
which leads to a large ledge. Step left to gain a good flake (bolt). Sharp pockets
enable a good hold to be reached (bolt); then move up to a bolt belay. Abseil
descent.

12.   Fusion   15m   E3   6a   (1967/1986)
Follow Sniffin' to the large ledge, then climb the fine, thin, snaking crack above
to a bolt belay. Abseil descent.

13.   Girdle Traverse   38m   E1   5b,5a,–   (1968/1979-83)(1966)
1.   10m.   As Sniffin' to the large ledge.

2.   18m.   Traverse right crossing the Main Wall to a deep recess containing a fierce thorn bush. Fight past this to belay on the loose pinnacle.

3.   10 m.   Move right and climb loose rock to the top.

3a.   10 m.   **The Fertility Variation**: climb the steep wall above the belay with two pegs for aid and loose rock to safe ground above.

★★★ **14.   Triggerfinger**   18m   E3   6a   (1978)
Probably the best route at the crag, but hard for its grade. Necky at the top, where a long reach helps. Start at a shallow scoop behind the ash tree which grows nearest the crag. From the scoop, swing round right to gain a small ledge with a stalactite above (twin bolts), move up and left over a bulge (peg) and gain the ledge above by a tricky move. Climb up to a peg, then take the upper wall direct to the bolt belay. Abseil descent.

★★ **15.   Shot by Both Sides**   18m   E3   6b   (1986)
A powerful route that takes the bulge at its steepest. Start immediately right of the ash tree and climb past a bolt to the first ledge on Triggerfinger, then continue to the bulge (twin bolts). Pull over the bulge and continue directly to a peg below the overlap. Grab the flake in the middle of the upper wall and make a fingery move left for the last obvious pocket on Triggerfinger, just below the bolt belay.

★★ **16.   The Firing Squad**   19m   E5   6b   (*F7a+*)   (1984/1989)
A hard start and a bold finish, with some interesting moves between. Start three metres to the right of the ash tree at a slightly lower level and climb the steep wall past two bolts to a small resting ledge. Continue to a pair of bolts, then make a long reach to gain a ledge and a jug. Easier climbing above leads to a shallow crack; pump up this to the top, bolt belay. Abseil descent.

● **17.   Hammerlock**   22m   E4   5c   (1968/1988)
The loose left-trending grooveline that starts about three metres up Virility is probably best left well alone.

★ **18.   Virility**   24m   E1   5b   (1966)
Start five metres right of the ash trees at an obvious right-slanting gangway. Follow this to its end at a shallow niche. Step up (bolt) and go right round the arête, then boldly climb the loose wall above to a bolt belay out on the right (as for Humphrey Hymen). Abseil descent.

★ **19.   Live Rounds**   20m   E4   6a   (*F7b*)   (1989)
From immediately left of where the path meets the Main Crag, climb to a bolt in the bulging wall. Continue in a direct line passing a peg in the first break and two bolts. Abseil descent.

20.   Shooting the Load   20m   E5   6a   (*F7a*)   (1989)
Start two metres right of the point where the path meets the crag. Climb directly to the shallow niche at the end of the gangway on Virility then continue up and left past bolts to the belay on Live Rounds.

★★★ **21.   Humphrey Hymen (Met a Sly Man)**   16m   E5   6b   (*F7b+*)   (1986)
Excellent fingery climbing up the steep, grey wall. Start one metre to the right and climb the bulging rib (Rock 3 below first bolt) to a pair of bolts. Continue

up the steep wall above, past two more pairs of bolts, to a bolt belay. Abseil descent.

★ **22. Stymen** 16m E3 5c (*F6b*) (1991)
Start one metre left of the sentry-box on Noda and climb the wall past two bolts to gain a scoop. Continue up the wall above passing two more bolts to a bolt belay. Abseil descent.

23. Noda 16m E1 5a (1967)(1967-68)
A loose and rather serious climb. Start below a sentry-box in the right end of the wall. Climb to the sentry-box, move left using a hollow flake, then go up and right into a short groove. Follow the crack above to a loose finish by a small bush. Finish up loose rock.
Variation Start (5b): climb Humphrey Hymen to a right-leading ramp, then follow this to the short groove.

★ **24. Pork Pie** 16m E2 5c (*F6a+*) (1991)
From the sentry-box on Noda, move up and right, then climb the wall directly past three bolts to a two bolt belay. Abseil descent.

25. Humphrey Bogart 16m E4 6b (*F7b*) (1991)
Start four metres to the right and surmount the initial overhang (thread immediately above), then continue up the scooped wall above via three bolts. Bolt belay. Abseil descent.

26. Sunflake 15m HVS 5a (1968-75)
Start behind the large ash tree at the right end of the buttress and climb the wall to the obvious wide flake. Finish up this.

Humphrey Dumphrey Buttress
This is the shallow depression high on the hillside 40 metres right of the Main Crag. It is best approached from its right. The main feature of this buttress is a deep cave at the left side, which is split by a prominent column.

27. Humphrey Dumphrey 8m E1 5a (*F5*) (1992)
The bolt line on the left of the deep cave. Abseil descent.

28. Englebert Humphreding 8m E5 6b (*F7b*) (1994)
The bolt line starting immediately right of the column in the cave. Abseil descent.

29. Mr Self-destruct 12m E5 6b (*F7b*) (1997)
Start two metres farther right and follow the line of four bolts on the right. Abseil descent.

Edgar's Arch
Edgar's Arch is the prominent archway (an old blowhole) 100 metres right of Main Wall. At the time of writing, the arch can be reached from the shore by a collapsing path. Alternatively, it can be reached more safely from the top, just below the trig point, by an easy scramble down on the landward side. The routes are described in a clockwise direction facing the rock, starting from the landward side of the left column.

★★ **30. Mindfields** 15m E5 · 6b (*F7a+*)   (1998)
Start just right of the seaward side of the arch and climb past two bolts to the
roof, then follow an obvious line of pockets running up rightwards beneath the
roof and across Hollow Lands, to gain the deep hole on Slightly Shoddy. Finish
up this route.

★ **31. Hollow Lands** 12m E4 6a (*F6c*)   (1989)
Start beneath the landward edge of the arch and climb past an old bolt to
another bolt and a peg. Move up and go left over the roof and, from the corner
above, step left to a large, deep hole. Move up slightly to a two bolt belay at
the top of the landward side of the arch itself. Abseil descent.

32. Slightly Shoddy 11m E4 6b (*F7a*)   (1991)
Start in the corner, two metres to the right of Hollow Lands, and climb the
rounded tufa pillar past a bolt to gain a deep hole above. Continue up the
overhanging wall past bolts to a bolt belay. Abseil descent.

33. The Job 8m E1 5c   (1986)
Start at the landward side of the right column, immediately right of the easy
way to the top and climb the short, left-leaning crack above.

★★ **34. Back into the Future** 11m E7 6c (*F7c+*)   (1977/1991)
A fun route, which climbs down under the right side of the arch and then up its
seaward face. Start just to the right of The Job and climb up to a bolt, then
follow an obvious line of holds under the arch along a prominent flake crack,
past three bolts to an obvious hanging flake on the lip. The crux involves using
this flake to change from climbing downwards to pull back into the vertical.
Bolt belay above. Abseil descent.

35. Sir Edgar's Crack 10m VS 4c   (1997)
The left-slanting crack, that starts at the seaward side of the right-hand column,
proves entertaining. There are no belays at the top and so it is advisable for the
leader to be lowered down the inside of the blowhole, whilst the second should
be lowered down the seaward face. About 30 metres of rope are necessary to do
this.

Forgotten Walls

*To the right of the arch the rock steadily increases in height and there is
currently one final wall about 20 metres right of the arch itself. It is easily
identified by a prominent, right-facing corner at its centre and there is a large
grassy terrace directly below this. Unfortunately, despite the quality of the rock
and the routes, this part of the crag has been overlooked by climbers in the
past. This is a pity, because the rock is good and from midday it forms a
natural suntrap.*

*The first two climbs start from trees at a higher level. To reach them, start from
the left side of the grassy terrace and scramble up and leftwards over rock and
grass, then go back right.*

Steven Rowan sings **A Song for Europe** (E4 6b), Chapel Head Scar.   *Photo: Dave Kells*

36. Wolfman 17m E2 5b (1997)
From the trees at a higher level, climb a short groove and poor rock to a small overhang. Climb this via the obvious crack and continue until thin right-leading flake holds can be used to gain a good flake above. Pull up on this and make a long step right (bolt) to a small, high footledge and a peg and bolt belay. An abseil descent is recommended to avoid the poor top.

⋆⋆ **37. Adela** 18m E2 5c (1997)
This airy route makes the best use of the rock left of January. Start as for Wolfman and climb the groove to a large ledge on the right, then walk along this to a small, pinnacle flake. Step left from the flake and climb past a bolt to the horizontal break. Continue up (bolt), then leftwards using sharp pockets to reach a thin diagonal crack on the left. This can also be climbed more direct from the second bolt at a similar grade. Step up to a good jug on Wolfman, then make a long step right (bolt) to a small, high footledge and a peg and bolt belay. An abseil descent is recommended to avoid the poor top.

⋆⋆ **38. January** 22m HVS 4b,5a (1975-79/1981)(1997)
Well worth doing for the unique top wall on excellent, bubbly rock. Start below a deep, right-facing corner and climb this to a ledge on the left. Finish up the shallow depression in the bubbly wall above, past an in-situ thread to reach a short slab and peg. Belay just above this at two pegs in the little outcrop above. **September Arête** (4b): the sharp, left arête of the corner gives a pleasant start.

⋆ **39. Where Bolters Fear to Tread** 23m HVS 5a (1997)
Gain the arête on the right by a flake crack on its right, then step into a groove and follow this to easier-angled rock above. Just above a prominent flake crack on the right, step left to a peg and climb boldly up the right side of the top arête, until it is possible to swing round to a good foothold on the left. Finish past a peg in a short slab and belay at two pegs as for January.

⋆ **40. Oktoberfest** 30m HVS 5a (1997)
10 metres right there is a large flake at ground level. From the left side of this, climb the slab and shallow groove above to a large ledge. Step left and climb up to an in-situ thread, then traverse left on sloping footholds to a peg and round the overhang. Scramble up to a two peg belay on the left.

There is an excellent traversing wall at the very southerly end of the point, above a sloping rock platform, which gives a sustained 6a problem.

First Ascents at Humphrey Head Point

1966 Nov	**The Fertility Variation** Mick Goff, Des Marshall	
	Originally called West Wall Traverse	
1966	**Virility** Ken Woods, Tony Greenbank	
1967 Oct 20	**Noda** Mick Goff, Jim Duff, with 2 pts of aid	
1967 Oct 29	**Fusion** Mick Goff, Frank Booth	
	First free ascent by Al Phizacklea, John Topping, Aug 1986.	
1967-68	**Noda: Variation Start**	

Above: Mick Lovatt stretched out on **Maboulisme Merveilleux** (E6 6c), Chapel Head Scar.
Photo: Rollo Simey

Below: Hand it to Tom Walkington – look no feet on **The Hand Traverse** (6a), Woodwell.
Photo: Barry Rogers

1968 autumn   **Girdle Traverse**   Originally pegged, by Mick Goff and members of
Lancaster MC
First free ascent, 1979-83.
1968   **Hammerlock**   Mick Goff
First free ascent by Tony Brindle, Adrian Moore, 1988.
1968-75   **Sunflake**   Tony Greenbank
1976   **Roobarb's Corner, Earthworm, The Decent Thing**   Al Evans, Jean Horsfall
1977   **Back into the Future**   (A2)   Andy Hyslop, Jenny Hyslop
First free ascent by John Dunne, Apr 1991.
1978   **The Left Hand of Darkness**   Mark Danson, Andrew Cock, Peter Butterworth
1978   **Triggerfinger**   Pat McVey, Mark Danson
1975-79   **January**   Originally climbed as Pleasant Corner
1981 Jan   **January**   Top pitch added by Iain Greenwood, Angie Widowson

1984 May 9   **The Firing Squad**   Al Phizacklea, Rob Knight
*Independent start as now described, Luke Steer, Rick Graham, Bill Birkett,
29 Mar 1989.*
Originally climbed with 1 bolt runner. 2 more added later.
1986 Aug   **Fusion**   Al Phizacklea, John Topping
First free ascent,
1986 Aug 19   **The Job**   Paul Pritchard, Phil Kelly
1986 Sep 6   **Shot by Both Sides**   John Topping, Al Phizacklea
1986 Sep 7   **Sniffin' the Saddle**   Al Phizacklea, John Topping
1986 Sep 7   **Shooting the Load**   Al Phizacklea, John Topping
Retrobolted: 5 bolts added.
*Superseded Humphrey Cushion by Al Phizacklea, John Topping, Paul
Cornforth, Aug 1986*
1986 Sep   **Humphrey Hymen (Met a Sly Man)**   (3 bolts)   Paul Cornforth (unseconded)
1988   **Hammerlock**   Tony Brindle, Adrian Moore
First free ascent.
1989 Mar 31   **Live Rounds**   (2 bolts)   Rick Graham, Luke Steer
1989 Apr   **3-2-1**   Ted Rogers, Ken Forsythe
1989 Nov 12   **Shooting the Load**   (5 bolts)   Luke Steer, Ted Rogers, Ken Forsythe
1989 Nov 25   **Hollow Lands**   (3 bolts)   Mark Radtke, Jason Metcalf
1991 Apr   **Back into the Future**   (4 bolts)   John Dunne
First free ascent.
1991 Apr 16   **Slightly Shoddy**   (3 bolts)   Andy Hyslop
1991 May   **Sniffin' the Saddle Direct, Stymen** (4 bolts), **Pork Pie** (3 bolts)   Rick
Graham
1991   **Humphrey Bogart** (3 bolts)   Ken Forsythe
1992 Sep 7   **Humphrey Dumphrey** ((3 bolts)   Iain Greenwood
1994 Mar 29   **Englebert Humphreding** (3 bolts)   Iain Greenwood
1997 June 29 **Sir Edgar's Crack**   Dave Cronshaw, Les Ainsworth
1997 July 8   **Mr Self-destruct** (4 bolts)   John Gaskins
1997 July 13 **Oktoberfest**   Dave Cronshaw, Les Ainsworth
1997 Sep 6   **Right-hand Man**   Dave Cronshaw, Les Ainsworth
1997 Sep 19   **Where Bolters Fear to Tread**   Dave Cronshaw, Les Ainsworth
1997 Sep 20   **Wolfman, Adela, September Arête**   Dave Cronshaw, Les Ainsworth
1998 Mar 6   **Pocketman**   Les Ainsworth, Dave Cronshaw
1998 Mar 6   **Headwall Crack, Boneless Beef**   Dave Cronshaw, Les Ainsworth
1998 May 27   **Mindfields** (7 bolts)   John Gaskins

Millside Scar

Situation and Character

The crag lies at the western corner of the southern end of the Whitbarrow escarpment, directly above the hamlet of Mill Side. The routes are steep and of high quality and are generally adequately protected, mainly with bolts. Most of the loose skin of rock has now been removed from the existing routes, but there may still be a few places where care is necessary.

History

Les Ainsworth and Dave Cronshaw opened the door to the crag in 1972 after a fruitless day at White Scar by climbing *Pioneers' Cave*. Attempts to get anywhere on the central section were abandoned because they were doubtful about the rock quality and concerned about the lack of natural protection. Two years later Al Evans with Dave Parker put up the partly-aided *Pathfinder*.

It was not until 1982 that the crag received any further interest, when Ed Cleasby and Al Phizacklea climbed *Cadillac Cruiser*. This name was later shortened to *Cadillac* after Ed realized he had not 'cruised' the route; in fact he had taken a spectacular 12-metre dive off it whilst attempting the route on-sight! In the same year Iain Greenwood soloed two new routes on the upper crag, *Fossil Groove* and *Fossil Crack* then in 1983 Ian Conway and Dick Baker put up *Enter the Neutron*.

To complete the crag's history, in 1985, Paul Ingham and Pete Botterill (who had made the first free ascent of *Pathfinder* with Steve Howe earlier in the year) climbed the steep and unrelenting piece of rock right of *Cadillac* to give *Countach*.

In 1991 Rick Graham climbed *Mustang* by mistake, thinking that it was Pathfinder, but his error did not become apparent for another four years when Keith Phizacklea blitzed the crag in early 1995 to create *Firebird, Proton* and *The Green Route*, whilst Dom Donnini added *Integrali*.

Approach

From the A590 drive into the hamlet of Mill Side and park about 200 metres into the village just before a steep '*No through road*' on the right. Please park carefully and in particular avoid parking at the bottom of the hill, because this can cause problems for the milk tankers. Walk up the road on the right for about 500 metres past the Beck Head path to a permissive footpath on the left. Follow this path for a little over 200 metres to a marker post where the main path turns right. Turn left at this point and continue past a scree to the foot of the crag. About fifteen minutes from the bottom of the hill.

The Climbs

These are described from RIGHT to LEFT.

Main Crag

1.   Pioneers' Cave   19m   S   4a   (1972)
Start at the right side of the crag at a cave. Deserves a black spot after nine metres.

1. 10m.   Climb the higher cave, then exit right on to a large ledge and tree belay.
2. 9m.   The continuation gully. Now completely overgrown and best avoided.

★★ **2.   Countach** 23m E5 6b   (1985)
Retrobolted! A very strenuous route up the hanging scoop right of Cadillac. Three metres left of the cave climb the groove and step left to the ledge. Follow the thin crack through the overhang, pull over the next bulge to gain better holds and a resting place before tackling the steep flake in the scoop above. Follow this flake rightwards, then pull out left to finish. Well-protected by bolts.

★★ **3.   Cadillac** 24m E4 6a   (1982)
Retrobolted! Sustained and technical climbing, with well spaced bolts. Climb the crack six metres left of the cave to the top of a pedestal. Continue up a shallow scoop (bolt) to a smaller ledge on the left, then move up and right to a bulge (bolt). Move right on a steep wall below an overhang to reach a fine hanging groove (bolt) which leads to the top.

4.   Integrali 22m E5 6b (*F7a*)   (1995)
Six metres left. Climb easily up the short corner to the horizontal break (thread). Surmount the bulge immediately above (bolt) to enter a right-leaning, yellow groove, which leads past three bolts to the top.

★ **5.   Mustang** 21m E2 5c   (1991)
Retrobolted! Climb the wall just to the left of the short pedestal to the horizontal break (thread). Climb up to a bolt, then left to a small tree. Follow ledges rightwards to a line of bolts up the steep top wall.

6.   Firebird 20m E4 6a (*F7a+*)   (1995)
Start four metres to the left and about three metres right of a tree on the horizontal break. Climb to a bolt at the horizontal break, then enter the short, pink groove directly above and continue up the steep wall above past more bolts.

7.   The Green Route 20m E4 6a (*F7a+*)   (1995)
Start about one metre to the left and climb the short wall to the horizontal break, then continue up the left-leading line of bolts above.

★ **8.   Pathfinder** 18m E2 5c   (1974/1985)
Retrobolted! Start directly below a prominent, hanging groove high on the crag and climb a short wall to the horizontal break. Cross the gnarly wall (three bolts) to gain the groove; follow this to its top before finishing out right.

9.   Proton 8m E1 5b (*F6a*)   (Pre-1995)
Farther left the bottom section to the horizontal break becomes short and vegetated. The next route starts two metres right of an ash tree on the break. From an obvious thread and unnecessary bolt belay, climb the bulging wall (bolts) to gain grooves above.

10.   Enter the Neutron 17m E1 5b   (1983)
Climb the wall just left of the ash tree until overhanging rock bars the way. Traverse diagonally up and right to a good runner, go down and round the bulge then continue traversing to the foot of the groove. Climb this groove, exiting right at the top then climb the wall above bearing left to a small holly.

Upper Right Tier
The Upper Tier lies above and right of the Main Crag, and is reached by scrambling from the path, or by the first pitch of Pioneer's Cave.

11. Fossil Groove 9m E1 5b   (1982)
Retrobolted! Start roughly in the centre of the wall and climb a short wall to a little yew, pull on to the slab above then step right into a fine flake groove to finish.

12. Fossil Crack 12m E2 5c   (1982)
Retrobolted! Two metres to the right climb the hanging crack, passing (gently!) a doubtful block en-route.

First Ascents at Millside Scar
1972	**Pioneers' Cave** Les Ainsworth, Dave Cronshaw	
1974	**Pathfinder** (A1) Al Evans, Dave Parker	
	First free ascent by Pete Botterill, Steve Howe, Mar 1985.	
1982 Apr 12	**Cadillac** Ed Cleasby, Al Phizacklea	
	Retrobolted: 4 bolts added.	
1982	**Fossil Groove, Fossil Crack** Iain Greenwood (solo)	
	Both routes retrobolted: 3 bolts added.	
1983	**Enter the Neutron** Ian Conway, Dick Baker	
1985 Mar	**Countach** Paul Ingham, Pete Botterill	
	Retrobolted: 4 bolts added.	
1985 Mar	**Pathfinder** Pete Botterill, Steve Howe	
	First free ascent. Later retrobolted: Pegs replaced with 4 bolts.	
1991 June 28	**Mustang** Rick Graham, Ted Rogers	
	Retrobolted: 4 bolts added.	
1995 Jan	**Firebird** (4 bolts), **Proton** (4 bolts) Keith Phizacklea,	
1995 Feb	**Integrali** (4 bolts) Dom Donnini, Keith Phizacklea	
1995	**The Green Route** (5 bolts) Keith Phizacklea (unseconded)	

Raven Lodge Crag   O.S. ref. SD 463 856

**Please read the Access section before visiting
Raven Lodge Crag**

Situation and Character
This is the small limestone crag (shrouded in trees) that lies 300 metres right of White Scar, on private land, and is somewhat dwarfed by its big brother.

History
The first two routes on the crag, *Cryptic Cripple Club* and *Dry Gin*, were put up in 1986 by Dave Bates. Mark Liptrot then visited later in the year and claimed the remainder of the routes.

Approach and Access
Leave the A590 as if approaching White Scar, but turn right just after the farm (before entering the quarry proper). Follow the track for about 50 metres to a lay-by on the left. The crag lies ahead on the left.

The crag is owned by the Landowners of Crosthwaite and Lyth, who are keen to conserve the area for flora and fauna. At the time of writing, access is not permitted.

The Climbs
The routes are described from RIGHT to LEFT.

1.   Cryptic Cripple Club   10m   E3   6a   (1986)
Start at the right-side of the main cliff. Climb a wall (bolt) and move left into a short groove (tape). Ascend this to a bolt and peg belay. Abseil descent.

⋆ **2.   Dry Grin**   10m   E5   6b   (1986)
Start four metres left of Cryptic Cripple Club; climb directly up the wall passing two bolts to the belay of Cryptic Cripple Club. Abseil descent.

3.   Wodwo   17m   E5   6b   (1986)
Start six metres left of Dry Grin and climb a blind flake to its end. Move left to the central groove and climb it (peg). Continue in the same line and make a hard move over the bulge (bolt) to jugs. Continue to a large tree.

4.   Cain   21m   E4   6b   (1986)
Start 15 metres left of Wodwo, beneath a pocket with a tiny pine, go to the right of a small holly. Climb up to the second of two bolts, move right for two metres and climb a clean wall to a bolt belay. Abseil descent.

5.   Cain Direct   20m   E5   6b   (1986)
From the second bolt of Cain, climb directly over a bulge (bolt) to a peg belay. Abseil descent.

First Ascents at Raven Lodge Crag
1986   **Cryptic Cripple Club, Dry Grin**   Dave Bates
1986 Aug   **Wodwo, Cain, Cain Direct**   Mark Liptrot (unseconded)

Scout Scar   O.S. ref.   SD 486 915

Situation and Character
Scout Scar is the limestone escarpment five kilometres west of Kendal, which has been known improperly as Underbarrow Scar in previous editions of the guidebook. The rock is fairly sound with little seepage. It is quite sheltered and provides excellent training for 'the pump'. The crag provides a mixture of traditional and sport climbs.

History
The crag saw its first action way back in the last century, by a local horseman called Hodgson. The story goes that he was riding back from the pub in Brigsteer (obviously drunk), when his horse apparently decided to go back for another one and promptly leapt off the summit, taking poor Hodgson with him; the crag is known locally as 'Hodgson's Loupe'.

Development did not really catch on in this mode and it was not until the late 1970s that the Kendal Mountaineering Club started to climb. Bill Birkett and Iain Greenwood put up a few routes around that time; Cliff Brown was responsible for *Cliff's Route*, whilst Derek Jewell, Ed Cleasby and Mike Lynch added *Born Free* in 1975. The next cherry then seemed to be the free-climbing of the old aid route *Ivy League*. Numerous parties attempted the ascent, and aid was whittled down to one point. Meanwhile, Tom Walkington arrived at the crag and as he was unable to locate Ivy League, he proceeded to climb another line, *Cro-Magnon*, which freed past the peg on Ivy League. However, he reverted back to the original name, when he discovered a few weeks later that his new route was actually a free ascent of Ivy League.

1984 saw Peter Short and Alan Towse's *Kathleen* then, in 1985, Paul Carling and Mark Glaister began a new wave of activity by climbing *First Blood*. Jim Bird and Dave Seddon began to get acquainted with the crag, adding *Born to Run*. 1986 saw the crag transformed, mainly by Bird; he speckled it with shiny bolts and decorated it with red, white and blue streamers (no doubt in preparation for a visit by royalty). Bird linked the lines of bolts, producing a vast crop of routes such as *Sylvester Strange, A Fistful of Steroids, Crimes of Passion, Spectral Wizard* and *Poetry in Commotion*. Seddon joined in the fun and put up *Beers for Fears* and *Grave New World*.

Carling returned to the crag with Glaister and went away again having made the first ascent of *Telegraph Road* then Tony Mitchell added *A Vision of Things Gone Wild*, taking Bird's developments into the next dimension. Nick Conway added a real heart-stopper called *Kathleen's Nightmare* because that is what it feels like – a bad dream! Conway returned later to put up *Bar Six*.

On the nearby Barrowfield Buttress, Glen Sutcliffe and Carling put up the well-named *Crumblefoot*, whilst *Blue Screw* was the work of Carling with Stew Wilson in tow. The ubiquitous Mark Liptrot then took the trouble to tramp the short distance to the buttress and made an ascent of the obvious open and heinous-looking central groove; *Toirdealbach*.

Bird was still busy in 1987, beavering away for *$9^1/_2$ Weeks*. There was then a short lull in developments at the crag, but the calm was not to last long and by the early 1990s the drills were in action again. In 1991 the most notable additions were Andy Hyslop's impressive *Leather Pets* and Stuart Halford's popular *Ropearse*, whilst Andy Tilney established *Poetry in Motion*, an easier variation to Poetry in Commotion. Other routes to be constructed at this time were Mark Lardner's *Meet the Wife* and Jim Bird's *Born Again*.

Approach
To reach Scout Scar from Kendal, turn left from the main one-way system (A6) immediately before the Town Hall and follow the Underbarrow road to a car park just past the police radio mast on top of the hill. Cross the road to a gate and follow the path along the top of the hill. About 300 metres past the mushroom-topped shelter, immediately before the start of the first field directly below the scar, a rough path leads down to the foot of the crag.

The Climbs
The routes are described from LEFT to RIGHT.

1.   Descent Route   12m   M   (Traditional)
About eight metres to the left of Scarfoot Chimney an easy scramble at the left
side of a short buttress leads to the top of the crag. This provides a useful
DESCENT, but care should be taken on the grassy top when it is wet.

Undercut Buttress
*The first main buttress of the crag is undercut on its left side and overlaps also
guard most of its right side.*

2.   Scarfoot Chimney   15m   D   (Pre-1975)
The obvious chimney with a chockstone at its top on the left of the first buttress.

3.   9^1/$_2$ Weeks   12m   E4   6b   *(F7a)*   (1987)
Start just left of a flake in the ground and climb past two overlaps (bolts) to
enter a flake-cum-groove, then finish up this.
Variation: at the bottom it is possible to move right then back left to gain the
groove at a similar grade.

4.   First Blood   14m   E4   6b   *(F7a+)*   (1985)
From the right side of the flake in the ground, surmount the roof at its widest
point by strenuous and gymnastic moves, to a thin crack and a good hold.
Finish up the wall above past a convenient tree.

★ **5.   Sylvester Strange**   12m   E5   6c   *(F7c)*   (1986)
Λ very hard problem that surmounts the roof towards its right-hand end. It has
several bolts.

6.   Meet the Wife   12m   E6   6b   *(F7b+)*   (1992)
Start directly below the right extremity of the roof then trend right above the
roof to gain Telegraph Road and finish up this.

★ **7.   Telegraph Road**   15m   E3   6b   *(F6c+)*   (1986)
Start at the right side of the wall and climb to a bolt below a small overlap,
then step left and go up into a shallow depression. Follow this trending right
past a bolt on Sylvester Strange to a tree belay. Abseil descent.

Tower of Babel Area
*Just right of this buttress is a deep, tree-filled gully with a yew tree at 10
metres, which provides the start for the next routes. This area is further
identified by a prominent tower near the top of the crag at its right, which is
reminiscent of the Tower of Babel at Stoney Middleton in Derbyshire.*

8.   Gilmin Groove   14m   M   (Pre-1975)
Previously incorrectly named Gimlin Groove and Grimlin Groove. The obvious
grassy left-slanting break from the tree.

9.   Arête Finish   12m   VD   (Pre-1975)
The pleasant rib above the tree.

10.   Red Rock Gully   18m   S   4a   (Pre-1975)
From the tree move right into the main gully and ascend this over several bulges.

★ **11. Cliff's Route** 30m VS 4c (1975)

Ascend the gully to a clean layback crack on the right, then climb this to reach a steep groove. Climb the right arête of the groove to gain an easy-angled slab, then cross this to the right to gain the top.

12. Brain Salad Surgery 18m VS 4a (1977)

Start just right of the gully and scramble to a tree stump below an obvious broken groove, then go up this to finish up the top wall.

13. Grass Roots 21m E2 5b (1985)

A little to the right a sideways-growing tree arches over the path. Climb to the right of a bolt to a ledge, then continue into the grassy groove above and finish up this. For climbers who are intimidated by the groove itself, it is possible to climb up and left to a bolt belay and an abseil descent at HVS, 5b.

14. Born Again 24m E1 5b *(F6a)* (1992)

Start three metres farther right and climb directly through the centre of the obvious overlap, then climb rightwards until it is possible to finish up the centre of the wall above a bolt about two metres left of the crack, which is very reminiscent of The Tower of Babel' at Stoney.

★★ **15. Born Free** 26m E1 5b (1960-62/1975)

The traditional classic of the crag. Remember to carry a rack. Start three metres to the right and climb past a flake at the right side of the overlap. Trend slightly left up a vague groove then traverse right to the prominent crack on the left of the tower and follow this to the top.

★ **16. Born to Run** 24m E3 6a (1985)

Retrobolted! A direct start to Born Again. Start one metre right and climb a blunt rib past several bolts, then finish up the top wall as for Born Again. **Variation** (E2, 5c): start up Born Free to a tape thread, then step right into Born To Run.

★★ **17. A Fistful of Steroids** 24m E3 6a (1986)

Retrobolted! The line of the crag – a central pillar that just begs to be climbed. Variety and interest of this order perhaps might even give sport climbing a good name! Start two metres right and climb directly over the roof (bolts) to bushes at the left side of a ledge. Finish up the front face of the pillar, past widely-spaced bolts.

There is now a gap of about 10 metres before climbable rock re-appears.

18. Ropearse 16m E2 5b *(F6a)* (1992)

Climb the right-hand side of a yellow flake to the right-hand side of a bushy ledge, then climb the wall above, trending slightly right. Abseil descent.

★ **19. Beers for Fears** 15m E4 6b *(F7a)* (1986)

An awkward, strenuous route that starts two metres farther right. Climb through bulges, then up the wall above towards a sapling and a bolt on the left and a bolt belay a little higher up. Abseil descent.

★★ **20. Crimes of Passion** 15m E4 6a (*F7a*) (1986)
An excellent route up the centre of the wall. The explosive start is followed by intricate and sustained climbing. Start two metres to the right. Climb past a bolt to a jug, go up left past another bolt to gain a flat hold above (bolt), then ascend to the bolt belay on Beers for Fears.

★ **21. Grave New World** 12m E4 6b (*F7a+*) (1986)
Start immediately to the right of a short vegetated groove and climb the wall to a bulge, then pull straight over this to the belay. Abseil descent.

★ **22. Kathleen's Nightmare** 12m E4 6a (*F7a*) (1986)
Start two metres to the right and climb the arête direct past a bolt to finish up the loose groove above.

Ivy League Area
The wall to the right is characterized by a shallow cave at its left side.

23. Kathleen 15m E2 6b (1984)
Start below the corner with a holly in it, that rises directly above the left side of a cave. Climb awkwardly past the shallow cave to gain the stumps, move out right to gain a '*porthole*' then finish at a tree above. Abseil descent. Often wet.

★ **24. Spectral Wizard** 18m E4 6b (*F7a+*) (1986)
Pull over the roof three metres right of Kathleen (unless she moves!), past a bolt, to an obvious hold, then crank up left past two bolts to the '*porthole*' on Kathleen. Finish at the tree above.

25. Bar Six 23m E5 6b (*F7b*) (1986)
Climb the wall between Spectral Wizard and Ivy League, to finish up the pillar right of the latter.

★★ **26. Ivy League** 16m E5 6b (Pre-1975/1975/1982)
Retrobolted! The classic sport climb of the crag is short, but fierce. You NEED to do this route. From the right side of the shallow cave, climb up the obvious series of pockets (threads) then continue past a small overhang above to gain a small, left-trending corner. Climb this to the belay. Abseil descent.

★★ **27. A Vision of Things Gone Wild** 15m E5 6b (*F7b*) (1986)
A very pumpy route which is nearly a classic of the crag. Start immediately right of the shallow cave. Climb a black streak then go up to the small roof. Pull over this and climb the wall above to a bolt belay. Abseil descent.

★ **28. Idle Times** 15m E4 6b (1986)
Retrobolted! Climb the vague groove on the right then go over a bulge to gain a small corner. Climb this to finish up the wall on the right. Abseil descent.

★ **29. Leather Pets** 15m E4 6a (1991)
Start at a slightly higher level and climb the right-hand edge of the wall past a bolt to reach a short crack. Step left through the bulge, then trend slightly left and continue to the belay on Idle Times. Abseil descent.

★ **30. Stepping Out** 15m E2 5c (1975)
Climb a shallow groove just to the right of Leather Pets, then pull left on to the wall and finish up Idle Times. Abseil descent.

Poets' Corner
This is the name given to the area that starts at a big corner on the right.

31.   Broken Zipper   27m   HS   4a   (1977)
Climb the big right-facing corner past a tree to the top. Rather loose in places.
Thread belay on top.

★★ **32.   Cross of Lorraine**   25m   VS   4c   (1975)
A surprising climb, crossing rock that is much more solid than it appears from
below. Start immediately left of a left-facing, hanging groove. Follow the groove
for a short way until it is possible to stand on a flake on the left. Continue up
the slab until about one metre below an obvious hanging block it is possible to
traverse right to twin bolts (Poetry in Motion). Step up and right past a low
bolt, then go up to twin bolts below an overlap. Either finish directly at this
point, or traverse right to a tree (on Icicle), then go up to the top. Belay well
back round a bush.

33.   Poetry in Motion   12m   E1   5b   (*F5+*)   (1991)
Climb the wall one metre right, starting behind a group of hazel bushes and
continue past three bolts to the left side of an obvious overlap at half-height.
Continue, avoiding the overlap itself to a twin bolt belay, then move up right
and finish as for Cross of Lorraine.

★ **34.   Poetry in Commotion**   12m   E4   6b   (*F7a*)   (1986)
Start three metres to the right and climb up and left past three bolts, then finish
up Poetry in Motion.
Direct Finish (6b, *F7a*): continue directly to the twin bolts below an overlap on
Cross of Lorraine.

35.   Icicle   15m   HVS   5b   (1975)
Climb the obvious groove directly behind a large tree, passing a tree three
metres below the top. Better than it looks. Belay well back round a bush.

36.   Pits Stop   9m   VD   (1986)
Start about 35 metres farther right, just left of the second yew and climb
pleasantly up a wide, open groove. Exit left past a holly at the top.

Barrowfield Buttress   O.S. ref.   SD 487 908
Five minutes walk south of Scout Scar is a crag directly above the farm. The
DESCENT *is to the south of the crag. The climbs are described from RIGHT to*
LEFT.

1.   Crumblefoot   18m   E2   5c   (*F6a+*)   (1986)
Climb the right-hand side of the wall to an area of broken rock. Go up steeply
past three bolts to the top.

2.   Blue Screw   18m   E4   6b   (*F6c+*)   (1986)
A fine, sound route. Climb the centre of the wall past four bolts.

3.   Toirdealbach   18m   E3   5c   (1986)
The obvious large overhung scoop/corner on the left, direct.

First Ascents at Scout Scar

1960-62	**Born Free** (A1) Frank Booth, Jim Duff, Mick Goff	

Started further to the left than the current route.
First free ascent by Ed Cleasby, Cliff Brown, Mike Lynch, summer 1975.

Pre-1975   **Scarfoot Chimney, Gilmin Groove, Arête Finish, Red Rock Gully**

Pre-1975   **Ivy League** (A1)

Reduced to 1pt aid by Iain Greenwood, Dave Knighton, 1975.
Aid completely eliminated by Tom Walkington, 1982.

1975 Apr 6   **Cross of Lorraine**   Ed Cleasby, Mike Lynch, Cliff Brown

1975 summer   **Born Free**   Ed Cleasby, Cliff Brown, Mike Lynch

First free ascent.

1975 Nov   **Cliff's Route**   Cliff Brown, Dave Goodwin, Derek Jewel

1975 Nov   **Steppin' Out**   Iain Greenwood, Bill Birkett

1975 Nov 29   **Icicle**   Bill Birkett, Iain Greenwood

1975   **Ivy League**   Iain Greenwood, Dave Knighton

Aid reduced to 1pt.
Aid completely eliminated by Tom Walkington, 1982.

1977   **Brain Salad Surgery, Broken Zipper**   M. Robinson, Dave Parker

1982   **Ivy League**   Tom Walkington

Aid completely eliminated. Later retrobolted, 4 bolts added.

1984   **Kathleen**   Peter Short, Alan Towse

1985 Mar 11   **Born to Run**   Jim Bird, Dave Seddon

Retrobolted: 6 bolts added.

1985 Nov 13   **First Blood**   (4 bolts)   Paul Carling, Mark Glaister

1985 Dec   **Grass Roots**   Glen Sutcliffe, Paul Carling

1986 Apr 23   **Telegraph Road**   (4 bolts)   Paul Carling, Mark Glaister

1986 May 21   **A Fistful of Steroids**   Jim Bird (unseconded)

Retrobolted: 8 bolts added.

1986 May 14   **Poetry in Commotion**   (4 bolts)   Jim Bird

1986 May 21   **Pits Stop,** *The Rocky Horror Show*   Jim Bird (solo)

1986 May 21   **Grave New World**   (4 bolts)   Dave Seddon, Jim Bird

1986 May 22   **A Vision of Things Gone Wild**   (6 bolts)   Tony Mitchell, Dave Bates

1986 June 17   **Crimes of Passion**   (4 bolts)   Jim Bird, Frank Booth

1986 July 4   **Spectral Wizard**   (5 bolts)   Jim Bird, Frank Booth

1986 July 10   **Beers for Fears**   (4 bolts)   Dave Seddon (unseconded)

1986 Dec 7   **Crumblefoot**   (3 bolts)   Glen Sutcliffe, Paul Carling

1986 Dec 13   **Blue Screw**   (4 bolts)   Paul Carling, Stew Wilson

1986   **Sylvester Strange**   (4 bolts)   Jim Bird

1986   **Kathleen's Nightmare**   (4 bolts), **Bar Six**   (4 bolts)   Nick Conway

1986   **Idle Times**   Dave Bates

Retrobolted: 4 bolts added.

1986   **Toirdealbach**   Mark Liptrot

1987 July   **9$^{1}/_{2}$ Weeks**   (3 bolts)   Jim Bird

1991 Apr 21   **Leather Pets**   (4 bolts)   Andy Hyslop

1991 Aug 4   **Ropearse**   (5 bolts)   Stuart Halford

1991   **Poetry in Motion**   (3 bolts)   Andy Tilney

1992 Aug   **Meet the Wife**   (4 bolts)   Mark Lardner

1992 Dec   **Born Again**   (5 bolts)   Jim Bird

Slape Scar

Situation and Character

The crag lies on top of the Whitbarrow escarpment in a wooded area about a kilometre south-east of Lord's Seat. It is a small, south-west-facing limestone scar of generally excellent rock up to 11 metres in height, which provides some good climbing in a very pleasant environment. The crag extends northwards for several hundred metres from the main climbing area but, though the rock is often excellent, it is generally shorter and so no routes have been described. Nevertheless, there are some pleasant problems to be found on these outlying buttresses.

A visit to the crag can easily be combined with a pleasant walk to Lord's Seat or elsewhere on Whitbarrow.

History

Most of the routes that have been recorded are the work of John Shepherd, Karl Lunt, Tom Phillips and Andrew Hinton during 1991 and 1992. The only exceptions are *White Groove* in 1996 and *Worlds Apart* in 1997, both by Dave Cronshaw and Les Ainsworth.

Approach and Access

The crag is owned by Forest Enterprise whose managers are happy to permit climbing.

The crag can be reached in about 40 minutes from the car-parking space about 100 metres past that for White Scar.

From the car park continue along the track for about 400 metres to a barn just past Raven Close Scar. About 100 metres farther on, cross a ladder stile on the left and follow the track that rises first left then back right. After some way this merges with a slightly larger track (note this point, because it can be harder to find on returning) which continues upwards to a small clearing with small limestone scars on the right. Take the more distinct right fork at the start of this clearing and then about 100 metres further on, take the left fork, then fork right about 80 metres farther on. Follow the track through a gateway and about 500 metres past this there is a right-hand bend and the track starts to descend to a cairn on the right side of the track about 100 metres from the bend. Follow the path that leads right over a slight rise to meet another grassy track. Turn left along this for about 150 metres to a small 'gargoyle' boulder on the left side of the track. At this point turn right and head directly through the trees for a few metres to reach the scar at the obvious Fallen Block.

The crag can also be reached from Chapel Head Scar in about 45 minutes, or a visit can be combined with a walk to Lord's Seat.

The Climbs

The climbs are described from LEFT to RIGHT.

Roof Area

This is the rock about sixty metres left of the large, fallen block, and which is characterized by a large roof at half-height. The first route starts just to the left of this roof where a yew tree grows from the rock near the base of the scar.

★ **1.   Uclid**   8m   VS   5a   (1992)
Start just to the left of the yew. Climb the wall leftwards to a crack then move right and finish direct.

2.   The Slickrock Trail   9m   E1   5b   (1992)
Climb the bulging lower wall then move left and pull into the hanging corner at the left of the large roof to finish.

3.   Big Job   9m   E2   5c   (1992)
Ascend the broken groove leading to the obvious roof crack (crux) and a less-demanding wall above.

4.   First Past the Post   9m   VS   4b   (1992)
The wall and right-facing groove which bound the roof on its right.

5.   Party Politics   9m   HVS   5a   (1992)
Two metres to the right is another groove with a small tree near the top. Use flake cracks on the right to enter the groove.

6.   White Groove   8m   HS   4b   (1996)
The deep groove on the right.

7.   Crusher Run   8m   VS   4c   (1992)
Start just to the right and climb to a small overlap, then finish up the cracked wall above.

★ **8.   Slim Groove**   8m   HS   4b   (1997)
Climb the slim groove on the right and finish up the wall above.

Overlap Wall

About eight metres farther right there is a large square block at the foot of the crag and, about 10 metres past this, there is a wall with a small, square-cut overlap near its top.

★ **9.   Type One**   8m   VS   4c   (1992)
The left side of the overlap is marked by a shallow groove rising from a small block. From this block climb the short groove, then finish up the continuation crack.

★ **10.   Pole Position**   8m   HVS   5b   (1992)
Gain and follow a thin crack which leads to the right-hand end of the overlap. Pull out right to finish.

Fallen Block Area

The Fallen Block forms the most obvious landmark of the scar. The first routes in this area lie about eight metres to the left of it, and 12 metres right of Overlap Wall, at a short wall with a long overhang at its top.

11.   Late Scoop 6m   VD   (1998)
Start two metres left of a yew at the foot of the crag and about four metres left
of Cat 955. Climb a scoop and finish up the crack on the left.

12.   Loose Pinnacle 6m   VD   (1998)
Climb the V-groove and arête directly behind the yew.

13.   Cat 955 6m   VS   5a   (1992)
Climb a shallow groove to a long overhang, then finish up a crack above and to
the right.

14.   Easy Groove 7m   VD   (1997)
The V-groove on the right.

15.   D6 6m   VS   4c   (1992)
Start just left of a yew that grows at the foot of the crag a couple of metres left
of the Fallen Block. Climb into the depression behind the tree, then continue up
the rib on the left.

16.   Zzzz! 9m   VS   4c   (1991)
Bridge up the gap between the scar and the right edge of the Fallen Block. Pull
on to the face and finish directly.

17.   Geryon 10m   E1   5b   (1991)
Three metres right of the Fallen Block behind a straight yew tree. Climb the
wall. Move left then pull over the bulge (crux) to reach a good crack. Finish on
the right.

Main Overhang Area
*This area starts at the large roof on the right of the Fallen Block and continues
to the right end of the scar.*

★★ **18.   Pingora** 10m   HVS   5a   (1991)
Not as monumental as its namesake in Wyoming perhaps, but likewise well
worth the walk in. It is the prominent, capped groove six metres right of the
Fallen Block, which bounds the Main Overhang on its left. Ascend the bulging
lower wall to gain the groove, then pull out left round the roof.

★★ **19.   Treeline Traverse** 23m   HVS   5a   (1992)
A surprisingly impressive route for such a small crag. It combines the best of
Pingora with an airy but amenable amble into spectacular territory. Follow
Pingora to the roof, then traverse right above the overhangs on excellent rock
until it is possible to finish on the prow above the widest part of the big roof.

★★ **20.   Icarus** 10m   HVS   5b   (1997)
A good, but improbable line where blind moves lead to good but sharp holds
but the difficulties are soon overcome. Start three metres left of Spike, directly
below another flake which splits the top wall. Climb to a peg in the roof, then
use a good hold on the lip to gain an even better one and finish up the groove
on the left.

21.   Spike   10m   HS   4b   (1991)
About a quarter of the way along the Main Overhang, the roof is split by a
prominent flake. Climb this.

*Farther right the Main Overhang is split by an obvious roof crack, but this has
not yet been climbed.*

★ **22.   Amazon**   11m   E2   5b   (1991)
Four metres right of Spike is a short corner below the big roof. Climb the
corner to an awkward stance on a ledge on the left. Climb strenuously over the
roof to gain better holds above. Finish up the big crack on the right.

23.   RB22   9m   VS   4c   (1992)
The Main Overhang ends at a hanging groove and immediately right of this is
another groove capped by a small overhang. Climb this direct.

24.   Stone Rose   8m   HS   4b   (1997)
Two metres to the right is an open, slabby groove. Gain this and either finish
direct or move right and finish up the next groove.

25.   Little Yosemite Rib   8m   VS   4c   (1992)
On the right is a jutting prow. Climb the hanging corner right of this and finish
up the prow.

26.   On Line   8m   HVS   5a   (1997)
Start two metres to the right at the right side of a bulge. Ascend to a good flake
hold with difficulty then finish direct.

27.   Worlds Apart   7m   HVS   5a   (1997)
Start immediately left of a low cave at ground level. Climb to the bulge, then
move right and finish just to the left of the blunt rib.

28.   The Colostomy Kid   8m   E2   5b   (1992)
From the right-hand edge of the low cave, climb up to a flake crack on the right
of the rib. Move left (hard) and finish on good holds.

29.   Broken Groove   7m   VD   (1997)
The broken groove on the right gives a poor route.

30.   Scaredy Cat   8m   E1   5b   (1992)
Right again is another groove (shattered) with a crack to its right. Climb
dubious rock to reach and follow the crack. Move right below the tree to finish.

★ **31.   The Badger**   8m   HVS   5a   (1992)
Five metres to the right is a birch tree. Climb up and left to finish up the
square-cut groove on the right of the roof.

To the right the crag loses height and a short corner provides a useful
DESCENT.

First Ascents at Slape Scar

1991 Dec 27	**Zzzz!** Andrew Hinton, John Shepherd, Karl Lunt
1991 Dec 27	**Geryon, Pingora** Karl Lunt, John Shepherd, Andrew Hinton
1991 Dec 27	**Spike, Amazon** John Shepherd, Andrew Hinton, Karl Lunt
1992 Jan 11	**Uclid, Big Job** John Shepherd, Karl Lunt
1992 Jan 11	**The Slickrock Trail** Karl Lunt, John Shepherd

1992 Apr 5	**First Past the Post, Party Politics** Karl Lunt, John Shepherd
1992 Apr 5	**Crusher Run, Type One, Cat 955, D6** John Shepherd, Karl Lunt
1992 Apr 5	**Pole Position, Slape Victim, RB22** John Shepherd, Karl Lunt
1992 June 23	**Treeline Traverse, Little Yosemite Rib** Tom Phillips, Karl Lunt
1992 June 23	**The Colostomy Kid, Scaredy Cat** Karl Lunt, Tom Phillips
1992 June 23	**The Badger** Tom Phillips, Karl Lunt
1996 Nov	**White Groove** Dave Cronshaw, Les Ainsworth
1997 Jan 19	**Worlds Apart** Dave Cronshaw, Les Ainsworth
1997 Jan	**Slim Groove** Dave Cronshaw, Les Ainsworth
1997 July	**Easy Groove, Broken Groove** Les Ainsworth (solo)
1997 July	**Icarus, Stone Rose, On Line** Dave Cronshaw, Les Ainsworth
1998 May 14	**Late Scoop, Loose Pinnacle** John Mason, Sheilgh Vigano

White Scar

O.S. ref.   SD 459 853

**Please read the Access notes before visiting
White Scar**

Situation and Character

White Scar is the prominent natural limestone crag at the southern end of the Whitbarrow escarpment, which dominates the view from the A590 as it passes about two kilometres west of Gilpin Bridge. The climbing is steep and sustained, but even though some of the climbs are bolt-protected, without exception the routes are all serious undertakings.

The slopes to the foot of the crag have been extensively quarried to leave steep tiers of shattered rock separated by steep grass slopes and unstable scree. Nevertheless, access to the foot of the natural crag is possible, though it is a serious venture, which makes it probably one of the most difficult inland crags to get to in England. However, those climbers who are willing to negotiate this somewhat hazardous approach will be rewarded by some good climbing.

History

Many brave men have visited White Scar in the past, even before quarrying ceased. Al Atkinson, amongst others, is reputed to have paid a short visit in the mid-50s, and to have climbed directly up the scree slope (which was still being quarried at the time!) to gain the base of the crag proper. Still not intimidated he then climbed a route somewhere in the vicinity of *The Turin Shroud* utilizing a couple of pegs for aid. He made this ascent totally on-sight and has not returned to the crag, claiming that a shiver goes down his spine every time the crag is mentioned. An unknown pair of climbers from Vickers Shipbuilders is also rumoured to have made aided ascents of *The Book of Invasions* and much of *Air City*.

The first free route was added in 1973 by Dave Cronshaw and Les Ainsworth who, hungry for adventure, put up *Stride Pinnacle*. The same pair returned in 1977 and after numerous abortive attempts to gain the base of the crag via the scree slope, they finally made it, only to discover that the only means of escape was by climbing *Puppy Dog Pie*, the name of which reflects perfectly the non-quality of the climbing involved.

Development then ceased for a few years until Cronshaw introduced Dave Knighton to the crag on Boxing Day 1978 when together they made the first free ascent of *Aqualung*.

Encouraged by this significant breakthrough, they then launched a full-frontal attack on the centrepiece of the crag, the majestic and forbidding Space Buttress. Knighton took the lead for most of the routes on Space Buttress and in July of 1979 he made a free ascent of *Book of Invasions*, though retaining one point of aid to gain entry into the exit groove. A couple of months later Knighton was back with Angie Widowson to attempt a line up the smooth wall left of Book of Invasions. They only managed to complete the first pitch however, so Knighton dragged Cronshaw back screaming the following month to complete *The Prometheus Crisis*, which finished up the same groove as Book of Invasions and used the same point of aid. The two Daves then swung leads on *T.M.A.* (Tycho Magnetic Anomaly); the easiest route up Space Buttress.

Attention then changed to the Left Wing, which seemed to suit Cronshaw's style of climbing more, and so he took the lead to produce *The Turin Shroud* in December of 1981, which was completed in a huge blizzard, Knighton having completed *Torn Curtain* and *The Malacia Tapestry* the previous year.

Interest waned once again, only for Ed Cleasby to eradicate the mutual point of aid from *The Prometheus Crisis* and *Book of Invasions* in 1982 whilst making the second ascent of the former. Cleasby found that the aid move was in fact easier than the crux of Book of Invasions, six metres lower, though in a more terrifying position. Adrian Moore and Tony Brindle worked on the crag in 1987, but it was not until February 1988 that Mick Lovatt and Dave Kenyon managed to force the sustained and impressive *Introducing the Hardline*, which finished past Kelly's line of bolts through the bulges in the headwall.

Returning to White Scar in 1996 Lovatt produced the brilliant *Zona Norte*, bolted-up during a lightning storm, and the aptly named *Ten Years Gone*, with Steve Wilcock. Maintaining the scary tradition of the crag and the vertiginous nature of the climbing, Lovatt completed this trio of high-quality, extreme climbs by conjuring up *Men at Work* with Tim Whitely. During an intensive year of activity Lovatt's perseverance had succeeded in exorcising White Scar as the pariah of the crags.

Access

The crag is owned by the Landowners of Crosthwaite and Lyth, and is managed by English Nature. The landowners are keen to conserve the area for flora and fauna. The crag is an important site for peregrines, ravens and buzzards, and in the past, there were seasonal climbing restrictions during the nesting season from March to June. However, climbing is no longer permitted at White Scar due to the over-enthusiasm of climbers to develop access to this impressive crag in recent years.

It is hoped that this situation will be reviewed and that an agreement for managed climbing at the crag will be developed. Notices on site will inform climbers if the access situation changes.

Approach

From the A590, follow a track which leads directly towards Raven's Lodge Farm at the right-hand side of the crag. Follow the bend round to the left of the farm and park about 15 metres past the old quarry track. A short walk then leads past a locked gate to an old quarry building on the left, near the foot of a long, very easy-angled, black slab, up which it used to be possible to drive.

All the climbs can be reached by abseil from the top of the crag, which is reached by continuing up the obvious track above the black slab until it is possible to strike back right. However, any abseils from the top are long, serious and for most climbers are utterly frightening. Therefore, abseil approaches are only recommended for the routes on Stride Pinnacle.

For the remainder of the routes on the main crag, the preferred approach is via a steep path which leads diagonally right towards the foot of the barrel-shaped buttress at the right-hand side of the crag, known as Space Buttress. The foot of this path is reached by continuing for about 50 metres past the old quarry building then striking directly for the foot of the scree at the right-hand side of the long black slab that forms the quarry floor. Scramble on to the small terrace above, then follow an obvious ramp rightwards for about 50 metres to a point just after a short squeeze behind a small boulder and about twelve metres below the solid rock.

For many years a short length of hanging rope at this point was used to gain access to the main terrace past a very loose section. However, at the time of writing, all fixed equipment has been removed from the base of the crag at the request of the landowners. A similar, but shorter rope about 20 metres farther along the path was used to reach Puppy Dog Pie. If access is reinstated by this approach, climbers are advised that the rock is unstable and so it will be necessary to proceed with great caution.

The Climbs
The routes are described from RIGHT to LEFT as one faces the crag from the quarry floor.

Space Buttress
Space Buttress is the large barrel-shaped buttress at the right-hand side of the crag, where the rock reaches its lowest point. The climbers' path leads directly to its centre and this forms a useful reference point.

1.   Puppy Dog Pie 29m VS 4c,4c   (1977)
Start at the right-hand side of Space Buttress, about 25 metres right of the fixed rope.
1.   12m.   Climb the deep crack for eight metres, then move diagonally right to a ledge and belay.
2.   17m.   Climb the corner and chimney above to a tree belay.

2.   Air City 51m E2 5b,5a   (Pre-1970/1979)
1.   27m.   Start just right of the top of the fixed rope and climb a groove to a small ledge (peg). Continue up to a larger ledge (peg belay).
2.   24m.   Swing left on to the wall, then move up for three metres and traverse right to a shallow groove. Climb this and the steep wall above, then traverse easily left to the top.

3.   T.M.A. 59m E1 5a,5a,4c   (1979)
The easiest way up Space Buttress. An interesting outing.
1.   27m.   As for the first pitch of Book of Invasions.
2.   8m.   Traverse right along a fragile break to a peg belay on Air City.

3. 24m. Follow Air City for nine metres to below the shallow groove, then traverse right across the steep wall to an easier-angled groove and follow this to the top.

4.   The Book of Invasions   42m   E3   4c,6a   (Pre-1970/1979/1982)
An exciting route up the centre of Space Buttress.
1. 21m. From just left of the top of the fixed rope, climb the big curving groove to a hanging stance beside a holly tree.
2. 21m. Move left to a ledge, then climb the wall and overhang to a flat hold (peg and threads), reach up left to a small hidden sidepull and climb the wall (peg) to a depression below a final bulge (poor peg). Climb the thin crack above which fades out, and make a hard move right to gain the easy groove above.

5.   Zona Norte   42m   E5   6a,6b   (1996)
A superb route consisting of two contrasting pitches. The first, steep and fingery, the second bulging and powerful. The climbing is adequately protected by good but spaced resin anchors which make the route a Resin Erection Shuffle.
1. 21m. From the start of Book of Invasions, follow a line of bolts three metres leftwards to reach the holly tree belay, ignoring any opportunity to traverse off the line onto easier ground above the last bolt.
2. 21m. Attack the overhang above (crux) utilizing small flakes and layaways to reach a break. Gain a standing position over the roof above, then continue to layback the shallow groove to the final bulge. A thin rockover to the right brings the belay within reach. Abseil descent.

6.   Introducing the Hardline   42m   E5   6b,6a   (1988)
A complete contrast to the other routes. Approach as for The Book of Invasions, bolt belay.
1. 21m. From the first bolt on Zona Norte, trend diagonally left to a line of bolts. Follow this steeply (crux) to the sixth bolt and enter the hanging groove above, which slants rightwards to the hanging belay on The Book of Invasions.
2. 21m. Move up and right (peg) from the tree to a tape and pass it to gain a bolt. Climb through the bulge above to a second bolt then traverse right for two metres and pull over a second bulge to a third bolt. Step up and right (peg on left) and finish up the right arête.

7.   Men at Work   42m   E5   6b,6b   (1996)
Another excellent route taking a direct, uncompromising line up the crag. The climbing is sustained and exciting. Protection is again provided by good but spaced resin anchors.
1. 21m. Start at the left end of the large ledge, five metres left of the fixed rope. Climb the shallow groove to a bulge and turn this on the right, then step left and make a fingery pull up to better holds (crux). Continue in a direct line, crossing Prometheus Crisis on the way, to a bolt belay at the break.
2. 21m. Pull over the bulge directly above the belay. Continue trending right for about nine metres (Prometheus Crisis) to where that route escapes rightwards. Step straight up, then steep fingery climbing leads to the top. For maximum enjoyment, be sure to climb past the bolt belay to the bucket finish about one metre above and to the left. Abseil descent.

8. Ten Years Gone 42m E6 6c,6a (1996)

A truly magnificent route. Two contrasting pitches, the first is long, hard, and sustained, the second is easier but more exposed. Protection is again provided by good but spaced resin anchors.

1. 21m. From the start of Men at Work stumble leftwards for three metres on poor rock to the sanctuary of the first of six bolts. Get established on the bulging wall above and sprint for six metres (crux) to a rest in a shallow groove. Follow the groove to where it peters out at the traverse of Prometheus Crisis and continue up the smooth wall above to the mid-height belay ledge. Thin and technical.

2. 21m. Traverse right for three metres and pull over the bulge above as for Prometheus Crisis. Once established, continue straight up a thin, intermittent crack, following a line of bolts to the belay. Abseil descent.

9. The Prometheus Crisis 48m E3 5b,5c (1979/1982)

A superb, intricate line on the left side of Space Buttress. Start about 10 metres below the bolt belay on Aqualung. This is best reached by a precarious scramble, or a short abseil from Aqualung.

1. 24m. Step right round the rib and climb a short groove to a horizontal break. Follow this rightwards for eight metres (peg), then move up to a shallow depression (thread) and go up to a spike below the overhang on The Book of Invasions. Move right to a hanging belay.

2. 24m. Move left past the spike for six metres to a thread, then pull over an overhang to a good flake. Move up for three metres, then traverse right round a vague rib to the junction with The Book of Invasions. Follow the thin crack above with a hard move rightwards to finish up a groove (as for Book of Invasions). Abseil descent.

10. Aqualung 30m VS 4c (1978)

This is the deep chimney which bounds Space Buttress on its left. Note that fifty metres of rope are needed to enable the leader to reach the belay. From the path at the base of the crag, traverse easily rightwards to the chimney to a bolt belay in the cave at its foot. Climb the chimney on good holds to the cave at its top (possible belay). Traverse right across the wall to instant exposure and move round the lip of the roof to finish easily, then belay at a stake well back.

Tapestry Buttress

Immediately left of Aqualung there is a long wall, which juts forward a little and then arcs left to form the right side of a large amphitheatre. The left side of this buttress is dominated by a prominent overhang and below the central part of the buttress there is a spacious terrace.

11. The Turin Shroud 36m HVS 4c,4c (1981)

1. 24m. From the extreme right edge of the broad terrace, climb the groove/corner (currently some ivy in) to a small ledge below an arched overhang (in-situ peg belay).

2. 12m. Climb the crack to the overhang and traverse right, then pull over on to a short headwall. Belay to a tree further back.

12. The Malacia Tapestry 51m E2 5b,5c,5c (1980)

Start at a bolt belay at the left-hand end of the broad terrace.

1.   12m.   Move left to an obvious groove and follow this past a bulge to a small stance (nut belay).
2.   24m.   Traverse easily right to a perched block at the foot of a steep wall. Climb this on small holds, then trend right to below an overhang, pull round (peg on left) to a superb jug, then move right (crux) to a *porthole*. Climb up to a horizontal break and hand-traverse left (peg – hard to clip) to a ledge around the arête. Large nut belay.
2a.   24m.   Continue straight up to the bulge, level with the large roofs on the left, then traverse right along the break to the peg below the superb jug. Easier than the original pitch, but the crux is still to come.
3.   15m.   Step right and climb a short wall to the top.

13.   Torn Curtain   27m   HVS   5b   (1980)
Start about 20 metres farther left, at a higher level below the left side of the long roof. Climb delicately to the ledge, then pull over an overhang into the long flake which is followed strenuously to the top. Abseil descent.

Stride Pinnacle Area
The next route goes intricately up the centre of the Left Wing. It is reached by a difficult abseil from the top of the crag.

14.   Big Strides   25m   E1   5b   (1996)
From the left side of a ledge at the right-hand side of Stride Pinnacle, a wide crack runs up to a roof (final pitch of Sidewinder). Move left from the ledge to a loose spike level with the ledge and follow a crack running up the front of the pinnacle. The crack widens near its top, then easy climbing leads to the top of the pinnacle.

15.   Stride Pinnacle   70m   VS   4b,4a,–   (1973)
The route takes the left side of a large pinnacle on the left of the main amphitheatre of the crag, which is almost directly below a tree which overhangs the crag. Approach by an abseil over this tree (N.B. it may be preferable to tie to a tree farther back; and a sling placed round the tree may later prove useful to regain terra firma). There is a large tree belay six metres left of the foot of the route.
1.   34m.   Climb a short wall which leads to the deep crack which forms the left side of the pinnacle, and then climb this to a belay at the saddle.
2.   12m.   Step onto the wall behind on the left, then follow the obvious right-slanting weakness to a tree.
3.   24 m.   Climb steep grass to a short friable rock band just below the top. Although this can be climbed it is very unstable and it is recommended that a sling on the tree at the top is used. (If you forgot to place it earlier, then panic).

16.   Sidewinder   255m   E3   4c,5b,5b,5b,5a,4c,5a   (1996)
A girdle traverse of the right-hand side of White Scar. There is some loose rock and this is a serious expedition.
1.   35m.   From a ledge below the overhangs at the far right-hand side of Space Buttress, traverse left into a bramble-filled depression at Puppy Dog, before gaining rock and a belay at the other side.
2.   30m.   Continue leftwards to the blunt arête, then reverse the traverse on T.M.A. to reach the holly tree complete with a visitors' book. Continue at this level to a ledge below the bulge and belay on bolts as for Men at Work.

3. 45m. Continue to Aqualung at the large cave, then climb up for about three metres and traverse left at a vague break to the skyline rib and belay in the area of Turin Shroud. A loose and serious pitch.

4. 25m. Continue easily along an overhung ledge for about 10 metres, until the ledge narrows and becomes more overhung. Protection can be found below foot-level in a narrow groove. Drop down, then hand-traverse the ledge into a good, short corner and belay directly above the first pitch of Malacia Tapestry.

5. 45m. Climb down slightly, then traverse left at this level until a flake allows down-climbing to a good belay ledge at the start of Torn Curtain.

6. 45m. Traverse just above bramble height until just right of the large pinnacle (Stride Pinnacle) then climb down to a good ledge at its base, which is scattered with the remains of racing pigeons.

7. 30m. Climb the wide crack at the left end of the ledge to a recess at the right of the pinnacle. Continue to the top of the pinnacle.

Wilf's Crag
At the top of the long black slab which forms the quarry floor, there is a short, nondescript tier of compact rock that leads to a terrace below the main scree.

17. Tormented Shower 8m HVS 5a (*F5+*)   (1993)
The deep crack that forms a groove at the right side of the crag.

18. Summer Lightning 8m E2 5c (*F6a*)   (1993)
Two metres left follow a line of bolts to a bolt belay.

19. Anniversary Waltz 6m E2 6a (*F6a+*)   (1993)
At the left side of the buttress at a higher level, a line of three bolts leads rightwards.

20. Anaconda Adams 6m E2 6a (*F6a+*)   (1993)
Climb the three-bolt ladder immediately to the right of the angle of the crag.

First Ascents at White Scar

Pre-1970	**The Book of Invasions** (A2) Unknown climbers from Barrow, possibly Frank Hunsperger and Tony Dunn in early 1968	
	Reduced to 1pt aid by Dave Cronshaw, Dave Knighton, 2 June 1979.	
Pre-1970	**Air City** (A2) Unknown climbers from Barrow, possibly Frank Hunsperger and Tony Dunn in mid-1968	
	First free ascent by Dave Cronshaw, Dave Knighton, 29 Sep 1979.	
1973	**Stride Pinnacle** Dave Cronshaw, Les Ainsworth, Brian Lodge	
	One big step into the unknown!	
1977 Jan	**Puppy Dog Pie** Dave Cronshaw, Les Ainsworth	
1978 Dec 26	**Aqualung** Dave Cronshaw, Dave Knighton	
1979 June 2	**The Book of Invasions** (1pt aid) Dave Cronshaw, Dave Knighton (alts)	
	A heroic onslaught with a total disregard to the meaning of the word 'fear'.	
	Aid eliminated by Ed Cleasby, 1982 when he freed Prometheus Crisis.	
1979 Sep 29	**Air City** Dave Knighton, Dave Cronshaw (alts)	
	First free ascent.	
1979 Sep 30	**The Prometheus Crisis** (Pitch 1) Dave Knighton, Angie Widowson	
1979 Oct	**The Prometheus Crisis** (Pitch 2 – 1pt aid) Dave Knighton, Dave Cronshaw, John Gridley	
	Aid eliminated by Ed Cleasby, 1982.	
	Cleasby's ascent also cleaned up the aid point from The Book of Invasions, because the routes shared the same aid move!	
1979	**T.M.A.** Dave Knighton, Dave Cronshaw (alts)	
1980	**The Malacia Tapestry** Dave Knighton, Bernie Woodhouse	

1980 Jan	**Torn Curtain** Dave Knighton, Dave Cronshaw, Angie Widowson
1981 Dec 13	**The Turin Shroud** Dave Cronshaw, Dave Knighton
1986-87	*Wombling Way* Tony Brindle, Adrian Moore
1988 Feb	**Introducing the Hardline** Mick Lovatt, Dave Kenyon
1993 July	**Tormented Shower** (3 bolts) James Bumby, Wilf Williamson
1993 July	**Summer Lightning** (3 bolts) Wilf Williamson, James Bumby
1993 Aug	**Anniversary Waltz** (3 bolts), **Anaconda Adams** (3 bolts) Wilf Williamson, Gareth Jones
1996 July 27	**Sidewinder** Nick Green, Brian Davison
1996 Aug 25	**Zona Norte** Mick Lovatt, Steve Wilcock
1996 Aug 29	**Big Strides** Nick Green, Brian Davison
1996 Sep 8	**Men at Work** Mick Lovatt, Tim Whiteley
1996 Sep 22	**Ten Years Gone** Mick Lovatt, Steve Wilcock

Whitestones Crag   O.S. ref. SD 387 849

Situation and Character
Whitestones is a small but pleasant crag, which is situated about three kilometres south-east of Newby Bridge just above the A590.

The main crag is bounded on its left by a long broken ridge, **Long Ridge**, which gives many pleasant variations at around Diff. If the ridge is followed in its entirety, it gives the longest vertical route in the area covered by this guidebook.

History
Little is known about the early easier routes, though it is likely that Arthur Hassall did many of them, including the classic *Moose*. Iain Greenwood soloed *Missing Words* and Al Phizacklea soloed *Wild Winds* with a knotted rope alongside. During 1987 Les Ainsworth cleaned and climbed *Cartmel Groove* then returned in 1988 with his daughter Aly to add *Jess*. In 1992, Brian Davison visited the crag and climbed the last obvious line, which, for some unexplained reason, had been completely overlooked by locals, to give the interesting *W*.

Approach
The crag can be reached in about ten minutes' walk from the Newby Bridge side of the lay-by which is about 300 metres on the Kendal side of the road which is signed '*Cartmel 4*'. From a gate and stile on the opposite side of the road a direct path leads up to the crag. Visitors should beware of adders during the summer months.

The Climbs
The climbs are described from LEFT to RIGHT.

Lower Crag
Below the left-hand side of the Main Crag there is a sprawling yew at a lower level. The first climbs start about 15 metres left of this on a wall that is bounded on its left by the broken arête of **Long Ridge** *(D). These climbs are easily gained by scrambling left above the yew about ten metres below the foot of the Main Crag.*

★ 1.   Two Overhang Route 17m HS   4a   (1979-83)
Start at the lowest point on this part of the crag, midway between Long Ridge
and the yew. Climb a short, easy, right-slanting groove to the first overhang,
then follow a flake crack leftwards to a large ledge. Step right below the second
overhang on to the slab above the first overhang and continue rightwards to a
shallow groove. Ascend this to a small ledge, then follow the leftward-leading
break to the arête, and finish up this.

2.   Cartmel Groove 14m VS   4b   (1987)
From the top of the initial groove of Two Overhang Route, continue over the
overhang with difficulty then follow the continuation groove past the small ledge
on Two Overhang Route, until it is possible to step left on to the arête at the
top.

3.   Elk 15m VD   (1986-87)
Five metres farther right, above the left side of the broken rocks, is a flat ledge
at three metres. The climb takes a direct line up the wall from this ledge.

Main Crag
*The crag now becomes a little broken, but to the right of the yew and two trees,
the Main Crag starts at a higher level. The main feature of this part of the crag
is an overhang that splits much of the crag at mid-height.*

4.   Stag 26m S   4a,4a   (Pre-1969)
1.   12 m.   At the left side of the terrace below the Main Crag there is an
obvious, short, awkward corner. Climb this to a tree, then continue over grassy
ledges to a spike belay below an obvious groove.
2.   14 m.   Just to the right of the belay is a bulging wall which is split by two
cracks. Climb this wall using the cracks to reach a slab, then continue easily to
the top.

★ 5.   Missing Words 24m HVS   5b   (1979-83)
Start one metre to the right, and climb direct past two ledges to two small
blocks below a short, blunt arête. Go up this to the break, then ascend the
overhang above on its left. Continue on pockets to the top, with an interesting
move over the next overhang.

★ 6.   The V 26m VS   4c   (Pre-1969)
At its centre, the prominent overhang is split by a deep V-notch. Start below the
right-hand side of the overhang and climb up the left side of a large block to
the overhang, then move left for about three metres to a smaller block directly
below the notch. Climb into the notch on good holds to reach a slab, then finish
up the wide crack above.

★ 7.   W 25m HVS   5a   (1992)
One metre farther right is another, smaller, notch in the overhang. Climb to
below this, either via the block on the right, or up the short pocketed wall
immediately below. From the smaller block on The V, use a hidden hold in a
pocket on the left (this can be difficult to find, but it is good) to make a
spectacular pull up into the shallow groove above. Continue up this, then finish
on good holds. The move over the roof is interesting and is not as hard as it
appears, nevertheless a long reach is extremely helpful.

8.   Direct Route   24m   HS   4a   (Pre-1969)
Climb the left-hand side of the large block to the overhang, as for The V. Step
right on to the block itself, then pull on to the slab at the left-hand groove and
follow this to the top.

9.   Jess   37m   S   –,4a   (1988)
A rising traverse directly below the prominent overhang which splits the Main
Wall. Should get easier with traffic.
1.   23 m.   Climb Chimney Route for five metres then traverse left immediately
below the overhang and continue to the block below the roof of The V. Swing
round this block, then continue to a blunt arête and cross a grassy bay to reach
the spike belay on Stag.
2.   14 m.   Climb the obvious groove passing an awkward bulge at half-height.

10.   High-level Girdle   29m   S   4a   (1987)
Follow Chimney Route on to the slab then continue horizontally left until a
rising line of small holds can be followed to reach Missing Words. Step down a
little and continue past Stag to the groove on its left. Step across this, then
climb diagonally left for a few metres to finish.

11.   Chimney Route   25m   VD   (Pre-1969)
Climb up to a cave below a deep, wide crack, then step left on to the slab and
go back right to the crack. Continue for a couple of metres, then either finish up
the chimney, or more pleasantly up the slab on the left.

12.   Wild Winds   24m   HVS   4c   (1981)
Climbs the sharp arête right of the chimney. Follow Chimney Route to just
below the chockstone above the cave, step right, then climb the arête on its right
side. Easier than it might appear.

★★ **13.   Moose**   25m   HS   4b   (Pre-1969)
An excellent route, with a bold top half, which may intimidate some leaders.
One of the classics at its grade. Climb the block which forms the right side of
the cave on Chimney Route, to the overlap, then make an awkward step right
on to the nose and finish up the steep wall.

14.   Cracked Wall   23m   HS   4b   (Pre-1969)
The aptly-named wall on the right. Climb to a recess just below the nose of
Moose, then step up and move right up the wall and shallow groove. It can be
made slightly easier by climbing the wall farther right.

15.   Easy Chimney   14m   D   (Pre-1969)
Start two metres to the left of the obvious rowan tree which grows from a split
block at the right side of the crag. Climb the left wall of the obvious groove,
then climb the obvious groove/chimney.

16.   Ridge   15m   VD   (Pre-1969)
Climb the ridge directly behind the rowan tree to a ledge with a small tree on it.
Step right and go up, then regain the ridge and follow it to the top.

First Ascents at Whitestones Crag

Pre-1969	**Stag, The V, Direct Route, Chimney Route, Moose, Cracked Wall, Easy Chimney, Ridge**
1981 Sep 20	**Wild Winds** Al Phizacklea (solo with a knotted rope alongside)
1979-83	**Two Overhang Route**
1979-83	**Missing Words** Iain Greenwood (solo)
1987	**Cartmel Groove** Les Ainsworth (unseconded)
1986-87	**Elk**
1986-87	**High-level Girdle**
1988	**Jess** Les Ainsworth, Aly Ainsworth
1992 May 30	**W** Brian Davison (unseconded)

Minor Crags

Barker Scar   O.S. ref   SD 334 783

A low broken crag next to the Leven estuary just north of the railway viaduct.
It is reached by turning left about one kilometre north of Holker Hall along a
road that leads to a caravan site by the sea. Walk along the beach to the crag.

Crocodile   (9m, E2, 6b) follows the centre of the first big clean wall – a
'snappy' route, one bolt.

Farther right is a conspicuous cave. An aid route – **Harry Worth Goes to
Hollywood**   (A2) – crosses the roof crack (big Friends). An unusual route, it
finishes on the floor!

There are several boulder problems on the wall outside the cave.

Black Yews Scar   O.S. ref.   SD 439 867

It has been agreed not to climb on this crag, which is a northward continuation
of Chapel Head Scar, in order to obtain access to Chapel Head. It is mostly
broken, but reaches nine metres in places.

Bow Marble Breast   O.S. ref   SD 428 938

A steep slate crag above the hamlet of Thorneyfields, three kilometres north of
Crosthwaite. One route of 5a has been reported up the groove high up in the
centre of the diamond-shaped buttress.

Brant Fell   O.S. ref.   SD 409 962

Reached from Bowness on the B5284 Kendal road, the fell is the first open
ground on the left, just above the steep hill. The crag is near the summit of the
fell and commands the finest view of any crag in this guidebook. It is a popular
bouldering area for local climbers; short steep slate with a sustained test-piece
traverse (6b).

High Newton Crag   O.S. ref. SD 404 828

This is a small quarry situated adjacent to the A590 just south of High Newton.
It has two climbs which are well worth 20 minutes effort on the way to, or out
of, The Lake District. Climbers are asked not to park on the grass verge below
the crag.

The climbs lie on a steep slab at the north end of the quarry. Some doubtful
holds exist due to the nature of the rock. Now overgrown.

1.   Cat o' Nine Tales   12m   HVS   5b   (1981)
Climb the obvious right-slanting crack.

2.   The Wall   12m   E1   5c   (1981)
Takes the wall to the left. It is easier if started from the left, rather than direct.

Some other routes include the deep groove right of Cat o' Nine Tails (VD), and
the sharp arête just right (5a). The slab in the lower part gives routes of VD and
S, and the broken arête right of this is VD.

First Ascents at High Newton Crag
1981 Jan   **The Wall**   Mark Danson
1981 Mar 28   **Cat o' Nine Tales**   Ed Cleasby, Al Phizacklea

Kettlewell Crag   O.S. ref. SD 504 933

A short limestone crag on the north-west side of Kendal provides some
interesting bouldering. Park just off the Windermere road into Kendal, opposite
Fairfield Lane, then follow a footpath up the hillside to a derelict building. Skirt
round this, then head diagonally left to the corner of the next field and walk
back for about 200 metres to the crag.

Latterbarrow Crag   O.S. ref. SD 440 830

A steep limestone outcrop 10 metres high, which is hidden in the wooded
hillock opposite the Derby Arms Hotel. Ask permission from the farmer at
Latterbarrow Farm.

Lindale Slabs   O.S. ref. SD 418 817

These clean, open, slate slabs are clearly seen from the Lindale bypass on the
slopes of Newton Fell. They are reached from Lindale by taking the narrow
road next to the pub at the bottom of the hill. The slabs are 15 metres high and
there are several cracks running up them. These hold routes of D/VD grade,
which are used by a local outdoor centre. Bolt belays at the top. In order to
prevent congestion at the crag, any groups intending to visit the crag are asked
to ring Castle Head Field Centre, (Grange 34300) prior to their visit. Individuals
should ask permission from the farmer who lives just north of the crag.

Meathop Quarry   O.S. ref SD 433 798

This limestone quarry lies directly above the railway about two kilometres
north-east of Grange-over-Sands. To reach it from the A590, drive to Meathop
village, turn right, then continue to a sharp bend at a bridge over a small river.
Park in the broken quarry and follow a path round to the right into the main
quarry.

Although much of the quarry is well over 20 metres high, it is generally stepped and broken by ledges. About two dozen climbs have been recorded, but the lack of vertical features makes them difficult to identify and, as it is possible to climb at VD to HS throughout most of the quarry, it has been decided not to include detailed descriptions. For visitors who like bouldering, there is also some good traversing on the beach side of the railway line, on natural rock.

In some parts of the quarry there are interesting possibilities in the harder grades, but some cleaning will generally be necessary.

Yewbarrow   O.S. ref.   SD 405 782

Yewbarrow is a small limestone crag in the woods above Grange-over-Sands, which gives about ten climbs of up to nine metres. From the library in the centre of Grange, it is reached by following Grange Fell Road towards Cartmel for about 600 metres to Eden Mount Road on the right. Turn up this to a T-junction (Charney Well Lane). From this junction a path leads diagonally right across the wooded fellside past some small outcrops, then go down slightly to the foot of the main crag.

Furness Area

The Furness Peninsula is conveniently identified as the land lying to the south of the A5092 Broughton to Greenodd Road. Apart from Goldmire Quarry, which provides some excellent, longer climbs, the crags in this area are relatively small and only of interest to locals.

Goldmire Quarry   O.S. ref.   SD 219 739

Situation and Character

Goldmire is an extensive limestone quarry which lies about one kilometre west of Dalton-in-Furness and five kilometres from Barrow-in-Furness, which can be seen from the Dalton bypass.

Much of the quarry comprises shattered and loose walls of unstable blocks, but amongst them there is the stunning Black Slab, which is a solid sweep of black-stained limestone, 30 metres high, and set at an angle which increases from 60° to 80° at its steepest end. This slab is a natural fault line laid bare by the quarrying, which displays few features and is quite unlike any other limestone wall in the North. The face of the slab, at one time buried deep in the earth, is covered in some areas by calcite crystal formations. These are loose and brittle, often snapping off with alarming results, but the underlying rock is basically sound.

History

Although Goldmire Quarry is clearly visible from Barrow, it was neglected by climbers until June 1993, when Al Phizacklea, John Holden and Andy Rowell decided to make a visit. They immediately dismissed all thoughts of climbing on the loose, lower tier which was still being worked, but were impressed by one section of the upper tier, on which they staked their claim with *Insular Peninsular*. By the end of the month, Phizacklea returned and added *Black Gold* over the prominent roof at the right-hand side, whilst Holden introduced John Martindale, who climbed *Neibelheim*.

A week later all four climbers returned and spent a memorable evening on the crag, during which the honours were equally shared. The two plum routes of the evening were Phizacklea's companion route to Black Gold, which he called *Welcome to Barrow, Gateway to Oblivion* and the obvious winding runnel on the left, which Holding claimed as *Baedecker for Metaphysicians*. However, *Paranoid Man* by Rowell was also worthwhile and Martindale's *Gold Digger* opened up more rock at the left-hand side. This was a particularly busy night for Holden – He arrived at the crag well after 8 o'clock, but only two and a half hours later he was in the pub, having participated in four first ascents. A few days later, Phizacklea caught *The Last Train to Millom*, which marks the current leftward extent of developments at the quarry.

Towards the end of July, Phizacklea climbed *Goodbye, Cruel World*, to complete a fine trio of routes over the roof at the right-hand side of the crag, whilst Holding and Martindale claimed *The Glass Bead Game* and *Hunding* respectively.

A couple of weeks later Phizacklea returned to the quarry and started off by climbing *Bypass to Nowhere*. He was well into his second route of the day, when the police arrived to evict the climbers. A somewhat dispirited Phizacklea finished *Caught by the Fuzz* and then left. However, there was still a route that had been cleaned, but not climbed and so just over a week later, he returned with Rowell fairly late in the evening by a more circuitous route, in the hopes that their approach would be unnoticed. The pair kept out of sight at the top of the crag and remained hidden whilst they donned all their gear. They abseiled down already roped up and Rowell started to climb even before Phizacklea had finished his abseil. They claim that they were both at the top within slightly over five minutes, then they quickly merged into the night, coiling their ropes as they went. They named their route *Arrested Development*, but though quarrying at Goldmire ceased a few months later, this was to be the last visit by climbers for almost five years.

During the final stages of the preparation of this guidebook, Dave Cronshaw and Les Ainsworth decided that the time was ripe to revisit the quarry, which had been abandoned by the quarrymen since the Dalton bypass was completed in early 1994. They were impressed by what they saw and promptly repeated several of the routes, which confirmed the quality of the climbing. During the first weekend in August 1998, Cronshaw discovered *Au* and then they spent some time cleaning the grass from an obvious diagonal break that split the crag. This gave a pleasant route, which they called *The Pipe*, because of a curious fossil near its top – Goldmire was back in business.

Approach and Access

Since the completion of the Dalton bypass in 1994 the quarry has been closed and the buildings have been demolished, so further quarrying operations in the near future seem highly unlikely. However, there is currently no access agreement and the quarry owners did evict climbers when it was active. So please keep a low profile, as the local residents have been known to report climbers to the police.

To reach Goldmire, follow the A590 towards Barrow-in-Furness, to the roundabout at the end of the Dalton by-pass. This is at the foot of a long downhill section that curves through a cutting and is about five kilometres before Barrow. Turn left at this roundabout, then turn left towards Thwaite Flat after nearly a kilometre, take the next road on the right and park carefully at a gate by the railway. Walk along to the lower tier of the quarry, then follow the obvious path that rises up on the right to reach the foot of the upper tier.

The Climbs

All the climbs that are described lie on a prominent black wall on the upper tier and are described from RIGHT to LEFT. The first route starts about 50 metres left of the main shattered corner of the upper tier, where the wall is characterized by a prominent curving overlap and roof halfway up the crag. It is hoped that there will soon be some belay stakes at the top of the crag.

DESCENT is by walking at the right-hand side by walking along the top, but please take care at the point where the top of a collapsed corner has to be crossed.

★ 1.   Goodbye, Cruel World   30m   E3   5c   (1993)
Start at the left edge of the steep spoil-heap at the foot of the wall and scramble
up the edge of the spoil to reach a thin flake in the wall to the left. Follow this
to a horizontal crack at 12 metres, then step left to a good hold. Stand on this
then delicately climb leftwards to reach an excellent crack below the roof. A
fingery swing directly over the roof leads to a good break (Friend $2^1/_2$), step
right and continue up the headwall to finish on good holds.

★ 2.   Welcome to Barrow, Gateway to Oblivion   30m   E2   5c   (1993)
Start five metres to the right of Black Gold and gain a shallow groove using
good pockets, then continue up a crack to the overlap. Pull through this
strenuously on brilliant holds to reach a fine crack system above. Follow this,
slightly right to the final roof. and pull carefully over this to reach the top.

★★ 3.   Black Gold   30m   E2   5c   (1993)
In the past, climbers driving down the Barrow cul-de-sac were probably lost.
However, this route now provides a good reason to travel into Furness. It is a
fine climb with some good positions, which is sustained at a reasonable grade
throughout and is reasonably protected. The overlap is easier than it appears
from below and there is a delicate crux high up. Follow the prominent crack
system at the left-hand side of the curving overlap to the top overlap. Continue,
using the wall on the left and the wide crack, to gain a shallow snaking runnel
in the wall above. Climb this delicately past an excellent nut slot to reach a
horizontal crack below the final scoop and finish up this. It is also possible to
finish up a nose on the left side of the scoop.

4.   Caught by the Fuzz   30m   E1   5b   (1993)
Start 15 metres to the left and three metres right of an obvious winding runnel.
Climb up a clean slab to a flake, move up and right to about three metres below
a grassy pock-marked overlap, then trend diagonally right into a small vague
scoop. Continue up and right, past two good runners to a ledge. Climb leftwards
on calcite flakes to the diagonal break of The Pipe and step on to the wall
above. Pull up to a thin crack and climb this directly to the top.

★ 5.   Baedecker for Metaphysicians   28m   E1   5a   (1993)
This pleasant route that follows the obvious winding runnel 18 metres left of
Black Gold. Enter the rounded niche at three metres and continue, crossing the
diagonal line of The Pipe, following the runnel until it fades. Climb the wall
above, keeping right of the grassy area, then trend left to a dirty finish.

6.   The Pipe   35m   HVS   4c   (1998)
This climb is named after a curious fossil formation in a pocket on the right
about a metre below the top. It should improve and become slightly easier with
traffic. Follow the obvious diagonal break that runs rightwards across the face.
About three metres after passing the curving runnel on Baedecker, it is
necessary to step right to a small ledge, then climb the wall for a short way to
regain the break.

An unknown climber makes some magical moves on **Spectral Wizard** (E4 6b), Scout Scar.

Photo: Dave Cronshaw

★ 7.   The Insular Peninsula   28m   E2   5b   (1993/1998)
Start just left of the foot of The Pipe, below a smooth slab, and climb up then
left to a good hidden pocket at five metres. Balance up to gain a thin crack and
follow this and the centre of the clean slab above to a bolt. Continue to the top
via interesting quartz crystals. The crack/runnel on the left gives an easier start,
though it is destined to become an independent line.

8.   Au   27m   VS   4c   (1998)
Start 13 metres left of the foot of The Pipe at a short, broken runnel. Climb this
and the continuation flake past a slight bulge until it is possible to step left and
climb the short wall to the crack above. Climb this and finish up a short
depression at the top.

9.   The Glassbead Game   29m   VS   4b   (1993)
Climb the runnel on Au, then go left and up a pocketed slab directly to reach a
good hold. Continue straight up a vague depression to a steepening, then step
left and climb straight up to a dirty finish.

★ 10.   Paranoid Man   28m   HVS   4c   (1993)
Climb the scalloped crack six metres left to a small ledge and continue direct,
passing a prominent white rock scar at its left edge. Move up a delightful slab
to the foot of a shallow runnel, climb this to its top, then exit carefully above.

★ 11.   Arrested Development   28m   E1   5b   (1993)
Follow the thin crack up the slab about six metres to the left, and just right of a
prominent narrow runnel, to a peg, where thin moves lead to a small overlap.
Pull over on to the slab, and climb the delicate scoop above, pulling over the
final block to finish on top.

12.   Gold Digger   28m   HS   4a   (1993)
Climb the prominent narrow runnel until it deepens, and continue to where the
angle eases. Avoid the deep grassy continuation by taking a shallow line on the
right, parallel to the grass, to a slab below the headwall. Stride left across the
grass and move up past a spike and an easy corner to the top.

13.   Hunding   25m   VS   4c   (1993)
Start two metres to the left and scramble up three metres of grass, then follow a
narrow vertical runnel to a horizontal line at eight metres, just below the peg on
Neibelheim. Make a long step right across the peach-coloured streak on the slab,
then climb directly over the rounded grey bulge then step right and finish easily
as for Gold Digger.

14.   Neibelheim   26m   HS   4a   (1993)
Climb into an open hole one metre farther left and continue directly to reach a
thin crack at eight metres. Follow this slightly rightwards, past an ancient peg
until the angle eases, then cross delicately right to join the upper section of Gold
Digger, and finish up this.

Unknown climber shoots up **Triggerfinger** (E3 6a), Humphrey Head Point.

Photo: Al Phizacklea

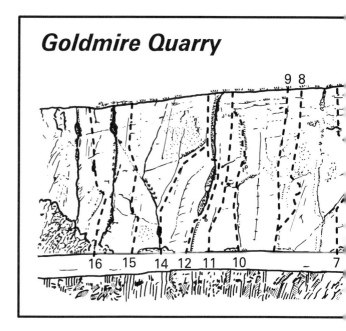

Goldmire Quarry

15.   Bypass to Nowhere   27m   E1   5b   (1993)
Start from a small block below the smooth slab on the left. Climb directly up
the slab to a nut slot, then follow a short ramp on the left to a clean wide crack.
Continue straight up the easier slab to a spike just left of a grassy crack. Climb
the wall above to a nut slot, then move left and go up to a peg. Finish directly
up the headwall on good holds.

16.   The Last Train to Millom   26m   E2   5c   (1993)
Start five metres farther left at the base of a stack of blocks resting against the
face. Climb on to the lower right edge of the blocks and pull on to the wall to a
flake pocket (Friend 3). Climb up and slightly right, following a shallow groove,
to reach a nut by the right-hand crack. Traverse diagonally left into the centre of
the face to a conspicuous hole, then climb the fine wall above, past a peg, to
reach the short finishing crack.

First Ascents at Goldmire Quarry

1993 June 24   **The Insular Peninsula**   Al Phizacklea, John Holden, Andy Rowell
                      Extended by Dave Cronshaw, Les Ainsworth, 4 May 1998.
1993 June 27   **Black Gold**   Al Phizacklea, John Holden
1993 June 28   **Neibelheim**   John Martindale, John Holden
1993 July 5   **Paranoid Man**   Andy Rowell, John Martindale, Al Phizacklea, John Holden
1993 July 5   **Welcome to Barrow Gateway to Oblivion**   Al Phizacklea, John Holden
1993 July 5   **Baedecker for Metaphysicians**   John Holden, John Martindale, Andy Rowell
1993 July 5   **Gold Digger**   John Martindale, John Holden
1993 July 9   **The Last Train to Millom**   Al Phizacklea, John Holden
1993 July 20   **Goodbye Cruel World**   Al Phizacklea, John Holden, Andy Rowell
1993 July 22   **The Glassbead Game**   John Holden, Andy Rowell
1993 July 28   **Hunding**   John Martindale, John Holden, Al Phizacklea
1993 Aug 14   **Caught by the Fuzz, Bypass to Nowhere**   Al Phizacklea, Brian McKinley
1993 Aug 22   **Arrested Development**   Andy Rowell, Al Phizacklea

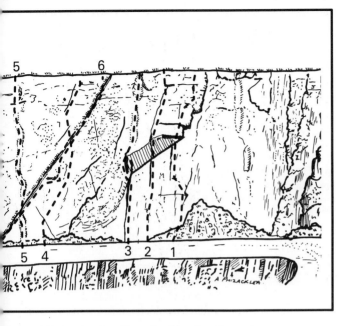

1998 Aug 1   **Au**   Dave Cronshaw, Les Ainsworth
1998 Aug 2   **The Pipe**   Dave Cronshaw, Les Ainsworth

Minor Crags

Birkrigg Quarry
O.S. ref.   SD 282 747

This quarry is on Birkrigg Common, a low rounded hill three kilometres south of Ulverston. The best rock is in the low quarry, below the road level just left of the main face, is a popular bouldering and training area, often viewed from the 'galleries' by the public. The rock is limestone, up to nine metres high. It has become highly polished in some areas, but the rock is of reasonable quality. However, much of the unpolished stone is friable and loose.

The usual test-piece is the low-level traverse which runs from left to right (5c). There is also a very bold upper traverse along the horizontal break near the top of the quarry, along the left and central walls (5c).

Of note are the superb boulder problems on the left wall. Use your imagination and fingers!

Donkey Rocks
O.S. ref   SD 211 867

This is a steep quarry, about 700 metres south of Broughton beside the Foxfield road. The rock is a geological curiosity, with very smooth slate which has a most unusual blistered structure and is stained with hematite. There are only three 'asinine' routes at present.

1.   Hee Haw   20m   E2   5b   (1978)
The widest of the cracks in the right end of the wall, which is further identified
by some shallow drill holes.

2.   Muffin' the Mule   20m   A2   (1983)
The thin crack about two metres left of Hee Haw, climbed on knife-blades and
crack 'n ups.

3.   No Sheep 'till Broughton   18m   E3   5c   (1991)
Climb the steep finger crack in the centre of the left-hand section of the quarry,
which lies slightly forward of the rest of the main wall.

First Ascents at Donkey Rocks
1978   **Hee Haw**   Ian Cooksey
1983 Dec 30   **Muffin' the Mule**   Al Phizacklea, Rob Knight
1991   **No Sheep 'till Broughton**

Dunnerholme   O.S. ref.   SD 211 799
A curious limestone plug in the Duddon Estuary, which is visible from the
A595. Approach is via Grange Marsh Farm, and care is needed with parking to
prevent blocking access.

On the left is a set of short friction slabs with several eliminate problems
marked in blue paint, as well as a delicate girdle. Around the back is a
continuously overhanging low wall with a desperate monster girdle.

The routes that are described are located in a cove on the edge of the estuary,
which faces Millom and Black Combe. These are described from RIGHT to
LEFT.

1.   La Villa Strangiato   8m   E1   5b   (1993)
Climb directly up the short wall on the right to the upper arête.

2.   Different Strings   9m   HVS   5a   (1985)
Surmount overhangs to reach the horizontal break, then finish slightly rightwards.

3.   Natural Science   10m   E2   5c   (1996)
The thin crack in a short white wall is gained by a rising traverse from the left.
It is also possible direct.

4.   Centre Wall   9m   VS   4c   (Pre-1994)
Climb directly up the centre of the short, wall that lies in the angle of the cove.

5.   Permanent Waves   9m   E3   6b   (1994)
The right-hand boltline up the overhanging left wall.

6.   Caress of Steel   9m   E4   6c   (1996)
The central boltline is very fingery to start.

Mandarin (E2 5b,5b), Hoghton Quarry.   *Photo: Leo Dickinson*
Christeena (VS 4c), Wilton One.   *Photo: Ken Wilson*

7.   Grace Under Pressure 9m E2 5c   (1993)
The overhanging crack system on the left.

8.   Power Windows 9m E2 6a   (1993)
Start one metre farther left and climb over the roof passing three bolts.

First Ascents at Dunnerholme
1985   **Different Strings** Rob Southall, Tony Thompson
1993 July 31   **Grace Under Pressure** Rob Southall, Tony Thompson
1993 Aug 1   **La Villa Strangiato** Rob Southall
1993 Sep 25   **Power Windows** (3 bolts) Tony Thompson, Rob Southall
Pre-1994   **Centre Wall**
1994 June 5   **Permanent Waves** (4 bolts) Tony Thompson
1996 May 19   **Caress of Steel** (4 bolts) Tony Thompson
1996 Aug 8   **Natural Science** Rob Southall, Tony Thompson

Hoad Slabs   O.S. ref. SD 296 790
Clearly seen from the A590 just north of Ulverston, these clean slate slabs are a
popular practice ground. Park in the steep lane below the hill. The slabs
themselves lie halfway up the hill about 150 metres from the gate at the end of
the lane. From the gate, keep parallel to the A590 for about 50 metres, then
strike directly up the hillside to the prominent, steep slabs, directly above a
bench on a tarmac path.

The routes start behind a short protecting flake and are described from RIGHT
to LEFT. The rock on top of the slabs has been vandalised by the needless
insertion of an over-abundance of belay bolts.

1.   Railway 20m HS 4a   (Pre-1976)
Climb the right side of the slab, then finish up the right-hand side of the top
arête.
2.   Devil's Armchair 20m S 4a   (Pre-1976)(Pre-1976)
Climb the central crack to the sentry-box near the top and finish direct. Classic.
Armchair Variant (HS, 4c): move left from the sentry-box and finish up the
slab.

3.   Hoad Road 22m HVS 5a   (1978)
A straight eliminate starting midway between Devil's Armchair and Airway.
Climb the slab directly via a very vague crack. The thin top slab is the crux.

4.   Airway 22m VS 4b   (Pre-1976)
Start six metres to the left of Devil's Armchair and climb the thin crack to the
large ledge. Move right on good holds and either finish directly up the left arête
of the top slab, or, move left and climb the short slab and overhang direct.

5.   Hoad Way 25m D   (Pre-1976)
Start from the lowest point of the slab and climb up to the large ledge, move
right and up an easy-angled groove to an obvious, slightly rising footledge and
follow this across the slab to the sentry-box on Devil's Armchair. Move right
round the top arête and finish up a groove.

Martin Boysen leads The Golden Tower (E2 5a,5c), Anglezarke Quarry.   *Photo: Ken Wilson*
Martin Boysen on Cameo (E1 5a), Wilton One.   *Photo: Ken Wilson*

First Ascents at Hoad Slabs

Pre-1976   **Railway, Devil's Armchair, Armchair Variant, Airway, Hoad Way**
1978   **Hoad Road**   Mark Danson

Stainton Quarry   O.S. ref.   SD 243 727

This quarry lies near to Stainton Village, just south-east of Dalton-in-Furness.
Although six routes existed in the old quarry, it has now been filled, leaving
only the left-hand side. The Main Quarry is still being worked and climbers are
most unwelcome.

Stott Park Heights Crag   O.S. ref.   SD 368 894

Approach is direct through the woods from the lay-by on the Newby
Bridge–Hawkshead road, just south of the south entrance of the YMCA camp.
Short but pleasant.

Previous Editions

1969 *Lancashire. A Guide to Rock Climbs.* **Ainsworth, L. and Watkin, P.**
Rocksport. Writers included: Les Ainsworth, Allan Allsopp, Arthur
Hassall, Paul Horan, J Ingham-Riley, Hank Pasquill, Michael Pooler,
Tony Sainsbury, Walt Unsworth and Stew Wilson.

1972 *Lancashire Update. Vols 1, 2 and 3.* **Ainsworth, L. and Meakin, R.**

1975 *Lancashire. Rock Climbs in the North West.* **Ainsworth, L.** Cicerone
Press. Writers included: Chris Calow, G. Harrison, J. Holmes, Ken
Lathom, S. Nicholson, Stu Thomas and John Yates (all for Liverpool
Area); Allan Allsopp, Les Ainsworth, Dave Cronshaw, Al Evans, Phil
Garner, Bob MacMillan, Dave Parker, Hank Pasquill, David
Powell-Thompson, Walt Unsworth and Bob Whittaker.

1979 *Rock Climbs in Lancashire and the North West. Supplement.*
Ainsworth, L., Cronshaw, D. and Evans, A. Cicerone Press.

1983 *Rock Climbs in Lancashire and the North West,. Including the Isle of
Man* **Ainsworth, L.** Cicerone Press. Writers included: Phil
Davidson (Liverpool Area); Malc Baxter (Tameside Area); Miles
Peters and Ron Yuen (Isle of Man); Les Ainsworth, Roger Bunyan,
Ian Conway, Dave Cronshaw, Mark Dansen, Kev Glass, Alec
Greening, Bruce Goodwin, Geoff Haigh, Nigel Holmes, Steve
Hubbard, Dave Knighton, Ian Lonsdale, Dave Sanderson and Bob
Whittaker.

1986 *Rock Climbs in Lancashire and the North West. Supplement.* **Kelly, P.
and Cronshaw, D.** Cicerone Press. Writers included: Joe Healey,
Ken Lathom (Liverpool Area); Malc Baxter, Harry Venables
(Tameside Area); Dave Cronshaw, Andrew Easton, Bruce Goodwin,
Andrew Gridley, Malc Haslam, Nigel Holmes, Geoff Hibbert, Owain
Jones, Phil Kelly, Mark Liptrot, Al Phizacklea and Paul Pritchard.

1987 *Rock Climbs in Lancashire and the North West.* **Kelly, P. and
Cronshaw, D.** Cicerone Press. Writers included: Les Ainsworth,
Goi Ashmore, Dave Bates, Malc Baxter, Chris Booth, Mick Bullough,
Al Cameron, Ian Conway, Paul Cornforth, David Craig, Dave
Cronshaw, Brian Davison, Carl Dawson, Dennis Gleeson, Bruce
Goodwin, Andrew Gridley, Geoff Haigh, Chris Hardy, Geoff Hibbert,
Steve Hubbard, Paul Ingham, Jason Kaushal, Phil Kelly, Tim Lowe,
John Mason, Andy Moss, Tony Nichols, Al Phizacklea, John Ryden,
Dave Sanderson, Rob Smitton, Jon Sparks, Rob Scott, Phil Stone,
Bob Whittaker, Ian Vickers and Roger Vickers.

Selected Bibliography

1913   *Some Gritstone Climbs* **Laycock, J.**

1937   Cadshaw Rocks. **Allsopp, A.** *Mountaineering Journal,* Pp. 5/4, 213–215.

1947   Guide to the Problems in the Brownstone Quarry. **Parr, E.** *Journal of Lancashire Climbing & Caving Club.*

1949   Guide to the Problems in the Brownstone Quarry. **Parr, E.** *Journal of Lancashire Climbing & Caving Club*, Pp. 21/1, 28–33.

1951   Cadshaw Rocks. **Allsopp, A.** *Journal of Lancashire Climbing & Caving Club*, 1/3, 30–35.

1951   *Kinder, Roches and Northern Areas: Climbs on Gritstone, Vol 3.* **Allsopp, A.** Pp. 148–150.

1957   *Kinder and Roches Area: Climbs on Gritstone, Vol 3.* **Allsopp, A.** Pp. 53–55.

1960   *Cadshaw Rocks.* **Allsopp, A.** Duplicated guide.

1961   *Guide to Climbs on the Prow at Wilton.* **Kilner, G. and Taylor, H.** (Duplicated guide)

1964   *Denham Quarry.* (Typescript)

1965   *Shooter's Nab Quarry* **West, G.T.W. and Howard, A.** In *The Saddleworth–Chew Valley Area: Rock Climbs in the Peak, Vol 2.* (Ed.) Byne, E. Pp. 18–28.

1965   *Pule Hill Rocks* **Howard, A.** In *The Saddleworth–Chew Valley Area: Rock Climbs in the Peak, Vol 2.* (Ed.) Byne, E. Pp. 29–41.

1966   *Guide to Wilton Quarries Number One and Number Two.* **Evans, R.** Alpine Sports, Bolton.

1966   *Guide to Wilton Quarries Number Three.* **Evans, R.** Alpine Sports, Bolton.

1967   The Unrealised Climbing Potential of Lancashire. **Ainsworth, L.** *Climber and Rambler*, August, Pp. 326–329.

1968   *Rock Climbing Guide to the Wilton Quarries.* **Evans, R. and Black, A.B.** Alpine Sports, Bolton.

1968   Climbing on Humphrey Head. **Goff, M.** *Kendal M C Journal*, Pp. 6–9.

1968   Interim Guide to Hoghton Quarry. **Hamer, P.** *Rocksport*, April/May, Pp. 15–21.

1968   *Bellmanpark Quarry* **Vickers, R.** (Typescript)

1969   *Blackstone Edge* **Horan, P.** In *Yorkshire Gritstone.* (Ed.) Bebbington, M. Pp. 237–239. Yorkshire Mountaineering Club.

Stevie Whittal on **Countach** (E5 6b), Millside Scar.   *Photo: Al Phizacklea*

1969 Off the Beaten Track: Warton Crags and Trowbarrow Quarry. **Lounds, B.** *Rocksport*, April/May, P. 23.

1971 Guide to Longridge Quarry. **Hill, D.** *Manchester University MC Bulletin*, June.

1972 *Bellmanpark Quarry* **Haslam, M.** (Typescript)

1974 Stronstrey Bank Quarry **Dickinson, C.** *Rocksport*, August, Pp. 22–23.

1974 *Hutton Roof Crags – 'Birkber Edge'* **Parker, J.** (Typescript)

1974 *Blackstone Edge* **Horan, P.** In *Yorkshire Gritstone*. (Ed.) Bebbington, M. Pp. 237–239. Yorkshire Mountaineering Club.

1975 Tremadocthwaite. **Evans, A.** *Climber and Rambler*, March, Pp. 106–107.

1976 *Shooter's Nab Quarry* **Hart, J.** In *Chew Valley: Rock Climbs in the Peak, Vol. 2.* (Ed.) Whittaker, B. Pp. 22–31.

1976 *Pule Hill Rocks* In *Chew Valley: Rock Climbs in the Peak, Vol. 2.* (Ed.) Whittaker, B. Pp. 32–42.

1976 Lancashire Hot Pot. **Ainsworth, L.** *Crags* 3, Pp. 30–32.

1977 What's New in Lancashire. **Knighton, D. and Cropper, B.** *Climber and Rambler*, February, Pp. 22–24.

1977 Egerton Quarry. **Holmes, N.** *Lancashire Climbing & Climbing Caving Bulletin*, Summer, Pp. 15–20.

1979 *Facit Quarries.* **Conway, I., and Goodwin, B.** Duplicated guide to Britannia Quarry.

1982 Early Days at Anglezarke. **Unsworth, W.** *Climber and Rambler*, January, Pp. 33–36.

1982 *Blackstone Edge* **Berzins, M.** In *Yorkshire Gritstone*, (Ed.) Lesniak, E. Pp. 76–79. Yorkshire Mountaineering Club.

1985 Cold Stones. *Gritstone Club Journal*, New Series, No. 6, P. 39.

1989 *Blackstone Edge* **Goodwin, B.** *In Yorkshire Gritstone, (Ed.) Desroy, G.* Pp. 76–79. Yorkshire Mountaineering Club.

1990 Rock Climbing in Northern England Birkett, White, J. Pp. 1–58. Constable.

1992 Provisional Guide to Slape Scar, Whitbarrow, Cumbria. **Lunt, K.** *Lancashire Climbing & Caving Club Journal,* Pp. 31–34.

1993 Metamorphosis – The Transformation of Scout Scar. **Birkett, B.** *Climber*, November, Pp. 16–20.

1996 Recent Developments at Fairy Steps, Beetham, South Cumbria. **Lunt, K.** *Lancashire Climbing & Caving Club Journal,* Pp. 15–16.

1996 White Scar **Wilcock, S.** *High* 168, Pp. 8–10.

1997 Trowbarrow. **Sparks, J.** *High* 172, Pp. 38–42.

Mick Lovatt and Chris Gore spaced out on Space Buttress during **Men at Work** (E5 6b), White Scar.   *Photo: Steve Wilcock*

Index